Climate Change and Agriculture in Europe

Assessment of impacts and adaptation

Edited by
P.A. Harrison, R.E. Butterfield and T.E. Downing

Research Report No. 9

December 1995

ENVIRONMENTAL CHANGE UNIT
University of Oxford
1a Mansfield Road
Oxford OX1 3TB, UK

First published 1995 by
Environmental Change Unit
University of Oxford

ISBN: 1 874370 09 5

The Administrator
Environmental Change Unit
University of Oxford
1a Mansfield Road
Oxford OX1 3TB, UK
Tel: +44 1865 281180
Fax: +44 1865 281181

Photograph on front cover courtesy of Oxford Picture Library/Chris Andrews.

CONTENTS

Preface..vii

1. **Climate change and agriculture in Europe: Study aims and methods**...........1
    P.A. Harrison

2. **Construction of scenarios of climate change and climatic variability
    at the site and regional scales**

    Summary..15

    2.1 Introduction..17
         E. Barrow, M. Hulme and M.A. Semenov

    2.2 General circulation models..17
         E. Barrow and M. Hulme

    2.3 Construction of regional scenarios..21
         E. Barrow and M. Hulme

    2.4 Construction of site-specific scenarios...30
         E. Barrow, M.A. Semeonv and M.Hulme

3. **Modelling the effects of agriculturally significant climatic extremes at
    the site and regional scales**

    Summary..51

    3.1 Introduction..53
         T.S. Karacostas and R.E. Butterfield

    3.2 Site-specific extreme events for wheat..53
         T.S. Karacostas

    3.3 Regional drought characterisation for wheat in Europe.....................68
         T.S. Karacostas

    3.4 Crop-specific climatic extremes for wheat and maize in Hungary.....75
         Zs. Harnos

PREFACE

The Environmental Change Unit (ECU) is an interdisciplinary unit at the University of Oxford, dedicated to collaborative research on the nature, causes and impacts of environmental change, and to the development of management strategies for dealing with future changes. The Unit focuses on the following research areas: environmental impacts modelling; energy and the environment; legal and policy aspects of environmental change; land use change; monitoring of environmental change; information retrieval and collation.

The Research Report series of the Environmental Change Unit is designed to present current research spanning a range of formats from research summaries with a policy focus to technical documentation of data, models and results.

The research reported here was conducted over the period 1 October 1993 to 31 December 1995 under the European Commssion's ENVIRONMENT Programme (Contract number: EV5V-CT92-0294). It was coordinated by the Environmental Change Unit at the University of Oxford and was implemented as a collaborative project by the following research institutions:

- Agricultural Research Centre of Finland, Finland.
- Centre for Computer Science Applications in Agriculture, University of Florence, Italy.
- Climatic Research Unit, University of East Anglia, U.K.
- Danish Institute of Plant and Soil Science, Research Centre Foulum, Denmark.
- Department of Agricultural Sciences, Royal Agricultural and Veterinary University, Denmark.
- Department of Mathematics and Informatics, University of Horticulture and Food Industry, Hungary.
- Department of Meteorology and Climatology, University of Thessaloniki, Greece.
- Departments of Meteorology, Horticulture and Agriculture, University of Reading, U.K.
- Department of Soil Science, Swedish University of Agricultural Sciences, Sweden.
- Department of Theoretical Production Ecology, Wageningen Agricultural University, The Netherlands
- Environmental Change Unit, University of Oxford, U.K.
- IACR - Long Ashton Research Station, University of Bristol, U.K.
- INIA - Area de Informatica Cientifica, Spain.
- INIA - Department de Sistemas Forestales, Spain.
- INRA - Station de Bioclimatologie, France.
- Institut für Pflanzenbau, Friedrich Wilhelms Universität, Germany.

This report presents the final results of the project. An overview of the study's aims and methodology are provided in Chapter 1. This should be read to ascertain how the detailed methods and results reported in Chapters 2 to 6 relate to the overall research strategy. Chapters 2 to 6 consist of a number of associated papers on the same theme. These chapters are self-contained with a summary of key findings from all papers. Chapter 7 draws together selected results from the project and discusses their relevance to European climate change policy.

The editors and authors are grateful to the staff of the EPOCH programme, in particular, Dr. Roberto Fantechi and Mr. Denis Peter, and to Ms. Megan Gawith for the design and layout of the report.

CHAPTER 1

Climate change and agriculture in Europe:

Study aims and objectives

1.1   Aims

This project, funded under the European Commission's Environment Programme, involved fourteen institutions in ten member countries of the European Union and one eastern European research centre. This interdisciplinary team of scientists has undertaken a thorough assessment of the potential impacts of climate change on agriculture and horticulture in Europe.

The work had four main research initiatives:

- To compile a database of relevant environmental data and state-of-the-art climate scenarios for Europe.
- To assess the impact of climate change (namely elevated carbon dioxide and altered weather) on crop development, growth, yield and yield quality through controlled experiments and simulation models.
- To evaluate appropriate farm-level adaptive responses and prospects for sustainability.
- To develop a geographical information system (GIS) for climate change impact assessment for European agriculture that integrates the project components and spans spatial and temporal scales.

1.2   Methods

The research approach sought to develop robust impact models for a wide variety of crops at different spatial and temporal scales (Figure 1.1). Site-based and spatial models have been developed in parallel and the results integrated within a GIS framework. Experiments on the interactive effects of elevated carbon dioxide and increased temperature on selected crops were conducted to improve parameterization of mechanistic models. The foundation for the project's activities was the development of a geographically referenced European database of current climatological, agricultural and other relevant environmental data. This database facilitated consistent links between scenarios of climate change, experimental results and models of crop responses. Changes in climate which exert a critical effect on crop yields and/or

spatial shifts in crop potential were compared with projections of future climate from coupled ocean-atmosphere general circulation models (GCMs). Structured comparisons of simulation models were conducted to quantify the uncertainties associated with crop responses to climate change. Emphasis was placed on integrating scales of analysis, from site applications of crop simulation models to region-wide spatial assessments using less data-intensive models. The output from the project is the design of a framework for assessing the risk and impact of climate change, and evaluating rates and levels of adaptive strategies available to farmers and policy makers.

1.2.1   Database development

A consistent database of relevant environmental variables was essential for the integration of model results and comparison of models and modelling methods. High quality geographically referenced observed data on present climatic, agronomic and edaphic conditions in Europe provided a solid foundation for the crop impact modelling activities. A number of derived variables, which are key inputs to the models, were also incorporated in the database. These included a range of climate change scenarios and calculated values of potential evapotranspiration.

1.2.1.1   *Climatic data*

Baseline climate

Two datasets of current (1961-1990) climatic data were compiled for use in the project:

- spatially gridded monthly variables; and
- site-specific daily variables.

A 1961-90 mean monthly climatology for the European region extending from 11°W to 42°E and from 35 to 71.5°N has been constructed at a resolution of 0.5° latitude/longitude for a suite of nine surface climate variables: minimum, maximum and mean air temperature; precipitation totals; sunshine hours; vapour pressure; wind speed; and (ground) frostday and rainday (>0.1mm) frequencies (Hulme *et al.*,

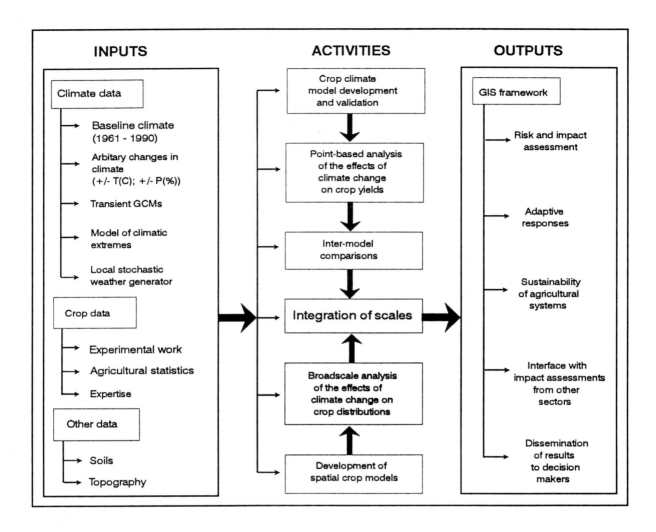

Figure 1.1   Research strategy of the project.

1993). This climatology was constructed from observed station data distributed across the region.

The interpolation of the station data to the grid used elevation as one of the predictor variables and, thus, enabled three climate surfaces to be produced for each variable, reflecting the minimum, mean and maximum elevation within each 0.5° cell. The accuracy of the various interpolations was assessed using validation sets of independent station data (i.e., those not used in the interpolation). Estimated mean absolute errors (MAE) ranged from under 5% for vapour pressure to about 15% for wind speed to up to 20% for precipitation in some regions. The accuracy of the interpolated surface for maximum temperature was greater (MAE ~

0.4°C) than for minimum temperature (MAE ~ 1.0°C). Mean surface air temperature for January and July averaged over the period 1961-90 is shown in Figure 1.2.

Observed daily climatic data have been collected for the time series 1961-90 for a number of sites in Europe. The sites were chosen to represent different agricultural and climatic zones throughout Europe and included Jokioinen (Finland), Rothamsted (UK), Oxford (UK), Wageningen (The Netherlands), Bonn (Germany), Mannheim (Germany), München (Germany), Debrecen (Hungary), Györ (Hungary), Montpellier (France), Bologna (Italy), Sevilla (Spain) and Athens (Greece). The dataset consists of nine variables: minimum, maximum and mean surface air temperature,

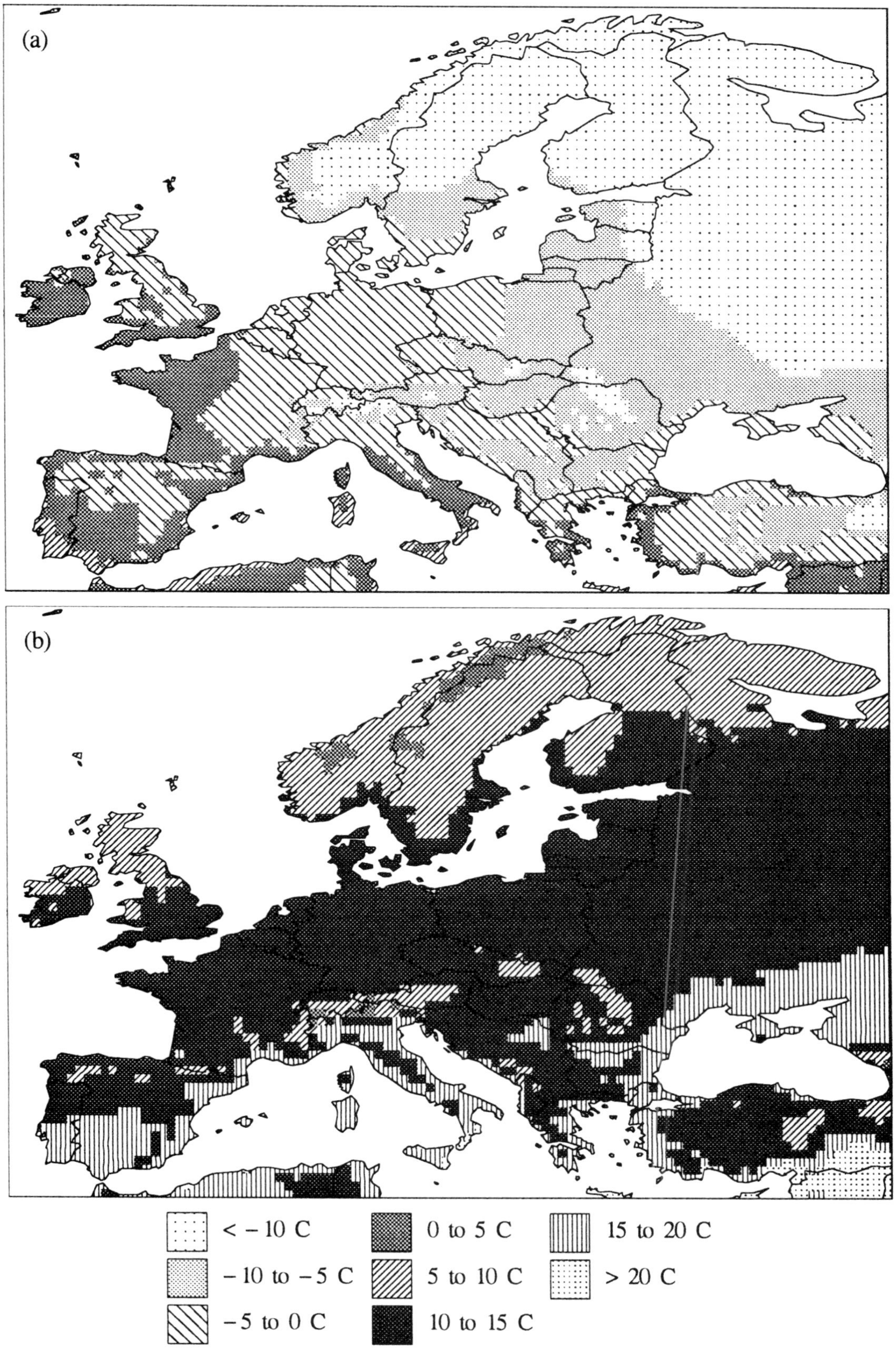
(a)
(b)
< −10 C
−10 to −5 C
−5 to 0 C
0 to 5 C
5 to 10 C
10 to 15 C
15 to 20 C
> 20 C

Figure 1.2 (a) January and (b) July mean surface air temperature for 1961-90.

total precipitation, sunshine hours, global radiation, vapour pressure, relative humidity and wind speed. All data were error checked and transferred to a consistent format within the geographically referenced database.

Scenarios of climate change

Projections of future climate from a range of general circulation models (GCMs) have been used in conjunction with crop models to assess the potential impacts of climate change. Two types of GCM scenarios were constructed:

- transient scenarios from two coupled ocean-atmosphere GCM experiments (the United Kingdom Met. Office (UKTR) experiment and the Geophysical Fluid Dynamics Laboratory (GFDL) experiment) for two time periods to investigate rates of change; and
- equilibrium scenarios from two previous generations of GCM experiments (the United Kingdom Met. Office's low resolution (UKLO) experiment and the United Kingdom Met. Office's high resolution (UKHI) experiment) to ensure results can be compared with previous studies and to assess how projections of climate change have altered as GCMs have evolved.

The change fields were calculated at each GCM's original resolution and then interpolated to the finer 0.5° latitude/longitude resolution. A pilot study investigating methodologies for downscaling GCM grid-box information to specific sites was undertaken at two sites, Rothamsted (UK) and Sevilla (Spain). At the remaining sites GCM grid-box data was used in conjunction with a stochastic weather generator to produce scenarios at the daily time scale. Use of a stochastic weather generator permitted changes in temperature and precipitation variability to be considered in the site-specific scenarios.

The transient scenarios were related to two Intergovernmental Panel on Climate Change (IPCC) emissions scenarios (Leggett *et al.*, 1992): IS92a (the 'business-as-usual' scenario) and IS92d (a low, but plausible, emissions

scenario). Based on the greenhouse gas emissions associated with IS92a and IS92d, approximate calender years have been assigned to the decades of the transient climate change experiments using a simple climate model. The climate model was run for three values of climate sensitivity to generate a range of uncertainty about each global-mean temperature projection. Details of the scenarios are shown in Table 1.1.

All scenarios have been incorporated within the GIS database in a format consistent with the baseline climatic data.

1.2.1.2   *Agronomic data*

Agronomic data was collected to aid with model development, calibration and validation. Statistics on agricultural production in Europe have been obtained from the FAO, EUROSTAT and individual countries. Statistics collated include yield (t/ha) and area planted ('000 ha) for total cereals, wheat, barley, grain maize, rice, potatoes, oilseed, rapeseed, sunflower, sugar beet, fodder maize and tobacco. Data covers the period 1975-1991 and is held at NUTS level 2 (level 1 in UK and former East Germany).

Data have been reformatted by allocating the statistics within each NUTS region to 0.5° latitude/longitude cells in the European Union to allow direct comparison with model results. As the statistics are represented by administrative unit, detailed local deviations in the data are not apparent. The resampled dataset did not improve this: for example, in southwest France the region extending into the Pyrenees shows equal distribution and performance of crops, whereas in reality large differences occur due to effects of topography and associated changes in environmental conditions.

A database of observed phenology for winter wheat has been compiled for Europe. This contains information gleaned from a literature review covering the average and earliest dates of eight developmental stages: sowing, emergence, double ridge, terminal spikelet, anthesis, beginning of grain filling, end of grain filling and harvest. Information can be identified by NUTS region, with the ability to display discrete

Table 1.1   GCM scenarios used with the impact models.

Emissions scenario	GCM	Model decade	Equivalent year based on climate sensitivity (°C)			Global-mean temperature change (°C)	CO$_2$ concentration (ppmv)
			1.5 (low)	2.5 (best guess)	4.5 (high)		
IS92a	UKTR	31-40	2036	2023	2013	0.68	454
IS92a	GFDL	25-34	2036	2023	2013	0.68	454
IS92a	UKTR	66-75	after 2100	2064	2042	1.76	617
IS92a	GFDL	55-64	after 2100	2064	2042	1.76	617
IS92d	UKTR	66-75	after 2100	2099	2054	1.76	545
IS92d	GFDL	55-64	after 2100	2099	2054	1.76	545
2 x CO$_2$	UKHI	-	-	-	-	3.5	560
2 x CO$_2$	UKLO	-	-	-	-	5.2	560

point observations. The average date of winter wheat harvest is shown in Figure 1.3. The coverage is built up hierarchically as only a few regions have detailed (NUTS level 3 resolution) information. All point sources are shown as regions in this map. The non-E.U. country information can be resolved to region, but is shown at country level in this example.

1.2.1.3   *Other data*

Other data which were required for the project's research activities include edaphic, topographic and administrative data.   Specific details of these data held within the GIS are:

- Soils data (soil type, texture, slope, stoniness, lithic contact and derived available water-holding capacity) for three predominant soil types in a 0.5° latitude/longitude grid for Europe (Groenendijk, 1989);
- 10' resolution altitude data from NOAA;
- 1:1 million Digital Chart of the World from ESRI, including country boundaries, rivers, roads, urban areas etc.;

- 1:3 million Nomenclature Unitare Territorial Statistiques (NUTS) boundary from EUROSTAT; and
- 1:10 million NUTS equivalent information for non-E.U. countries from EUROSTAT.

1.2.1.4   *Potential evapotranspiration data*

Potential evapotranspiration (PET) is a climatically derived variable which is an integral part of crop models. There are many different methods of calculating PET which can lead to significant differences in crop model output. Within the project it was desirable to choose a single standard method of calculation and, thus, the majority of models used the Penman formula (Penman, 1948). However, standardization was not possible in all cases due to data limitations or poor performance of this method in certain regions of Europe. For example, insufficient climatic variables were available to calculate Penman PET for two of the GCM scenarios (GFDL and UKLO). In these cases, the less data demanding methods of Priestley-Taylor (Priestley and Taylor, 1972) or Thornthwaite (Thornthwaite and Mather, 1955) were used,

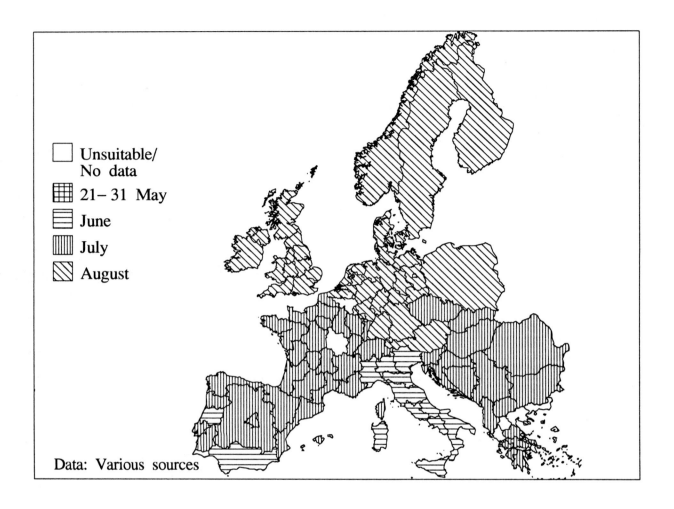

Figure 1.3   The average date of winter wheat harvest in Europe.

depending on the array of available climatic variables.

A comparison of the three methods used in the project (Penman, Priestley-Taylor, Thornthwaite) was undertaken to quantify relative differences using the common dataset. Each method has different data requirements. Penman is the most data demanding method requiring temperature, net radiation, vapour pressure and wind speed data, Priestley-Taylor requires temperature and net radiation data, whilst Thornthwaite requires only mean temperature data. Penman and Priestley-Taylor are physically-based formulas and, as such, may be more accurate, particularly under climate change scenarios. Further, since the Thornthwaite method is empirical, and

calibrated for present conditions, it is likely that it will have to be re-calibrated if changes in climate occur in the future. It should be noted that of the three methods only Thornthwaite is intended for use with monthly data, whilst the others require daily input.

The comparison of results was based on examination of maps and transects across Europe. Comparison of PET estimates on a latitudinal transect from southeast England to central Russia (50.75°N) indicated that the methods produce relatively similar values for western Europe, with Thornthwaite being the lowest. Values become increasingly different towards eastern Europe as Penman and Priestley-Taylor PET increase across the transect, while Thornthwaite PET changes only marginally. These variations with longitude can be explained by the increasing continentality of the climate to which Thornthwaite is the least sensitive. Comparisons for a longitudinal transect from northern Norway to Crete (25.75°E) showed greater variation, reflecting differences in radiation receipt from north to south. PET estimates were more similar in northern Europe than in southern Europe; values varied by approximately 100 mm at 55°N and increased progressively to approximately 600 mm at 35°N. Thornthwaite PET was always lower than both Penman and Priestley-Taylor PET across this latitudinal range. The calculated values of PET were mapped across Europe on the 0.5° latitude/longitude grid to identify spatial differences in the three methods. Figure 1.4 shows annual values of PET calculated using the Penman, Priestley-Taylor and Thornthwaite methods. The Penman method produces the most variable results across the European region, Priestley-Taylor produces similar values for PET but with less spatial variation, whilst Thornthwaite produces lower PET values with little spatial variation. This may reflect the relative simplicity of the methods. For example, Penman is the most successful in identifying the presence of water bodies, as indicted by the relatively lower values over the Caspian and Aral Seas, due to the inclusion of wind speed and vapour pressure functions. These variables are replaced by a constant in the Priestley-Taylor method and ignored in the Thornthwaite method.

In summary, results showed that Penman and Priestley-Taylor produce the highest values of PET and usually differ by less than 100 mm per year. Thornthwaite produces similar values of PET to Penman and Priestley-Taylor in northwest Europe, but differs by up to 600 mm per year in southern Europe and by up to 400 mm per year in eastern Europe.

1.2.2 Experimental and modelling activities

A range of crops were studied using a number of experimental and modelling approaches to investigate impacts on crop phenology, yield, agricultural risk and distribution (Table 1.2). Crop modelling activities spanned a hierarchy of scales: detailed crop simulation models were applied at individual sites located in different agricultural and climatic zones throughout Europe; and spatial models assessed regional impacts on either a 10 x 10 km grid at the country scale or a 0.5° latitude/longitude grid at the continental scale. Experiments on the effects of elevated concentrations of carbon dioxide and/or increased temperature were performed where possible to support model development and validation.

Recent research has made considerable progress in assessing the potential impacts of climate change for a number of cereal crops. However, it is critical that research is extended to cover a much wider range of crops to allow fuller assessments of the agricultural implications of a warmer climate. Hence, within the project experimental and modelling activities were extended to include new crops, such as vegetables, perennial fruit crops and non-food crops, as well as continuing work on the major European cereal crops.

Guidelines were established to provide a coherent structure to the crop modelling research. Firstly, models were developed and validated against independent observed data. They were then applied to the baseline climate for the period 1961-90. This baseline run acted as a reference against which the impacts of climate change were appraised. Following the baseline run, the sensitivity of each model to a range of systematic changes in mean climate was investigated (sensitivity tests). The quantification of crop model responses to independent changes in individual climatic variables, as well as changes in CO_2 concentration, allowed a more informed interpretation of predicted impacts from GCM scenarios. In addition to changes in mean climate, the effects of changes in the variability of climate were evaluated at the site scale. Each model was then used to assess the effects of climate change on the specific crop with the set of scenarios described in Table 1.1. Finally, a number of possible farm-level adaptive strategies were evaluated using the models, including changes in sowing date and changes in crop variety.

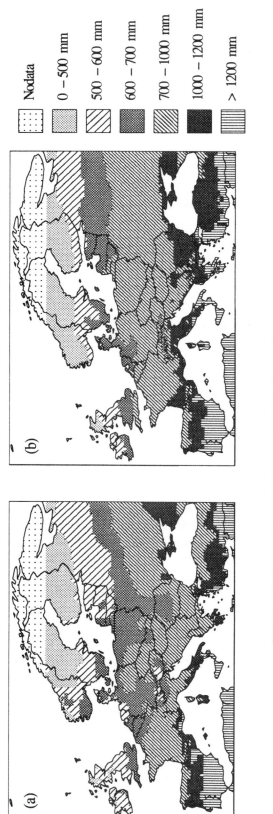

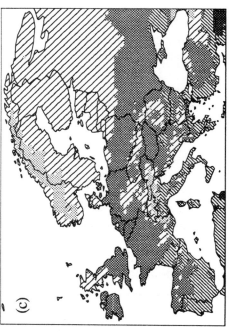

Figure 1.4 Annual PET calculated according to the (a) Penman, (b) Priestley-Taylor and (c) Thornthwaite methods.

Table 1.2 Crops and subjects studied in the project.

Crop	Models	Modelling domain				Experiments
		Phenology	**Yield**	**Risk**	**Distribution**	
Winter wheat	[1] AFRCWheat	✓	✓	✓		
	[1] SIRIUS	✓	✓	✓		
	[1] NWHEAT	✓	✓	✓		
	[1] SOILN-Wheat	✓	✓	✓		
	[1] CERES	✓	✓	✓		
	[3] EuroWheat	✓	✓		✓	
Spring wheat	[2] FinWheat	✓			✓	✓
Spring barley	[2] FinBarley	✓			✓	
Maize	[1] CERES	✓	✓	✓		
Sunflower	[3] EuroSunfl	✓	✓		✓	
Sugar beet						✓
Cauliflower	[1] CauliSim	✓	✓	✓		✓
Broccoli	[1] BroccoSim	✓	✓	✓		✓
Onions	[1] PELonion	✓	✓	✓		✓
	[3] EuroOnion	✓	✓		✓	
Faba bean						✓
Grapes	[1] CeSIAgrape	✓	✓	✓		✓
Non-food	[1] SOILN-Willow	✓	✓	✓		

[1] Site-specific crop models
[2] Country scale crop models on a 10 x 10 km grid
[3] Continental scale crop models on a 0.5° latitude/longitude grid

A major focus of the crop modelling activities was to undertake a comparison of models. Adopting a methodology consistent with that of the GCTE Crop Modelling Working Group, the project conducted a thorough comparison of wheat models for different agroclimatic conditions in Europe. The aim was to quantify which models, or model components, most accurately simulate crop behaviour under altered climatic conditions.

1.2.3 Integration of crop model results across scales

Within the project work took place at four scales:

- crop models were developed for application at a number of sites throughout Europe;

- spatial crop models were developed for application at the regional/national scale;
- spatial crop models were developed for application at the continental scale with a 0.5° latitude/longitude resolution; and
- scenarios of climate change were generated from general circulation models which operate on a global scale with resolutions varying from 2.5 to 7.5° latitude/longitude.

A hierarchical GIS was designed to integrate the Europe-wide analyses with results from the site-specific crop simulation models. This system allows for graphical and tabular presentation of results at different scales of detail for a specific crop. For example, results from site-based models and experiments for wheat can be examined within a spatial overlay of broadscale wheat suitability.

This multi-level framework, linking together all project activities, enables researchers and decision-makers to compile climate change impact assessments for European agriculture at a range of spatial and temporal scales for various climate scenarios and adaptive strategies.

1.3   Structure of the report

The report has been structured to give a coherent presentation of research methodology and results. Construction of scenarios of climate change was central to all of the research and is presented in Chapter 2. It is followed by the analysis of crop-specific climatic extremes which is both climatically and agriculturally orientated (Chapter 3). An essential component of any crop modelling activities is a sound research programme on the combined effects of changes in climate and atmospheric carbon dioxide on crops. Results from six experiments conducted within the project are reported in Chapter 4. The crop modelling work is divided into two chapters: Chapter 5 discusses results from mechanistic models run at a range of sites in Europe, whilst Chapter 6 presents some spatial implications of climate change on crop suitability. Finally, methodologies for the integration of the different temporal and spatial scales employed in the project are examined in Chapter 7. Results are also drawn together in Chapter 7 to provide recommendations for policy and further research.

References

Hulme, M., Jiang, T., Turney, C. and Barrow, E. (1993). *A 1961-90 baseline climatology and future climate change scenarios for Great Britain and Europe. Part II: 1961-90 European baseline climatology.* Climatic Research Unit, University of East Anglia, 49pp.

Leggett, J., Pepper, W.J. and Swart, R.J. (1992). Emissions scenarios for the IPCC: An update. In: Houghton, J.T., Callander, B.A. and Varney, S.K. (Eds.) *Climate change 1992: The supplementary report to the IPCC scientific assessment*, Cambridge University Press, Cambridge, pp.69-96.

Penman, H.L. (1948). Natural evaporation from open water, bare soil, and grass. *Proceedings of the Royal Society, London A.*, **193**: 120-146.

Priestley, C.H.B. and Taylor, R.J. (1972). On the assessment of surface heat flux and evaporation using large scale parameters. *Monthly Weather Review*, **100**: 81-92.

Thornthwaite, C.W. and Mather, J.R. (1955). The water balance. *Climatology*, **8**: 1-104.

CHAPTER 2

Construction of scenarios of climate change
and climatic variability
at the site and regional scales

SUMMARY

To investigate the impacts of future climate change on agriculture in Europe, several scenarios of climate change were constructed and provided as inputs to crop-climate models at both regional and site-specific scales. Scenarios were based on results from a number of general circulation model (GCM) experiments, including both equilibrium and transient climate change experiments. These included the UK Met. Office low and high resolution GCM equilibrium experiments (UKLO and UKHI, respectively), the UK Met. Office high resolution GCM transient climate change experiment (UKTR) and the Geophysical Fluid Dynamics Laboratory GCM transient climate change experiment (GFDL). All models provide internally consistent scenarios of climate change, but at different horizontal spatial resolutions. Results from equilibrium experiments give no indication of the rate of climate change, whereas the transient experiments simulate time-dependent climate change and also simulate feedbacks between ocean and atmosphere circulation changes. By combining the global-mean temperature changes of the two decades used from each transient experiment with information from a simple climate model (MAGICC), a range of possible future dates was allotted to these scenarios.

Regional climate change scenarios for Europe were constructed at a 0.5° latitude/longitude resolution using a simple Gaussian space-filtering routine. Site-specific scenarios were constructed using both downscaling techniques and a simpler methodology. A pilot study investigating the use of regression techniques to downscale GCM changes in temperature and precipitation to those of specific sites was carried out at Rothamsted, UK and Sevilla, Spain.

Regression relationships were determined using observed areal temperature, precipitation and a number of pressure variables as predictors. The GCM grid-box changes in the predictor variables were then used to derive site changes in temperature and precipitation, provided that the grid-box values were within the anomaly ranges over which the relationships had been constructed. Downscaling was more successful for temperature than for precipitation at both sites. For Sevilla, in particular, there were problems determining reliable relationships for summer precipitation. At both sites, downscaled temperatures were warmer than the corresponding grid-box values. For a number of other European sites where crop-climate models were being run a simpler methodology was used to construct the climate change scenarios.

Climate change information at the daily timescale was prepared for each site. This was achieved using a stochastic weather generator rather than daily data from the GCMs themselves. The weather generator was initially calibrated for each site using at least 20 years of daily weather data. The parameters produced in this exercise were used to generate synthetic data, the statistics of which were then compared with those of the observed data. The weather generator performed sufficiently well at each site to enable it to be used without any modifications. Parameter files were modified according to each climate change scenario and then used to generate the daily scenario data. Use of a weather generator also enabled changes in climatic variability to be incorporated in the scenarios. Analysis of daily data from UKHI and the last decade of the UKTR experiment enabled changes in both temperature variability and the length of wet and dry spells to be incorporated into the weather generator parameter files. Thirty years of simulated daily data were produced for each climate change scenario.

Scenarios based on results from an equilibrium experiment, which represents climate at some unspecified point in the future, will give much greater changes compared to those from an early decade of one of the transient experiments (for example, 5.2°C for UKLO, 3.5°C for UKHI, compared to 0.68°C for the earlier decade of the transient experiments used), which represent climate in the earlier years of the twentyfirst century. Crop model results should only be directly compared if the climate change scenarios used as input have the same global-mean warming, e.g., UKTR years 31-40 and GFDL years 25-34.

In order to investigate the inter-model differences and similarities in the patterns of climate change the spatial pattern correlation coefficients between the different model change fields were calculated for mean temperature and precipitation.

2.1 Introduction

Scenarios of climate change were constructed at two spatial scales, the Europe-wide regional scale and the site-specific scale, to assess the impacts of such changes on European agriculture and in the determination of possible adaptation strategies.

A number of GCMs were used to construct regional change fields at the 0.5° latitude/longitude resolution for a number of climate variables at the monthly timescale. The change fields were calculated at each model's original horizontal spatial resolution (see Table 2.1) and then interpolated to the finer resolution using a simple Gaussian space-filtering routine. Two equilibrium (UKLO and UKHI) and two transient GCM experiments (UKTR and GFDL) were used. Equilibrium GCM experiments were included to provide the link between the present work and that of the previous project investigating the impacts of climate change on the agricultural and horticultural potential of Europe (Kenny *et al.*, 1993). These scenarios were used in the regional extreme events analysis (Chapter 3), the investigation of regional impacts on a variety of crop species (Chapter 6) and the integration of the project results into a geographical information system (Chapter 7).

Site-specific climate change information was required as input to a number of crop growth simulation models in order to examine the sensitivity of a number of crop species to climate change (Chapter 5). A pilot study investigating the feasibility of downscaling GCM grid-box information to specific sites was undertaken at two sites, Rothamsted, UK, and Sevilla, Spain. At the remaining European sites GCM grid-box data were used in conjunction with a stochastic weather generator to produce scenarios at the daily timescale necessary for the crop-climate models. Use of a stochastic weather generator permitted changes in temperature and precipitation variability to also be considered.

Not all the crop model results from the different climate change scenarios can be directly compared. This is because differences in the crop model results may be due to different global-mean warmings of the individual scenarios rather than due to different patterns of climate change. Crop model results should only be directly compared if the climate change scenarios used as input have the same globlal-mean warming. This point is discussed more fully in Section 2.5

Detailed descriptions of the construction of the climate change scenarios and the summarised results are presented in the following sections.

2.2 General circulation models

GCMs are the tools which are most widely used to generate scenarios of climate change for impacts assessment (Giorgi and Mearns, 1991;

Table 2.1 Characteristics of the GCMs used in the construction of climate change scenarios.

GCM	CO$_2$ concentration (ppmv)		Type of model	Atmospheric resolution (°latitude by °longitude)	Climate sensitivity (ΔT_{2x})
	Control	Perturbed			
UKLO	323	646	Gridded	5 x 7.5	5.2°C
UKHI	323	646	Gridded	2.5 x 3.75	3.5°C
UKTR	323	1% yr^{-1} compounded	Gridded	2.5 x 3.75	
GFDL	300	1% yr^{-1} compounded	Spectral	4.5 x 7.5	

Carter *et al.*, 1995). In GCMs the climatological conditions of the Earth are represented at a finite number of discrete grid points[1] (a grid point model) or by a finite number of mathematical functions (a spectral model). The fundamental physical equations describing the conservation of momentum, mass and energy are solved using numerical computational methods and using values specified either at the grid points or by the mathematical functions. The horizontal resolution of the GCM depends either on the number of grid points or on the number of mathematical functions used. The limiting factor for running GCMs is computational power; a compromise must be reached between the spatial resolution and the computer time required to perform an experiment. This means that most GCMs tend to have a coarse spatial resolution, which leads to approximations in the model representation of meteorological variables across a region. The coarser the resolution, the greater the approximation of local and regional weather phenomena. These so-called 'sub-grid scale' processes have to be parameterised in the model rather than solved realistically as a function of the fundamental equations. However, despite these limitations, GCMs provide an opportunity to examine the nature of both past and possible future climates under a variety of conditions (Gates *et al.*, 1990).

Two types of climate studies have been undertaken using GCMs, namely equilibrium and transient climate change experiments. The latter is a direct result of the progress made in computer technology in recent years. Equilibrium experiments have studied the response of climate to an instantaneous doubling of CO_2[2]. In such experiments, the GCM is integrated with a control concentration of CO_2 (usually approximately 300 ppmv) until a steady-state climate is reached; the CO_2 concentration is then instantaneously doubled (i.e., to 600 ppmv) and the model re-integrated until equilibrium is again achieved. The differences between this 'perturbed' climate and the control are indicative of the climate changes which would eventually result from this instantaneous doubling of CO_2. In such experiments representation of the oceans is usually very simplistic. In transient experiments, on the other hand, the atmospheric GCM is usually coupled to a full ocean GCM, thus allowing the representation of the feedbacks between atmosphere and ocean circulation. This permits the vertical heat transfer within the oceans to be modelled and a more realistic response of the climate to CO_2 forcing to be obtained. The thermal inertia of the oceans delays and reduces the surface climatic responses to radiative forcing. Transient experiments also allow for the fact that concentrations of atmospheric CO_2 do not change abruptly, but rise gradually over time.

2.2.1   Characteristics of the GCMs used in the construction of climate change scenarios

In this project, results from both types of GCM experiment have been used. Climate change scenarios have been constructed from equilibrium and transient climate change experiments undertaken at the UK Met. Office.

---

[1]   The term 'grid-point' is somewhat misleading. Within a GCM the boundary conditions for the grid (elevation, albedo, surface vegetation, etc.) are areally-averaged values, therefore the resulting model climate is also an areally-averaged value. 'Grid box' is therefore a more appropriate term to use and, conceptually, is what is assumed in this study. Skelly and Henderson-Sellers (in press) provide a fuller discussion of this issue.

[2] CO_2 is used in most GCM experiments as a surrogate for other GHGs and, hence, this 'equivalent' CO_2 concentration represents all the greenhouse gases rather CO_2 alone. In the equilibrium scenarios constructed here, for use in crop-climate models, a CO_2 concentration of 560 ppmv has been used. This value represents a doubling of pre-industrial CO_2 concentrations and also approximates to the actual CO_2 concentration when the equivalent value is approximately 600 ppmv.

Results from the Geophysical Fluid Dynamics Laboratory (GFDL) transient GCM climate change experiment were also used. Table 2.1 illustrates the main characteristics of these GCMs.

The UK Met. Office low resolution GCM equilibrium experiment (UKLO; Wilson and Mitchell, 1987) is an eleven-layer atmospheric GCM with sea surface temperatures, sea ice limits and cloud dynamics prescribed. The spatial resolution is 5° latitude by 7.5° longitude. The high resolution GCM used for the study of the equilibrium response of climate (UKHI; Mitchell *et al.*, 1990) is similar to UKLO, but has an enhanced horizontal spatial resolution of 2.5° latitude by 3.75° longitude. Other improvements include a better representation of cloud dynamics and processes. The UK Met. Office GCM transient experiment (UKTR; Murphy, 1995; Murphy and Mitchell, 1995) has the same horizontal spatial resolution as UKHI, but has been coupled to a 17 unequally spaced vertical layer ocean GCM which includes a thermodynamic sea-ice model. In this experiment the equivalent atmospheric CO_2 concentration was increased by 1% per year compounded, which resulted in an effective CO_2 doubling after 70 years. The GFDL GCM transient experiment (GFDL; Manabe *et al.*, 1991; Manabe *et al.*, 1992) consists of a nine-layer atmospheric GCM coupled to an eleven-layer GCM of the World Ocean. GFDL has a coarser horizontal spatial resolution than both UKHI and UKTR, but, like UKTR, the CO_2 concentration is increased by 1% per year compounded in its perturbed integration.

2.2.2 Construction of climate change scenarios

2.2.2.1 *Scenarios using GCM equilibrium experiments*

Climate change scenarios were produced from both UKLO and UKHI by calculating the $2xCO_2$-$1xCO_2$ difference fields for maximum and minimum temperature, precipitation, vapour pressure, incident solar radiation and wind speed. For all climate variables except precipitation and wind speed the absolute difference was used, whereas for these two

variables the percentage difference was calculated. These fields represent the difference between the 'present' climate and the equilibrium climate at some point in the future; the exact date is unknown because the lag between the radiative forcing of the atmosphere and the ocean response may be many centuries and is not directly simulated by the GCM. These equilibrium changes in climate are not expected to occur before the latter years of the 21st century at the earliest, and probably not until the 22nd century.

2.2.2.2 *Scenarios using GCM transient experiments*

Construction of climate change scenarios from GCM transient experiments is not so straightforward. One problem of GCM transient experiments is drift in the control integration. The control integration of, for example, UKTR, produces a noticeable deviation (approximately 1°C) from the initial ten-year average over the 75 year period of the simulation. There are a number of reasons for this drift (see Viner and Hulme, 1993), although none are sufficient for a full explanation. How control integration drift is handled affects the way in which scenarios are constructed from these transient models. There are three ways of calculating the change fields, each of which makes assumptions about climate variability and drift in the GCM (Viner and Hulme, 1993). These are outlined in Figure 2.1.

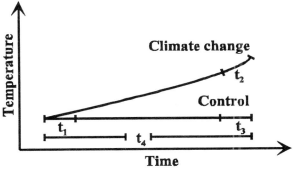

Figure 2.1 Different methods for the calculation of change fields from transient climate change experiments.

1)   The change is defined as the difference between a period in the climate change integration and the first corresponding length of the control integration. This

definition is appropriate if one assumes that there is no serious drift within the control simulation and that any drift is caused by short-term climate variability.

$$\Delta T_{(1)} = T_{change(t2)} - T_{control(t1)}$$

2) The change is defined as the difference between a period in the climate change integration and the corresponding years of the control integration. This definition is appropriate if one assumes that both the control and climate change integrations exhibit similar drift and long-term variability.

$$\Delta T_{(2)} = T_{change(t2)} - T_{control(t3)}$$

3) The change is defined as the difference between a period of the climate change integration and the mean of the entire control simulation. This definition is appropriate if one assumes that the variability is constant throughout the control integration and that the drift that exists is due to the long-term variability of the coupled ocean-atmosphere system.

$$\Delta T_{(3)} = T_{change(t2)} - T_{control(t4)}$$

Definition (2) was used to construct the climate change fields from both UKTR and GFDL.

Data from UKTR were available only as decadal time-slices, so two decades were selected: the years 31-40 as representative of the climate about half-way through the model experiment, and years 66-75, the last decade of the experiment. The global-mean temperature changes associated with these decades are 0.68°C and 1.76°C respectively. In the case of the GFDL experiment a 100-year monthly time series was available; decades were selected which had the same global-mean temperature change as those of the two UKTR decades, namely the years 25-34 and 55-64.

The climate change scenarios constructed from the GCM transient experiments were linked to the global-mean temperature changes associated with two Intergovernmental Panel on Climate Change (IPCC) emissions scenarios (Leggett *et al.*, 1992), namely IS92a and IS92d. Both emissions scenarios include the changes in government policies aimed at mitigating climate

change which have been adopted as of December 1991. IS92a incorporates only those emissions controls internationally agreed upon and national policies enacted into law, such as the London Amendment to the Montreal Protocol. IS92d is a low, but plausible, emissions scenario. Figure 2.2 illustrates the estimated global-mean temperature changes associated with these two emissions scenarios (Wigley and Raper, 1992).

Although the CO_2 forcing scenarios of transient experiments are more realistic than in equilibrium integrations it is still not possible to ascribe actual calendar years to the years of the perturbed integration for a number of reasons. The initial concentration of 323 ppmv is equivalent to the observed CO_2 concentration of the early 1950s (or a CO_2-equivalent concentration of about 1940), so a literal translation of, for example, UKTR may assume that the control integration represents the climate of the mid-20th century and the climate change integration from about 1950 to 2025. However, such a literal translation must not be made for a number of reasons. First, the 1% per year compounded increase in CO_2 imposed by the model is not the observed forcing since 1950. If one assumes that the control integration represents the 'current' (i.e., 1990) climate and that the perturbed integration starts with a 1% increase in CO_2 concentration from 1990 through to 2065 then again a 1% increase in CO_2 does not correspond to the IPCC scenarios. Second, and more important, the perturbed

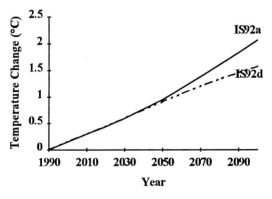

Figure 2.2 Global-mean temperature changes (°C) associated with emissions scenarios IS92a and IS92d. Results derived from MAGICC (Version 1.2) using a climate sensitivity of 2.5°C.

integrations of UKTR and GFDL assume that the climate is in equilibrium in year 1 (e.g., 1990), which is not the case since the real climate system in 1990 is responding to a long history of greenhouse gas (GHG) forcing. Hence, transient experiments have what is known as a 'cold start', i.e., for the first few decades of the perturbed integration global warming is strongly inhibited by the inertia of the coupled ocean-atmosphere system. This problem has been more fully investigated in Hasselmann *et al.* (1993).

It is possible, however, to assign approximate calendar years to the decades of the transient (and equilibrium) climate change experiments by using a simple climate model, e.g., MAGICC (Model for the Assessment of Greenhouse gas Induced Climate Change; Wigley and Raper, 1992; Wigley, 1994; Hulme *et al.*, in press). MAGICC provides internally consistent estimates of global-mean CO_2 concentration, temperature and sea level change between 1990 and 2100 resulting from scenarios of anthropogenic emissions of carbon dioxide, methane, nitrous oxide, the halocarbons and sulphur dioxide. MAGICC consists of an upwelling-diffusion climate model (Wigley and Raper, 1987), a sea level rise model (Raper *et al.*, 1993) and a number of gas cycle models integrated into one software package (as used in Houghton *et al.*, 1995). Emissions of the various GHGs are converted into radiative forcings using radiative transfer models following Shine *et al.* (1990). The resulting total global-mean radiative forcing drives the upwelling diffusion energy balance climate model. In this model there are four parameters which determine the rate at which heat is taken up by the ocean. The most important of these parameters is the climate sensitivity, i.e., the equilibrium warming

for a doubling of atmospheric CO_2, the IPCC best estimate of which is 2.5°C, with a range of 1.5°C to 4.5°C. By running MAGICC with the associated GHG emissions of IS92a and IS92d and for each of the three values of climate sensitivity, a range of uncertainty is generated about each global-mean temperature projection.

The best estimates of global-mean temperature change for IS92a and IS92d are illustrated in Figure 2.2, whereas Table 2.2 indicates possible dates when global-mean temperature changes of 0.68°C and 1.76°C may occur, given the uncertainty related to the climate sensitivity. For example, a global-mean temperature change of 1.76°C may occur as early as 2042 or as late as the beginning of the 22nd century under emissions scenario IS92a. The equivalent dates for IS92d are 2054 and later in the 22nd century. The mitigating effect of sulphate aerosols on global-mean temperature has been omitted since it was not considered as a forcing mechanism in any of these GCM climate change experiments (see Jonas *et al.*, 1995). Table 2.2 also indicates the actual CO_2 concentrations associated with the global-mean temperature change of each emissions scenario. This CO_2 concentration is also a best-estimate value. A particular scenario will be represented by a range of possible concentrations, depending on a number of assumptions, rather than a single value. Hence, as well as being distinguished by timing, the two IS92 scenarios are also characterised by different CO_2 concentrations. This is important for the crop-model runs.

2.3 Construction of regional scenarios

The absolute or percentage difference fields were interpolated from their original horizontal spatial resolutions to a resolution of 0.5° latitude

Table 2.2 The range of calendar years by which the global-mean warmings of 0.68°C and 1.76°C may be realised. Results are from MAGICC Version 1.2. Changes are expressed with respect to 1990.

Forcing scenario	Global-mean temperature change (°C)	Equivalent year based on climate sensitivity (°C)			UKTR years	GFDL years	CO_2 conc. (ppmv)
		1.5	2.5	4.5			
IS92a	0.68	2036	2023	2013	31-40	25-34	454
	1.76	after 2100	2064	2042	66-75	55-64	617
IS92d	1.76	after 2100	2099	2054	66-75	55-64	545

by 0.5° longitude using a Gaussian space-filtering routine (Santer, 1988). Changes in mean temperature (°C) and precipitation (%) are illustrated in Figures 2.3-2.6.

Figure 2.3(a)-(f) illustrates the changes in mean temperature (°C) for the winter season for UKLO, UKHI, UKTR decade 31-40, UKTR decade 66-75, GFDL decade 25-34 and GFDL decade 55-64 respectively. The two equilibrium model change fields, UKLO and UKHI, indicate the change in climate at some point in the future in response to an instantaneous doubling of CO_2. UKLO exhibits the largest temperature changes, with increases of greater than 7°C over central and eastern Europe and the Scandinavian countries. The increase in spatial horizontal resolution and improvements to some of the parameterisation procedures in UKHI result in smaller increases in mean temperature; over central Europe changes in excess of 5°C may occur, but in general they are less than this, especially in coastal areas. The two decades of the UKTR model exhibit similar patterns of change to each other, but with larger increases apparent in decade 66-75. Maximum increases of 7°C may occur in eastern Europe, whereas in western Europe increases of between 1°C and 4°C may be experienced. Although the two decades chosen in the GFDL model have identical global-mean temperature changes compared to the UKTR decades, they have different patterns of change, both when compared to UKTR and to each other. In the first model decade, years 25-34, the northern European and southern Scandinavian countries may experience an increase in temperature of the order of 1°C. In the second decade, years 55-64, these areas experience increases of between 2°C and 3°C. A similar pattern of change is repeated in spring, summer and autumn (not shown). In summary, the equilibrium experiments, UKLO and UKHI, exhibit the largest temperature changes, the two UKTR decades exhibit similar patterns of change, with the changes being more intense in the second decade, whereas the two decades of the GFDL experiment indicate different patterns of change. The GFDL temperature changes for the two decades generally tend to be less than those of UKTR; the same is true for changes in precipitation.

Changes in winter precipitation are illustrated in Figure 2.4(a)-(f). Precipitation changes indicated by UKLO and UKHI can be summarised as increases in northern Europe and decreases in the countries bordering the Mediterranean Sea. The two UKTR decades also indicate a similar pattern, but the changes are not as intense as in the equilibrium models. Areas of precipitation increase are apparent in central and northern Europe, with decreases in the southern Mediterranean area. As with temperature, the pattern of precipitation change is different between the two GFDL decades. In the earlier decade, a central band of precipitation increase is bordered by bands of precipitation decrease to the north and the south. In the latter decade, most of Europe experiences a precipitation increase of up to 10%; there are only small areas where precipitation decreases. In spring (Figure 2.5(a)-(f)), most models indicate decreases in precipitation in the Mediterranean area, which, in the case of UKHI, are in excess of 20%. Central and northern Europe generally exhibit increases in precipitation, the largest of which are indicated by UKLO and UKHI. The two UKTR decades indicate differing patterns of change in this season. It is interesting to note that in this season the earlier GFDL decade exhibits larger changes in precipitation than in the later model decade. In the southern European countries these changes are comparable to those of UKHI and the latter decade of the UKTR experiment. In summer (Figure 2.6(a)-(f)), UKHI and the two UKTR decades exhibit very similar patterns of precipitation change. Decreases in precipitation occur as far north as central UK, northern France and Germany. Increases in precipitation tend to occur further north in the Scandinavian countries. A band of precipitation decrease extends from central northern UK through France, Germany, Italy and Greece in the earlier decade of GFDL, which is flanked by two areas of precipitation increase extending over Spain in the west and Russia in the east. In autumn (not shown), both UKLO and UKHI exhibit similar patterns of change, but the precipitation decreases in southern Europe are more intense in the UKHI experiment. The pattern of change for the latter decade of the UKTR experiment is also very similar to that of UKHI, namely increases in precipitation in northern Europe and decreases

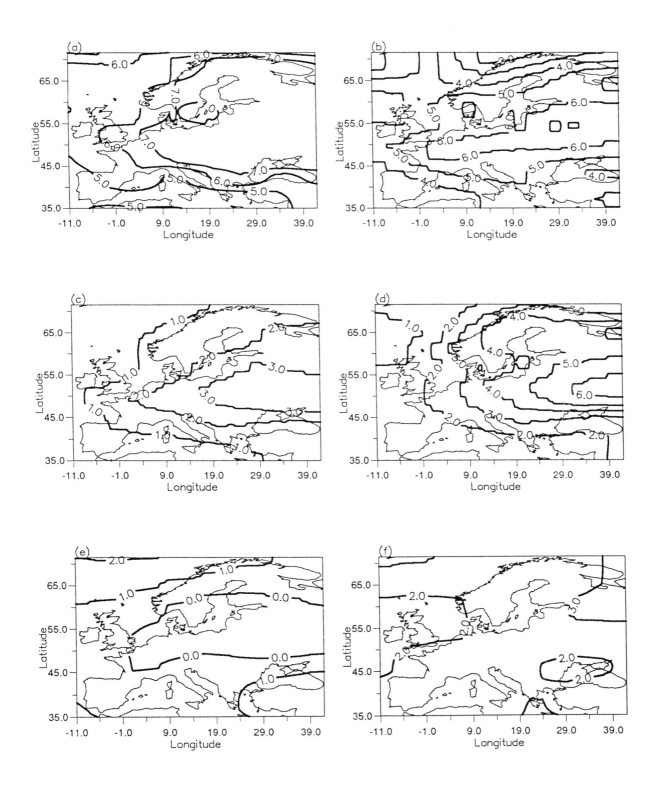

Figure 2.3 Winter (DJF) mean temperature change (°C): (a) UKLO, (b) UKHI, (c) UKTR decade 31-40, (d) UKTR decade 66-75, (e) GFDL decade 25-34, (f) GFDL decade 55-64.

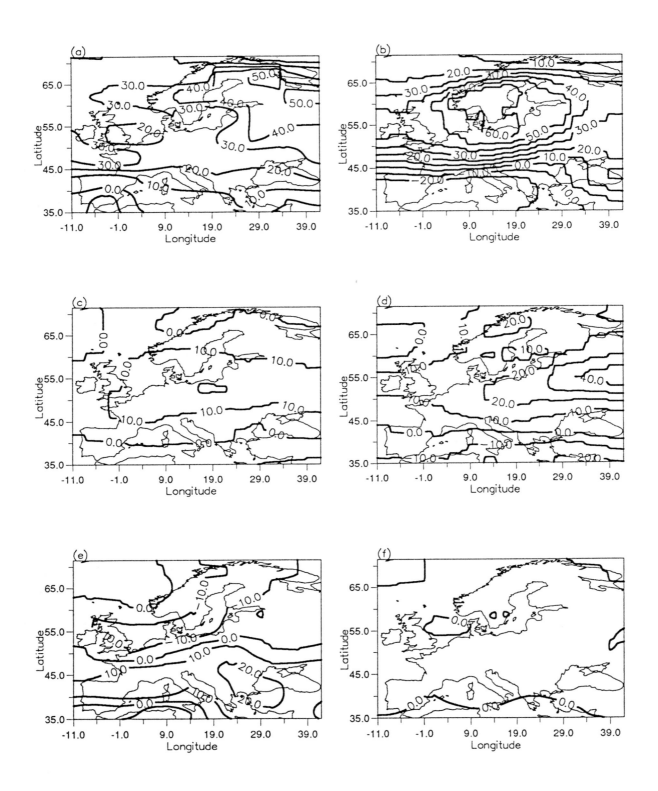

Figure 2.4   Winter (DJF) precipitation change (%): (a) UKLO, (b) UKHI, (c) UKTR decade 31-40, (d) UKTR decade 66-75, (e) GFDL decade 25-34, (f) GFDL decade 55-64.

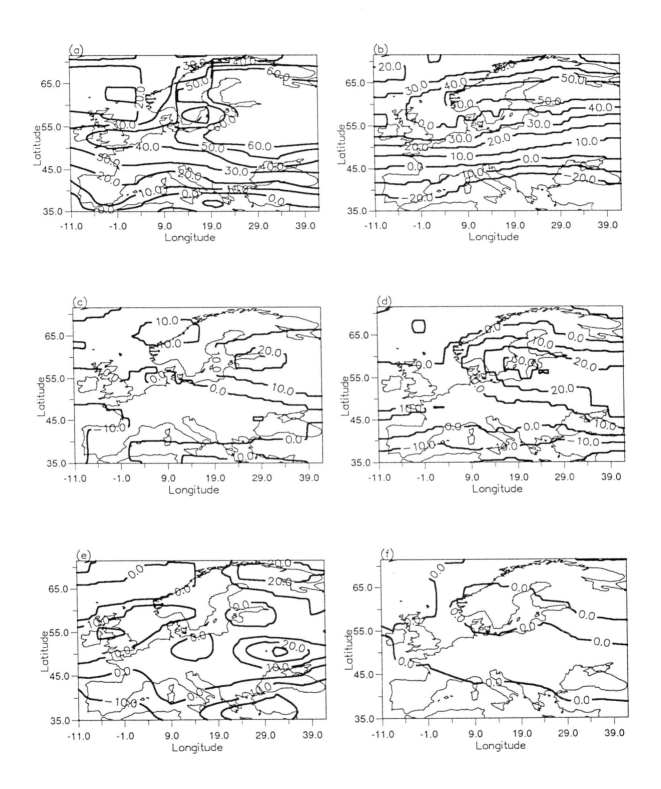

Figure 2.5 Spring (MAM) precipitation change (%): (a) UKLO, (b) UKHI, (c) UKTR decade 31-40, (d) UKTR decade 66-75, (e) GFDL decade 25-34, (f) GFDL decade 55-64.

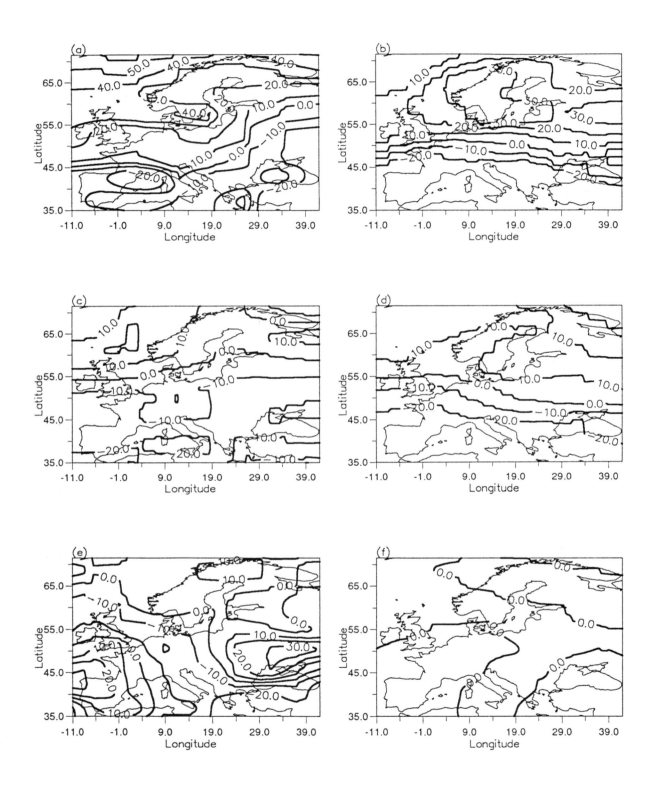

Figure 2.6   Summer (JJA) precipitation change (%): (a) UKLO, (b) UKHI, (c) UKTR decade 31-40, (d) UKTR decade 66-75, (e) GFDL decade 25-34, (f) GFDL decade 55-64.

in the south. The two decades from the GFDL transient experiment exhibit different patterns, with the changes in the earlier decade again being greater than those of the latter decade.

2.3.1 Intermodel comparison of the patterns of climate change

In order to quantify the intermodel differences and similarities described above, the spatial pattern correlation coefficients between pairs of change fields were calculated. First, the change fields were standardised with respect to their climate sensitivity in the case of the equilibrium models (cf. Table 2.1), and the global-mean temperature change of the appropriate decade for the transient models (cf. Table 2.2). The Pearson correlation coefficients were then calculated. Seasonal pattern correlation coefficients for mean temperature change are shown in Table 2.3 and for precipitation change in Table 2.4.

In general, Table 2.3 indicates that the spatial pattern correlation coefficients tend to be higher amongst the UK Met. Office models than between the two decades of the GFDL experiment. The two decades of the UKTR

Table 2.3 Intermodel spatial pattern correlation coefficients: mean temperature change.

(a) Winter

DJF	UKLO	UKHI	UKTR 31-40	UKTR 66-75	GFDL 25-34	GFDL 55-64
UKLO	1.000					
UKHI	0.534	1.000				
UKTR 31-40	0.777	0.676	1.000			
UKTR 66-75	0.895	0.525	0.882	1.000		
GFDL 25-34	-0.523	-0.650	-0.677	-0.642	1.000	
GFDL 55-64	0.427	0.234	0.198	0.365	-0.120	1.000

(b) Spring

MAM	UKLO	UKHI	UKTR 31-40	UKTR 66-75	GFDL 25-34	GFDL 55-64
UKLO	1.000					
UKHI	0.419	1.000				
UKTR 31-40	0.831	0.187	1.000			
UKTR 66-75	0.881	0.539	0.887	1.000		
GFDL 25-34	0.069	0.332	0.035	0.171	1.000	
GFDL 55-64	-0.121	0.437	-0.284	-0.077	0.491	1.000

(c) Summer

JJA	UKLO	UKHI	UKTR 31-40	UKTR 66-75	GFDL 25-34	GFDL 55-64
UKLO	1.000					
UKHI	0.296	1.000				
UKTR 31-40	0.430	-0.115	1.000			
UKTR 66-75	0.550	0.020	0.849	1.000		
GFDL 25-34	0.138	0.167	0.346	0.323	1.000	
GFDL 55-64	0.277	0.036	0.267	0.419	0.233	1.000

(d) Autumn

SON	UKLO	UKHI	UKTR 31-40	UKTR 66-75	GFDL 25-34	GFDL 55-64
UKLO	1.000					
UKHI	-0.013	1.000				
UKTR 31-40	0.540	0.014	1.000			
UKTR 66-75	0.634	0.131	0.943	1.000		
GFDL 25-34	0.191	0.512	0.217	0.351	1.000	
GFDL 55-64	0.166	-0.391	0.424	0.324	-0.016	1.000

model appear to be highly correlated in all seasons, indicating that there is little difference in the pattern of mean temperature change between these two decades (see also Figure 2.7). These high correlations suggest that in this experiment the greenhouse gas signal may be evident as early as decade 31-40. Both decades of the UKTR experiment also appear more highly correlated with the UKLO experiment than with UKHI. There does not appear to be any consistent pattern between the GFDL decades themselves, or amongst these model decades and any of the UK Met. Office experiments. The pattern of mean temperature change is most similar between the two GFDL decades in spring (see also Figure 2.8). In the case of precipitation change, Table 2.4 indicates broadly similar results although the correlation coefficients are not as high as those of mean temperature change. The two UKTR decades are again well correlated except in the spring (see also Figure 2.9). The UKLO experiment

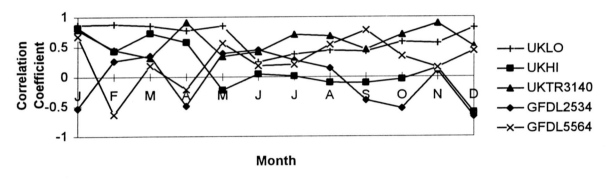

Figure 2.7   Spatial pattern correlations coefficients between UKTR decade 66-75 and the five other model experiments: mean temperature change.

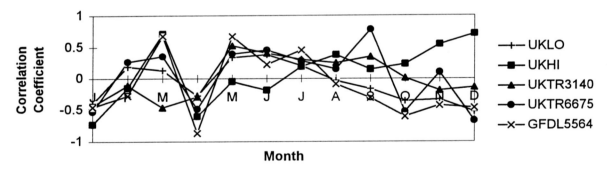

Figure 2.8   Spatial pattern correlations coefficients between GFDL decade 25-34 and the five other model experiments: mean temperature change.

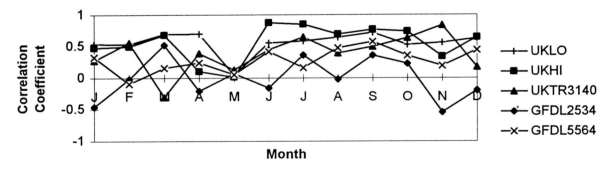

Figure 2.9   Spatial pattern correlations coefficients between UKTR decade 66-75 and the five other model experiments: precipitation change.

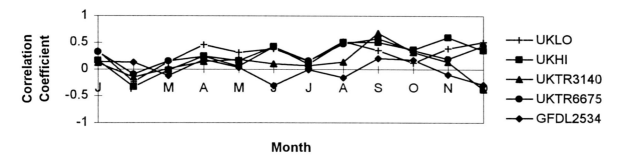

Figure 2.10 Spatial pattern correlations coefficients between GFDL decade 55-64 and the five other model experiments: precipitation change.

Table 2.4 Intermodel spatial pattern correlation coefficients: precipitation change

(a) Winter

DJF	UKLO	UKHI	UKTR 31-40	UKTR 66-75	GFDL 25-34	GFDL 55-64
UKLO	1.000					
UKHI	0.756	1.000				
UKTR 31-40	0.574	0.709	1.000			
UKTR 66-75	0.731	0.665	0.737	1.000		
GFDL 25-34	-0.338	-0.466	-0.244	-0.400	1.000	
GFDL 55-64	0.404	0.226	0.233	0.358	0.081	1.000

(b) Spring

MAM	UKLO	UKHI	UKTR 31-40	UKTR 66-75	GFDL 25-34	GFDL 55-64
UKLO	1.000					
UKHI	0.649	1.000				
UKTR 31-40	0.448	0.451	1.000			
UKTR 66-75	0.718	0.448	0.170	1.000		
GFDL 25-34	0.583	0.614	0.020	0.368	1.000	
GFDL 55-64	0.409	0.230	-0.016	0.234	0.427	1.000

(c) Summer

JJA	UKLO	UKHI	UKTR 31-40	UKTR 66-75	GFDL 25-34	GFDL 55-64
UKLO	1.000					
UKHI	0.658	1.000				
UKTR 31-40	0.760	0.650	1.000			
UKTR 66-75	0.701	0.933	0.700	1.000		
GFDL 25-34	0.018	0.259	-0.139	0.281	1.000	
GFDL 55-64	0.336	0.263	0.203	0.279	-0.285	1.000

(d) Autumn

SON	UKLO	UKHI	UKTR 31-40	UKTR 66-75	GFDL 25-34	GFDL 55-64
UKLO	1.000					
UKHI	0.835	1.000				
UKTR 31-40	0.672	0.711	1.000			
UKTR 66-75	0.817	0.764	0.689	1.000		
GFDL 25-34	0.031	0.131	0.152	0.055	1.000	
GFDL 55-64	0.489	0.645	0.571	0.535	0.275	1.000

correlates well with both UKHI and the last decade of the UKTR experiment. Correlations amongst the equilibrium models and the earlier decade of UKTR are also relatively high, but generally lower than those with the latter decade of this experiment. There is little consistency in the pattern of precipitation change between the two GFDL decades except in spring, when the correlation coefficient is 0.43 (see also Figure 2.10). The pattern of precipitation change in the earlier decade of the GFDL experiment is most consistent with the other five experiments in spring. The latter decade of this experiment is most consistent with the pattern of change of the UK Met. Office models in the autumn.

2.3.2   Comparison of European and global climate sensitivities

In order to compare European- and global-mean temperature changes the weighted European-average mean temperature changes were calculated and compared to the global-mean temperature change of each of the scenarios. Weighting was based on the cosine of each latitude band and was introduced to take into account the latitudinally-varying grid box areas. In all scenarios the European-mean temperature change is greater than or equal to that of the global-mean (Table 2.5). One reason for this is that the European window used (11°W - 43°E, 35°N - 71.5°N) has a larger land:ocean ratio than that of the globe and, in general, land areas warm more rapidly than ocean areas.

2.4   Construction of site-specific scenarios

2.4.1   Scenarios with downscaling

GCMs have a coarse spatial resolution which leads to approximations in the spatial representation of meteorological variables and, hence, the masking of local and regional weather phenomena. In order to produce scenarios of climate change at the site scale, it is necessary to 'downscale' the coarse resolution data to the scales required in regional impacts work. This procedure involves the development of relationships between the coarse- and local-scale data for the climate variables concerned. There are a number of methodologies currently in use, including circulation patterns (e.g., Bardossy and Caspary, 1991; Matyasovszky *et al.*, 1993; Jones and Conway, 1995) and regression techniques (e.g., Kim *et al.*, 1984; Wigley *et al.*, 1990; Karl *et al.*, 1990; Von Storch *et al.*, 1993). Both methods use existing instrumental data to determine the relationships between large-scale and local climate. Regression techniques develop statistical relationships between local station data and grid-box scale, area average values of say, temperature and precipitation and other meteorological variables. The circulation pattern approach classifies atmospheric circulation according to type and then determines links between the pattern and climate variable, for example, precipitation.

Table 2.5   Comparison of European- and global-mean temperature change (°C)

Scenario	Mean temperature change (°C)	
	European	Global
UKLO	5.3	5.2
UKHI	4.3	3.5
UKTR, decade 31-40	1.3	0.7
UKTR, decade 66-75	2.5	1.8
GFDL, decade 25-34	0.7	0.7
GFDL, decade 55-64	1.9	1.8

Work by Hulme *et al.* (1993) has shown, however, that there are a number of reservations to be considered when using circulation patterns as part of climate change studies. An assessment was made of the ability of the control simulations of two GCM experiments (UKHI and the Max Planck Institute for Meteorology large-scale geostrophic experiment [ECHAM; Cubasch *et al.*, 1992]) to produce realistic 'real world' weather. Their results illustrated that not only do these two GCMs have problems simulating the correct frequencies of weather types (for example, both GCMs are too cyclonic in winter), but they also fail to simulate some of the observed relationships between particular circulation patterns (in this case the Lamb weather types [Lamb, 1972]) and temperature and precipitation. This is especially the case in summer when both models fail to reproduce any of the observed relationships correctly. In this sense, these two GCMs can be shown to possess a different internal consistency to that of the real world. Another point to be considered is that the relationships between circulation patterns and, for example, temperature and precipitation, in one area of Europe may not be applicable in another location. As a result of these concerns it was decided to use the regression approach to downscaling.

A pilot study was undertaken at two sites in Europe (Rothamsted, UK and Sevilla, Spain) using the regression relationship approach to downscaling. Regression relationships were calculated between local station data (mean temperature and precipitation) and grid-box scale data (monthly anomalies of mean sea level pressure (MSLP), the north-south and east-west pressure gradients, temperature and precipitation). The regression relationships were based on anomalies from the long-term mean, rather than actual data; this facilitated the use of the GCM change fields in the equations. The regression models were used to calculate site-specific changes in temperature and precipitation, using the GCM-derived grid-box information, if the regression models explained a high proportion of the variance in the observed data and provided that the scenario changes in these variables were within the observed range.

The first step in this approach was to develop observed areal averages of mean temperature and precipitation for both Rothamsted and Sevilla. Areal averages were calculated to correspond to the grid box area of the UKHI and UKTR models.

2.4.1.1 *Rothamsted*

Figure 2.11 illustrates the location of the sites used to calculate the observed areal means. Five sites, including Rothamsted, were used, all approximately equally distributed throughout the grid box. For each site the anomalies from the 1961-90 mean were calculated for mean temperature and precipitation for each month. The site anomalies were then simply averaged to produce an areally-averaged value. No weighting of the sites was necessary because of their approximate even distribution throughout the grid and the likely homogeneity of temperature and precipitation anomalies in this particular area. Anomalies for the three pressure variables were also calculated for this grid box.

Once the anomalies had been calculated, the data were split into two time periods, 1961-83 and 1984-90. The first period was used to calibrate the regression equations, whilst the latter period was used to verify their performance. Regression analyses were then

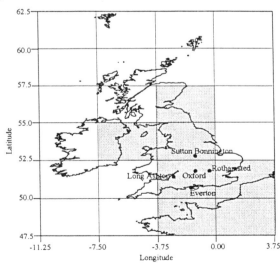

Figure 2.11 Location of the sites used to calculate observed areal means for the Rothamsted grid box. The shaded area illustrates UKTR land grid boxes. Unshaded cells represent ocean area.

undertaken for each month using Rothamsted mean temperature and precipitation anomalies as predictands and the regionally-averaged anomalies of temperature, precipitation, MSLP, north-south and east-west pressure gradients as predictors. The performance of the regression models is illustrated in Table 2.6. As would be expected, the models generally perform better for temperature than for precipitation, especially in spring and summer. The correlations shown in Table 2.6(b) may be misleadingly high because of the small number of data points available for this verification exercise.

The next step in this procedure was the calculation of the changes in mean temperature and precipitation at this site corresponding to UKHI and to the two decades of the UKTR experiment. The UKLO and GFDL GCM data were not downscaled because the resolution of these models was less than that of UKHI and UKTR. Downscaling for UKLO and GFDL would have entailed calculation of observed areal means at the appropriate coarser resolution and then recalculation of the regression models. Since the downscaling exercise was undertaken as a pilot study, and also because of problems of obtaining sufficient observed data to calculate areal means, this process was not undertaken.

The grid box changes in mean temperature, precipitation, MSLP and the north-south and east-west pressure gradients were extracted for the UKHI experiment and for both decades of the UKTR experiment. On comparison of these data with the anomaly ranges used to calculate the regression models and derived from the observed data, it was apparent that for UKHI most of the mean temperature changes were

outside the range used to calculate the regression equations. For the two decades of the UKTR experiment this was the case on only four occasions. Changes in precipitation were always within the observed anomaly range, whilst there was only one occasion when one of the pressure variables was outside the observed range. Thus, in the case of temperature, more confidence can be placed in the downscaled results from the two UKTR experiments than in those for the UKHI experiment. However, given that there is little difference between the site and areal changes in mean temperature at this location and that the regression models do explain most of the variance in the data at this site (the most important variable in the regression models is areal temperature), the fact that most of the changes in temperature for UKHI are outside the anomaly range is not necessarily important. Table 2.7 illustrates the grid box changes in temperature and precipitation for this site and also the downscaled values. It is apparent that there are no large deviations in site mean temperature compared to the UKHI grid box values.

2.4.1.2 *Sevilla*

As for Rothamsted, the first step in the regression exercise was to derive areal anomalies of mean temperature and precipitation from the observed station data. Figure 2.12 illustrates the location of the sites used in this process; station 7 corresponds to Sevilla. For temperature, the procedure involved the calculation of the monthly anomalies from the 1961-90 means for each station in the grid box. These anomalies were then averaged to produce areal values. For precipitation the procedure was

Table 2.6   Performance of the regression models

(a) Calibration of regression models for Rothamsted based on 1961-83 observed data: Variance explained (%).

	Jan	Feb	Mar	Apr	May	Jun	Jul	Aug	Sep	Oct	Nov	Dec
Temp	99.2	99.1	98.6	98.0	97.3	98.3	98.5	98.5	96.8	99.1	97.9	99.0
Precip	85.9	90.3	88.2	73.9	76.4	81.9	79.7	80.9	90.3	90.1	93.5	93.7

(b) Verification of regression models for Rothamsted using 1984-90 data: Correlation coefficients between observed data and those predicted by the regression models.

	Jan	Feb	Mar	Apr	May	Jun	Jul	Aug	Sep	Oct	Nov	Dec
Temp	0.99	0.99	0.99	0.99	0.99	0.99	0.99	0.98	0.98	0.94	0.99	0.99
Precip	0.96	0.96	0.90	0.99	0.86	0.95	0.92	0.96	0.98	0.99	0.99	0.99

Table 2.7 Grid box and downscaled mean temperature changes and precipitation anomalies for the Rothamsted site. Precipitation anomalies indicate relative changes ((perturbed/control)-1).

(a) Mean temperature (°C)

	UKHI		UKTR, decade 31-40		UKTR, decade 66-75	
	Downscaled	**Grid box**	**Downscaled**	**Grid box**	**Downscaled**	**Grid box**
January	8.2	8.1	0.4	0.4	3.5	3.4
February	7.0	6.7	7.2	7.0	1.0	1.0
March	5.6	5.3	0.7	0.8	2.5	2.4
April	3.6	3.8	0.7	0.8	0.5	0.5
May	4.8	4.1	0.8	0.6	1.9	1.6
June	3.3	2.9	1.6	1.2	1.6	1.4
July	3.7	3.5	0.9	0.8	2.3	2.2
August	5.1	4.8	1.9	1.8	3.7	3.6
September	4.6	4.4	1.9	1.9	3.8	3.7
October	4.1	4.0	0.7	0.7	1.5	1.5
November	3.0	2.9	1.5	1.6	2.0	2.0
December	4.6	4.2	-1.0	-1.0	2.3	2.2

(b) Precipitation

	UKHI		UKTR, decade 31-40		UKTR, decade 66-75	
	Downscaled	**Grid box**	**Downscaled**	**Grid box**	**Downscaled**	**Grid box**
January	0.29	0.63	-0.01	-0.07	-0.07	0.13
February	0.42	0.49	0.45	0.51	0.25	0.30
March	0.42	0.46	-0.13	-0.12	0.08	0.03
April	0.21	0.21	-0.12	-0.12	-0.12	-0.14
May	-0.42	-0.09	0.02	0.01	-0.07	0.09
June	-0.06	0.04	-0.20	-0.10	-0.02	0.04
July	-0.02	-0.03	-0.32	-0.30	-0.10	-0.11
August	-0.07	0.39	-0.34	-0.16	-0.59	-0.33
September	0.03	0.08	-0.31	-0.25	-0.31	-0.25
October	0.14	0.22	0.09	0.14	-0.06	0.12
November	-0.01	0.00	0.40	0.33	0.45	0.35
December	0.46	0.40	0.00	-0.02	0.13	0.12

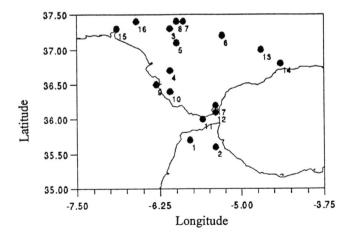

more complicated because of the distribution pattern of the sites in the grid box, the fact that part of the area is ocean and also because of the large amount of missing data. To overcome these problems a Thiessen fitting procedure was used. This method produces grid-box estimates of precipitation and fills in missing values by considering precipitation amounts of neighbouring sites within a specified search radius. Once the grid-box precipitation values had been calculated the anomalies from the 1961-90 means were determined.

Figure 2.12 Location of the sites used to calculate observed areal means for the Sevilla grid box. Number 7 corresponds to Sevilla.

Calibration and verification of the regression equations were carried out using data from 1961-90 and 1951-60 respectively. Table 2.8(a) illustrates the performance of the regression models in relating Sevilla mean temperature and precipitation to the grid box variables. It is apparent that the regression models perform better for temperature than for precipitation, with modelling of precipitation being particularly poor in July. This result is also reflected in the verification results shown in Table 2.8(b). However, as precipitation is small in July, the poor performance of the model in this month is not necessarily important; more worrying is the negative correlation obtained in October. Further examination of the 1951-60 observed precipitation data for this month indicates that there is a high positive anomaly which the regression model completely fails to pick up. Furthermore, for six of the ten years, the model predicts anomalies of the opposite sign compared to the actual observed data. This indicates that although the regression model explains 67.4% of the 1961-90 observed data in this month, the majority of the 1951-60 data falls outside the range explained by the models. Although there were reservations about using a number of these regression models in the downscaling procedure because of their poor performance, the process was completed in order to produce scenarios of climate change for Sevilla.

The grid box changes in mean temperature, precipitation, MSLP and the north-south and east-west pressure gradients were then extracted for UKHI and the two decades of UKTR. On comparison of these data with the anomaly ranges used in the calculation of the regression models, it was apparent that all the UKHI grid-box changes in mean temperature were outside this range. For each decade of the UKTR experiment about half of the temperature values were outside the observed anomaly range. For the other predictors in the regression equations the grid-box changes were within the observed anomaly ranges. Hence, there is less confidence in the downscaled results at this site, both for mean temperature and precipitation. In the case of mean temperature this is because of a combination of the grid-box changes being outside the anomaly ranges and the regression models explaining less of the variance in the observed data compared to the Rothamsted site. In the case of precipitation, the grid-box changes are within the observed anomaly ranges, but the regression models do not perform as well in explaining the variance in the observed data. As the Sevilla site is on the northern edge of the area defining the grid-box used, improvements in the regression models may be possible by relating site precipitation changes to the changes in areal precipitation of the adjacent grid box and, hence, relating precipitation at Sevilla to a more continental area, rather than to the coastal region, as at present. Unfortunately, however, the necessary observed data were not received in time to undertake this work and to ascertain whether this was in fact the case. Table 2.9 indicates the grid box and downscaled changes in mean temperature and precipitation for Sevilla. In the case of mean temperature, site changes are greater than the corresponding areal values in all months except April. Changes in precipitation are not so consistent. In some cases decreases in areal precipitation become increases

Table 2.8   Performance of the regression models.

(a)   Calibration of regression models for Sevilla based on 1961-90 observed data: Variance explained (%).

	Jan	Feb	Mar	Apr	May	Jun	Jul	Aug	Sep	Oct	Nov	Dec
Temp	93.8	91.3	84.5	81.9	84.9	90.3	85.4	77.9	94.0	87.4	95.6	97.5
Precip	82.3	84.6	65.8	81.7	77.3	68.2	20.0	64.8	54.4	67.4	79.4	86.5

(b)   Verification of the regression models for Sevilla using 1951-60 observed data: Correlation coefficients between observed data and those predicted by the regression models.

	Jan	Feb	Mar	Apr	May	Jun	Jul	Aug	Sep	Oct	Nov	Dec
Temp	0.95	0.99	0.82	0.94	0.87	0.87	0.85	0.93	0.97	0.73	0.96	0.98
Precip	0.91	0.96	0.92	0.97	0.67	0.64	0.0	0.83	0.72	-0.07	0.64	0.89

Table 2.9 Grid box and downscaled mean temperature changes and precipitation anomalies for the Sevilla site. Precipitation anomalies indicate relative changes ((perturbed/control)-1).

(a) Mean temperature (°C)

	UKHI		UKTR, decade 31-40		UKTR, decade 66-75	
	Downscaled	Grid box	Downscaled	Grid box	Downscaled	Grid box
January	5.1	4.4	2.3	1.8	2.8	2.3
February	6.8	6.0	2.5	2.2	4.5	3.9
March	7.1	6.2	0.6	0.6	2.7	2.4
April	4.8	5.4	1.2	1.4	1.3	1.5
May	5.5	5.3	1.1	0.9	2.6	2.6
June	7.5	7.2	4.0	3.9	4.6	4.4
July	7.8	6.5	3.5	3.1	5.8	4.9
August	6.8	6.4	2.4	2.1	5.7	5.3
September	7.0	6.6	2.4	2.2	6.9	6.5
October	7.9	7.2	2.8	2.6	5.0	4.5
November	7.2	5.5	2.8	2.1	4.3	3.2
December	7.6	5.7	0.5	0.3	2.4	1.8

(b) Precipitation

	UKHI		UKTR, decade 31-40		UKTR, decade 66-75	
	Downscaled	Grid box	Downscaled	Grid box	Downscaled	Grid box
January	-0.43	-0.81	-0.09	-0.11	-0.19	-0.33
February	-0.12	-0.83	-0.04	-0.30	0.29	-0.02
March	0.19	-0.85	-0.10	-0.29	0.07	-0.31
April	-0.05	-0.09	0.34	0.59	-0.07	-0.02
May	-0.70	-0.52	1.17	1.21	-0.84	-0.78
June	-2.13	-0.66	-1.46	-0.92	-1.27	-0.42
July	2.84	-0.58	0.63	-0.75	2.29	-1.00
August	-0.47	-0.81	-2.18	-0.20	-0.29	-0.42
September	0.50	-0.62	0.29	-0.28	0.53	-0.69
October	0.60	-0.88	0.24	-0.28	0.60	-0.12
November	0.13	-0.66	0.13	-0.15	-0.07	-0.67
December	-0.32	-0.63	-0.12	-0.17	-0.22	-0.34

when downscaled to the site, but whether or not this occurs seems to be dependent on the magnitude of the areal decrease.

2.4.2 Scenarios without downscaling

For those sites not included in the downscaling pilot study, scenarios of climate change were constructed using the appropriate GCM grid-box changes in conjunction with a stochastic weather generator. Scenarios for the following sites were required: Jokioinen (Finland), Oxford (UK), Wageningen (The Netherlands), Mannheim (Germany), München (Germany), Debrecen (Hungary), Györ (Hungary), Bologna (Italy), Montpellier (France), Athens (Greece) and Bonn (Germany). These non-downscaled scenarios represent an improvement on previous site-specific studies, for example those as produced for the previous project investigating the impacts of climate change on the agricultural and horticultural potential of Europe (Kenny *et al.*, 1993).

2.4.3 Production of daily climate change data

In order for the climate change scenarios to be of use in site-specific crop-growth simulation models, the information produced must be at the daily timescale. To do this for both the downscaled and simple scenarios of climate change use of a stochastic weather generator was necessary. The stochastic weather generator used in this project (LARS-WG) was based on that described in Racsko *et al.* (1991). Modifications were made to LARS-WG in order to match the weather generator output to the meteorological input required by crop simulation models.

2.4.3.1   *Description of LARS-WG*

LARS-WG is based on distributions of the length of continuous sequences, or series, of wet and dry days. Long dry series are simulated better using this approach (Racsko *et al.*, 1991) compared to the Markov chain method (e.g., Richardson, 1981) of simulating precipitation occurrence. A long dry series significantly affects crop growth and can dramatically decrease yields. Hence, in order to be able to assess agricultural risk, it is important that such events are modelled well. The distribution of other weather variables, in this case maximum and minimum temperature and solar radiation, is based on the current status of the wet or dry series. Mixed exponential distributions were used to model dry and wet series so that LARS - WG would be applicable to a wide range of European locations. Daily minimum and maximum temperature and radiation were considered as stochastic processes with daily means and standard deviations conditioned on the wet and dry series. The techniques used to

analyse the processes are very similar to those presented in Richardson (1981). The seasonal cycle of means and standard deviations was removed from the observed record and the residuals approximated by a normal distribution. These residuals were used to analyse a time correlation within each variable. Fourier series were used to interpolate seasonal means and standard deviations.

2.4.3.2   *Calibration of LARS-WG*

The first step in the production of daily weather data using a stochastic weather generator is the calibration of the generator itself. In this process observed daily data are used to calculate the site-specific parameters of the generator; these parameters are then used to generate synthetic data. At least twenty years of observed daily data must be used in order to determine robust parameters. Various statistics of the observed and generated data are compared in order to ensure that the generator performs well. Figures 2.13-2.18 illustrate some statistics for five European sites. It is apparent that LARS-WG generally performs well in simulating the magnitude and seasonal cycle of the main parameters and consequently it was used at all the European sites without any modifications.

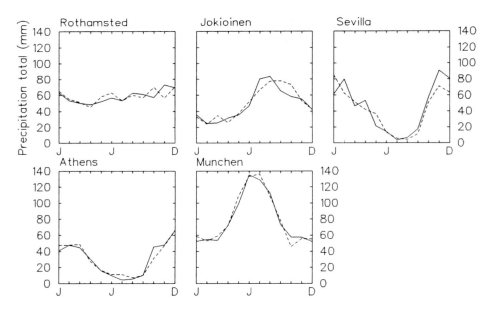

Figure 2.13   Comparison of observed (solid line) and generated (dashed line) monthly mean precipitation (total, mm).

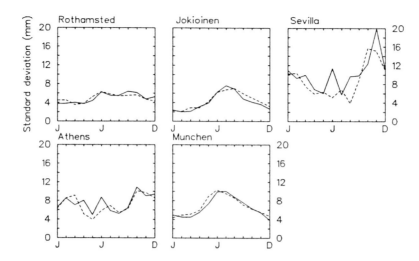

Figure 2.14 Comparison of observed (solid line) and generated (dashed line) precipitation standard deviations (mm).

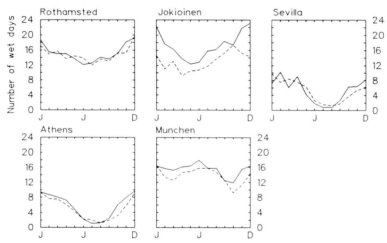

Figure 2.15 Comparison of observed (solid line) and generated (dashed line) mean number of wet days (days).

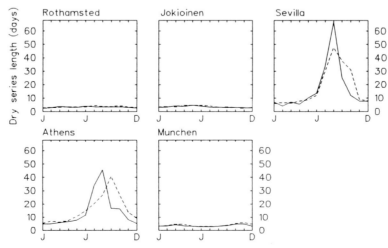

Figure 2.16 Comparison of observed (solid line) and generated (dashed line) mean dry series length (days).

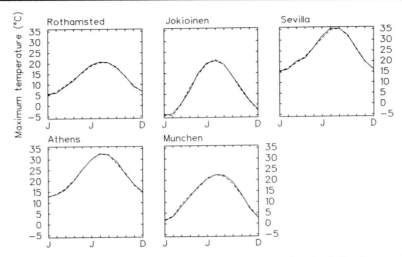

Figure 2.17 Comparison of observed (solid line) and generated (dashed line) mean daily maximum temperature (°C)

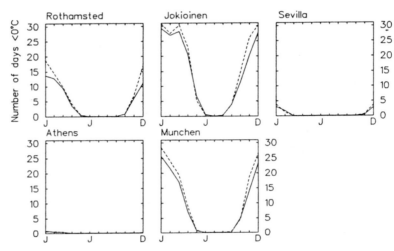

Figure 2.18   Comparison of observed (solid line) and generated (dashed line) mean number of days with Tmin < 0°C

2.4.3.3   *Adjustment of LARS-WG parameters for climate change scenarios*

The parameters of LARS-WG were adjusted according to the GCM-derived changes in temperature and precipitation. However, information about changes in temperature and precipitation means is not enough to define precisely the changes in all of the LARS-WG parameters, especially changes in daily temperature variability and the duration of wet and dry spells. Additional information is required. Possible changes in temperature variability and in the duration of wet and dry spells were derived from analyses of daily grid box data, where available, i.e., from UKHI and the last decade of the UKTR experiment. In these cases two types of scenario were constructed, with and without changes in temperature variability and wet and dry spell length, in order to determine the impact of changing variability on crop development and yield.

2.4.4   Description of site-specific scenarios

Scenarios of climate change were constructed for all the sites listed in Section 2.4.2 but, because of space limitations, results are presented for only the two downscaled sites, Rothamsted and Sevilla, and for two sites without downscaling. Changes in variability were included in those scenarios without downscaling by analysing daily data from the UKHI and UKTR GCM experiments to determine changes in, for example, precipitation intensity and dry spell length. A 'hybrid' scenario was also produced for the downscaled scenarios which included changes in variability. However, this is inconsistent as the monthly grid-box changes in temperature and precipitation were downscaled to the individual sites, whilst the variability changes (determined from daily data) were not. All the following tables are based on 30 years of daily data generated by LARS-WG.

2.4.4.1 *Sites including downscaling*

Table 2.10 illustrates the effect of downscaling on mean monthly precipitation totals at Rothamsted. If downscaling is not carried out, then all scenarios, except UKTR years 31-40, indicate an increase in precipitation amount at this site. Downscaling results in a larger decrease in precipitation in the earlier decade of the UKTR experiment and also in a decrease in precipitation for the latter decade of this experiment. The shaded cells in Table 2.10 indicate where the downscaled results are opposite to those without downscaling when compared with the 'observed' precipitation generated by LARS-WG (indicated in the column entitled 'Base'). These values were generated using the weather generator parameters calculated from the observed daily data.

Mean minimum temperature for each climate change scenario is illustrated in Table 2.11 for Rothamsted. Downscaling generally appears to result in higher mean minimum temperatures. All scenarios indicate warming in all months with only one exception; the early decade of the UKTR experiment exhibits a temperature decrease in December in both the downscaled and non-downscaled scenarios. This scenario also exhibits an anomalously high warming in February and this is reflected in the mean values for this month being about three times warmer than those of the succeeding March.

Table 2.12 indicates similar results for precipitation at the Sevilla site to those at Rothamsted. Of the scenarios without downscaling only the scenarios based on information from UKLO and GFDL years 25-34 indicate an increase in precipitation amount at this site. For both of these scenarios the increase in precipitation amount generally occurs in the autumn and winter months. Including downscaling actually results in an increase in precipitation amount over the generated base values for the two decades of the UKTR experiment. Although the downscaled UKHI scenario precipitation amounts are less than those of the generated base, they are almost three times greater than for the same scenario

Table 2.10 Mean monthly precipitation totals (mm) at Rothamsted with and without downscaling. Shaded cells indicate where downscaling has resulted in a change of the opposite sign compared to the corresponding scenario without downscaling. Changes in variability not included.

| | Without downscaling | | | | | | | With downscaling | | |
	Base	UKLO	UKHI	UKTR 31-40	UKTR 66-75	GFDL 25-34	GFDL 55-64	UKHI	UKTR 31-40	UKTR 66-75
Jan	64.8	98.8	105.6	59.9	72.7	67.0	57.9	83.4	64.3	60.3
Feb	55.1	74.1	82.1	83.3	71.3	55.1	56.6	78.0	79.6	68.9
Mar	50.9	67.3	74.2	44.9	52.3	56.2	42.9	72.4	44.3	55.1
Apr	44.9	61.5	54.3	39.7	38.6	56.3	54.6	54.3	39.7	39.5
May	57.9	75.3	52.7	58.7	62.9	58.9	88.4	33.5	58.9	53.9
Jun	62.9	55.3	65.5	56.6	65.5	80.6	86.6	59.5	50.6	61.9
Jul	53.5	72.0	51.9	37.7	47.6	61.1	45.8	52.3	36.7	48.1
Aug	60.0	78.4	83.5	50.5	40.4	52.8	31.0	55.7	39.7	24.5
Sep	56.9	75.1	61.2	42.6	43.0	71.5	51.4	58.7	39.1	39.5
Oct	69.6	85.0	85.0	79.3	77.6	76.3	65.4	79.5	75.8	73.7
Nov	56.4	73.0	56.6	74.7	76.2	57.8	54.9	56.0	79.0	81.5
Dec	69.9	96.1	98.1	68.7	78.4	67.8	83.8	102.1	69.9	79.2

without downscaling. Part of the increase in precipitation amount as a result of downscaling is directly attributable to the high July precipitation amounts predicted by the regression model. It is worth noting that the July regression model explained only 20% of the variance in the observed data, and hence these results should be treated with caution. If precipitation is assumed to be zero in this month, precipitation totals for the two decades of the UKTR experiment are still higher than when downscaling is not included.

Mean maximum temperatures for each scenario are presented in Table 2.13 for Sevilla. Downscaling appears to generally increase mean maximum temperatures at this site compared to the grid-box changes.

Table 2.11   Mean minimum temperature (°C) at Rothamsted with and without downscaling. Changes in variability not included.

		Without downscaling						With downscaling		
	Base	UKLO	UKHI	UKTR 31-40	UKTR 66-75	GFDL 25-34	GFDL 55-64	UKHI	UKTR 31-40	UKTR 66-75
Jan	-1.2	4.2	6.9	-0.8	2.2	-0.5	1.0	7.0	-0.8	2.3
Feb	-0.4	4.8	6.3	6.6	0.6	0.0	1.0	6.6	6.8	0.6
Mar	1.3	6.7	6.6	2.1	3.7	1.6	2.7	6.9	2.0	3.8
Apr	3.1	8.7	6.9	3.9	3.6	4.3	4.9	6.7	3.8	3.6
May	6.3	11.9	10.4	6.9	7.9	6.6	7.8	11.1	7.1	8.2
Jun	9.0	14.6	11.9	10.2	10.4	9.4	10.0	12.3	10.6	10.6
Jul	10.5	16.1	14.0	11.3	12.7	10.9	12.7	14.2	11.4	12.8
Aug	11.1	16.6	15.9	12.9	14.7	12.2	13.3	16.2	13.0	14.8
Sep	9.3	14.7	13.7	11.2	13.0	9.3	11.5	13.9	11.2	13.1
Oct	6.0	11.4	10.0	6.7	7.5	7.2	7.6	10.1	6.7	7.5
Nov	2.1	7.5	5.0	3.7	4.1	2.0	4.3	5.1	3.6	4.1
Dec	-0.5	4.8	3.7	-1.5	1.7	-0.1	1.9	4.1	-1.5	1.8

Table 2.12   Mean monthly precipitation totals (mm) at Sevilla with and without downscaling. Shaded cells indicate where downscaling has resulted in a change of the opposite sign compared to the corresponding scenario without downscaling. Changes in variability not included.

		Without downscaling						With downscaling		
	Base	UKLO	UKHI	UKTR 31-40	UKTR 66-75	GFDL 25-34	GFDL 55-64	UKHI	UKTR 31-40	UKTR 66-75
Jan	84.9	69.4	15.8	75.3	56.7	94.4	99.9	48.1	77.2	68.8
Feb	62.3	64.4	10.7	43.3	61.4	58.2	58.4	54.9	60.0	80.4
Mar	51.6	49.3	7.9	36.4	35.5	53.9	46.6	61.6	46.6	55.2
Apr	41.8	48.7	38.3	66.5	41.1	30.6	37.5	39.7	56.0	39.0
May	36.5	40.2	17.4	80.5	7.8	31.1	22.5	11.0	79.3	5.7
Jun	13.2	12.1	4.5	1.1	7.6	20.6	4.7	0.0	0.0	0.0
Jul	5.5	5.7	2.3	1.4	0.0	2.8	1.8	21.0	9.0	18.0
Aug	4.0	3.2	0.7	3.2	2.3	3.6	3.0	2.1	0.0	2.8
Sep	11.4	10.8	4.3	8.2	3.6	13.9	8.8	17.1	14.6	17.4
Oct	51.0	59.1	6.0	36.6	44.8	67.7	36.9	81.3	63.1	81.3
Nov	71.1	80.5	24.1	60.4	23.4	92.8	78.3	80.2	80.2	66.0
Dec	63.2	61.2	23.6	52.3	41.5	51.8	63.4	42.9	55.5	76.9

2.4.4.2 *Sites without downscaling*

For these scenarios, the grid box changes for each of the GCMs were extracted and applied to the weather generator parameters for each site. Analysis of the daily GCM data from UKHI and the last decade of the UKTR experiment permitted the inclusion of changes in temperature variability and wet and dry spell length. Where no changes in variability were imposed, the number of wet days and the length of the wet and dry spells remains the same as in the observed case. This means that increases in precipitation amount are a result of increases in precipitation intensity, rather than from an increase in the number of wet days in a given month. Where changes in variability are included, the number of wet days and the length of wet and dry spells change, so increases in precipitation amount may be spread over more days in the month in addition to possible changes in precipitation intensity.

Table 2.14 indicates mean monthly precipitation totals for Jokioinen, Finland. Only the early decade of the GFDL transient experiment

Table 2.13 Mean maximum temperature (°C) at Sevilla with and without downscaling. Changes in variability not included.

	Without downscaling							With downscaling		
	Base	UKLO	UKHI	UKTR 31-40	UKTR 66-75	GFDL 25-34	GFDL 55-64	UKHI	UKTR 31-40	UKTR 66-75
Jan	15.1	19.7	19.5	16.9	17.4	16.2	18.1	20.2	17.4	17.9
Feb	17.0	21.6	23.0	19.2	20.9	18.7	17.9	23.8	19.5	21.5
Mar	19.2	23.7	25.4	19.8	21.6	20.4	21.8	26.3	19.8	21.9
Apr	22.2	26.6	27.6	23.6	23.7	22.9	24.0	27.0	23.4	23.5
May	26.4	30.6	31.7	27.3	29.0	27.0	28.6	31.9	27.5	29.0
Jun	30.6	34.6	37.8	34.5	35.0	31.8	36.3	38.1	34.6	35.2
Jul	34.5	38.7	41.0	37.6	39.4	35.9	40.0	42.3	38.0	40.3
Aug	35.2	39.6	41.6	37.3	40.5	35.4	38.3	42.0	37.6	40.9
Sep	31.8	36.3	38.4	34.0	38.3	31.9	35.2	38.8	34.2	38.7
Oct	26.0	30.6	33.2	28.6	30.5	27.2	28.2	33.9	28.8	31.0
Nov	19.8	24.3	25.3	21.9	23.0	20.0	21.9	27.0	22.6	24.1
Dec	16.1	20.7	21.8	16.4	17.9	15.9	19.4	23.7	16.6	18.5

Table 2.14 Mean monthly precipitation totals (mm) at Jokioinen with and without changes in variability.

	No changes in variability							Variability included	
	Base	UKLO	UKHI	UKTR 31-40	UKTR 66-75	GFDL 25-34	GFDL 55-64	UKHI	UKTR 66-75
J	33.1	40.8	64.5	37.0	33.6	28.8	36.9	98.0	60.3
F	23.7	26.3	38.8	30.3	27.2	32.3	28.2	47.0	36.5
M	34.7	40.9	59.1	45.7	47.2	42.0	35.9	75.8	42.3
A	25.7	29.1	52.2	37.0	32.8	19.6	23.6	90.4	33.5
M	37.4	38.3	43.9	36.0	46.2	33.8	30.6	25.6	54.7
J	51.6	94.0	60.9	43.4	77.4	69.0	53.1	15.6	95.5
J	66.2	115.4	97.2	62.8	67.4	71.7	82.7	111.9	83.3
A	77.2	113.2	78.1	68.0	85.9	53.0	85.0	157.9	76.6
S	77.7	89.4	99.2	88.8	75.0	81.3	79.5	83.5	65.5
O	72.8	76.4	120.7	80.4	88.7	61.4	112.7	106.1	99.3
N	52.9	67.6	70.7	62.9	62.5	52.5	56.8	105.7	98.5
D	42.4	48.3	80.7	47.2	60.7	34.1	34.6	99.7	58.0

indicates an overall decrease in precipitation amount at this site. For the scenarios without changes in variability, this implies an increase in precipitation intensity as the number of wet days per month is unchanged. Where changes in variability are included, whether the increases in precipitation amount will result in an increase in precipitation intensity depends on the change in the number of wet days. This is illustrated in Table 2.15. It is apparent that increases in precipitation amount under the UKHI scenario are generally accompanied by increases in the number of wet days in every month except for September and October. For October, in particular, it is probable that precipitation intensity may increase as there is a small decrease in the number of wet days, but a large increase in precipitation amount (45% compared to the base precipitation). For UKTR decade 66-75, decreases in the number of wet days occur in April, May and June without a concomitant decrease in precipitation and, hence, precipitation intensity will increase. In August and September a decrease in the number of wet days is associated with a decrease in

precipitation amount and it is therefore difficult to conclude the effects upon precipitation intensity.

Tables 2.16-2.17 illustrate similar results for Athens, Greece. As well as information about precipitation amount (Table 2.16) and mean number of wet days (Table 2.17), information about the mean length of dry spells is also included (Table 2.18). It is apparent from Table 2.16 that all scenarios indicate a decrease in precipitation totals at this site. When changes in variability are included these decreases become more severe. Table 2.17 indicates that the mean number of wet days per month also generally decreases for both scenarios including changes in variability. Changes in variability lead to increases in the length of dry spells under the UKHI scenario in all months, and general increases for the latter decade of the UKTR experiment. Slight decreases are indicated in May, June and October. The largest increases in dry spell length for this scenario occur in August and September.

Table 2.15   Mean number of wet days for Jokioinen.

	J	F	M	A	M	J	J	A	S	O	N	D
Base	14.6	11.0	13.0	9.2	10.5	10.7	11.7	13.6	15.2	17.3	15.2	14.2
UKHI	19.5	12.9	17.4	14.7	4.4	3.7	12.8	19.4	13.8	15.3	18.5	19.1
UKTR 66-75	21.0	12.1	11.5	7.6	10.2	10.6	13.2	10.9	12.1	18.2	21.0	14.8

Table 2.16   Mean monthly precipitation totals (mm) for Athens with and without changes in variability.

	No changes in variability							Variability included	
	Base	UKLO	UKHI	UKTR 31-40	UKTR 66-75	GFDL 25-34	GFDL 55-64	UKHI	UKTR 66-75
J	47.3	54.1	40.2	47.8	43.9	54.2	38.4	38.2	29.0
F	47.9	40.0	26.0	36.8	40.9	47.6	50.3	12.9	27.8
M	48.7	43.5	29.8	56.3	33.3	34.1	46.4	8.6	17.5
A	26.9	21.1	18.3	23.7	27.3	18.7	28.9	16.9	22.1
M	16.3	15.4	11.9	17.5	16.1	12.1	15.2	18.0	25.0
J	11.1	11.0	6.9	10.2	9.3	6.3	9.0	5.1	12.7
J	11.1	9.9	7.2	8.7	5.4	8.3	11.2	6.1	0.6
A	6.8	4.7	6.2	4.1	4.2	1.9	3.4	4.4	2.0
S	10.0	8.9	7.8	5.6	6.2	3.5	2.8	17.8	8.8
O	30.9	29.4	32.7	19.4	26.4	37.7	25.7	18.7	20.6
N	46.8	55.4	59.0	42.1	32.3	51.5	39.4	40.9	17.1
D	65.2	71.9	64.9	82.2	49.8	83.1	48.4	17.5	32.7

Table 2.17   Mean number of wet days for Athens.

	J	F	M	A	M	J	J	A	S	O	N	D
Base	9.3	7.6	7.5	6.1	4.3	2.2	2.0	1.2	1.9	3.1	5.7	9.0
UKHI	5.7	3.4	2.5	5.3	4.0	1.3	1.3	0.6	2.1	2.5	4.4	2.5
UKTR 66-75	5.3	4.6	3.7	3.8	5.6	2.6	0.2	0.5	1.5	2.8	3.0	5.5

Table 2.18   Mean dry spell length (days) for Athens.

	J	F	M	A	M	J	J	A	S	O	N	D
Base	5.3	6.8	6.2	7.4	10.5	14.7	20.2	26.7	40.7	26.8	14.0	8.9
UKHI	8.8	19.3	17.7	7.6	11.5	19.5	41.5	42.5	44.3	27.2	18.9	14.0
UKTR 66-75	9.3	12.5	16.9	25.4	9.0	11.4	25.8	73.7	66.7	25.4	26.2	17.3

The effects of changes in variability on minimum temperatures are shown in Table 2.19 for Jokioinen, Finland. This table indicates the mean number of days per month when minimum temperature is below 0°C. All scenarios generally indicate a decrease in the number of days below freezing point, as would be expected under a warmer climate. The impact of changes in variability can be seen in late winter/early spring and in the autumn months when, in the case of the UKHI scenario with changes in variability, the number of days below 0°C does not decrease as fast as in the equivalent scenario without variability changes. Similar results are obtained in late winter/early spring for the UKTR years 66-75 scenarios. The length of the frost-free season generally increases under all scenarios.

Table 2.20 illustrates the mean number of days when maximum temperature exceeds 30°C at Athens, Greece. Including the effects of temperature variability indicates that this maximum temperature will be exceeded at some time in almost all months of the year. In July and August the maximum temperature on almost every day, on average, will exceed this value. For the scenarios which do not include changes in variability, this table indicates that this threshold temperature will be exceeded both earlier and later in the year.

Table 2.19   Mean number of days per month when Tmin < 0°C for Jokioinen.

	Base	**UKLO**	**UKHI**	**UKTR 31-40**	**UKTR 66-75**	**GFDL 25-34**	**GFDL 55-64**	**UKHI**	**UKTR 66-75**
		No changes in variability						Variability included	
J	30.8	27.9	22.0	29.6	28.6	30.8	29.4	20.0	27.8
F	27.5	25.1	23.6	25.8	25.4	27.3	27.4	23.8	26.8
M	30.3	20.4	15.2	27.8	24.4	30.4	28.6	16.3	26.3
A	23.0	8.6	4.9	17.4	16.8	18.0	21.1	3.5	15.8
M	5.3	0.2	0.0	5.6	0.7	4.2	1.6	0.0	3.8
J	0.4	0.0	0.0	0.2	0.1	0.2	0.0	0.5	0.9
J	0.0	0.0	0.0	0.0	0.0	0.0	0.0	0.0	0.0
A	0.3	0.0	0.0	0.0	0.0	0.2	0.0	0.0	0.2
S	3.8	0.3	1.0	1.8	2.0	1.5	1.3	0.6	2.2
O	14.7	3.8	0.6	7.9	3.4	15.2	7.4	2.1	2.0
N	26.0	13.6	3.9	15.9	17.5	26.0	11.4	10.9	16.6
D	30.2	24.8	18.3	30.6	22.2	30.9	25.5	18.2	22.6

Table 2.20   Mean number of days when Tmax > 30°C for Athens.

	No changes in variability							Variability included	
	Base	UKLO	UKHI	UKTR 31-40	UKTR 66-75	GFDL 25-34	GFDL 55-64	UKHI	UKTR 66-75
J	0.0	0.0	0.0	0.0	0.0	0.0	0.0	0.5	0.2
F	0.0	0.0	0.0	0.0	0.0	0.0	0.0	0.2	0.0
M	0.0	0.4	0.0	0.0	0.0	0.0	0.0	0.6	0.8
A	0.0	2.9	0.7	0.0	0.2	0.1	0.2	0.8	1.7
M	2.9	18.1	9.0	3.6	4.7	3.4	8.2	9.5	5.2
J	14.3	27.8	24.4	17.7	20.7	18.9	23.1	26.6	20.2
J	26.0	30.9	30.7	28.6	29.4	26.9	30.1	30.9	29.8
A	24.8	30.6	30.3	27.2	29.2	27.7	29.5	30.8	27.1
S	8.6	21.7	20.3	11.9	14.4	11.4	17.5	24.6	17.1
O	2.0	8.9	7.4	2.6	3.3	3.4	4.0	7.0	5.5
N	0.0	0.4	0.2	0.0	0.0	0.0	0.1	0.8	0.1
D	0.0	0.0	0.0	0.0	0.0	0.0	0.0	0.3	0.0

2.5   Summary

Scenarios of climate change have been produced at both the regional and site-specific scales. Both equilibrium and transient GCM experiments have been used to construct these scenarios. Scenarios based on equilibrium climate change experiments are not indicative of climate in the near future, but they can be used to determine the likely range of changes in climate that may occur towards the end of the twenty-first century and beyond, depending on future greenhouse-gas emissions. Transient climate change experiments, however, enable us to examine the pattern and magnitude of climate change in response to a continuous change in forcing, i.e., the 1% per year compound increase in CO_2 concentration. Two decades were used from both the UKTR and the GFDL experiments. The global-mean temperature changes of the GFDL decades were selected to correspond to those of the decades used from the UKTR experiment. Examination of the patterns of change for each experiment indicated that the two UKTR decades were similar, whereas the GFDL decades exhibited more variation over time.

Site-specific scenarios were produced using both downscaling techniques and a more simple approach. Downscaling involved the determination of regression relationships between the broad-scale and site-specific climate. These relationships were then used to determine the site changes in temperature and precipitation by using the GCM grid box changes as predictors. Downscaling of temperature was more successful than for precipitation; precipitation was especially problematic for Sevilla in summer. The disadvantage of using this downscaling methodology is that it is rather data intensive; observed data from several sites are required in order to calculate observed areal anomalies. This amount of data was not available for the other European sites. For the remaining sites, therefore, simpler scenarios were constructed using the corresponding GCM grid-box changes.

For both types of site-specific scenarios, data were produced at the daily timescale. This was achieved using a stochastic weather generator. This also meant that changes in temperature and precipitation variability could be included in the scenarios. The variability of climate has important effects on the occurrence of extreme events, which may have more of an impact on crop growth than changes in mean climate alone (Semenov and Porter, 1994).

In the future, construction of site-specific scenarios of climate change may be aided by the current development of the high resolution limited area models. These models are embedded within GCMs and operate at a resolution of approximately 50km. Validation of the models will indicate whether the data are reliable and can be used alone to produce local scenarios of climate change. If this is the case, the need for further development of downscaling techniques may be reduced.

Both the regional and site-specific climate change scenarios reflect different global-mean temperature changes and therefore not all the crop model results from the different scenarios can be directly compared. The differences in the crop model results may be due to the different global-mean warmings rather than due to the different patterns of climate change. There are four possible types of comparison between the climate change scenarios:

i)   those constructed from different GCM experiments but where the global-mean temperature change is the same. For example, the two decades of each of the transient GCM experiments (i.e., UKTR years 31-40 with GFDL years 25-34 or UKTR years 66-75 with GFDL years 55-64);

ii) those constructed from the same GCM experiment, but where the global-mean warming is different, i.e., UKTR years 31-40 with UKTR years 66-75 or GFDL years 25-34 with GFDL years 55-64;

iii) those constructed from the same type of GCM experiment but where the global-mean temperature change is different, e.g., the equilibrium experiments, UKLO and UKHI; and

iv) those constructed from different GCM experiments which have different global-mean temperature changes, e.g., an equilibrium (e.g., UKHI) and a transient experiment (e.g., UKTR years 66-75).

Acknowledgements

The UK Met. Office GCM data were provided by the Climate Impacts LINK Project (Department of the Environment Contract PECD 7/12/96) on behalf of the UK Met. Office. The GFDL data were provided by Dr. R.J. Stouffer of the Geophysical Fluid Dynamics Laboratory at Princeton University, USA. We would also like to thank The Finnish Meteorological Institute, Institut National de la Recherche Agronomique, Departement de Bioclimatologie, The Danish Institute of Plant and Soil Science and the Radcliffe Observatory, Oxford for provision of climate data as well as those colleagues involved in this project who provided climate data for their countries.

References

Bardossy, A. and Caspary, H.J. (1991). Conceptual model for the calculation of the regional hydrologic effects of climate change. In: *Hydrology for the Water Management of Large River Basins*. Proceedings of the Vienna Symposium, August 1991. IAHS Publ. no. 201.

Carter, T.R., Parry, M.L., Harasawa, H. and Nishioka, S. (1995). *IPCC technical guidelines for assessing climate change impacts and adaptations*. UCL/CGER, London/Tsukuba, 59pp.

Cubasch, U., Hasselmann, K., Höck, H., Maier-Reimer, E., Mikolajewicz, U., Santer, B.D. and Sausen, R. (1992). Time-dependent greenhouse warming computations with a coupled ocean-atmosphere model. *Climate Dynamics*, **8**, 55-69.

Giorgi, F. and Mearns, L.O. (1991). Approaches to the simulation of regional climate change: a review. *Reviews of Geophysics*, **29**, 191-216.

Gates, W.L., Rowntree, P.R. and Zeng, Q.-C. (1990). Validation of climate models. In: Houghton, J.T., Jenkins, G.J. and Ephraums, J.J. (Eds.) *Climate Change: The IPCC Scientific Assessment*, Cambridge University Press, Cambridge, pp. 93-130.

Hasselmann, K., Sausen, R., Maier-Reimer, E. and Voss, R. (1993). On the cold start problem in transient simulations with coupled atmosphere-ocean models. *Climate Dynamics*, **9**, 53-61.

Houghton, J.T., Meira Filho, L.G., Bruce, J., Hoesung Lee, Callander, B.A., Haites, E., Harris, N. and Maskell, K. (1995). *Climate Change 1994: Radiative forcing of climate change and an evaluation of the IPCC IS92 emission scenarios*. Cambridge University Press, Cambridge, 339pp.

Hulme, M., Briffa, K.R., Jones, P.D. and Senior, C.A. (1993). Validation of GCM control simulations using indices of daily airflow types over the British Isles. *Climate Dynamics*, 9, 95-105.

Hulme, M., Raper, S.C.B. and Wigley, T.M.L. (in press). An integrated framework to address climate change (ESCAPE) and further developments of the global and regional climate modules (MAGICC). *Energy Policy*.

Jonas, P.R., Charlson, R.J. and Rodhe, H. (1995). Aerosols. In: Houghton, J.T., Meira Filho, L.G., Bruce, J., Hoesung Lee, Callander, B.A., Haites, E., Harris, N. and Maskell, K. (Eds.) *Climate Change 1994: Radiative forcing of climate change and an evaluation of the IPCC IS92 emission scenarios*. Cambridge University Press, Cambridge, pp. 127-62.

Jones, P.D. and Conway, D. (1995). The use of weather types for GCM downscaling. In: Proceedings of International Conference on Statistical Climatology, Galway, Ireland, June 1995.

Karl, T.R., Wang, W.-C., Schlesinger, M.E., Knight, R.W. and Portman, D. (1990). A method of relating general circulation model simulated climate to the observed local climate. Part I: Seasonal statistics. *Journal of Climate*, 3, 1063-1079.

Kenny, G.J., Harrison, P.A. and Parry, M.L. (Eds.) (1993). *The effect of climate change on agricultural and horticultural potential in Europe*. Research Report No. 2, Environmental Change Unit, University of Oxford, 224pp.

Kim, J.-W., Chang, J.-T., Baker, N.L., Wilks, D.S. and Gates, W.L. (1984). The statistical problem of climate inversion: Determination of the relationship between local and large-scale climate. *Monthly Weather Review*, 112, 2069-2077.

Lamb, H.H. (1972). British Isles weather types and a register of daily sequence of circulation patterns, 1861-1971. *Geophysical Memoir*, 116, HMSO, London, 85pp.

Leggett, J., Pepper, W.J. and Swart, R.J. (1992). Emissions scenarios for the IPCC: An update. In: Houghton, J.T., Callander, B.A. and Varney, S.K. (Eds.) *Climate Change 1992: The Supplementary Report to the IPCC Scientific Assessment*, Cambridge University Press, Cambridge, pp. 69-96.

Manabe, S., Spelman, M.J. and Stouffer, R.J. (1992). Transient responses of a coupled ocean-atmosphere model to gradual changes of atmospheric CO_2. Part II: Seasonal response. *Journal of Climate*, 5, 105-126.

Manabe, S., Stouffer, R.J., Spelman, M.J. and Bryan, K. (1991). Transient responses of a coupled ocean-atmosphere model to gradual changes of atmospheric CO_2. Part I: Annual mean response. *Journal of Climate*, 4, 785-818.

Matyasovszky, I., Bogardi, I., Bardossy, A. and Duckstein, L. (1993). Space-time precipitation reflecting climate change. *Hydrological Sciences*, 38, 539-558.

Mitchell, J.F.B., Manabe, S., Meleshko, V. and Tokioka, T. (1990). Equilibrium climate change and its implications for the future. In: Houghton, J.T., Jenkins, G.J. and Ephraums, J.J. (Eds.) *Climate Change: The IPCC Scientific Assessment*, Cambridge University Press, Cambridge, pp. 131-172.

Murphy, J.M. (1995). Transient response of the Hadley Centre coupled ocean-atmosphere model to increasing carbon dioxide. Part I: Control climate and flux adjustment. *Journal of Climate*, 8, 36-56.

Murphy, J.M. and Mitchell, J.F.B. (1995). Transient response of the Hadley Centre coupled ocean-atmosphere model to increasing carbon dioxide. Part II: Spatial and temporal structure of the response. *Journal of Climate*, 8, 57-80.

Racsko, P., Szeidl, L. and Semenov, M. (1991). A serial approach to local stochastic weather models. *Ecological Modelling*, 57, 27-41.

Raper, S.C.B., Wigley, T.M.L. and Warrick, R.A. (1993). Global sea level rise: past and future. In: Milliman, J.D. (Ed.) *Proceedings of the SCOPE Workshop on Rising Sea Level and Subsiding Coastal Areas*, John Wiley and Sons, Chichester.

Richardson, C.W. (1981). Stochastic simulation of daily precipitation, temperature and solar radiation. *Water Resources Research*, **17**, 182-190.

Santer, B.D. (1988). *Regional validation of general circulation models*. PhD Thesis. Climatic Research Unit Publication No. 9.

Semenov, M.A. and Porter, J.R. (1994). The implications and importance of non-linear responses in modelling of growth and development of wheat. In: Grasman, J. and van Straten, G. (Eds.) *Predictability and non-linear modelling in natural sciences and economics*, Wageningen.

Shine, K.P., Derwent, R.G., Wuebbles, D.J. and Morcrette, J.-J. (1990). Radiative forcing of climate. In: Houghton, J.T., Jenkins, G.J. and Ephraums, J.J. (Eds.) *Climate Change: The IPCC Scientific Assessment*, Cambridge University Press, Cambridge, pp. 41-68.

Skelly, W.C. and Henderson-Sellers, A. (in press). Grid-box or grid-point: what type of precipitation do GCMs deliver? *International Journal of Climatology*.

Viner, D. and Hulme, M. (1993). *The UK Met. Office High Resolution GCM Transient Experiment (UKTR)*. Technical Note 4 prepared for the UK Department of the Environment Climate Change Impacts/Predictive Modelling LINK, Contract Reference Number PECD 7/12/96. Climatic Research Unit, Norwich, 18pp.

von Storch, H., Zorita, E. and Cubasch, U. (1993). Downscaling of global climate change estimates to regional scales: an application to Iberian rainfall in wintertime. *Journal of Climate*, **6**, 1161-1171.

Wigley, T.M.L. (1994). *MAGICC (Model for the Assessment of Greenhouse-gas Induced Climate Change) User's Guide and Scientific Reference Manual*. Climatic Research Unit, Norwich. 23pp.

Wigley, T.M.L. and Raper, S.C.B. (1992). Implications for climate and sea level rise of revised IPCC emissions scenarios. *Nature*, **357**, 293-300.

Wigley, T.M.L. and Raper, S.C.B. (1987). Thermal expansion of sea water associated with global warming. *Nature*, **330**, 127-131.

Wigley, T.M.L., Jones, P.D., Briffa, K.R. and Smith, G. (1990). Obtaining sub-grid-scale information from coarse-resolution general circulation model output. *Journal of Geophysical Research*, **95**, 1943-1953.

Wilson, C.A. and Mitchell, J.F.B. (1987). Simulated climate and CO_2-induced climate change over Western Europe. *Climatic Change*, **10**, 11-42.

CHAPTER 3

**Modelling the effects of
agriculturally significant climatic extremes
at the site and regional scales**

SUMMARY

The occurrence and effects of agriculturally significant extreme meteorological events have been assessed for present and future climatic conditions at three scales: site; country; and Europe-wide.

The site-based assessment analysed the risk of extreme events on winter wheat at a range of sites located in different agricultural and climatic zones throughout Europe. A number of methodologies were developed to quantify extremes during specific developmental phases. These included crop-specific alarm criteria, an extreme statistical model and percent normalised growing degree days. The three methods were applied, using daily data for the 1961-90 time series, to the sites of: Athens, Sevilla, Montpellier, Bologna, Debrecen, Györ, München, Mannheim, Bonn, Wageningen, Rothamsted, Oxford and Jokioinen.

The study identified particular wheat growing seasons in the period 1961 to 1990 which suffered extreme 'high' temperature events according to all three methodologies, ie. meteorological alarm criteria were exceeded at most sites, the extreme event model calculated a 95-100% probability of occurrence of the highest temperature in the series and the highest growing degree day accumulations occurred. These were the 1975-1976, 1968-1969 and 1983-1984 seasons. Specific sites indicated a greater risk from extreme 'high' temperature events during specific development phases, eg. Sevilla experienced extreme 'high' events during the phase leading up to anthesis during all seasons from 1987 to 1990. Under the climate change scenarios the total number of extreme events increased considerably. The cumulative number of extreme 'high' events over a 30 year time series at Bologna increased from 2 with the baseline climate to 7, 8, 18 and 19 for the GFDL2534, GFDL5564, UKTR6675 and UKHI scenarios respectively. The length of the frost free period increased dramatically at most sites under the scenarios (with the exception of those with almost year round frost free conditions at present, ie. Sevilla and Athens) shifting from a mean of about 50 days at Jokioinen with the baseline climate up to 150 and 200 days for the UKTR6675 and UKHI scenarios respectively.

The Europe-wide study assessed meteorological drought and excess wet conditions during the growing season of winter wheat using three models: the Soil Water Deficit; the Palmer Drought Severity Index; and the Hydrothermal Coefficient. The models were applied, using monthly data for the 1961-90 time series, to a spatial climatic database at a 0.5° latitude/longitude resolution.

Areas of extreme dry conditions were identified for the baseline climate in the Iberian Peninsula, southern Italy, Sicily and southern Greece where frequencies of drought were as high as 30% of months. Moderate dry conditions occurred in a very similar spatial pattern to extreme dry conditions. The occurrence of extreme wet conditions is very limited throughout Europe. Moderately wet areas occurred throughout Europe with a frequency of at least 20% of months, except in the Iberian peninsular, central and southern Italy and southern Greece. Changes in the spatial distribution of extreme dry and wet conditions with the climate change scenarios will be assessed in future analyses.

The country study examined climatic variability and crop-specific extreme events for winter wheat and maize in Hungary. Analyses were conducted for two sites in different agricultural zones (Debrecen and Győr) and at the county scale. There were four stages to the assessment. Firstly, the variability of temperature and precipitation was determined using historic quarterly and annual temperature and precipitation time series data. Secondly, the effects of climatic variability on wheat and maize production was assessed by the characterisation of climate year types and the use of expert opinion to determine yield differences between each type and the average climate. Thirdly, a number of specific extreme thresholds for wheat and maize were investigated, including extreme cold days, long dry periods, the length of the frost free period and extreme hot days. Finally, a statistical model was developed which characterises deviations from expected yields for maize and wheat using a function of probability of yield loss and expert opinion of yields with climate year type.

Analysis of historic climatic time series data revealed that cooling, rather than warming, has been observed in Hungary over the last century. However, during the last 20 to 30 years precipitation has decreased which has resulted in significant crop yield losses. The UKTR climate change scenarios predict this trend in decreasing precipitation to continue, which might further exacerbate agricultural losses. The characterisation of climate year types for the UKTR scenarios fall into the dry-warm category, which is the most unfavourable, in terms of expected yield decrease, for wheat production. Conditions for maize production are also predicted to worsen due to considerable increases in the maximum temperature sum in conjunction with decreased precipitation.

Analysis of sites common to both the country study and the site-based study (i.e. Debrecen and Győr) were consistent in identifying extreme 'high' temperature seasons in the historic climate data and in trends in extremes under climate change scenarios.

3.1   Introduction

Crop growth and yield quality are very sensitive to extremes of weather such as very high temperature, severe frost and persistent drought. However the amount of damage a crop suffers often depends on the development stage the crop has reached when the extreme conditions occur, for example, extreme high temperatures occurring immediately prior to anthesis will reduce the number of grains set due to male and female sterility, therefore, lowering final grain number per ear and reducing yields. Most current research on extremes concentrates on their probability of occurrence. The work described in this chapter aims to focus on the risk of extremes, which also includes consequences to the crop. To achieve this the work needs to be fully integrated with crop modelling activities.

Meteorological definitions of extreme events have not been emphasised, rather the consequences to crop yield and quality. This involves investigating the interaction of climate with soil characteristics and crop development stage. For example, drought may be classed as an extreme event if there is a severe soil moisture deficit over a long run of days during flowering. On the other hand, dry weather can be beneficial during grain filling as protein is increased and grain quality improved. Also excess precipitation may only have an extreme consequence for crop yield if it occurs during grain filling or at harvest. Site specific models often do not include direct responses to short-term extreme events (such as high temperatures or intense rainfall) and for broadscale models, extreme events at sites will be hidden in the spatially and temporally averaged climatology. This analysis aims to quantify the current risks of climatic extremes to production at the site and regional scales and to anticipate how these may change in the future using scenarios of climate change.

There are three main components to the study on agriculturally significant climatic extremes: (i) the identification and characterisation of extreme events for wheat, at thirteen sites in Europe (Section 3.2); (ii) analysis of the variability of European climate at the

broadscale, in particular, the spatial distribution of drought and wet conditions during the wheat growing season (Section 3.3); and (iii) analysis of the occurrence of, and yield response to, extremes in Hungary in order to produce a probability model of yield losses in maize and wheat for future climates in Hungary (Section 3.4).

The first objective was accomplished by: (i) the use of the Extreme Statistical Model, (ii) the application of meteorological alarm criteria during specific wheat developmental phases, and (iii) the use of the percent normalised degree anomaly of the agroclimatic index Growing Degree Days (GDD). These three methodologies have been implemented at the following sites: Athens, Sevilla, Montpellier, Bologna, Debrecen, Győr, München, Mannheim, Bonn, Wageningen, Rothamsted, Oxford and Jokioinen.

Three models were used for the identification of meteorological drought and wet conditions, both in space and time for 5085 European grid boxes in order to determine the broadscale distribution of extreme and moderate drought and wet events during the wheat growing season. These are soil water deficit (SWD), the Palmer Drought Severity Index (PDSI) and the Hydrothermal Coefficient (HTC).

The third objective was achieved through the analysis of quarterly and annual historic temperature and precipitation time series data at sites in Hungary, the characterisation of climatic year-types (in terms of the productivity of wheat and maize by region) using a Ward type cluster analysis, an analysis of the frequency and yield consequences of severe, medium and light drought by county and an assessment of the probability of yield losses based on a statistical model by county.

3.2   Site-specific extreme events for wheat

Site-specific extreme events for wheat were analysed at thirteen sites for which times series of daily climatic data were available. Appropriate extreme threshold values known to cause damage to the development and growth of wheat were selected based on information in a wheat knowledge base (Russell and Wilson, 1994). The damage caused by a particular extreme event is highly dependent on the development stage of the wheat plant. Hence, a wheat phenological model (AFRCWHEAT) was run using daily data for each site to ascertain dates of the various development stages of wheat for each year of the baseline climate period. The extreme statistical model, the meteorological alarm criteria and the growing degree day index were then used to identify the risk of agriculturally significant climatic extreme events in specific developmental stages of wheat at each site.

3.2.1   The extreme statistical model

The extreme statistical model was used to identify agriculturally significant climatic extreme events based on the construction of time series of extreme values from the baseline site datasets. Statistical information was obtained from the time series to specify asymptotic distributional characteristics and, thus, provide a complete description of the behaviour of the extreme events.

Three parameters of the Generalised Extreme Value (GEV) distribution were estimated: the location (ξ), scale (α) and shape (k), parameters. The methods of Sextiles, L-moments and Maximum Likelihood were used to estimate parameter values (Hosking, 1990).

The asymptotic approximation was assessed using simulated data, drawn from a controlled GEV population, according to Monte-Carlo

methodology. The characteristics of the simulated datasets vary in respect to the length and shape of the parental GEV and to the serial correlation within the datasets. The statistical model for the identification of meteorological extreme events was derived from the best estimating method. This consisted of: the density function (3.2.1), the cumulative density function (3.2.2) and the quantile function (3.2.3):

$$P(X = x) = f(x) = a^{-1}e^{-(1-k)y}e^{-y} \qquad (3.2.1)$$

$$P(X \le x) = F(x) = e^{-e^{-y}} \qquad (3.2.2)$$

$$x(F) = x + a\{1 - (-\log F)^k\} / k \qquad (3.2.3)$$

where $y = -k^{-1}\log\{1 - k(x - x) / a\}$, $k \ne 0$

$x + a / k \le x \le \infty$ if $k < 0$,

$-\infty < x < x + a / k$ if $k > 0$

Some of the results produced by the statistical model are shown in Figure 3.2.1(a), where the probabilities of occurrence of maximum air temperature values for the site of Wageningen, The Netherlands, are depicted on a cross section obtained at the 80% probability level for each development phase of wheat, during the 30-year climate baseline period. The developmental phases of wheat are coded in Table 3.2.1. Figure 3.2.1 (b) demonstrates the probabilities of occurrence of extreme maximum temperature conditions, during the entire wheat growing season. Good agreement exists between Figures 3.2.1 (a) and (b), in spite of the fact that more information is depicted in (a) where the analysis was conducted for each development phase.

Table 3.2.1   Wheat developmental phases modelled by the AFRCWHEAT phenological model.

Phases	Description
1	Sowing to emergence
2	Emergence to double ridges
3	Double ridges to terminal spikelet
4	Terminal spikelet to anthesis
5	Anthesis to start of grain filling
6	Start of grain filling to end of grain filling
7	End of grain filling to maturity

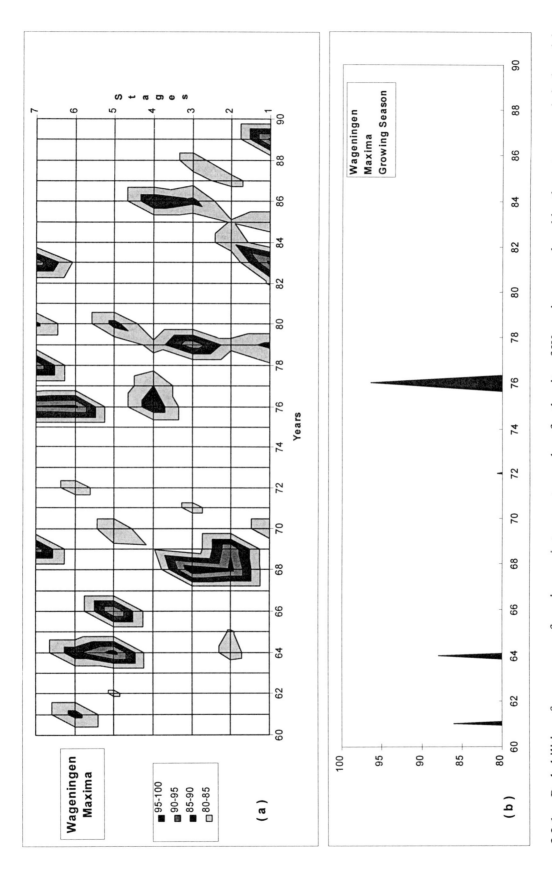

Figure 3.2.1   Probabilities of occurrence of maximum air temperature values for the site of Wageningen produced by the extreme statistical model. They are depicted: (a) on a cross section, obtained at the 80% probability level, for each developmental stage of wheat, and (b) for the whole growing season of wheat, during the climate baseline period, 1961-90.

The 1975-76 growing season was a climatic extreme period for wheat, since it was very hot for a long and almost continuous period, particularly during the development phases from terminal spikelet to anthesis and start of grain filling to maturity (phases 4, 6 and 7) (Table 3.2.1).

Comparable analyses have been conducted for all sites. A synthesis of results for all sites during the entire baseline growing season, is shown in Table 3.2.2. Note that this type of information may lead to some discrepancies in the identification of extreme 'high' events, since maximum air temperature values were used. All the bullet-marked cells characterise extreme events, some with higher probabilities than others. It is apparent that the 1975-76 growing season is the most extreme, both in intensity and spatial extension. This becomes more evident during the last two development phases (start of grain filling to maturity) where it appears as an extreme event at almost all sites, except Sevilla and Jokioinen.

Table 3.2.2   Probabilities of occurrence of extreme 'high' events for the thirteen sites examined, produced by the extreme statistical model, based on maximum temperature values, during the baseline growing season.

Year	ATH	SEV	MON	BOL	DEB	GYO	MUN	MAN	BON	WAG	ROT	OXF	JOK
60-61		□	□			□			•	••	•••	□	□
61-62		□	•••	••••	•	••••							
62-63		□	•••		•	•							••
63-64	•••	□							•	••			
64-65		□		•••		•							
65-66		□											
66-67		□				•••	•••						
67-68	•••	□			••	••					•••	•••	
68-69	••	□					••••	••••	••••		••	••	
69-70		□									••	•••	
70-71		□											
71-72		□					••			•			••
72-73		□							•				
73-74		□											
74-75		□											
75-76			•••			•	•••	••••	••••	••••	••••	••••	
76-77													•••
77-78													
78-79													
79-80	•					••••							
80-81		••••	••••				□	□					
81-82				••			□	□					
82-83							□	□				•••	
83-84				••••	•••	••	□	□	••		•	••	
84-85							□	□					
85-86							□	□					
86-87	••••				•••	•	□	□					
87-88				••••		•	□	□					••••
88-89							□	□					
89-90	••				•••	••	□	□			•		

Legend	•	••	•••	••••	□
%	80-85	85-90	90-95	95-100	Missing

Minimum air temperature values were used to identify 'low' temperature climatic extreme events. Table 3.2.3 depicts the probability of occurrence of 'low' extreme events during the wheat growing season as a function of site. The 1962-63 growing season appears to be the coldest for all stations, except for Mannheim and Jokioinen. This characterisation mostly occurs during developmental phase 2 (emergence to double ridges), which is the longest and usually the coldest period of the wheat growing season.

Three sequential growing season periods (1984-85, 1985-86 and 1986-87) appear to characterise extreme cold events for the majority of sites, with the exception of Athens and Sevilla. Cold conditions are more intense over the central European stations and less severe in northern Europe. The 1984-85 season is the most intense, while the 1985-86 the weakest of the three seasons.

Similar analyses have been performed for each station for each developmental phase.

Table 3.2.3 Probabilities of occurrences of extreme 'low' temperature events for the thirteen stations, produced by the extreme statistical model, by using the minimum temperature values for the baseline growing season.

Year	ATH	SEV	MON	BOL	DEB	GYO	MUN	MAN	BON	WAG	ROT	OXF	JOK
60-61		□	□			□						□	□
61-62		□										●	
62-63	●●	□	●●●●	●●●	●●●	●●●●	●●●		●●●●	●●●	●●●●	●●●●	
63-64		□		●●	●●●●	●●							
64-65		□									●●		
65-66		□	●	●●●●								●	●●●●
66-67		□				●							●●●
67-68	●●●●	□		●●		●●●		●		●●			●●●
68-69		□				●				●●●			
69-70		□											
70-71		□	●●				●●			●●			
71-72		□											
72-73	●	□											
73-74		□					●●			●●●			
74-75		□											
75-76								●●●					
76-77													
77-78								●●●●					
78-79	●●●			●●●				●●	●●	●●	●●	●	●●●
79-80		●●●											
80-81		●●					□	□					
81-82					●●		□	□	●		●●●●	●●●●	
82-83	●●●●						□	□					
83-84							□	□					
84-85			●●●	●●●	●●●	●●●	□	□	●●●	●●●		●	●●
85-86			●	●●●			□	□	●●		●●	●●	
86-87			●●●		●●●●	●●●	□	□		●		●●	●●
87-88							□	□					
88-89							□	□					
89-90							□	□					

Legend	●	●●	●●●	●●●●	□
%	80-85	85-90	90-95	95-100	Missing

3.2.2   The meteorological alarm criteria

The most critical environmental factors influencing crop development and yield are temperature and precipitation and, hence the extreme events are defined in terms of these variables. Meteorological alarm criteria were selected, which define the susceptibility of wheat to extreme environmental conditions during specific developmental phases from Russell and Wilson (1994) (Table 3.2.4).

Since the length of the growing season varies from year to year and depends greatly on the latitude of the station, the growing seasons and the various development stages of wheat were calculated using the AFRCWHEAT phenology model, for each of the years of the baseline period and for all stations. The developmental phases of wheat are coded in Table 3.2.1.

The frequency of occurrence of each alarm criteria and its intensity were calculated in terms of the mean value of the particular variable. For the purposes of spatial and temporal comparison, normalised values of the mean deviations were calculated as follows:

$$D_i^* = 100.\,|D_i|\,/max\{D_i\}, \text{for } i=1,.......,N \quad (3.2.4)$$

where, D_i is the critical value deviation for the examined meteorological alarm criteria, i is the year of the interest and N is the total number of years.

The meteorological alarm criteria may be divided into two categories. The first group includes those criteria which are based on temperature (criteria 2 to 8 in Table 3.2.4), while the other group includes criteria concerning wet or dry conditions (criteria 1 and 9 in Table 3.2.4). High temperature conditions during grain filling lead to the production of small grains, resulting in low grain weight. Hence, the threshold of 25°C on more than 14 days and the threshold of 28°C on 3 successive days were adopted for development phase 5-6 covering anthesis to end of grain filling (criteria 7 and 8, respectively). For the week before anthesis, a critical value of 30°C was used (criterion 6).

Similar meteorological alarm criteria based on minimum temperature have been adopted. Winter wheat is sensitive when it is exposed to low temperatures during early vegetative growth. Temperatures of -20°C, which can cause frost damage to the developing apex, during the period from emergence to terminal spikelet were defined as an extreme threshold (criterion 3) (Petr, 1991).

Sowing dates often depend on the suitability of soil conditions. In southern Europe the soil must not be too dry, whilst in northern Europe it must not be too wet. Hence, for sites with latitudes south of 45°N a critical value of 25 mm of precipitation was required to fall during the period a month before and after the date of sowing (criterion 1).

Harvesting is a critical operation and depends on the reliability of good drying weather. Ideally, wheat is harvested at 15% grain moisture content. A threshold of 10 dry days was chosen (criterion 9) assuming that with

Table 3.2.4   The selected meteorological alarm criteria for winter wheat, used for the identification of agriculturally significant extreme events. T_{min} = minimum temperature (°C) ; T_{max} = (°C); Precip = mm.

Number	Meteorological alarm criteria	Period
1	Precip< 25, latitude <45°N	Sowing - 30 days to sowing + 30 days
2	$T_{min} < -8$	Emergence
3	$T_{min} < -20$	Emergence to terminal spikelet
4	$T_{min} < -4$	On either side of terminal spikelet
5	$T_{min} < 5$	Anthesis -7 days
6	$T_{max} > 30$	Anthesis -7 days
7	$T_{max} > 25$, on more than 14 days	Anthesis to end of grain filling
8	$T_{max} > 28$, on 3 successive days	Anthesis to end of grain filling
9	Dry days < 10	End of grain filling to maturity

fewer dry days during the period from the end of grain filling to maturity, the grain will not reach the optimal moisture content.

An example of the use of the alarm criteria is shown in Table 3.2.5. This depicts the probability of occurrence of alarm criterion 7, as a function of the examined sites and the developmental phases 5 and 6 of Table 3.2.1. Once again, the 1975-76 growing season is highlighted, demonstrating its extreme character.

3.2.3   The growing degree day index

Several agroclimatic indices were calculated to investigate the effects of different climatic parameters on the development and growth of wheat. The effect of temperature on the rate of phenological development of wheat can be estimated in terms of the accumulated temperature required from germination to maturity.

Table 3.2.5   Probabilities of occurrence of more than 14 days with daily maximum temperature > 25°C during the phase end of grain filling to maturity (alarm criteria 7) for the thirteen sites.

Year	ATH	SEV	MON	BOL	DEB	GYO	MUN	MAN	BON	WAG	ROT	OXF	JOK
60-61													
61-62													
62-63					●●●●								
63-64					●								
64-65													
65-66													
66-67													
67-68					●●●●								
68-69	●●●●												
69-70													
70-71													
71-72					●								
72-73													
73-74			●●●●										
74-75													
75-76					●●●●	●●●●	●●●●	●●●●		●●●●	●●●●	●●●●	
76-77													
77-78													
78-79		●●●●		●	●●●●								
79-80													
80-81		●●●											
81-82		●		●●●●									
82-83													
83-84													
84-85													
85-86		●							●●●●				
86-87		●			●●●●								
87-88		●											●●●●
88-89													
89-90		●											

Legend	●	●●	●●●	●●●●
%	80-85	85-90	90-95	95-100

The agroclimatic index growing degree days (GDD) uses daily temperature measurements and is expressed as the accumulated excess of mean daily temperature above a base temperature, during the growing season. This index has been used for the identification of temperature extreme weather years (Karacostas and Flocas, 1993). The literature indicates that a wide range of lower and upper temperature threshold values have been used in the calculation of GDD (Rosenzweig, 1985; Blonet *et al.*, 1984; Dagneaud *et al.*, 1979; Del Pozo *et al.*, 1985; Parry *et al.*, 1988). In this study, 5°C and 32°C were used, respectively.

The arithmetic mean values of the GDD and their standard deviations were calculated, for each development phase and for the entire growing season for all sites, throughout the baseline climate period. The percent normalised degree of anomaly of an extreme GDD-year was defined as follows:

$$e_i = \frac{(d_i \cdot 100)}{d^*} \qquad (3.4.5)$$

where d_i is the arithmetic mean deviation of the calculated GDD value, and d^* is the maximum value of the mean deviations throughout the examined period. Positive and negative values of the mean deviations indicate 'high' and 'low' agriculturally significant extreme years, respectively.

A gradual decrease in GDD units is observed with increasing geographical latitude. Southern areas around the Mediterranean indicate GDD units as high as 1750 at Athens whereas the far northern areas exhibit only 900 GDD units at Jokioinen, thus giving a very large range value of 850 GDD units. The meridianal distribution of the GDD analyses is fairly uniform, with slightly higher GDD values at the southern sites (Sevilla = 1625 °C days and Athens = 1750 °C days).

The quantitative characteristics of each year for the sites under consideration were calculated and the percent normalised anomalies estimated. This information was then used to identify the extreme GDD-years for each site of interest.

Figure 3.2.2(a) depicts the probabilities of occurrence of the GDD values for Wageningen, on a cross section obtained at the 60% probability level, for each developmental phase of wheat, during the 30-year climate baseline period. Figure 3.2.2(b) shows the probabilities of occurrence of extreme high GDD values, over the whole wheat growing season. The structure of Figure 3.2.2 is similar to that of Figure 3.2.1, to allow for direct comparison between the two methodologies. The patterns depicted in Figure 3.2.2 correspond well with those demonstrated in Figure 3.2.1. This is very important, as the two methodologies were not expected, a priori, to reach comparable results. The discrepancies between the figures, particularly for the whole growing season, can be explained by the fact that the GDD methodology relies upon the sum of mean air temperature values, while the extreme statistical model uses only maximum temperature values. Moreover, the GDD approach does not take into consideration temperatures higher than the adopted upper limit of 32°C, which may explain the fewer number of cells encountered in Figure 3.2.2. The agreement between Figures 3.2.1 and 3.2.2 is valid for the majority of sites.

3.2.4   Results and discussion

The results produced by the extreme statistical model, the meteorological alarm criteria and the GDD approach were combined to produce the final conclusions. Although the three methodologies have the same objective, a direct comparison among these was not possible, due to their different internal structures. Inputs to the extreme statistical model are actual maximum and minimum temperature values, which probably are not inclusive in the GDD calculations, due to the ceiling and base temperature limits. The alarm criteria are specific to the development phase of wheat and by their nature are based on short-term extreme events, whereas GDD is an accumulated calculation of temperature alone. Nevertheless, the alarm criteria and the GDD approaches can be used as additional methods to verify the results obtained from the extreme statistical model.

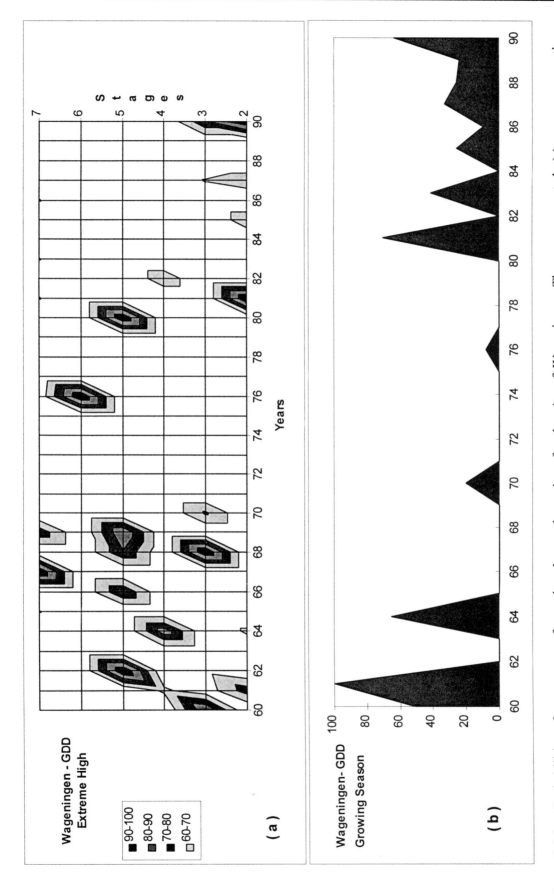

Figure 3.2.2 Probabilities of occurrence of growing degree day values for the site of Wageningen. They are presented: (a) on a cross section, obtained at the 60% probability level, for each developmental stage of wheat, and (b) for the whole growing season of wheat, during the climate baseline period, 1961-90.

3.2.4.1 *Baseline analysis*

Table 3.2.6 illustrates the extreme 'high' events in terms of growing season and development phase for regions and sites.

The 1975-76 growing season is the most extreme 'high' season, due to its spatial distribution. It is extreme for almost all sites, except for the two most spatially separated stations, Sevilla and Jokioinen. It is also the most severe 'high' extreme with a 95 to 100% probability of occurrence. A thorough examination of the developmental phases of the 1975-76 growing season suggests that the latest phases of the growing season were responsible for this characterisation. Based on alarm criteria 7 and 8 (from anthesis to end of grain filling), 76% of stations indicated extreme 'high' events.

Further analysis of criterion 7 (Tmax > 25°C on more than 14 days) revealed that 10 sites

indicated extreme 'high' events with durations of 17 to 24 days. Moreover, criterion 8 (Tmax > 28°C on 3 successive days) was satisfied by all sites, except Athens and Jokioinen.

The next most extreme 'high' growing seasons were 1968-69 and 1983-84. 1968-69 was extreme during most developmental phases, indicating its significant duration. Developmental phases 1 and 2 (sowing to double ridges) experienced the major extreme conditions. From terminal spikelet to anthesis (developmental phase 4) the extreme 'high' events are more pronounced for the area of central Europe. Extremes in the 1983-84 growing season were more intensive during latter developmental phases where four sites indicated extreme values as high as 95 to 100%. The highest probabilities of occurrence of alarm criteria 7 and 8 were encountered in the Mediterranean area.

Table 3.2.6   Synthesised results produced by the extreme statistical model, alarm criteria and GDD approach. The extreme 'high' temperature events are displayed under the headings of growing seasons, developmental phases and sites.

Growing season		1975-76	All except Sevilla and Jokioinen
		1968-69	Almost all
		1983-84	"
Developmental phase:	**Phases 1 & 2**	1967-68	All except Athens and Oxford
		1968-69	"
		1969-70	"
	Phase 4	1963-64	Central Europe
		1968-69	"
		1978-79	"
		1981-82	"
	Phases 6 & 7	1975-76	Almost all
Site:	**Athens**	1960-66	Phases 1 & 2
	Sevilla	1980-83	Phase 3
		1987-90	Phase 4
	Bonn	1979-83	Phase 5
	Wageningen	1975-79	Phase 4
	München	1961-64	Phase 4
		1964-65	Phase 5

Analyses performed for each developmental phase sometimes characterised results in a regional sense. Extreme 'high' conditions appeared to be pronounced for developmental phase 4, during the growing seasons of 1963-64, 1968-69, 1978-79 and 1981-82. The higher probabilities were located over central Europe. The 1978-79 growing season was the most severe, whilst the 1963-64 season was the least severe. Taking into consideration criterion 6 (Tmax > 30°C during the last week before anthesis), the Hungarian and German stations showed extreme 'high' conditions.

Extreme 'high' conditions were identified over the three consecutive periods of 1967-68, 1968-69 and 1969-70, during the early developmental phases (1 and 2). The growing season of 1968-69 was the most severe, whilst that of 1969-70 was the least severe.

Site analyses highlighted consecutive periods of extreme events. For example, extreme 'high' conditions were apparent during developmental phases 1 and 2 at Athens for almost five consecutive growing seasons, showing warm winters during 1960 to 1966. Sevilla indicated extreme 'high' conditions during developmental phase 3 for the three consecutive growing seasons: 1980-81, 1981-82 and 1982-83, and during developmental phase 4 for the three consecutive growing seasons: 1987-88, 1988-89 and 1989-90.

Four consecutive growing seasons: 1979-80, 1980-81, 1981-82 and 1982-83 indicated extreme 'high' conditions at Bonn during phase 5 (anthesis to start of grain filling). In the last two seasons the probability reached 95 to 100%. According to alarm criterion 8, extreme 'high' temperature events were encountered during these two most extreme growing seasons and the average duration of events was three and four successive days, respectively.

The four consecutive growing seasons, 1975-76, 1976-77, 1977-78 and 1978-79 were characterised as extreme 'high' events for Wageningen during developmental phase 4 (terminal spikelet to anthesis). Criterion 6 supports this finding by indicating extreme 'high' temperature events during the pre-

anthesis period during the 1975-78 growing seasons.

At München, the growing seasons of 1961-62, 1962-63 and 1963-64 showed extreme 'high' events during developmental phase 4, while the growing season of 1964-65 appeared to be more severe during developmental phase 5. The results, according to criterion 6, indicated that the first three growing seasons could be characterised as extreme 'high', since high temperature events (Tmax > 30°C) were observed during the growing seasons of 1961-64. Concerning developmental phase 5 of growing season 1964-65, extreme 'high' temperature events were identified with the use of criterion 8, with a mean duration of three days.

The extreme 'low' events are depicted in Table 3.2.7. Over the baseline climate period, the 1962-63 growing season was identified as the most pronounced extreme event for all examined sites, except Jokioinen and Mannheim. Results for Sevilla are inconclusive since no data was available for that growing season. Extreme 'low' temperatures are most severe in developmental phase 2 (emergence to double ridges) which covers the cold period of the season. Criterion 3 supports this finding, since the period from emergence to double ridge is characterised by high frequencies of cold events for the majority of the sites in central and northern Europe.

The three consecutive growing seasons of 1984-85, 1985-86 and 1986-87 indicated extreme cold conditions for all sites, except for the two southern most stations (Athens and Sevilla) and the two German stations because of missing data. This characterisation is particularly evident in developmental phase 2. The most intense cold conditions are focused over central Europe, with the north less severely affected. A similar classification was found through the assessment of criterion 3, where the central European sites were coldest. The 1986-87 growing season was the most severe, while the 1985-86 the least severe. Moreover, the 1984-85 growing season was characterised by its persistence of extreme 'low' temperature events.

Table 3.2.7   Synthesised results produced by the extreme statistical model, alarm criteria and GDD approach. The extreme 'low' temperature events are displayed under the headings of growing seasons, developmental phases and sites.

Growing season		1962-63	All except Mannheim and Jokioinen
		1984-85	All except Athens and Sevilla
		1985-86	"
		1986-87	"
Developmental phase:	Phase 1	1969-72	Northern Europe
	Phase 6	1963-65	Northern Europe
	Phases 5 & 6	1988-90	Almost all
Site:	Rothamsted	1963-65	Phase 6
		1965-68	Phase 3
		1969-72	Phase 1
		1986-90	Phase 4
	Györ	1970-74	Phase 1
	Bologna	1978-81	Phase 1
	Montpellier	1968-71	Phase 3

Considering regional similarities the northern European region, identified by the sites of Oxford, Rothamsted and Jokioinen, is notable. Extreme 'low' events are indicated for this region, during the three consecutive growing periods 1969-70, 1970-71 and 1971-72 in developmental phase 1, and during two consecutive growing seasons, 1963-64 and 1964-65, in developmental phase 6. Moreover, 'low' conditions were identified at almost all sites, except Sevilla, Montpellier and Jokioinen, during developmental phases 5 and 6 for the two consecutive growing seasons: 1988-89 and 1989-90.

Extreme 'low' events were identified at each site for each developmental phase. Rothamsted is characterised by cold conditions during several consecutive time periods, under different growing phases. The growing periods of the years 1986 to 1990 are characterised as extreme 'low' events at developmental phase 4 (terminal spikelet to anthesis). According to criterion 5, the growing season of 1989-90 was the most severe. The highest frequencies of 'low' temperature events was during the 1988-

89 growing season, where five occurrences of criterion 5 were observed during the pre-anthesis period. Moreover, developmental phases 6 and 3, appeared to be extreme 'low' temperature events during the two-year 1963-65 and three-year 1965-68 consecutive growing seasons, respectively.

Extreme 'low' temperature conditions were also identified, during the developmental phase 1, for three (1969-70, 1970-71 and 1971-72), four (1970-71, 1971-72, 1972-73, and 1973-74) and three (1978-79, 1979-80 and 1980-81) consecutive growing seasons for the sites of Rothamsted, Györ and Bologna, respectively. Developmental phase 3 was characterised by extreme 'low' temperature events for Montpellier during the three consecutive growing seasons of 1968-69, 1969-70 and 1970-1971.

Three consecutive growing periods, 1965-68, indicated extreme 'low' temperature conditions for the northern site of Jokioinen. The criterion 3 analysis indicated that the growing season 1966-67 was the coldest within the period 1961-

90, while 1965-66 and 1967-68 were characterised by a high frequency of extreme cold events.

Agriculturally significant events common to all stations are few. The scarcity of sites throughout Europe is probably the main reason for this limited similarity. Synoptic or sub-synoptic scale meteorological phenomena, which are usually responsible for similar weather conditions, cover areas much smaller than the area defined by the thirteen sites. In spite of this, the growing season of 1975-76 ('high') and the growing season of 1962-63 ('low') appear to be the most extreme for the majority of the examined sites.

It must also be recognised that experience of one 'extreme' event during development may affect any reaction to further extreme events. This could come about in one of two ways. Firstly, the timing of developmental phases could be altered such that an extreme event using, say, the baseline climate, occurs in a different phase of development than it would have done in the absence of the extreme event. This could move developmental phases both into and out of extreme events. Secondly, the occurrence of two or more extreme events in a single growing season could have interactive effects on crop growth. For example, an autumn with above average rainfall followed by very hot conditions around flowering or during grain-filling would have the combined effect of firstly reducing and delaying emergence leading to a lower main stem leaf number and plant population. Then high temperatures at flowering would amplify these effects for the final effect on yield since leaf area would senesce earlier. There may be a compensatory increase in grain protein content following such a sequence. The important conclusion is to link such extreme event analysis with both crop modelling and crop experimental work. This will be investigated in future analyses.

3.2.4.2 Scenario analyses

Changes in the frequencies of the identified agriculturally significant extreme events with climate change were analysed using the scenarios described in Chapter 2. The scenarios

used were: UKTR decade 66-75, UKHI, GFDL decade 25-34 and GFDL decade 55-64. The UKHI and UKTR scenarios were constructed both with and without changes in climatic variability (daily temperature variability and length of wet and dry series). The GFDL scenarios include only mean changes in climate. Scenarios including changes in climatic variability are dnoted by 'v', ie. UKHIv. Detailed descriptions of the methods used for constructing these scenarios are presented in Chapter 2. Figure 3.2.3 depicts the cumulative number of agriculturally significant extreme 'high' events as a function of the growing season. These extreme events were identified and predicted by the extreme statistical model probabilities, for the baseline climate period and the four scenarios, calculated at six of the sites. The methodology used for these calculations, which was applied for a probability threshold of 80%, was as follows:

Let p_1^c be the critical probability value for which the Tmax threshold x is calculated. Thus, $x = x_b(p_1^c)$, where x_b is the Quantile Function (QF) for the baseline data (QF is defined as the inverse function of the Cumulative Density Function (CDF)). If the threshold value x is applied to each one of the CDFs derived from the scenario data, then: $p_j^c = F_j(x)$, where F_j is the CDF of the jth scenario, and $j \varepsilon S = \{$UKHI, UKTR6675, GFDL5564, GFDL2534$\}$. Now, if $\overline{P}_j = \{p_1^j, p_2^j, ..., p_N^j\}$ are the extreme statistical model probability sets for $j \varepsilon S* = \{$Baseline$\}$ U S, then the sets $\overline{C}_j$, are created using the following formula:

$$\overline{C}_j = \{c_i^j = \sum_{k=1}^{i} p_k^*, i = 1..N, j \in S^* , \quad (3.2.6)$$

where

$$p_i^* = \begin{cases} 1 & p_i \geq p_j^c \\ 0 & p_i < p_j^c \end{cases}, j \in S^*, i = 1..N \quad (3.2.7)$$

The results show a considerable increase in the total number of extreme events for all scenarios. From Figure 3.2.3 and for the randomly selected growing season of 1980-81, the cumulative number of the extreme 'high' events for the site of Bologna increase from 2 for the

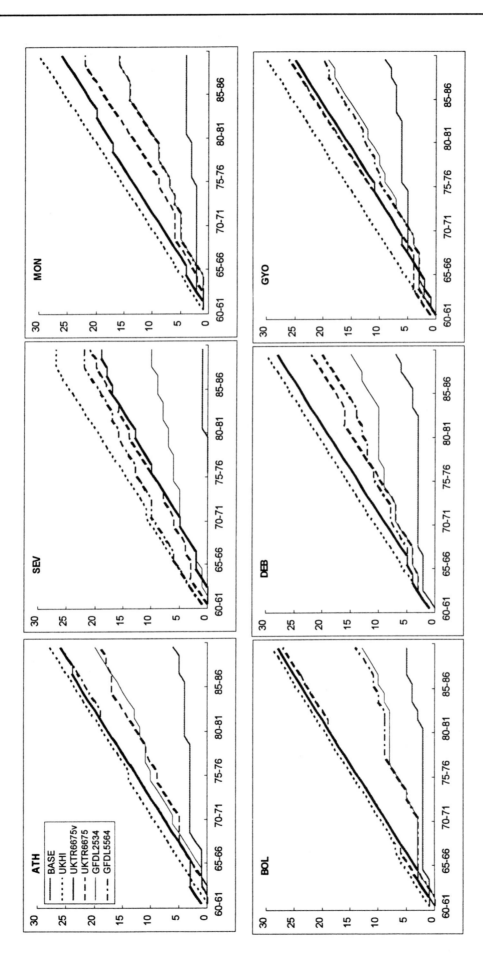

Figure 3.2.3 Cumulative number of agriculturally significant extreme 'high' temperatures events, as a function of the growing season, for the baseline climate period and the four specific scenarios, calculated for a probability threshold of 80%.

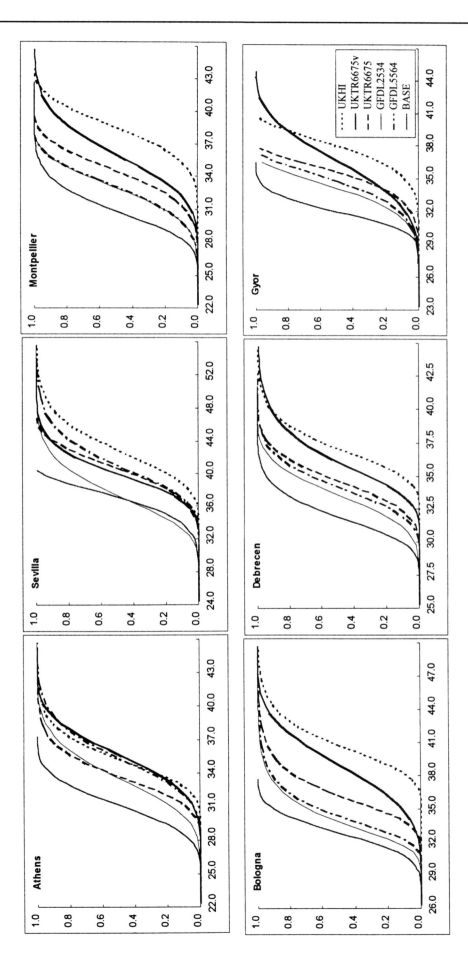

Figure 3.2.4   GEV cumulative distribution functions of the baseline climate period and the four specific scenarios, against maximum temperature threshold values.

baseline climate to 7, 8, 18 and 19 for the GFDL2534, GFDL5564, UKTR6675 and UKHI scenarios respectively. Similar increases, which reach one order of magnitude, are encountered for all sites.

Figure 3.2.4 shows the GEV cumulative distribution functions against maximum temperature threshold values for six sites for the baseline and the scenarios. The cumulative distribution functions of the scenarios show a shift of up to $10°C$, towards higher maximum temperature threshold values. It is worth noting that although the rate of change among the scenarios is variable, the order of change among them remains almost the same.

Figure 3.2.5 (a and b) illustrates the frost free periods for twelve of the examined sites during the baseline climate period and according to the scenarios UKHI and UKTR6675. The important feature is the geographical latitude dependence of the length of the frost-free period. The sites of Athens and Sevilla, the two southern stations, experience the longest frost-free periods, while Jokioinen has the shortest. The frost-free periods, calculated by the predictions of the two scenarios, indicate a remarkable increase with respect to the baseline, of up to 150 to 200 days. The UKHI scenario shows persistently higher values of frost-free periods than the UKTR6675 scenarios (both with and without changes in climatic variability).

From the presented material and conclusions, it is implied that the extreme statistical model, coupled with the meteorological alarm criteria and the GDD approach, is a powerful tool for the identification and analysis of agriculturally significant extreme events.

3.3   Regional drought characterisation for wheat in Europe

Drought is a unique natural hazard which differs from others in that it is a 'creeping phenomenon' which is 'pervasive in nature' (Meyer, 1990). The effects of drought accumulate gradually and may persist over long periods of time, making it difficult to determine when a drought has begun or ended. To some, a drought starts when the rains are delayed or fail altogether, and ends when the rains return. Others suggest that drought can only be identified in retrospect.

Drought severity is also difficult to determine, mainly because droughts differ from other natural hazards in three essential characteristics: intensity, duration and spatial coverage. However, the severity of a drought also depends on the demands made by human activities and by vegetation on a region's water supply. Drought is therefore relative to the demands placed on water as a resource, and occurs when water supplies fall below the requirements of a particular user.

There have been many attempts to monitor or define drought in terms of an index derived from meteorological and hydrological variables, or as a period of deficit in water supply or precipitation. At the same time, attention should also be paid to wet conditions. Three well known and widely used indices, the soil water deficit (SWD), the Palmer Drought Severity Index (PDSI) and the Hydrothermal coefficient (HTC) have been applied in an attempt to systematically characterise severe drought conditions, moderate and severe wet conditions and excessive humid conditions in time and space. The indices have been applied to a spatial climatic database which has been constructed for Europe at a resolution of $0.5°$ latitude by $0.5°$ longitude (Hulme *et al.,* 1993). The database contains 30 year time series for mean monthly temperature and total precipitation for the period 1961 to 1990.

3.3.1   Soil water deficit

Soil water deficits (SWD) have been used as a measure of dry or wet conditions. The approach is based on a simple water balance approach and on any day in the growing season, during the climate baseline period, SWD is calculated by:

$$SWD_1 = PET_1 - PREC_1 \qquad \text{for N} = 1$$
$$SWD_N = PET_N - PREC_N + SWD_{N-1} \quad \text{for N} > 1$$

If $SWD < 0$, then $SWD = 0$ and $EXW = - SWD$
If $SWD > AWC$, then $SWD = AWC$ or $EXW = SWD-AWC$ where PET = potential evapotranspiration, $PREC$ = precipitation, $N =$

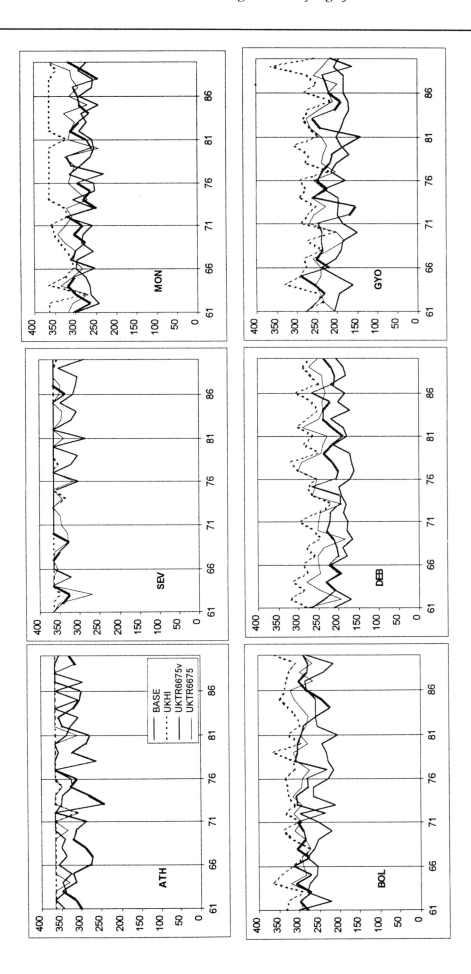

Figure 3.2.5a   Frost free periods for six stations for the baselin climate period and the four specified scenarios.

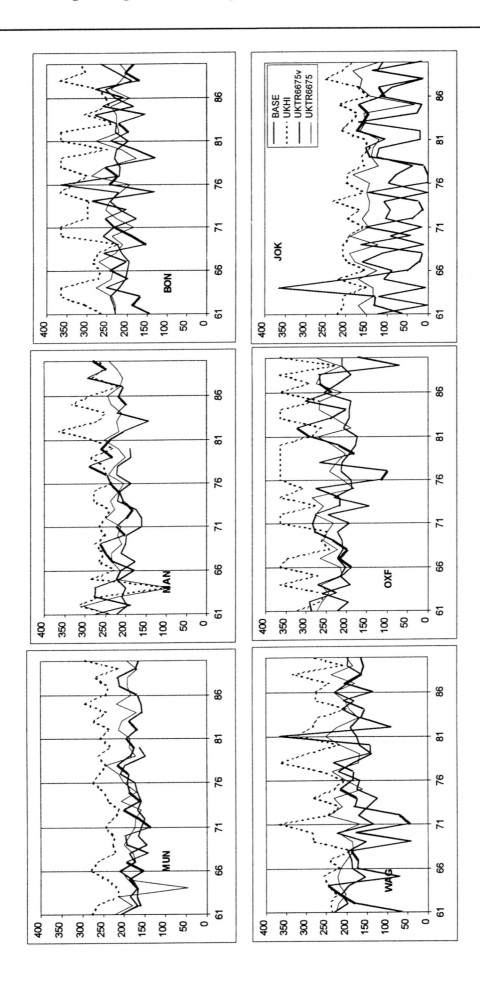

Figure 3.2.5b Frost free periods for six stations for the baselin climate period and the four specified scenarios.

day number and AWC = available water holding capacity of the soil.

Extreme drought conditions are defined when SWD reaches AWC (or higher) value. On the other hand, extreme and moderate drought conditions are achieved, when the SWD reaches or exceeds 75% of the AWC value, at each site. Moreover, the extreme, moderate and mild drought conditions are encountered when the SWD reaches or exceeds 50% of the AWC value, in any 0.5°C cell.

3.3.2 The Palmer Drought Severity Index

The Palmer Drought Severity Index (PDSI) is one of the few general indices for describing meteorological drought intensity and is frequently used to assess conditions of meteorological drought. It is readily available and is standardised to facilitate direct comparisons of PDSI in a temporal and spatial sense. The PDSI has been widely used by many researchers, amongst them: Palmer (1965), Alley (1984), Karl (1986) and Soule (1992).

Palmer's methodology calculates a water balance, usually on a monthly or weekly basis, using historic records of precipitation and temperature. Soil moisture storage is handled by dividing the soil into two layers and assuming that 25 mm of water can be stored in the surface layer. The underlying layer has an available capacity that depends on the soil characteristics of the 0.5°C cell being considered. Data on the available water-holding capacity (AWC) of the soil for the European region were obtained from Groenendijk (1989).

3.3.3 The Hydrothermal Coefficient

The Hydrothermal Coefficient (HTC) has been widely used (Parry *et al.*, 1988) for the characterisation of dry and humid conditions of an area. The HTC value describes the climatic conditions of the months of the wheat growing season. It is calculated from the ratio of total precipitation amount over effective accumulated temperature, assuming a base temperature of 10°C. Since potential evaporation is not included in the calculation of HTC, effective

accumulated temperature is reduced by a factor of 10 to compensate.

3.3.4 Analysis and discussion

Monthly values of SWD were calculated for 5085 grid cells over Europe. The frequency of months characterising different degrees of drought are depicted in Figure 3.3.1. The extreme dry conditions are demonstrated in Figure 3.3.1(a), defined as the percent normalised number of months of the 30-year baseline climate period which satisfy the condition that calculated SWD values reach those of the AWC of the soil. In an analogous way, the compiled, extreme and moderate dry conditions, are depicted in Figure 3.3.1(b), where the percent normalised number of months of the 30-year baseline climate period satisfy the condition that the calculated SWD value reaches 75% of the AWC of the soil. The dry conditions, i.e. extreme, moderate and mild dry conditions, are shown in Figure 3.3.1(c), where the satisfied condition is that the calculated SWD values reached only 50% of the AWC of the soil.

The highest relative frequencies of extreme dry conditions are encountered over the southern European area. It is apparent that the central and southern Iberian peninsula, southern Italy and southern Greece indicate frequencies as high as 30% of months. A general decline in the relative frequency of extreme dry conditions is noted northwards. However, some isolated pockets of extreme dry conditions, as high as 15%, are encountered over central, southeast and northeast Europe. It is worth mentioning the strong (30%) isolated pocket of extreme dry conditions over northeast UK. Similar and quite consistent patterns are also demonstrated for the extreme and moderate dry conditions (Figure 3.3.1(b)) and the extreme, moderate and mild dry conditions, (Figure 3.3.1(c)), implying that the addition of moderate events and moderate and mild events does not change the pattern over Europe. In summary, the most extreme dry episodes are detected over the Iberian peninsula, southern Italy, Sicily and southern Greece.

Extreme and moderate wet episodes, during the changeable wheat growing season within the climate baseline period, were calculated using

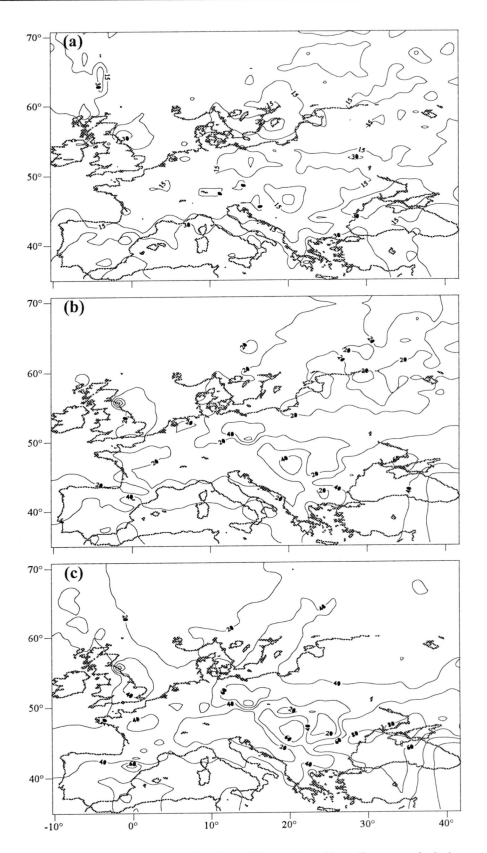

Figure 3.3.1   Relative frequencies of months of the 30-year baseline climate period characterising: (a) extreme dry (SWD = AWC), (b) extreme and moderate dry (SWD = 75% AWC), and (c) extreme, moderate and mild dry (SWD = 50% AWC) conditions.

the PDSI values for 5085 grid cells over Europe.

The percent normalised number of months of the 30-year baseline climate period, which satisfy the condition PDSI ≥ 3, characterise the extreme wet events (Figure 3.3.2a). Moderate wet situations were defined as: 2 ≤ PDSI < 3, and are depicted in Figure 3.3.2(b). The occurrence of extreme wet conditions is very limited throughout Europe. The lowest percentages are found in southern Europe and the Iberian peninsula, as expected. Although similar patterns are illustrated between the two maps, it is obvious that moderate wet episodes are more frequent than extreme episodes. The Iberian peninsula, central and southern Italy and southern Greece have the fewest wet (extreme and moderate) episodes. In summary, the areas around the Mediterranean are not affected by extreme and moderate wet conditions as much as the rest of Europe.

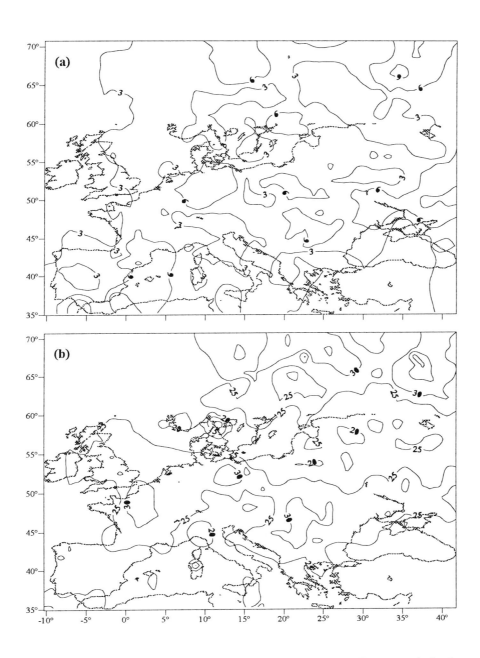

Figure 3.3.2   Relative frequencies of months of the 30-year baseline climate period, characterising: (a) extreme wet (PDSI ≥ 3), (b) extreme and moderate wet (PDSI ≥ 2) conditions.

The percentage of months of the growing season, characterised by extremely dry and excessively humid conditions, according to the HTC, are illustrated in Figures 3.3.3(a) and 3.3.3(b), respectively. It is evident that the areas around the Mediterranean indicate extremely dry conditions in 20% to 30% of months, whilst in central and northern Europe less than 10% are encountered. On the other hand, excessively humid conditions occur in about 30% of months over the Iberian peninsula, less than 50% in central and eastern Mediterranean areas, 80% over the Alps, and more than 50% to 80% across northern Europe.

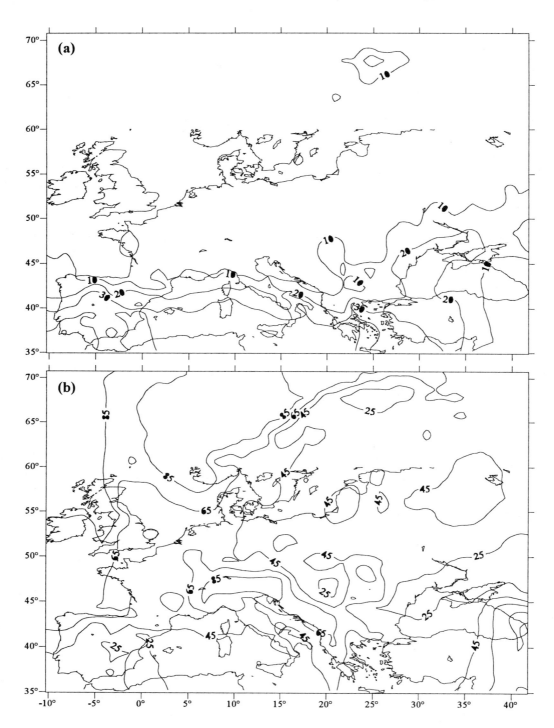

Figure 3.3.3   Relative frequencies of months of the 30-year baseline growing season characterising: (a) extreme dry and (b) extreme wet conditions according to the HTC calculations.

3.3.5   Conclusions

An attempt has been made to develop and apply methodologies for the identification of agriculturally significant climatic extreme events for wheat, and to analyse and study the broadscale features of the spatial distribution of drought and wet conditions over Europe.

In spite of the inherent limitations and deficiencies encountered in the computational procedures of the SWD, PDSI and HTC, their application illustrates their ability to identify severe dry and wet conditions in a temporal and spatial sense. The results are quite realistic, confirming their use as an efficient tool for the detection of drought and wet conditions.

Acknowledgements

The author gratefully acknowledges the valuable assistance of the following staff members: Chris Mitas, Christina Rizou, Olga Kakaliagou, Anthony Karageorgos, Helena Flocas and Michael Papadopoulos. Thanks are also due to John Porter for input concerning the consequences of extremes on crops.

3.4   Crop specific climatic extremes for wheat and maize in Hungary

3.4.1   Background

Hungary is located on the boundaries of the Atlantic, the Mediterranean and the continental climatic zones. As a result the weather is highly variable and extremes events which pose risks to agriculture are common (Faragó, 1992). However, climatic conditions in Hungary can generally be considered favourable for agriculture despite these risk factors. High quality grain production is possible, including wheat and maize, and conditions are also favourable for temperate-zone vegetable, fruit and grape production (Harnos *et al.*, 1990).

The last decade of the UK Met. Office high resolution transient GCM experiment, UKTR6675, indicates temperature increases of 3 to 4°C in the Hungarian region with accompanying increases in precipitation of 10-

15%. Such changes in climate would move existing agricultural zones northwards. Further, an increase in the arid nature of the climate would increase the risks for cultivation.

The following methodological steps were undertaken to assess the impacts of the UKTR6675 climate change scenario on Hungarian agriculture:

(i)   identification of historic events of similar magnitudes to those of the climate change scenario and the impact of those events on agriculture;
(ii) identification of how production conditions for important crops are changing; and
(iii) identification of how risks to cultivation may change, and by what means the risks can be reduced.

These issues are examined in this paper. Firstly, long term climatic variability was analysed and compared with GCM predictions of climate change for Hungary. Secondly, favourable conditions for the production of wheat and maize were determined by characterising climatic year types. Finally the effects of climatic extremes (in particular drought) on wheat and maize yield were investigated.

3.4.2   Long-term climatic variability

To analyse historic changes in climate, the longest time series of meteorological data available was used. Daily maximum and minimum temperature has been recorded in Budapest since 1785 and precipitation since 1845.

Figures 3.4.1 to 3.4.3 illustrate three year moving averages of annual and winter and summer half year mean temperatures. There has been a 2°C variation in annual mean temperature over the period 1785-1985; fluctuations of between 3 and 4°C have been experienced in the mean temperature of the winter and summer half years over the same time period. The temperature data indicate, however, that cooling has taken place rather than warming. Further examination of the summer (April-September) and the winter

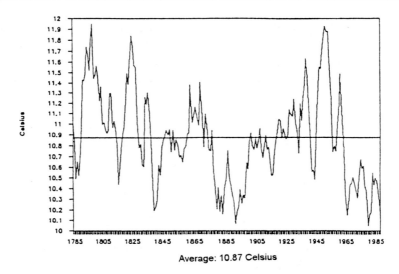

Average: 10.87 Celsius

Figure 3.4.1   Historic annual mean temperature record at Budapest (1780-1988).

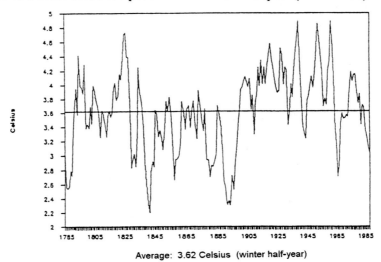

Average: 3.62 Celsius (winter half-year)

Figure 3.4.2   Historic mean temperature for the winter half year (October - March) at Budapest (1780-1988).

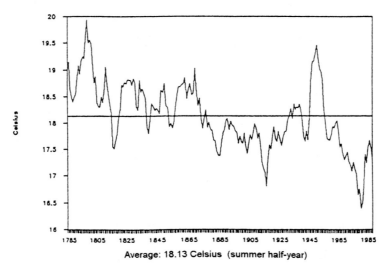

Average: 18.13 Celsius (summer half-year)

Figure 3.4.3   Historic mean temperature for the summer half year (April - September) at Budapest (1780-1988).

(October-March) half-year averages, indicates that the apparent temperature decrease is mainly in the summer half year, though at the end of the last century the winter half year was also lower than normal. The decrease in annual average temperatures is reflected in the average temperatures of the last four decades (10 year averages). On the basis of this it can be determined that the average temperature for the entire country was 1°C higher in the middle of this century than at present.

These changes in the historic record create problems for scenario forecasts, since the UKTR scenarios indicate a different result depending on the selected base period. According to the UKTR scenarios annual average temperature in Hungary will be 3°C higher than the present average, which is significantly higher than the current maxima (Table 3.4.1).

In most areas of Hungary the warmest years in the historic record were 1951 and 1952. From the point of view of the vegetative period of crop growth the hottest year was 1952 in which the whole country experienced severe drought. Yields in this year were less than 50% of average values at that time.

The amount of precipitation and its distribution is the most important limiting factor for crop production in continental climates. Hungary is classified as a semi-arid zone and during the last 20-30 years the arid nature has become more severe. Droughts have been more common and this has resulted in significant yield losses. Figures 3.4.4 - 3.4.6 show annual precipitation and fluctuations in the half-year averages from the mid-19th century to present in Budapest. The variability of precipitation even when calculated as three year averages is very large. During the 1860s and the 1980s annual average precipitation totals barely reached 450mm. At the end of the last century the annual average was close to 850mm. Even with large fluctuations, a downward trend in annual precipitation from the middle of this century can be observed. This is particularly notable during the winter months.

Both decades of the UKTR scenario predict a small increase in precipitation. In this case the selected base period is especially important, since Figures 3.4.4 - 3.4.6 show that over the last forty years there has been more than a 200mm difference in the annual averages, indicating a decreasing trend. The UKTR forecasts are compared to observed data for the cities of Györ and Debrecen in Table 3.4.2.

Table 3.4.1 Three month and annual mean temperatures at Debrecen and Györ for historic data for 1951-1990 and for the scenarios UKTR3140 and UKTR6675.

Site	Temperature (°C)				
	Jan-Mar	**Apr-Jun**	**Jul-Sep**	**Oct-Dec**	**annual average**
Debrecen					
1951-1990 average	0.9	15.2	18.9	5.1	10.1
minimum	-3.3	13.2	16.7	2.8	8.8
maximum	4.2	16.8	21.2	8.2	11.8
UKTR3140	4.1	16.3	20.4	7.0	11.9
UKTR 6675	5.6	17.1	21.8	9.1	13.4
Györ					
1951-1990 average	1.7	14.8	18.7	5.5	10.2
minimum	-2.8	12.8	17.3	4.0	9.0
maximum	4.9	16.1	20.2	7.9	11.5
UKTR3140	4.6	15.9	20.1	7.0	11.9
UKTR6675	5.7	16.5	21.6	9.2	13.2

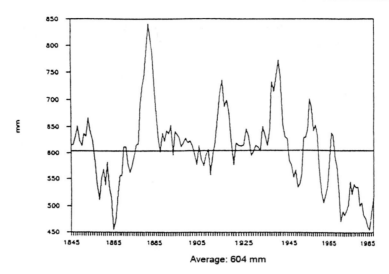

Average: 604 mm

Figure 3.4.4   Historic annual precipitation total at Budapest (1841-1988).

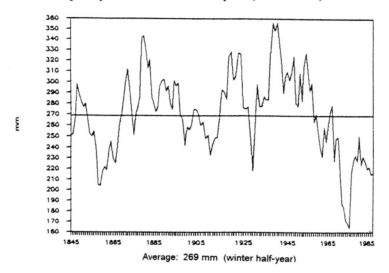

Average: 269 mm (winter half-year)

Figure 3.4.5   Historic precipitation totals for the winter half year (October - March) at Budapest (1841-1988).

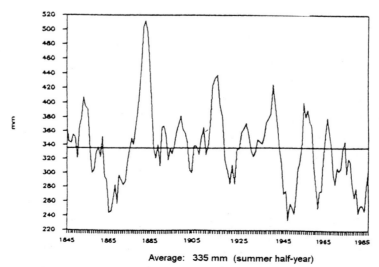

Average: 335 mm (summer half-year)

Figure 3.4.6   Historic precipitation totals for the summer half-year (April - September) at Budapest (1841-1988).

Table 3.4.2   Three month and annual mean precipitation at Debrecen and Győr for historic data for 1951-1990 and for the scenarios UKTR3140 and UKTR6675.

Site	Precipitation (mm)				
	Jan-Mar	**Apr-Jun**	**Jul-Sep**	**Oct-Dec**	**annual average**
Debrecen					
1951-1990	96	179	155	126	556
minimum	39	80	35	43	321
maximum	208	333	376	272	950
UKTR3140	160	170	90	150	570
UKTR6675	130	190	150	155	625
Győr					
1951-1990	92	158	158	138	540
minimum	35	68	69	49	353
maximum	162	308	271	264	778
UKTR3140	150	160	90	170	570
UKTR6675	130	160	170	170	630

Maximum precipitation currently occurs in the second and third quarters of the year (Table 3.4.2), which strongly determines wheat and maize yields. Based on the UKTR scenarios it is expected that there will be significant changes in the amount of precipitation in the winter and summer. Winter precipitation significantly increases whereas summer precipitation decreases in the UKTR3140 scenario, worsening the conditions for growing maize. Precipitation in the second half of the year is expected to be about 10 to 15% higher than at present.

The extreme values (minimum and maximum) also deviate from the present when looking at the annual average (Table 3.4.2). A downward historic trend is observed in the summer half-year precipitation at Győr. The slope of the linear trend shows an annual decrease of approximately 2.4 mm, which over 43 years totals more than 100mm, which is one third of the average. The rate of the downward trend in Debrecen is in contrast only 0.2 mm per year, and is thus a negligible change.

Figures 3.4.7 and 3.4.8 show the monthly breakdown for temperature and precipitation distribution at present and the expected changes under the UKTR3140 and UKTR6675 scenarios. From the point of view of crop production, the predicted decrease in precipitation distribution will be critical since the current May-June maximum precipitation falls to a lower level and July-August may also be very dry.

3.4.3   Effects of climatic variability on wheat and maize production

The two most important crops in Hungary are wheat and maize. The area of land cultivated is between 1.1 - 1.2 million hectares, and these two crops together account for half of all arable land. Hence, the examination of the scenario changes in climate and its variability focused on these two crops.

Yields of wheat and maize are determined by many climatic factors. The effects of climate, including extreme severely damaging events, are not easy to classify and because of this two methods were used in the analysis. Firstly, wheat and maize productivity was determined by the characterisation of important climatic year types and their effects on yield. Secondly, a number of specific extreme climatic thresholds for wheat and maize were assessed.

3.4.3.1 *Climatic year-types*

Methodology

Climatic year types were characterised in terms of the productivity of crops by regions using

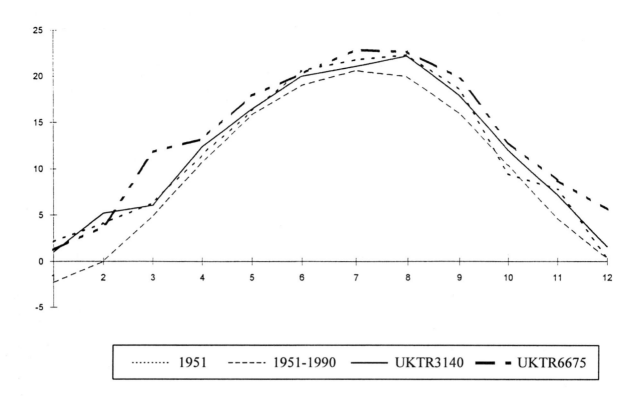

Figure 3.4.7   Monthly mean temperature in 1951, mean 1951-90, UKTR3140 and UKTR6675.

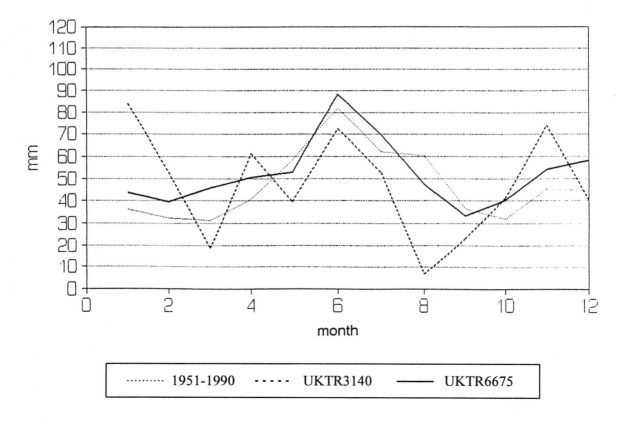

Figure 3.4.8   Monthly precipitation for 1951-90, UKTR3140 and UKTR6675.

statistical analysis and expert opinion. For wheat and maize the following parameters were used:

Wheat: - April and May precipitation total (mm)
- the effective temperature of May and June (°C days)

Maize: - summer half year precipitation total (April to September, mm)
- the effective temperature of the summer half year (°C days)

Climatic year types were determined using Ward type cluster analysis of 1951-75 data by agro-ecological region. The characterisation of climatic year types for maize is shown in Table 3.4.3. Differences in yield compared to the country average were estimated by expert opinion for each climate year type and the most important soil types for each agroecological region. The data for maize are illustrated in Table 3.4.4 for Hajdúság (Debrecen district).

If it is accepted that the expert estimations accurately reflect maize productivity by climatic year types, then the following questions may be considered:

- how do the climatic year types change over time for the regions?
- what effect do the changes in climatic year types have on crop productivity in the regions?

Baseline results

The effect of historical climatic variability on the frequency of individual year types throughout a 110 year time series was determined. The climatic year types calculated using 110 years of data differed somewhat from those calculated using 1951-1975 data, but the differences were not so significant that the expert's estimation was not appropriate. The results of the calculations are shown in Table 3.4.5.

The years 1881-1990 were split into four classes of climate type. Classes were characterised according to average temperature and precipitation values. After clustering, the frequency of the climatic year types in each 20-year period was calculated. It was readily observed that the cold year types, i.e., the occurrence of both the dry-cold and the wet-cold categories, have significantly increased in the second half of this century (Table 3.4.5). During the period before 1960 the wet-warm year type was characteristic for both crops.

Table 3.4.3 Classification of climatic year types for maize

Climatic year type	Total precipitation summer half year	Temperature sum above 10°C	Frequency of occurrence for each year type
A : dry - cold	300	1260	28
B : dry - warm	200	1400	12
C: wet - cold	530	1210	16
D: wet - warm	300	1500	44

Table 3.4.4 Characterisation of maize productivity in terms of climatic year type and soil type for Hajdúság (Debrecen district). Yields are presented relative to the country average of 1.0.

Soil type	Climatic year type			
	A	B	C	D
Prairie limestone based tsernozom	1.23	1.18	1.51	1.59
Field tsernozom	1.23	1.18	1.51	1.59
Field tsernozom, salty at depth	1.01	0.98	1.21	1.31
Steppe field szolonyec	0.80	0.78	0.96	0.16
Field soils with szolonyec	0.80	0.78	0.96	0.16
Field soils	1.01	0.98	1.21	1.31

Based on the characterisation of the climatic year types and the expert estimation the dry-cold year types are the most unfavourable for wheat and maize production. In the event that the dry-cold year type becomes dominant, the evaluation by the experts is a decrease in yield potential of 5-10 %. This can be seen in the last row and column of Table 3.4.5.

Scenario results

The values for the selection criteria of climatic year types for wheat and maize at Debrecen and Györ were predicted for the UKTR3140 and UKTR6675 scenarios and compared to the present values (Table 3.4.6).

Table 3.4.5   Frequency of the four climatic year types in 20 year periods for wheat and maize.

Wheat	dry cold	dry warm	wet cold	wet warm	
Year type characteristics:					
(i) Total precipitation April-May (mm)	76	59	152	122	
(ii) Temperature sum (above 5°C) of May-June (°C days)	436	522	383	511	
Period					Expected yield (t/ha)
1881-1900	11	0	3	6	5.80
1901-1920	7	2	4	7	5.85
1921-1940	4	2	2	12	5.97
1941-1960	5	4	1	10	5.85
1961-1980	9	4	5	2	5.71
1971-1990	7	1	7	5	5.88
Expert estimation (t/ha)	5.48	5.36	6.12	6.21	5.84 (1881-1980 base)
Maize	**dry cold**	**dry warm**	**wet cold**	**wet warm**	
Year type characteristics:					
(i) Total precipitation April-September (mm)	267	217	445	362	
(ii) Temperature sum (above 10 °C) of April-September (°C days)	1302	1693	1133	1412	
Period					Expected yield (t/ha)
1881-1900	7	0	3	10	7.47
1901-1920	6	0	6	8	7.49
1921-1940	3	1	3	13	7.77
1941-1960	2	4	10	4	7.34
1961-1980	10	0	6	4	7.08
1971-1990	10	0	7	3	7.05
Expert estimation (t/ha)	6.25	6.1	7.68	8.27	7.37 (1881-1980 base)

The expected year types for wheat fall into the current dry-warm category, which gives the lowest yields in the historic analysis of climate year types (Table 3.4.6). Maize production is determined by the summer half year temperature sum and since the UKTR6675 prediction is considerably higher than the maximum observed temperature sum over the period 1951-90, and as precipitation is not forecast to increase, unfavourable conditions will be created for maize production. For comparison the maximum temperature sum in the record is included in Table 3.4.6, which in the case of maize occurred in 1952. In this year the yield was very low. Two factors came into play besides the economic problems: (i) the high summer temperature, which included a record number of extremely hot days (daily maximum $\geq 30^{\circ}C$) and (ii) drought.

Climatic year types by their nature hide extreme events, since the cluster centre for the given class element is represented by its average. The recorded data is highly variable, shown in Figures 3.4.9 - 3.4.10. The April-May precipitation extreme low values occur more than seven times at Győr. It must also be noted that too much precipitation can also result in a significant reduction in crop yield. In the 1970s almost 700mm of precipitation in the summer

half year resulted in a noticeable decrease in yields for wheat and maize.

3.4.3.2 Climatic extremes

Drought

To characterise the relationship between yield and weather various statistical methods were applied but no reasonable correlation could be found between yield loss and meteorological parameters. For maize different degrees of drought help explain yield loss in most cases. Three degrees of drought were defined:

(i) Severe drought occurs if there is a winter drought and if the precipitation of May, June, July is at least 30% less in each of these months than the long-term average for the region.

(ii) Drought occurs if there is a summer drought and also if precipitation for each of the months May, June, July is at least 30% less than the long-term average for the region.

(iii) Mild drought occurs if for the months May, June, July there is less than a 30% decrease in precipitation when compared to the long-term average for the region.

Table 3.4.6 Values for selection criteria used in identifying climatic year types for wheat and maize at Debrecen and Győr for the historic data and the UKTR3140 and UKTR6675 scenarios.

	Debrecen		Győr	
	Temperature sum ($^{\circ}C$ days)	Precipitation (mm)	Temperature sum ($^{\circ}C$ days)	Precipitation (mm)
Wheat				
1951-90	450	99	425	92
maximum	571	-	525	-
UKTR3140	499	101	477	90
UKTR6675	551	103	524	91
Maize				
1951-90	1287	340	1233	322
maximum	1525	-	1491	-
UKTR3140	1529	256	1468	239
UKTR6675	1734	342	1660	313

(a)   (b)

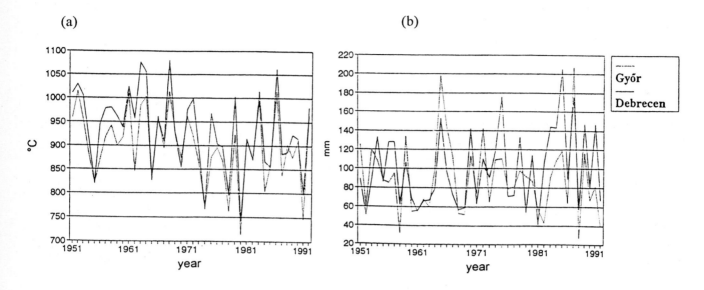

Figure 3.4.9   Historic time series for the selection criteria used in identifying climatic year types for wheat at Györ and Debrecen: (a) temperature sum (base 5°C) over April to June period; and (b) precipitation total for April to May.

(a)   (b)

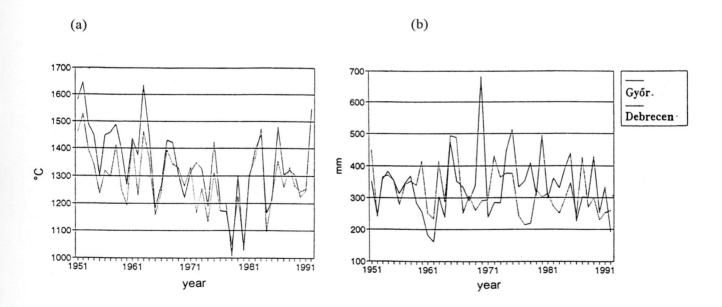

Figure 3.4.10   Historic time series for the selection criteria used in identifying climatic year types for maize at Györ and Debrecen: (a) temperature sum (base 10°C) over April to September period; and (b) precipitation totals for April to September.

The analysis showed that severe drought caused considerable yield loss almost everywhere in the country, even in the wetter counties of West Transdanubia. Table 3.4.7 illustrates drought years and the resulting reductions in yield in the Hajdú-Bihar county. Mild drought in Hajdú-Bihar county generally occurred in every fourth year. In 80% of the mild drought years there was some yield loss. The degree of yield loss from drought is significant. However, in drought years there was almost always one case in each county when the actual recorded yield exceeded the long-term mean, if only by a small amount. The frequency of drought was between 9% (severe) and 17% (mild) over the period 1951-1980.

Figures 3.4.11 (a) and (b) show the frequency of dry and very dry summers respectively in the period 1981-1992. A dry summer is defined as occurring if the amount of summer half-year precipitation is more than 30mm less than the long-term average. If the summer half-year precipitation is more than 60mm less than the long-term average, then the summer is defined as very dry. The frequency of very dry summers exceeded 1 in 3 years in 6 out of 19 counties during the period 1981-92.

Other extremes

An analysis of daily climate data at Debrecen and Győr for the period 1951-1990 has been conducted to investigate the frequency and magnitude of extreme events for winter wheat and maize.

The most important limiting factors for wheat and maize production in Hungary are:

For wheat: - cold winters without snow cover (number of frost days with daily minima $\leq$ -5°C, -10°C, -15°C)
- long dry periods (daily precipitation less than 1.0mm)

For maize: - a short vegetative period (determined by the length of the frost free period)
- the number of very hot days (daily maximum temperature $\geq$ 30°C)

There has been no significant change in the number of frosty days in the last four decades, in Debrecen (Figure 3.4.12a) and Győr (Figure 3.4.12b). The two sites show similar occurrences of daily minima < -5°C, -10°C, -15°C for each year between 1951 and 1990.

Table 3.4.7 Identification of severe drought, drought and mild drought years in Hajdú-Bihar county and the estimated yield loss as a percentage of the long-term yield. + denotes an increase in yield.

	Severe drought years		Drought years		Mild drought years	
	Year	Yield loss as a % of the expected yield	Year	Yield loss as a % of the expected yield	Year	Yield loss as a % of the expected yield
			1952	43	1952	43
			1960	+5	1960	+5
			1961	16	1961	16.5
					1962	11
					1963	+12
	1964	6	1964	6.3	1964	6
	1968	3			1968	3
					1972	6.8
	1976	20			1976	20
Frequency (1951-80)	9%		11%		17%	

(a)

(b)

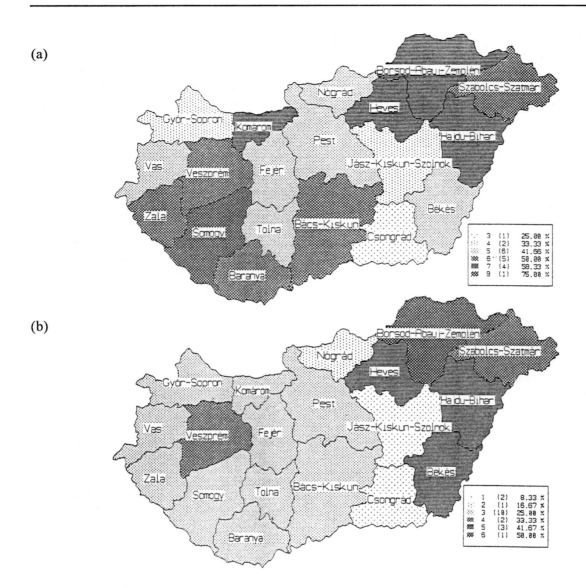

Figure 3.4.11   Number and percentage of (a) dry summers (April to September precipitation 30mm less than long term mean) and (b) very dry summers (April to September precipitation 60mm less than long term mean) for 1981-1992 by county.

(a)   (b)

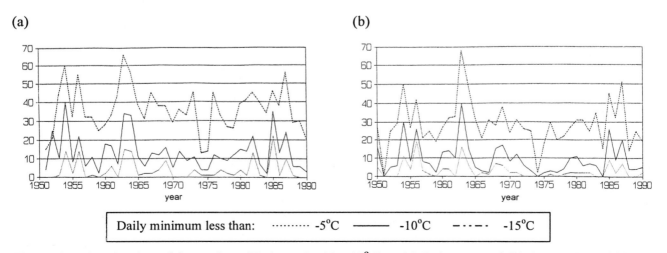

Figure 3.4.12   Number of frosty days (Tmin < -5; -10; -15°C) at (a) Debrecen and (b) Györ, 1951-1990.

The longest dry period (consecutive days with daily precipitation < 1.0 mm) in Hungary was observed in Heves county and was 80 days in length. Table 3.4.8 shows that the longest dry periods occur in winter. Significant damage can occur in the case of autumn sown crops suffering long dry spells if spring precipitation is also deficient.

A significant change can be observed in the frost free period, which largely determines the vegetative period of both maize and wheat, as shown in Figure 3.4.13. The average start of the frost free period has shifted from the end of February to mid-March (Figure 3.4.13a). The end of the frost-free period varied from the beginning of November to the beginning of December (Figure 3.4.13b). The end also shows a shift in mean date from early December to the middle of November (1990) during 1951-93. The length of the frost-free period has, thus, become 8-10 days shorter according to the trend (Figure 3.4.13c).

In the case of extreme hot days an increasing trend has been observed (but only since 1975), as shown in Figure 3.4.14. In the 1990s there were record values observed in many regions (these figures are not shown on the diagram).

3.4.4 Risk analysis

To characterise deviations from expected yields a statistical model was developed. This determines the expected yield against which risks of crop damage can be compared (Harnos *et al.*, 1995). In the statistical analysis a relatively simple, but widely accepted hypothesis was used in which the development of yield was based on two factors:

(i) genetic and agrotechnical development; and

(ii) the stochastic character of the weather.

This means that for a fixed agrotechnology yield is expressed in the following form:

$$\eta(t,\xi) = y_1(t) + \eta_2(t,\xi) \qquad (3.4.1)$$

Table 3.4.8 Timing and length of dry periods for counties. The dry period given is the longest within the time series of climatic data available in the county.

| County | Longest dry spell | | |
	Start date	End date	Length of spell (days)
Bács-Kiskun	24.11.1972	15.01.1973	53
Baranya	05.10.1978	25.11.1978	52
Békés	07.01.1989	18.02.1989	43
Borsod-Abaúj-Zemplén	17.08.1961	19.10.1961	64
Csongrád	13.12.1988	25.02.1989	75
Fejér	08.11.1953	05.01.1954	59
Györ-Sopron	30.10.1956	03.01.1957	66
Hajdú-Bihar	30.01.1976	06.04.1976	68
Heves	31.07.1961	18.10.1961	80
Komárom-Esztergom	07.10.1953	26.11.1953	51
Nógrád	13.02.1961	17.04.1961	64
Pest	10.01.1959	06.03.1959	56
Somogy	09.01.1989	23.02.1989	46
Szabolcs-Szatmár-Bereg	07.02.1974	25.04.1974	78
Jász-Nagykun-Szolnok	23.08.1961	28.10.1961	67
Tolna	08.11.1953	30.12.1953	53
Veszprém	11.03.1974	24.04.1974	45
Zala	05.10.1978	25.11.1978	52

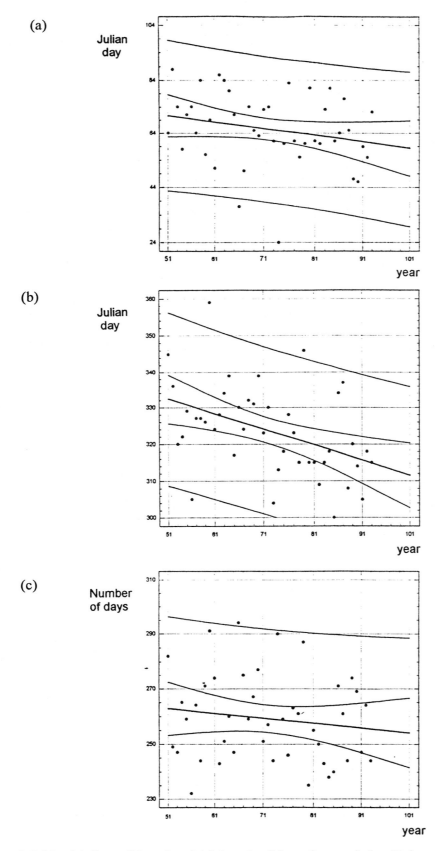

(a)

(b)

(c)

Figure 3.4.13   (a) Start, (b) end and (c) length of frost-free period at Debrecen, 1951-1993. The central line is a linear regression and the curved lines show the 95% confidence that the fitted line lies between them. The outlier lines are the 95% confidence limits of the point.

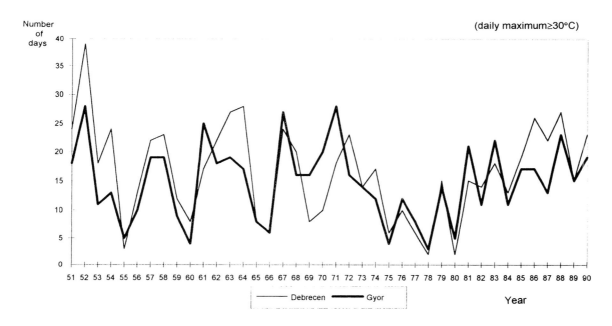

Figure 3.4.14 Number of days with maximum temperature exceeding 30°C at Debrecen and Győr, 1951-1990.

At the regional level agrotechnology did not explicitly play a role in this function as no direct observations were available. The development of agricultural technology was, however, a part of the base hypothesis, which was implicitly expressed in $y_1(t)$. $y_1(t)$ depends on the ecological capacity of a given region and $\eta_2(t,\xi)$ expresses the effects of the weather. It is assumed that $y_1(t)$ behaves asymptotically and is a solution of the following differential equation:

$$\frac{dy(t)}{dt} = \alpha y(t)(1-\beta y(t)) \qquad (3.4.2)$$

where $\quad y(0) = y_0$

The asymptotic nature of $y_1(t)$ assumes that in the process of development there are no changes in varieties, but considerable changes in agrotechnology. For Hajdú - Bihar county the fitted curves for wheat and maize yield are illustrated in Figure 3.4.15.

From $y(t)$ the conditional expected values of $\eta(t,\xi)$ in the t-th year, i.e.: a regression function $y(t) = E(\eta(t,\xi)|t)$, can be determined. The

risk can be characterised by the $\eta(\xi_t) = \eta_2(t,\xi) = y_r(t)-y_1(t)$ probability variable, and its distribution function $F(y)=P(\eta(\xi_t)<y)$, where $F(y)$ expresses the probability that the $\eta(\xi_t)$ yield fluctuations are not larger than y. From the point of view of risk, this is not a relevant indicator but rather, how the yield loss is characterized.

The yield loss function can be defined as:

$$\eta^l(\xi) = \begin{cases} 0 & \text{if } \eta(\xi)\geq0 \\ -\eta(\xi) & \text{if } \eta(\xi)<0 \end{cases} \qquad (3.4.3)$$

and its distribution function is:

$$F^l(y) = P(\eta^l(\xi)\leq y) \qquad (3.4.4)$$

By using $^l(y)$ the yield certainty of the regions can be compared and the terms of the risk can be defined. For example, it can be implied that in the j region a given crop is better than in the

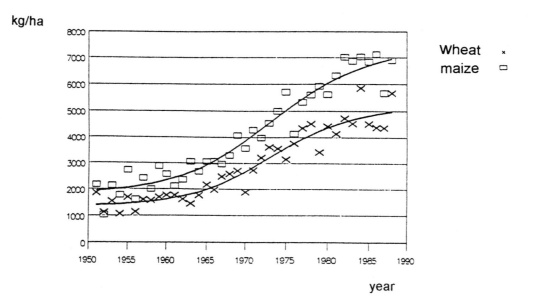

Figure 3.4.15 Observed yields and fitted statistical model for wheat and maize yields in Hajdú-Bihar county.

k region, if

$$P(\eta l_j^!(\xi) \geq y) \leq P(\eta l_k^!(\xi) \geq y) \qquad (3.4.5)$$

for every y, i.e. the probability of the yield loss being larger than y in the j region is less than in the k region for every y. This comparison is illustrated in Figure 3.4.16.

In Figure 3.4.16

$$p_j = F_j^!(y) = P(\eta_j^! \leq y) \qquad (3.4.6)$$

and

$$p_k = F_k^!(y) = P(\eta_k^! \leq y) \qquad (3.4.7)$$

represent the probability that the yield loss is not more than y.

If

$$1 - p_j = P(\eta_j^!(\xi) \geq y) \leq P(\eta_k^!(\xi) \geq y) = 1 - p_k$$

is true for every y, then the yield certainty of j region is better than the k indexed ones. The distribution functions are not comparable with each other.

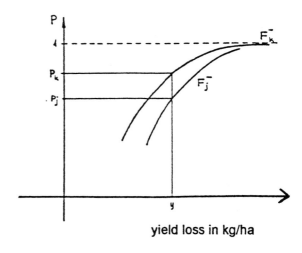

Figure 3.4.16 Cumulative probability functions of yield loss at site k (Fk) and j (Fj). The probability of loss of a specific yield (y) is always higher at k (Pk) than at j (Pj).

To determine crop certainty for a comparison of cultivated areas there is no need to use a distribution function. In practice it is enough to decide on the given probability level. This is made possible by the following notion. The y_p p-percentile is determined by the formula:

$$F^l(y_p) = P(\eta^l \langle y_p) = p \qquad (3.4.8)$$

Using this notion the different regions can be compared in the following manner. It is said that the crop certainty of the j region is better than the k region on the p probability level if the p-percentiles satisfy the $y_p^j \rangle y_p^k$ inequality, where

$$P(\eta_j^l \langle y_p^j) = p = P(\eta_j^l \langle y_p^k) \qquad (3.4.9)$$

The comparison of distribution functions can be given by the p-percentilies.

If $y_p^j \rangle y_p^k$ for every $p \in (0,1)$ then for the F distribution function:

$$1 - F_j^l(y) = P(\eta_j^l \geq y) \leq P(\eta_k^l \geq y) = 1 - F_k^l(y)$$
$$(3.4.10)$$

is true for every y.

The relative yield loss functions of wheat and maize are shown in Figure 3.4.17 for the counties of Györ-Sopron and Hajdú-Bihar. From these graphs it can be read that in the Györ-Sopron county wheat, and in the Hajdú-Bihar county maize, can be grown with a greater certainty. The graph in Figure 3.4.18 shows the yield average for wheat and maize for various probability levels for each of the counties.

Using the climatic year types and the expert estimation of yields the changes in risk for wheat and maize production were analysed (Tables 3.4.9 and 3.4.10). First the distributions of climatic year types for 20 year periods were determined. Then the expected value of the yield loss was calculated. Table 3.4.9 shows the theoretical yield. Significant changes in the risk can be detected only after the 1960s (Table 3.4.10). The expected averages losses can be considered constant.

Table 3.4.9 Forecast yields of wheat and maize by climatic year types for 20 year periods for the agroecological region Hajdúság.

Forecast yield by climatic year type	dry cold	dry warm	wet cold	wet warm
wheat	5.48	5.36	6.12	6.14
maize	6.25	6.10	7.68	8.27

Table 3.4.10 Probability of yield loss for 20 year periods for the agroecological region Hajdúság

	Wheat		Maize	
	(%)	(t/ha)	(%)	(t/ha)
1881-1900	55	0.36	35	1.12
1901-1920	45	0.39	30	1.12
1921-1940	30	0.40	20	1.15
1941-1960	45	0.41	30	1.14
1961-1980	65	0.40	50	1.12
1971-1990	40	0.38	50	1.12
expected value of yield (t/ha) for years 1881-1980	5.84		7.37	

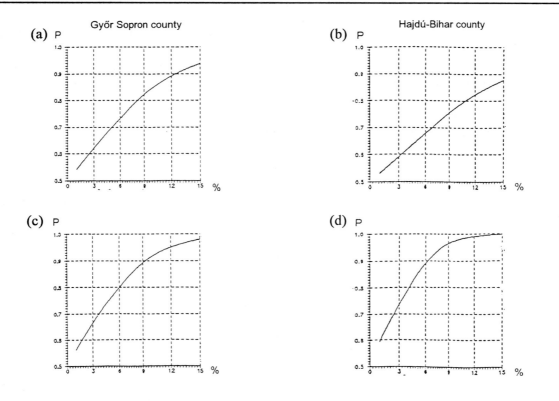

Figure 3.4.17 Probability yield loss functions for wheat (a, b) and maize (c, d) in Győr Sopron (a, c) and Hajdú-Bihar (b, d) counties.

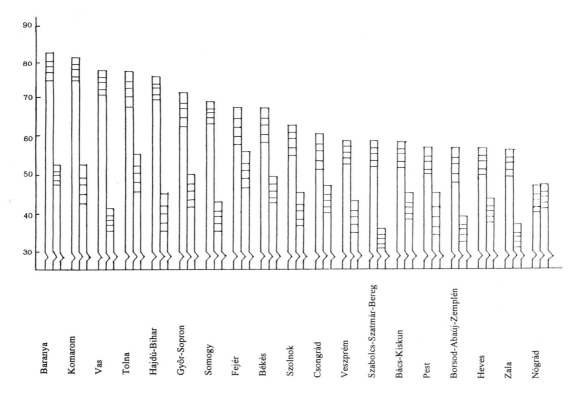

Figure 3.4.18 Percentiles of yield of maize and wheat, 1950-1989 by county. The first column of the pair is maize and the second wheat. The lowest line in each column is the 70th percentile, followed by the 80th, 90th, 95th and 99th percentiles.

3.4.5 Conclusions

Climatic conditions in Hungary can be considered favourable for crop production. High quality grain production is possible and conditions are also favourable for temperate zone vegetable, grape and fruit production.

As a consequence of climate change agricultural zones will move northwards and the climate will become drier, hence, increasing risks for cultivation. Analysis of long time series of climatic data indicate that over the last century a cooling process has taken place rather than warming. This is occurring particularly in the summer half year. The amount of precipitation and its unfavourable distribution is the most important limiting factor for crop production in Hungary. A downward trend in precipitation can be observed in the historic record particularly in the winter months. During the last 20 to 30 years the arid nature of the climate has become more severe and droughts more common resulting in significant yield losses.

Under the UKTR climate change scenarios this tendency will continue and therefore the characterisation of the weather risk and extreme meteorological events are now the focus of researchers. Using comparative analysis of climatic year types the following conclusions can be drawn.

- The unfavourable year types have become increasingly dominant in the last two to three decades and evaluation by the experts is a decrease in yield potential of 5-10%.

- The expected year type for wheat predicted by the UKTR scenarios will fall into the dry warm category that is the most unfavourable for wheat production.

- The conditions for maize production will also be unfavourable under the UKTR scenarios because the summer temperature sum is considerably higher than the maximum observed temperature sum over the period 1951-1990, particularly as precipitation is not forecast to increase.

One of the most important factors in Hungary is the uncertainty of agricultural production. The yield loss function makes a relatively good comparison of regional yield security and helps to identify a given crop/land use with the lowest risk as well as the optimal land use at a given risk.

References

Alley, W. M. (1984). The Palmer Drought Severity Index: Limitations and Assumptions. *Journal of Climate and Applied Meteorology*, **23**, 1100-1109.

Blonet, A., Gaillard, B. and Masse, J. (1984). Le Gel et les cereales: Exemple d' etude des risques de gel hivernal en Loraine. *Perspectives Agricoles*, **No. 85**.

Dagneaud, J. R., Courreur, F. and Tranchefort, J. (1979). Variabilite des rendements de ble' tendre d' hiver sous l'effet du climat. Exemple du Loiret. *Perspectives Agricoles*, **No. 26**.

Del Pozo, A. H., Garcia-Huidobro, J., Noroa, R., and Villaseca, S. (1987). Relationship of base temperature to development of spring wheat. *Experimental Agriculture*, **23**, 21-30.

Faragó, T. (1992). *Climatic Variability, Impacts and Sustainability: Generalization from Regional Climate Impact Studies*. Hungarian Meteorological Service, Hungary.

Füstös, L., Mcszéna, Gy. and Simon, N. (1986). *Statistical Methods of Multivariable Data Analysis*. Academic Public House, Budapest.

Groenendijk, H. (1989). *Estimation of the waterholding-capacity of soils in Europe. The compilation of the soils data sets*. Simulation Report CABO-TT No. **19**, Wageningen.

Harnos, Zs. (1991). *Adaptive Agricultural Systems: Methodological Research*. AKAPRINT, Budapest.

Harnos, Zs., Racskó, P. and Szeidl, L. (in press). *Risk Analysis of Crop Production in Hungary Biometrics*.

Harnos, Zs., Racskó, P., Szeidl, L., Semenov, M. and Svirezhev, I. (1990). *Risk Analysis of Crop Production*. OTKA-report No. 400-713. In Hungarian.

Hosking, J. R. M. (1990). L-moments: Analysis and estimation of distributions using linear combinations of order statistics. *Journal of the Royal Statistical Society*, **52,** 105-205.

Hulme, M., Jiang, T., Turney, C. and Barrow, E. (1993). *A 1961-90 baseline climatology and future climate change scenarios for Great Britain and Europe. Part II: 1961-90 European baseline climatology*. Climatic Research Unit, University of East Anglia, 49pp.

Karacostas, T. S., and Flocas A. A. (1993). The Identification and characterisation of extreme weather years in Europe. In G. J. Kenny, P. A. Harrison and M. L. Parry, eds., *The Effect of Climate Change on Agricultural and Horticultural Potential in Europe*. University of Oxford, 224 pp.

Karl, T. R. (1986). The sensitivity of the Palmer Severity Index and Palmer's Z-Index to their calibration coefficients including potential evapotranspiration. *Journal of Climate and Applied Meteorology*, **25,** 77-86.

Meyer, S. J. (1990). *The development of a crop specific drought index for corn*. Ph. D. Dissertation, University of Nebraska, Lincoln, Nebraska, U.S.A., 165pp.

Palmer, W. C. (1965). Meteorological drought. U. S. Weather Bureau, Washington D. C. Research Paper **No. 45**, 58 pp.

Parry, M. L., Carter, T.R. and Konijn, N.T. (1988). *The impact of climate variations on Agriculture. Vol.1*. Kluwer Academic Publishers, Dordrecht. 876 pp.

Petr, J. (ed.) (1991). *Weather and Yield. Developments in Crop Science*, 20. Elsevier, Amsterdam. 288pp.

Rosenzweig, S. (1985). Potential CO_2 included climate effects on North American wheat-producing regions. *Climatic Change*, **7,** 367-389.

Russell, G. and Wilson, G.W. (1994). *An agro-pedo-climatological knowledge-base of wheat in Europe*. Publication EUR 15789 EN of the Office for Official Publications of the European Communities; Series 'Agriculture', Luxembourg, 158 pp.

Soule, P. T. (1992). Spatial patterns of drought frequency and duration in the contiguous USA based on multiple drought event definitions. *International Journal of Climatology*, **12,** 11-24.

Weir, A.H., Bragg, P.L., Porter, J.R. and Rayner, J.A. (1984). A winter wheat crop simulation model without water or nutrient control limitations. *Journal of Agricultural Science*, **102,** 371-382.

CHAPTER 4

Experiments on the effects of increased temperature and / or elevated concentrations of carbon dioxide on crops

SUMMARY

Introduction

A series of experiments on the effects of changing environmental conditions on crop growth and development have been conducted in greenhouses, growth chambers, open top chambers and in the field. The main intentions of the experiments were:

- to provide basic information about plant responses to future increasing atmospheric CO_2 and climatic warming;

- to improve understanding of the plant mechanisms involved; and

- to provide data sets for validation and improvement of existing crop growth models to be used for predicting crop growth in a future climate.

The experimental programme consisted of three types of C_3 crops: spring wheat (an annual cereal crop), grapevine (a perennial fruit crop), and onion, cauliflower and broccoli (vegetable crops).

Nearly all experiments were combined with activities in crop growth modelling (Chapter 5). This demonstrates the close link between the measurement and interpretation of crop variables, and the structures and algorithms used in the models for the same crop. Consequently, the experimental results are summarised and discussed in the context of mechanistic crop modelling. For this a crop growth schema was used which includes the main plant processes involved in phenological development, growth and assimilate partitioning and can be considered as the basis of the structure of most crop growth models.

Cauliflower and broccoli

Both cauliflower and broccoli are important field grown vegetable crops in Europe. It is known from earlier experiments that reproductive growth of cauliflower and broccoli is very sensitive to temperature and, hence, these experiments were designed to obtain estimates of the risk of temperature induced quality defects.

Three experiments in growth chambers were conducted at the Research Centre Foulum (Denmark) with various temperature and illumination regimes. The dry matter of the individual organs, as well as leaf area and light interception, was measured at 3 to 7 day intervals.

Field-based portable enclosures were used to investigate the optimum temperature for vernalization and the cardinal temperature for curd quality defects on cauliflower.

Finally, field experiments on three varieties of broccoli were conducted to obtain data required for model validation and calibration, each variety planted at different dates and at two densities. Phenological development, dry matter, leaf area and light interception were recorded in weekly intervals.

A major result of these experiments was that the date of curd initiation of cauliflower and broccoli was found to be strongly influenced by temperature but was unaffected by light level. The calculated light extinction coefficient (Monsi and Saeki, 1953) decreased with increasing leaf area in both crops, but was lower in broccoli. In many models the extinction coefficient, which is needed to calculate radiation interception by the canopy, is assumed to be constant during growth. The experiments demonstrated that this parameter declined with increasing plant age and therefore this change should be considered in the models. Two reasons for the decrease in light extinction coefficient, namely changes in leaf inclination and clustering of leaves, are discussed in Section 4.2.5.

An exponential growth equation was used to describe dry matter accumulation and a logistic equation to describe the development of leaf area, both of which fitted the experimental data well. The radiation use efficiency (RUE), calculated from plant dry matter and intercepted photosynthetically active radiation, was temperature dependent and increased up to a maximum at about 14°C for both cauliflower and broccoli. Differences in the optimum temperature for curd initiation of cauliflower were found between the varieties. Models have, therefore, to consider this optimum to be genotype dependent.

Onion

Experiments in the literature report that the percentage yield increase with CO_2 enrichment is usually greater in root crops, such as carrots and sugar beet, than the average increase reported for a broad range of crops. As the response of bulbing species to enriched CO_2 has not yet been reported, an experiment was set up at Reading (UK). This experiment made use of a CO_2 fumigation technique in field tunnels, where plants were imposed to a temperature gradient along each tunnel (Hadley et al., 1995). The main aims were to quantify the effects of temperature, CO_2 and possible interactions on development, yield, rate of increase in the number of leaves and leaf area expansion, as well as to examine the implications for onion production in a future climate. Two onion varieties were grown which were subjected to the following treatments: ambient and elevated CO_2 and a mean temperature increase along the tunnels of 2 to 4.5°C.

As expected, higher temperatures shortened the duration of crop growth; a close linear relation between the rate of crop development and temperature was found for both varieties. CO_2 decreased the rate of development from transplanting to bulbing, but increased it from bulbing to maturity. It was assumed that conditions favouring carbohydrate accumulation promoted the swelling of bulb scale leaves so that the stage of bulbing was reached earlier.

In this experiment, mean plant leaf number was described as a linear function of thermal time. CO_2 had only a slight effect on leaf emergence but this differed between genotypes. Temperature also influenced the plant leaf area; highest values were measured at the warmer ends of the tunnels. For the calculation of RUE the duration of the leaf area (LAD) in a crop stand is relevant. From bulbing to maturity LAD was lower with higher temperatures. A positive effect of CO_2 on RUE was found only during the early growth stages from transplanting to bulbing, but not during bulbing to maturity. It was assumed that the stimulation of growth by elevated CO_2 was predominantly during early stages of growth.

Grapevine

A sophisticated technique has been used to investigate the effects of elevated CO_2 on plant growth and yield performance in grapevine, a perennial crop, in Siena (Italy). This system (mini-FACE) offers the opportunity to raise the CO_2 concentration in crops under field conditions. The technique and the accuracy of the CO_2 fumigation device is extensively documented in Section 4.4.2. Growth parameters measured were RUE, specific leaf area, partitioning between organs, leaf water relations and photosynthetic capacity.

Fruit weight increased by about 20% with elevated CO_2 and total dry weight by 35%. However, this increase in dry matter accumulation had no effect on the harvest index (HI). In both CO_2 environments the same slope of increase in HI over time was found.

An increase in sugars and leaf starch content with elevated CO_2 was found in leaves and consequently specific leaf area decreased. The accumulation of extra carbohydrates, mainly starch, may act as a source of carbon which can be remobilized when the carbon gain from photosynthesis is low, e.g. during drought stress or during low radiation receipts in cloudy weather.

Quality aspects play a special role in grapevine cultivation. It is expected that elevated atmospheric CO_2 would influence the quality of wines depending on their type. The observed increase in the dimensions of the berries is important because of its direct relationship with must components. The lower sugar concentration and increased acidity in the must under elevated CO_2 would improve the quality of light or sparkling wines but be detrimental to the quality of high quality wines.

Spring wheat

Experiments on spring wheat have been conducted at three Institutes: the Agricultural University in Wageningen (The Netherlands); the University of Bonn (Germany) and the Agricultural Research Centre at Jokioinen (Finland).

Elevated CO_2 resulted in a higher rate of net photosynthesis and, hence, a higher total dry matter yield for wheat crops in most experiments. Although a large number of such experiments with winter wheat have been carried out, little information is available on the effects of elevated CO_2 on wheat growth under limited nutrient availability. As nutrient supply is strongly limiting for crop growth in most arable areas of the world, the interaction between elevated CO_2 and nutrient limitation is of broad interest. The limited amount of experimental results showed that the positive CO_2 effect on crop growth is less with a decreased nutrient supply. A greenhouse experiment was conducted to test this hypothesis (Section 4.5).

The carbon that is translocated to the growing grains during grain growth is derived from two sources: the assimilates from photosynthesis (mainly in leaf tissue) and the labile pool of carbon assimilated before anthesis and temporarily stored in the stems and leaves. Assuming that vegetative growth is stimulated by elevated CO_2, the question arises, what effect would this have on the redistribution of carbon in vegetative organs during grain filling and what consequences would this have for managing the vegetative growth in wheat fields? A ^{13}C labelling technique was used to trace the carbon redistribution during grain filling (Section 4.6).

For the third wheat experiment a northern site under long photoperiod conditions at high latitudes was chosen. From simulation runs with wheat growth models it was concluded that increasing CO_2 would partly compensate for the negative effect of early ripening and lower yields with rising temperatures. Open top chambers, some of them enriched with CO_2, were used in greenhouses with a temperature regime 3°C above outside, to investigate the temperature and CO_2 effects on a Swedish spring wheat variety. Plants grown outdoors were kept under the same plastic cover as that used for the greenhouse, to achieve comparable radiation and water supply. Additionally the temperature effects on domestic and non-domestic spring wheat varieties in greenhouses were tested (Section 4.7).

In these wheat experiments the following information has been determined:

- phenological development, tillering and leaf emergence;
- photosynthetic rate and dry matter accumulation of vegetative and reproductive organs;
- uptake and nutrient use efficiency of N, P, K;
- fraction of carbon and nitrogen actually partitioned within the plant during grain filling;
- water use efficiency; and
- harvest index and the quality of the grain fraction.

Following the crop modelling schema in Figure 4.1, light interception occurs at the beginning of the plant processes involved. Although direct effects of CO_2 on light interception have not been investigated in the experiments it is assumed that an increase in dry matter caused by elevated CO_2 may produce higher plant densities of the canopy and, hence, improve the absorption of photosynthetically active radiation.

The rate of net photosynthesis (next process in Figure 4.1) in flag leaves, measured throughout three years of experiments at Jokioinen, Finland was found to increase by up to 40% with doubling of ambient CO_2. In both CO_2 environments the temperature effect on carbon assimilation was not significant.

In the high CO_2 treatments at Bonn additional carbon was accumulated in the leaves and, hence, a decreasing specific leaf area was observed. These results correspond well with a decrease in specific leaf area and increases in leaf sugar content, as a primary assimilation product, and leaf starch accumulation measured in the FACE experiment on grapevine.

As a consequence of increased carbon availability with elevated CO_2, total dry matter production increased with elevated CO_2 when nutrient supply was unlimited in all wheat experiments. This increase was a consequence of both a higher number and dry mass of tillers, leaves and roots as well as an increased grain mass. This positive effect was not significant in all observations, however, natural variation of parameters between and within individual plants was large.

The impact of increasing temperature on dry matter accumulation in wheat has been investigated in the Finnish experiment only. As a mean over three years of observation the total biomass per plant significantly increased with temperature in elevated CO_2 but not at ambient CO_2. Again under elevated CO_2 the total biomass per m^2 increased when temperatures were maintained at 3°C above outdoors, but the temperature effect was negative at ambient CO_2.

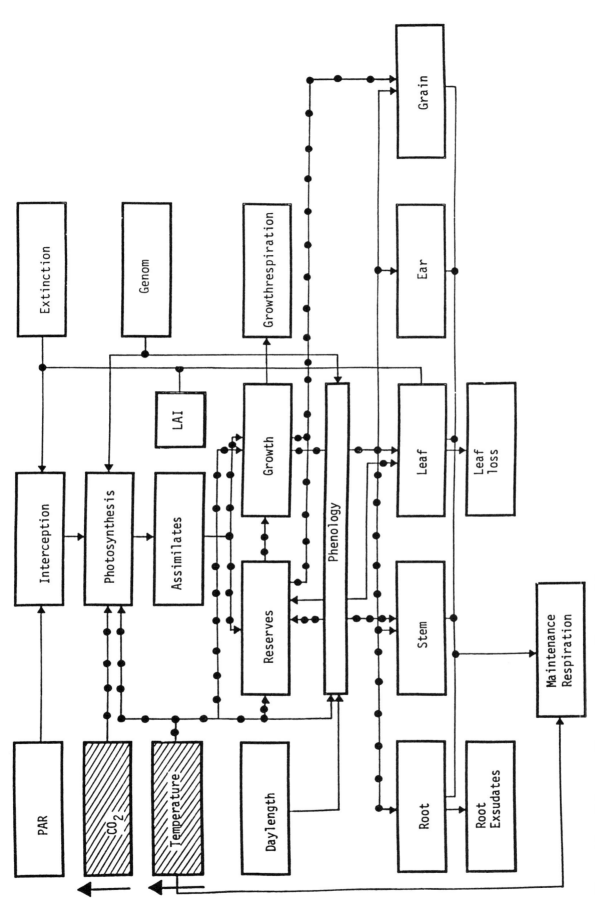

Figure 4.1   Schema to illustrate structure of crop models.

The CO_2 effect on dry matter production of wheat was strongly influenced by N, P and K supply and was strongly positive without any nutrient limitation. In the Wageningen experiment with K limitation a considerable positive CO_2 effect was retained, but with 90% reduction of P supply the growth was limited to such an extent, that this effect became nil.

The partitioning of dry matter reserves in Figure 4.1 during grain filling was not affected by CO_2 concentration; the relative carbon mass in mature grains from pre-anthesis assimilation was nearly the same in both CO_2 treatments. However, as the total grain mass increased with elevated CO_2, stems and leaves contributed more carbon to the grain compared to ambient conditions. Additionally carbon availability from photosynthesis increased during grain filling, documented by the leaf assimilation rates measured in the experiments in Finland.

As a result of the plant processes of vegetative growth illustrated in Figure 4.1, grain growth commences a few days after flowering in cereals. It is important to note that the leaf area and reserve pools do influence the grain mass and harvest index. Grain yield was affected by both CO_2 and temperature. In fully fertilized treatments in Finland the yield per plant was higher with high CO_2 than with ambient CO_2. Elevated temperature had the opposite effect; grain yield per plant and per area was lower at elevated temperature. This would mean that individual wheat plants in the field would not benefit from a global 3°C increase of temperature at this northern site but may benefit from a prolonged growing season due to elevated temperatures.

Conclusions for further work

The two years of research in the project clearly could not provide the necessary experimental data to explain all the effects of CO_2 and temperature on crop growth and development. The climatic conditions and light quality in growth chambers, open top chambers (OTC's) and greenhouses could never completely meet 'true' outdoor conditions. In addition, in many experiments plants were grown in pots where the limited rooting volume influenced many plant processes, e.g. water and nutrient uptake and dry matter partitioning (Arp, 1991). OTC's and greenhouse experiments are useful, however, because an exact treatment can be applied and tested unlike in the field where many factors may be contributing to the variation in results. Experiments in field tunnels seem to be an optimal solution for temperature and CO_2 interaction experiments where true field conditions are required. However, sampling of roots, which is important in such experiments, cannot be managed easily in the field without considerable effort. For future activities on climate change more technical equipment is needed to ensure conditions resemble reality in the field.

There is a strong demand for information about how agricultural practices (fertilization, irrigation, variety) need to be changed if future climates change both the mass and quality of yield. Some parameters measured with spring wheat show contrasting results. CO_2 concentrations have been altered together with temperature and nutrient supply, but interactions are not yet clear. It seems, that for any combination of CO_2 and temperature with nutrients and water an individual optimum curve exists, which can only be derived from experiments with CO_2 and temperature gradients, including a stepwise increase in fertilization. A more detailed study is required, to find out response curves for CO_2 and temperature in combination with treatments relevant for agricultural practices and climate change, which can later be integrated into growth models.

4.1 Introduction

Crop experiments were integrated into the project to provide information about plant responses to changes in temperature, atmospheric CO_2 concentration and irradiance. These are needed to validate crop models and to verify the algorithms that are being used in models.

Although many experiments on plant responses to possible future climates have been published, the physiological mechanisms of the responses are not well understood. Hence, the experiments presented here not only provide data sets for model validation, but permit a more thorough understanding of the plant processes involved. All crops investigated are C_3 crops, in which the CO_2 effect is known to be more prominent compared with C_4 plants.

The crop species investigated and the facilities used are presented in Table 4.1.1. Spring wheat was chosen as one of the most important crops in Europe, which has been modelled intensively over many years by the project scientists. A selection of vegetable crops (onion, broccoli, cauliflower) have been investigated for two reasons: firstly because little is known about the responses of changing environmental conditions on these species, and secondly because quality aspects - mainly influenced by temperature and light - play a dominant role in commercial vegetable production. Additionally, from the response of root crops to elevated CO_2 it was assumed that the response of bulbing species like onion would be greater compared with others, possibly because the below ground plant fractions are stronger sinks for assimilates. Grapevine, which covers about 4 M.ha in the EU countries, was chosen as a perennial crop with special emphasis on quality.

A general problem for crop experiments on climate change is to create an experimental environment in which plants can be grown without 'chamber-effects': any shelter or chamber that is needed to control temperature, CO_2 concentration and precipitation, influences wind speed, air humidity and light quality in the system and may affect plant growth and development. Consequently, the conditions within controlled environments may also influence the crop characteristics measured. Field-based experiments go some way to reducing this effect and giving more realistic growing conditions.

Spring wheat was grown in greenhouses (Section 4.5), growth chambers (Section 4.6) as well as in greenhouse-based open top chambers (Section 4.7). The greenhouses allowed accurate regulation of temperature and CO_2 concentrations. In some of the experiments plants were grown directly into soil, to overcome the problem of limited soil volume on root growth in pots. In the ^{13}C labelling technique experiment, it was necessary to grow spring wheat plants in growth chambers, in order to carefully regulate the concentration and constant turnover of CO_2, and to control the fraction of ^{13}C in the CO_2 added to the artificial atmosphere.

Different environments have been chosen to study temperature effects on cauliflower and broccoli (growth chambers, open top chambers, and the field) (Section 4.2). Comparison of the different experimental approaches helps to interpret environmental effects on plants and to improve the interpretation of agronomic variables measured under different conditions.

Onions were grown in near-field conditions under polyethylene tunnels in which a temperature gradient was imposed and different CO_2 concentrations were maintained (Section 4.3). This technique was optimal for a combined temperature-CO_2 experiment on a short stature crop that demands only small plot sizes and a small volume of air to be enriched with CO_2.

Mini free-air carbon dioxide enrichment (FACE) facilities have been used for grapevine experiments in Italy (Section 4.4). The FACE technique offers the opportunity to grow plants under real field conditions, but needs an enormous CO_2 input. The CO_2 used in the grapevine experiment was available free from an uncontaminated natural source and, hence, the season-long fumigation of CO_2 was less costly. It is obvious that a perennial crop like grapevine can be best investigated in an open field system under real daylength and temperature conditions, whereas in long-term experiments in controlled environments (greenhouse, tunnel, chamber) plants would suffer greatly from artificial conditions.

In all experiments ambient CO_2 was maintained at 353 ppmv and was elevated to 700 ppmv, except for the onion experiment, where 560 ppmv was used to permit comparisons with vegetable experiments in the previous project (Kenny *et al.*, 1993). The day-night cycles of ambient and elevated temperature were not unique and varied between the experiments.

In Europe the growth of arable crops is widely limited by the availability of nutrients. Section 4.5 describes a wheat experiment where N, P and K fertilization was varied to determine the significance of nutrient availability to the CO_2 effect.

In the following chapters the experiments are described in detail, each of them including implications for modelling, which are strongly linked to the site specific crop modelling chapters for wheat, vegetables and grapevine (Chapter 5). This demonstrates the integration and close interaction of the experimental and modelling activities within the project.

Table 4.1.1   Crops investigated and experiment information

Crop	Experimental design	Treatments	Year	Experimentalists	Country
Spring wheat	greenhouse	CO_2 N/P/K	1994	Wolf	Netherlands
	OTC in greenhouse OTC in field	CO_2 Temperature	1992-94	Hakala *et al.*	Finland
	growth chamber	CO_2 Nitrogen	1994-95	Wilbois, Schellberg	Germany
Broccoli	growth chamber	temperature radiation	1992-94	Olesen, Grevsen	Denmark
	field	cultivar planting date plant density	1992-94	Olesen, Grevsen	Denmark
Cauliflower	growth chamber	temperature radiation	1994	Olesen, Grevsen	Denmark
	field based portable enclosure	temperature	1994	Olesen, Grevsen	Denmark
Onion	field tunnels	variety CO_2 temperature	1994	Wheeler *et al.*	England
Grapevine	free-air CO_2 enrichment	CO_2	1994	Bindi *et al.*	Italy

4.2 Growth chamber and portable enclosure experiments on cauliflower and broccoli

4.2.1 Background

Cauliflower and broccoli (*Brassica oleracea* L. var. *botrytis* and var. *italica*) are important vegetables especially in European countries. Compared to most other vegetables, they are unusual because it is the generative stage, the flower, and not a vegetative plant organ that is the edible part. The duration and success of different developmental phases in cauliflower and broccoli are very dependant on climatic factors, especially temperature and light (Wiebe, 1972abc, 1973, 1974, 1989; Wurr *et al.*, 1990, 1991, 1993; Grevsen and Olesen, 1994a, b).

Cauliflower and broccoli development can be divided into three phases from transplanting to harvest: a juvenile phase, a curd/flower induction phase, and a curd/inflorescence growth phase. The juvenile phase is an early growth phase during which the plant is unable to respond to flower inductive conditions (Wiebe, 1989). Flower or curd induction is promoted by a period of relatively low temperatures during the curd/flower induction phase. High temperature periods during the curd/flower induction phase will prolong the time to curd/flower initiation and, therefore, also of time to harvest (Salter, 1960; Booij, 1987; Wurr *et al.*, 1990, 1991). The temperature response of the curd/flower induction process is very important in modelling plant development.

Morphological investigations of the cauliflower apex show that the apex begins to develop bracts and secondary meristem in the axil at an apex diameter of 0.4 to 0.6 mm (Salter, 1969; Wiebe, 1972c). Salter concluded that a mean apex size of 0.6 mm marked curd initiation and the change to reproductive growth. The apex diameter of 0.6 mm as the point of curd/flower initiation is used here for both cauliflower and broccoli.

In the period around curd initiation a kind of de-vernalization or 'over'-vernalization can occur resulting in the development of abnormal curds. If temperatures immediately following curd initiation are high the bracts (leaves) subtending the flower primordia in the inflorescence may begin to grow (Wiebe, 1973; Fujime, 1983). This gives either a hairy or 'fuzzy' appearance because of small white bracts on the surface of curds - so called 'bracting' or 'bractedness' - or in more severe cases results in green leaves penetrating the surface of the curd - called 'green bracts'. The effect can be viewed as a kind of devernalization of the plant and a return to vegetative growth due to high temperatures. On the other hand when temperatures during curd induction phase are very low an abnormality called 'riceyness' can evolve in the maturing curd. Riceyness refers to the premature development of small flower buds on the curd surface. Riceyness gives a granular or mossy surface appearance (Wiebe, 1973; Fujime, 1983). Riceyness is a kind of 'over'-vernalization where the cauliflower plant goes on to flower development instead of stopping at 'immature' inflorescence. Both quality defects will cause the product to be discarded and are therefore important to include in modelling effects of climate change on cauliflower production.

The objectives of the experimental work was to obtain improved parameter estimates for growth and development of cauliflower and broccoli in relation to temperature and light and to obtain estimates of cardinal temperatures for the risk of temperature induced quality defects. The effects of elevated CO_2 were not investigated in the experiments. The parameter estimates are used for improving crop models. In addition experiments have been performed to provide validation data for the models.

4.2.2 Experimental approach

Experiments have been conducted under various degrees of control of the temperature environment, from growth chamber experiments to portable enclosures used in the field to traditional factorial field experiments.

4.2.2.1 *Growth chamber experiments on cauliflower and broccoli*

Three experiments with both cauliflower and broccoli were conducted in growth chambers at Research Centre Foulum. The growth chambers enabled control of air temperature, air humidity and light intensity. Air temperature was varied in the two first experiments and radiation level was varied in the third experiment. All experiments were carried out at ambient CO_2 concentration.

The growth chambers were illuminated using sets of Osram HQI T400/D lamps placed in a separately cooled section above the plants. Two of the growth chambers had five light levels and one had six levels. The PPFD (Photosynthetic Photon Flux Density) at 75 cm above the floor at the various light levels was: 152, 307, 468, 649, 1041, 1430 $\mu E\ m^{-2}\ s^{-1}$.

Three growth chambers were used in each experiment. All growth chambers had different treatments. Seeds of summer cauliflower (*Brassica oleracea* L. *botrytis* cv. Plana F1) and broccoli (*Brassica oleracea* L. *italica* cv. Shogun) were sown in nutrient enriched peat soil in rectangular pots with a surface of 30 x 40 cm and a depth of 40 cm. The top of the pots were placed 65 cm above the cabinet floor, and the effective height of the canopy was assumed to be 75 cm above the floor. The soil was watered to full capacity at time of sowing and subsequently watered every second day. After sowing all pots were placed under identical conditions until the plants had reached about ten initiated leaves. During this period air temperature was kept at 14°C during an 8 hour long night and at 16°C during a 16 hour long day, and with a daily PAR of 12.1E m^{-2}.

At about ten initiated leaves the plants were thinned to a density of about six plants per pot in experiments 1 and 2 and about ten plants per pot in experiment 3. Small and untypical plants were also removed at this point. The pots were then distributed among the three growth chambers giving five pots of each crop in each chamber. The experimental treatments included different air temperatures in experiments 1 and 2 and different radiation levels in experiment 3 (Table 4.2.1). All treatments received an 8 hour long night and a 16 hour long day.

Table 4.2.1   Summary of experimental treatments in the growth chambers, i.e. night and day air temperatures, mean daily air and leaf surface temperature and daily photosynthetically active radiation. The duration of the experiment is the number of days from start of experimental treatment until the last sampling.

Experiment		Growth chamber		
		1	**2**	**3**
1	Night / day air temperature [°C]	5 / 8	11 / 16	17 / 24
	Mean air / surface temperature [°C]	7.0 / 5.6	14.3 / 12.9	21.7 / 20.3
	Daily PAR [E m^{-2}]	20.4	19.1	19.1
	Duration of experiment [days]	43	35	20
2	Night / day air temperature [°C]	8 / 12	14 / 20	20 / 28
	Mean air / surface temperature [°C]	10.7 / 9.2	18.0 / 16.5	25.3 / 23.9
	Daily PAR [E m^{-2}]	20.4	19.1	19.1
	Duration of experiment [days]	27	27	27
3	Night / day air temperature [°C]	11 / 16	11 / 16	11 / 16
	Mean air / surface temperature [°C]	14.3 / 15.0	14.3 / 13.7	14.3 / 12.1
	Daily PAR [E m^{-2}]	50.8	32.7	9.3
	Duration of experiment [days]	38	38	38

Samples were taken of the plants in the pots once or twice per week. This meant that the plant density in the pots was successively reduced. The first sample was taken at onset of the experimental treatments. Each plant was dissected into stems, leaf blades, midribs and stalks. Leaf area was measured and the weight of the individual organs was determined before and after oven-drying at 80°C for 24 hours. Curd/flower initiation was measured as the time when the apex had reached a diameter of 0.6 mm (Salter, 1969; Wiebe, 1972c). The light interception of the crops was determined in experiment 3 by using a modified LICOR line quantum sensor eight times during the experiment.

4.2.2.2   *Field-based portable enclosure experiment on cauliflower*

Four portable enclosures for applying temperature treatments in field plots were constructed and applied in experiments at Årslev Research Centre (55°18'N, 10°27'E). The compartment wall was made of insulating double layer acrylic material allowing about 70 % light transmission (PPFD). The dimensions of the compartments were: length 240 cm, width 120 cm, and height 100 cm. The possible temperature treatment range was about 5 to 30°C, controlled by cooling, heating and ventilation. Ventilation units ensured near ambient CO_2 concentrations. The temperature was regulated by simple on/off thermostats (± 1°C) with the possibility of different day/night set points.

Optimum temperatures for vernalization

Field experiments with four constant temperature regimes of 8, 12, 16 and 20°C were performed with cv. Plana in 1994. The temperature treatments were given in portable enclosures for a duration of ten days after the end of the juvenile phase, i.e. at about 15 to 20 leaves initiated and at an apex diameter of 0.2 to 0.3 mm (Wiebe, 1972c; Wurr *et al.* 1993; Grevsen and Olesen, 1994a). The experiment was repeated four times during the season from mid April to August 1994. Samples of 20 plants were taken once or twice per week to determine the end of juvenility. Samples of nine plants were taken at the start and end of the temperature treatment and again 14

days after the end of the treatment to determine the vernalization stage, i.e. the diameter of the shoot apex by dissection, total number of leaves initiated and later the curd growth.

Cardinal temperatures for curd quality defects

Field experiments with four constant temperature regimes of 8, 13, 18, 24°C were performed with cv. Plana in 1994. The temperature treatments were given in portable enclosures for a duration of ten days after curd initiation, i.e. apex diameter just over 0.6 mm. Samples of 20 plants were taken once or twice per week to determine when the curd was initiated and to record plant weight (cut at ground level) and total number of leaves initiated. After the temperature treatments the remaining plants were allowed to finish growth under prevailing weather conditions. At harvest the temperature treated plants were assessed for plant weight, curd weight, curd diameter and curd height, total number of leaves and curd quality defects such as bracting, green bracts and riceyness.

4.2.2.3   *Field experiments on broccoli*

Data for calibration and validation of the broccoli model were obtained from field experiments during three years (1991-1994) with three cultivars (Caravel, Shogun and Emperor). The experiments had four plantings per year and two plant densities of 5 and 10 plants m^{-2}. Seedlings were raised in peat blocks and transplanted into a sandy loam soil at Årslev Research Centre when the plants had about 9 to 10 leaves. The water regime and fertilization were held as constant as possible throughout the experiments. The experiment had a complete randomised block design with four replicates. Weekly samples of about 20 plants were used for monitoring apex diameter (0.6 mm set as flower initiation), and further recording of plant weight, total leaf number, head (inflorescence) weight and diameter and longest flower stalk length. The harvested heads were always cut 17 cm from the top of the head. The developmental stages in terms of maturity and quality were also evaluated. In 1994 light interception was measured several times in the crops with a LICOR line quantum sensor. Together with the light measurements, plant samples (3 plants per replicate) were taken to measure leaf area and dry weight production of leaf, stalk and stems.

4.2.3   Results

4.2.3.1   *Growth chamber experiments on cauliflower and broccoli*

The date of curd initiation was found to be strongly influenced by temperature but was unaffected by light level in both cauliflower and broccoli.

For each treatment and for each day of measurement of canopy light transmission, the mean of the measured light level without plants I_o and beneath plants I_p was calculated. The extinction coefficient was then calculated by applying the following equation:

$$k = -\ln(I_p/I_o)/LAI \tag{4.2.1}$$

where *LAI* is total leaf area index calculated by multiplying number of plants per pot with an estimated plant total leaf area and dividing by an assumed surface area of 40 cm x 50 cm. The estimated extinction coefficients are shown in Figure 4.2.1 versus total plant leaf area. The extinction coefficient declined with increasing leaf area for both crops, but it was generally 0.1 units lower for broccoli.

Growth of above gound dry matter is illustrated in Figure 4.2.2 for experiment 3. The dry matter growth in the various treatments could be described by an exponential growth equation, which indicates a constant relative growth rate. The only exceptions from this were plants from chambers 1 and 2 in experiment 3. These plants were grown under high radiation and showed a purpling of the leaves and more or less stopped producing both new leaf area and dry matter. This was most pronounced for broccoli, whereas cauliflower plants tended to develop a more yellow/orange appearance.

A logistic equation was used to describe development of leaf area with time in the experiments:

$$A = \frac{A_{max}}{1 + \exp(a-bt)} \tag{4.2.2}$$

where A is leaf area per plant, t is number of days after start of the experiment, A_{max} is maximum leaf area, and a and b are parameters. The a parameter may be substituted by $\ln[(A_{max}-A_i)/A_i]$, where A_i is leaf area at onset of the experiment. The b parameter describes the rate of leaf area growth. b parameters from different treatments are, however, only comparable if the A_{max} parameter is kept constant. The parameters were therefore estimated using a common A_{max} value of 6000 cm^2 (Figure 4.2.3). This value fitted the data well, partly because the last sample was taken before any plants attained their final leaf area.

The accumulated photosynthetically active radiation (PAR) intercepted by the crops was estimated by summing daily contributions. These were calculated by using the extinction coefficients from Figure 4.2.1 and the leaf area index calculated by multiplying plant leaf area by number of plants per pot and dividing by effective pot surface area. Plant above ground dry matter was linearly related to intercepted PAR, and radiation use efficiency was calculated as the slope of this line. There was a tendency for a lower initial radiation use efficiency, especially in experiment 3. Figure 4.2.4 shows the response of radiation use efficiency to air temperature and to PAR. Radiation use efficiency for cauliflower increased with temperature up to about 14°C. A similar response was observed for broccoli, but with slightly higher coefficients.

4.2.3.2   *Field-based portable enclosure experiment on cauliflower*

Optimum temperature for curd induction

Figure 4.2.5 shows the effects of the different temperature treatments on the curd induction of cauliflower cv. Plana. An optimum temperature of about 16°C, with respect to increase in apex diameter, was obtained as a mean of four experiments. A more detailed analysis of the data showed that the leaf number at the end of the juvenile phase has to be at least 16, but it can vary up to about 25 leaves initiated under

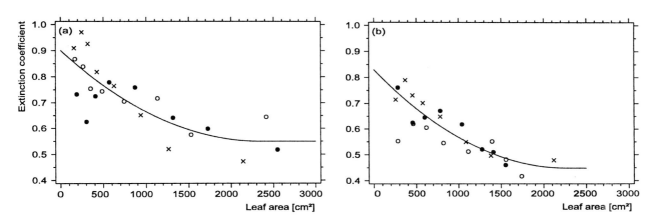

Figure 4.2.1 Estimated extinction coefficient versus plant leaf area for (a) cauliflower and (b) broccoli in growth chamber experiment 3. The symbols indicate daily PAR treatment (•: 50.8 E m^{-2}, o: 32.7 E m^{-2}, ×: 9.3 E m^{-2}). Fitted second order polynomia are also shown.

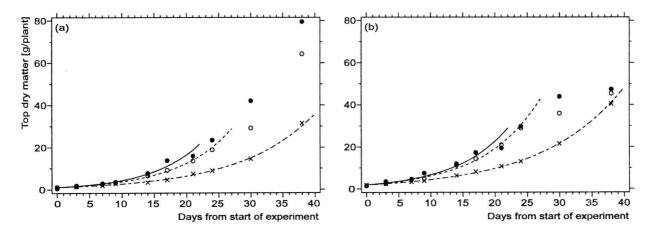

Figure 4.2.2 Mean plant above ground dry weight over time in growth chamber experiment 3 for (a) cauliflower and (b) broccoli. The points and lines indicate the daily PAR treatment (•— •: 50.8 E m^{-2}, o---o: 32.7 E m^{-2}, ×--×: 9.3 E m^{-2}). The lines show the fitted exponential functions.

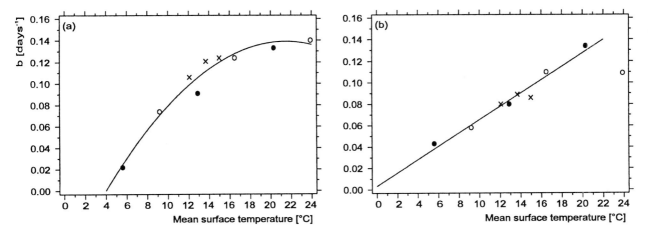

Figure 4.2.3 Estimated *b* parameter (rate of leaf area growth) versus mean leaf surface temperature for (a) cauliflower and (b) broccoli in the growth chamber experiments. The *b* in the logistic equation describing leaf area was estimated assuming an A_{max} value of 6000 cm^2. The symbols indicate experiment (•: 1, o: 2, ×: 3). A fitted second order polynomium (a) and a regression line (b) is also shown.

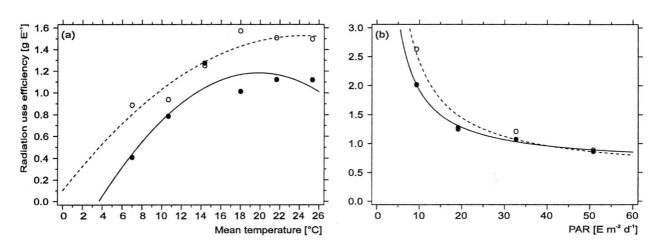

Figure 4.2.4   Radiation use efficiency of cauliflower (•) and broccoli (o) versus (a) mean air temperature and (b) daily PAR. The points in (a) only comprise treatments with a daily PAR of about 20 E m^{-2}, and (b) only concerns treatments with a daily mean air temperature of 14.3°C. Fitted second order polynomia (a) and inverse linear functions (b) are also shown for cauliflower (-) and broccoli (---).

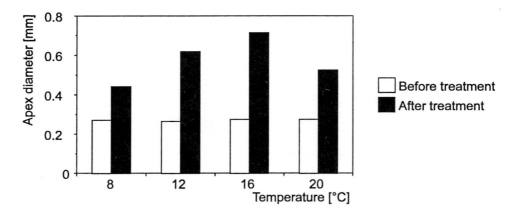

Figure 4.2.5   Temperature effects on curd induction - increase in apex diameter - in cauliflower cv. Plana. Temperature treatments applied in portable enclosures for 10 days (day 10) after end of the juvenile phase (day 1). Average of four experiments in 1994.

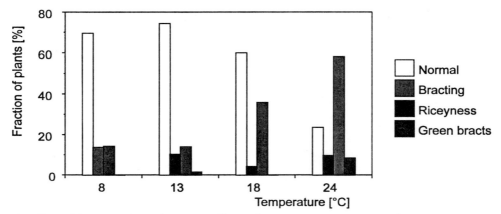

Figure 4.2.6   Quality of harvested curds as an effect of temperature treatment for ten days immediately following curd initiation. Average of four experiments in portable enclosures in 1994.

warm conditions. The apex diameter must be over 0.25 mm to respond to temperature treatments. By observing curd diameter increase 14 days after the treatments the plants which received 20°C are delayed by about 4 to 8 days compared to the 12 and 16°C temperature treatments.

Figure 4.2.6 and Table 4.2.2 show the effects of the temperature treatments on the quality of the harvested curds. The average results of four experiments show that the risk of bracting increases severely when the temperature in the days after curd initiation are higher than 18°C (Figure 4.2.6). Table 4.2.2 shows that the riceyness defect was only observed in the first planting from early June, but this was not an effect of the temperature treatment given just after curd initiation. The period from transplanting to curd initiation was cool

(average temperature 11.1°C) and the riceyness may be caused by the early cold conditions before curd initiation.

Cardinal temperatures for curd quality defects

Bracting is a result of high temperatures just after curd initiation. There is, however, a variation in the extent of bracting between the different plantings (Table 4.2.2). This indicates that the necessary period for inducing bracting has to be longer than strictly 10 days immediately following curd initiation, as used in the experiment.

The experiments have been continued in 1995 with treatments both before and after curd initiation and the results will be available during the summer of 1995.

Table 4.2.2 Quality defects in cauliflower cv. Plana as a result of temperature treatment just after curd initiation. Treatments were applied in field based portable enclosures in 1994.

Planting number	Start diameter [mm]	Treatment period	Temp. before and after treatment [°C]	Treatment temperature [°C]	Percent curds with			
					Normal or other	Ricey-ness	Brac-ting	Green bracts
1	2.0	10/6-17/6	before 11.1 after 15.0	8	45	55	0	0
				13	59	41	0	0
				18	83	17	0	0
				24	61	39	0	0
2	0.6	28/6-8/7	before 13.4 after 19.4	8	50	0	50	0
				13	44	0	56	0
				18	0	0	100	0
				24	0	0	100	0
3	0.7	29/7-8/8	before 18.4 after 15.1	8	93	0	7	0
				13	100	0	0	0
				18	72	0	28	0
				24	33	0	33	34
4	0.9	24/8-8/9	before 14.8 after 11.6	8	100	0	0	0
				13	94	0	0	6
				18	85	0	15	0
				24	0	0	100	0

4.2.3.3   *Field experiment on broccoli*

Figure 4.2.7 shows the relationship between floret diameter and temperature sum from flower initiation. The plant density has a great influence on the floret diameter and in modelling broccoli growth it is necessary to include plant density. A quadratic relationship between floret diameter and temperature sum from flower initiation including effects of plant density and cultivar can account for over 95 % of the variation in the data with respect to floret diameter. The time of transplanting in the year also had a significant effect on floret diameter probably caused by differences in temperature and radiation.

Plant density also influenced leaf area of the broccoli plants. The leaf area of plants grown at a density of 10 plants m^{-2} compared to 5 plants m^{-2} was considerably lower. In mature plants the leaf area per plant in the high density crop was reduced to about 50 to 60 % of the low density. The light interception of the crop as a whole was, however, the same in the later stages for both densities. The radiation use efficiency changed with crop development and was higher during early growth for the high plant densities.

4.2.4   **Implications for modelling**

Most crop models simulate leaf area expansion by assuming a constant specific leaf area. Examples are the SUCROS model (Spitters *et al.*, 1989) and the cauliflower model of Johnsen (1990). The growth chamber experiments demonstrate that this may lead to large errors in simulation of leaf area under varying temperature and radiation conditions. The specific leaf area varied from about 300 cm g^{-1} in the high temperature treatments to about 40 cm g^{-1} in the high radiation treatment. Similar but less pronounced effects can be anticipated under changed atmospheric CO_2 concentration.

In the experiments temperature appeared to be the main environmental determinant of leaf area, and the relationship between temperature and leaf area growth rate is given in Figure 4.2.3. The use of successive sampling gradually reduced plant density and the leaf area index, therefore, never exceeded 3. It is possible that other factors will influence leaf area growth under field conditions where leaf area index may exceed 3. In models temperature should, however, be incorporated as the main driving variable for leaf area expansion.

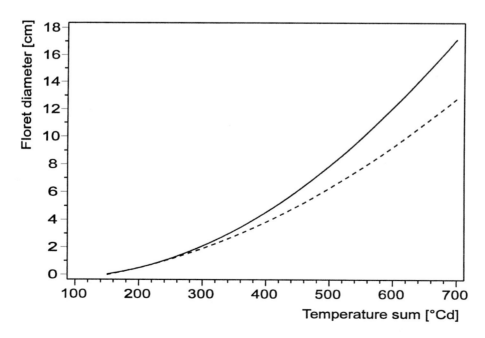

Figure 4.2.7   The relationship between floret diameter in broccoli and temperature sum (base 0°C) from flower initiation. The impact of two plant densities is shown as quadratic regression lines (— : 5 plants m^{-2}, ---: 10 plants m^{-2}). The results are average of three cultivars in three years with four plantings per year.

Most crop models assume that the extinction coefficient for calculating light interception by the crop canopy is constant throughout the crop life cycle. The results in Figure 4.2.1 clearly demonstrate that the extinction coefficient declines with increasing plant age in cauliflower and broccoli. This should be incorporated in models of these and other crops where average leaf angle changes considerably during crop development.

The effect of temperature on radiation use efficiency shown in Figure 4.2.4 is roughly in agreement with the temperature function for adjusting assimilation rate at light saturation as suggested for temperate C_3-crops by Versteeg and van Keulen (1986). Both temperature relations may therefore be used for modelling effects of temperature on assimilation.

The optimum temperature of about 16°C observed for progress towards curd initiation in cauliflower cv. Plana confirms the results of 15.5°C in Grevsen and Olesen (1994b) and Wheeler *et al.* (1995) for this cultivar. This means that the optimum temperature is higher for cv. Plana than for cv. Delira and cv. Elgon (Grevsen and Olesen, 1994a) and also higher than the optimum of 9.5°C for cv. White Fox found by Wurr *et al.* (1993). Models should therefore consider the optimum temperature for curd induction to be cultivar dependent.

4.2.5 Discussion and conclusions

A reduction in expansion of leaf area and in rate of dry matter accumulation was seen for both cauliflower and broccoli plants in growth chamber experiment 3 under high radiation. The observed discolouring of the leaves are consistent with symptoms of nitrogen and possibly phosphorous deficiency (Scaife and Turner, 1983). It is possible that the plants developed nitrogen deficiency despite watering with nutrient solutions. The symptoms may, however, also be caused by the large accumulation of reserves in the leaves (Arp, 1991). The results may thus imply a sink limitation of the plants. The plants were, however, not analysed for nitrogen content and it is impossible to determine the exact cause of the observed reduction in growth.

The observed reduction in extinction coefficient of the crop canopy may be explained partly by a gradual change from horizontal leaves to more erect leaves (Trenbath and Angus, 1975), and partly by increased clustering of leaves over time. A similar decline in extinction coefficient was observed for napier grass by Kubota *et al.* (1994). Wheeler *et al.* (1995) found a slightly lower extinction coefficient of 0.4 in cauliflower. This estimate was, however, based on measurements of total shortwave radiation, which will result in a lower extinction coefficient.

The estimated radiation use efficiency for cauliflower was in the order of 1.1 g E^{-1}. Assuming 2.0 E MJ^{-1} global radiation (Hansen *et al.*, 1981) a radiation use efficiency of 2.2 g MJ^{-1} is obtained, which is somewhat higher than the values of 1.42 g MJ^{-1} and 2.01 g MJ^{-1} found by Wheeler *et al.* (1995) for cauliflower plants grown under atmospheric CO_2 concentrations of 328 ppmv and 531 ppmv, respectively. The observed coefficient of 2.2 g MJ^{-1} is also higher than the values found for field grown agricultural crops in Denmark (Christensen and Goudriaan, 1993). There are two possible explanations of the high radiation use efficiencies found in the growth chamber. Firstly a constant effective canopy height was assumed, but during plant development plants will grow higher and thus intercept more radiation because the radiation intensity increases with height in the growth chamber. Secondly plants also received radiation reflected from the walls of the growth chamber and thus received more radiation than anticipated in the calculations. The higher estimates of radiation use efficiency in broccoli compared with cauliflower may partly be due to the lower extinction coefficient of the broccoli crop canopy. The difference thus becomes nil at high radiation levels (Figure 4.2.4).

The temperature effect on curd quality in cauliflower cv. Plana may as a first approximation be estimated as 40 % crop loss due to bracting if the mean temperature during a period 15 days after curd initiation exceeds 18°C (Figure 4.2.6). The temperature limit for riceyness is not clear and awaits the completion of the 1995 experiments. Probably average temperatures well below 10°C prior to curd initiation gives a high risk of crop loss because of riceyness (Table 4.2.2).

The experimental results demonstrate the presence of optimal temperatures for a wide range of crop processes, including development, growth of leaf area, dry matter growth and development of quality defects. The actual yield and quality of a field grown crop is a function of all these processes integrated over time.

4.3   Field tunnel experiments on onion

4.3.1   Background

Elevated CO_2 concentrations generally result in greater crop yields, primarily due to increases in the rate of photosynthesis (Bowes, 1991). Differences in temperature also affect crop yields through, for example, changes in the duration of crop growth and biomass partitioning (Ellis *et al.*, 1990). Therefore, to assess the response of crops to potential climate change it is important to consider the impact of both elevated CO_2 concentrations and warmer temperatures, and their possible interaction. Idso *et al.* (1987) found that the proportional increase in the dry weight of five species due to CO_2 enrichment was greater at warmer temperatures. Such an observation is expected from studies on photosynthesis (Long, 1991). In contrast, no interaction between the effects of CO_2 and temperature on the biomass of carrot (*Daucus carota* L.) (Wheeler *et al.*, 1994), cauliflower (*Brassica oleracea* L. *botrytis*) (Wheeler *et al.*, 1995a) or wheat (*Triticum aestivum* L.) (Mitchell, 1993; Wheeler *et al.*, 1995b) was reported with up to a 4°C difference in mean seasonal temperature.

Yield increases at elevated CO_2 are usually greater in root crops than the average increase in yield of 33% reported for a wide range of crops grown under doubled current CO_2 (Kimball, 1983); possibly because the harvestable portion of root crops are larger sinks for photosynthetic assimilates (Clough *et al.*, 1981). For example, Sionit *et al.* (1982) observed an increased yield of 56% in sugar beet (*Beta vulgaris* L.) and Wheeler *et al.* (1994) observed an increase of 80% in carrot at elevated (675 and 551 ppmv CO_2, respectively) compared with ambient CO_2 (350 ppmv). The response of bulbing species, such as onion (*Allium cepa* L.), to CO_2 enrichment and temperature has not been reported.

The rate of crop developmental events is usually independent of CO_2 concentration. For example, no consistent effect of CO_2 enrichment on the rate of apical development of cauliflower (Wheeler *et al.*, 1995a) and of wheat (Batts *et al.*, 1995; Mitchell *et al.*, 1993) was reported, despite large effects on the growth and yield of these crops. The main developmental stage in onion is the onset of bulbing. The rate of onion bulbing is affected by both temperature and photoperiod (Brewster, 1990). However, because bulbing consists primarily of growth, rather than developmental, processes (Brewster, 1990), it is possible that bulbing is affected by an increase in CO_2 enrichment. Thus, the effects of interactions between warmer temperatures and elevated CO_2 on bulb formation presents a potentially complex response. The existence of both long and short-season varieties of onion provides a further complication to assessments of the impacts of future climates on onion crop production.

An improved understanding of crop responses to potential climate change is provided by experiments conducted in near-field conditions (Lawlor and Mitchell, 1991). To achieve this, crop stands may be grown within double-walled polyethylene tunnels, along which a temperature gradient is imposed, and in each of which a different CO_2 concentration is maintained (Rawson, 1992; Wheeler *et al.*, 1993a, 1994, 1995a,b; Hadley *et al.*, 1995). This technique has been developed as part of a previous EC-funded project in which the effects of differences in temperature and CO_2 were studied on both a flower and root crop (cauliflower and carrot, respectively) (Wheeler *et al.*, 1993b). To complete our investigations of the potential impacts of climate change on crop yields for the main categories of horticultural crops, the experimental protocol developed using temperature gradient tunnels was used here to study the effects on a further horticultural crop, the bulb onion.

4.3.1.1 *Aims*

The aims of the study were to:

- impose a difference in temperature on field-grown crops of onion from transplanting to bulb maturity at either normal or elevated CO_2;
- quantify the effects of temperature, CO_2 and any possible interaction on the development, biomass accumulation and yield of two contrasting varieties of onion;
- quantify the effects of temperature and CO_2 on the rate of increase in the number of leaves and leaf area expansion before bulbing;
- examine the implications of these experimental results for onion production under future climates.

4.3.2 Experimental approach

4.3.2.1 *Crop husbandry*

Seeds of onion (*Allium cepa* L.) cv. 'Hysam' and 'Sito' were sown on 3 March 1994 in modular trays filled with multipurpose compost and maintained in an unheated glasshouse. In accordance with prior soil analysis, fertilizer was applied to a site at the Plant Sciences Field Unit near Reading (51°27'N, 0°56'W) in order to give a target of 100 kgha^{-1} N, 200 kgha^{-1} P$_2$O$_5$ and 60 kgha^{-1} K$_2$O. Fifty-two days after sowing, the seedlings were transplanted at a density of 64 plants per m^2 (square planting) to four 20 x 2m areas, each of which were subsequently covered with a double-walled polyethylene tunnel. The short-season cv. 'Sito' was planted along one side of the tunnel whilst the longer season cv. 'Hysam' was planted along the other side. The crops were irrigated by means of a network of porous pipes in order to maintain the soil at near field capacity.

4.3.2.2 *Temperature gradient tunnels*

The tunnel construction is described in detail in Hadley *et al.* (1995). In order to achieve a temperature gradient along the tunnels, cool air was passed along the inner tunnel over the crop whilst warm air was passed in the opposite direction between the inner and outer tunnels. Additional air circulation around the crop was provided by seven axial fans centrally placed at 3 m intervals in areas corresponding to discard rows. Air temperature was monitored at seven locations 3 m apart within each tunnel using double-screened molybdenum resistance sensors positioned 0.2 m above the ground. Two tube solarimeters were positioned above the crop in the central region of each tunnel in order to monitor incident radiation and one solarimeter was placed beneath the crop at both ends of each tunnel to measure transmitted radiation.

Two of the tunnels were enriched to a target concentration of 560 ppmv CO_2 whilst the other two were maintained at a target of 350 ppmv CO_2. These treatments are subsequently referred to as 'elevated' and 'normal', respectively. To minimise variation in CO_2 concentration along the temperature gradient, CO_2 was injected along a plastic tube at points above each in-crop fan. For each pair of tunnels, air was continually sampled to a reservoir in a nearby shed using a pump. The CO_2 concentration of the air was continually measured using a single-beam infrared gas analyser and controller. Carbon dioxide was injected into the fan of the cold heat exchanger; CO_2 enrichment was intermittant before, and continuous from, 21 days after transplanting.

4.3.2.3 *Crop harvests*

The crop in each tunnel was divided along the temperature gradient into six 3 m x 2 m plots (each variety occupying an area of 3 m x 1 m). Each of these plots was divided into eight guarded sub-plots of nine plants. Three sub-plots were harvested at bulbing (when the ratio of bulb to pseudostem diameter was 2:1) and three at bulb maturity (when the foliage of 80% of the plants had fallen over, or when 30% of plants had flowered). Fresh weights of all the leaves, senesced leaves, pseudostems, bulbs and roots in each plot were determined immediately and the diameter of individual bulbs measured. Any flowering plants in harvested plots at bulb maturity were excluded from the growth analysis. The dry weights of each sample were determined after oven-drying at 80°C for 96 hours. Also, the number of leaves on each plant at bulbing were counted and the total leaf area measured using a video-based leaf area machine. Due to problems with disease, all of the plots harvested from one of the elevated CO_2 tunnels were excluded from the analysis, as were the coolest two plots in the other elevated CO_2 tunnel for cv. Sito at bulb maturity.

The length and width of each leaf on nine plants in the warmest, coolest and middle plots of one tunnel maintained at normal and one tunnel maintained at elevated CO_2 were measured non-destructively at weekly intervals between 23 and 87 days from transplanting. The leaf area of each leaf was calculated as the area of a cone using these measurements of leaf width and length. The accuracy of this calculation was checked using destructive harvests of extra plants. The fraction of radiation transmitted to the bottom of the crop canopy was measured at the same time using a sunfleck ceptometer. Logistic functions were used to describe the relationship between fractional intercepted radiation (where intercepted radiation is one minus transmitted radiation) and time. Fractional intercepted radiation was estimated for each day using these functions.

4.3.2.4   *Growth and radiation-use*

The following growth parameters were calculated from the destructive harvests: leaf area index, specific leaf area, leaf area duration and radiation use efficiency. Between transplanting and bulbing, radiation use efficiency was calculated from six plots for each variety (three in each CO_2 concentration, one at either end and one in the middle of one tunnel). For this, the product of daily fractional intercepted radiation and above crop incident radiation was accumulated for this period. Between bulbing and bulb maturity it was assumed that the fraction of intercepted radiation was constant (Brewster, 1990) and this was calculated using the leaf area determined at bulbing with the Monsi-Saeki equation (Monsi and Saeki, 1953):

$$\ln(I_t) = -k * L \qquad (4.3.1)$$

where I_t is fraction transmitted radiation, L is leaf area index and k is a light extinction coefficient which was calculated from the leaf study.

4.3.2.5   *Statistical analysis*

The temperature at any given position along the gradient was not identical in different tunnels. Therefore, the relationship between growth parameters and mean temperature was determined and the effects of CO_2 and variety examined by comparing these regressions. The effect of temperature and CO_2 on the light extinction coefficient (k in equation 4.3.1) was determined by comparing regressions of the logarithm of transmitted radiation with leaf area index for each variety.

The reciprocal of the duration (t) from transplanting to bulbing, and from bulbing to bulb maturity, was quantified as a linear function of mean temperature (T), such that:

$$1/t = a + bT \qquad (4.3.2)$$

In accordance with the concept of thermal time (Monteith, 1977), equation 4.3.2 can be rearranged to give:

$$1/t = (T-T_b) / Q \qquad (4.3.3)$$

in which T_b is the base temperature for the rate of progress to bulbing or bulb maturity ($-a/b$) and Q is the thermal time requirement ($1/b$). The effect of CO_2 on the duration from transplanting to bulbing was examined by comparing regressions of equation 4.3.2 at each CO_2 concentration. For the duration from bulbing to bulb maturity, initial estimates of T_b and Q were determined for each CO_2 treatment. Then, the change in the residual sum of squares with a common value of T_b for both CO_2 concentrations was examined over a range of T_b and the optimal model selected on the basis of minimised residual sum of squares.

4.3.3   Results

4.3.3.1   *Environmental conditions*

Differences in mean air temperature from transplanting to bulb maturity between the coolest and warmest plot in each tunnel were between 4.4°C and 6.1°C, with mean air temperature ranging from 12.3°C in the coolest plot to 18.6°C in the warmest plot. The mean CO_2 concentration from transplanting to the last harvest in each pair of tunnels was 532 ppmv CO_2 in the enriched pair of tunnels and 374 ppmv in the normal tunnels.

4.3.3.2   *Duration of crop growth*

The entire crop duration ranged from 122 days at the warmest temperature to 192 days at the coolest temperature for cv. Hysam and from 100 to 175 days for cv. Sito in the warmest and coolest plots, respectively. The rate of progress from transplanting to bulb maturity was a positive linear function of temperature for both varieties (P < 0.01 for each) with no significant effect of CO_2 (P > 0.25 for cv. Hysam and P > 0.05 for cv. Sito; Figure 4.3.1a, b). The entire crop duration can be divided into the period from transplanting to the onset of bulbing and the subsequent period from the onset of bulbing to bulb maturity. For the former period, the rate of progress from transplanting to bulbing was also a positive linear function of mean temperature for each variety at normal and elevated CO_2 (Figure 4.3.1c, d). Differences in CO_2 concentration affected the intercept (P < 0.01 for cv. Hysam and P < 0.05 for cv. Sito) but not the slope (P > 0.25 for each variety) of these relationships. From these fitted relationships, the time to bulbing in cv. Hysam was reduced by between 8 and 11 days with an increase from normal to elevated CO_2 concentration (Figure 4.3.1c). In cv. Sito, time to bulbing at a given temperature was also reduced at elevated CO_2; by 4 to 5 days with an increase from normal to elevated CO_2 (Figure 4.3.1d). The time of bulbing was significantly earlier (P < 0.01) in cv. Sito than in cv. Hysam in the same environment. The rate of progress from the onset of bulbing to bulb maturity was a positive linear function of mean temperature over this period (Figure 4.3.1e, f). Plots in which more than 30% of the plants flowered were omitted from the analysis. Estimates of T_b (equation 4.3.3) for each variety were not affected by CO_2 concentration (P > 0.25 for cv. Hysam and P > 0.1 for cv. Sito) but Q was greater at elevated compared with normal CO_2 in both varieties (P < 0.01). For cv. Hysam, T_b was 7.0°C and Q was 624°C d and 803°C d at normal and elevated CO_2, respectively

(Figure 4.3.1e) and for cv. Sito, T_b was 10.5°C and Q was 324°C d and 445°C d at normal and elevated CO_2, respectively (Figure 4.3.1f).

4.3.3.3   *Leaf growth during canopy expansion*

The mean number of leaves on each plant could be described as a linear function of thermal time in each variety up to 1000°C d. The residual sums of these functions was minimal when a base temperature of 0°C was assumed (the range -5 to 5°C was tested). In cv. Hysam there was a small effect of CO_2 concentration on this linear relationship (P < 0.001) such that plants grown at elevated CO_2 had 0.7 leaves more than those grown at normal CO_2 at a given thermal time from transplanting (Figure 4.3.2a). In cv. Sito the effect of CO_2 on leaf number was just significant, but plants grown at elevated CO_2 had, on average, 0.3 leaves less than plants grown at normal CO_2 (Figure 4.3.2b). The number of senesced leaves could also be described as linear functions of thermal time (above 0°C), similar to those for total leaf number although with more scatter among these data. Differences in CO_2 concentration only affected this relationship in cv. Sito (P < 0.01). The number of senesced leaves at a given thermal time was greater at normal compared with elevated CO_2 in cv. Sito; this difference was more evident for the earliest senescing leaves. No effect of CO_2 concentration on the number of senesced leaves at a given thermal time could be detected in cv. Hysam.

Increase in total plant leaf area from transplanting until near to the onset of bulbing was clearly affected by differences in temperature (Figure 4.3.3). Maximum leaf area was attained earlier in the crops grown in the warmest compared with the coolest of the three plots studied for each variety and at either CO_2 concentration. For example, in cv. Sito crops grown at normal CO_2 (Figure 4.3.3b) maximum leaf area was recorded 65 days from transplanting in the warmest plot and mean leaf area was still increasing at 87 days in the coolest plot in this treatment. Within the same tunnel, increase in leaf area at the two coolest temperatures was similar (Figure 4.3.3).

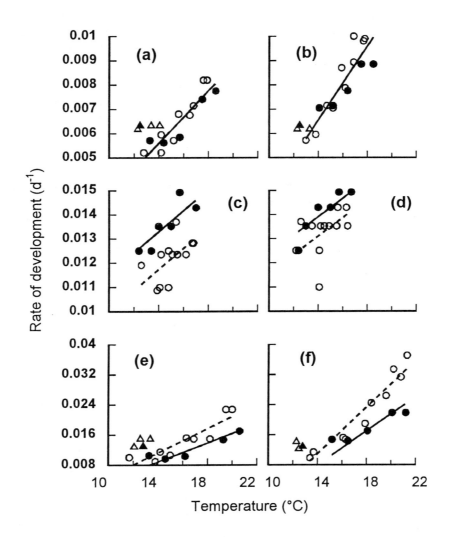

Figure 4.3.1   Relationship between rate of developmental progress and mean temperature at 372 (O, ······) and 532 (●,——) ppmv CO_2 in cv. Hysam (a, c, e) and cv. Sito (b, d, f), between transplanting and maturity (a, b), transplanting and bulbing (c, d), bulbing and maturity (e, f). Plots in which plants flowered (Δ, ▲) were omitted from analyses.

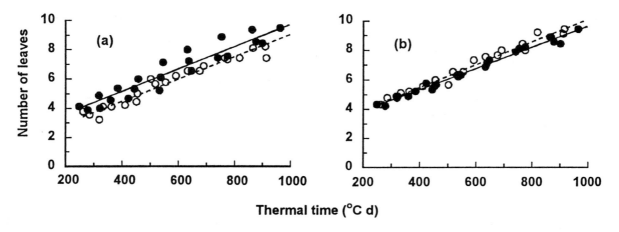

Figure 4.3.2   Relationship between the number of leaves and thermal time (above $0^{o}C$) from transplanting at 372 (O,·····) and 532 (●,——) ppmv CO_2 in (a) cv. Hysam and (b) cv. Sito.

Estimates of the light extinction coefficient (k in equation 4.3.1) for each variety were not affected by differences in either temperature or CO_2 concentration. Thus, estimates of k common to all these growing environments were 0.26 (s.e. = 0.011) and 0.24 (s.e. = 0.008) for cvs. Sito and Hysam, respectively.

4.3.3.4   *Crop canopy and radiation use efficiency*

Leaf area index at bulbing was slightly greater in crops grown at elevated compared with normal CO_2 but the differences were not significant in either variety (Table 4.3.1). In contrast, the number of leaves at bulbing was similar in crops grown at either CO_2 concentration.

Leaf area duration between transplanting and bulbing was not affected by temperature or CO_2 concentration, but between bulbing and bulb maturity leaf area duration was a negative linear function of temperature ($P < 0.01$ for each variety) with a significant effect of CO_2 on the intercept of this relationship($P < 0.05$ for cv. Hysam and $P < 0.01$ for cv. Sito; Table 4.3.1). Radiation use efficiency between transplanting and bulbing (analysed with data from the two varieties combined) was greater at elevated compared with normal CO_2 ($P < 0.01$). In contrast, radiation use efficiency from bulbing to bulb maturity (analysed with data from the two varieties treated separately) was not affected by temperature or CO_2 in either variety (Table 4.3.1).

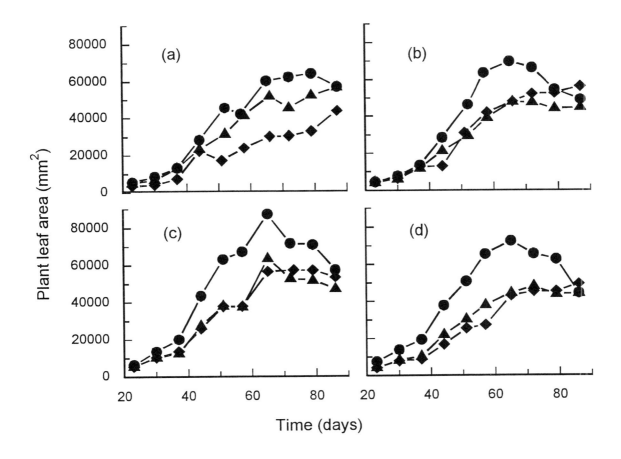

Figure 4.3.3   Increase in plant leaf area before bulbing in crops grown at the warmest (●) coolest (▲) and central (◆) plot in cv. Hysam (a, c) and cv. Sito (b, d) at either 372 (a, b) or 532 (c, d) ppmv CO_2. Each symbol is the mean of nine observations.

Mean plant specific leaf area at bulbing was a positive linear function of temperature (P < 0.01 for both varieties; Figure 4.3.4). The effect of CO_2 on the intercept of this relationship was significant (P < 0.01 for cv. Hysam and P < 0.05 for cv. Sito) such that specific leaf area was greater at normal than at elevated CO_2 at a given temperature.

4.3.3.5   *Total dry weight*

No significant effect of temperature on the total dry weight per m^2 of both varieties was detected at bulbing (P > 0.1 for cv. Hysam and P > 0.25 for cv. Sito). Total dry weight was greater at elevated than at normal CO_2 (P < 0.01 for each

variety; Figure 4.3.5a, b). At bulb maturity, a negative linear relationship between total dry weight and temperature was detected (P < 0.01 for both varieties: Figure 4.3.5c, d). The positive effect of CO_2 on the intercept of this relationship was significant (P < 0.01 for cv. Hysam and P < 0.05 for cv. Sito). When data from the two CO_2 concentrations at bulb maturity were analysed separately, total dry weight was not significantly affected by differences in temperature at elevated CO_2, but total dry weight was still a negative function of temperature at normal CO_2. Plants of cv. Hysam were on average 16% greater than those of cv. Sito at the same temperature and CO_2 concentration (P < 0.05).

Table 4.3.1   Summary of the effects of CO_2 and temperature on crop canopy characteristics. Means over all temperatures are given where only the effects of CO_2 concentration were significant, and means for a cool and warm temperature are given in addition to each CO_2 concentration when the effects of CO_2 and temperature were significant. Estimates of leaf area (LAI) and leaf number (LN) are for the end of the period shown, whilst those of leaf area duration (LAD) and radiation use efficiency (RUE) are for the duration of the period shown. The effects of differences in temperature or CO_2 concentration were only significant where indicated (* = P < 0.05, ** = P < 0.01). nd indicates not determined.

Harvest	Variety	CO_2 or temperature	LAI (s.e)	LAD (s.e.) (days)	LN (s.e.)	RUE (s.e.) (g MJ^{-1})
From	Hysam	normal	3.3 (0.14)	136.8 (7.26)	7.3 (0.11)	1.12** (0.34)
transplanting		elevated	3.6 (0.24)	133.0 (12.6)	7.0 (0.19)	2.21** (0.45)
to the onset	Sito	normal	3.2 (0.18)	122.3 (7.3)	6.8 (0.1)	1.12** (0.34)
of bulbing		elevated	3.5 (0.31)	126.4 (12.6)	6.8 (0.2)	2.21** (0.45)
	Hysam	normal	nd	240.9* (28.3)	nd	1.69 (0.16)
		elevated	nd	304.6* (47.4)	nd	1.55 (0.32)
From the		13°C	nd	340.0** (20.15)	nd	nd
onset of		20°C	nd	182.8** (21.02)	nd	nd
bulbing to	Sito	normal	nd	159.0** (19.7)	nd	1.78 (0.20)
bulb		elevated	nd	213.6** (53.9)	nd	1.80 (0.27)
maturity		15°C	nd	233.1** (17.41)	nd	nd
		21°C	nd	119.5** (17.96)	nd	nd

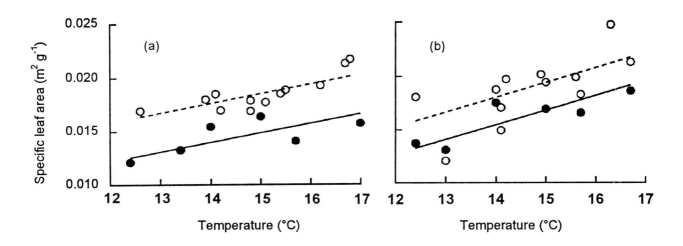

Figure 4.3.4 Relationship between mean plant specific leaf area at bulbing and mean temperature at 372 (O,·····) and 532 (●,——) ppmv CO_2 in (a) cv. Hysam and (b) cv. Sito.

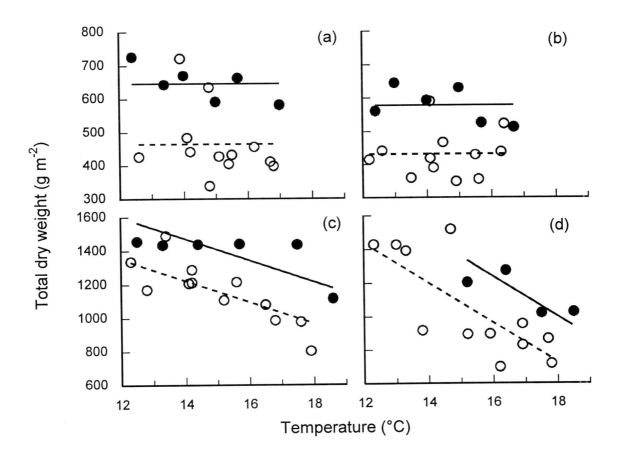

Figure 4.3.5 Relationship between total dry weight and mean temperature at 372 (O,·····) and 532 (●, ——) ppmv CO_2 in cv. Hysam (a, c) and cv. Sito (b, d), at bulbing (a, b) and at bulb maturity (c, d).

4.3.3.6   *Yield*

At harvest maturity, bulb dry weight was a negative linear function of mean temperature in both varieties (P < 0.01, Figure 4.3.6). The positive effect of CO_2 on the intercept of the relationship between bulb dry weight and temperature was significant (P < 0.01 for both varieties, Figure 4.3.6a, b). As for total dry weight, when data from the two CO_2 concentrations at bulb maturity were analysed separately, total dry weight was not significantly affected by differences in temperature at elevated CO_2. Dry matter yields of mature plants were on average 18% greater in cv. Hysam than in cv. Sito (P < 0.05). The effects of differences in temperature and CO_2 concentration on the total fresh weight yields (of ungraded bulbs) followed the same trends as those shown for dry weight. At normal CO_2, fresh weight bulb yields ranged from 46.4 to 86.8 tonnes ha^{-1} in cv. Hysam and from 41.1 to 88.2 tonnes ha^{-1} in cv. Sito. In comparable plots at elevated CO_2, bulb yields were 73.5 to 90.4 and 70.5 to 80.6 tonnes ha^{-1} for cv. Hysam and Sito, respectively. A summary of

the proportional effects of CO_2 and temperature on onion growth and yield is presented in Table 4.2.2.

4.2.4   Implications for modelling

The results of this experimental programme have some specific implications for crop simulation models of onion growth for application to future climates of warmer temperatures and elevated concentrations of CO_2, and some implications for crop modelling in general. Experimental evidence supports the absence of an effect of CO_2 concentration on the rate of developmental processes in crops other than onion. However, it was clear that the timing of both bulbing and bulb maturity in onion were affected by CO_2 concentration, although the reduced time to bulbing at elevated CO_2 was counteracted by the longer period of bulb maturity in these crops. Therefore, the effects of CO_2 concentration on the entire crop duration can also be omitted from a general model of onion crop growth, but may be justified in a more detailed model of time to bulbing or the period of bulb maturity. The effect

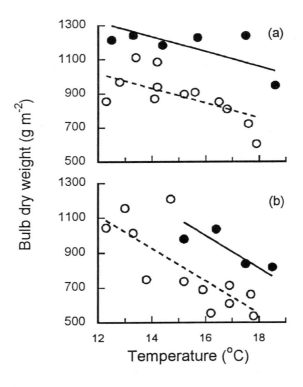

Figure 4.3.6   Relationship between bulb dry weight at harvest maturity and mean temperature at 372 (O ;·····) and 532 (●,——) ppmv CO_2 in (a) cv. Hysam and (b) cv. Sito.

Table 4.3.2 Summary of results from the onion experiment at Reading in 1994 expressed as percentage change with respect to either normal CO_2 or temperature 1°C cooler where significant. nd indicates not determined. [1] = 372 ppmv CO_2; [2] = 532 ppmv CO_2.

Parameter	At bulbing		At harvest maturity	
	+CO₂ (532 ppmv)	+1°C	+CO₂ (532 ppmv)	+1°C
cv. Hysam				
Specific leaf area	-18 to -23%	+5 to +6%[1] +6 to +7%[2]	nd	nd
Total Biomass	+39%	0	+19 to +27%	-5 to -7%[1] -5%[2]
Bulb Dry Weight	+35%	0	+30 to +41%	-4 to -6%[1] -3 to -4%[2]
cv. Sito				
Specific leaf area	-12 to -17%	+7 to +9%[1] +8 to +11%[2]	nd	nd
Total Biomass	+34%	0	+16 to +24%	-9 to -15%[1] -7 to -11%[2]
Bulb Dry Weight	+45%	0	+24 to +51%	-9 to -16%[1] -7 to -11%[2]

of elevated CO_2 concentration on crop biomass was not constant during ontogeny, as assumed in crop models which describe the effects of elevated CO_2 on biomass accumulation using a constant increase in radiation use efficiency throughout crop growth. In crop models which include a submodel of photosynthesis, such an observation can be modelled as acclimation of the rate of photosynthesis to elevated CO_2. Models in which the increase in leaf area is calculated as the product of estimated specific leaf area and the biomass partitioned to leaves, need to consider that, in onion, specific leaf area at a given time was affected by differences in both temperature and CO_2 concentration. An experimental finding that simplifies the modelling of onion growth in future climates is that the leaf light extinction coefficient was independent of both temperature and CO_2 concentration in onion.

4.3.5 Discussion and conclusions

Warmer temperatures hastened the duration of onion crop growth. An increase in mean temperatures of between 2 and 4.5°C resulted in more rapid bulbing and earlier bulb maturity; a response similar to that found in previous studies of onion (Steer, 1980; Terabun, 1981). The shorter period of bulb growth at warmer temperatures resulted in smaller leaf area durations such that the amount of incident radiation received by plants growing in the warmest conditions was 21 to 27% less than in the coolest conditions. Therefore, the principal effect of differences in temperature on final crop weights could be explained by the influence of temperature on crop durations.

The timing of developmental stages in onion was also affected by CO_2 concentration, in addition to the considerable effects of temperature. Bulbing involves a change from the expansion of leaf blade leaves to the swelling of bulb scale leaves (Brewster, 1990) and is thought to be promoted by conditions favouring carbohydrate accumulation (Mondal *et al.*, 1986a). Thus, our observations of earlier bulbing at elevated compared with normal CO_2 are in accordance with the conclusions of Mondal *et al.* (1986a). Changes in apical development of onion sometimes occurs after sheath swelling (Mondal *et al.*, 1986b). Therefore, earlier bulbing at high CO_2 does not necessarily imply earlier bulb scale initiation at the apex. Thus, our results do not necessarily contradict evidence that the rate of apical development in several crops is independent of CO_2 concentration (for example, Batts *et al.*, 1995, Mitchell *et al.*, 1993, Wheeler *et al.*, 1995a,b).

The greater total biomass at bulbing at elevated compared with normal CO_2 was not associated with a significant increase in leaf area index as has often been observed in a number of other crops (for example, Morison and Gifford 1984; Goudriaan and de Ruiter, 1983; Baker *et al.*, 1989). Neither was a large effect of elevated CO_2 on the number of appeared leaves or senesced leaves found. The observation of a lower specific leaf area at elevated CO_2 is compatible with other studies (for example, Leadley and Reynolds, 1988; Lawlor and Mitchell, 1991, Wheeler *et al.*, 1994, 1995a) and has been shown to be associated with increased non-structural carbohydrate concentration (Sionit *et al.*, 1982; Ehret and Joliffe, 1985) providing further evidence for photosynthetic stimulation. The observation that radiation use efficiency between bulbing and maturity was not affected by CO_2 suggests that there was little stimulation of photosynthesis during this period and that there may have been photosynthetic acclimation to a high-CO_2 environment. Thus, in onion the greater biomass at elevated CO_2 of mature plants was a result of higher growth rates during the early developmental stages as well as a longer duration between bulbing and maturity.

The heavier yield with enrichment to 532 ppmv CO_2 of 24 to 51% (0.16 to 0.34% per 1 ppmv) for cv. Sito is greater than the 0.10% per 1 ppmv CO_2 average crop response assembled by Kimball (1983) but is not dissimilar to studies on root crops which found a 64% increase (0.19% per 1 ppmv rise) in yield of radish (*Raphanus sativus* L.) and a 71% (0.22% per 1 ppmv rise) increase in soybean (*Glycine max* L.) with a doubling of ambient CO_2 concentrations (in the studies reviewed by Poorter, 1993). Thus, it would appear that the magnitude of the yield response to elevated CO_2 of onion, as representative of bulbing species, is similar to that of root crops. This enhanced response may be because the yield component in these crops is a relatively large sink (Clough *et al.*, 1981). The range of harvest indices observed here in onion (78 to 86%) are certainly comparable to those of 65 to 70% for carrot in the experiment of Wheeler *et al.* (1994), both of which are greater than the 31% to 54% range reported for wheat (Hay, 1995).

Although total biomass was affected by both temperature and CO_2, no interaction between these two variables was detected. Whilst a temperature and CO_2 interaction is expected from studies on photosynthesis (Long, 1991) this has not always been found in experimental studies with relatively small differences in mean temperature (for example, Wheeler *et al.*, 1994). Since an increase in temperature is expected to have the opposite effect to that of CO_2 in determinate crops such as onion, greater crop dry weights will be partially offset by increases in temperature; an increase from 372 to 532 ppmv CO_2 was offset by a 3.9°C temperature increase in cv. Hysam and by a 2.3°C increase in cv. Sito. Similarly, the increase in bulb yield from 372 ppmv CO_2 to 532 ppmv was offset by an increase in temperature of 6.9°C in cv. Hysam and 2.8°C in cv. Sito.

The absence of an interaction between CO_2 and temperature over these ranges of temperature simplifies an assessment of the impact of climate change on onion crops. Thus, assuming that an increase in atmospheric CO_2 concentration to about 560 ppmv is accompanied by a rise in temperature of 2.1°C (Viner and Hulme, 1993), this climatic change scenario would result in an increase in dry matter yield of 25% in cv. Hysam and 8% in cv. Sito.

A simple response to any future changes in climate is to change the variety of crop grown (Parry and Carter, 1990). The results of this experiment suggest that a future climate of warmer temperatures and elevated CO_2 would allow a long season variety to be grown in place of a short season variety without a loss in yield.

4.4   Mini Free Air Carbon dioxide enrichment (FACE) experiment on grapevine

4.4.1   Background

Changes in the concentration of CO_2 in the atmosphere have the potential to alter both the physiological functioning and growth of plants and the structure of plant communities. Hundreds of experiments on the effects of CO_2 enrichment on many species of plants have been performed using various types of enclosure chambers (see reviews by Kimball, 1983; Strain and Cure, 1985; Allen, 1992; Lawlor and Mitchell, 1991). For the most part, these studies have been carried out on annual crops, and in general, have found that increased atmospheric CO_2 increases net photosynthesis, biomass, seed yield, light use efficiency, nutrient use efficiency, plant water potential and water use efficiency. A few studies have been carried out on woody perennial crops (Idso and Kimball, 1992) but the response of fruit trees, such as grapevine, to CO_2 enrichment has not been evaluated.

The growth and development of grapevine are influenced by environmental factors such as temperature and radiation (Mullins *et al.*, 1992). Further, fruit and total biomass accumulation are affected by an increase in CO_2 enrichment through the stimulation of photosynthesis and growth. Thus, changes in climatic and atmospheric conditions will have a significant impact on the growth of grapevine and it is important to analyse and model the range of possible future impacts.

Several methods exist for studying the effects of elevated CO_2 on plant growth (Allen, 1992), amongst which sunlit controlled-environment chambers (e.g. soil plant atmosphere research, SPAR, units) and open- top chambers (OTCs) are probably the most popular. However, the free air CO_2 enrichment (FACE) approach is advantageous because it can produce plants under conditions of field realism. An opportunity to organise a FACE experiment over an existing vineyard in Tuscany was offered by a CO_2 producer that currently extracts CO_2 from geothermal sources. CO_2 production costs and, therefore, CO_2 prices were very low and a FACE experiment was affordable.

The objective of the FACE experiment was to collect information on growth parameters (such as radiation use efficiency, specific leaf area, partitioning between plant organs) which can be used in models to predict the effects of climate change on grapevine production. Moreover, since this FACE experiment provides a unique opportunity for evaluating the response of grapevine to elevated CO_2 concentration, further measurements were made on the main components of must (sugars, acids, etc.) and also gas and water exchanges between the crop and the atmosphere.

4.4.2   Experimental approach

When evaluating the effects of gases on crops or other ecosystems, researchers are faced with the problem of trying to produce an exposure regime in which only the variables to be investigated are altered, while other features remain in a natural state. This type of experiment has often been hampered by the inability to create an experimental environment free of artificial conditions introduced by the structures and equipment used to expose the crop to the test gas. These are generally described as 'chamber effects' and include changes in wind speed, humidity, temperature, light quality and intensity. In seeking a more realistic experimental design, researchers have replaced their studies in the highly controlled and unnatural environment of greenhouses, growth chambers or open top chambers with free air carbon dioxide enrichment (FACE) facilities. FACE has successfully achieved a series of innovative experiments on cotton and wheat in the USA. These experiments made use of a sophisticated FACE technology developed by the Brookhaven National Laboratory of the United States Department of Energy (Lewin *et al.*, 1994).

The Mini-FACE facility developed for this experiment was a much simpler system that made use of the same concepts adopted by FACE technology but on a smaller scale.

4.4.2.1   *Description of the system*

The fumigation system consisted of 22 vertical pipes, each pipe containing multiple gas emitter ports. Each pipe was connected with a common 24 m horizontal plenum positioned at the soil surface (Figure 4.4.1). The 24 m plenum was assembled from polyvinyl chloride (PVC) pipe with an internal diameter of 20 cm. The vertical pipes were made from PVC pipe with an internal diameter of 4 cm and were 2 m long. Each vent pipe had four emission holes having a 2 cm diameter. The holes were placed in two groups of two holes each. The grouped holes were arranged so that the angles between the centre of each of the two holes and the perpendicular to the vineyard row was 60 degrees. The two rows of holes were positioned approximately 100 and 170 cm above the soil surface.

Figure 4.4.1   Photograph of the Mini-FACE fumigation devices positioned in the vineyard.

A high-volume fan (OMIE, Florence) drew ambient air into the plenum at a rate of approximately 30 $m^3 min^{-1}$. The pure CO_2 was mixed with the ambient air by placing the outlet from the CO_2 flow controller directly in front of the blower outlet.

An infra-red gas analyser (IRGA) (PPS EMG1, Hitchin) was used to continuously monitor the gas concentration of experimental plots. Air was sampled from the centre of the array with the inlet height at 1.5 m above the soil surface. The

sampled air was pumped at 10 min^{-1} through approximately 50 meters of 4 mm polyethylene tubing before reaching the analyser. The time taken for the sample to traverse this distance, along with measurement delays inherent in the analyser, resulted in a total delay of 5 to 8 seconds from when the air sampled entered the sampling tube and when the resulting concentration was measured by the gas analyser.

The amount of CO_2 metered into the plenum was based on wind speed and gas concentration sampled at the centre of the array. A computer-controlled system was used to keep the CO_2 concentration constant inside the Mini-FACE array. The program controlled CO_2 injection rates into the plenum by means of computer-controlled valves. Injection rates were at first calculated from wind velocity measured by an anemometer located near the treatment areas and these measurements were then corrected using a feedback control algorithm. This algorithm calculated a feedback coefficient which was a function of the difference between the target CO_2 concentration (700 ppmv) and CO_2 concentration measured at the centre of each treatment array. Wind speed and CO_2 injection were respectively read and re-calculated every second. The feedback coefficient was calculated every one minute by averaging the IRGA readings taken every second. The whole Mini-FACE set-up was operated by a single IRGA and air sampling was alternatively made at the centre of each CO_2 treatment array using a multiport sampler (ACME, Florence).

4.4.2.2   *Description of experiment*

The Mini-FACE experiment was conducted in an existing vineyard near Rapolano, Siena (43°35', 10°45') where the availability of large quantities of pure geologic CO_2 provided an inexpensive source of gas for experiments (Miglietta *et al.*, 1993). The *Vitis Vinifera* L. (cultivar Sangiovese) vines were chosen for the experiment for consistency with the grapevine physiological model described in Section 5.4. Vines were trained with a mixture of different pruning systems (traditional cordon, single curtain and vertical cordon). All the vines were abundantly fertilized and were not irrigated.

The Mini-FACE fumigation devices were placed in the vineyard in three different rows in order to produce an experimental design with three replicates for both treatment and control areas. To minimise contamination of control areas by CO_2 released from treatment areas, control samples were collected in areas situated at least 10 m from the nearest treatment area (Figure 4.4.2).

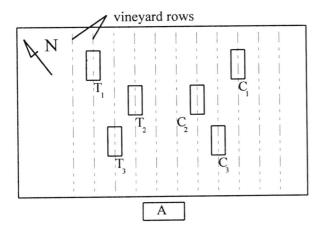

Figure 4.4.2 Scheme of the Mini-FACE facility. A represents the system control; T_1 through T_3 represent the treatment areas and C_1 through C_3 represent the control areas.

The Mini-FACE experiment was performed to collect information on a number of growth parameters (such as radiation use efficiency, specific leaf area and partitioning between plant organs). These data were used to validate the model presented in Section 5.4. Moreover since this Mini-FACE system provides a unique opportunity for evaluating the response of grapevine to elevated CO_2 concentration, measurements were also made on the main components of must (sugars, acids, pH) as well as gas and water exchanges between the crop and the atmosphere (leaf water relations and photosynthetic capacity).

Biomass samples were taken four times during the growth season, final fruit production was harvested at the date of ripening, and measurements of leaf water relations and photosynthetic capacity were made during the season. Biomass components were estimated from two shoots harvested from each replicate.

Individual shoots were separated into stems, fruit and leaf components, dried in a ventilated oven for at least 72 hours and weighed. Harvest index (HI) was computed as the ratio of dry berries biomass to the total biomass of the shoot. Specific leaf area was estimated from 15 small discs (each of 7 cm^2) punched from fully expanded leaves. The samples were placed into ice for transport to the laboratory. Leaf discs were stored and weighed in the laboratory.

Solar radiation data was measured at hourly intervals in an automatic weather station located on the farm to calculate radiation use efficiency (RUE).

4.4.3 Results and Discussion

4.4.3.1 *System performance*

There are two general areas of system control. The first is reliability of subsystems and components. The second is maintenance of temporal and spatial control of the CO_2 concentration within the experimental plot. As regards the former, system control, with the exception of the first month of the growing season where some problems with the system hardware (multiport scanner and main board of the computer) were experienced, there were only two interruptions to the fumigation due to equipment maintenance and power supply failure during the season. These, however, were not longer than one day. An evaluation of the system performance was made in 1994 by continuously recording one minute average values of wind velocity, CO_2 injection rates and CO_2 concentration measured in the arrays. Moreover, detailed measurements of horizontal concentration gradients were made during the growing season. These measurements were made using a multiport sampler (ACME, Florence) connected to pipes placed along the vineyard rows and perpendicular to the rows (Figure 4.4.3). Air was repeatedly sampled for one minute from each pipe and analysed by an IRGA. IRGA readings taken every second were recorded on a portable data logger (Delta T Devices, Cambridge).

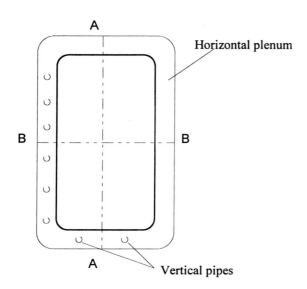

Figure 4.4.3   Direction of gas concentration measurements. A-A along vineyard rows, B-B perpendicular to vineyard rows.

Table 4.4.1   Seasonally averaged CO_2 exposure (ppmv).

	Array T1	Array T2	Array T3
Target	700.00	700.00	700.00
Array conc.	707.00	712.44	717.09

Table 4.4.2   Fraction of time that average CO_2 concentrations deviated from the set point for 1 and 15 minute averages.

	1 minute average			15 minute average		
Array	<10%	<20%	<30%	<10%	<20%	<30%
T1	0.459	0.762	0.899	0.699	0.913	0.978
T2	0.403	0.683	0.826	0.667	0.865	0.933
T3	0.393	0.683	0.840	0.704	0.924	0.966

Over the course of the season the CO_2 concentration was between 707 and 717 ppmv depending on the array (Table 4.4.1). Daily average CO_2 treatment was very close to the set point (700 ppmv) for most of the running period. Only in the middle of June were daily average CO_2 levels higher due to software problems (Figure 4.4.4).

The Mini-FACE system maintained the CO_2 concentration very close to the set point when calculated over long time periods (day or season) (Table 4.4.1). However, fluctuations of CO_2 over shorter time periods may be of biological significance. Short-term performance was measured by calculating the fraction of time that measured CO_2 concentrations (e.g. 1 minute average and 15 minute average) was smaller than a certain amount (10%, 20%, 30%) from the set point. In this experiment, with a set point at 700 ppmv, 10%, 20% and 30% from the set point corresponds to 70 ppmv (630 to 770 ppmv), 140 ppmv (560 to 840 ppmv) and 210 ppmv (490 to 910 ppmv) respectively. The design criterion was to hold the 1 minute average within 20-30% for over 80% of time. Table 4.4.2 shows the fraction of time 1 minute and 15 minute average gas concentrations were lower than 10%, 20% and 30% from the set

point. The 1 minute average deviation was greater than 30% for less than 20% of the time, and it was within the 20% limit for more than 70% of the time. Hence, the design criterion was fulfilled. Since all the arrays demonstrated similar short-term control capability under all conditions, the remaining results are presented for combined data from all three arrays.

Control performance varied with wind speed (Table 4.4.3). Control was worse under low and high wind speeds than for the other wind speed categories. Above 1 m s^{-1}, average performance improved up to 2 m s^{-1} after which it decreased. In general, low wind speeds were associated with relatively greater variability in wind speed and direction during the daytime, causing relatively higher vertical turbulence; whereas high wind speeds caused increased vertical turbulence inside the vineyard rows.

In general, control was worse in the early morning and afternoon hours (Table 4.4.4). This was due to a high frequency of low wind speeds in the early morning and a high frequency of high wind speeds and increased vertical turbulence induced by solar energy during the daytime.

Plot T1

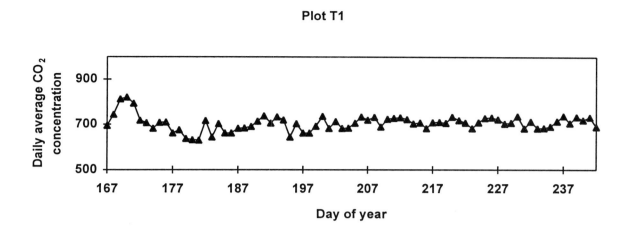

Plot T2

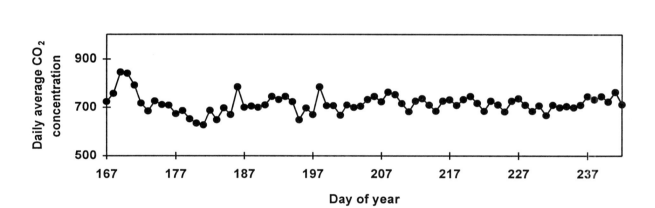

Plot T3

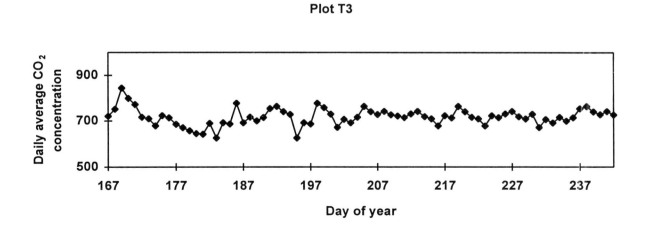

Figure 4.4.4   Daily average of 1-minute integral CO_2 concentrations (ppmv).

Table 4.4.3   Fraction of time that average CO_2 concentrations deviated from the set point for 1 and 15 minute averages versus wind speed.

wind (m s^{-1})	1 minute average			15 minute average		
	<10%	<20%	<30%	<10%	<20%	<30%
0-0.625	0.406	0.688	0.836	0.682	0.889	0.952
0.625-1.25	0.502	0.835	0.976	0.770	0.957	0.980
1.25-1.875	0.461	0.813	0.977	0.613	0.968	1.000
1.875-2.5	0.355	0.739	0.975	0.313	0.750	0.950
>2.5	0.232	0.526	0.916	0.000	1.000	1.000

Table 4.4.4   Fraction of time average CO_2 concentrations deviated from the set point for 1 and 15 minute averages versus hour of day.

hour	1 minute Average			15 minute Average		
	<10%	<20%	<30%	<10%	<20%	<30%
6-7	0.290	0.518	0.676	0.545	0.783	0.874
7-8	0.350	0.587	0.740	0.863	1.258	1.427
8-9	0.444	0.718	0.851	0.690	0.875	0.945
9-10	0.497	0.816	0.939	0.796	0.938	0.979
10-11	0.492	0.822	0.957	0.790	0.948	0.984
11-12	0.465	0.799	0.951	0.781	0.965	0.982
12-13	0.459	0.774	0.943	0.757	0.965	0.996
13-14	0.454	0.758	0.993	0.713	0.952	0.996
14-15	0.431	0.742	0.912	0.677	0.900	0.969
15-16	0.423	0.734	0.890	0.677	0.886	0.961
16-17	0.409	0.723	0.875	0.643	0.884	0.960
17-18	0.408	0.721	0.871	0.601	0.860	0.938
18-19	0.434	0.741	0.877	0.603	0.882	0.926

Data on the gas distribution within the Mini-FACE were taken during 2 days in July (20-21). Figure 4.4.5a shows CO_2 concentration as a function of distance from the centre of the array along the vineyard row direction (see Figure 4.4.3). The data indicate that on average, CO_2 concentration slowly increased to about 10% and 20% above the target at 2 and 4m respectively. Figure 4.4.5b displays the same information sampled perpendicular to the rows. On average, CO_2 concentration was essentially constant out to a distance of 50 cm and decreased to about 20% below target at 70 cm. On this basis the usable area within the Mini-FACE array where CO_2 concentration was maintained with the design criteria of the target concentration was estimated to be 8m by 1.4m. This area was used for the biomass harvest.

4.4.3.2   *Crop performance*

Harvest index (HI)

There is no extensive information about the effect of elevated CO_2 concentration on the rate of change in HI (dHI/dt) in grapevines. However, a recent experiment on soybean suggested that elevated atmospheric CO_2 concentration, which largely enhanced biomass accumulation and final yield, had a positive effect on dHI/dt. It is likely that this reflected increased resource allocation to growing seeds. Biomass components sampled in the treatment and control areas of the Mini-FACE experiment were analysed to verify whether elevated atmospheric CO_2 concentrations affect the rate of change in harvest index in grapevine.

Analysis of fruit growth data showed that growth in both treatments follows the typical double sigmoid pattern (Figure 4.4.6) with three stages: I, the initial phase of rapid growth; II, the so-called lag phase of slow growth; and III, the final phase of resumed growth. Despite the fact that biomass accumulation was substantially affected by CO_2 (Table 4.4.5), dHI/dt remained constant during the fruit growth period (Figure 4.4.7). The dHI/dt was, however, higher than that calculated for developing the model, due essentially to the differences in age of the plants, rootstock and training system.

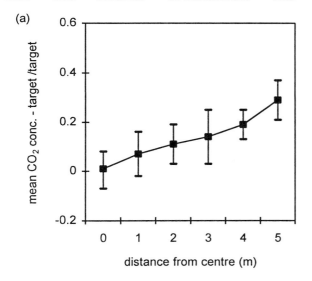
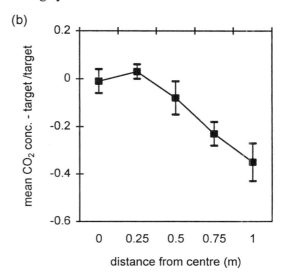

Figure 4.4.5 Average distribution of CO_2 with the Mini-FACE array: a) along the row (A-A); b) perpendicular to the row (B-B).

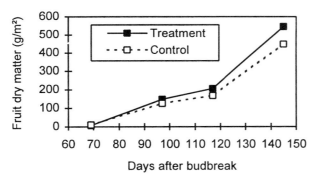

Figure 4.4.6 Accumulation of fruit biomass in treatment and control areas for cultivar Sangiovese. Data are the means of six observations.

Table 4.4.5 CO_2 effects on leaf number, leaf area and biomass (dry weight). Values within a row followed by the same letter are not significantly different at the 5% level using LSD multiple range test.

Plant parameters	Treatment	Control	Ratio*
Leaf number (m^{-2})	150.333a	125.888a	1.194
Leaf area ($cm^2 m^{-2}$)	30872.917a	21427.309a	1.440
Stem and leaf weight (gm^{-2})	706.866a	472.45a	1.496
Total weight (gm^{-2})	1252.343a	922.686a	1.357
Fruit weight (gm^{-2})	545.477b	450.236a	1.211

*Ratio of parameters from treatment and control CO_2 levels.

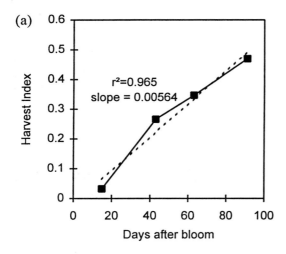
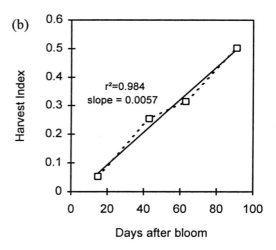

Figure 4.4.7   Harvest index observed during the season in (a) treatment and (b) control arrays for cultivar Sangiovese. Data are the means of six observations.

Specific leaf area (SLA)

Many studies have shown that leaf weight per unit surface area (SLA) increases in high CO_2 concentrations (Acock, 1990, Goudriaan and Unsworth, 1990). This increase in weight could be caused by either the accumulation of starch and sugar in the leaf or increasing structural growth. Hence, to quantify the increase in grapevine leaf weight under elevated CO_2 concentrations and to understand the nature of this increase (change in tissue volume or density), the SLA of plants in treatment and control areas was calculated throughout the season and analyses of starch and sugar contents of leaves were carried out at the end of the growing season.

The values of leaf weight throughout the season showed that SLA in treatment areas was significantly lower than those in control areas, with a mean reduction of 12% (Figure 4.4.8). Accordingly, leaf starch content was significantly increased in treatment leaves (Figure 4.4.9). Soluble sugars exhibited a similar pattern, but it was not as pronounced as for leaf starch. This higher accumulation of non structural carbohydrates in grapevine leaves grown in elevated CO_2 concentration increased the ability of these plants to export carbon during periods of cloudy weather, water stress and heavy metabolic demand, such as at fruit set, allowing these plants to tolerate stress periods better than plants grown in ambient CO_2.

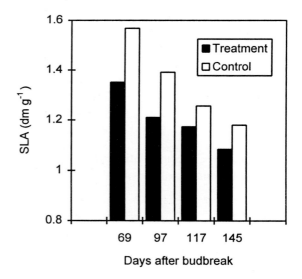

Figure 4.4.8   Specified leaf area (SLA) of treatment and control plots. Data are the means of 15 observations.

(a)

(b)

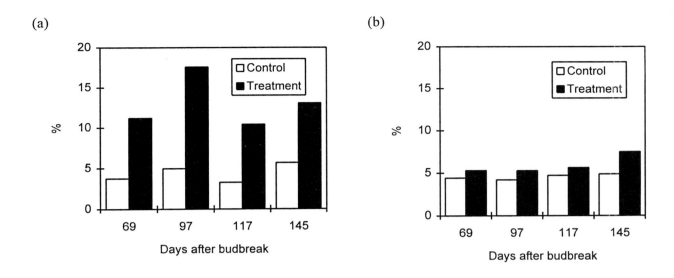

Figure 4.4.9 (a) Starch and (b) soluble sugar (glucose, fructose and sucrose) in grapevine leaves exposed to two levels of CO_2. Data are the means of four observations.

Radiation Use Efficiency (RUE)

Crop photosynthetic activity was expressed in the grapevine model as RUE (see Section 5.4). Crop modelling studies performed on different crops (Sinclair and Rawlins, 1993) assume increases in RUE under increased CO_2 concentration that range from 10% (maize) to 40% (soybean). Hence, in order to use the grapevine model for evaluating the impact of future climate on grapevine production, biomass samples were taken in both control and treatment arrays to calculate the increase in RUE for grapevine. Figure 4.4.10 shows the values of RUE and its standard error (SE) calculated for the cv. Sangiovese in an experiment at Lampeggi-Mondeggi farm (used to develop the grapevine model) and in the Mini-FACE experiment. The values of RUE for current CO_2 concentrations are similar, whereas the RUE calculated for treatment areas is higher by approximately 35%. The higher SE of the RUE values found for the Mini-FACE data is due to a lower number of samples harvested (2 shoots with respect to 10 shoots in Lapeggi-Mondeggi).

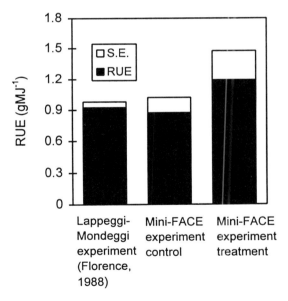

Figure 4.4.10 Radiation use efficiency (±SE) of the Lappeggi-Mondeggi experiment (used to develop the model) and the Mini-FACE experiment.

Final production and must components

The final harvest of the grapevine was made on 30 September 1994. Total fruit production was harvested from each replicate. Individual production of each replicate was divided into nine samples (one per plant) and the fresh weight of each sample and of 100 berries were measured. This latter weight can be used as an indicator of the dimensions of the berries. Then for each replicate four samples were extracted to analyse must components and the rest of the harvest was used to produce wine.

The results showed that CO_2 concentration has a significant effect on both fruit production and the dimensions of berries (Table 4.4.6). The ratio between treatment and control values was 1.23 and 1.37 respectively. Based on the current relationship between berry dimensions and must components, the increase in the dimensions of berries in plants exposed to elevated CO_2 affected all must components (Table 4.4.7). Specifically, total sugar content and pH were higher under ambient CO_2 levels than under CO_2 enrichment, whereas total acid content was lower under ambient CO_2 levels.

These effects on must components could be considered positive or negative, depending on the type of wine produced. For example, these effects would be positive for the production of light wine or sparkling wine where a higher acidity level is necessary but they would be negative for the production of high quality wine where the sugars are the most important component.

Leaf water relations

In general, elevated CO_2 slows transpiration and reduces the severity of water stress in plants. As a result, CO_2 enrichment exerts a larger stimulatory effect on water-stressed plants than unstressed plants (Dahlmann *et al.*, 1984; Dahlmann, 1992). This subject is, however, complex because of the dual effect of CO_2 enrichment on photosynthesis assimilation and transpiration.

Predawn and midday measurements on leaf total water, osmotic potential and hydraulic conductivity were made during the growing season. Total water and osmotic potential were measured with a pressure chamber following the techniques proposed by Tyree and Jarvis (1982), and hydraulic conductivity was measured on shoots samples using the technique described by Sperry *et al.* (1988).

Both the leaf water potentials were affected by CO_2. In particular, with an overcast sky, CO_2 enriched plants showed predawn and midday water potential values that were consistently higher than those from control areas. On the other hand, with a clear sky the midday

Table 4.4.6 CO_2 effects on final yield. Values within a row followed by the same letter are not significantly different at the 5% confidence level using LSD multiple range test.

	Treatment	Control	Ratio *
Total fresh weight (g.m^{-2})	1292.10 (a)	1054.50 (b)	1.23
100 berry fresh weight (g)	54.48 (a)	39.76 (b)	1.37

* Ratio of the values in treatment and control CO_2 levels.

Table 4.4.7 CO_2 effects on yield quality. Values within a row followed by the same letter are not significantly different at the 5% confidence level using LSD multiple range test.

	Treatment	Control	Ratio *
Total sugars (g.l^{-1})	218.70 (a)	256.4 (b)	0.85
Total acidity (g.l^{-1})	6.98 (a)	6.57 (b)	1.06
pH	2.93 (a)	3.03 (b)	0.97

* Ratio of the values in treatment and control CO_2 levels.

potentials were maintained at lower levels (more negative) in plants grown and monitored in elevated CO_2 than those exposed to ambient CO_2 (Figure 4.4.11). Measurements on hydraulic conductivity, however, showed that the percentage loss of hydraulic conductivity was higher in plants grown in ambient CO_2 concentration than in those exposed to elevated

CO_2 (Figure 4.4.12). So, these lower values of midday potential in days with high irradiance of plants exposed to elevated CO_2 can be attributed to a combination of osmotic adjustment in the chloroplasts, as showed by the lower values of osmotic potential in treatment plots (Figure 4.4.13). Osmotic adjustment in leaves of plants in above-ambient CO_2 treatments were credited

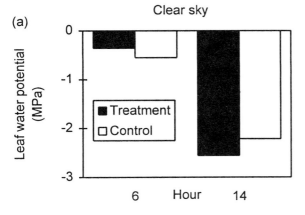
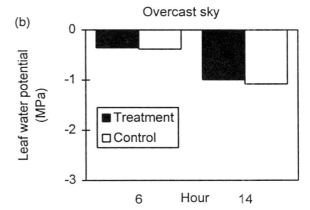
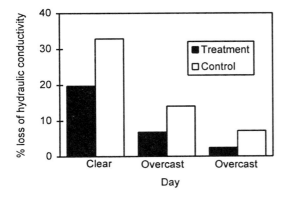

Figure 4.4.11 Leaf water potential for two levels of CO_2 and different sky conditions. (a) - clear sky; (b) and (c) - overcast sky.

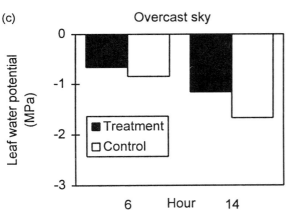

Figure 4.4.12 Percentage loss of hydraulic conductivity for two levels of CO_2 and different sky conditions.

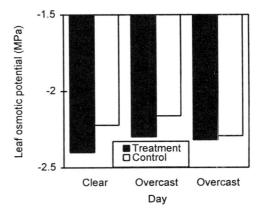

Figure 4.4.13 Osmotic potential for two levels of CO_2 and different sky conditions.

with the maintenance of higher relative water content (RWC) and turgor pressure, and prevention of full stomatal closure, allowing net photosynthesis to proceed. This differential osmotic response creates a differential response in turgor pressure (Kramer, 1983), and thus greater calculated turgor in plants exposed to equal water stress but higher CO_2 (Thomas and Harvey, 1983). The occurrence of similar osmotic adjustments has been reported by many authors (Conroy *et al.*, 1988; Sasek and Strain, 1989).

Photosynthetic capacity

Acclimatory downward regulation of photosynthetic capacity has been often, but not always, observed in C_3 plants after long-term exposure to elevated CO_2 (Sage *et al.*, 1989; Long and Drake, 1992), and it is now accepted that photosynthetic acclimation under conditions of elevated CO_2 is not simply an artefact due to growing conditions (Arp, 1991; Stitt, 1991; Sage, 1994). Several potential mechanisms leading to acclimation under conditions of elevated CO_2 have been extensively reviewed (Stitt, 1991; Woodrow, 1994), but the excessive accumulation of carbohydrates in leaves is accepted to be one of the most important determinants of acclimation (Stitt, 1991; Sage, 1994; Webber *et al.*, 1994). Several studies in controlled environments have been performed (Mitchell *et al.*, 1993; Petterson and McDonald, 1994; Mckee and Woodward, 1994), but it is uncertain if results obtained in laboratory experiments can be directly extrapolated to plants grown under field conditions.

In the Mini-FACE experiment assimilation versus intercellular CO_2 concentration (A:Ci) was measured by gas exchange using an open portable photosynthesis system during the growing season. The biochemical model developed by Farquar *et al.* (1980) was fitted to each measured A:Ci curve to obtain the values of the maximum RuBP rate of carboxylation (Vcmax, μmol m^{-2} s^{-1}) and the light saturated rate of electron transport (Jmax, μmol m^{-2} s^{-1}).

Gas exchange measurements showed that elevated concentrations of CO_2 had a significant positive effect on Jmax and a negative, but not significant, effect on Vcmax (Table 4.4.8). This type of acclimation response, involving an increase in Jmax and a reduction in Vcmax, has been observed previously in elevated CO_2 experiments (Sage, 1994). Upward regulation of electron transport capacity can be related in this case to a reallocation of nitrogen resources within the leaf away from Rubisco and to the light harvesting complex. However, in the specific case of the grapevines grown in the Mini-FACE experiment, increased Jmax could also be the result of an overall improvement in water relations due to decreased stomatal conductance.

4.4.4   Implications for modelling

Following the results obtained from the Mini-FACE experiment the major implications for the processes included in the grapevine model presented in Section 5.4 are that:

- ontogeny: none of the three periods into which crop ontogeny of grapevine is divided seem to be affected by an increase in CO_2[1];

Table 4.4.8 CO_2 effects on photosynthetic capacity. Values within a row followed by the same letter are not significantly different at the 5% confidence level using LSD multiple range test.

	Treatment	Control	Ratio*
Jmax (μmol m^{-2} s^{-1})	175.2 (a)	152.8 (b)	1.15
Vcmax (μmol m^{-2} s^{-1})	54.9 (a)	57.8 (b)	0.95

* Ratio of the values in treatment and control CO_2 levels.

[1] Weekly observations of the phenological stages were made from budbreak according to the scheme of Eichhorn and Lorenz (1977).

- leaf area: the relationship between the total number of appeared leaves and leaf area seems not to be affected by an increase in CO_2;

- biomass accumulation: RUE calculated for treatment areas is 35% higher than that observed for current CO_2 concentrations; and

- fruit growth: the daily increase in harvest index (dHI/dt) is not affected by an increase in CO_2.

Moreover, with regard to implications for other models, the values of leaf weight throughout the season show that SLA is significantly lower (mean reduction of 12%) in high CO_2 concentrations.

4.4.5 Conclusions

Analysis of biomass accumulation showed that all the biomass components (leaf, shoot and fruit) were substantially affected by CO_2 with increases ranging between 21 and 49%, whereas no differences in the rate of change in harvest index were detected among the CO_2 treatments. Crop photosynthetic activity, expressed as radiation use efficiency (RUE), showed an increase of 35% under increased CO_2 concentration (700 ppmv). The values of leaf weight throughout the season showed that the specific leaf area (SLA) in treatment areas was significantly lower with a mean reduction of 12%. Accordingly, leaf starch and sugar content were significantly increased in leaves of enriched plants.

CO_2 enrichment had a significant positive effect both on the final fresh fruit production and the dimensions of berries, with increases of 23% and 37% respectively. All the must components were affected by CO_2. Total sugar content and pH revealed higher values under ambient CO_2 levels than under CO_2 enrichment whereas total acid content revealed lower values under ambient CO_2 levels.

Measurement of leaf water relations showed a significant effect of CO_2 on leaf water potential which could be related to osmotic adjustment, as shown by hydraulic conductivity and osmotic potential measurements.

Gas exchange measurements showed an acclimatatory downward regulation of photosynthetic capacity of plants exposed to elevated CO_2 (positive effect on Jmax and a negative, but not significant, effect on Vcmax) which can be related in this case to a reallocation of nitrogen resources within the leaf away from Rubisco and to the light harvesting complex.

4.5 Greenhouse-based pot experiments on spring wheat, faba bean and sugar beet

4.5.1 Background

Increasing concentrations of atmospheric CO_2 appear to increase the rate of photosynthesis and to suppress photorespiration of most (i.e. C_3) plants (Goudriaan and Unsworth, 1990). This generally stimulates crop growth and leads to a much higher level of plant production (Cure, 1985; Cure and Acock, 1986; Kimball, 1983). Simultaneously dry matter allocation within the plant may change with increasing CO_2 (Stulen and Hertog, 1993) which may affect the amount of harvestable crop parts. Another effect of increasing CO_2 is an increased closure of stomata in the epidermis of leaves. This causes a higher exchange resistance between leaf and ambient air to gases such as CO_2 and water vapour which results in lower water losses by crop transpiration and in a much higher water use efficiency (Goudriaan and Bijlsma, 1987; Morison, 1993).

Growth of natural vegetation and of arable crops is mainly limited by the availability of nutrients in large parts of the world. If the nutrient use efficiency in crops at increased atmospheric CO_2 changes, this may affect crop growth and the attainable level of production (van Keulen and van Heemst, 1982), soil organic matter decomposition and nutrient cycling (Kuikman and Gorissen, 1993; van de Geijn and van Veen, 1993; Zak *et al.*, 1993). The effects of atmospheric CO_2 on crop growth, dry matter allocation and crop transpiration may be different if severe nutrient shortage occurs. To study the effects of increased atmospheric CO_2 on crop growth and their interaction with nutrient shortage pot experiments have been carried out. These experiments have been conducted with spring wheat, sugar beet and faba bean for a limited supply of nitrogen (N), phosphorus (P) and potassium (K), respectively. The results for spring wheat are reported in this section. Results for the other crop species and more detailed information on the spring wheat experiment are reported in Wolf (1995).

4.5.2   Experimental approach

4.5.2.1   *Design of the experiment*

The plants were grown in two similar glasshouses, presumed to differ only in CO_2 concentration (315 and 695 ppmv). In each glasshouse all plant species were subject to seven nutritional treatments: a control without nutrient limitation (NPK), 10% (0.1N) and 30% (0.3N) of optimum nitrogen supply, 10% (0.1P) and 30% (0.3P) of optimum phosphorus supply, and 10% (0.1K) and 30% (0.3K) of optimum potassium supply with the other elements sufficiently supplied. For a sound statistical analysis of the CO_2 effect more glasshouses would be required in order to assess the variability between the glasshouses. In this experiment the variability between the CO_2 plus nutrient treatments is used to determine the significance of the CO_2 effect. This may have influenced the significance of differences. For the NPK and the 0.1N treatments there were six replicates of which half were used for an intermediate harvest. For the other treatments there were three replicates, all used in the final harvest.

The plants were grown on coarse sand. They received nutrient solution and additional tap water. During the first four weeks after sowing (12 October 1993) all plants received the same treatment (315 ppmv CO_2, same glasshouse, identical nutrient supply). On 8 November the plants were distributed between the two glasshouses (having different CO_2 concentrations) and from that date the pots received different nutrient solutions. In each glasshouse there were three blocks (i.e. replicates). Each block consisted of three separate

rows of sugar beet, faba bean and spring wheat, respectively. The rows were situated perpendicular to the main wind direction in the glasshouse. For each replicate of each plant species seven pots with different nutritional treatments and two pots for the intermediate harvest were distributed at random within one row. The pots were standing apart.

4.5.2.2   *Soil and nutrient treatments*

Plants were grown on coarse sand with a low water holding capacity and an almost nil organic matter content in black plastic pots of about 10 l (spring wheat, faba bean) and 20 l (sugar beet). The pots received nutrient solution weekly. For the control (NPK) a Hoogland solution was used, which consisted of 5 mmol/l KNO_3, 2 mmol/l $MgSO_4.7H_2O$, 5 mmol/l $Ca(NO_3)_2.4H_2O$ and 1 mmol/l KH_2PO_4. For the 0.1 N and 0.3N treatments 90% and 70% of the NO_3^- in this solution was replaced by SO_4^{2-}; for the 0.1P and 0.3P treatments 90% and 70% of $H_2PO_4^-$ was replaced by SO_4^{2-}; and for the 0.1 K and 0.3K treatments 90% and 70% of K^+ was replaced by Ca^{2+}. The nutrient solution also contained the necessary microelements and FeEDTA to allow sufficient iron uptake.

The pots had holes in the bottom so that excess water could drain from the pots into a saucer but remained available for the plants. The soil surface in all pots was covered with white plastic grains to prevent surface evaporation and crust formation. Water stress was prevented by regularly adding tap water. In each glasshouse, pots without plants but with the soil covered by plastic grains, were weighed to allow a correction for surface evaporation.

4.5.2.3   *Air/light conditions*

Plants were grown almost completely under artificial light from sodium high-pressure agro-lamps, as during the main period of crop growth (November until February) the amount of natural light was almost nil. To attain sufficient light for plant growth the daylength in the glasshouses was set at 16 hours. The total amount of radiation (during 16 day hours) was determined to be 3.64 and 2.60 $MJm^{-2}d^{-1}$ in the glasshouse with present CO_2 and doubled CO_2, respectively, if the amount of natural light was nil. The temperature was set at $20^{\circ}C$ during the day and $15^{\circ}C$ during the 8 hours of night time, resulting in an average daily temperature over the whole growth period of $18.5^{\circ}C$. The relative humidity was set at 70% in both glasshouses, but turned out to be 60%, on average, during the growth period in the glasshouse with present CO_2 and 75% in that with doubled CO_2. The large differences in relative humidity and in amount of radiation may have resulted in different growing conditions and water use efficiency of plants between glasshouses.

The CO_2 concentration in the doubled CO_2 glasshouse was on average 695 ppmv ($\pm$ 60 ppmv for $P < 0.05$). The concentration was maintained by monitoring the CO_2 concentration with an IRGA and by injecting pure CO_2 into the glasshouse, whenever the CO_2 concentration was less than a pre-set value. In the other glasshouse CO_2 concentration was not controlled and was on average 315 ppmv ($\pm$ 30 ppmv for $P < 0.05$). CO_2 enrichment started in the doubled CO_2 glasshouse at the date that the plants were distributed over the two glasshouses (8 November).

4.5.2.4 *Plant material and methods*

Table 4.5.1 shows data on plant variety, dates of sowing, intermediate and final harvest, and number of plants per pot. At intermediate and final harvests the fresh and dry weights (after 24 hours in an oven at $70^{\circ}C$) were determined of leaves, stems and roots, plus chaff and grains for spring wheat, beets for sugar beet and pods and seeds for faba bean. To determine the root weights roots were separated from the sand by washing carefully above a fine mesh. Leaf area of the harvested plants was measured. At four intermediate dates leaf area was also determined in a non-destructive way. For spring wheat the number of ears and grains was counted.

By weighing the pots and adding sufficient tap water to bring them back to their initial weights, the total amount of water used by the plants during their growth periods was determined. Identical pots without plants were weighed to make a correction for surface evaporation. Subsamples of dried plant tissue from the different plant organs were analysed for their nitrogen, phosphorus and potassium concentration. The nitrogen concentrations were determined using the Dumas method, the phosphorus concentrations colorimetrically and the potassium concentrations with atomic absorption.

Table 4.5.1   Some characteristics of the plant material.

Crop	Cultivar, Number of plants per pot	Sowing date	Emergence date	Flowering date	Intermediate harvest date	Final harvest date (1x/2xCO$_2$)	Ripening date
Faba bean (*Vicia Faba* L.)	Minica, 1	12 Oct.	19 Oct.	from 20 Nov.	6 Jan.	25/26 Jan.	-
Spring wheat (*Triticum aestivum* L.)	Minaret, 3	12 Oct.	17 Oct.	20-30 Dec.	6 Jan.	8/22 Feb.	5/12Feb.
Sugar beet (*Beta vulgaris* L.)	Univers, 1	12 Oct.	21 Oct.	-	6 Jan.	14/15 Feb.	-

4.5.3   Results

4.5.3.1   Phenological development

Dates of emergence, flowering and ripening were recorded for the three crops (Table 4.5.1). For spring wheat the date of flowering appeared to be some days later in the doubled CO_2 glasshouse. The date of ripening for spring wheat was also later in the doubled CO_2 glasshouse, about 7 days for pots with NPK treatment but about nil for pots with strongly limited N and P supply. This is in contrast with results from Goudriaan and de Ruiter (1983) and Sionit *et al.* (1981a) who found an acceleration of flowering for wheat at increased CO_2. As there were not only differences in the CO_2 concentration but also in the amount of radiation and relative humidity between the glasshouses, these may have caused the unexpected changes in rate of phenological development.

4.5.3.2   Yields

The CO_2 effect on total above-ground dry matter yield was greatest in the control treatment without nutrient limitation (NPK) and was highly significant, and the ratio between the yield at doubled CO_2 and that at present CO_2 (i.e. ratio $2xCO_2/1xCO_2$) was 1.7 (Figure 4.5.1a; Table 4.5.2). In the K limited treatments (0.1K, 0.3K)

where growth reduction only occurred to a limited degree, the CO_2 effect was also highly significant and the yield ratio $2xCO_2/1xCO_2$ was about 1.4. In the 0.1N treatment the CO_2 effect was significant and the yield-ratio $2xCO_2/1xCO_2$ was about 1.3 . In the 0.1P treatment, P supply limited growth to such extent that the CO_2 effect on yield became nil. In the 0.3P treatment the CO_2 effect was highly significant, but it was probably overestimated as a result of the very low yield level at present CO_2.

The CO_2 effect on grain yield was also highest in the NPK control treatment with a grain yield-ratio $2xCO_2/1xCO_2$ of 2.1 (Table 4.5.2; Figure 4.5.1b). In the 0.3N, 0.3P, 0.1K and 0.3K treatments the CO_2 effect was also highly significant but the ratio $2xCO_2/1xCO_2$ decreased to about 1.4 to 1.6 because of increasing nutrient limitation. For the same reason as mentioned in the previous paragraph the CO_2 effect in the 0.3P treatment was probably overestimated. In the 0.1N treatment the ratio $2xCO_2/1xCO_2$ was about 1.3 but was not significant, and in the 0.1P treatment the CO_2 effect on grain yield was very small and not significant.

For both present and doubled atmospheric CO_2 concentration the average effect of a limited nutrient supply on yield was determined. In comparison to the NPK treatment, a limited

(a)

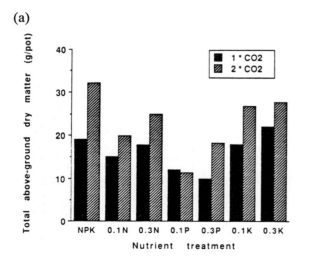

(b)

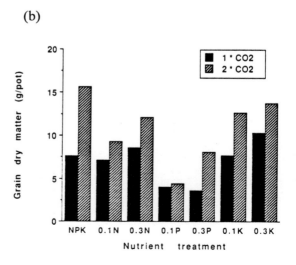

Figure 4.5.1   Average values for (a) total above-ground dry matter and (b) grain dry matter (g/pot) of spring wheat plants grown in pots at different nutrient treatments (with three replicates) at present and doubled atmospheric CO_2 concentrations.

Table 4.5.2   The ratio between average dry matter yields at doubled atmospheric CO_2 and those at present CO_2 for spring wheat plants grown in pots at different nutrient treatments (with three replicates) and the level of significance of CO_2 and nutrient effect on yield for each nutrient treatment.

	Nutrient treatment						
	NPK	0.1N	0.3N	0.1P	0.3P	0.1K	0.3K
Total above ground dry matter							
Ratio 2xCO_2/1xCO_2	1.69	1.33	1.40	1.07	1.84	1.49	1.26
Level of significance							
- of CO_2 effect[1]	**	*	**	-	**	**	**
- of nutrient effect[2]	-	** n	** n	** n	** n	* n	-
Grain dry matter							
Ratio 2xCO_2/1xCO_2	2.07	1.31	1.41	1.10	2.25	1.64	1.34
Level of significance							
- of CO_2 effect[1]	**	-	**	-	**	**	**
- of nutrient effect[2]	-	** n	-	** n	** n	-	-

[1]   The level of significance is indicated by * for $P < 0.05$, ** for $P < 0.01$ and - for not significant. Significance of CO_2 effect is based on inter-pot variance and significance of nutrient effect is determined in comparison to NPK treatment.

[2]   p indicates positive nutrient effect on dry matter yield in comparison to NPK treatment and n indicates negative effect.

supply of nitrogen and phosphorus generally resulted in a highly significant decrease in total above-ground dry matter yield (Table 4.5.2). Compared to the NPK treatment the grain dry matter yield was significantly lower in the 0.1P, 0.3P and 0.1N treatments. In the other treatments the nutrient effect on grain yield was not significant.

4.5.3.3   Dry matter partitioning

In the NPK treatment the root/shoot ratio at doubled CO_2 was about 0.8 of the ratio at present CO_2 (Figure 4.5.2a; Table 4.5.3). In the 0.1P, 0.3P and 0.1K treatments identical decreases in root/shoot ratio by CO_2 doubling were found. The inter-pot variance, however, was such that

(a)

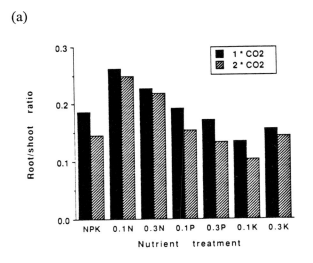

(b)

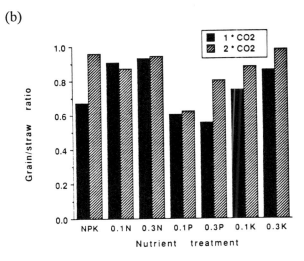

Figure 4.5.2   Average values for (a) root/shoot ratio and (b) grain/straw ratio of spring wheat plants grown in pots at different nutrient treatments (with three replicates) at present and doubled atmospheric CO_2 concentrations.

these CO_2 effects were not significant. In the other nutrient treatments the root/shoot ratio also decreased by CO_2 doubling but to a very limited and non-significant extent. Root/shoot ratio also changed as a result of limited nutrient supply. In comparison to the NPK treatment, the 0.1N and 0.3N treatments caused highly significant increased in root/shoot ratio and the 0.1K treatment a very significant decrease.

In the NPK and 0.3P treatments the grain/straw ratio at doubled CO_2 was significantly higher than in the ratio at present CO_2 (Figure 4.5.2b; Table 4.5.3). As these ratios at $1xCO_2$ were relatively low, this CO_2 effect was uncertain. In the other nutrient treatments the CO_2 effect on the grain/straw ratio was nil to small (0 to 15% increase) and not significant. Limited P supply caused a significant decrease in grain/straw ratio.

4.5.3.4 *Transpiration*

From the date that the plants were distributed over the two glasshouses and CO_2 and nutrient treatments were started, until the date of final harvest the water use by the plants was determined. Crop transpiration was calculated based on total water use corrected for surface evaporation. The transpiration coefficient, calculated as total transpiration per total above-ground dry matter yield, was about 260 g/g at present atmospheric CO_2 for the NPK treatment and slightly but not significantly higher for the N and K limited treatments (Figure 4.5.3a; Table 4.5.4). Limited P supply resulted in significantly higher transpiration coefficients.

By doubling atmospheric CO_2 the transpiration coefficient decreased to about 160 g/g in the NPK

Table 4.5.3   The ratio between average dry matter distribution at doubled atmospheric CO_2 and that at present CO_2 for spring wheat plants grown in pots at different nutrient treatments (with three replicates) and the level of significance of CO_2 and nutrient effect on distribution for each nutrient treatment.

| | Nutrient treatment | | | | | | |
	NPK	0.1N	0.3N	0.1P	0.3P	0.1K	0.3K
Root/shoot ratio							
Ratio $2xCO_2/1xCO_2$	0.78	0.95	0.96	0.80	0.77	0.77	0.92
Level of significance							
- of CO_2 effect[1]	-	-	-	-	-	-	-
- of nutrient effect[2]	-	** p	** p	-	-	** n	-
Grain/straw ratio							
Ratio $2xCO_2/1xCO_2$	1.43	0.96	1.01	1.04	1.44	1.18	1.14
Level of significance							
- of CO_2 effect[1]	**	-	-	-	**	-	-
- of nutrient effect[2]	-	-	* p	** n	* n	-	-

[1] The level of significance is indicated by * for $P < 0.05$, ** for $P < 0.01$ and - for not significant. Significance of CO_2 effect is based on inter-pot variance and significance of nutrient effect is determined in comparison to NPK treatment.

[2] p indicates a positive nutrient effect on root/shoot and grain/straw ratios in comparison to NPK treatment and n indicates a negative effect.

treatment (Figure 4.5.3a). In the nutrient limited treatments again slightly higher values were found. For the 0.1P treatment a significantly higher value was determined which corresponded with a relatively high total leaf fraction. The ratio between the transpiration coefficient at doubled CO_2 and that at present CO_2 was about 0.6 for both the NPK and the nutrient-limited treatments (Figure 4.5.3b). This ratio was determined by the difference in CO_2 concentration between both glasshouses and the difference in relative humidity and level of radiation (see section 4.5.2.3). For these reasons the significance of the CO_2 effect cannot be determined and a statistical analysis of the nutrient effect on transpiration coefficients has been conducted separately for each CO_2 treatment (Table 4.5.4).

Transpiration rates have been calculated for the conditions in each glasshouse using the Penman formula (Frère & Popov, 1979). The ratio between transpiration rates has been used to make a correction for the difference in glasshouse conditions (except CO_2 concentration level). The direct effect of CO_2 doubling on the transpiration coefficient (Table 4.5.4: ratio 2xCO_2/1xCO_2 with Penman correction) was a 10% lower transpiration coefficient at optimum or almost optimum nutrient supply (NPK, 0.3N and 0.3K treatments); a 5 to 7% lower coefficient for 0.1N

and 0.1K treatments; and a 2% lower coefficient for the 0.1P treatment. The result for the 0.3P treatment differed strongly from the other treatments because of the high transpiration coefficient at present CO_2.

To overcome the problem of the different conditions in the glasshouses and to allow a statistical analysis of the significance of the CO_2 effect for each nutrient treatment, the transpiration coefficients have been standardised. This was done by dividing transpiration coefficients for each treatment by the average transpiration coefficient for the NPK treatment and the same CO_2 treatment. The ratio 2xCO_2/1xCO_2 of these relative transpiration coefficients indicates the extent to which the decrease in transpiration coefficient at optimum nutrient supply as a result of CO_2 doubling was also found at limited nutrient supply. For the 0.3N and 0.3K treatments the decrease in transpiration coefficient was almost identical to that for NPK treatment and for the 0.1N and 0.1K treatments the decrease was smaller. Only for the 0.1P treatment was the CO_2 effect significant, resulting in about a 10% smaller decrease compared to the NPK treatment. This means that the transpiration coefficient in the 0.1P treatment almost did not change with CO_2 doubling.

(a)

(b)

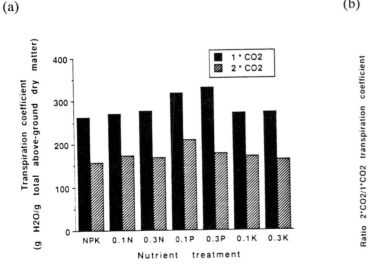
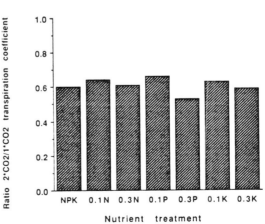

Figure 4.5.3   Average values for (a) transpiration coefficient (i.e. total transpiration divided by total above-ground dry matter yield (g/g)) at present and doubled atmospheric CO_2 concentrations and (b) the ratio of the transpiration coefficient at doubled to that at present atmospheric CO_2 concentration of spring wheat plants grown in pots at different nutrient treatments (with three replicates).

Table 4.5.4   Average values (AVG) of transpiration coefficients of spring wheat plants grown in pots at different nutrient treatments (with three replicates) and at present ($1xCO_2$) and doubled ($2xCO_2$) atmospheric CO_2 concentrations, the ratio between average transpiration coefficients at doubled CO_2 and those at present CO_2, and the level of significance of nutrient effect on transpiration coefficients.

	Nutrient treatment						
	NPK	0.1N	0.3N	0.1P	0.3P	0.1K	0.3K
Transpiration coefficient (per total[1], g/g)							
AVG ($1xCO_2$)	263	271	277	319	331	272	274
Level of significance - of nutrient effect $(1xCO_2)$[2]	-	-	-	**	**	-	-
AVG ($2xCO_2$)	157	173	168	210	177	171	163
Level of significance - of nutrient effect $(2xCO_2)$[2]	-	*	-	**	*	-	-
Ratio $2xCO_2/1xCO_2$	0.60	0.64	0.61	0.66	0.53	0.63	0.59
AVG ($2xCO_2$) with Penman correction[3]	233	258	250	313	263	254	243
Ratio $2xCO_2/1xCO_2$ with Penman correction[3]	0.89	0.95	0.90	0.98	0.79	0.93	0.89

[1] Total transpiration during the growth period divided by total dry matter (above ground) yield.

[2] The level of significance is indicated by * for $P < 0.05$, ** for $P < 0.01$ and - for not significant. It indicates the difference in transpiration coefficient from that of the NPK treatment.

[3] To allow comparison of transpiration coefficients at the two CO_2 treatments, total transpiration at doubled CO_2 has been multiplied with the ratio between the transpiration rate in the glasshouse at present CO_2 and that in the glasshouse at doubled CO_2, both calculated with the Penman formula for the climate conditions in the glasshouses.

4.5.3.5 *Nutrient concentrations and nutrient use efficiency*

The concentrations of N, P and K in plant tissue from the different plant organs were determined at final harvest. In the treatment with strongly limited N supply (0.1N) the N concentration decreased with CO_2 doubling by 11% in roots, about 30% in leaves and chaff, and 25% in grains, but these CO_2 effects were not significant (Table 4.5.5). In the stems the N concentration increased with CO_2 doubling, contrary to expectations. This resulted in a very small decrease in N concentration in straw with CO_2 doubling, differing from the considerable decrease in N concentration in the grains (Figure 4.5.4a). In the NPK and the 0.3N treatments where N supply was not or slightly limiting, the N concentrations decreased in all plant organs with CO_2 doubling except for the roots (Table 4.5.5).

In these treatments N concentrations were higher than those in the 0.1N treatment and decreased considerably with CO_2 doubling (Figure 4.5.4a), probably because of dilution of N in the larger amount of biomass produced at doubled CO_2.

In the 0.1P treatment the P concentration decreased with CO_2 doubling by 5% in chaff and grains and increased by 6% and 30% in roots and leaves, respectively and much more strongly and significantly in stems (Table 4.5.5). This resulted in a small increase in P concentration in straw with CO_2 doubling (Figure 4.5.5a), as opposed to the small decrease in P concentrations in grains. In the NPK and 0.3P treatments where P was not or slightly limiting, the P concentrations decreased slightly in roots and decreased considerably in chaff and grains, slightly increased in leaves or were strongly variable in stems (Table 4.5.5). In these treatments the P concentrations were higher than in the 0.1P treatment and decreased considerably with CO_2 doubling (Figure 4.5.5a), probably because of dilution of P in the larger amount of biomass.

In the 0.1K treatment the K concentration decreased significantly with CO_2 doubling in leaves and stems (by about 30%) and in chaff and grains (by about 20%) (Table 4.5.5). This resulted in a considerable decrease in K concentration in straw which was stronger than that in grains (Figure 4.5.6a). In the NPK and 0.3K treatments the K concentrations decreased considerably in leaves, stems, chaff and grains (Table 4.5.5). In these treatments the K concentrations in straw were higher than in the 0.1K treatment and

decreased considerably with CO_2 doubling (Figure 4.5.6a), probably because of dilution of K in the larger amount of biomass. In the grains the K concentrations were almost the same for the different treatments and almost did not change with CO_2 doubling.

The ratio between total above ground yield and nitrogen uptake was highest, and significantly increased (28%), with CO_2 doubling if nitrogen supply was strongly limiting (0.1 N), both for nitrogen uptake in total plant material and in total above ground plant material (Figure 4.5.4b; Table 4.5.6). This probably indicates a decrease in the minimum N concentrations with CO_2 doubling.

Table 4.5.5   The ratio between average concentrations of nitrogen (N), phosphorus (P) and potassium (K) in different plant organs at doubled atmospheric CO_2 and those at present CO_2 for spring wheat plants grown in pots at different nutrient treatments (with three replicates) and the level of significance of CO_2 effect on nutrient concentration for each nutrient treatment.

	Nutrient treatment								
	NPK			0.1N	0.3N	0.1P	0.3P	0.1K	0.3K
Nutrient	N	P	K	N	N	P	P	K	K
Roots									
Ratio $2xCO_2/1xCO_2$	1.17	1.00	1.37	0.89	3.47	1.06	0.91	0.33	0.53
Significance of CO_2 effect[1]	-	-	-	-	*	-	-	-	-
Leaves									
Ratio $2xCO_2/1xCO_2$	0.72	1.09	0.82	0.65	0.78	1.30	1.04	0.68	0.84
Significance of CO_2 effect[1]	*	-	*	-	-	-	-	*	-
Stems									
Ratio $2xCO_2/1xCO_2$	0.45	1.10	0.95	1.35	0.62	2.34	0.73	0.74	0.85
Significance of CO_2 effect[1]	-	-	-	-	-	*	*	*	-
Chaff									
Ratio $2xCO_2/1xCO_2$	0.39	0.67	0.89	0.71	0.77	0.94	0.72	0.78	0.86
Significance of CO_2 effect[1]	*	*	*	-	-	-	-	**	*
Grains									
Ratio $2xCO_2/1xCO_2$	0.83	0.90	0.80	0.75	0.94	0.96	0.81	0.84	0.91
Significance of CO_2 effect[1]	-	-	**	-	-	-	*	**	-

[1]   The level of significance is indicated by * for $P < 0.05$, ** for $P < 0.01$ and - for not significant. Significance of CO_2 effect is based on inter-pot variance.

(a)   (b)

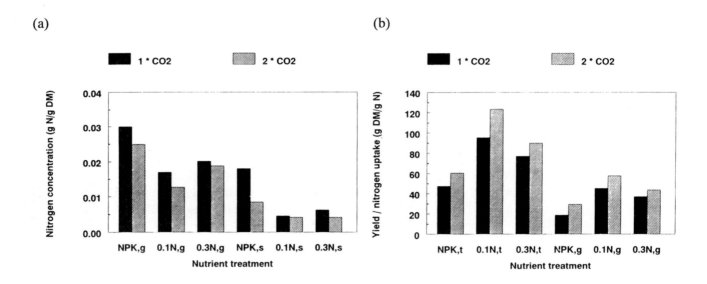

Figure 4.5.4   Average values for (a) nitrogen concentrations in grains (NPK,g etc.) and straw (NPK,s etc.) and for (b) total above ground yield to nitrogen uptake (NPK,t etc.) and grain yield to nitrogen uptake ratios (NPK,g etc.) of spring wheat plants grown in pots at different nutrient treatments (with three replicates) at present and doubled atmospheric CO_2 concentrations (nitrogen uptake in ratios applies to total above ground plant material).

(a)   (b)

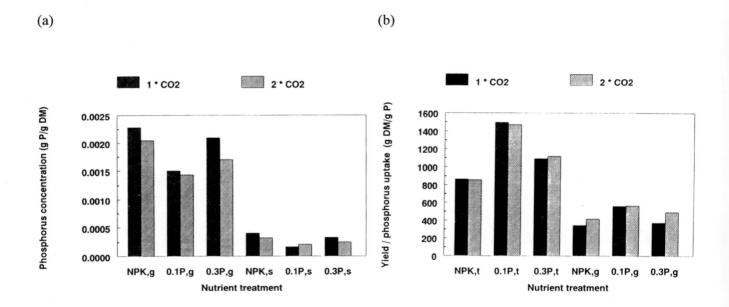

Figure 4.5.5   Average values for (a) phosphorus concentrations in grains (NPK,g etc.) and straw (NPK,s etc.) and (b) total above ground yield to phosphorus uptake (NPK,t etc.) and grain yield to phosphorus uptake ratios (NPK,g etc.) of spring wheat plants grown in pots at different nutrient treatments (with three replicates) at present and doubled atmospheric CO_2 concentrations (phosphorus uptake in ratios applies to total above ground plant material).

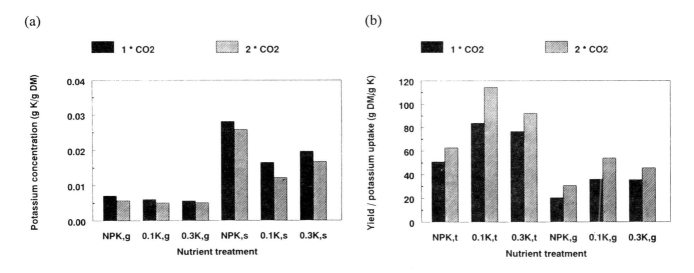

Figure 4.5.6   Average values for (a) potasssium concentrations in grains (NPK,g etc.) and straw (NPK,s etc.) and (b) total above ground yield to potassium uptake (NPK,t etc.) and grain yield to potassium uptake ratios (NPK,g etc.) of spring wheat plants grown in pots at different nutrient treatments (with three replicates) at present and doubled atmospheric CO_2 concentrations (potassium uptake in ratios applies to total above ground plant material).

Table 4.5.6   The ratio between average yield to nutrient (N, P or K) uptake at doubled atmospheric CO_2 and present CO_2 for spring wheat plants grown in pots at different nutrient treatments (with three replicates) and the level of significance of CO_2 effect on yield to nutrient uptake ratio for each nutrient treatment.

| | Nutrient treatment | | | | | | | | |
	NPK			0.1N	0.3N	0.1P	0.3P	0.1K	0.3K
Nutrient	N	P	K	N	N	P	P	K	K
Total above ground yield / nutrient uptake ratio A[1]									
Ratio $2xCO_2/1xCO_2$	1.27	1.01	1.23	1.28	1.01	1.00	1.05	1.38	1.22
Significance of CO_2 effect[2]	-	-	-	*	-	-	-	**	*
Total above ground yield / nutrient uptake ratio B[1]									
Ratio $2xCO_2/1xCO_2$	1.27	0.99	1.23	1.29	1.17	0.98	1.02	1.37	1.20
Significance of CO_2 effect[2]	-	-	-	*	-	-	-	**	*
Grain yield / nutrient uptake ratio A[1]									
Ratio $2xCO_2/1xCO_2$	1.56	1.23	1.50	1.26	1.02	1.02	1.34	1.51	1.30
Significance of CO_2 effect[2]	-	-	*	-	-	-	*	**	*
Grain yield / nutrient uptake ratio B[1]									
Ratio $2xCO_2/1xCO_2$	1.57	1.21	1.50	1.27	1.17	1.01	1.32	1.50	1.28
Significance of CO_2 effect[2]	*	-	*	*	-	-	*	**	*

[1]   A : ratio calculated for nutrient uptake in total plant material with roots included; B : ratio calculated for nutrient uptake in total above ground plant material.

[2]   The level of significance is indicated by * for $P < 0.05$, ** for $P < 0.01$ and - for not significant. Significance of CO_2 effect is based on inter-pot variance.

In the 0.3N and NPK treatments the ratio between total above ground yield and nitrogen uptake was much lower (i.e. higher N concentration) than that in the 0.1N treatment (Figure 4.5.4b) and increased slightly and moderately respectively with CO_2 doubling (Table 4.5.6). This can probably be explained from the dilution of N in the larger amount of biomass produced at doubled CO_2. In the 0.1N and 0.3N treatments the change in ratio between grain yield and nitrogen uptake with CO_2 doubling was identical to that between total above ground yield and nitrogen uptake (Table 4.5.6). In the NPK treatment, however, the change in ratio between grain yield and nitrogen uptake with CO_2 doubling was higher than that between total above ground yield and nitrogen uptake, which was a result of the increase in harvest index with CO_2 doubling.

The ratio between total above ground yield and phosphorus uptake did not change with CO_2 doubling (Table 4.5.6; Figure 4.5.5b) both if phosphorus was strongly limiting (0.1P) and if phosphorus was slightly or not limiting (0.3P, NPK). This constant ratio for the 0.3P and NPK treatments was caused by both a decrease in P concentration and an increase in harvest index with CO_2 doubling. Results from the 0.1P treatment probably indicate that minimum phosphorus concentrations do not change with CO_2 doubling. The ratio between grain yield and phosphorus uptake did not change with CO_2 doubling in the phosphorus limited treatment (0.1P) and increased in the other treatments (0.3P, NPK). This increase was a result of the increase in harvest index with CO_2 doubling.

The ratio between total above ground yield and potassium uptake increased very significantly with CO_2 doubling (Table 4.5.6; Figure 4.5.6b) if potassium supply was strongly limiting (0.1K). This probably indicates a decrease in the minimum potassium concentrations with CO_2 doubling. In the treatments (0.3K, NPK) where K supply was slightly or not limiting for crop growth, the ratio between total above ground yield and potassium uptake was lower (i.e. higher K concentration) than the ratio in the 0.1K treatment (Figure 4.5.6b) and increased considerably with CO_2 doubling (Table 4.5.6). This can be explained from dilution of K in the larger amount of biomass produced at doubled

CO_2. The change in ratio between grain yield and potassium uptake with CO_2 doubling was larger than that between total above ground material and potassium uptake (Table 4.5.6) both for the 0.1K treatment and the other treatments (0.3K, NPK). This was a result of the increase in harvest index with CO_2 doubling.

The recovery fraction of applied N changed little with CO_2 doubling if nitrogen supply was strongly limiting crop growth (0.1N treatment; Table 4.5.7). The recovery fractions of applied P and K also did not change with CO_2 doubling in the 0.1P, 0.1K and 0.3K treatments. In the treatments with larger N supply (0.3N, NPK) the recovery fraction of applied N was higher at doubled CO_2 which was a result of the increased biomass production with CO_2 doubling. In the treatments with larger P and K supply the recovery fractions of applied P and K were significantly higher at doubled CO_2 which also was a result of the increased biomass production.

For both applied N, P and K the recovery fraction became higher, if its supply became more limited (Table 4.5.7). The recovery fraction of applied P was much lower than for applied N and K because a large part of the applied amount of this element became less available by absorption and precipitation. The very high recovery fraction in the 0.3N treatment at doubled CO_2 cannot be explained. If the K supply was clearly limiting (0.1K treatment) the recovery fraction of applied K was higher than 1, indicating that some potassium was also supplied by the sandy soil.

4.5.4   Implications for modelling

The positive effect of CO_2 enrichment on the rate of CO_2 assimilation becomes smaller when crops are grown under severe nutrient stress. Models should incorporate this interaction between nutrient limitation and CO_2 enrichment. Increased CO_2 results in larger biomass production and, thus, in more dilution of available nutrients in plant tissue when nutrient supply is limiting. If the assimilation rate decreases with decreasing nutrient concentrations in the leaves, CO_2 enrichment and nutrient stress interactions, such as those used in the NWHEAT model (Groot, 1987), can be incorporated into models.

Table 4.5.7   Average recovery fractions (g/g) of applied nutrients (N, P and K) for spring wheat plants grown in pots at different nutrient treatments (with three replicates) and at present and doubled atmospheric CO_2 concentrations, the ratio between average recovery fraction at doubled CO_2 and that at present CO_2, and the level of significance of CO_2 effect on the recovery fraction for each nutrient treatment.

	Nutrient treatment								
	NPK			0.1N	0.3N	0.1P	0.3P	0.1K	0.3K
Nutrient	N	P	K	N	N	P	P	K	K
Recovery fr., 1 x CO_2	0.65	0.23	0.49	0.93	0.87	0.29	0.23	1.09	0.92
Recovery fr., 2 x CO_2	0.81	0.39	0.67	0.99	1.30	0.31	0.41	1.18	0.96
Ratio 2xCO_2/1x CO_2	1.25	1.70	1.37	1.06	1.49	1.07	1.78	1.08	1.04
Significance of CO_2 effect[1]	-	**	*	-	*	-	**	-	-

[1]   The level of significance is indicated by * for $P < 0.05$, ** for $P < 0.01$ and - for not significant. Significance of CO_2 effect is based on inter-pot variance.

Increased CO_2 results in lower transpiration coefficients but the effect becomes smaller if nutrient shortage occurs. The decrease in transpiration coefficient with increased CO_2 is mainly determined by the larger biomass production while the transpiration roughly remains the same. If models are able to calculate biomass production under the interacting effects of CO_2 enrichment and nutrient stress as described above, they may also simulate the smaller decrease in transpiration coefficient under nutrient stress. In simpler models fixed values for transpiration coefficients are often used to calculate crop production in a water-limited situation. Such values should be corrected for both increased CO_2 and nutrient supply.

To calculate crop yields on unfertilized soils or the fertilizer requirements for attaining a specified yield level, elaborate models use plant-specific nutrient concentrations and simpler models (Janssen *et al.*, 1990) use yield-nutrient uptake ratios. Increased CO_2 concentrations result in lower nutrient concentrations (with the exception of P), so higher yield to nutrient uptake ratios should be incorporated into models for application in situations with increased CO_2.

Baking quality of wheat grains is determined by variety, growing conditions and the rate and timing of nitrogen application. To attain a high

protein content in the grains, which is a requirement for good baking quality, the wheat crop should be able to accumulate large amounts of nitrogen during its growth (van Keulen and Seligman, 1987). Conversely, Darwinkel (1987) showed that baking quality was mainly variety-specific and although protein content in the grains increased with the rate of nitrogen application, baking quality improved little with increasing protein content. Elevated CO_2 concentrations resulted in lower nutrient concentrations in the grains in this experiment. This may reduce baking quality. Simulation models can be used to calculate recommendations for fertilizer rates and timing in a changed climate with increased CO_2, to prevent a reduction in yield quality.

4.5.5   Discussion

In the control (NPK) treatment without nutrient limitation the ratio between total yield at doubled CO_2 and that at present CO_2 (i.e. ratio 2xCO_2/1xCO_2) was 1.7. In the K limited treatment which reduced growth to a limited extent, the ratio 2xCO_2/1xCO_2 was 1.4. In the 0.1N and 0.1P treatments where growth was strongly limited by nutrient supply, the ratio was 1.3 and 1.1, respectively. For the grain yield the CO_2 effect was also highest in the control treatment. This corresponds well with results from other experiments with wheat under nutrient limitation. For example, Sionit *et al.* (1981b) found a decrease in the ratio $2xCO_2/1xCO_2$ for total yield if the nutrient solution was diluted and Goudriaan and de Ruiter (1983) measured a ratio $2xCO_2/1xCO_2$ for total yield of 1.4 at optimum nutrient supply, 1.2 at severe N shortage and 1.0 at severe P shortage.

The ratio $2xCO_2/1xCO_2$ for total yield in the NPK treatment was much higher than the values that are generally found. In this experiment the pots were placed apart and shading did not occur. In such conditions a higher rate of CO_2 assimilation at doubled atmospheric CO_2 results in more assimilates, more leaves, more light interception, even more CO_2 assimilation and so on. In two other experiments where spring wheat was grown in pots that were placed apart, the ratio $2xCO_2/1xCO_2$ for total yield was also high, i.e. 1.93 and 1.83 respectively (Sionit *et al.*, 1981a; Morrison and Gifford, 1984). In a dense crop canopy a larger leaf area caused by CO_2 doubling results in a slightly higher light interception and a much smaller yield increase. For example, in crop enclosures under normal agricultural practice and plant density and with optimum nutrient supply the ratio $2xCO_2/1xCO_2$ for total yield was 1.35 for spring wheat (Dijkstra *et al.*, 1993) and in a pot experiment at an almost identical plant density the ratio was 1.15 for winter wheat (Mitchell *et al.*, 1993).

In the NPK treatment root/shoot ratio decreased with CO_2 doubling but this effect was not significant. In the P and K limited treatments the root/shoot ratio decreased to approximately the same extent, but in the N limited treatments the decrease in root/shoot ratio with CO_2 doubling was negligible. According to a survey of experimental information on the direct effect of increasing CO_2 for crop growth and dry matter partitioning (Cure, 1985; Stulen and den Hertog, 1993), increasing CO_2 may cause either an increase or a decrease in the root/shoot ratio of a wheat crop. The increases are generally found in situations with a limiting nutrient supply. This corresponds well with results found in this experiment for the N limited treatments but not with those for the P limited treatments.

Grain/straw ratio did not increase with CO_2 doubling if nitrogen or phosphorus were strongly limiting and slightly increased in the other treatments. Slight increases which become nil with the nutrient limitation, were also found in a survey of experimental information for wheat by Cure (1985). Compared to the control, P limited treatments resulted in significantly lower grain/straw ratios.

The ratio between the transpiration coefficient at doubled and present CO_2 was about 0.6, both in the control and the nutrient limited treatments. This corresponds well with an increase in water use efficiency of 80% with CO_2 doubling which was determined for single wheat plants growing in pots (Morison, 1985). This high value only applies to single plants. If wheat plants are grown in stands, water use efficiency increases by only 25 to 35% (Morison, 1993). This difference can be explained from the micro-meteorological feedback in the crop canopy (Goudriaan and Unsworth, 1990). If a correction for the difference in glasshouse conditions (except CO_2 concentration level) is taken into account, the ratio $2xCO_2/1xCO_2$ became 0.89 for the control. This decrease in transpiration coefficient is very small compared to literature data, particularly because pots in this experiment were standing apart.

In nutrient limited conditions the decrease in transpiration coefficient with CO_2 doubling was smaller than that in the control and close to zero if the supply of nutrients, in particular the supply of P, was severely limiting. This can be explained mainly by the fact that CO_2 enrichment did not lead to increases in yield with severe P shortage. This was also found for seedlings of *Pinus radiata* (Conroy *et al.*, 1988). However, the literature survey of Cure and Acock (1986) indicates for corn, soybean and cotton that the reduction in transpiration by CO_2 doubling is almost identical in both non-limited and nutrient limited conditions.

In situations where nutrient supply is limiting for crop growth, nutrient concentrations in plant tissue may gradually decrease during the growth cycle and at harvest nutrients appear to be diluted to a plant-specific minimum concentration level. Such levels will only be attained if all required nutrients are supplied sufficiently and only one nutrient strongly limits crop growth. Further dilution appears to be impossible. It is feasible that minimum concentrations may change with CO_2 doubling. In general, experiments with doubled CO_2 have been carried out with diluted nutrient solutions which cause a limited supply of more than one nutrient (e.g. Sionit *et al.*, 1981b). This means that complete dilution of nutrients down to the minimum concentration will not occur (Janssen *et al.*, 1990) and minimum concentration levels cannot be established.

For a large number of fertilizer experiments van Keulen and van Heemst (1982) and van Keulen (1986) have analysed relations between yield and nutrient uptake. From these relations they have derived minimum concentration levels for a large number of crop species. For a wheat crop the minimum concentrations are as follows: 0.0110 g N/g dry matter in grains, 0.0030 g N/g mattter in crop residues (above-ground), 0.0016 g P/g dry matter in grains, 0.0004 g P/g dry matter in crop residues (above-ground), 0.0030 g K/g dry matter in grains, 0.0070 g K/g dry mater in crop residues (above-ground) (van Diepen *et al.*, 1988).

The concentrations of nitrogen, phosphorus and potassium in plant tissue were determined in the present experiment at final harvest. This was done for different organs of the wheat crop. When nitrogen was strongly limiting for crop growth (0.1N treatment), the average N concentration was 0.0046 g N/g dry matter in crop residues (without roots) and 0.0170 g N/g dry matter in grains at present CO_2 and 0.0042 g N/g and 0.0127 g N/g, respectively at doubled CO_2. These concentration levels are slightly higher than the minimum concentration levels reported and probably indicate that CO_2 doubling causes a decrease in minimum N concentration by 9% in crop residues and by 10 to 25% in grains (dependent on the assumed degree of dilution by increased biomass production with CO_2 doubling). This resulted in an increase in the ratio between total above-ground yield and N uptake in above-ground yield by 10 to 30% (lower value applies if the dilution effect is removed).

When phosphorus was strongly limiting for crop growth (0.1P treatment), the average P concentration was 0.00017 g P/g dry matter in crop residues (without roots) and 0.00150 g P/g dry matter in grains at present CO_2 and 0.00021 g P/g and 0.00143 g P/g, respectively at doubled CO_2. These concentrations are at the minimum level and, hence, indicate that CO_2 doubling causes a decrease in minimum P concentration by 5% in grains and an increase by 24% in crop residues. This resulted in a decrease in the ratio between total above-ground yield and P uptake in above-ground yield by 2%, which indicates that minimum P concentrations remain almost constant with CO_2 doubling.

When potassium was limiting for crop growth (0.1K treatment), the average K concentration was 0.0164 g K/g dry matter in crop residues (without roots) and 0.0060 g K/g dry matter in grains at present CO_2 and 0.0121 g K/g and 0.0050 g K/g, respectively at doubled CO_2. These concentrations are rather high compared with the minimum concentration levels (van Diepen *et al.*, 1988) and, hence, potassium was not completely diluted in plant tissue. The decrease in K concentration with CO_2 doubling by 26% in crop residues and by 17% in grains only indicates the degree of dilution by increased biomass production as a result of CO_2 doubling and not the change in minimum K concentration.

Literature data indicate that with CO_2 enrichment nutrient concentrations in plant tissues may decrease, in particular for nitrogen, somewhat less for potassium and only slightly or not at all for phosphorus (Cure *et al.*, 1988a, 1988b; Goudriaan and de Ruiter, 1983; Overdieck, 1993). This corresponds well with results in this experiment for nitrogen and phosphorus.

4.5.6   Conclusions

A broad survey of the effects of doubling atmospheric CO_2 as determined in this study, are given in Table 4.5.8. Doubling of atmospheric CO_2 resulted in a strong increase in total dry matter and grain yield for spring wheat if the nutrient supply was optimal. In the 0.1N and 0.1K treatments the CO_2 effect was approximately halved and in the 0.1P treatment it became negligible.

Table 4.5.8 Summary table of the effects of doubling atmospheric CO_2 for yield, transpiration coefficient, nutrient concentrations and nutrient use efficiency of spring wheat plants grown in pots at different nutrient treatments and for the recovery fraction of applied nutrients.

	Nutrient treatment			
	NPK	0.1N	0.1P	0.1K
Total above-ground dry matter	+	+	0	+
Grain dry matter	+	+	0	+
Root/shoot ratio	-	0	-	-
Grain/straw ratio	+	0	0	+
Transpiration coeficient	-	-	0	-
Nutrient concentration straw	- - -[1]	-	0	-
Nutrient concentration grains	- - -[1]	-	0	-
Total biomass/nutrient uptake	+ 0 +[2]	+	0	+
Grain yield/nutrient uptake	+ + +[2]	+	0	+
Recovery fraction	+ + +[3]	0	0	0

[1] Change in N, P and K concentration respectively.
[2] Ratio between yield and N uptake, P uptake and K uptake respectively.
[3] Recovery fraction of applied N, P and K respectively.

Doubling of atmospheric CO_2 resulted in a decrease in the transpiration coefficient for spring wheat by 11% if the nutrient supply was optimal. In the 0.1N and 0.1K treatment this decrease was approximately halved and in the 0.1P treatment it became negligible. Doubling of atmospheric CO_2 resulted in an approximately 10% lower minimum N concentration and no change in the minimum P concentration. The supply of potassium appeared to be too high to derive a change in minimum concentration level.

With increasing limitation of nutrient supply for crop growth, in particular severe P deficiency, the effects of CO_2 enrichment on yield and transpiration coefficient disappeared in most cases. The change in minimum N concentration in plant tissue with CO_2 doubling should be incorporated in wheat models and evaluation systems of soil fertility. This will result in lower fertilizer N requirements for a given yield level at doubled CO_2.

For other varieties of wheat which might have other nutrient concentration levels and for other crop species the change in minimum concentration levels of macro-nutrients with CO_2 doubling should be determined. Such information is practically not available and is required to adjust fertilizer recommendations to future conditions with a higher atmospheric CO_2 concentration. This is of interest from both an economic and an environmental point of view.

Acknowledgements

Many thanks are due to J. Goudriaan (Dept. of Theoretical Production Ecology, Wageningen Agricultural University) for support and valuable comments and to J.C.M. Withagen (AB-DLO, Wageningen) for carrying out the statistical analysis.

4.6 Growth chamber experiments on spring wheat

4.6.1 Introduction

Under elevated CO_2 an increased rate of photosynthesis raises the amount of carbon available to the plant. As a consequence, in many C_3-plants a significant increase of dry matter accumulation in roots, shoots and leaves has been found (Musgrave and Strain 1988, Chaudhury *et al.* 1990, Hocking and Meyer, 1991).

Following flowering in cereals, grains are the main sink of carbon. Experiments at the 'Institut für Pflanzenbau' with ^{13}C labelled CO_2 have shown that during grain filling a considerable amount of carbon stored temporarily in the stems and leaves is transferred to the growing grains. As increasing atmospheric CO_2 promotes vegetative growth, changes in the CO_2 environment may also have some consequences for the pattern of carbon partitioning in wheat.

Carbon partitioning is directly linked to nitrogen supply. Acock (1990) concluded that an increase in CO_2 supply to plant increases nitrogen demand and uptake, because CO_2 enriched plants accumulate more nitrogen than the controls. However, the increase in N accumulation was observed to be less than that in dry matter and N concentration became lower in all organs of enriched plants (Hocking and Meyer, 1991). Hence, nitrogen use efficiency was observed to increase under elevated CO_2. Nitrogen supply affects the carbon economy of wheat and the question arises: will this effect differ in an elevated CO_2 environment?

Although the effects of CO_2 enrichment on growth parameters of wheat have been observed in many experiments, it is not yet clear how plants use the extra carbon and with what priority the carbon is translocated to different organs. To address this matter it seems necessary to investigate plant species separately, C_3-plants vs. C_4- plants, annuals vs. perennials, monocots vs. dicots. Such differences in sink-source relations of plant species in CO_2 enriched environments have been described by Farrar and Williams (1991) who recommended studies with enrichment throughout the growth cycle of individual species.

The present study focuses on the C- and N-economy of wheat in growth chamber experiments, using steady state ^{13}C labelling of CO_2 and ^{15}N labelling of nitrogen. This labelling system is used in order to follow the uptake and distribution of carbon and nitrogen during different phases of crop development in elevated CO_2 environments compared with ambient CO_2. Experiments were conducted over two growing seasons, 1994 and 1995.

4.6.2 Experimental approach

Plants of spring wheat (cv. Munk) were grown in washed sand in plastic pots, 33.5 cm deep and 10 cm in diameter (five plants per pot). A total of 120 plants were grown outside to be sampled at double ridge (DR), ear emergence (EA), anthesis (A) and maturity (M). Another 180 plants were grown outside and transfered to the growth chambers in batches of 60 plants during the following phases: DR to EA, EA to A and A to M. Hence, 60 plants per batch were sampled at the end of the given phases. In parallel, 240 plants were permanently grown in growth chambers with 353 and 700 ppmv CO_2 concentration and sampled at the same stages as those outside. The main intention of this procedure was to identify the effect of environmental conditions in the growth chambers compared with outside conditions. Technical details of the growth chambers and the long-term steady state labelling system of $^{13}CO_2/^{12}CO_2$ were described in detail by Schnyder (1992). With this system the CO_2 entering the chambers is marked with stable isotopes of carbon.

Temperatures during the hours of light and dark in the growth chambers were adjusted to the actual day and night temperatures outdoors. Light intensity in the chambers was constant at 450 μmol m^{-2} s^{-1} PAR during the whole experiment. The day/night cycle was varied in steps of 30 minutes from 12/12h at emergence to 14/10h at anthesis and 13/11h at maturity. As the plants grown outdoors had to be protected from rainfall by a polyethylene shelter, the intensity of incident PAR on the plants was reduced by up to 40%. Daylong runs of incident PAR measurements underneath the shelter were conducted during 18 days of the experiment. The daily radiation sum in the growth chamber was the same as the mean radiation outside when the illumination in the chamber was adjusted to 450 μmol m^{-2} s^{-1}.

Plants were supplied with nitrogen in solutions with different N concentrations: 10.5 ppm in the N1 treatment and 105 ppm in the N2 treatment. Solutions supplied to the plants grown in the chambers were enriched with ^{15}N (1%). The amount of nitrogen supplied to the plants was steadily increased from emergence until ear emergence (100 ml to 500 ml per day) and thereafter reduced to 400 ml per day until maturity. Pots were flushed with deionized water twice a day to avoid salt accumulation in the rooting medium.

With each sampling the following parameters were determined:

- dry weight of roots of all plants per pot;
- dry weight of stem, individual leaves and the ear of the main tiller;
- dry weight of all leaves and the stem separately of 1st, 2nd and 3rd order side tillers;
- total grain dry weight per ear separately of 1st, 2nd and 3rd order side tillers;
- dry weight of stems, leaves, ears and grains each accumulated for higher order side tillers;
- area of individual leaf blades and the stem of the main tiller (green and senesced);
- leaf area per tiller and the stem separately of 1st, 2nd and 3rd order side tillers;
- accumulated leaf area and stem area of higher order side tillers;
- length of individual leaves exclusively on main tiller;
- number of tillers per plant;
- number of leaves of main tiller and of 1st, 2nd and 3rd order side tillers;
- accumulated number of leaves of higher order side tillers;
- number of ears per individual plant; and
- mean plant height per pot.

All plant samples were oven dried (55°C, 72 hours) and stored for analysis of relative water content, relative C and N content and the isotope composition of plant carbon and nitrogen.

In the second experiment (1995) a number of changes were made to avoid difficulties encountered during the first experiment (1994):

- The light regime was altered to a 13/11h day/night cycle at emergence to 16/8h at maturity. During the first 15 minutes of the light period plants only received infrared light emitted by incandescent bulbs (6 m^{-2}; 60W). Following this, light intensity was increased to 200 μmol m^{-2} s^{-1} for another 30 minutes. At the end of the light period the same but reverse procedure was applied;
- Only four plants per pot were grown instead of five;
- The base of plants was shaded by a frill surrounding the pots; and
- N concentration in the nutrient solution of the low N treatment (N1) was increased to 26.25 ppm N. The nutrient solution was supplied only twice a day instead of four times a day. To prevent a loss of nutrients by run off the amount of applied solution was halved and the concentration of nutrients in the solution doubled. Furthermore the amount of nutrient solution was incrementally reduced to nil by 20 days after anthesis.

4.6.3   Results and discussion

In the 1994 experiment the whole growth cycle of plants in the growth chambers was prolonged by about 40 days compared to outdoor crop stands independent of CO$_2$ treatment. The reason for this was the light condition in the growth chambers. It is presumed that the day/night cycle of 12/12h up to 14/10h and the lack of an infrared phase of sunrise and sunset caused this delay in development. In the 1995 experiment the light regime was altered (see Section 4.6.2) and plant development coincided with that of the outdoor plants.

There was a growth chamber effect with respect to tillering in both experiments but less so in the 1995 experiment when plant bases were shaded by frills. Tillering continued until the plants reached anthesis. In this experiment the low-N plants developed fewer tillers than high-N plants but had a stronger main shoot.

Table 4.6.1 shows the dry matter development of spring wheat grown in the growth chambers under different CO_2 concentrations from emergence to maturity. At every growth stage (DR to M) there was a large positive effect of N supply. At both stages of N supply the plant dry matter responded positively to the elevated CO_2 concentration and was greatest with sufficient N. The really severe N-stress in the 1994 experiment prevented a higher CO_2 response. Only at maturity was the total plant dry matter of the low N treatment 10% less under elevated CO_2 levels. These observations are in agreement with results for wheat reported by Sionit *et al.* (1981), who found a 20% decrease in dry weight when severe N stress was imposed on enriched plants. In this study the reason for the negative effect on dry weight was the strong stimulation of root growth under high CO_2 and low N until anthesis (see root to shoot ratio at anthesis in Table 4.6.2) and a subsequent decrease of root dry weight which is probably due to root decay after anthesis. In the 1995 experiment the relative stimulation of dry matter formation by elevated CO_2 was highest in the low N treatment. This effect has also been reported in the literature (e.g. Hocking and Meyer, 1991) and is mainly due to a proportionally higher stimulation of dry matter formation under a shortage of N supply. Although high N supply caused roughly a doubling of plant dry weight in both CO_2 treatments the surplus of CO_2 could not be fully transformed into additional plant dry matter. The reason for this might be a self shading effect by increased leaf dry matter. Thus, reduced light absorption might have hampered the transformation of additional atmospheric CO_2 into plant material.

The dry weight of the main tiller and side tillers was positively affected by CO_2 and N treatment, except in the low N treatment in the first experiment. Here the total dry weight of side tillers decreased under elevated CO_2 although

the number of tillers was strongly increased (see Table 4.6.2). This is because the majority of side tillers remained small and in the vegetative stage. The more than proportional investment of dry matter into the root system under elevated CO_2 in earlier growth stages led to less above ground plant material in this treatment at maturity.

With high N supply the grain weight rose with total plant dry weight, but the increase was far less than proportional in the 1994 experiment. Only a few side tillers reached the generative phase and contributed to grain weight. In the 1995 experiment the enhancement in grain weight through higher N supply was less than that of the total dry weight under low CO_2 but more than proportional under elevated CO_2. In the high N/low CO_2 treatment in the first experiment grain yield failed because of an aphid attack.

These results are in good agreement with the literature although the values for dry matter increase at maturity are generally higher (Kimball, 1983; Idso and Idso, 1994). It must be taken into consideration that growing conditions in most investigations vary from one experiment to another. In addition, in the present study root growth restrictions by pot size may have caused the lower response to CO_2 enrichment (Arp, 1991; Lawlor and Mitchell, 1991). However, recent research using FACE equipment found that former greenhouse and growth chamber experiments have overestimated dry matter enhancement by elevated CO_2.

In Table 4.6.2 selected growth parameters at anthesis are given. As expected under N stress the root to shoot ratio in the low N treatment was much higher than with high N. Under elevated CO_2 this effect was even stronger. In the high N treatment in Experiment 1 there was no effect of CO_2 on the root to shoot ratio under elevated CO_2. Here the shoot dry matter increased proportionally to root dry matter. The enhancement of root to shoot ratio due to elevated CO_2 is in broad agreement with values reported in the literature (Hocking and Meyer, 1991; Larigaudarie *et al.*, 1988; Sionit *et al.* 1980).

Table 4.6.1   Dry matter (DM) development [g/plant] of different organs at double ridge (DR), ear apperance (EA), anthesis (A) and maturity (M) and the relative effect of doubled CO_2 concentration in the 1994 experiment (Experiment 1) and in the 1995 experiment (Experiment 2); plants were permanently grown in the growth chambers. N- is the low N treatment and N+ is the high N treatment.

Experiment 1

| | Ambient CO_2 | | Elevated CO_2 | | Rel. effect of $2xCO_2$ | | Results of ANOVA | | |
| | | | | | | | Sources of variance | | |
	N-	N+	N-	N+	N-	N+	N	CO_2	$NxCO_2$
Growth parameters									
Total DM at DR	0.11	0.23	0.13	0.29	+18%	+26%	**	ns	ns
EA	2.10	7.91	2.28	9.37	+9%	+18%	**	ns	ns
A	3.67	11.35	5.06	13.06	+38%	+15%	ns	ns	ns
M	6.29	17.25	5.67	21.86	-10%	+27%	**	ns	ns
Main tiller	1.57	2.25	1.22	3.01	-22%	+34%	**	ns	ns
Side tillers	3.17	12.24	2.98	16.62	-6%	+36%	**	ns	ns
Grain DM (g.plant)	1.71	1.55[1]	1.21	3.50	-29%	126%	ns	ns	ns
Vegetative ear	0.51	2.36	0.62	4.11	+22%	+74%	ns	ns	ns
Leaf blades	0.92	5.71	0.87	6.37	-5%	+12%	**	ns	ns
Stem	1.60	4.87	1.49	5.64	-7%	+16%	**	ns	ns
Root	1.55	2.75	1.47	2.23	-5%	-19%	ns	ns	ns

* = P < 0.05; ** P < 0.01; ns = not significant.
[1]   Grain weight was reduced because of an aphid attack.

Experiment 2

| | Ambient CO_2 | | Elevated CO_2 | | Rel. effect of $2xCO_2$ | | Results of ANOVA | | |
| | | | | | | | Sources of variance | | |
	N-	N+	N-	N+	N-	N+	N	CO_2	$NxCO_2$
Growth parameters									
Total DM at DR	0.41	0.49	1.81	2.16	+341%	+341%	ns	ns	ns
EA	2.30	7.81	3.51	8.52	+53%	+9%	**	*	ns
A	3.30	9.05	4.67	10.85	+42%	+20%	**	ns	ns
M	6.15	13.96	8.65	15.62	+18%	+12%	**	ns	ns
Main tiller	2.67	3.41	3.06	3.68	+15%	+8%	*	ns	ns
Side tillers	2.29	9.41	2.79	10.59	+22%	+13%	**	ns	ns
Grain DM (g. plant)	1.89	3.51	2.32	4.54	+26%	+29%	**	ns	ns
Vegetative ear	0.77	2.46	0.97	2.11	+26%	-14%	**	ns	ns
Leaf blades	0.65	2.42	0.44	2.90	-32%	+20%	**	ns	ns
Stem	1.78	4.85	2.29	5.11	+29%	+5%	**	ns	ns
Root	1.19	1.15	2.80	1.35	+135%	+17%	*	**	*

* = P < 0.05; ** P < 0.01; ns = not significant.

Table 4.6.2 Selected growth statistics for spring wheat at anthesis permanently grown in growth chambers under ambient and elevated CO_2 in the 1994 experiment (Experiment 1) and the 1995 experiment (Experiment 2); parameters are given on a per plant basis. N- is the low N treatment and N+ is the high N treatment.

Growth parameters	Ambient CO_2		Elevated CO_2		Rel. effect of 2xCO_2	
	N-	N+	N-	N+	N-	N+
Experiment 1						
Root:shoot ratio	0.52	0.15	0.91	0.15	+75%	±0%
Tiller number	4.10	8.80	10.70	14.60	+161%	+66%
GLA [cm^2]	82.00	489.00	100.00	197.00	+22%	-60%
SLA [dm^2 g^{-1}]	1.21	1.79	1.12	0.91	-7%	-47%
Leaf N-conc. [%]	1.64	2.91	1.46	2.99	-11%	+3%
Experiment 2						
Root:shoot ratio	0.54	0.13	0.78	0.23	+44%	+77%
Tiller number	3.00	6.50	3.00	7.20	±0%	+11%
GLA [cm^2]	126	516	106	463	-16%	-10%
SLA [dm^2 g^{-1}]	2.17	1.85	1.89	1.72	-15%	-9%
Leaf N-conc. (%)	3.23	4.39	2.80	3.61	-13%	-18%

The green leaf area (GLA) at anthesis was very sensitive to N supply (Table 4.6.2). This was partly due to larger single leaves and partly due to a higher number of tillers with high N supply. Elevated CO_2 also had an effect on GLA. However, under high CO_2 conditions stronger tillering led not only to increased leaf number but also to a self shading effect, and thus to an earlier decrease of leaf area by decaying leaves. Examining all stages of development and the leaf area on a single shoot basis there was no clear effect of elevated CO_2 on green leaf area. Moreover it seemed to be rather an effect of competition for light. This is in good agreement with Larigauderie et al. (1988) and Acock et al. (1982) who found no effect on leaf area. On the other hand, many authors (e.g. Morison and Gifford, 1984; Sionit et al., 1981; Wong, 1979) found GLA increased owing to a higher tiller number under elevated CO_2. Nevertheless, this effect might disappear when there are self shading effects by upper leaves.

In Experiment 1 the effect of elevated CO_2 on specific leaf area (SLA) was highest with ample supply of N. However, in this case the decay of green leaves caused an underestimation of SLA. The relatively low SLA in the low N treatments under both CO_2 levels might be an effect of strong N stress leading to reduced cell

production and hence to an accumulation of assimilates in leaves (Williams et al., 1981). In Experiment 2 the low N treatment exhibited a stronger relative effect of CO_2 on SLA than with high N, although the absolute figure is lowest. The reason for this may be the same as for total plant dry weight, ie. as the self shading effect prevented an accumulation of starch in some lower leaves. This effect has also been described by Smart et al. (1994) who found lower concentrations of non-structural carbohydrates in lower canopy layers. The data presented in Table 4.6.2 show SLA to decrease by about 10% which is in agreement with other observations (e.g. Goudrian and de Ruiter, 1983; Rogers et al., 1980; Schönfeld et al., 1989). The underlying cause is starch accumulation (Goudrian and de Ruiter, 1983) but could also partly be due to an increased leaf thickness (Acock and Pasternak, 1982; Rogers et al., 1980; Schönfeld et al., 1989).

Table 4.6.3 shows that in the first experiment the relative effect of doubled CO_2 on both grain number and weight was similar. By contrast, in the 1995 experiment the number of grains in the low N treatment were more strongly increased by high CO_2 than grain dry weight, whilst in the high N treatment the grain number was proportionally lower. Consequently with low N

Table 4.6.3   Grain dry weight and number per plant and grain-N concentration at maturity permanently grown in growth chambers under ambient and elevated CO_2 in the 1994 experiment (Experiment 1) and the 1995 experiment (Experiment 2); N- is the low N treatment and N+ is the high N treatment.

Growth parameters	Ambient CO_2		Elevated CO_2		Rel. effect of 2x CO_2	
	N-	N+	N-	N+	N-	N+
Experiment 1						
Grain DM (g.plant)	1.71	1.55[1]	1.21	3.50	-29%	+126%[1]
Grain number	48.40	79.50[1]	37.50	183.00	-23%	+130%[1]
Grain-N-conc. [%] (M)	2.48	2.35	2.53	2.40	+2%	+2%
Experiment 2						
Grain DM (g. plant)	1.89	3.51	2.32	4.54	+26%	+29%
Grain number	51.30	176.50	76.70	180.50	+50%	+2%
Grain-N-conc. [%] (M)	2.64	2.66	1.95	2.76	-26%	+4%

[1] Grain number was reduced because of plant disease.

supply the single grain weight declined under high CO_2 but was increased with high N supply.

The leaf N concentration has often been found to decrease (e.g. Billes *et al.*, 1993; Hocking and Meyer, 1991; Larigauderie *et al.*, 1988) under CO_2 enrichment due to a higher nitrogen use efficiency (NUE). The present study confirms these observations. However, there is some evidence that not only the vegetative but also the generative organs respond to elevated CO_2 with lower N concentrations which might have an impact on grain quality (Hocking and Meyer, 1991). In this study no decrease in grain N concentration by elevated CO_2 was found in Experiment 1 but a decrease was observed in the low N treatment of Experiment 2 (Table 4.6.3). The reason for this was the gradual reduction of N supply after anthesis imposed only in the second experiment. Without additional soil N there was not enough nitrogen stored in vegetative tissues (because of lower N concentrations) to mobilize which would satisfy the demand of growing grains. Hence, it is assumed that the grain N concentration under CO_2 enrichment was more dependent on post anthesis soil N availability than directly affected by CO_2.

A specific objective of this experiment was to investigate the relocation of carbon and nitrogen during different phases of plant growth, especially during grain filling. To do this a

labelling technique with stable isotopes of carbon and nitrogen was used. Tables 4.6.4 to 4.6.7 show how C and N in different organs was composed of pre-anthesis and post-anthesis fixed C and N when exposed to different environments from anthesis to maturity. In the 1994 experiment the relative contribution of pre-anthesis fixed C was only affected by the supply of N, whereas the CO_2 concentration caused no significant difference in this respect. Under elevated CO_2 and high N supply there was a higher loss (relocation into the growing grains) of C from the vegetative organs, but simultaneously a higher replacement of C by current photosynthesis. The surplus of C fixed by the high photosynthesis under elevated CO_2 exceeded the sink-size of growing grains and instead filled up the reserve pools in vegetative organs. A thinning effect of soluble carbohydrates in the reserve pools could explain why the percentages of pre-anthesis C in vegetative organs are relatively low although the absolute C contents are high.

Under normal CO_2 and high N the turnover of carbon in vegetative organs was far less than under high CO_2. Obviously the weaker current photosynthesis did not supply much to vegetative organs but rather to growing grains directly. Thus, no great turnover took place in this treatment and, hence, the portion of pre-anthesis carbon remained relatively high during grain filling.

With respect to nitrogen the ambient CO_2/high N treatment had a much higher relative portion of pre-anthesis N in the grain than the elevated CO_2/high N treatments, however the absolute content of N was one third higher. The relatively high amount of post-anthesis N under ambient CO_2 was obviously due to an 80% lower uptake of nitrogen after anthesis owing to available carbohydrates. Despite the larger N-contribution of the vegetative organs of elevated CO_2/high N-plants there remained

about 90% more N in these organs than in those of the low CO_2/high N treatment. With low N supply there was only a small difference concerning N economy between ambient and elevated CO_2 treatments.

In the 1995 experiment no data for the high-N plants were available because of crop failure in this treatment. Furthermore, the N-stress imposed on low-N plants in 1995 was far less severe than in 1994. Thus the results of low N

Table 4.6.4 Percentage of pre-anthesis carbon[B] of total main tiller carbon[A] [mg] in different organs at maturity and the change in pre-anthesis-C[C] [mg] during grain filling in the 1994 experiment. N- is the low N treatment and N+ is the high N treatment.

Organ	Ambient CO_2		Elevated CO_2		Results of ANOVA		
					Sources of variance		
	N-	N+	N-	N+	N	CO_2	NxCO$_2$
Grain	175[A] (27%)[B]	293 (20%)	143 (27%)	421 (21%)	*	ns	ns
	+44[C]	+59	+39	+87			
Veg. Ear	69 (74%)	68 (86%)	68 (67%)	126 (32%)	ns	**	**
	-0.4	-80.0	-4.7	-99.0			
Stem (+ leaf sheaths)	103 (67%)	270 (84%)	98 (76%)	363 (47%)	*	**	**
	-52	-123	-57	-181			
Leaf blades	55 (73%)	147 (85%)	42 (79%)	200 (62%)	ns	**	**
	-32	-52	-39	-52			
Root	81 (77%)	129 (84%)	67 (76%)	322 (47%)	**	*	**
	-53	-232	-61	-198			

* = P < 0.05; ** P < 0.01; ns = not significant.

Table 4.6.5 Percentage of pre-anthesis nitrogen[E] of total main tiller nitrogen[D] [mg] in different organs at maturity and the change in pre-anthesis-N[F] [mg] during grain filling in the 1994 experiment. N- is the low N treatment and N+ is the high N treatment.

Organ	Ambient CO_2		Elevated CO_2		Results of ANOVA		
					Sources of variance		
	N-	N+	N-	N+	N	CO_2	NxCO$_2$
Grain	10.6[D] 55%)[E]	16 (89%)	8.2 (51%)	24 (49%)	**	**	**
	+5.8[F]	+14.4	+4.2	+11.8			
Veg. Ear	1.3 (67%)	1.6 (92%)	1.7 (67%)	2.5 (68%)	*	**	*
	-0.9	-5.2	-0.8	-5.0			
Stem (+ leaf sheaths)	1.4 (78%)	8.4 (71%)	1.2 (66%)	10.0 (59%)	**	**	ns
	-2.2	-5.8	-2.4	-6.0			
Leaf blades	1.8 (76%)	9.0 (84%)	1.1 (71%)	12.0 (67%)	ns	**	ns
	-1.7	-7.2	-2.3	-6.4			
Roots	2.4 (49%)	4.0 (49%)	1.9 (10%)	18.6 (32%)	**	**	**
	-2.0	-8.0	-1.7	-4.0			

* = P < 0.05; ** P < 0.01; ns = not significant.

treatment in 1995 are more like the high N treatment in 1994, particularly because considerations with respect to relocation of C and N refer only to the main tiller.

The amount of fixed carbon after anthesis was 36% higher in plants exposed to elevated CO_2 than in those at ambient CO_2. Consequently there was a higher amount of carbon in all vegetative organs as well as in the mature grain. As the percentages show there was less pre-anthesis carbon exported in the elevated CO_2 plants due to a lower demand by growing grains, which were better supplied by the higher photosynthesis in a high CO_2-environment. In addition the period of grain filling was shortened by improved light conditions and high temperatures. The lower relative portion of pre-anthesis C in the stem of the high CO_2-plants was due to a diluting effect caused by more incoming assimilates from current photosynthesis. In 1995 the roots did not loose much of the pre-anthesis C but gained carbon from post-anthesis assimilation. The reason for

Table 4.6.6 Percentage of pre-anthesis carbon[B] of total main tiller carbon[A] [mg] in different organs at maturity and the change in pre-anthesis-C[C] [mg] during grain filling in the 1995 experiment (dashes indicate there are no data available because of crop failure). N- is the low N treatment and N+ is the high N treatment.

Organ	Ambient CO_2		Elevated CO_2		Results of ANOVA Sources of variance		
	N-	N+	N-	N+	N	CO_2	$NxCO_2$
Grain	513[A] (7%)[B] +35[C]	-	573 (10%) +59	-	ns	ns	ns
Veg. Ear	137 (47%) -37	-	145 (54%) -21	-	ns	ns	ns
Stem (+ leaf sheaths)	400 (58%) -87	-	497 (53%) -56	-	ns	ns	ns
Leaf blades	140 (62%) -71	-	156 (70%) -46	-	ns	ns	ns
Root	43 (50%) -0.8	-	97 (22%) -1.7	-	ns	**	ns

* = $P < 0.05$; ** $P < 0.01$; ns = not significant.

Table 4.6.7 Percentage of pre-anthesis nitrogen[E] of total main tiller nitrogen[D] [mg] in different organs at maturity and the change in pre-anthesis-N[F] [mg] during grain filling in the 1995 experiment (dashes indicate there are no data available because of crop failure). N- is the low N treatment and N+ is the high N treatment.

Organ	Ambient CO_2		Elevated CO_2		Results of ANOVA Sources of variance		
	N-	N+	N-	N+	N	CO_2	$NxCO_2$
Grain	30.0[D] (75%)[E] +22.5[F]	-	25.2 (87%) +21.8	-	ns	ns	ns
Veg. Ear	2.5 (82%) -2.9	-	1.6 (90%) -3.5	-	ns	ns	ns
Stem (+ leaf sheaths)	4.6 (85%) -14.0	-	2.7 (90%) -15.5	-	ns	ns	ns
Leaf blades	7,0 (89%) -11.9	-	5,1 (94%) -13.2	-	ns	ns	ns
Roots	1.4 (76%) -0.4	-	1.8 (81%) -0.1	-	ns	ns	ns

* = $P < 0.05$; ** $P < 0.01$; ns = not significant.

this was probably the steep reduction of N supply after anthesis. Thus the plants enlarged the root system between anthesis and maturity in order to exploit the rooting medium for nutrients.

The partitioning and relocation of N was characterised by a lower relative N content in the grain although the dry mass of the grain was higher under elevated CO_2. As a consequence the C to N ratio was 22.7 compared to 17.1 in low CO_2. The vegetative plant parts, except those from the roots of the enriched plants, lost about 12% more pre-anthesis N during grain filling than non enriched plants, and hence a higher relative portion of pre-anthesis N was found in the grain. Otherwise the roots of high CO_2-plants stored 28% more N because of the strong post-anthesis enlargement of the root system in this treatment. Furthermore under CO_2 enrichment there was less total post-anthesis N in the whole plant although the roots exploited much more rooting medium than those of low CO_2-plants. The cause for this might be the strong enlargement of above and below ground material in these plants. Hence, the above ground material of the whole plant increased by 78% in the enriched CO_2 environment and the roots were 2.5 times bigger than those of non enriched plants. Thus, much of the diminishing amount of N could have been fixed by this extra material.

In the first experiment the stem, including leaf sheath, contributed the highest amount of carbon to grain filling. In terms of nitrogen the leaf blades of high N-plants contributed somewhat more than stems, with leaf sheath, but under low N supply the reverse effect occurred. Here, there was less N available for relocation because leaves remained small and chlorotic due to severe N stress. In the second experiment in which no data for the high N treatment were available these relations were confirmed.

There is very little reported in the literature about this subject. Unpublished investigations at the Institut für Pflanzenbau under ambient CO_2 exhibited a very similar pattern of carbon relocation into growing grains. The dependence of N supply was also found.

4.6.4 Implications for modelling

Available crop models do not include mechanistic submodels of carbon and nitrogen economy. Often no usage of plant reserves or only a fixed percentage of total vegetative plant biomass are calculated to contribute to grain weight. The literature (Gallagher *et al.*,1975; Pinter, 1977; Schnyder, 1993) and results from this experiment show that the contribution of pre-anthesis carbon and nitrogen reserves to grain filling is highly dependent on environmental conditions. If adverse conditions reduce current photosynthesis during grain filling the relocation of reserves into the growing grain becomes particularly important. In a future elevated CO_2 environment such adverse conditions (e.g. drought, reduced photosynthesis due to overcast skies) may occur more frequently. Detailed consideration needs to be taken of vegetative plant reserves for grain filling in crop models simulating future crop growth.

A submodel accomplishing these objectives should be able to calculate the different vegetative reserve pools of assimilates during vegetative and generative phases. In addition a hierarchy model which decides which sink is supplied with precedence within the different phases is required. The same applies to a nitrogen reserve model. Furthermore the submodels of C and N reserve pools should be connected to display the mutual influence of carbon and nitrogen economy.

Data from this experiment shows the importance of the contribution of vegetative reserve pools to grain filling. The relative amount varied between the two experiments: in Experiment 1 these figures were 27 and 20% of total grain carbon for low N and high N respectively and in Experiment 2 approximately 10% for moderate N shortage. In both cases the relative contribution was independent of CO_2, indicating that the mechanism of C-relocation is independent of the availability of carbohydrates. However, a dependence of carbohydrate relocation on nitrogen supply was found; N-stressed plants contributed a higher percentage of pre-anthesis carbon to grain filling than those supplied with ample N.

With respect to N economy the data indicate that with high carbohydrate availability after anthesis due to elevated CO_2 the assimilation of N is promoted, but if there is not enough N available in the rooting medium (e.g. drought, less fertile soil) the decrease of N concentration in enriched plants might lead to a lower absolute contribution to grain filling. Hence, a decrease of N concentration in the grain might result.

From these results it can be concluded that a calculation of C and N economy in an accurate way is necessary, especially under changing environmental conditions. But the mechanisms of translocation of C and N within the different reserve pools are, as yet, poorly understood. More detailed experiments on this subject will be needed to improve our knowledge and to build models displaying the carbon and nitrogen economy of cereal crops.

4.6.5   Conclusions

In the present study enrichment of CO_2 resulted in a positive effect on tillering, root to shoot ratio, total plant dry weight and grain yield. The specific leaf area (SLA) and the leaf N concentration decreased whereas the green leaf area (GLA) exhibited no clear effect under elevated CO_2. These findings are in good agreement with other observations.

The enlarged root system of enriched plants may be able to absorb more nutrients and water from the soil to an extent that plants may better overcome adverse growing conditions. Furthermore the higher availability of carbohydrates in storage pools and the increase in current photosynthesis of plants exposed to high CO_2 can (i) promote grain filling even under poor conditions and (ii) promote the energy dependent assimilation of nitrogen. This might lead to an improved N economy especially during the phase of grain filling during which carbohydrates are usually scarce because the demand of growing grain has the priority.

The percentage of relocated carbon into growing grain was found to be independent of CO_2 and varied only with N supply. So it is assumed that the mechanism of carbon relocation is unaffected by CO_2 concentration although enhanced absolute contributions of vegetative organs to grain filling occur.

To simulate crop growth in a future higher CO_2 environment it seems necessary to include detailed models of carbon and nitrogen economy. The contribution of vegetative reserve pools to grain filling may become more important when, for example, dry or overcast weather conditions limit photosynthesis. The assumption of fixed percentage of vegetative reserve carbon or nitrogen contribution to grain filling would not then be satisfactory.

4.7   Greenhouse-based open top chamber experiments on spring wheat

4.7.1   Background

Increases in growing season temperatures and CO_2 levels caused by the greenhouse effect are potentially beneficial for crop plants grown in the cool climate of Finland, since these conditions promote photosynthesis and growth. The plants that are commonly cultivated in Finland such as wheat, barley, oats and rye are C_3 plants. Unlike C_4 plants (e.g. maize and sugar cane) they do not have a CO_2 concentrating system in their cells, and therefore photosynthetic CO_2 assimilation is limited by the concentration of CO_2. As the key enzyme in photosynthetic carbon assimilation, Rubisco, is not solely for CO_2, but also binds its active center to oxygen (O_2), an increase in CO_2 concentrations would also decrease the occurrence of O_2 binding to the active centre of Rubisco and hence decrease photorespiration of C_3 plants (Bowes, 1991).

A steady increase in photosynthetic activity in elevated CO_2 is, however, only possible if other environmental factors, such as water, plant nutrients, light and temperature, are not limiting (Lawlor and Mitchell, 1991). Further, an increase in atmospheric CO_2 concentration, causes a decrease in the stomatal conductance of plant leaves and, hence, the plant is able to reduce water loss and to maintain a higher leaf temperature (Lawlor and Mitchell, 1991). In addition, factors limiting growth may cause a decline in photosynthesis in elevated CO_2 by reducing the sink size and thus causing accumulation of the end products of photosynthesis (Bowes, 1991; Farrar and Williams, 1991).

The effect of temperature on plant productivity in elevated CO_2 concentrations has been demonstrated in experiments, where plant growth response to elevated CO_2 concentrations was considerably higher when temperatures were also elevated (Krenzer and Moss, 1975). Moderate increases in temperature may promote grain crop cultivation in Finland through lenghtening of the growing period by providing more favourable conditions for photosynthesis and growth. However, larger increases in temperature may be disadvantageous, because crops cultivated in Finland at present are adapted to a short growing season and may mature too early under higher temperatures, thus reducing yields. Simulations with the CERES wheat growth model (Ritchie and Otter, 1985) have indicated that when wheat yields are reduced by elevating growing season temperatures, the gain in yield due to elevated CO_2 could compensate for the shorter growing time. However, according to the future climatic and atmospheric conditions predicted for Finland only a modest net gain in yield is anticipated (Mela *et al.*, 1994). Therefore, new varieties of grain crops with higher temperature requirements and longer growing times are needed to realise the considerable potential of rising temperatures and CO_2 concentrations. An increase in nitrogen fertilization will also be needed, in order to prevent plants from mobilising nitrogen in its photosynthesising leaves to support grain growth too early in the growing season.

This study seeks to evaluate, through direct experimentation, the possible impact of predicted climatic and atmospheric changes on the growth and development of a cereal crop,

spring wheat (*Triticum aestivum* L.) in Finland. Although many experiments have been conducted to study the effects of temperature and CO_2 in individual crop plants, fewer investigations have been made of crop stands, especially under the long photoperiod conditions experienced during the growing season at high latitudes. In the present investigation a wheat variety (Polkka, Sweden) has been grown according to the following four treatments: a) ambient air temperature and ambient CO_2 concentration; b) increased air temperature (3°C above ambient) and ambient CO_2; c) ambient air temperature and elevated CO_2 concentration (700 ppmv), and d) increased air temperature and elevated CO_2. In addition, the effects of increased temperature on different (non-domestic) cultivars of wheat have also been examined to investigate the adaptability of such cultivars to varying conditions in Finland.

4.7.2   Experimental approach

4.7.2.1   *Increased temperature*

In order to maintain air temperature at 3°C above ambient, a greenhouse (20 m x 30 m) was constructed in 1991 in the experimental field at Jokioinen (60°49'N, 23°30'E). The greenhouse was built with white pressure impregnated laminated wood arches in an east-west direction. The shape of the greenhouse was the pointed arch type. A standard ethyl vinyl acetate (EVA) antifog film (light transmission 60% at 350-800 nm) was used as the covering material. Air temperature was regulated by an automatic computer controlled system which was installed inside the greenhouse. This operated ridge ventilation hatches for cooling and heater fans for heating.

4.7.2.2   *Elevated CO_2*

Experiments in elevated CO_2 concentrations were conducted using open top chambers (OTCs). These are cylindrical in shape with a diameter of 3 m and a height of 2 m. They were constructed from colourless corrugated acrylate sheets (Vetricell, ER, photosynthetically active radiation transmission 90%) bolted together on an aluminium frame. The thickness of the sheets was 1.5 mm and corrugation depth 18 mm and width 76 mm. One side of the sheet was left unbolted to serve as a door for entering the chamber. The overhead frustrum running around the upper edge of the chamber was 35 cm wide and constructed from 1 mm thick polymethyl meta-acrylate sheets.

The experimental plot outside the greenhouse, at ambient temperature, was covered at the height of 3-4 m with the same plastic as that used in the construction of the greenhouse so as to achieve comparable radiation and rainfall (though not wind and humidity) conditions to those in the greenhouse.

The CO_2 gas was supplied to the chambers from a set of gas cylinders by vapour withdrawal. The gas was led through a heating device and a two stage pressure regulator into rubber tubing 12 mm in diameter, leading to a delivery stand inside the greenhouse. The main flow was divided into eight minor flows, stopped with separate main valves. From this point the gas was led to solenoid valves regulated by an automatic measuring-dosing feedback system (Itumic Oy, Jyvaskyla, Finland). From the solenoid valves the CO_2 gas was led to the chambers individually through separate flow metres and 7 mm diameter rubber tubing. Inside the chamber the rubber tubing was perforated and criss-crossed over the plant canopy, to make the gas flow even. The CO_2 source was placed above rather than within the plant canopy in order to avoid the problem of CO_2 depletion due to plant uptake in the canopy during photosynthesis. Standard measurements of ambient atmospheric CO_2 concentrations were made between the CO_2 source and plants as it is known that concentrations within a plant canopy can be significantly lower than those in free air. Overhead fans were attached to each chamber to mix the CO_2 gas with the chamber air and also to prevent the temperature in the chamber from rising above that outside the chamber.

In 1994 the system was improved so that CO_2 was led into a perforated plastic tunnel together with air from the overhead fans. In ambient CO_2 chambers a similar system was arranged but with no CO_2 added. The tunnel is a standard greenhouse ventilation tunnel comprising a thin plastic tube 24 cm in diameter. This configuration results in more uniform CO_2 levels and airflow inside the chambers.

Measurements of temperature and CO_2 concentrations were recorded by automatic control systems and transferred to a master unit, from which data files were obtained and the information was processed on a personal computer.

4.7.2.3   *Experimental plots*

Spring wheat (cv. Polkka) was sown at normal sowing density (600 germinating seeds m^{-2} in 1992 and 500 germinating seeds m^{-2} in 1993 and 1994) directly in the ground in both the greenhouse and the open field. Sowing was done three to four weeks earlier in the greenhouse in order to simulate expected management conditions in a changed climate. After emergence, the seedlings were enclosed in OTCs, four in the greenhouse and four in the open field, which gave two independent replicates per treatment. Irrigation was applied so that soil moisture would not be limiting for growth. Fertilizer was applied as required, according to normal farm recommendations, and pests and diseases were kept under control. Each chamber area was divided in half, one half of which was occupied by a meadow fescue stand and the other half by wheat. Thus the area of the wheat canopy in each chamber was approximately 4.5 m^2.

4.7.2.4   *Measurements*

Open top chamber experiments

Photosynthesis of the wheat flag leaves was measured regularly at saturating light (> 800 μmol photons m^{-2} s^{-1}) with a portable CO_2 exchange measuring system (LCA3 of ADC, England, with a Parkinson leaf cuvette). Samples were taken for dry weight and nitrogen content measurements of both roots and above ground plant organs at the 5-6 leaf stage (in 1992 and 1993) and at anthesis and maturity (in 1992-1994). The green leaf area of the flag leaves, the leaf beneath the flag leaf and the other main stem leaves were measured with a planimeter (Hayashi Denko Ltd., Japan) and leaf dry weight was determined after oven-drying. At maturity, dry matter of yield components was measured, but leaf area could not be determined. At the 5-6 leaf stage and anthesis, three samples were taken from each replicate (6 per treatment) while at maturity ten samples were taken in 1992-1993 and five samples in 1994. The sample size was 20 cm per row in 1992-1993 and 50 cm per row in 1994. The mean number of plants per row metre was 61 in 1992 and 56 in 1993-1994. In 1993, at ambient temperatures, only one replicate of each CO_2 treatment could be harvested; results for ambient temperatures

are means of ten samples. Plant development was observed throughout the experiments.

4.7.3   Results and discussion

4.7.3.1   *Seasonal temperatures*

Mean monthly temperatures recorded at Jokioinen Observatory during the growing seasons of 1992-1994 are shown alongside the long-term mean (1961-1990) in Figure 4.7.1. 1992 was warmer than average throughout the growing season, 1993 was generally cooler than average and 1994 was cool at first but

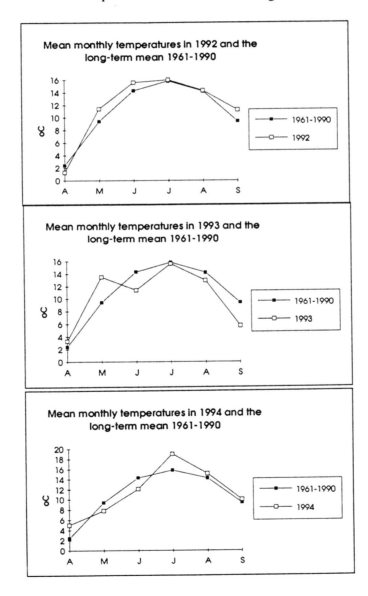

Figure 4.7.1   Mean monthly temperatures recorded at Jokionen Observatory during the growing seasons of 1992-94 and the long-term mean 1961-90.

warm later in the summer. Because of the different sowing dates for wheat inside the greenhouse (increased temperatures) and outside (ambient temperatures), the temperatures inside the greenhouse were not always higher than the ambient temperatures on a given day after sowing (DAS).

4.7.3.2   *Phenology*

In previous experiments, elevated CO_2 concentrations have been observed either to slightly increase the developmental rate by 2 to 3 days (Sionit *et al.*, 1981a) or to have no effect (Krenzer and Moss, 1975). In the present investigation, elevated CO_2 concentrations did not appear to affect the phenology of wheat, but increased temperatures either increased or decreased the development rate, the effect depending on the year.

Anthesis was reached 10 days earlier at increased temperatures in 1992 and 3 days earlier in 1993, but 3 days later in 1994. Maturity was reached 18 days earlier at increased temperatures in 1992, 8 days earlier in 1993 and in the same number of days after sowing as ambient conditions in 1994. The difference in the developmental rate was greatest in 1992, possibly because wheat was sown in the greenhouse about two weeks later than in 1993 and 1994 and growth started very quickly. The seedlings emerged 5 days after sowing in 1992, whilst in 1993 and 1994 the seedlings did not emerge until 10 to 11 days after sowing.

4.7.3.3   *Photosynthesis and biomass allocation*

Photosynthesis

Substantial increases in photosynthetic activity in elevated CO_2 have been detected in several previous experiments. because the current concentration of carbon dioxide is limiting for photosynthesis (Lawlor and Mitchell, 1991). In the present investigation, the photosynthesis of the flag leaves was higher at elevated CO_2 than at ambient CO_2 under both ambient and increased temperatures in all three seasons (Table 4.7.1).

Specific leaf area

Both elevated CO_2 and increased temperatures increased the specific leaf area ($cm^2.g^1$ dry weight) of the leaf beneath the flag leaf at anthesis. Elevated CO_2 also increased the specific leaf area of flag leaves, while temperature alone had no clear effect (Table 4.7.2). Elevated CO_2 has been observed to decrease rather than increase the specific leaf area in other experiments, possibly because of accumulation of starch or thickening of the cell walls (Lawlor and Mitchell, 1991), or have no effect (Sionit *et al.* 1981a; Hocking and Meyer, 1991) or an effect which varies during the course of development (Havelka *et al.*,1984).

Plant biomass

An increase in plant biomass as a consequence of the increased CO_2 assimilation rate in elevated CO_2 has been observed in several experiments (Lawlor and Mitchell, 1991; Sionit *et al.* 1981a; Havelka *et al.*, 1984). In the present investigation, wheat biomass was higher at elevated CO_2 at anthesis both at ambient and increased temperatures (Table 4.7.2). At maturity the total biomass per plant was considerably higher in elevated CO_2 than in ambient CO_2 at increased temperatures (Table 4.7.3). At ambient temperatures, the effect of elevated CO_2 on the total biomass per plant was not clear (Table 4.7.3), the biomass was lower in elevated CO_2 in 1992 and 1993 and in 1994 was clearly higher. When calculated on an area basis (biomass m^{-2}), the total biomass was always higher at elevated CO_2 (Table 4.7.3). The difference in the CO_2 effect when calculated on a per plant basis or per area basis can be explained by the differences in plant densities in the various treatments (Table 4.7.3). When the density is higher, the total biomass per plant is lower because of competition. However, higher plant densities may give higher biomass m^{-2}, due to the higher number of plants. The total biomass per plant was lower at ambient temperatures than at increased temperatures at anthesis (Table 4.7.2), while at maturity it was higher at ambient temperatures than at increased temperatures in 1992 and 1993, and lower in 1994 (Table 4.7.3).

Table 4.7.1 CO_2 assimilation (μmol m^{-2}s^{-1}) of spring wheat 'Polkka' in the different experimental conditions in 1992-1994. DAS = days after sowing, amb.T = ambient temperatures, inc. T = increased temperatures.

(a) 1992

DAS	2xCO$_2$, amb. T	1xCO$_2$, amb. T	DAS	2xCO$_2$, inc. T	1xCO$_2$, inc. T
43	18.8	11.9	40	23.5	20.0
53	23.5	15.1	41	22.7	18.8
55	26.2	15.0	54	15.7	13.2
56	27.5	15.6	56	17.0	14.1
69	20.6	14.1	61	19.7	13.4
70	24.6	17.8			
87	16.1	10.5			

(b) 1993

DAS	2xCO$_2$, amb. T	1xCO$_2$, amb. T	DAS	2xCO$_2$, inc. T	1xCO$_2$, inc. T
57	18.6	18.3	54	24.8	17.1
58	19.0	14.2	60	16.9	13.1
63	22.0	17.1	69	26.2	19.5
80	15.7	16.3	73	23.9	12.4
84	17.0	13.6	74	23.8	12.6
			77	23.6	11.3
			82	17.0	10.8

(c) 1994

DAS	2xCO$_2$, amb. T	1xCO$_2$, amb. T	DAS	2xCO$_2$, inc. T	1xCO$_2$, inc. T
56	33.1	19.2	55	30.1	20.7
58	23.6	18.4	59	25.8	22.1
63	27.9	16.7	61	27.5	19.6
72	24.1	14.8	67	25.0	18.6
77	26.9	15.2	75	23.4	18.1
80	22.8	12.6	80	24.0	13.7
			82	28.3	17.3
			87	18.3	11.6

Table 4.7.2 Biomass allocation in spring wheat at anthesis in the different experimental conditions, average of 1992-1994. SLA = specific leaf area, amb. T = ambient temperatures, inc. T = increased temperatures.

Parameter	2xCO$_2$, amb. T	1xCO$_2$, amb. T	2xCO$_2$, inc. T	1xCO$_2$, inc. T
SLA of flag leaf (cm^2 g^{-1})	302.60	276.70	298.20	278.00
SLA of leaf beneath flag leaf (cm^2 g^{-1})	348.30	319.70	367.60	343.90
number of plants per m^2	394.00	454.00	467.00	431.00
number of heads per plant	1.22	1.12	1.42	1.31
main shoot dry weight (g shoot^{-1})	1.42	1.35	1.52	1.37
whole plant dry weight (g plant^{-1})	1.65	1.5	2.01	1.76

Table 4.7.3   Biomass allocation in spring wheat at harvest in the different experimental conditions, average of 1992-1994. amb. T = ambient temperatures, inc. T = increased temperatures.

Parameter	2xCO$_2$, amb. T	1xCO$_2$, amb. T	2xCO$_2$, inc. T	1xCO$_2$, inc. T
number of plants per m^2	513.00	472.00	480.00	491.00
number of heads per plant	1.35	1.30	1.49	1.34
above ground biomass (g per plant)	2.77	2.66	3.20	2.51
grain weight per main shoot (g per plant)	0.98	1.02	0.93	0.82
grain weight per lateral shoot (g per plant)	0.20	0.17	0.26	0.16
above ground biomass (g per plant)	1395.00	1227.00	1465.00	1183.00
yield (g m^{-2})	596.00	551.00	549.00	458.00
grain number per main shoot	28.30	29.30	26.70	24.30
grain number per lateral shoot	18.70	15.00	15.70	14.00
1000 grain weight (g)	33.40	34.40	33.90	32.70
harvest index	0.42	0.45	0.38	0.38

Grain yield

Previous experiments with wheat have shown that an increase in yield at elevated CO_2 concentrations is brought about by an increase in the number of heads and/or grains rather than grain size (Lawlor and Mitchell, 1991; Havelka et al., 1984; Krenzer and Moss, 1975; Sionit et al., 1981a). In the present investigation, with wheat sown at normal density, the number of heads per plant was low (1.04 to 1.78) in all experimental conditions in all three seasons. There was, however, evidence of a positive effect of elevated CO_2 on the number of heads at anthesis at both increased and ambient temperatures (Table 4.7.2). The number of heads at maturity was also higher in elevated CO_2 and increased temperatures (Table 4.7.3). The grain number on the main shoots was higher in elevated CO_2 only at increased temperatures, while that of the lateral shoots was always higher in elevated CO_2 (Table 4.7.3). The grain biomass per main shoot was lower in elevated CO_2 at ambient temperatures during all experimental years and higher in elevated CO_2 at increased temperatures (Table 4.7.3). The grain biomass of the lateral shoots per plant was low, varying from 0.08 g plant^{-1} to 0.33 g plant^{-1} (Table 4.7.3). It was lower in elevated CO_2 at ambient temperatures except in 1994 and higher in elevated CO_2 at increased temperatures, except in 1994.

When calculated on an area basis, the yield m^{-2} was always higher in elevated CO_2 at increased temperatures, while at ambient temperatures the yield was considerably higher, the same or slightly lower in elevated CO_2 during the experimental years 1992, 1993 and 1994, respectively (Table 4.7.3). The grain yield was higher at ambient temperatures than at increased temperatures both when calculated on an area basis and when calculated on a per plant basis (Table 4.7.3). The grain number of both main shoots and lateral shoots was also higher at ambient temperatures (Table 4.7.3). The 1000 grain weight was slightly lower in elevated CO_2 at ambient temperatures and higher in elevated CO_2 at increased temperatures (Table 4.7.3). The harvest index was unchanged or slightly lower in elevated CO_2 at both ambient and increased temperatures (Table 4.7.3). This supports other studies which have observed no change in harvest index in wheat (Lawlor and Mitchell, 1991; Havelka et al., 1984). The harvest index and the 1000 grain weight were considerably higher at ambient temperatures than at increased temperatures (Table 4.7.3).

Nitrogen content

Increased nitrogen use efficiency in elevated CO_2 and, hence, decreased nitrogen content in the different shoot parts of wheat has been reported (Hocking and Meyer, 1991), as well as no change in nitrogen content in elevated CO_2 (Havelka *et al.*, 1984). In the present investigation, the nitrogen content of the leaves and stems of wheat was higher in elevated CO_2 at both ambient and increased temperatures during the early stages of development. However, while the nitrogen content of all shoots decreased with time, the rate of decrease was greater under elevated CO_2 and the final nitrogen content was smaller in elevated compared with ambient CO_2 (Table 4.7.4). Under increased temperatures, however, the main shoots and the main shoot chaff contained more nitrogen at harvest in elevated CO_2 than in ambient CO_2.

4.7.4 Implications for modelling

The experimental reults have been used to support crop modelling work in three ways. First, measurements for ambient CO_2 concentrations of phenology, leaf area, biomass and grain yield have been used to calibrate and validate the development and growth response of the CERES-Wheat model. The model performs poorly in simulating crop development under Finnish conditions when parameter values are selected following the documented recommendations for spring wheat. Therefore it has been necessary to substitute unique parameter values, optimised from the experimental material, that reflect the rapid development of domestic Finnish cultivars.

Second, the phenological observations have provided an independent test of development models used in national-scale suitability mapping (cf. Section 6.4). The results for increased temperatures are of particular interest as they represent conditions outside those observed in Finland during the period for which models were calibrated.

Third, measurements of net photosynthesis under ambient and elevated CO_2 concentrations (both at saturating and non-saturating light levels) are being used to modify the equation in CERES-Wheat describing the effect of radiation use efficiency on biomass accumulation. This formulation will be specific to the Polkka

Table 4.7.4 Nitrogen content (% of dry weight) in the different shoot parts of spring wheat 'Polkka' in the different experimental conditions in 1992. DAS = days after sowing, amb. T = ambient temperatures, inc. T = increased temperatures.

Plant part	DAS	$2xCO_2$, amb. T	$1xCO_2$, amb. T	DAS	$2xCO_2$, inc. T	$1xCO_2$, inc. T
5-6. leaf	42	4.76	4.21	33	5.44	5.42
flag leaf	67	4.13	4.12	54	4.47	4.56
other parts of main shoot	42	2.20	1.81	33	4.08	3.98
	67	1.07	1.16	54	1.46	1.51
	104-109	0.39	0.41	89-96	0.57	0.48
lateral shoot	42	2.74	2.21	33	4.80	4.62
	67	1.20	1.46	54	1.88	1.97
	104-109	0.58	0.68	89-96	0.85	0.87
head	55	2.13	2.07	54	2.05	2.07
	67	1.60	1.78	70	1.91	1.93
root	55	1.01	0.99	70	1.24	1.27
	104-109	1.03	1.08	89-96	1.35	1.39
main shoot grain	104-109	2.15	2.31	89-96	2.42	2.41
main shoot chaff	104-109	0.39	0.43	89-96	0.57	0.50
lateral shoot grain	104-109	2.25	2.31	89-96	2.51	2.40
lateral shoot chaff	104-109	0.53	0.99	89-96	1.06	1.04

variety used in the experiments, and is preferred to the current method of simulating growth response to CO_2 used in CERES-Wheat. This involves the application of a gross photosynthetic enhancement factor of 28% for a doubling of CO_2, based on empirical results from different genotypes. Further work is planned to develop more sophisticated schemes for simulating CO_2 effects on both photosynthesis and water use, using measurements of stomatal conductance and transpiration.

4.7.5   Conclusions

The photosynthetic rate measured at saturating irradiance levels was always higher at elevated CO_2. The CO_2 effect on the growth and yield of wheat varied from year to year, possibly because of the variation in other environmental factors, such as the temperature regime during the growing seasons. There were, however, some more or less constant effects of elevated CO_2: the specific leaf area was higher, the number of heads per plant was higher and the total biomass m^{-2} was higher at elevated CO_2 in both ambient and increased temperatures. The content of nitrogen in different shoot parts was higher in elevated CO_2 compared with ambient CO_2 in the early stages of development and lower at maturity. Increased temperatures resulted in lower yields, while elevation of CO_2 improved yields at increased temperatures. More information will be available when the experimental data have been fully analysed for scientific publications.

References

Acock, B. (1990). Effects of Carbon Dioxide on Photosynthesis, Plant Growth, and Other Process. In: *Impact of carbon dioxide, trace gases, and climate change on global agriculture.* ASA Special Publications **No. 53**. American Society Of Agronomy, Crop Science Society of America, and Soil Science Society of America, Madison, USA, 45-60.

Allen, L.H. (1992). Field techniques for exposure of plants and ecosystems to elevated CO_2 and other trace gases. *Critical Reviews in Plant Sciences*, **11**, 85-119.

Arp, W.J. (1991) Effects of source-sink relations on photosynthetic acclimation to elevated CO_2. *Plant, Cell and Environment*, **14**, 869-875.

Booij, R. (1987). Environmental factors in curd initiation and curd growth of cauliflower in the field. *Netherlands Journal of Agricultural Science*, **35**, 435-45.

Bowes, G. (1991). Growth at elevated CO_2: photosynthetic responses mediated through Rubisco. *Plant, Cell and Environment*, **14**, 795-806.

Christensen, S. and Goudriaan, J. (1993). Deriving light interception and biomass from spectral reflectance ratio. *Remote Sensing of Environment*, **43**, 87-95.

Conroy, J.P., Kuppers, M., Kuppers, B., Virgona, J., and Barlow, E.W.R. (1988a). The influence of CO_2 enrichment, phosphorus deficiency and water stress on the growth, conductance and water use of *Pinus Radiata* D. Don. *Plant, Cell and Environment,* **11**: 91-98.

Conroy, J.P., Virgona, J.M., Smillie, R.M. and Barlow, E.W.R. (1988b). Influence of drought acclimation and CO_2 enrichment on osmotic adjustment and chlorophyll a fluorescence of sunflower during drought. *Plant Physiology*, **86**, 1108-1115.

Cure, J.D. (1985). Carbon dioxide doubling responses: a crop survey. In: Strain, B.R. and Cure, J.D. (eds.). *Direct Effects of Increasing Carbon Dioxide on Vegetation.* DOE/ER-0238. US Department of Energy, Washington DC, USA, 99-116.

Cure, J.D. and Acock, B. (1986). Crop responses to carbon dioxide doubling: A literature survey. *Agricultural and Forest Meteorology,* **38**: 127-145.

Cure, J.D., Israel, D.W. and Rufty, T.W. (1988a). Nitrogen stress on growth and seed yield of nonnodulated soybean exposed to elevated carbon dioxide. *Crop Sience,* **28**, 671-677

Cure, J.D., Rufty, T.W. and Israel, D.W. (1988b). Phosphorus stress effects on growth and seed yield responses of nonnodulated soybean to elevated carbon dioxide. *Agronomy Journal,* **80**, 897-902.

Dahalman, R.C. (1992). CO_2 and plants: revisited. *Vegetatio,* **104**, 1-17.

Dahalman, R.C., Strain, B.R. and Rogers, H.H. (1984). Research on the response of vegetation to elevated atmospheric carbon dioxide. *Journal of Environmental Quality,* **14**, 1-8.

Darwinkel, A. (1987). Improvement of grain quality of winter wheat in arable farming in the Netherlands. In: Borgho, B. (Ed.) *Agriculture. Hard Wheat: Agronomic, Technological, Biochemical and Genetic Aspects.* CEC Report EUR 11172en, Brussels, p.73-84.

Diepen, C.A. van, Rappoldt, C., Wolf, J. and Keulen, H. van (1988). *Crop growth simulation model WOFOST version 4.1 .Documentation, SOW-88-01.* Centre for World Food Studies, Wageningen, The Netherlands, 299 pp.

Dijkstra, P., Schapendonk, A.H.C.M and Groenwold, J. (1993). Effects of CO_2 enrichment on canopy photosynthesis, carbon economy and productivity of wheat and faba bean under field conditions. In: Geijn, S.C. van de, Goudriaan, J. and Berendse, F. (Eds.). *Climate Change, Crops and Terrestrial Ecosystems.* Agro-biological themes part 9. AB-DLO, Wageningen, the Netherlands, 23-41.

Eichhorn, K.W. and Lorenz, D.H. (1977). Phanologische entwickungsstadien der rebe. *Nachichtenbl. Dtch. Pflanzenschutzdienstes (Braunschwieg),* **29**, 119-120.

Farquar, G.D., von Caemmerer, S. and Berry, J.A. (1980). A biochemical model of photosynthetic CO_2 assimilation in leaves of C_3 species. *Planta,* **149**, 78-90.

Farrar, J.F. and Williams, M.L. (1991). The effects of increased atmospheric carbon dioxide and temperature on carbon partitioning, source-sink relations and respiration. *Plant, Cell and Environment,* **14**, 819-830.

Frère, M. and Popov, G.F. (1979). *Agrometeorological Crop Monitoring and Forecasting.* FAO Plant production and protection paper 17. FAO, Rome, Italy, 64 pp.

Fujime, Y. (1983). Studies on thermal conditions of curd formation and development in cauliflower and broccoli, with special reference to abnormal curd development. *Memoirs of the Faculty of Agriculture Kagawa University,* **No 40**. Miki-tyo, Kagawa-ken, Japan.

Geijn, S.C. van de and Veen, J.A. van (1993). Implications of increased carbon dioxide levels for carbon input and turnover in soils. *Vegetatio,* **104/105**, 283-292.

Goudriaan, J. and Bijlsma, R.J. (1987). Effect of CO_2 enrichment on growth of faba beans at two levels of water supply. *Netherlands Journal of Agricultural Science,* **35**, 189-191.

Goudriaan, J. and Ruiter, H.E. de (1983). Plant growth in response to CO_2 enrichment, at two levels of nitrogen and phosphorus supply. 1. Dry matter, leaf area and development. *Netherlands Journal of Agricultural Science,* **31**, 157-169.

Goudriaan, J. and Unsworth, M.H. (1990). Implication of increasing carbon dioxide and climate change for agricultural productivity and water resources. In: *Impact of carbon dioxide, trace gases, and climate change on global agriculture.* ASA Special Publications **No. 53**. American Society of Agronomy, Crop Science Society of America, and Soil Science Society of America, Madison, USA, 111-130.

Grevsen, K. and Olesen, J.E. (1994a). Modelling cauliflower development from transplanting to curd induction. *Journal of Horticultural Science,* **69**, 755-766.

Grevsen, K. and Olesen, J.E. (1994b). Modelling development and quality of cauliflower. *Acta Horticulturae,* **371**, 151-160.

Groot, J.J.R. (1987). *Simulation of nitrogen balance in a system of winter wheat and soil.* Simulation reports CABO-TT **No. 13**, Centre for Agrobiological Research & Dept. of Theoretical Production Ecology, Agricultural University, Wageningen, Netherlands, 195 pp.

Hansen, S., Jensen, S.E. and Aslyng, H.C. (1981). *Jordbrugsmeteorologiske observationer, statistisk analyse og vurdering 1955-1979.* Hydroteknisk Laboratorium, The Royal Veterinary and Agricultural University, Copenhagen, 414 pp.

Havelka, U.D., Wittenbach, V.A. and Boyle, M.G. (1984). CO_2-enrichment effects on wheat yield and physiology. *Crop Science,* **24**, 1163-1168.

Hocking, P.J. and Meyer, C.P. (1991). Effects of CO_2 enrichment and nitrogen stress on growth and partitioning of dry matter and nitrogen in wheat and maize. *Australian Journal of Plant Physiology,* **18**, 339-356.

Idso, S.B. and Kimball, B.A. (1992). Above ground inventory of sour orange trees exposed to different atmospheric CO_2 concentrations for 3 full years. *Agricultural and Forest Meteorology,* **60**, 145-151.

Janssen, B.H., Guiking, F.C.T., Eijk, D. van der, Smaling, E.M.A., Wolf, J., and Reuler, H. van (1990). A system for quantitative evaluation of the fertility of tropical soils (QUEFTS). *Geoderma,* **46**, 299-318.

Johnsen, S. (1990). Modelling plant-herbivore interactions: Cauliflower (*Brassica oleracea* L. var *botrytis*) and cabbage maggot (*Delia radicum* (L.)). Ph.D. Thesis, University of California, Berkeley, 152 pp.

Kenny, G.J., Harrison, P.A. and Parry, M.L. (Eds.) (1993). *The effect of climate change on the agricultural and horticultural potential of Europe.* ECU Research Report **No. 2**, Oxford University, Oxford.

Keulen, H. van (1986). Crop yield and nutrient requirements. In: Keulen, H. van and Wolf, J. (Eds.). *Modelling of agricultural production: Weather, soils and crops.* Simulation Monographs, Pudoc, Wageningen, The Netherlands, 155-181.

Keulen, H. van and Heemst, H.D.J. van (1982). *Crop response to the supply of macronutrients.* Agricultural Research Reports 916, Pudoc, Wageningen, The Netherlands, 46pp.

Keulen, H. van and Seligman, N.G. (1987). Simulation of water-use, nitrogen nutrition and growth of a spring wheat crop. *Simulation Monographs.* Pudoc, Wageningen, pp. 309.

Kimball, B.A. (1983). Carbon dioxide and agricultural yield: An assemblage and analysis of 430 prior observations. *Agronomy Journal,* **75**, 779-788.

Kramer, P.J. (1983). *Water relations of plants.* Academic Press, New York.

Krenzer, E.G. Jr. and Moss, D.N. (1975). Carbon dioxide enrichment effects upon yield and yield components in wheat. *Crop Science,* **15**, 71-74.

Kubota, F., Matsuda, Y., Agata, W. and Nada, K. (1994). The relationship between canopy structure and high productivity in napier grass, *Pennisetum purpureum* Schumach. *Field Crops Research,* **38**, 105-110.

Kuikman, P.J. and Gorissen, A. (1993). Carbon fluxes and organic transformations in plant-soil systems. In: Geijn, S.C. van de, Goudriaan , J. and Berendse F. (Eds.), *Climate change; crops and terrestrial ecosystems.* Agrobiological Themes, AB-DLO, Wageningen, The Netherlands, 97-107.

Lawlor, D.W. and Mitchell, R.A.C. (1991). The effects of increasing CO_2 on crop photosynthesis and productivity: A review of field studies. *Plant, Cell and Environment,* **14**, 807-818.

Lewin, K.F., Hendrey, G.R., Hassinger, E. and LaMorte, R.L. (1994). FACE facility CO_2 concentration control and CO_2 use in 1990 and 1991. *Agricultural and Forest Meteorology*, **70**, 15-30.

Long, S.P. and Drake, B.G. (1992). Photosynthetic CO_2 concentrations. In: Baker, N.R. and Thomas, H. (Eds.) *Crop photosynthesis: Spatial and temporal determinants*. Elsevier Science Publisher BV, New York, 69-103.

McKee, I.F. and Woodward, F.I. (1994) The effect of growth at elevated CO_2 concentrations on photosynthesis in wheat. *Plant Cell and Environment*, **17**, 853-859.

Mela, T., Carter, T., Hakala, K., Hannukkala, A., Hannukkala, A., Kaukoranta, T., Laurila, H., Saarikko, R., Tahvonen, R., Tiilikkala, K. and Tuovinen, T. (1994). The effects of climatic change on crop production. In: Kanninen, M. and Anttila, P. (Eds.) *The Finnish Research Programme on Climatic Change. Second Progress Report*. Publications of the Academy of Finland **1/94**. Painatuskeskus OY, Helsinki, 233-243.

Miglietta, F., Raschi, A., Bettarini, I., Resti, R., and Selvi, F. (1993). Carbon dioxide springs in Italy: A resource for examining long-term response of vegetation to rising atmospheric CO_2 concentrations. *Plant Cell Environment*, **16**, 873-878.

Mitchell, R.A.C., Mitchell, V.J., Driscoll, S.P., Franklin, J. and Lawlor, D.W. (1993). Effects of increased CO_2 concentration and temperature on growth and yield of winter wheat at two levels of nitrogen application. *Plant, Cell and Environment*, **16**, 521-529.

Morison, J.I.L. (1993). Response of plants to CO_2 under water limited conditions. *Vegetatio*, **104/105**, 193-209.

Morison, J.I.L (1985). Sensitivity of stomata and water use efficiency to high CO_2. *Plant, Cell and Environment*, **8**, 467-474.

Morison, J.I.L and Gifford, R.M. (1984). Plant growth and water use with limited water supply in high CO_2 concentrations. II. Plant dry weight, partitioning and water use efficiency. *Australian Journal of Plant Physiology*, **11**, 375-384

Mullins, M.G., Bouquet, A. and Williams, L.E. (1992). *Biology of Grapevine*. Cambridge University Press, Cambridge, 239 pp.

Overdieck, D. (1993). Elevated CO_2 and the mineral content of herbaceous and woody plants. *Vegetatio*, **104/105**, 403-411.

Petterson, R. and McDonald, A.J.S. (1994). Effects of nitrogen supply on the acclimation of photosynthesis to elevated CO_2. *Photosynthesis Research*, **39**, 389-400.

Ritchie, J.T. and Otter, S. (1985). Description and performance of CERES-Wheat: A user-oriented wheat yield model. In: Willis, W.O. (Ed.). *ARS Wheat Yield Project*. Department of Agriculture, Agricultural Research Service. ARS-38. Washington, DC, 159-175.

Sage, R.F. (1994). Acclimation of photosynthesis to increasing atmospheric CO_2: The gas exchange perspective. *Photosynthesis Research*, **39**, 351-368.

Sage, R.F., Sharkey, T.D. and Seeman, J.R. (1989). Acclimation of photosynthesis to elevated CO_2 in five C_3 species. *Plant Physiology*, **89**, 590-596.

Salter, P.J. (1969). Studies on crop maturity in cauliflower. I. Relationship between the times of curd initiation and curd maturity of plants within a cauliflower crop. *Journal of Horticultural Science*, **44**, 129-40.

Salter, P.J. (1960). The growth and development of early summer cauliflower in relation to environmental factors. *Journal of Horticultural Science*, **35**, 21-33.

a

a

Sasek, T.W. and Strain, B.R. (1989). Effects of carbon dioxide enrichment on the expansion and size of kudzu (Pueraria lobata) leaves. *Weed Science*, **37**, 23-28.

Scaife, A. and Turner, M. (1983). *Diagnosis of mineral disorders in plants. Volume 2. Vegetables.* London, 96 pp.

Sinclair, T.R. and Rawlins, S.L. (1993) Inter-seasonal variation in soybean and maize yields under global environmental change. *Agronomy Journal*, **85**, 406-409.

Sionit, N., Strain, B.R and Hellmers, H. (1981a). Effects of different concentrations of atmospheric CO_2 on growth and yield components of wheat. *Journal of Agricultural Science, Cambridge,* **79**, 335-339.

Sionit, N., Mortensen, D.A., Strain, B.R. and Hellmers H. (1981b). Growth response of wheat to CO_2 enrichment and different levels of mineral nutrition. *Agronomy Journal,* **73**, 1023-1027.

Sperry, J.S., Donnelly, J.R. and Tyree, M.T. (1988). A method for measuring hydraulic conductivity and embolism in xylem. *Plant Cell and Environment*, **11**, 35-40.

Spitters, C.J.T., van Keulen, H. and Kraalingen, D.W.G. (1989). A simple and universal crop growth simulator: SUCROS87. In: Rabbinge, R., Ward, S.A. and van Laar, H.H. (Eds.) *Simulation and systems management in crop protection*, Pudoc, 147-181.

Stitt, M. (1991). Rising CO_2 levels and their potential significance for carbon flow in photosynthetic cells. *Plant Cell and Environment*, **16**, 341-349.

Strain, B.R. and Cure, J.D. (1985). *Direct effects of increasing carbon dioxide on vegetation.* DOE/ER-0238, US Department of Energy, Washington, DC, 286 pp.

Stulen, I. and Hertog, J. den (1993). Root growth and functioning under atmospheric CO_2 enrichment. *Vegetatio,* **104/105**, 99-115.

Thomas, J.F. and Harvey, C.N. (1983). Leaf anatomy of four species grown under continuos CO_2 enrichment. *Botanical Gazette*, **144**, 303-309.

Trenbath, B.R. and Angus, J.F. (1975). Leaf inclination and crop production. *Field Crop Abstracts*, **28**, 231-244.

Tyree, M.T. and Jarvis, P.G. (1982). Water in tissues and cells. In: Nobel, P.S., Osmond, C.B., Ziegler, H., (Eds.) *Encyclopedia of Plant Physiology* (N.S.). Springer-Verlag, Berlin, Heidelberg, New York, **12B**, 37-77.

Versteeg, M.N. and van Keulen, H. (1986). Potential crop production prediction by some simple calculation methods, as compared with computer simulations. *Agricultural Systems*, **19**, 249-272.

Webber, A.N., Nie, G.Y. and Long, S.P. (1994) Acclimation of photosynthetic proteins to rising atmospheric CO_2. *Photosynthesis Research*, **39**, 413-426.

Wheeler, T.R., Ellis, R.H., Hadley, P. and Morison, J.I.L. (1995). Effects of CO_2, temperature and their interaction on the growth, development and yield of cauliflower (*Brassica oleracea* L. *botrytis*). *Scientia Horticulturae*, **60**, 191-197.

Wiebe, H.-J. (1972a). Wirkung von Temperatur und Licht auf Wachstum und Entwicklung von Blumenkohl. I. Dauer der Jugendphase für die vernalization. *Gartenbauwissenschaft*, **37**, 165-78.

Wiebe, H.-J. (1972b). Wirkung von Temperatur und Licht auf Wachstum und Entwicklung von Blumenkohl. II. Optimale Vernalisationstemperatur und Vernalisationsdauer. *Gartenbauwissenschaft*, **37**, 293-303.

Wiebe, H.-J. (1972c). Wirkung von Temperatur und Licht auf Wachstum und Entwicklung von Blumenkohl. III. Vegetative Phase. *Gartenbauwissenschaft*, **37**, 455-69.

Wiebe, H.-J. (1973). Wirkung von Temperatur und Licht auf Wachstum und Entwicklung von Blumenkohl. IV. Kopfbildungsphase. *Gartenbauwissenschaft*, **38**, 263-80.

Wiebe, H.-J. (1974). Zur Bedeutung des Temperaturverlaufs und der Lichtintensitet auf den Vernalizationseffekt bei Blumenkohl. *Gartenbauwissenschaft*, **39**, 1-7.

Wiebe, H.-J. (1989). Vernalization von wichtigen Gemüsearten - Ein Überblick. *Gartenbauwissenschaft*, **54**, 97-104.

Wolf, J. (1995). *Effects of CO_2 enrichment and nitrogen, phosphorus or potassium deficiency on crop yield, dry matter partitioning, water use and nutrient use*. Report Department of Theoretical Production Ecology, Wageningen, The Netherlands.

Woodrow, I.E. (1994) Optimal acclimation of the C3 photosynthetic system under enhanced CO_2. *Photosynthesis Research*, **39**, 401-412.

Wurr, D.C.E., Fellows, J.R., Phelps, K. and Reader, R.J. (1993). Vernalization in summer/autumn cauliflower (*Brassica oleracea* var. *botrytis* L.). *Journal of Experimental Botany*, **44**, 1507-14.

Wurr, D.C.E., Fellows, J.R., and Hambidge, A.J. (1991). The influence of field environmental conditions on calabrese growth and development. *Journal of Horticultural Science*, **66**, 495-504.

Wurr, D.C.E., Fellows, J.R., Sutherland, R.A. and Elphinstone, E.D. (1990). A model of cauliflower curd growth to predict when curds reach a specific size. *Journal of Horticultural Science*, **65**, 555-64.

Zak, D.R., Pregitzer, K.S., Curtis, P.S., Teeri, J.A., Fogel, R., and Randlett, D.L. (1993). Elevated atmospheric CO_2 and feedback between carbon and nitrogen cycles. *Plant and Soil*, **151**, 105-117.

CHAPTER 5

Modelling the effects of
climate change and climatic variability
on crops at the site scale

SUMMARY

The development and application of models for a range of agricultural, horticultural and energy crops at specific sites is described. The aim was to investigate climate change impacts on crop phenology, crop yield, yield quality and agricultural risk. The interaction between a key weed species and the crops it infests is also described for present and climate change conditions.

All models were developed and calibrated for the sites of interest in Europe. Models were then validated against independent field datasets. The models were then applied to a baseline climate dataset, a series of sensitivity tests and a number of GCM climate change scenarios with concomitant changes in CO_2 concentration. In addition to changes in mean climate, the effects of changes in the variability of climate were also evaluated. Finally a number of possible farm-level adaptive strategies were examined using the models, including changes in sowing or transplanting date and changes in crop variety.

Crops modelled were cauliflower and broccoli (applied at the sites of Jokioinen, Oxford, Wageningen and München); onion (at Oxford and München); grapevine (at Bologna); willow (at Uppsala) and maize (at Sevilla). Five wheat models were applied to the sites of Rothamsted and Sevilla and a comparison of their performance was conducted. Lastly, the effects of the weed species *Avena sterilis* on wheat yields were analysed at the Spanish sites of Sevilla, Badojoz, Albacete, Lerida and Zamora.

Models of cauliflower (CauliSim) and broccoli (BroccoSim) growth and phenology have been developed and validated. The models aimed to describe variability between plants in time of curd/flower initiation and harvest. This allowed an evaluation of the effects of climate change on the variability of harvest duration, an important factor in cauliflower and broccoli production. The crop model has been restructured from an earlier version to incorporate results from experiments conducted in this project. The model calculates outputs of crop duration, length of the cutting period and fresh weight of the harvestable curd/floret. An increase in temperature caused a decrease in duration from transplanting to harvest. However, the curd/floret fresh weight was not influenced by temperature and increased only slightly. The influence of CO_2 was beneficial because higher dry matter contents diminish the risk of curds/florets becoming loose and, thus, make it possible to harvest curds and florets at higher weights. The length of the cutting period is very important in both cauliflower and broccoli production because the cost of harvesting increases with the length of this period. A short length of cut means that the crop can be machine harvested, reducing harvest costs. The equilibrium scenarios had large effects on the length of the cutting period. Both the mean length and the coefficient of variation increased in these scenarios. The effect was most pronounced with the later transplantings. The frequency of crop failure due to the quality defect bracting in cauliflower cv. Plana was low under current climatic conditions at all sites but increased dramatically in all equilibrium scenarios. These effects were much smaller in the transient scenarios. For some of the transient scenarios there was even a decline in length of the cutting period, which would be beneficial to growers. The frequency of crop failure due to bracting were, however, unacceptably high in the midsummer transplantings for most of the transient scenarios. This means that new cauliflower cultivars must be introduced to cope with this effect.

Simulation modelling of field-grown vegetable crops is not as advanced as that for the major cereal or legume crops and most models tend to be empirical production type models. The aim of the onion model development was to produce a functional response-based crop model of potential onion growth (PELonion). The model was validated using field experiments conducted in 1994 at Reading, UK and Arslev, Denmark. The large increases in temperature projected for the equilibrium scenarios decreased crop durations at all sites. The greatest reduction (of 48 and 56 days for Oxford and München respectively) was under UKLO. The shorter crop durations under the UKLO scenario resulted in a 9% and 13% reduction in bulb yields at Oxford and München respectively. However, bulb yield was greater with the UKHI scenario compared with the baseline at both sites. The lower yields expected as a result of shorter durations of crop growth were more than compensated by the increased CO_2 under UKHI but not under UKLO. Crop durations were reduced with all transient scenarios at both sites, compared with the baseline. However, the increased concentration of CO_2 predicted by the forcing scenarios was sufficient to result in greater total crop dry weight at bulbing and harvest maturity, and greater bulb yields for all scenarios at both sites compared with the baseline. The effect of changing climatic variability in the scenarios had a greater effect on bulb yields at Oxford than at München.

A simple mechanistic model has been developed to predict grapevine growth and yield using existing knowledge about the temperature and CO_2 dependence of growth and development processes (CeSIAgrape). Calibration and validation was conducted for cv. Sangiovese and cv. Cabernet Sauvignon using experimental data from field trials in the Chianti region over three seasons 1992-1994. The model simulations at Bologna showed an increase in the variability of both total and fruit biomass with all scenarios. The equilibrium scenarios caused fruit biomass to decrease, compared with the baseline and the transient scenarios showed increases for UKTR3140, GFDL2534 and GFDL5564 with emissions scenario IS92a. The UKTR6675 scenario led to a decrease with the same emissions scenario. The coefficient of variation of fruit biomass was higher under all scenarios. Under scenarios with altered climatic variability, average yield did not change substantially but the variability of production was increased. Changes in cultivar were analysed as a possible adaptive strategy. No consistent changes in average fruit production and coefficient of variation were found between the two varieties (Sangiovese and Cabernet Sauvignon). Cabernet Sauvignon showed better adaptation in terms of average production but poorer adaptation in terms of year-to-year production variability.

Willow energy forests are now recognised as providing a fuel source of considerable potential and large land areas may be taken up with energy forests in the future. An existing simulation model (SOILN-Willow) has been evaluated and preliminary sensitivity tests conducted. The model will be further developed in the future to enable application at a range of sites in Europe and for the series of climate change scenarios. Simulations of willow growth can be run over several years and with different types of management, for example, changes in harvest date, fertilization timing and defoliation. The model was used to perform sensitivity analysis, assuming optimal water and nitrogen conditions, over a 30 year period for Rothamsted, UK after successful calibration with a dataset from Uppsala, Sweden for the period 1985 to 1988. Harvest was assumed to occur every fourth winter. Results showed that an increase in mean temperature of 3°C produced an increase in mean yield (total dry matter) of 9.4 t/ha to 32.2 t/ha from the baseline mean of 22.8 t/ha. There was a reduction in the variability of yields, with the coefficient of variation decreasing from 14 to 9%. Doubling the variability of temperature caused a reduction in yield to 18 t/ha. Combining the two sensitivity tests led to a modest increase in both the mean yield and the yield variability.

A maize model (CERES) with an embedded water-balance was calibrated and validated with experimental field data from two sites that represent contrasting agroclimatic conditions in the Mediterranean region (Albacete and Sevilla). Low precipitation during the crop growing season makes irrigation a necessity. Evapotranspiration constitutes a crucial component of the hydrological balance and, hence, its accurate calculation is essential. Therefore, the calibration included an adjustment to the evapotranspiration calculation in the model. Results of crop simulations under the climate change scenarios depended on the balance between the severity of changes in climate and the physiological effects of CO_2 enrichment. Under present management practices maize yields were predicted to decrease under all scenarios at Sevilla. Yield decreases occurred as a consequence of the shortening of crop duration, especially the grain filling period, which occurs when temperatures rise. Evapotranspiration, summed over the entire period of crop growth, increased for all scenarios except UKTR6675 (with and without variability) compared with the baseline. The effect of climate change on crop evapotranspiration is mainly the result of two opposing factors: the shortening of the vegetative period and the direct effect of increased temperatures on daily evapotranspiration. A possible adaptive strategy under a warmer climate would be early sowing allowing the crop to develop during a period of the year with cooler temperatures thereby offsetting the yield losses. The yield reduction under the UKLO scenario was offset by planting the crop 30 days earlier in Sevilla. Earlier sowing dates also allowed the crop to develop during a time with lower evapotranspiration demand, which increased water use efficiency and reduced irrigation demand.

A comparison of the performance of five wheat models (AFRCWHEAT, CERES-Wheat, NWHEAT, SIRIUS and SOILN-Wheat) was carried out for two sites in Europe, Rothamsted, UK and Sevilla, Spain which have considerably different agroclimatic conditions. The models were calibrated and validated against independent field data sets from both sites. Observed time courses of crop growth, evapotranspiration and nitrogen uptake in wheat crops at Rothamsted were reproduced reasonably well by the different models, except for the time course of leaf area index. In Sevilla the experimental data set was insufficient for a detailed comparison and, thus, mainly simulated results were compared. Increases in temperature generally resulted in lower yields and increases in precipitation and atmospheric CO_2 concentration in higher yields in the model runs. The transient climate change scenarios generally resulted in considerable yield increases at Rothamsted and in nil to considerable yield increases at Sevilla. If the direct effect of increased atmospheric CO_2 was not taken into account, yield changes by climate change alone became nil or negative. The equilibrium scenarios resulted in small increases or moderate decreases in yield. Yield changes were much less positive than those calculated for the transient scenarios (with the inclusion of CO_2 direct effects). For most climate change scenarios the range of results between the simulation models did not differ widely.

Current simulations models of crop growth and development generally do not include the effects of weed competition. The final section of this chapter quantifies the effect of *Avena sterilis* on winter wheat in Spain in current and under climate change conditions. The environmental conditions required for the weed's germination and emergence were identified in laboratory experiments and a statistical model developed to simulate the response.

A model was chosen which best simulated the effects of weed density on crop grain yield for the zones considered (Sevilla, Badojoz, Albacete, Lerida and Zamora). The CERES-wheat model and the fitted statistical models were then used to calculate grain yield changes with and without weed infestation for the climate change scenarios at different sites in Spain. The crop-weed interaction produced a reduction in the grain yield under most scenarios and sites considered. The inclusion of weed competition in both equilibrium and transient scenarios resulted in a reduction of grain yield at all sites considered compared to scenario results without infestation. A relatively larger reduction in yield, up to 15%, was found at the northern sites (Lerida, Zamora), in comparison to a maximum reduction of 7% found at the central and southern sites (Sevilla, Badojoz, Albacete) under the transient scenarios.

In summary, maize at Sevilla showed the most detrimental response to climate change, showing yield losses under all scenarios. For all other crops modelled, i.e. cauliflower, broccoli, onion, grapevine and wheat, under the transient scenarios the beneficial effects of CO_2 on yield were sufficient to offset the shortening in season length due to increased temperature. However, the risk of damage due to quality defects is higher for cauliflower and broccoli and the coefficient of variation increased for fruit biomass in grapevine and bulb fresh weight in onion (particularly at München). In general yield benefits are fewer and risks to production greater at the more southerly sites, for example, water-limited wheat yields were predicted to increase more substantially at Rothamsted compared with Sevilla and yield variation was lower.

5.1 Introduction

A number of agricultural and horticultural crops have been modelled at the site-specific scale. These encompass a range of crop types: vegetable crops (cauliflower, broccoli, onion); perennial fruit crops (grapevine); energy crops (willow); and cereal crops (maize, wheat). The interaction between a key weed species (*Avena sterilis* L.) and the cereal crops which it infests have also been studied. Several modelling approaches have been developed to investigate climate change impacts on crop/weed phenology, crop yield, yield quality and agricultural risk.

The detailed mechanistic crop models have been applied at individual sites located in different agricultural and climatic zones throughout Europe (Figure 5.1.1).

Guidelines were established to provide a coherent structure to the crop modelling research. Firstly, models were either developed, if no existing model was available, or calibrated for the sites of interest in Europe. Secondly, all models were validated against independent field data sets.

Once the model was developed and validated it was applied to a series of synthetically generated weather data sets. Thirty years of daily weather sequences were generated using the LARS-WG stochastic weather generator for each crop model run (see Section 2.4 for a description and evaluation of LARS-WG). Three types of data set were generated: (i) a baseline; (ii) a series of sensitivity tests; and (iii) a number of GCM climate change scenarios.

The weather generator was calibrated against observed meteorological data for the period 1961-90 at all sites. All crop models were applied first to this baseline climate. The baseline run acted as a reference against which the impacts of the sensitivity tests and climate change scenarios were appraised. Following the baseline run, the sensitivity of each model to a range of systematic changes in mean climate was investigated (sensitivity tests). The quantification of crop model responses to independent changes in individual climatic variables as well as changes in CO_2 concentration allowed a more informed interpretation of the predicted impacts from GCM scenarios. In addition to changes in mean climate,

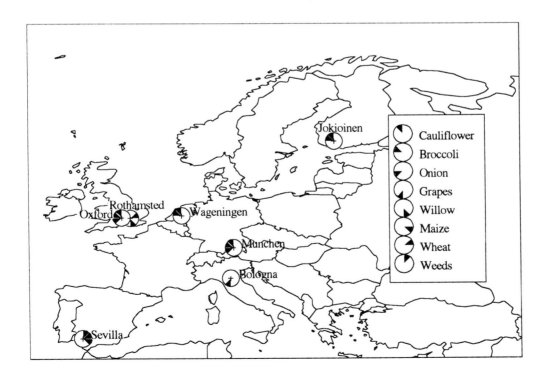

Figure 5.1.1 Sites at which the crop models have been applied.

the effects of changes in the variability of climate were evaluated. Specifically, a doubling of temperature variability and a doubling of the length of dry spells were examined.

Scenarios of future climate have been constructed for all sites (Table 5.1.1; see Section 2.4 for a detailed description). Two equilibrium (UKLO, UKHI) and two transient (UKTR, GFDL) GCM scenarios have been applied to the crop models. For each transient GCM, two model decades have been analysed (UKTR3140, UKTR6675, GFDL2534, GFDL5564). Mean changes in climate have been extracted from all the GCMs, whilst changes in climatic variability were only available for the UKHI and UKTR6675 scenarios. Appropriate concentrations of atmospheric CO_2 have been assumed for each scenario (Table 5.1.1). For the transient GCM scenarios, the model decades have been related to two IPCC greenhouse gas emissions scenarios (IS92a, IS92d).

Finally, a number of possible farm-level adaptive strategies were evaluated using the models, including changes in sowing or transplanting time and changes in crop variety.

Two aspects of the site-specific crop modelling research are particularly innovative. Firstly, uncertainties arising from different crop modelling approaches have been quantified through a comparison of five wheat models for different agroclimatic conditions in Europe in

Section 5.7. Secondly, competitive interactions between wheat and an important weed species (*Avena sterilis* L.) has been examined for current and future climates in Section 5.8.

5.2   Effects on cauliflower and broccoli

5.2.1   Background

The growth and development of cauliflower and broccoli plants are strongly influenced by environmental conditions such as temperature and radiation (Salter, 1960; Wurr *et al.*, 1990). CO_2 concentration also influences dry matter growth and hence curd/inflorescence weight (Wheeler *et al.*, 1995). These environmental conditions also determine the quality of the produce, and thus the marketable yield.

The time from transplanting to harvest can be divided into three phases: a juvenile phase, a curd/flower induction phase and a curd/floret growth phase. As shown in Section 4.2, environmental variables, especially temperature, influence growth and development differently in these growth phases. The final effect on yield and quality of the produce is obtained through integration of these nonlinear processes. Consequently the effect of climate change on cauliflower and broccoli production cannot be predicted without first quantifying the influence of such aspects of the environment on the crops.

Table 5.1.1   Details of climate change scenarios applied to the site-specific crop models.

Emissions scenario	GCM scenario	Climatic variability changed	CO_2 concentration (ppmv)
2 x CO_2	UKLO	no	560
2 x CO_2	UKHI	no	560
2 x CO_2	UKHI	yes	560
IS92a	UKTR3140	no	454
IS92a	UKTR6675	no	617
IS92a	UKTR6675	yes	617
IS92a	GFDL2534	no	454
IS92a	GFDL5564	no	617
IS92d	UKTR6675	no	545
IS92d	GFDL5564	no	545

The effect of climate change on the timing of cauliflower production has previously been studied for the UK by Wurr *et al.* (1995) and for several sites in Europe by Olesen and Grevsen (1993, 1994), who also used a model to simulate effects of climate change on yield and quality. Kenny *et al.* (1993) used a simplified model to map the agroclimatic suitability of cauliflower in Europe and possible effects of climate change.

This study expands upon and refines the previous work in several ways. The crop simulation model has been restructured to incorporate the results of the experiments described in Section 4.2, and the results of an experiment on CO_2 and temperature effects in cauliflower (Wheeler *et al.*, 1995). Broccoli is now also covered by the simulation model. Finally variability between plants in timing of development is now included in the model. This allows an evaluation of the effects of climate change on the variability of harvest duration, an important factor in cauliflower production.

5.2.2 Model development and validation

A model of cauliflower and broccoli growth and development has been developed and validated. The model consists of four linked processes: crop development, leaf area expansion, vegetative dry matter growth and curd/inflorescence growth. The model aims to describe variability between plants in time of curd/flower initiation and harvest.

5.2.2.1 *Model description*

The hourly crop developmental rate (r_d) is defined as (Grevsen and Olesen, 1994):

$$r_d = \begin{cases} f_{d1}(T) & P<1 \\ f_{d2}(T) & 1 \leq P<2 \\ f_{d3}(T) & 2 \leq P \end{cases} \quad (5.2.1)$$

where f_{d1}, f_{d2} and f_{d3} are temperature response functions for the juvenile, curd/flower induction and curd/inflorescence growth phases, respectively. *P* is the current developmental stage of the crop, ranging from 0 at transplanting to 1 at the end of juvenility, 2 at curd/flower initiation, and 3 at the end of curd/floret growth.

The aging of plants from transplanting to curd/flower initiation is described by a distributed delay procedure with *K* age classes (Manetsch, 1976). Plants move through the age classes from young to old. Separate delay procedures are used for the juvenile and the curd/flower induction phases. The model is updated using hourly steps, and the number of plants reaching curd/flower initiation is accumulated. When this number exceeds 0.2% of the total number of plants, a new cohort of curds/inflorescences is generated. The curd/inflorescence cohorts are all handled separately to simulate variability.

The expansion rate of leaf area (*L*) [m^2] per plant is described by:

$$\frac{dL}{dt} = r_l \; L(S_{ly}) \; f_{l1}(T) \; f_{l2}(\alpha) \; f_{l3}(R) \quad (5.2.2)$$

where r_l is the maximum expansion rate [day^{-1}], $L(S_{ly})$ is the area of young leaves [m^{-2}] i.e. leaves younger than a specified age (S_{ly}), $f_{l1}(T)$ is a function of daily mean temperature [0-1], $f_{l2}(a)$ is a function of the fraction of radiation intercepted by the crop canopy [0-1], and $f_{l3}(R)$ is a function of plant reserves [0-1]. The ageing of the leaf area is described by a distributed delay procedure.

Daily canopy gross assimilation (A_d) [g $CO_2 m^{-2}$ d^{-1}] is calculated by applying a Gaussian integration technique (Goudriaan, 1986). The effect of atmospheric CO_2 concentration on photosynthesis is modelled using the concepts of Goudriaan *et al.* (1985). The assimilation rate at light saturation (A_m) is a function of temperature and CO_2, i.e.:

$$A_m = A_{mr} \; \frac{C_a - \Gamma}{350 - \Gamma} \; f_A(T) \quad (5.2.3)$$

where A_{mr} is the assimilation rate at light saturation and at ambient CO_2 [g CO_2 m^{-2} d^{-1}], C_a is actual CO_2 concentration [ppmv], and $f_A(T)$ is a function dependent on daily mean temperature [0-1]. Γ is the CO_2 compensation point [ppmv].

The calculated gross assimilation is converted into a maximum amount of carbohydrates available for growth (P_g) [g CH_2O m^{-2} d^{-1}] assuming that 40% of the daily assimilation (A_d) goes to respiration (Gifford, 1995):

$$P_g = \frac{30}{44} 0.6 A_d \qquad (5.2.4)$$

The net production (P_n) [g DM m^{-2} d^{-1}] may be restricted by sink limitation (Gutierrez *et al.*, 1984):

$$P_n = D \left[1 - \exp \left(-\frac{\beta P_g}{D} \right) \right] \qquad (5.2.5)$$

where D is the demand for growth [gDM m^{-2}d^{-1}] and β is a response factor.

The demand for dry matter growth is assumed to be composed of three demands

$$D = D_s + D_c + D_r \qquad (5.2.6)$$

where D_s is the demand for growth of structural dry matter, D_c is the demand for curd/floret growth, and D_r is the demand for growth of reserves. The demand for structural growth is assumed to be proportional to the growth of leaf area, whereas demand for growth of reserves is proportional to the remaining capacity for reserve storage. The maximum rate of curd/inflorescence diameter growth is assumed to decline linearly with crop development. This growth rate determines the growth of curd/inflorescence volume, which in turn defines the demand for curd/floret dry matter growth. Growth of curd/inflorescence size is reduced if the demand cannot be met.

The assimilates available for partitioning to the various crop organs is the sum of net production plus a fraction (γ) of the reserves. Partitioning of assimilates is assumed to follow a priority scheme. The demand for structural growth and for growth of curds/florets is met first and scaled according to the supply-demand ratio. Any remaining assimilates will go to the reserves. The

broccoli florets were assumed to have a height of 17 cm at harvest.

The only quality defect currently included in the model is the occurrence of bracting in cauliflower cv. Plana. It is assumed that mean temperatures above 18°C during a period of 10 days after curd induction cause bracting (section 4.2). Climate inputs for the model are daily minimum and maximum temperature and global radiation.

5.2.2.2   *Model calibration and validation*

Model parameters were estimated primarily from results from the growth chamber experiments described in Section 4.2 and from the literature. The model parameters are shown in Table 5.2.1. A few parameters were estimated using data from tunnel experiments at Reading, UK (Wheeler *et al.*, 1995) and field experiments from Årslev, Denmark (Grevsen and Olesen, 1994). Data from Reading and Årslev were, however, mainly used for model validation.

An example of the validation is shown in Figure 5.2.1 for cauliflower with the first transplanting at Årslev in 1989. In general, very good agreement between the model results and the experimental data were obtained. There is, however, a tendency for overestimation of the total plant fresh weight. The standard deviation of the curd diameter increases with plant age up to a certain point and then decreases as the curds reach their maximum size. For some of the other transplantings agreement between simulated and observed values was less good, mainly due to problems in correctly simulating date of curd initiation. The validation of the broccoli model also showed a tendency for an overestimation of plant fresh weight.

5.2.3   Model sensitivity to systematic changes in climate

The sensitivity of the model to changes in temperature and atmospheric CO_2 concentration was examined for selected transplanting dates using 30 years of baseline climatic data from Oxford. The planting densities used were 3 plants m^{-2} in cauliflower and 5 plants m^{-2} in broccoli.

Table 5.2.1   Parameter estimates for the cauliflower and broccoli models.

Parameter	Cauliflower cv. Plana	Broccoli cv. Shogun
Development	$f_{d1}(T)=T_+/(83.3\times24)$	$f_{d1}(T)=T_+/(32.8\times24)$
	$f_{d2}(T)=(10.4-\mid T-15.5\mid)_+/(108.2\times24)$	$f_{d2}(T)=(6.9-\mid T-16.3\mid)_+/(60.2\times24)$
	$f_{d3}(T)=T_+/(917\times24)$	$f_{d3}(T)=T_+/(988\times24)$
	$K_{d1}=K_{d2}=30$	$K_{d1}=K_{d2}=30$
Leaf area	$r_l=0.164$	$r_l=0.144$
	$S_{ly}=320°Cd,\ S_l=620°Cd$	
	$f_{l1}(T)=(-0.644+0.143T-0.00311T^2)_+$	
	$f_{l2}(a)=1-a^3$	
	$f_{l3}(R)=1-(R/R_c)^2$	
	$T_{lb}=0°C,\ K_l=30,\ s_l=308\ cm^{-2}\ g$	
Light interception	$k_d=\begin{cases}0.9-3.28L+7.6L^2 & L<0.215\\ 0.55 & L\geq0.215\end{cases}$	$k_d=\begin{cases}0.83-3.73L+9.06L^2 & L<0.206\\ 0.45 & L\geq0.206\end{cases}$
Assimilation	$b=1.1$	
	$A_{mr}=5\ g\ CO_2\ m^{-2}\ h^{-1}$	
	$f_A(T)=(-0.145+0.1054T-0.00243T^2)_+$	
	$\gamma=0.1,\ d=0.08$	
	$a_r=3,\ b_r=0.15$	
Partitioning	$f_r=f_s=0.12,\ f_m=0.24,\ f_l=0.52$	
Curd/floret growth	$c_h=1.4$	$c_h=0.49\ m,\ c_b=0.27$
	$r_{cx}=0.0137\ (°Cd)^{-1}$	$r_{cx}=0.0130\ (°Cd)^{-1}$
	$a_c=0.015\ g\ cm^{-3}$	$a_c=0.01\ g\ cm^{-3}$
	$b_c=0.06\ g\ cm^{-3}$	$b_c=0.05\ g\ cm^{-3}$
	$c_c=0.9$	$c_c=0.9$

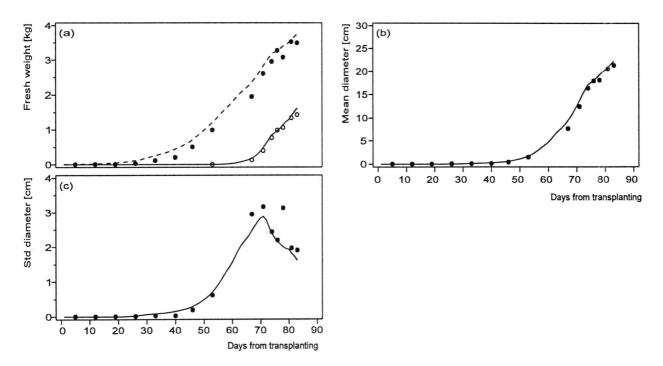

Figure 5.2.1   Measured (points) and simulated (lines) time course of cauliflower fresh weight and curd diameter for the first planting at Årslev in 1989. (a) Single plant total top fresh weight (•) and single curd fresh weight (o); (b) mean curd diameter; and (c) standard deviation of curd diameter.

The harvest criteria used was a curd diameter of 13 cm in cauliflower and a floret diameter of 12 cm in broccoli.

The simulated crop responses to changes in temperature and CO_2 are shown in Figures 5.2.2 and 5.2.3 for cauliflower and broccoli,

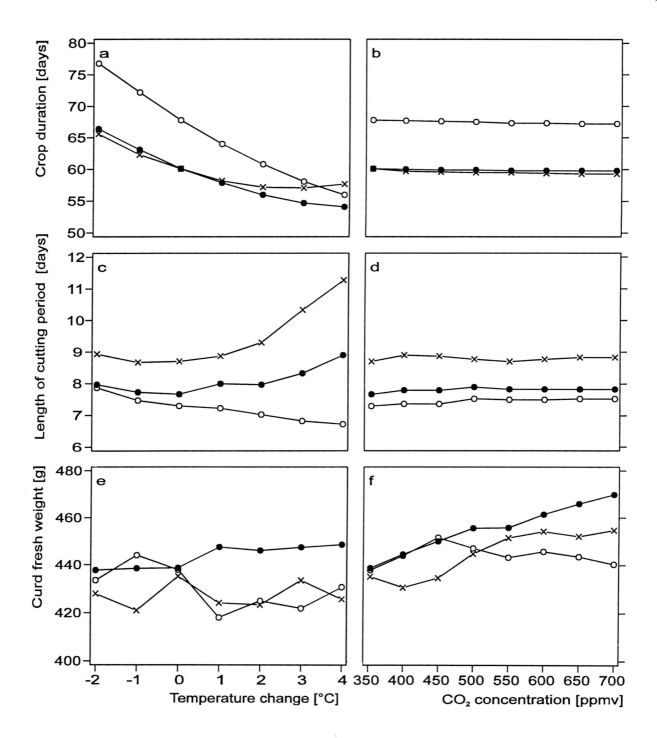

Figure 5.2.2   Simulated response of cauliflower cv. Plana to changes in temperature and CO_2 concentration at Oxford. The graphs show (a and b) mean duration from transplanting to 50% harvestable curds, (c and d) mean length of cutting period from 10% to 90% harvestable curds, and (e and f) mean curd fresh weight at 50% harvestable curds. Mean of 30 years are shown for three transplanting dates: 1 May (o—o), 1 June (•—•) and 1 July (×—×).

respectively. The crop response was quantified as time from transplanting to 50% harvestable curds/florets, as length of cutting period from 10% harvestable to 90% harvestable curds/florets, and as mean curd fresh weight at time of 50% harvestable curds/florets.

The simulated response to changes in temperature and CO_2 concentration was similar in the two crops. The duration from transplanting to harvest declined with increasing temperature. This response was largest for the May transplanting. There was little effect of temperature change on curd fresh weight.

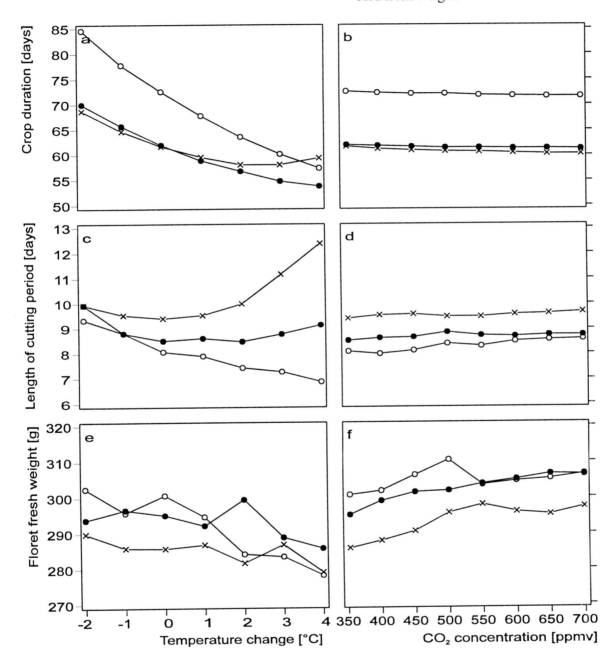

Figure 5.2.3   Simulated response of broccoli cv. Shogun to changes in temperature and CO_2 concentration at Oxford. The graphs show (a and b) mean duration from transplanting to 50% harvestable florets, (c and d) mean length of cutting period from 10% to 90% harvestable florets, and (e and f) mean floret fresh weight at 50% harvestable florets. Mean of 30 years are shown for three transplanting dates: 1 May (o—o), 1 June (•—•) and 1 July (×—×).

Similar results were found by Olesen and Grevsen (1993). There was a small increase in curd fresh weight with increasing CO_2 concentration, but no effect of CO_2 on crop duration or length of the cutting period.

Figures 5.2.2 and 5.2.3 show a large effect of temperature change on the length of the cutting period. A long cutting period is undesirable as this will increase the harvest costs. The mean length of the cutting period decreased with increasing temperature in the May transplanting, but increased dramatically in the July transplanting.

The simulated response of the frequency of severe incidents of bracting in cauliflower cv. Plana to changes in temperature is shown in Figure 5.2.4. A severe incident of bracting was considered to have occurred in a crop with more than 50% of the curds developing bracts, which implies that a large proportion of the crop will not be marketable as class 1 produce. Increasing temperature caused the number of years with crop failure due to bracting to increase markedly.

5.2.4   Application of climate change scenarios

The model was run for a number of sites and scenarios using 30 years of climatic data from each site and scenario. The selected sites were Jokioinen, Oxford, Wageningen and München. The planting densities and the harvest criteria used were as for the sensitivity study. Three different transplanting dates were used for each site and scenario: 1 May, 1 June and 1 July. The variables examined were the same as those in the sensitivity study.

Generated data from two equilibrium scenarios (UKLO, UKHI) and two transient scenarios (UKTR and GFDL) were used. For the transient scenarios two different model decades were used. For the UKTR scenario these were 31-40 and 66-75, and for GFDL 25-34 and 55-64. The scenario data were produced by a stochastic weather generator. For the UKLO and GFDL scenarios the baseline variability in temperature was retained in the scenario data, whereas for the UKHI and UKTR scenarios both the baseline

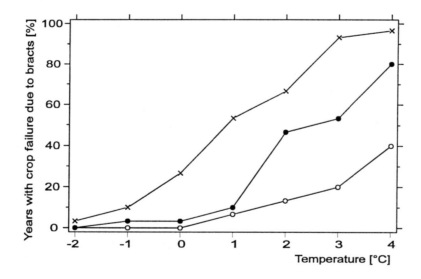

Figure 5.2.4   Simulated fraction of years with more than 50% of the cauliflower cv. Plana curds developing bracts at Oxford in response to changes in temperature. Results are shown for three transplanting dates: 1 May (o—o), 1 June (•—•) and 1 July (✕—✕).

variability and variability calculated from the GCM experiments were used. The scenarios with changed variability are denoted with a small 'v' in the scenario name, e.g. UKHIv.

The atmospheric CO_2 concentration was set to 353 ppmv for the baseline climate, and to 560 ppmv for the equilibrium GCM scenarios. The CO_2 concentration of the first transient model decade was set to 454 ppmv corresponding to the IS92a emissions scenario. For the second transient model decade two CO_2 concentrations

were used, 617 ppmv for the IS92a and 545 ppmv for the IS92d emissions scenarios. The emissions scenario is denoted with a small 'a' or 'd' in the scenario name, e.g. GFDL5564a. Details of the construction of the site-specific scenarios are given in Section 2.4.

5.2.4.1   *Equilibrium scenarios*

The simulated length of the cutting period for the baseline climate and the equilibrium scenarios is shown in Table 5.2.2 for three transplanting

Table 5.2.2   Simulated length of cutting period from 10% to 90% harvestable curds/florets in cauliflower cv. Plana and broccoli cv. Shogun for the baseline climate and equilibrium scenarios. Both the mean [days] and the coefficient of variation [%] is shown.

Transplanting date	Station	Baseline		UKLO		UKHI		UKHIv	
		Mean	c.v.	Mean	c.v.	Mean	c.v.	Mean	c.v.
Cauliflower									
1 May	Jokioinen	8.9	19	7.8	26	10.1	33	9.2	31
	Oxford	7.3	23	7.6	30	7.8	26	8.0	22
	Wageningen	7.4	16	8.4	25	7.7	22	8.3	29
	München	7.8	20	9.1	38	8.2	31	8.7	30
1 June	Jokioinen	9.3	16	11.5	39	10.2	47	9.7	26
	Oxford	7.7	19	10.5	33	8.3	22	9.5	29
	Wageningen	8.1	21	10.0	43	8.7	35	10.7	49
	München	8.7	29	12.1	40	10.8	33	10.2	43
1 July	Jokioinen	12.0	35	13.0	29	10.9	26	11.4	30
	Oxford	8.7	22	13.9	27	11.1	31	11.1	67
	Wageningen	8.2	29	10.6	32	8.8	30	10.4	47
	München	8.7	31	12.4	37	10.4	54	10.4	38
Broccoli									
1 May	Jokioinen	11.7	22	9.2	27	10.0	28	10.7	35
	Oxford	8.1	24	7.3	30	7.6	29	8.0	25
	Wageningen	8.7	22	8.8	30	8.5	26	8.9	32
	München	9.3	25	9.9	35	8.7	30	9.2	27
1 June	Jokioinen	11.2	26	12.2	42	10.6	30	11.1	47
	Oxford	8.5	20	10.7	39	8.6	23	10.1	35
	Wageningen	9.0	25	10.2	46	8.7	34	11.8	57
	München	9.6	26	12.5	60	8.7	37	10.1	41
1 July	Jokioinen	14.6	34	14.9	42	12.8	31	12.4	30
	Oxford	9.4	30	15.5	30	12.1	40	12.0	71
	Wageningen	9.1	31	11.0	29	9.0	40	12.3	60
	München	9.7	32	13.1	41	11.0	54	11.1	42

dates. The length of cut is generally slightly higher for broccoli cv. Shogun compared to cauliflower cv. Plana, and the coefficient of variation is also slightly higher for broccoli.

Under current climatic conditions the length of cut was longest at Jokioinen and shortest at Oxford or Wageningen. The length of cut increased with later transplanting. The coefficient of variation remained about the same at all sites and transplanting dates under current conditions.

The equilibrium scenarios had large effects on the length of cut. In general, both the mean length and the coefficient of variation increased in the equilibrium scenarios. The effect was most pronounced for the later transplantings. The large coefficients of variation may be due to only a few years giving very long cutting periods as illustrated in Figure 5.2.5. This graph shows the cumulative distribution function for length of cut in cauliflower in the July transplanting at Oxford for the various scenarios. The baseline climate had the lowest coefficient of variation which is clearly seen as a steep line in the graph. The

UKHI scenario without changes in the variability of temperature had the same mean length of cut as the UKHI scenario including changes in variability. The distribution function was, however, considerably different between these two scenarios. The inclusion of a change in temperature variability caused a much larger spread in the length of cut. This occurred for most of the stations in the June and July transplantings.

The frequency of crop failure due to bracting in cauliflower is shown in Table 5.2.3. Under current climate there was no severe incidence of bracts in the early transplanting. For the June and July transplantings the risk of crop failure was larger, especially at München and Oxford. All equilibrium scenarios caused a dramatic increase in risk of crop failure due to bracting, and it will not be possible to grow this cultivar in the midsummer at any station.

5.2.4.2   *Transient scenarios*

The simulated crop duration, length of cut and curd/floret fresh weight for the different transient

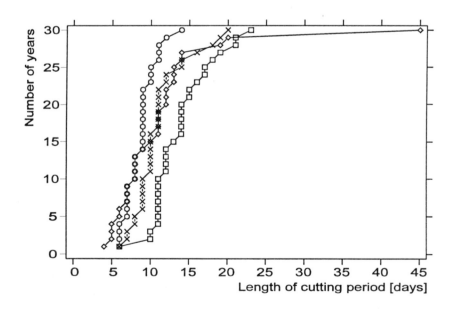

Figure 5.2.5   Simulated number of years with a length of cutting period less than a specified number of days. Results are from a transplanting of cauliflower cv. Plana on 1 July at Oxford with four scenarios: baseline (o——o), UKLO (□——□), UKHI (×——×) and UKHIv (◇——◇).

scenarios are shown in Tables 5.2.4 and 5.2.5 for cauliflower and broccoli, respectively. The results are only presented for the stations Jokioinen, Oxford and München for a June transplanting.

The crop duration declined in all transient scenarios when compared to the baseline climate. The decline was largest in the second transient model decade. The inclusion of temperature variability in the UKTR scenario reduced the decline in crop duration.

The mean length of the cutting period did not change markedly in the transient scenarios. There was, however, a tendency for a reduction in length of cut in the first model decade followed

by an increase in the second decade. This effect was most pronounced for the UKTR scenarios, whereas some of the smallest lengths of cut were actually obtained in the second model decade of the GFDL scenario. The coefficient of variation of length of cut remained about the same in the GFDL scenarios, but increased in the UKTR scenarios, especially when the variability was changed.

There was only a small increase in curd/floret fresh weight in the scenarios compared with the baseline conditions. The effect of changed CO_2 concentration on curd fresh weight was also marginal, as can be seen by comparing scenarios UKTRa and UKTRd.

Table 5.2.3 Simulated fraction of years [%] with more than 50% curds with bracts in cauliflower cv. Plana for the baseline climate and all climate change scenarios.

Transplanting date	Scenario	Jokioinen	Oxford	Wageningen	München
1 May	Baseline	0	0	0	0
	UKLO	40	67	63	57
	UKHI	60	33	33	33
	UKHIv	50	33	30	47
	UKTR 3140a	17	7	7	3
	UKTR 6675a	3	7	0	7
	UKTR 6675av	0	7	3	7
	GFDL 2534a	3	3	0	3
	GFDL 5564a	13	7	0	17
1 June	Baseline	7	3	13	27
	UKLO	90	93	90	100
	UKHI	53	57	63	97
	UKHIv	63	83	57	80
	UKTR 3140a	20	10	27	50
	UKTR 6675a	33	37	33	83
	UKTR 6675av	40	40	37	60
	GFDL 2534a	13	3	17	33
	GFDL 5564a	33	17	40	73
1 July	Baseline	7	27	10	33
	UKLO	97	100	87	93
	UKHI	70	97	80	80
	UKHIv	70	80	73	77
	UKTR 3140a	17	50	47	50
	UKTR 6675a	30	83	63	57
	UKTR 6675av	43	60	57	67
	GFDL 2534a	7	33	17	50
	GFDL 5564a	20	73	73	63

The frequency of crop failure due to bracting increased in most scenarios (Table 5.2.3). The increase was largest in the later transplantings, and the GFDL scenarios generally gave slightly higher frequencies of crop failure than the UKTR scenarios. There was no consistent effect of inclusion of variability in the UKTR model on risk of crop failure due to bracting.

5.2.5   Discussion and conclusions

The simulated effects of climate change on crop duration and harvestable fresh weight in cauliflower and broccoli are consistent with the results reported by Olesen and Grevsen (1993) and Wurr *et al.* (1995). An increase in temperature caused a decrease in duration from

Table 5.2.4   Simulated duration from transplanting to 50% harvestable curds, length of cutting period from 10% to 90% harvestable curds, and mean curd fresh weight at 50% harvestable curds. The results were simulated for cauliflower cv. Plana for the baseline climate and the transient scenarios at Jokioinen, Oxford and München with a transplanting date of 1 June. Both the mean and the coefficient of variation [%] is shown.

Station	Scenario	Crop duration [days]		Length of cut [days]		Curd fresh weight [g]	
		Mean	c.v.	Mean	c.v.	Mean	c.v.
Jokioinen	Baseline	66	6.0	9.3	16	440	7.5
	UKTR 3140a	63	5.1	8.9	20	453	8.7
	UKTR 6675a	60	4.5	8.7	22	457	11.7
	UKTR 6675av	62	6.8	9.4	38	470	12.6
	GFDL 2534a	64	5.4	9.1	19	452	9.1
	GFDL 5564a	60	4.7	9.2	21	469	12.2
	UKTR 6675d	60	4.5	8.6	23	451	11.6
	UKTR 6675dv	62	6.8	9.4	39	464	12.6
	GFDL 5564d	60	4.7	9.2	21	464	12.1
Oxford	Baseline	60	3.9	7.7	19	439	9.8
	UKTR 3140a	58	3.6	8.2	20	460	9.1
	UKTR 6675a	56	3.4	7.8	20	471	9.2
	UKTR 6675av	57	6.7	8.7	28	464	9.1
	GFDL 2534a	59	3.7	7.6	20	440	9.1
	GFDL 5564a	56	3.1	7.5	18	467	11.4
	UKTR 6675d	56	3.4	7.8	20	465	8.9
	UKTR 6675dv	57	6.7	8.7	27	455	9.2
	GFDL 5564d	56	3.3	7.4	21	465	10.5
München	Baseline	68	5.3	7.4	16	441	8.0
	UKTR 3140a	65	5.4	7.3	25	453	6.7
	UKTR 6675a	63	5.2	7.1	18	463	7.1
	UKTR 6675av	65	4.6	8.7	30	463	8.9
	GFDL 2534a	67	5.4	7.6	34	443	7.1
	GFDL 5564a	63	5.0	7.0	18	449	8.4
	UKTR 6675d	63	5.2	7.1	35	460	7.1
	UKTR 6675dv	65	4.6	8.7	22	461	9.4
	GFDL 5564d	63	4.9	7.0	18	451	8.7

transplanting to harvest. This effect was strongest for spring transplantings, whereas transplantings in midsummer only showed a small response to temperature.

The curd/floret fresh weight was not influenced by temperature and increased only slightly with increasing CO_2 concentration. Similar results were found by Wheeler *et al.* (1995) who observed that the main effect of increasing CO_2 was an increase in the curd dry matter content.

The harvest criterion used in this study was based on a fixed diameter of the curd or floret. In practise the harvest, especially in broccoli, is carried out just prior to the time when the curds/florets become too loose. This is probably also influenced by CO_2 concentration such that increasing CO_2 concentration and consequently higher dry matter contents will diminish the risk of looseness, and thus make it possible to harvest curds and florets at higher diameters and higher weights.

Table 5.2.5 Simulated duration from transplanting to 50% harvestable florets, length of cutting period from 10% to 90% harvestable florets, and mean floret fresh weight at 50% harvestable florets. The results were simulated for broccoli cv. Shogun for the baseline climate and the transient scenarios at Jokioinen, Oxford and München with a transplanting date of 1 June. Both the mean and the coefficient of variation [%] is shown.

Station	Scenario	Crop duration [days]		Length of cut [days]		Floret fresh weight [g]	
		Mean	c.v.	Mean	c.v.	Mean	c.v.
Jokioinen	Baseline	70	8.4	11.2	26	301	5.4
	UKTR 3140a	66	7.0	10.3	24	306	5.9
	UKTR 6675a	63	6.9	10.2	27	305	4.8
	UKTR 6675av	65	9.5	10.7	39	316	7.8
	GFDL 2534a	68	7.6	11.0	26	299	5.5
	GFDL 5564a	62	6.6	10.3	27	309	5.1
	UKTR 6675d	63	6.9	10.2	26	302	5.1
	UKTR 6675dv	65	9.5	10.7	39	313	8.0
	GFDL 5564d	62	6.6	10.2	26	306	5.1
Oxford	Baseline	62	5.5	8.5	20	295	5.9
	UKTR 3140a	59	5.0	8.8	25	301	7.2
	UKTR 6675a	56	4.7	8.4	23	310	7.5
	UKTR 6675av	58	7.8	9.8	31	304	7.7
	GFDL 2534a	61	5.0	8.3	22	294	6.7
	GFDL 5564a	57	4.7	8.2	24	304	6.5
	UKTR 6675d	56	4.7	8.5	23	309	6.8
	UKTR 6675dv	58	7.8	10.0	30	299	8.1
	GFDL 5564d	57	4.7	8.2	23	300	6.5
München	Baseline	63	7.0	9.0	25	290	6.1
	UKTR 3140a	59	6.5	8.3	27	294	6.1
	UKTR 6675a	57	6.5	8.1	26	302	7.0
	UKTR 6675av	58	9.5	9.8	47	300	7.2
	GFDL 2534a	62	6.6	8.4	24	291	6.2
	GFDL 5564a	55	6.1	7.5	28	295	7.1
	UKTR 6675d	57	6.5	8.1	25	300	6.8
	UKTR 6675dv	58	9.3	9.8	48	301	6.5
	GFDL 5564d	55	6.3	7.4	27	293	6.5

The length of the cutting period is very important in both cauliflower and broccoli production. A long cutting period means that only a small fraction of the plants can be harvested each time and the costs of harvesting will increase markedly. If the length of cut is very short then machine harvest can be used, which will reduce harvest costs even further.

The transient scenarios do not cause large changes in the length of the cutting period, and for some of the transient scenarios there is even a reduction in the length of cut, which will be beneficial for growers. The length of the cutting period and the coeffient of variation increased dramatically in the equilibrium scenarios. This effect occured at all stations and transplanting times and indicates that these climates are generally more unfavourable for producing cauliflower and broccoli.

The risk of crop failure due to bracts in the cauliflower cultivar Plana was simulated. The midsummer transplantings had a significant risk of crop failure from bracting even under current climatic conditions, and this risk increased considerably in all scenarios. This cultivar thus appears to be very finely tuned to current northern European climatic conditions, and it will be unsuitable under warmer climatic conditions. This is consistent with the conclusion by Olesen and Grevsen (1994) that the main detrimental effects of climate change on cauliflower production are caused by the effects of temperature on product quality, although they estimated the problems to occur at higher increases in temperature than observed in this study. The risk of bracting can probably be reduced by breeding for new cultivars, as there is a genetic variation in the occurence of this quality defect (Crisp *et al.*, 1975). Other quality defects are also important and are affected by changes in temperature, but these have not been included in this study because of lack of knowledge and data.

5.3   Effects on onion

5.3.1   Background

Differences in temperature and CO_2 concentration affect the growth and development of onion (*Allium cepa* L.). The rate of progress to

bulbing in onion (the reciprocal of time to bulbing) is increased by warmer temperatures and by longer photoperiods (Brewster, 1990). In the Reading tunnel experiment, a temperature gradient of around 5°C resulted in a difference in time to maturity of 70 to 75 days in two cultivars of onion (Section 4.3). Such a response of developmental duration is similar to that reported in previous studies on onion (e.g., Steer, 1980; Terabun, 1981). A 1°C rise in temperature reduced the total dry weight of mature plants by 4 to 14%. In contrast, elevated CO_2 increased total dry weights along the temperature gradient by 19 to 38% and bulb yields by 21 to 47% in the two onion cultivars (Section 4.3). The increased yield observed for onion at elevated CO_2 is greater than the average crop response typically observed (Kimball, 1983) but is not dissimilar to studies on root crops (Poorter, 1993; Clough *et al.*, 1981). Thus, the enhanced response of onion compared with grain crops may be because the harvestable fraction in onion is a relatively large sink.

The results of crop experiments can often be summarised in crop simulation models. Such models may then be run for a number of years using historical or artificial meteorological records at one or more sites and the possible impacts of future climates examined. Simulation modelling of field-grown vegetable crops is not as advanced as that for the major cereal and legume crops, nor to a lesser extent as that for glasshouse vegetable crops, for which many models have been developed. Most models of field-grown vegetable crops tend to be empirical production-type models (e.g., Wurr *et al.*, 1990; 1992). Such models do not include the effects of CO_2 concentration and are unlikely to simulate accurately crop production in future climates. Our aim in this study was to develop a functional response-based crop model of potential (i.e. neither water- or nutrient- limited) onion growth in parallel with field experiments at current and elevated CO_2 concentrations. This model was then validated and used to examine the impact of future climate scenarios on potential onion production at two sites in northern Europe.

5.3.2 Model development and validation

5.3.2.1 *Description of the model*

The model is of a functional type consisting of semi-empirical functions in which crop dry matter accumulation is determined by the response of crop growth to the environment within the constraints of the crop development processes. Model processes were initially calibrated using experiments reported in the literature, small experiments done in controlled environments at Reading and the Reading field tunnel experiment (Section 4.3). The model is divided into nine inter-connected sub-models (Figure 5.3.1a).

Meteorological functions

Standard meteorological data are processed to provide daily estimates of mean temperature and photosynthetically active radiation (PAR). Photoperiod was calculated as a function of day of year and latitude.

Development

The rate of seedling emergence was modelled as a function of temperature (Wheeler and Ellis, 1992). After seedling emergence, two developmental processes run concurrently: progress towards bulb formation and progress towards flowering. These two processes are modelled separately (Figure 5.3.1b). The rate of progress to bulbing is promoted by long days and warmer temperatures in temperate onion varieties (Brewster, 1990). Hence, the rate of bulb development was modelled using a photothermal-type approach for a long day flowering response (i.e. Roberts and Summerfield, 1987), calibrated using the data of Brewster (presented in Visser, 1994). The rate of subsequent progress to bulb maturity is assumed to be solely a function of temperature. The ratio of progress towards bulbing on any day to the final photothermal requirement for bulbing is used as a measure of plant "age" to modify processes in other sub-models. Progress to flowering is modelled as a temperature-sensitive juvenile phase, followed by

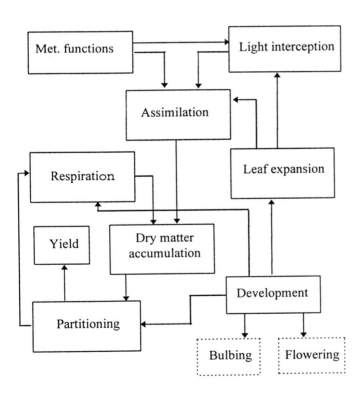

Figure 5.3.1a Diagram of the sub-models of the onion crop model and the connections between these sub-models.

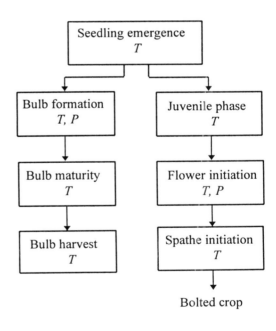

Bolted crop

Figure 5.3.1b Diagram of the phases within the development sub-model of the onion crop model. *T* and *P* denote temperature and photoperiod and indicate that progress through the phase is driven by that variable.

a photothermal-sensitive flower initiation phase, and then by a temperature-sensitive spathe initiation phase (calibrated using data of Brewster, 1983). If spathe initiation occurs before bulb maturity, then the crop is classified as having flowered and is not suitable for harvest. Otherwise, the time of bulb maturity determines the bulb harvest date.

Leaf appearance and expansion

The rate of leaf appearance is modelled as a simple function of temperature; the phyllochron interval in a field trial at Reading in 1994 was 131°C d above 0°C. The rate and duration of leaf area expansion, and of leaf senescence, are functions of both temperature and plant "age". Canopy establishment and growth are not determined by current assimilate supply (as in the SUCROS-87 type models (Spitters *et al.*, 1989)), and thus specific leaf area of a crop can be used as a sensitivity test of the balance between assimilatory processes and canopy growth as predicted by the model.

Light interception

The amount of PAR intercepted by the crop canopy is calculated in accordance with the Monsi-Saeki equation (Monsi and Saeki, 1953) using a value of the light extinction coefficient determined in the field experiments (Section 4.3). Since the onion leaf is a cylindrical shape, the canopy is divided into areas receiving full sunlight, shaded areas and lower surfaces.

Assimilation

The leaf model of gross photosynthesis developed by Acock (1991) and Charles-Edwards *et al.* (1986) was used to calculate the amount of CO_2 fixed per day. This photosynthesis model combines the two hyperbolic relationships between gross photosynthesis and each of irradiance and CO_2 into a single function. The effect of CO_2 concentration on the rate of photorespiration is also incorporated. It was necessary to add a dependence of leaf conductance to CO_2 on the current CO_2 concentration in order to avoid too large a stimulation of gross photosynthesis to elevated CO_2 (as suggested by Acock (1991)). Total canopy gross photosynthesis is calculated as the sum of assimilation by full sunlight, shaded and lower leaf fractions of the crop canopy.

Dry matter accumulation and respiration

Plant respiration is divided into growth respiration (modelled as a function of the chemical composition of current assimilates in each plant part (Penning de Vries and van Laar, 1982)) and maintenance respiration (modelled as a function of temperature (Hansen *et al.*, 1990)) per unit mass. Daily estimates of total respiration were then subtracted from those of daily gross dry matter accumulation.

Partitioning

Dry matter accumulated daily is divided among root (8% of daily dry matter), pseudostem (42%) and leaf (50%) fractions before bulbing, and root (2%), pseudostem (25%) and bulb (73%) fractions after bulbing. Dry matter is also relocated from senescing leaves (3% per day), and from the pseudostem (3%), to the bulb during bulb growth.

Yield

Dry weight yields are converted to fresh weight yields using the dry matter content of the bulbs determined in the field experiment (Section 4.3).

5.3.2.2   *Model validation*

Two field crops were grown in 1994 to provide independent data sets; one at Reading, UK, and one at Årslev, Denmark. At Reading (51°N), onion cv. Sito and Hysam were sown on 3 March 1994 at a density of 64 plants m^{-2}. Three sub-plots of each variety were harvested at bulbing (when the ratio of bulb to pseudostem diameter was 2:1) and three at bulb maturity (when the foliage of 80% of the plants had fallen over, or when 30% of plants had flowered). Fresh weights of all the green leaves, senesced leaves, pseudostems, bulbs and roots in each plot were determined immediately and the diameter of individuals bulbs measured. Any flowering plants in harvested plots at bulb maturity were counted but excluded from the growth analysis. The dry weights of each sample were determined after oven-drying at 80°C for 96 h. Also, the number of leaves on each plant at bulbing were counted and the total leaf area measured using a video-based leaf area machine.

The model was run with the meteorological data for the Reading field trial with most of the model parameters unaltered except for some parameters in the leaf and assimilation sub-models which were calibrated with these data. The model output and field data for the most important aspects of onion growth, development and yield are shown in Table 5.3.1. The development of the Reading crop was closely predicted by the model; the time of bulbing and harvest maturity were only 2 days earlier and 6 days later, respectively, than the field observations. Crop dry weight was overestimated at bulbing despite the leaf area index prediction exactly matching observations. Therefore, specific leaf area at bulbing was underestimated by the model. Both total dry weight and bulb yield at harvest maturity were predicted closely by the model (Table 5.3.1).

At Årslev (55°N), the same two cultivars were sown on 26 April 1994 at a density of about 50 plants m^{-2}. Two samples each of ten plants of each variety were harvested at bulbing and two areas of 19 m^2 harvested at bulb maturity (using the same harvesting criteria as at Reading). Leaf area and above-ground dry weight were measured at bulbing and the fresh weight of the bulbs was measured at bulb maturity. The values of all model parameters were the same as the previous simulation for Reading. Both the model output and field data are shown in Table 5.3.2. Unlike at Reading, the crop development predicted by the model did not compare well with field observations; the time of bulbing and harvest maturity were later than the model prediction. Leaf area index at bulbing was not greatly different in the model output compared with field data. The shorter durations predicted by the model contributed to the smaller crop weights at bulbing and harvest maturity predicted from the model compared with those observed; a 38% difference (14.7 t ha^{-1}) in final bulb yield resulted (Table 5.3.2).

Table 5.3.1 Model output and field observations for onion cv. Hysam sown at Reading, UK in 1994 on day of year (DOY) 62. n.d indicates not determined.

Crop parameter	Field observation	Model output	Difference (%)
Time of seedling emergence (DOY)	n.d.	89	-
Time of bulbing (DOY)	185	183	-1
Total dry weight at bulbing (g m^{-2})	382	460	+20
Leaf area index at bulbing	2.4	2.4	0
Specific leaf area at bulbing (m^2 g^{-1} x 10^{-3})	18.3	11.3	-38
Time of bulb maturity (DOY)	229	235	-3
Total dry weight at bulb maturity (g m^{-2})	851	873	+3
Bulb yield at bulb maturity (FW, t ha^{-1})	50.3	50.2	-0.2

Table 5.3.2 Model output and field observations for onion cv. Hysam sown at Årslev, Denmark in 1994 on day of year (DOY) 116. n.d indicates not determined.

Crop parameter	Field observation	Model output	Difference (%)
Time of seedling emergence (DOY)	134	133	+ 0.7
Time of bulbing (DOY)	200	184	+ 8
Total dry weight at bulbing (g m^{-2})	163	119	- 27
Leaf area index at bulbing	0.9	1.3	- 44
Specific leaf area at bulbing (m^2 g^{-1} x 10^{-3})	n.d.	25.3	-
Time of bulb maturity (DOY)	258	234	-9
Total dry weight at bulb maturity (g m^{-2})	n.d.	399	-
Bulb yield at bulb maturity (FW, t ha^{-1})	38.4	23.7	-38

The effect of environment on the balance within the development sub-model between the rate of progress to bulbing and the rate of progress to flowering was tested using observations from the tunnel experiment at Reading in 1994 (Section 4.3). At some of the cooler temperatures in that study the crops flowered before forming a bulb. The model was run for the 24 plots of cv. Hysam and cv. Sito and the predicted time of bulb maturity and spathe initiation recorded. The flowering functions correctly forecasted which plots flowered (i.e. spathe initiation was predicted to occur before bulb maturity) in the cooler plots, but some plots in which flowering was not observed were also predicted to flower (Figure 5.3.2), particularly for cv. Hysam. Nevertheless, model calibration was as good as the variation in crop responses within the tunnels and published quantitative data allowed.

5.3.3   Model sensitivity to systematic changes in climate

The effect of systematic changes in daily mean temperature and CO_2 concentration on model output was examined at Reading and Årslev using the 1994 season as the baseline climate. An increase in temperature shortened the time from sowing to seedling emergence, seedling emergence to bulbing and from seedling emergence to bulb maturity at both sites (Figure 5.3.3 a-c). At temperatures $2^{\circ}C$ cooler than the baseline, the crops at both Reading and Årslev were predicted to flower rather than form harvestable bulbs (Figure 5.3.3c). Consequently, further results for these $-2^{\circ}C$ sowings were omitted from the remaining graphs. Total dry weight at bulbing increased at warmer temperatures at Reading despite the shorter

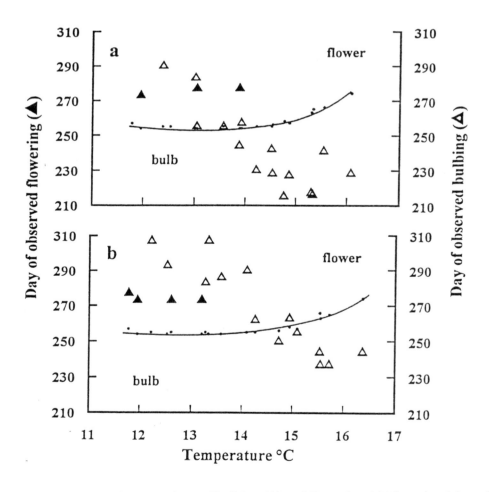

Figure 5.3.2   Comparisons of observations of bulbing (Δ) and flowering ($\blacktriangle$) in onion (a) cv. Sito and (b) cv. Hysam grown at different mean temperatures (Section 4.3) with predictions of spathe initiation from the development sub-model of the onion crop model (Figure 5.3.1b). Observations above and below the line shown are predicted to flower and bulb, respectively.

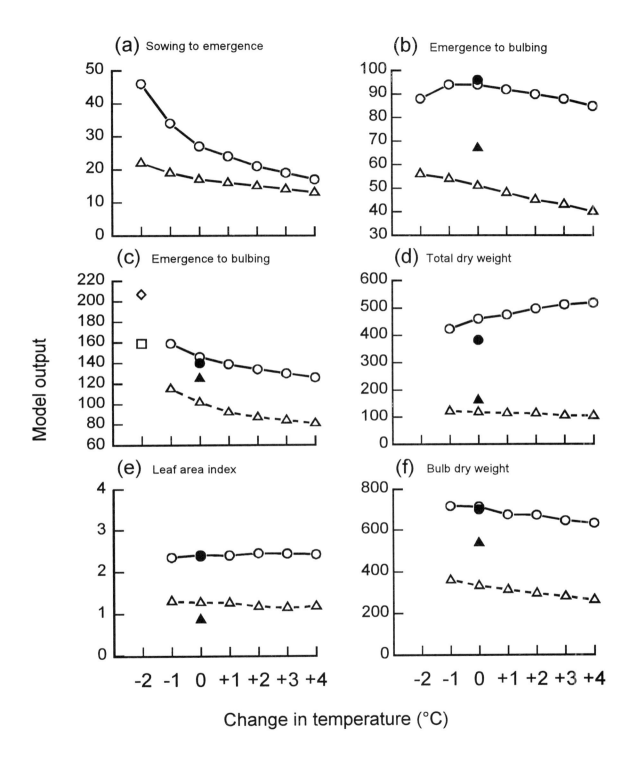

Figure 5.3.3 Sensitivity to systematic changes in mean temperature at Reading (O) and Årslev (Δ) of: (a) time from sowing to seedling emergence (days); (b) time from seedling emergence to bulbing (days); (c) time from emergence to bulb maturity (days); (d) total crop dry weight at bulbing (g m^{-2}); (e) leaf area index at bulbing; (f) bulb dry weight at bulb maturity (g m^{-2}). Some plots in (c) were predicted to flower before bulb maturity (◊,□). Data from field trials at these locations, where available, are also shown (●,▲).

duration of growth before bulbing (Figure 5.3.3d). At these temperatures the benefit of more rapid canopy establishment overcame the effects of the shorter duration on radiation interception. A different trend was observed at Årslev where total dry weight at bulbing declined slightly as temperature increased (Figure 5.3.3d). Leaf area index was relatively insensitive to differences in temperature (Figure 5.3.3e). Equally, no significant effect of temperature on leaf area index at bulbing was detected on the onion crops grown in the tunnels (Section 4.3, Table 5.3.1). At harvest maturity, an increase in temperature resulted in a progressive decline in bulb dry weight at both Reading and Årslev (Figure 5.3.3f), probably largely as a result of the shorter crop durations at these warmer temperatures.

Increase in CO_2 concentration from 355 to 700 ppmv progressively increased bulb dry weight at harvest maturity (Figure 5.3.4). To compare the magnitude of this increase in yield to the tunnel experiment at Reading (Section 4.3) the ratio of bulb dry weight at 560 ppmv to that at 355 ppmv was calculated for both model output at Reading and the experimental observations. This ratio was 1.3 - 1.41 in the experiment (depending on the temperature) compared with 1.22 from the model output.

5.3.4   Application of the climate change scenarios

The effects of climate change scenarios on potential onion production was studied at two northern European sites: Oxford, UK and München, Germany. The sowing date for each site was selected using the same criteria as in the broadscale onion modelling (Section 6.5.3). That is, the date of sowing was the first day of the year when mean air temperature reaches $6^{\circ}C$. Based on this criterion, sowing took place on DOY 85 and 92 at Oxford and München, respectively.

Generated data from two equilibrium scenarios (UKLO, UKHI) and two transient scenarios (UKTR and GFDL) were used. For the transient scenarios two different model decades were used. For the UKTR scenario these were 31-40 and 66-75, and for GFDL 25-34 and 55-64. The scenario data were produced by a stochastic weather generator. For the UKLO and GFDL scenarios the baseline variability in temperature was retained in the scenario data, whereas for the UKHI and UKTR scenarios both the baseline variability and variability calculated from the GCM experiments were used. The scenarios with changed variability are denoted with a small 'v' in the scenario name, e.g. UKHIv.

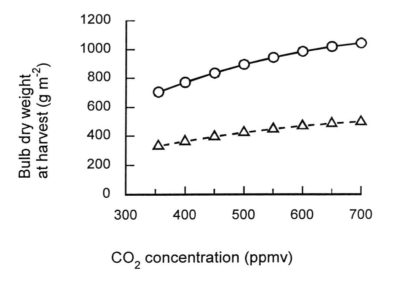

Figure 5.3.4   Sensitivity of onion (cv. Hysam) bulb dry weight at bulb maturity to systematic changes in CO_2 concentration at Reading (O) and Årslev (Δ).

The atmospheric CO_2 concentration was set to 353 ppmv for the baseline climate, and to 560 ppmv for the equilibrium GCM scenarios. The CO_2 concentration of the first transient model decade was set to 454 ppmv corresponding to the IS92a emissions scenario. For the second transient model decade two CO_2 concentrations were used, 617 ppmv for the IS92a and 545 ppmv for the IS92d emissions scenarios. The emissions scenario is denoted with a small 'a' or 'd' in the scenario name, e.g. GFDL5564a. Details of the construction of the site-specific scenarios are given in Section 2.4.

The mean duration from sowing to harvest maturity for the 30 years' baseline climate at Oxford was 162 days (Table 5.3.3), which was only 5 days shorter than the same duration observed, from an earlier sowing, in the field experiment at Reading (Table 5.3.1). Mean bulb yield at Oxford was 20% less than at Reading (Tables 5.3.1, 5.3.3). The mean duration from sowing to harvest maturity and bulb yield for the baseline climate at München were similar to those at Oxford (Table 5.3.3, 5.3.4). However, the variability about these means was greater at München than at Oxford; the coefficient of variation of the time from sowing to maturity was 7.6% at München compared with 4.5% at Oxford, and for bulb yield was 9.9% and 12.7% at Oxford and München, respectively (Table 5.3.3, 5.3.4).

5.3.4.1 *Equilibrium scenarios*

The large increase in temperature compared with the baseline climate in both equilibrium scenarios decreased crop durations at both sites (Tables 5.3.3, 5.3.4; Figures 5.3.5, 5.3.6, scenarios 1-4). The greatest reduction (of 48 and 56 days for Oxford and München, respectively) in the mean time from sowing to harvest maturity was for the UKLO scenario (Figures 5.3.5, 5.3.6) and was associated with the larger temperature changes predicted in this scenario compared with UKHI. The change in variability of this duration for both equilibrium scenarios was greater at München than at Oxford (Figures 5.3.5, 5.3.6). Changing the variability of climate in the UKHI scenario did not affect the mean crop duration but increased the coefficient of variation at both sites (Figures 5.3.5, 5.3.6).

The shorter crop durations with the UKLO scenario resulted in a 9% and 13% reduction in bulb yields at Oxford and München, respectively (Tables 5.3.3, 5.3.4). However, bulb yield was greater with the UKHI scenario compared with the baseline climate at both sites (Figure 5.3.5, 5.3.6). Thus, the lower yields expected as a result of shorter durations of crop growth in both equilibrium scenarios were more than compensated for by the increased CO_2 concentration in the UKHI, but not the UKLO, scenario.

5.3.4.2 *Transient scenarios*

Crop durations (from sowing to bulbing and from sowing to harvest maturity) were reduced with all eight transient scenarios compared with the baseline climate at both sites (Tables 5.3.3, 5.3.4; Figures 5.3.5, 5.3.6) due to warmer temperatures. However, the increased concentration of CO_2 predicted using these scenarios was sufficient to result in greater total crop dry weight at bulbing and harvest maturity, and greater bulb yields for all scenarios at both sites compared with the baseline yields (Tables 5.3.3, 5.3.4; Figures 5.3.5, 5.3.6).

Comparison of UKTR6675 (scenarios 6 and 10, Tables 5.3.4, 5.3.5) and GFDL5564 (scenarios 9 and 12, Tables 5.3.4, 5.3.5) permit the effects of different GCMs with the same global temperature change to be studied. With the IS92a emissions scenario, mean bulb yield was predicted to be 23% and 32% greater with the UKTR and GFDL GCM (scenarios 6 and 9, Table 5.3.3), respectively than the baseline climate at Oxford. However, the highest change in bulb yield at München was predicted with the UKTR (+13%) rather than the GFDL (+11%) scenario (scenarios 6 and 9, Table 5.3.4). Similarly, when the IS92d emissions scenario was used (scenarios 12 and 10, respectively, Tables 5.3.3, 5.3.4) the increase in bulb yield with the GFDL5564 GCM was only greater than that with the UKTR6675 scenario at München. Regardless of the emissons scenario, variability of mean bulb yields decreased at Oxford in the transient scenario compared with the baseline climate (scenarios 6, 10 and 9, 12, Figure 5.3.5), but increased at München (scenarios 6, 10 and 9, 12, Figure 5.3.6).

Table 5.3.3   Mean and coefficient of variation (cv) for several outputs of 30 year model runs with climate scenarios for onion crops (cv. Hysam) sown at Oxford on DOY 85.

Scenario	Sowing to bulbing (days)		Sowing to harvest (days)		Total dry weight at bulbing (g m^{-2})		Total dry weight at harvest (g m^{-2})		Bulb fresh weight at harvest (t ha^{-1})	
	mean	cv (%)	mean	cv (%)	mean	cv (%)	mean	cv (%)	mean	cv (%)
1. Baseline	97	3.6	162	4.5	257	13.4	654	9.8	40.1	9.9
2. UKLO	72	3.5	114	2.6	300	11.8	660	10.6	36.6	11.0
3. UKHI	79	4.0	127	2.8	354	12.7	811	7.8	46.5	7.9
4. UKHIv	79	4.9	128	3.4	330	18.1	754	11.7	43.5	11.8
5. UKTR 3140a	92	3.7	149	3.5	299	12.2	747	8.1	44.7	8.3
6. UKTR 66-75a	90	3.7	141	2.9	345	12.8	843	7.9	49.2	7.9
7. UKTR 6675av	90	4.9	141	4.4	332	16.2	785	12.9	45.7	14.2
8. GFDL 2534a	95	3.7	155	3.8	311	11.5	768	8.0	46.3	8.2
9. GFDL 5564a	90	3.8	143	3.3	375	11.6	900	6.9	52.9	7.1
10. UKTR 6675d	90	3.7	141	2.9	324	12.8	792	7.9	46.2	7.9
11. UKTR 6675dv	90	4.9	141	4.4	313	16.3	737	12.9	42.9	14.3
12. GFDL 5564d	90	3.8	143	3.3	353	11.6	845	6.9	49.6	7.2

Table 5.3.4   Mean and coefficient of variation (cv) for several outputs of 30 year model runs with climate scenarios for onion crops (cv. Hysam) sown at München on DOY 92.

Scenario	Sowing to bulbing (days)		Sowing to harvest (days)		Total dry weight at bulbing (g m^{-2})		Total dry weight at harvest (g m^{-2})		Bulb fresh weight at harvest (t ha^{-1})	
	mean	cv (%)	mean	cv (%)	mean	cv (%)	mean	cv (%)	mean	cv (%)
1. Baseline	100	4.5	165	7.6	295	16.3	644	11.7	39.2	12.7
2. UKLO	68	5.8	109	3.7	316	18.5	624	13.4	33.9	13.9
3. UKHI	76	4.9	121	4.2	372	13.4	746	11.1	41.5	12.7
4. UKHIv	73	4.6	119	5.4	368	13.1	740	12.2	41.3	13.3
5. UKTR 3140a	93	4.6	146	5.1	341	16.0	731	12.1	42.7	13.1
6. UKTR 6675a	91	4.2	137	4.6	369	15.6	783	13.8	44.2	15.2
7. UKTR 6675av	91	4.4	137	4.5	367	14.4	768	14.5	43.0	16.6
8. GFDL 2534a	96	4.4	148	5.7	339	16.9	726	13.6	42.2	14.9
9. GFDL 5564a	89	4.0	133	4.5	389	14.2	785	13.1	43.7	14.6
10. UKTR 6675d	91	4.2	137	4.6	347	15.6	737	13.9	41.6	15.3
11. UKTR 6675dv	91	4.4	137	4.5	346	14.5	723	14.5	40.5	16.7
12. GFDL 5564d	89	4.0	133	4.5	367	14.2	738	13.2	41.1	14.7

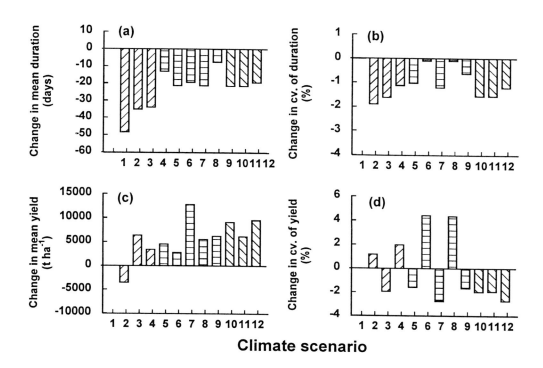

Figure 5.3.5 Changes in the (a) mean and (b) coefficient of variation of the duration from sowing to bulb maturity in onion (cv. Hysam) and the (c) mean and (d) coefficient of variation of fresh weight bulb yield from the baseline climate at Oxford as predicted by the climate scenarios. The equilibrium scenarios (///), transient scenarios with IS92a (≡) and IS92d (\\\) emissions scenarios are numbered as in Table 5.3.3.

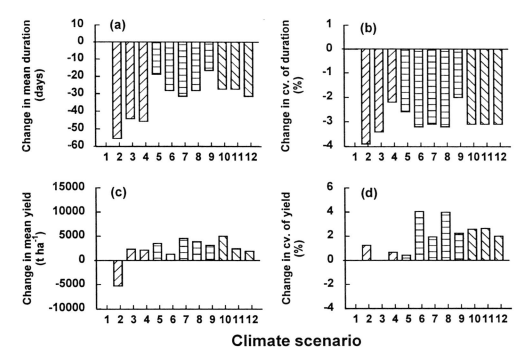

Figure 5.3.6 Changes in the (a) mean and (b) coefficient of variation of the duration from sowing to bulb maturity in onion (cv. Hysam) and the (c) mean and (d) coefficient of variation of fresh weight bulb yield from the baseline climate at München as predicted by the climate scenarios. The equilibrium scenarios (///), transient scenarios with IS92a (≡) and IS92d (\\\) emissions scenarios are numbered as in Table 3.5.4.

The effect of changed climatic variability with a given GCM scenario was clearly apparent at Oxford but not at München. For example, with the UKTR6675 GCM at München, mean bulb yields were predicted to be 10% and 13% greater than with the baseline climate with and without changed variability, respectively (scenarios 7 and 6, Figure 5.3.6). However, at Oxford, mean bulb yields were predicted to be 14% and 23% greater than with the baseline climate with and without changed variability, respectively (scenarios 7 and 6, Figure 5.3.5). The similar bulb yields at München with the UKTR6675 scenario with or without changed variability were also associated with small changes in the coefficient of variation (Table 5.3.4). In contrast, changing variability in the same scenario at Oxford changed the coefficient of variation of bulb yields from 2% less than the baseline (scenario 6, Table 5.3.3) to 4.3% more than the baseline (scenario 7, Table 5.3.3).

5.3.5   Possible adaptive responses

Higher bulb yields of onion in shorter growing seasons were predicted with all but one of the 11 climate change scenarios. Thus, adaptive responses are not necessary to either maintain or increase onion production at the two northern European sites studied. However, it would seem possible to use even longer duration varieties in these climates in order to maximise the increase in onion productivity.

5.3.6   Conclusions

The functional model of onion growth and yield developed in this project compared well with most of the field observations at two sites in northern Europe. This permitted the model to be used to study the effects of systematic changes in climate and climate change scenarios. Potential negative effects of the warmer temperatures predicted by the climate change scenarios, due to reduced opportunity for resource capture during the shorter crop growing period, were more than offset by the increased dry matter production at elevated concentrations of CO_2. This trend was apparent at both Oxford and München. However, differences between onion production at these two sites were apparent in the response of bulb yield to the transient scenarios (UKTR compared

with the GFDL GCM), and in the effects of changed climatic variability on the risk of onion production.

5.4   Effects on grapevine

5.4.1   Background

Grapevine is a woody perennial plant that reaches reproductive maturity after 4 to 5 years, and may remain economically productive for 50 to 60 years. Bud break occurs annually from March to April in Europe, over a characteristic range of variety-specific dates and is followed by a period of intensive vegetative growth during which the shoots arising from the buds elongate and produce leaves very rapidly. Vegetative growth usually slows after mid-May when flowering of the one to three clusters on each shoot begins. Relative earliness or lateness of bud break for a variety depends upon weather patterns. The number of viable fruits (berries) that continue development is determined shortly after flowering, at which time the maturing fruit clusters become the primary sinks for photosynthate. Maturing fruits undergo two phases of growth: (i) seed development and the building of the hard, green berry structure and (ii) sugar accumulation, colour change, and rapid enlargement of the fruit, the start of which is called varaison. Fruit maturity, depending upon the variety, is typically reached during August or September.

As is evident from the description of its biology, the growth and development of grapevine are influenced by environmental factors, such as temperature and radiation, which make the crop sensitive to changes in climate. Preliminary studies on the effects of climate change on the development and growth of grapevine have been carried out for Italy by Orlandini *et. al.* (1993) and by Bindi *et. al.* (1994) who also evaluated possible impacts on quality. Kenny and Harrison (1992a) used an empirically derived latitude-temperature index to provide a broad assessment of areas in Europe that are climatically suitable for grapevine and the possible effects of climate change.

This study aims to perform a more detailed analysis of the effects of climate change on grapevine production. For this reason a simple mechanistic model for grapevine growth and yield has been developed using existing knowledge about the temperature and CO_2 dependence of growth and development processes. An evaluation of the effects of climate change on grapevine production has been made using the model.

5.4.2 Model development and validation

A number of approaches have been developed to analyse the effects of environmental variables on crop growth. Statistical approaches were first used, in which regressions were obtained to correlate environmental variables and yield (Baier and Robertson, 1968). The problem with a statistical approach is that there is little confidence in extrapolating the results beyond the original limits of the data set. More recently, mechanistic models have been developed.

Usually, the difficulties in using these complex models arise from their use of many assumptions. An intermediate approach between statistical and complex methods, is the use of simplified mechanistic models which define crop behaviour using only a few relationships. Recently, this approach has been used to study the influence of environmental parameters on the growth and yield of many crop species: soybean (Spaeth *et al.*, 1987), maize (Muchow *et al.*, 1990), wheat (Amir and Sinclair, 1991).

Following this latter approach a model to simulate the growth and yield of grapevine under current climatic conditions has been developed. Model performance was compared to experimental data collected in field trials carried out in the Chianti region, Italy on the cv. Sangiovese.

5.4.2.1 *Field and weather data*

All field work was carried out in the 1992-94 seasons at the Mondeggi-Lappeggi Farm in the Chianti region, Italy (43.75° N). *Vitis vinifera* L. (cv. Sangiovese) vines were used to develop the model. The vines were grafted onto 420/A rootstock. Vines were trained with the traditional cordon pruned system and vines were not irrigated.

Monthly crop harvests of the current year growing parts of the vine were randomly sampled from the vineyard (ten shoots). All the vine parts harvested (berries, shoots, leaves) were separated, leaf area was determined with a LI-COR area meter, and samples were dried in forced air ovens at 75°C for 72 hours. After drying, the harvest index was calculated as the ratio of weight of berries to the total biomass harvest weight.

Daily minimum and maximum temperature and solar radiation were recorded in an automatic weather station located in the vineyard.

5.4.2.2 *Model description*

Relatively few relationships are used in this model to describe the development, growth and yield of grapevine (Figure 5.4.1). The major processes simulated are crop ontogeny, development of leaves, biomass accumulation and fruit growth.

Ontogeny

Crop ontogeny is divided in two periods: the development period between bud break and bloom and a fruit growth period between bloom and maturity. Several simulation studies of grapevine phenology have been conducted. In particular, different indicators, such as degree days or temperature summations, have been used to predict development stages. Unfortunately, few studies have simultaneously considered a wide range of varieties and years. In order to evaluate the reliability of different indicators (climatic and biological) for the prediction of development stages, a study has been performed on a wide range of varieties and years. Phenological observations made during the years 1965 to 1970 on 123 cultivars of *Vitis vinifera* L. grown in an experimental vineyard at the station of Conegliano, Italy were collected and classified on the basis of precocity of varieties in two data sets (early and late cultivars). Meteorological data were obtained from a recording station located less than one kilometre from the vineyard.

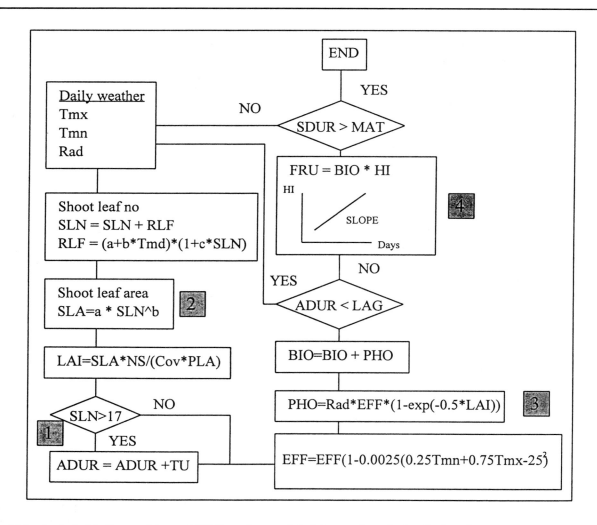

Variables included in the model are:

ADUR	=	Accumulated degree days during the lag phase
BIO	=	Total biomass
Cov	=	Plant cover
EFF	=	Radiation use efficiency
FRU	=	Fruit biomass
HI	=	Harvest index
LAG	=	Duration of lag phase in TU
LAI	=	Leaf area index
MAT	=	Duration of fruit growth phase in TU
NS	=	Number of shoot
PHO	=	Daily photosynthesis
PLA	=	Plant density
RAD	=	Solar radiation
RLF	=	Leaf number rate
SDUR	=	Accumulated degree days during the fruit growth phase
SLA	=	Shoot leaf area
SLN	=	Shoot leaf number
Tmd	=	Mean temperature
Tmn	=	Minimum temperature
Tmx	=	Maximum temperature
TU	=	Thermal unit

Figure 5.4.1   Flow diagram of the model for simulating growth and yield of grapevine. The main processes simulated are: 1. Crop ontogeny; 2. Leaf development; 3. Biomass accumulation; 4. Fruit growth.

For each data set the average (AVG), standard deviation (SD, expressed in equivalent days) and coefficient of variation (CV) of the various indicators of the development stages were calculated. The CV can be considered as an useful measure of the indicator's consistency. In Table 5.4.1 the average, standard deviation and CV of the various indicators of the development stages for early and late cultivars are reported. The reliability of the first five indicators (number of days, degree days, etc.) has been evaluated for all three phases, whereas the reliability of leaf number has been evaluated only for the interval from bud break to bloom and the Pouget-formulae[1] (Pouget, 1988) from 1 January to bud break.

In summary, the results of this analysis suggest that:

- for the 1 January to bud break interval, none of the indicators provide a better indication than the number of days.
- for the bud break to bloom interval, degree-days and leaf number are the best indicators, and
- for the bloom to maturity interval, all the indicators show a low reliability (high CV) due to the influence of vine management practices. However, cumulative degree-days is the most reliable indicator for this development stage.

Table 5.4.1 Various indicators of development stages for early and late vine cultivars. AVG is the average, SD is the standard deviation (expressed in equivalent days) and CV is the coefficient of variation.

Cultivar	Indicator	1 January to Bud break			Bud break to bloom			Bloom to maturity		
		AVG	SD	CV	AVG	SD	CV	AVG	SD	CV
Early										
	Number of days	103.5	6.7	6.4	54.7	7.6	13.9	101.7	7.8	7.6
	Degree Days	27.4	40.9	39.5	314.5	2.5	4.5	1135	5.2	4.9
	Cum. max. temperature	1003.3	10.7	10.3	1169.4	5.1	9.3	2718.4	8	7.9
	Cum. radiation	9418.2	8.2	7.9	10682.7	5.5	10.1	20804.7	8.8	8.7
	Cum. temperature diff.	894.7	8.0	7.7	630.3	5.9	10.8	1133.6	10.3	9.2
	Leaf number	-	-	-	16.8	2.8	5.1	-	-	-
	Pouget model	1495.5	13.6	13.1	-	-	-	-	-	-
Late										
	Number of days	107.5	7.8	7.2	53.2	6.6	12.4	119.5	6.4	5.3
	Degree Days	34.1	40.8	37.9	330.4	1.9	3.5	1242	4.7	4.2
	Cum. max. temperature	1067	11.1	10.3	1167.8	4.3	8.2	3088.2	5.1	4.2
	Cum. radiation	9981.8	10.0	9.3	10648.5	5.2	9.9	22950.5	7.4	6.2
	Cum. temperature diff.	933.1	7.7	7.2	620.6	5.7	10.8	1307.8	8.8	8.0
	Leaf number	-	-	-	17.2	2	3.8	-	-	-
	Pouget model	1163	14.3	13.3	-	-	-	-	-	-

☐ best indicator

---

[1] The method predicts the date of bud break on the basis of the effects of temperature on rate of bud break and the sum of the daily minimum and maximum temperature values from a fixed date during ecodormancy (e.g. 1 January).

Since none of the indicators provides a better indication than the number of days, the onset of the growing season is set as equal to the observed date in the model validation and is fixed as equal to the number of days from 1 January in the sensitivity analysis. In the scenario experiments the onset of the growing season is calculated as a function of cumulative temperature differences to take account of the effects of increasing temperature on the start of active growth. The duration of the period between bud break and bloom is calculated by setting the number of leaves on a shoot equal to 17 at bloom as a function of the rate of appearance of leaves. The duration of the period between bloom and maturity is calculated as a function of accumulated degree days during this period. The thermal units required to progress from bloom to maturity were held constant at 1200 °C days (base temperature 10°C).

Leaf area

Leaf area is estimated from the total number of actively growing shoots per unit surface, the rate of leaf appearance and leaf expansion. The total number of actively growing shoots per unit surface can be obtained if the variety cultivated and the training and pruning systems are known. The rate of leaf appearance is calculated using a model recently proposed by Miglietta *et al.* (1992). This model calculates the daily rate of leaf formation and emission after bud break on the basis of mean daily temperature, assuming that the rate of leaf appearance declines during ontogeny with constant temperature. The leaf area growth on a vine shoot is estimated as a function of the total number of appeared leaves using an empirical relationship. Many authors have found that simple exponential regressions adequately describe the correlation between leaf number and area per plant (Baker, 1985; Amir and Sinclair, 1991). In the model, data collected during the 1992 growing season were used to define the total leaf area per shoot as a function of the number of appeared leaves (Figure 5.4.2).

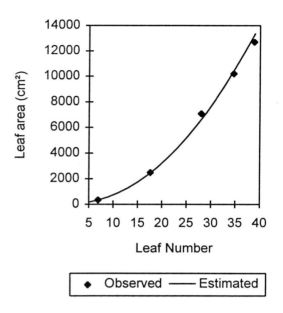

Figure 5.4.2 Exponential regression describing the correlation between leaf number and leaf area per shoot for cv. Sangiovese.

Biomass accumulation

Leaf area, as calculated using the relationship described in the previous section, is used to calculate the solar radiation intercepted by the leaf canopy. The exponential equation for radiation interception as a function of leaf area index (LAI) has been well established for many crops including grapevine. Crop biomass accumulation is calculated from radiation interception using estimates of crop radiation use efficiency (RUE, biomass accumulated per unit of solar radiation intercepted). An assumption that crop biomass accumulation can can be approximated by RUE is supported by observations in many studies in which a linear correlation was found between canopy CO_2 uptake rates and the fraction of intercepted radiation. The value of RUE was calculated from samples taken during the period June to September, 1992. In the model, RUE was set equal to 0.966 g MJ^{-1} throughout the whole growth period. Moreover, in order to take into account the effect of high temperatures on photosynthetic activity, a function which decreases RUE for high temperatures was introduced (Figure 5.4.1).

Fruit growth

Daily fruit growth rate is calculated on the basis of the empirical observation, found in many other crop species, that harvest index increases linearly during fruit growth. Although the progression in harvest index during fruit growth for grapevine has not been reported, calculation of the harvest index indicates that a linear response also exists in grapevine (Orlandini *et al.*, 1994). Field data collected in 1992 and 1993 provided direct evidence for the linear increase in harvest index during fruit growth (Figure 5.4.3). The rate of increase in harvest index was set to 0.00473 d^{-1} in the model. Daily fruit growth is calculated from the assumed change in harvest index.

5.4.2.3 *Model validation*

Model performance was compared to independent experimental data obtained from the field trials conducted in 1993 and 1994. These sets of data were not used for the development of the model. Daily values of minimum and maximum temperature and solar radiation for the two years were used to simulate crop growth and yield. All model parameters defining crop characteristics, which were set using the 1992 field data, were held constant for the validation.

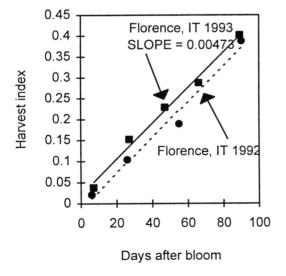

Figure 5.4.3 Harvest Index of grapevine cv. Sangiovese observed at monthly intervals during 1992 and 1993.

Observed total biomass and fruit accumulation were simulated satisfactorily (Figure 5.4.4). Small differences were found between simulated and observed total biomass and fruit production that were not systematic but, in most cases, these were within 10%.

To investigate the effects of climate change on grapevine production for a large range of climatic conditions the model was calibrated and validated for another cultivar (cv. Cabernet Sauvignon). This cultivar has a wider world distribution and experimental data were available for most European viticultural regions. As for the cv. Sangiovese, calibration and validation of the model were performed using experimental data from field trials in the Chianti region for three seasons: 1992-1994. Specifically, field data from the first season were used to calibrate the model and data from the remaining two seasons were used for validation. Results of the validation showed that biomass and fruit accumulation in both years were simulated well (Figure 5.4.5), with mean bias differences always within 10 g m^{-2}.

In conclusion, results of the validation demonstrated that the model was able to simulate the growth and yield of both cultivars. Thus it could be used, in combination with the data obtained from the Mini-FACE experiment, to investigate the impact of future climate on grapevine production.

5.4.3 Model sensitivity to systematic changes in climate

Sensitivity analysis of the model to independent changes in the three driving variables (temperature, solar radiation and CO_2 concentration) were made. Baseline conditions were those from the station of Bologna for the 28-year period 1961-1988. Simulated mean fruit and total (fruit + leaf + shoots) biomass for the baseline case were 6.62 t/ha and 15.09 t/ha, respectively. Simulated CVs were 0.13 for fruit and 0.11 for total biomass. Continuous grapevine experiments conducted at an experimental station located near Bologna (40 km) from 1965 to 1970 observed a mean fruit and total biomass of 5.9 t/ha and 14.3 t/ha respectively and CVs of 0.15 and 0.13 respectively. The model slightly underestimates the observed year-to-year variability, although CVs were calculated for different locations.

5.4.3.1 *CO$_2$ concentration*

The model predicted a positive and almost linear response of fruit and total dry matter to an increase in CO_2 concentration from 350 to 700 ppmv (Figure 5.4.6a) with about a 35% increase in fruit yield. The CVs of fruit and total biomass remained almost unchanged (Figure 5.4.6b). The predicted CV for total dry matter was always lower than that for fruit dry matter.

(a)

(b)

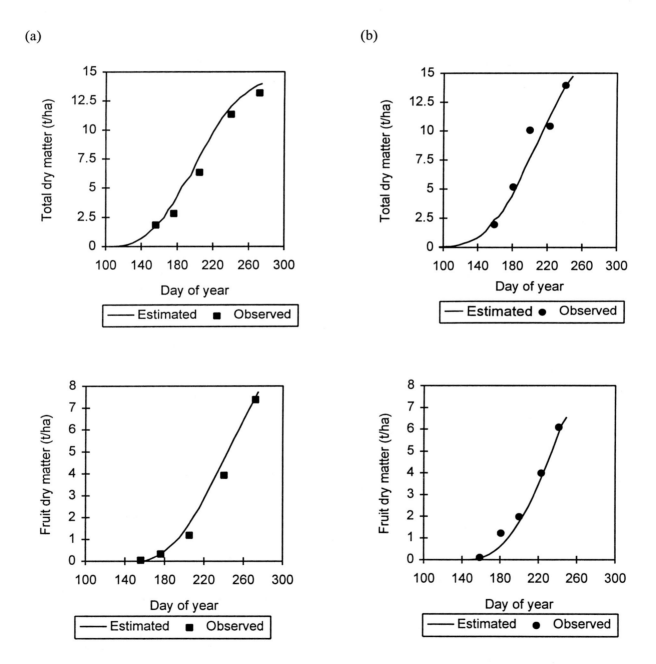

Figure 5.4.4   Simulated and observed total and fruit biomass in (a) 1993 and (b) 1994 for cv. Sangiovese.

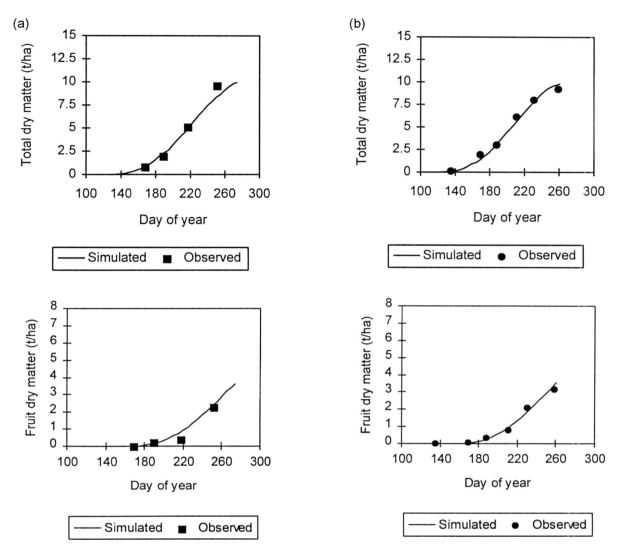

Figure 5.4.5   Simulated and observed total and fruit biomass in (a) 1993 and (b) 1994 for cv. Cabernet Sauvignon.

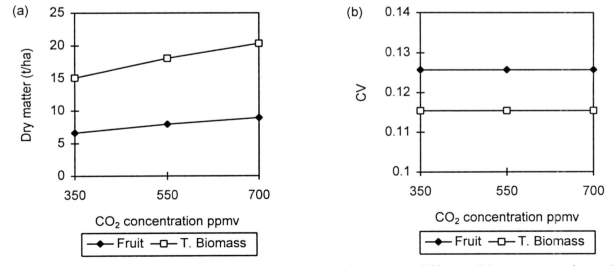

Figure 5.4.6   Response of grapevine model (cv. Sangiovese) to different CO_2 concentrations. (a) average dry matter production; (b) coefficient of variation (CV).

5.4.3.2   *Temperature*

The model predicted that increased temperature had a substantial negative effect on fruit and total dry matter (Figure 5.4.7a). The CV for both fruit and total biomass increased with temperature, with the CV of fruit biomass being larger than that for total biomass (Figure 5.4.7b). These predictions from the model can be explained in terms of the various effects temperature has on plants, as increases in

temperature shorten the growing season and, in particular, the fruit-filling period.

5.4.3.3   *Radiation*

The response of the model to ±20% changes in daily radiation was positive and almost linear (Figure 5.4.8a). The CVs of both the biomass components remained virtually unchanged (Figure 5.4.8b).

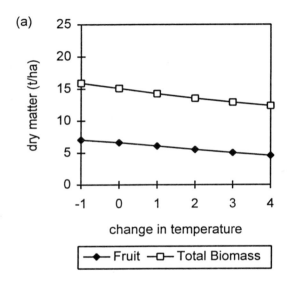
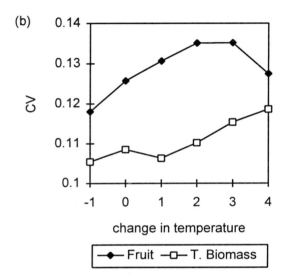

Figure 5.4.7   Response of grapevine model (cv. Sangiovese) to changes in temperature. (a) average dry matter production; (b) coefficient of variation (CV).

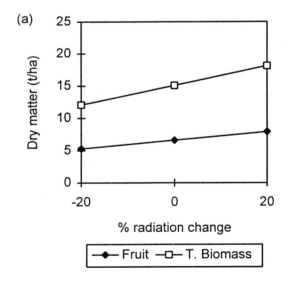
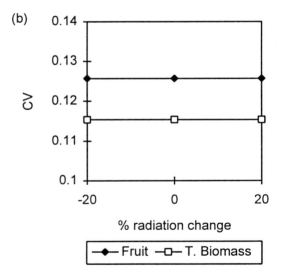

Figure 5.4.8   Response of grapevine model (cv. Sangiovese) to changes in radiation. (a) average dry matter production; (b) coefficient of variation (CV).

5.4.4 Application of the climate change scenarios

The model was run for the site of Bologna using 31 years of climatic data for each scenario. Generated data from two equilibrium scenarios (UKLO, UKHI) and two transient scenarios (UKTR and GFDL) were used. For the transient scenarios two different model decades were used. For the UKTR scenario these were 31-40 and 66-75, and for GFDL 25-34 and 55-64. The scenario data were produced by a stochastic weather generator. For the UKLO and GFDL scenarios the baseline variability in temperature was retained in the scenario data, whereas for the UKHI and UKTR6675 scenarios both the baseline variability and variability calculated from the GCM experiments were used. The scenarios with changed variability are denoted with a small 'v' in the scenario name, e.g. UKHIv.

The atmospheric CO_2 concentration was set to 353 ppmv for the baseline climate, and to 560 ppmv for the equilibrium GCM scenarios. The CO_2 concentration of the first and second transient model decades were set to 454 and 617 ppmv respectively corresponding to the IS92a emissions scenario. The emissions scenario is denoted with a small 'a' in the scenario name, e.g. GFDL5564a. Details of the construction of the site-specific scenarios are given in Section 2.4.

The direct effect of increasing atmospheric CO_2 concentration on the CO_2 assimilation and growth of grapevine was incorporated in the model by altering the radiation use efficiency (RUE). On the basis of results obtained from the Mini-FACE experiment (Section 4.4), the RUE was linearly increased up to a maximum of 35% for a CO_2 concentration of 700 ppmv. All other parameters in the model defining crop characteristics, which were set during calibration, were held constant.

5.4.4.1 *Equilibrium scenarios*

The two main factors which affect crop growth and development, namely temperature and CO_2 concentration, act in opposing ways. In general, an increase in CO_2 concentration stimulates fruit yield (Figure 5.4.6), whereas an increase in temperature decreases fruit yield (Figure 5.4.7).

The simulation runs showed a decrease in fruit biomass for all equilibrium climate change scenarios over the baseline up to a maximum loss of 18% for scenario UKHI (Figure 5.4.9a). Average total biomass showed a slight increase in all the scenarios up to a maximum of 8% for scenario UKHIv (Figure 5.4.10a). The CV for fruit and total biomass were always higher than the baseline and the CV of fruit was generally 15 to 60% higher than that for total biomass (Figure 5.4.9b and Figure 5.4.10b).

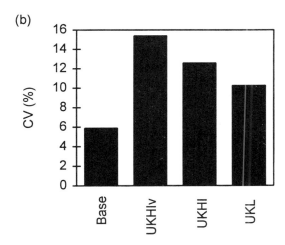

Figure 5.4.9 Simulation experiment for equilibrium scenarios for Bologna (cv. Sangiovese): (a) mean and (b) CV of fruit biomass.

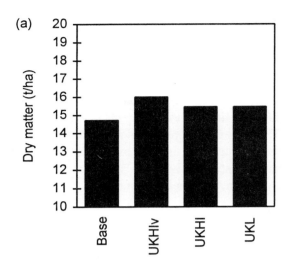
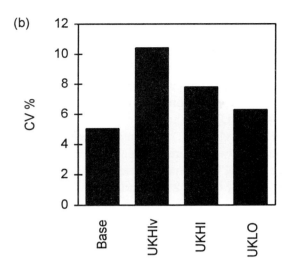

Figure 5.4.10 Simulation experiment for equilibrium scenarios for Bologna (cv. Sangiovese): (a) mean and (b) CV of total biomass.

5.4.4.2 *Transient scenarios*

Fruit production was lower for the UKTR6675a scenarios (both with and without variability) than for the baseline climate, but higher for the other three scenarios (UKTR3140a, GFDL2534a and GFDL5564a) (Figure 5.4.11a). Total biomass increased in all scenarios up to a maximum of 31% for scenario GFDL2534a (Figure 5.4.12a). The CV for fruit was always higher than the baseline (Figure 5.4.11b); whereas there were no consistent changes in the CV of total biomass for the different scenarios (Figure 5.4.12b). For UKTR3140a and the GFDL scenarios there were no changes in the CV, but for the scenarios UKTR6675a (with and without variability) the CVs of total biomass substantially increased.

The outcome of these simulations are summarized in qualitative terms in Table 5.4.2. The main implications of these results are that the average fruit production for the different scenarios are variable and uncertain; whereas

the predictions of average total biomass and the CV for both the components are less variable and uncertain. For example, for fruit production, four models predicted decreases in the average production, but the remaining models predicted the opposite situation; whereas, except for one case, all the scenarios predicted an increase in average total biomass and in the variability of both biomass components.

5.4.5 Possible adaptive responses

5.4.5.1 *Variety adaptation*

A comparison between the cultivars Sangiovese and Cabernet Sauvignon was made to examine the possibility of variety adaptation to climate change. The varieties chosen were a high productive variety (cv. Sangiovese), used in general for producing light wine, and a low productive variety (cv. Cabernet Sauvignon) used for producing high quality wine.

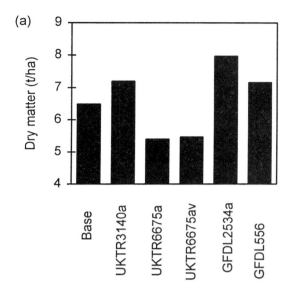
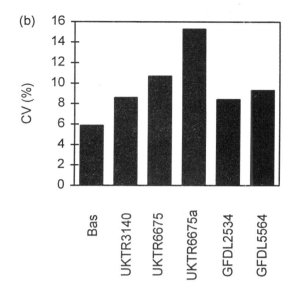

Figure 5.4.11 Simulation experiment for transient scenarios for Bologna (cv. Sangiovese): (a) mean and (b) CV of fruit biomass.

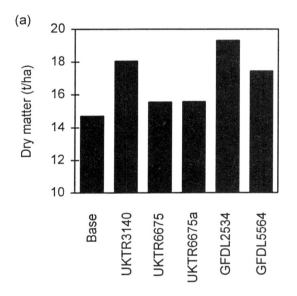
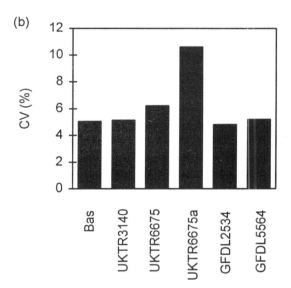

Figure 5.4.12 Simulation experiment for transient scenarios for Bologna (cv. Sangiovese): (a) mean and (b) CV of total biomass.

Table 5.4.2 Qualitative predictions of biomass components for the different scenarios. + or -M indicates an increase or decrease in mean values, and + or -V indicates an increase or decrease in variability (expressed by CV).

Biomass components	UKHIv	UKHI	UKLO	UKTR 3140a	UKTR 6675a	UKTR 6675av	GFDL 2534a	GFDL 5564a
Fruit	-M;+V	-M;+V	-M;+V	+M;+V	-M;+V	-M+V	+M;+V	+M;+V
Total	+M;+V	+M;+V	+M;+V	+M;+V	+M;+V	+M;+V	+M;-V	+M;+V

The two cultivars showed different adaptation, in terms of fruit production, to climate change. Both cultivars showed roughly similar changes in terms of fruit production for the various scenarios, but for Sangiovese the fruit production changes were more negative or less positive (Figure 5.4.13). However, there was no correspondence between changes in the CV of the cultivars (Figure 5.4.14). For cv. Sangiovese CV slightly decreased or increased, whereas for cv. Cabernet Sauvignon CV consistently increased.

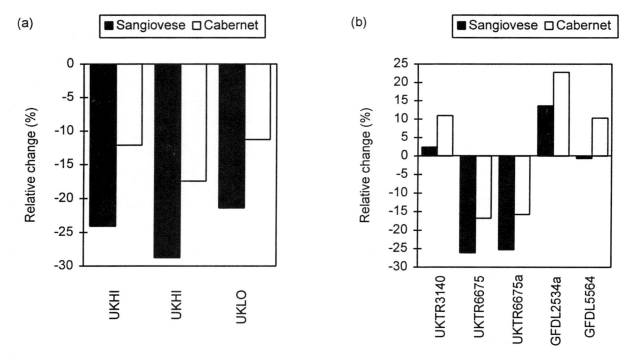

Figure 5.4.13   Relative change in mean of fruit biomass for the (a) equilibrium and (b) transient scenarios.

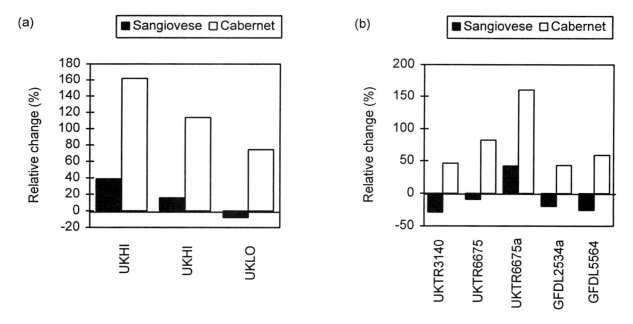

Figure 5.4.14   Relative change in CV of fruit biomass for the (a) equilibrium and (b) transient scenarios.

Both the adaptations could cause negative effects on grapevine production. In the first case the reduction in fruit production of cv. Sangiovese would reduce the production of light wine; whereas the combined increase in the mean and variability of Cabernet Sauvignon production would not guarantee the high quality of the wine and, in some years, would not meet the demand for wine.

5.4.5.2   *Agricultural risk assessment*

As illustrated in many studies, crop growth models have shown important alterations in mean crop yield as a result of a changed global environment. Such adjustments have important economic implications. However, in addition to changes in mean crop yield increases in season-to-season variability of crop yields are also detected. These latter changes could induce yield instability that might have much greater impacts on economic, sociological and political activities than a simple shift in mean crop yields.

For the purposes of analysing the risk of an increase in year-to-year variability associated with climate change, it is necessary to know detailed information not only on the effect of changes in climatic conditions on mean yield, but also on the distribution of yield (Semenov *et al.*, 1993).

The cultivar Sangiovese was chosen to describe in detail the possible changes in inter-seasonal variations in grapevine yield resulting from environmental changes. Simulation results for the various scenarios were plotted as cumulative distribution plots (CDP) (Figure 5.4.15). The CDP for these data were obtained by graphing the number of years exceeding a fruit production level against fruit production. As production increases on the abscissa in the plots, the number of years exceeding that production level declines. At very low levels of fruit production all years exceeded the production on the abscissa, while at very high levels few, if any, years exceeded the production on the abscissa. Consequently, the CDP has a negative

slope, with a less steep negative slope indicating greater variability in production among years. A constant slope with a shift to the right or left means production variability was unchanged, but the mean yield has changed. An overall shift to the right in the CDP indicates an increase in mean yield.

Fruit production increased or decreased with climate change, depending on which climate change scenario was used. In addition to these changes in average fruit production the shape of CDP also changed. Slopes of CDP for future scenarios were less steep than that for baseline climate indicating an increase in the variability in production. The fruit production range was larger because there was either an increase in years with good production or an increase in years with low production. Moreover, if the variability in climate changed (UKHIv and UKTR6675av scenarios), this also substantially affects the variability of production (less negative slope), but has little affect on the mean production (little shift of CDP).

5.4.6   Conclusions

The validation exercise suggests that the model simulates grapevine growth and yield well for the two varieties analysed. Simulation runs used to explore the sensitivity of the model showed the model to be more sensitive to changes in CO_2 concentration and temperature than to changes in radiation. The CVs were affected by changes in temperature only.

The model predicted a general increase in total biomass of cv. Sangiovese for the equilibrium scenarios, but there were no consistent changes in fruit production for these scenarios. The variability of both fruit and total biomass increased for all scenarios. A more detailed examination of the yield distribution for scenarios with and without changes in variability of weather sequences showed that a change in the variability of weather sequences did not greatly affect the average values (little shift of CDP), but substantially affected the variability of production (less negative slope).

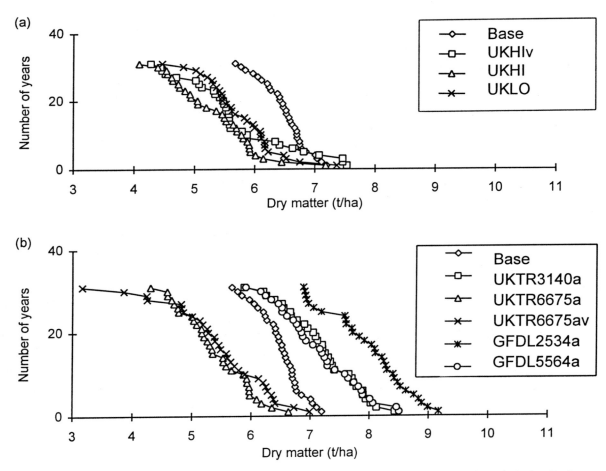

Figure 5.4.15   Cumulative distribution plot (CDP) of fruit biomass (cv. Sangioverse) for Bologna: (a) equilibrium and (b) transient scenarios.

The variety adaptation analysis showed that there were no consistent changes in the average fruit production and CV of the two varieties. Cabernet Sauvignon showed a better adaptation in terms of average production, but a worse adaptation in terms of production variability.

5.5   Effects on willow

5.5.1   Background

Willow energy forests are now recognised as providing a fuel source of considerable potential and large land areas may be taken up with energy forests in the future (Eckersten *et al.*, 1987). The stands contain deciduous trees intensively managed over a short rotation. The most commonly used trees are willows and one to two cuttings are planted every square metre. Such forests are now being planted on surplus agricultural soils as well as the nutrient-poor soils, such as peat, where they were originally grown. However, even with better soils, it is necessary to add nutrients for high and sustainable production. Growth above ground is slow in the first year and weed control is required, however the growth rate increases in the second year as the plants become more firmly established. Harvest of the stems (the above-ground woody parts) for fuel occurs after three to five years growth. The stumps resprout the following spring after harvest in the winter. The whole rotation time is thought to be about 20-30 years.

An existing site-specific simulation model has been evaluated in this study and preliminary sensitivity tests conducted. The model will be redeveloped in future analyses to enable its application at a range of sites in Europe and for the series of climate change scenarios.

5.5.2   Model description

The simulation of the growth of short-rotation forests as a function of environmental conditions was initially based on modelling photosynthesis without considering nitrogen uptake and use (Eckersten *et al*., 1983). This model was then coupled with a nitrogen turnover submodel (Eckersten and Slapokas, 1990) which assumes that growth rate determines the rate of uptake of nitrogen. Into this model a simulation of several-year-old shoots, using a pool of easily available assimilates, was introduced (Eckersten, 1991). In this WIGO (Willow Growth) model, the soil is treated as one layer from the ground surface to the deepest root depth and the litter is divided into age classes. In order to model the soil dynamics more accurately, WIGO was coupled with a more complex soil model, SOILN (Johnsson *et al*., 1987) to form the model SOILN-FORESTSR. The multi-layered soil model, SOILN, allows for differences in leaching, denitrification, mineralization and plant uptake between different layers in the soil.

SOILN-FORESTSR assumes a daily time-step. Simulations of willow growth can be run over several years and different types of management, for example, changes in harvest date, fertilization timing and defoliation can be included. The model has been developed specifically for willow stands but can also be used for other deciduous species.

5.5.2.1   *Plant submodel*

Tissues are separated into the current year's growth and growth older than one year. The young tissues are divided into leaf, stem, root and easily available assimilate compartments. Old tissues are divided into stem and root compartments only. Each plant compartment is divided into a biomass and a nitrogen part which interact daily. In calculating growth, the leaf nitrogen content (estimated from the nitrogen turnover calculations) is used as an input variable. Likewise in the nitrogen turnover calculations, the input variables are the daily growth of leaves etc., estimated from the growth calculations. In this way, internal input variables are passed between the different model components (plant and soil).

The plant growth calculations are described in detail in Eckersten and Slapokas (1990). Daily growth is mainly determined by photosynthetic rate which changes with light interception, air temperature, plant nitrogen, water status and leaf thickness. The photosynthesis of a semi-cloudy day is calculated from hourly photosynthesis from typical clear and overcast skies. Daily sums from these conditions represent the maximum and minimum photosynthesis, respectively. By interpolating between these values using actual radiation, daily photosynthesis is determined.

The proportion of total daily growth allocated to the roots is high when the nitrogen concentration in the canopy is low, and vice versa. The relation between stem and leaf growth is based on the balance between leaf area and above-ground biomass. The current year's growth can lose tissue through roots (which die at a rate proportional to their growth rate) and leaves (leaf fall is dependent on the amount of light at the bottom of the canopy and the rate also increases at the end of the season).

The easily available assimilate pool in the plant increases in proportion to total growth rate and the leaf fall. Its use in structural growth is directly related to the air temperature and the maximum daily release rate (which increases with stem biomass). The pool is used during flushing (restart of growth in spring or after harvest) until it is empty.

Newly formed tissue takes up nitrogen in proportion to its growth rate (this may be limited by the amount of nitrogen available) and is supplied from a pool in the soil. The amount of mineral nitrogen in the soil pool is increased by mineralization of litter and humus, fertilization, and a small amount of leaching from fallen leaves. Decreases in the pool are caused by leaching and denitrification. Allocation of nitrogen for daily uptake is exclusively to the roots until they reach their maximum nitrogen concentration and thereafter remaining nitrogen is supplied to the stems and then the leaves.

Old tissues have less effect on growth than young tissues. Direct effects from older tissues include the use of assimilates for maintenance respiration and for increasing the flushing rate during spring. An indirect effect is through the death of stems with low nitrogen concentration which reduces the mineralization rate in the soil.

5.5.2.2 *Soil submodel*

The soil is divided into layers which in turn are separated into compartments for litter, humus and mineral (ammonium and nitrate) nitrogen. The litter is assumed not to decompose until a year after it fell from the plant. The rate of decomposition is determined by microbial activity, soil temperature and soil water content. After several years the litter is transferred to the humus compartment where the mineralization rate is slower. A full description of the soil model can be found in Johnsson *et al.* (1987).

5.5.3   Model sensitivity to systematic changes in climate

The SOILN-FORESTSR model has been used for simulating data from willow stands in Uppsala, Sweden (Eckersten, 1994). An updated version of this model (SOILN-WILLOW) was used to perform sensitivity analyses for Rothamsted, UK after calibration with the Uppsala data set. Error checking has been added

to SOILN-WILLOW and the model uses radiation use efficiency instead of the more complex photosynthetic sub-model used in SOILN-FORESTSR.

5.5.3.1 *Calibration*

The model was calibrated for Uppsala using data from four years growth (1985-1988). The results were good with improved data fitting for the stem and leaf biomass, leaf area and standing stem biomass compared to the previous version of the model, SOILN-FORESTSR (see Eckersten, 1994). The predictions of yield (standing stem biomass) were accurate for all four years.

5.5.3.2 *Sensitivity analyses*

The model, calibrated for Uppsala, was used to perform sensitivity tests for Rothamsted, assuming optimal water and nitrogen conditions over the full 30 year period. Harvest was assumed to occur every fourth winter.

The effects of a range of temperature sensitivity tests on potential yield are shown in Figure 5.5.1. Results for Rothamsted showed that an increase in mean temperaturee of 3°C produced an increase in the mean yield (total dry matter) of 9.4 t/ha to 32.2 t/ha from the baseline mean of 22.8 t/ha. There was a reduction in the variability of predicted yields; the coefficient of

(a)

(b)

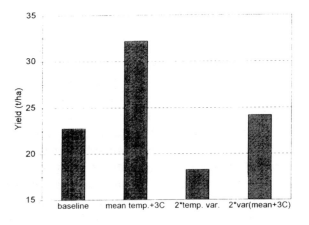
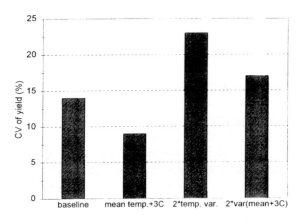

Figure 5.5.1   Effects of temperature sensitivity analysis for Rothamsted on (a) mean potential yield, and (b) CV of yield.

variation decreased to 9 from 14%. Doubling the variability of the temperature caused a reduction in the mean yield to 18.3 t/ha accompanied by an increase to 23% in the predicted yield variability. Combining the two temperature scenarios led to a modest increase in both the mean yield (to 24.2 t/ha) and the predicted yield variability (to 17%).

5.5.4   Discussion

The results from the calibration of the SOILN-WILLOW model were good, with accurate predictions of yield. In the sensitivity analyses, the model predicted a significantly higher mean yield with the increased temperature scenario (mean temperature increased by 3°C) compared to baseline (present conditions). In contrast, the mean predicted yield was reduced with doubling of the temperature variability. The coefficient of variation for this scenario was increased, indicating greater uncertainty in the yield predictions. The results from the analysis combining changes in both the mean and variability of temperature were close to the results from the baseline analyses.

The future aim of this work is to re-implement the willow model in the more user-friendly Windows environment, combining the plant growth model with the soil/nitrogen model from the SIRIUS wheat model (Jamieson *et al.*, 1995). In doing so, the complete model will be simplified which will also improve user access. The planned program structure will allow an expert system software platform to be built which will provide a generic model where different crops can be modelled within the same program.

5.6   Effects on maize

5.6.1   Background

A changing warmer climate would increase present uncertainties over water availability in southern European regions (IPCC, 1992). Possible future climatic conditions may have large effects on the distribution of crops, such as maize, that are presently limited by low spring temperatures in northern Europe and by water

availability in southern Europe. A few studies have evaluated changes in the suitability of grain maize in Europe using low resolution models over large geographical areas (Carter *et al.*, 1991; Kenny and Harrison, 1992b). This study uses a site-specific mechanistic maize model to analyse changes in crop variables with a series of climate change scenarios.

A crop model with an embedded water-balance model (CERES-Maize; Jones and Kiniry, 1986) was calibrated and validated with experimental field data from two sites that represent contrasting agroclimatic conditions in the Mediterranean Region (Albacete in the Central Plateau and Sevilla in the Guadalquivir Valley (Spain)). Low precipitation during the crop growing season in these regions (less than 100 mm) makes irrigation a necessity (Bignon, 1990; Minguez and Iglesias, 1995). Evapotranspiration (ET) constitutes an important component of the hydrologic balance and therefore its accurate calculation is essential. Hence, the calibration also included an adjustment to the ET calculation in the CERES-Maize model. The calibrated model was then used to calculate changes in crop growth and yield for an important area of maize production in the Mediterranean region (Sevilla, Spain) under different climate change scenarios.

5.6.2   Model description and calibration

5.6.2.1   *Model description*

The CERES-Maize model (Jones and Kiniry, 1986) is a simulation model for maize which describes daily phenological development and growth in response to environmental factors (soil, weather and management). Modelled processes include phenological development, (i.e. duration of growth stages), growth of vegetative and reproductive plant parts, extension growth of leaves and stems, senescence of leaves, biomass production and partitioning among plant parts, and root system dynamics. The model includes subroutines to simulate the soil and crop water balance and the nitrogen balance, which includes the capability to simulate the effects of nitrogen deficiency and soil water deficit on photosynthesis and carbohydrate distribution in the crop.

Development

The primary variable influencing phasic development rate is temperature. The thermal time for each phase is modified by coefficients which characterise the response of different genotypes. The timing of crop phenological stages can be calibrated by modifying the coefficients that characterise the duration of the juvenile phase (P1), photoperiod sensitivity (P2) and duration of the reproductive phase (P5).

Dry matter production

Potential dry matter production is a linear function of intercepted photosynthetically active radiation (PAR). The percentage of incoming PAR intercepted by the canopy is an exponential function of leaf area index (LAI). Dry matter allocation is determined by partitioning coefficients which depend on phenological stage and degree of water stress. Final grain yield is the product of plant population, kernels per plant and kernel weight. The number of kernels per plant is a linear function of stem weight (at anthesis) and coefficients that account for the variation between genotypes in potential kernel number (G2) and kernel growth rate (G3).

Water balance

Precipitation is a daily input to the model. Runoff is calculated as a function of soil type, soil moisture and precipitation; infiltration is precipitation minus runoff; drainage occurs when soil moisture is greater than the soil water holding capacity of the bottom soil layer. Potential evapotranspiration is calculated by the Priestley-Taylor relation. Actual transpiration is modified by LAI, soil evaporation and soil water deficit. Actual evaporation is a function of potential evaporation, LAI and time as described by Ritchie (1972). Daily changes in soil moisture are calculated as precipitation minus evaporation minus runoff minus drainage.

Carbon dioxide sensitivity

The CERES-Maize model has been modified to simulate changes in photosynthesis and evapotranspiration caused by higher CO_2 concentrations. The modifications are based on published experimental results (see Rosenzweig and Iglesias (1994) for a description of the methodology).

Input data

The model requires daily values for solar radiation, maximum and minimum temperature and precipitation. Soil data are needed for the functions of drainage, runoff, evaporation and radiation reflection. Soil water holding capacities and rooting preference coefficients are required for each soil layer, and for initial soil water contents.

5.6.2.2   *Model calibration and validation*

Field experimental data

Input data for the calibration and validation exercise were obtained from published field experiments conducted at the Agricultural Research Stations of Lora del Rio and Montoro (Sevilla, Spain, 37.42°N, 5.88°W, 31m altitude; Aguilar, 1990; Aguilar and Rendon, 1983), and Las Tiesas and Santa Ana (Albacete, Spain, 38.95°N, 1.85°W, 704m altitude; ITAP, 1985-1993). The maize hybrids selected for the calibration represent highly productive simple hybrids grown in the different agricultural regions. Local daily climatic data and soils information for the Sevilla site were provided by the Department of Agronomy of the University of Córdoba (Córdoba, Spain) and for the Albacete site by the Instituto Agronomico Tecnico Provincial de Albacete (ITAP, Albacete, Spain). Daily observed crop evapotranspiration data are from field experiments in Las Tiesas (Albacete, Spain, Martin de Santa Olalla *et al.*, 1990). In all field experiments the crop was irrigated and nitrogen-fertilized to meet total crop requirements.

Calibration of crop phenology, biomass and yield

The model was calibrated and validated with independent field data sets (which included information on yield components, phenology and crop ET) for maize hybrids of different crop growth duration (Table 5.6.1). The coefficients which define a maize hybrid in the CERES model refer only to rate of development and accumulation of dry matter; many other hybrid characteristics are not defined by these coefficients (such as drought resistance, pest and disease resistance, etc). Therefore one set of coefficients may be representative of a group of hybrids of similar characteristics grown in a particular geographical area. A set of coefficients were estimated for the most widely used hybrids in Spain and other Mediterranean regions. Table 5.6.1 shows the coefficients that define representative maize hybrids of different crop-cycle duration grown in southern Europe.

The coefficients were first calibrated in relation to phenology based on the thermal integrals of the juvenile period and the reproductive period. Once the phenology coefficients were calibrated, and therefore the simulated number of days available for grain filling, the yield component coefficients were adjusted to represent as accurately as possible the number of grains ear^{-1}, the final grain yield (t/ha), and the final biomass (t/ha). In the experiment crop nitrogen and water requirements were fully supplied and pests and diseases were controlled.

Nevertheless, these experimental yields are not potential yields, as they include some effect of losses by diseases and suboptimal management. Observed and simulated data are compared in

Table 5.6.2. Crop responses to changes in planting date and density under non-limiting conditions were also analysed. Figure 5.6.1 shows an example of the ability of the CERES-Maize model to simulate grain yields for long cycle hybrids (700 and 800). The different values in Figure 5.6.1 correspond to experiments with different sowing dates (March 4 to 20) and planting densities (5.5 to 11.5 plants m^{-2}).

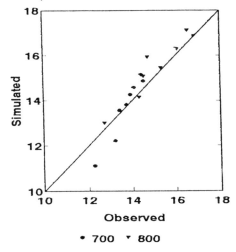

Figure 5.6.1 Simulated and observed yield (t/ha) for hybrids with long crop growth duration (700 and 800). Each point represents simulation versus observation at different planting dates and densities in Lora del Rio (1986).

Table 5.6.1   Values of the calibrated genetic coefficients used as input for the CERES-maize model. P1: Juvenile phase coefficient. P2: Photoperiodism coefficient. P5: Grain filling duration coefficient. G2: Kernel number coefficient. G3: Kernel weight coefficient.

Hybrid[1]	Thermal units[2]	Cycle length[3]	P1	P2	P5	G2	G3
200	2000	90-100	200	0.30	600	825	9.0
400	2000-2300	100-110	200	0.76	750	650	9.0
600	2500	120	200	0.70	800	800	8.0
700	2800	130	220	0.52	910	700	7.0
800	3000	150	260	0.50	980	600	8.5

[1]   Hybrids used in the calibration and validation are: FURIO (200), DEMAR (400), LUANA (600), AE703 (700) and PRISMA (800).

[2]   Accumulated total thermal units during the growing cycle (sum of degree days above 8°C).

[3]   Average duration of the growing cycle (days) in Albacete and Sevilla.

Table 5.6.2   Calibration: Comparison of phenology and yield data observed and simulated in Lora del Río (1986, sowing day 75) and in Las Tiesas (1993, sowing day 137). Day 1= January 1.

LORA DEL RIO	HYBRID	Observed	Simulated
Flowering date	600	175	169
	700	175	171
	800	179	177
Physiological maturity date	600	223	216
	700	223	224
	800	230	232
Grain filling period (days)	600	48	47
	700	48	53
	800	51	55
Grain yield (t/ha)	600	13.26	14.90
	700	13.43	14.25
	800	15.05	15.74
LAS TIESAS	**HYBRID**	**Observed**	**Simulated**
Flowering date	200	205	201
	400	207	204
Physiological maturity date	200	245	240
	400	255	255
Grain filling period (days)	200	40	39
	400	48	51
Grain yield (t/ha)	200	12.86	12.64
	400	13.38	13.51

Table 5.6.3 shows the agreement between simulated and observed crop data from an independent second set of field experiments used for validation.

Calibration of the water balance

Potential evapotranspiration is calculated in the CERES model using the Priestley-Taylor relation (Priestley and Taylor, 1972). Potential transpiration is directly related to potential evapotranspiration by a coefficient (alpha) whose value is fixed to 1.1 in CERES-Maize v2.1 (Jones and Kiniry, 1986). In many areas of the Mediterranean region, maximum temperatures higher than $35°C$ occur in the summer months of July and August. When short cycle maize crops are following another crop in late June or July, the crop is subject to high temperatures before reaching full ground cover. In this situation advective and micro-advective (between rows) processes occur, increasing crop

Table 5.6.3   Validation: Comparison of phenology and yield data observed and simulated in Lora del Río (1987, sowing day 63), Montoro (1981, sowing day 65), Santa Ana (1991, sowing day 151) and Las Tiesas (1991, sowing day 126). Day 1= January 1.

LORA DEL RIO	HYBRID	Observed	Simulated
Flowering date	600	162	156
	700	166	158
	800	170	164
Physiological maturity date	600	210	203
	700	220	212
	800	224	220
Grain filling period (days)	600	48	47
	700	54	54
	800	54	56
Grain yield (t/ha)	600	15.05	16.21
	700	14.21	14.51
	800	15.63	16.50
MONTORO	**HYBRID**	**Observed**	**Simulated**
Flowering date	700	168	165
	800	169	168
Grain yield (t/ha)	700	16.36	16.19
	800	16.27	16.76
SANTA ANA	**HYBRID**	**Observed**	**Simulated**
Grain yield (t/ha)	400	11.54	11.20
	600	13.97	14.84
	700	15.07	15.06
LAS TIESAS	**HYBRID**	**Observed**	**Simulated**
Flowering date	400	217	212
Grain yield (t/ha)	400	9.94	9.83

ET. Such conditions were not represented in the original ET formulation of the CERES-Maize model, and therefore, simulations of crop ET with the original model underestimated field-observed values (Figure 5.6.2). When advective conditions prevail the alpha coefficient should be higher (Shouse *et al.*, 1980; Rosenberg *et al.*, 1983; Pereira and Villa-Nova, 1992). The coefficent was set at 1.26 when maximum temperatures were below 35°C and 1.45 above 35°C. The result of these changes is a better estimate of total crop ET in Mediterranean conditions (Figure 5.6.2).

5.6.3   Model sensitivity to systematic changes in climate

5.6.3.1   *Methodology*

Crop responses to temperature changes are non-linear. A sensitivity analysis was carried out to characterise changes in crop yield, evaporative demand and crop growth duration with rising temperature. Generated weather data sets for Sevilla (see Section 2.4) included 30 years of weather data for the baseline climate (BS), a climate with doubled temperature variability (TM), and a climate with doubled length of dry spells (PR). In addition, these weather data sets were combined with stepwise increments of daily maximum and minimum temperature (BS+1°C to BS+3°C and TM+3°C).

Representative soil and crop management variables for these simulations were determined in accordance with information on current practices (soil deep silt loam, well drained; planting date 15 March; maize hybrid 700; planting density 8.5 plants m^{-2}, Lopez-Bellido, 1991). In all experiments nitrogen and water supply were considered non-limiting (as in practice). Initial soil water conditions were not specified and it was assumed that initial soil water was equal to field capacity.

Irrigation water requirements were calculated assuming 100% efficiency of the irrigation system, 1 m depth of soil wetted by irrigation, automatic irrigation when the available amount of soil water was 50% of soil water capacity and 100% of soil water capacity available at the start of each growing season. Because of these assumptions, only relative changes in water requirements result from this study.

5.6.3.2   *Results*

Table 5.6.4 shows simulated crop variables under the baseline climate and the sensitivity tests. A temperature increase of 1°C and a doubling in the length of dry spells (PR) had little effect on crop yield. A 3°C increase in mean temperature implied an average increase by 7% in daily ET and a decrease by 1% in total crop ET, associated with a shortening of crop duration by 8 days and a yield decrease by 8%. An increase in temperature variability (TM) had more negative effects on crop yield than an increase in average temperature. An increase in both average temperature and temperature

(a)

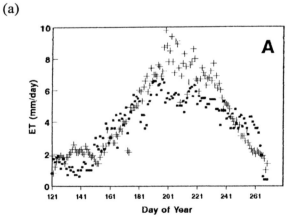

(b)

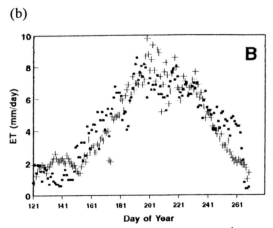

Figure 5.6.2   Simulated (■ SIM) and observed (+ OBS) daily evapotranspiration (mm day^{-1}) with (a) the original water balance and (b) the modified water balance.

variability (TM+3°C) had the largest negative effects on crop yield. This analysis did not include changes in average precipitation since all simulations were carried out under irrigated conditions during the entire growth cycle.

Changes in the demand for irrigation water are the result of two contrasting factors: increases in daily ET and shortening of the crop growth duration at higher temperatures (Table 5.6.4).

5.6.4 Application of the climate change scenarios

5.6.4.1 *Methodology*

The calibrated CERES-Maize model was run for a number of scenarios using 30 years of climatic data from each scenario at Sevilla. Generated data from two equilibrium scenarios (UKLO, UKHI) and two transient scenarios (UKTR, GFDL) were used. For the transient scenarios the last model decade was used. For the UKTR scenarios this was 66-75, and for the GFDL 55-64. The scenario data were produced by a stochastic weather generator. For the UKLO and GFDL scenarios the baseline variability in temperatures was retained in the scenario data, whereas for the UKHI and UKTR scenarios both the baseline variability and variability calculated from the GCM experiments were used. The scenarios with changed variability are denoted with a small 'v' in the scenario name e.g. UKHIv.

The atmospheric CO_2 concentration was set to 353 ppmv for the baseline climate, and to 560 ppmv for the equilibrium GCM scenarios. The CO_2 concentration for the second transient model decade was set to 617 ppmv corresponding to the IS92a emissions scenarios. The emissions scenario is denoted with a small 'a' in the scenario name, e.g. GFDL5564a. Details of the construction of the site-specific scenarios are given in Section 2.4.

Simulations were also made for climate change alone (without the direct CO_2 effect on the crop) for the UKTR6675 scenario. Results from the scenario runs were means and standard deviation of yield, evapotranspiration, water applied for irrigation and crop maturity date.

In this approach a number of yield limiting factors are not considered including nutrient limitation, negative effects of weed competition, diseases and insect pests and incidence of catastrophic weather events. Hence, simulated yields may overestimate the actual yield potential. In addition, maize hybrids and crop management are not adapted to future climatic conditions but are held constant even though both are likely to change.

5.6.4.2 *Results*

Results of crop growth simulations in the various scenario climates depend on both the severity of climate change and the physiological

Table 5.6.4 Sensitivity of maize grain yield, season length (SL), evapotranspiration (ET), water use efficiency (WUE= crop yield/crop ET) and irrigation water demand (IRR) to changes in temperature (BASE+1°C to BASE+3°C), temperature variability (TM and TM+3°C) and doubling of dry spells (PR) in Sevilla (Spain). CV= coefficient of variation.

Climate data sets	Yield (t/ha)	CV of yield	SL (days)	ET (mm)	WUE (kg m^{-3})	IRR (mm)
BASE	14.70	6.80	140	678	2.17	552
BASE+1°C	13.82	7.09	136	664	2.08	536
BASE+3°C	12.94	10.20	132	684	1.89	595
TM	10.32	29.65	111	495	2.09	589
TM+3°C	6.62	43.81	102	549	1.21	502
PR	14.69	6.74	140	653	2.25	582

effects of CO_2 enrichment. Although carried out under present management practices they suggest that maize yields are likely to decrease in the region under all scenarios considered (Table 5.6.5). Yield decreases are a consequence of the shortening of the crop growth duration, especially the grain filling period, which occurs if temperatures rise (Table 5.6.5).

Evapotranspiration was summed over the entire period of crop growth for the current and climate change simulations. ET increased in all scenarios except UKTR6675 (both with and without changes in variability). The effect of climate change on crop ET is mainly the result of two opposing factors: the shortening of the vegetative period caused by higher temperatures and the direct effect of the temperature rise on daily ET (see UKTR6675a* simulation in Table 5.6.5).

Changes in irrigation requirements are not only the result of changes in crop evapotranspiration but also because of changes in precipitation mainly during spring. Because of the assumptions made for the irrigation calculation, these changes should not be considered as absolute values. In general, irrigation demand varied with the scenario considered due to the combination of precipitation and crop ET.

Decreases in irrigation requirements have to be interpreted carefully, since they may reflect the decrease in crop ET due to the significant shortening of the crop growth duration which is accompanied with a significant yield reduction.

5.6.5   Possible adaptive responses

Changes in crop variables calculated for the climate change scenarios do not represent a realistic future situation since farmers and agricultural institutions will adapt to changing climatic conditions. A combination of adaptation strategies (such as changes in crop varieties and sowing dates) can be applied to the model to analyse possible farm-level adaptations to a warmer climate. An important adaptation strategy under a warmer climate is early sowing allowing the crop to develop during a period of the year with cooler temperatures, thereby partially offsetting crop yield reductions. As an example, the yield reduction in the warmer climate (as simulated with the UKLO scenario) can be offset by planting the crop 30 days earlier in Sevilla (Spain). Furthermore, earlier sowing dates allow the crop to develop during a period of lower ET demand, implying an increase in water use efficiency and a reduction in irrigation demand.

Table 5.6.5   Crop variables for the equilibrium and transient climate change scenarios in Sevilla (Spain): Grain yield, season length (SL), evapotranspiration (ET), water use efficiency (WUE= crop yield/crop ET) and irrigation water demand (IRR). CV= coefficient of variation.

Scenario	Yield (t/ha)	CV of yield	SL (days)	ET (mm)	WUE (kg m^{-3})	IRR (mm)
BASE	14.70	6.80	140	678	2.17	552
UKLO	13.04	10.97	123	691	1.89	519
UKHI	10.66	8.67	118	773	1.38	596
UKHIv	10.43	8.72	117	769	1.76	593
GFDL5564a	13.97	10.16	133	639	2.19	492
UKTR6675a*	12.31	9.10	129	705	1.75	584
UKTR6675a	13.19	9.17	129	587	2.25	450
UKTR6675av*	12.66	9.24	130	683	1.85	622
UKTR6675av	13.56	9.37	130	567	2.39	489

*   Simulations conducted for climate change alone (without the direct CO_2 effect)

5.6.6   Discussion and conclusions

This study evaluated and calibrated the CERES-Maize model for use in regions with a Mediterranean climate, with special emphasis on the simulation of the water balance and crop water demands. The study used the model to calculate the effects of various climate change scenarios on crop yields, water use and other crop variables in a major production area of the Mediterranean region (Sevilla). The scenarios always had a negative effect on grain yield and often a negative effect on crop water use but the magnitude of the changes depended on the counteracting effects between higher daily ET rates, shortening of the crop growth duration, changes in precipitation and the effects of CO_2 enrichment. Similar results were previously obtained with a different set of climate change scenarios (Iglesias and Minguez, 1995; Minguez and Iglesias, 1995). In an European context, the region considered may be one of the most negatively affected in terms of crop water availability with future changes in climate (Kenny and Harrison, 1992).

5.7   Effects on winter wheat: A comparison of five models

5.7.1   Background

Differences in modelling approach may cause significant differences in output from crop growth simulation models. This is an important consideration in the context of climate change research as the tendency has been to apply individual crop models using scenarios constructed from a range of GCMs. This provides a useful assessment of the uncertainty surrounding possible future climates. However, uncertainties arising from different modelling approaches also need to be quantified.

Crop models are developed for widely varying environmental conditions and for different objectives and, hence, emphasize different parts of the plant/soil/climate system. This leads to very different models which vary in their description of various processes, input requirements and sensitivities to environmental conditions. A truely mechanistic crop model should be able to reproduce experimental results

for a range of environmental conditions. Such robust and reliable models are critical for predicting the response of agriculture to changing climatic conditions. However, the description of processes and the parameters in models are often highly related to their testing conditions and are less universal than expected.

Recently the performance of three wheat models was tested against observed crop data in New Zealand (Porter *et al.*, 1993). In this detailed analysis the time courses of absorbed radiation, total and grain dry matter production and other plant characteristics were compared. The study indicated where the models differed from reality or from each other and where the models might be improved.

In the Global Change and Terrestrial Ecosystems (GCTE) Focus 3 Wheat Network eight wheat models were run for two climate data sets, one from Minnesota, U.S.A. and one from the Netherlands. The wheat models differed greatly in complexity, structure and parameterisation conditions (GCTE, 1994). Model results differed to a surprising degree. A detailed growth analysis was not undertaken and field data sets were not used for comparison. This made it difficult to trace the cause of the large differences because of the complexity and many feedbacks in the models. The conclusion from this modelling exercise was that crop growth models are not yet at a stage of development where they can be used for strongly different environmental conditions. They need at least a calibration of their parameter set against detailed field experiments before they can be applied (Goudriaan, 1994).

In this study a thorough comparison of the performance of five wheat models has been carried out for different agroclimatic conditions in Europe. Models have been compared for both current climatic conditions and a range of possible future climates. The approach was consistent with that of the GCTE Wheat Network but was more extensive in order to avoid some of the problems previously mentioned. A complementary activity within the GCTE Wheat Network has recently started which includes a comparison of wheat models on the basis of their process descriptions (Goudriaan and Porter, pers. comm., 1995). Such detailed analyses of similarities and differences in calculation routines in different wheat models will be extended in the future.

A number of possible future climates, climate change scenarios, were applied to the wheat models. These included both changes in the mean and variability of climatic variables. The majority of climate change impact assessments have used only average changes in climate and have kept the variability of weather parameters unchanged (Santer *et al.*, 1990; Giorgi and Mearns, 1991; Kenny *et al.*, 1993). However, information about changes in climatic variability are also required to build a complete picture of likely impact distributions. The relative importance of changes in climatic variability compared with changes in mean values has been investigated in sensitivity analyses by Semenov and Porter (1995). This study clearly demonstrates that plausible changes in the variability of temperature or precipitation can sometimes have larger negative effects on average yield and yield stability than changes in means. Moreover, simultaneous changes in the mean and variance of temperature can amplify the decrease in yield and thus the overall effect cannot be viewed as a simple arithmetic sum of the individual decreases. These effects have been assessed in this study, using climate data sets generated with a stochastic weather generator (see Section 2.4 for more information). There have been other attempts to incorporate changes in climatic variability into climatic scenarios (Mearns *et al.*, 1992). This approach however, using a weather generator instead of historical weather data, in conjunction with a crop simulation model, appeared to be methodologically more consistent (Semenov and Porter, 1995).

5.7.2   Methodology for model comparison

Five models (AFRCWHEAT, CERES-Wheat, NWHEAT, SIRIUS and SOILN-Wheat) were evaluated. The complexity and many feedbacks included in these models meant that it was very difficult to explain the results and sensitivities of different models on the basis of differences in model structure, source code and input data. Hence, the model comparison was based mainly on results. There were four main steps to the comparison. Firstly, models were calibrated and

validated against field data sets. Secondly, the sensitivity of wheat growth and development to independent changes in temperature, precipitation and atmospheric CO_2 concentration was investigated. Thirdly, models were run for a number of possible future climatic conditions, using the climate change scenarios described in Chapter 2. Fourthly, models were run for the same climate data sets used in the sensitivity and scenario analyses, but with changed variability in rainfall distribution and temperature. All analyses have been conducted for two European sites, Rothamsted, U.K. and Sevilla, Spain.

The following crop characteristics are produced as output by most of the models and were used to characterise the sensitivities of, and the differences between, the models:

- day of year of emergence, anthesis and maturity: [DE, DA, DM];
- grain yield and total above-ground biomass as dry matter (1000 kg DM/ha): [GR, TB];
- maximum green leaf area index (m^2 leaf/m^2 ground surface): [LAM];
- cumulative evapotranspiration from emergence to maturity (mm): [ET];
- water use efficiency, i.e. total above-ground biomass / cumulative evapotranspiration (g DM/kg H_2O) [WUE];
- cumulative intercepted photosynthetically active radiation (PAR) from emergence to maturity (MJ/m^2): [RI];
- radiation use efficiency, i.e. total above-ground biomass / cumulative intercepted PAR (g DM/MJ PAR): [RUE];
- harvest index, i.e. grain yield / total above-ground biomass (kg DM/kg DM) : [HI];
- amount of nitrogen in total above-ground biomass (kg N/ha): [NB];
- nitrogen use efficiency, i.e. total above-ground biomass / amount of nitrogen in total above-ground biomass (kg DM/kg N): [NUE].

5.7.3   Model description

A short description of the main routines of each wheat model is given. For more information on the main plant, soil and weather processes incorporated in these models, their input requirements and output produced, see the literature mentioned in the various model descriptions and the model database of the GCTE Wheat Network (GCTE, 1994).

5.7.3.1 *AFRCWHEAT 3S model*

AFRCWHEAT is a complex model of the growth and development of a wheat crop that describes its phenological development, dry matter production and partitioning in response to the environment using a daily timestep (Porter, 1984, 1993; Weir *et al.*, 1984). The model includes subroutines which describe crop transpiration and soil evaporation, the movement of water and nitrogen in the soil profile and their uptake and effects on growth.

Crop phenology

Timing of phenological stages follows calculation of a succession of phases whose thermal duration is modified by the crop's response to daylength and vernalization. Phenology sets the time frame for other developmental processes such as leaf production and tillering (Porter, 1984).

Crop growth

Production of dry matter depends mainly on the rate of photosynthesis. The photosynthesis routine describes the response of carbon fixation by the canopy to both CO_2 concentration and photosynthetically active radiation (PAR) absorbed by the leaf canopy. The partitioning of dry matter between leaves, stems, roots, ears and grains is determined by partitioning factors whose values vary with phenological stage. As the crop approaches the start date of grain filling, some dry matter is diverted from stems and leaves to a labile pool that is potentially available to the grains. During grain-filling all new dry matter goes to the grains, and the labile pool can also contribute to grain mass at a temperature-determined rate. Leaf production is calculated as a function of temperature, modified by the rate of change of daylength at emergence. The upper limit to leaf expansion is set by temperature and the availability of assimilate, water and nitrogen determines whether or not this maximum is reached.

Water balance

Simulation of soil water movement is based on the Solute Leaching Intermediate Model (SLIM) (Addiscot, 1977; Addiscot *et al.*,1986; Addiscot and Whitmore, 1987). The model simulates the daily movement of water through a layered soil and estimates how much is available for the crop. Water in each layer is treated as either mobile or retained. Excess water (when mobile water content is greater than the saturated level) is lost via rapid drainage to the bottom of the profile, bypassing the main body of the soil. The crop uptake of water is limited by availability in the rooting zone and the ability of the roots to absorb it. Evaporation from the soil and crop transpiration are calculated using the Penman equation. Crop transpiration is reduced when soil moisture is less than 65% of the available soil water in the rooting zone. A shortage of water is translated into two factors: SWDF1 hastens leaf senescence; SWDF2 reduces the leaf expansion rate and the life span of leaves, and increases specific leaf weight and the labile pool that is potentially available to the grains.

Nitrogen uptake and soil nitrogen

The SLIM model simulates the mineralization of organic nitrogen to ammonium and subsequent nitrification to nitrate as well as the distribution and movement of nitrogen throughout the soil profile. Added fertilizer is included in the top soil layer. The uptake of nitrogen by the crop is limited by its availability in the rooting zone and the ability of the roots to absorb it. The demand for nitrogen by the crop is calculated as the difference between current nitrogen concentration in the shoots and roots and their maximum value for the current development stage. Nitrogen shortage is translated into four factors: DEFN1 increases the death rate of tillers; DEFN2 reduces the leaf expansion rate; DEFN3 reduces the tiller production rate; DEFN4 increases leaf senescence, partitioning of dry matter to roots and the labile pool that is potentially available to the grains.

Direct effect of increases in atmospheric CO₂

In the model, increasing atmospheric CO_2 concentration increases both the maximum photosynthetic rate (Weir *et al.*, 1984) and the quantum yield (Gaastra, 1962; Goudriaan and van Laar, 1978).

5.7.3.2   CERES-Wheat model

CERES-Wheat describes phenological development and growth of a wheat crop in response to environmental factors (soil, climate and management) using a daily timestep (Godwin *et al.*, 1990; Ritchie and Otter, 1985). Modelled processes include phenological development, crop growth and dry matter partitioning among plant organs, extension growth of leaves and stems, senescence of leaves, and root system dynamics. The model includes subroutines to simulate water and nitrogen balances. This enables the effects of nitrogen deficiency and soil water deficit on biomass production and yield to be estimated.

Crop phenology

The primary variable influencing phasic development is temperature. The thermal time for each phase is modified by coefficients that characterise the response of different wheat genotypes. The timing of crop phenological stages can be calibrated by modifying coefficients that characterise vernalization (P1V), photoperiod response (P1D), duration of grain filling (P5) and phyllocron interval (PHINT) of a particular variety.

Crop growth

Potential dry matter production is a linear function of intercepted photosynthetically active radiation (PAR), modified by temperature. The percentage of incoming PAR intercepted by the canopy is an exponential function of leaf area index. Dry matter allocation is determined by partitioning factors that depend on the phenological stage and the degree of water stress. Final grain yield is the product of plant population density, grains per plant and grain weight. The number of grains per plant is a linear function of stem weight and coefficients that

account for the variation between genotypes in the number of grains per ear (G1) and spike number (G3). The maximum grain growth rate is an input coefficient that depends on the wheat genotype (G2).

Water balance

Precipitation is a daily input. Runoff is a function of soil type, soil moisture and precipitation. Infiltration is equal to precipitation minus runoff and drainage occurs when soil moisture exceeds the water-holding capacity of the bottom soil layer. Potential transpiration is calculated using the Priestly-Taylor approach. Actual transpiration is modified by leaf area index, soil evaporation and soil water deficit. Actual evaporation is a function of potential evaporation, LAI and time as described by Ritchie (1972). Daily change in soil moisture is calculated from precipitation minus transpiration, evaporation, runoff and drainage.

Direct effect of increases in atmospheric CO₂.

The model has been modified to simulate changes in dry matter production and transpiration as a result of changes in atmospheric CO_2 concentration. These modifications have been based on information from the literature as described by Rosenzweig and Iglesias (1994).

5.7.3.3   NWHEAT model

NWHEAT simulates the growth of a wheat crop and its response to environmental conditions. The simulation of growth and water and nitrogen dynamics is carried out in timesteps of one day. The model comprises submodels that simulate crop growth, phenological development, nitrogen uptake by the crop, soil nitrogen dynamics and soil moisture dynamics. The principles underlying this model have been discussed by Groot and de Willigen (1991) and Groot and Spiertz (1991). The model has been described completely by Groot (1987, 1993).

Crop phenology

Phenological development depends on the ambient temperature and is modified to account for the effects of vernalization and photoperiod.

This description of crop development is based on the model described by Porter (1984) and Weir *et al.* (1984), but has been adapted for Dutch conditions on the basis of results from wheat trials described by Reinink *et al.* (1986). From anthesis, phenological development is determined only by ambient temperature.

Crop growth

Simulation of crop growth is based on the model described by Spitters *et al.* (1989). Gross assimilation of the canopy is calculated as a function of leaf area index, radiation distribution in the canopy and the photosynthesis-light response curve of individual leaves. Maintenance requirements for the different plant organs, calculated as a function of their weight and chemical composition (Penning de Vries, 1975), are subtracted from daily gross assimilation. The remaining assimilates are allocated to leaves, stems and roots depending on the phenological development of the crop. Allocated assimilates are converted to structural plant material by taking into account conversion losses. After anthesis no vegetative growth occurs and all assimilates and stem reserves are allocated to grains.

Water balance

The soil is treated as a multilayered system. For each layer, changes in soil moisture content are the result of infiltration, water losses as a result of soil evaporation and crop transpiration, and downward movement to the lower layer. If precipitation occurs, the first layer is filled to field capacity. Excess water drains to the next layer which is also filled to maximum field capacity. This procedure is repeated for the deeper layers as long as there is excess water. Upward movement of water, for example capillary rise from ground water, is not calculated by the model. Potential soil evaporation is calculated using the Penman approach (Frère and Popov, 1979) and potential crop transpiration by the Penman-Monteith approach (Smith, 1992). Maximum rates of evaporation and transpiration are calculated from potential rates by correction for the degree of light interception by the canopy. Actual evaporation becomes lower than the maximum if the soil moisture content in the top

layer decreases, and actual transpiration is lowered if the moisture content in the root zone decreases. When actual transpiration is smaller than maximum transpiration, gross canopy assimilation is reduced proportionally.

Nitrogen uptake and soil nitrogen

Soil nitrogen supply depends on fertilizer nitrogen application, nitrogen in rainfall, decomposition of old (humus) and fresh organic matter (crop residues), crop nitrogen uptake and downward movement of nitrogen by leaching. Denitrification and ammonia volatilization are not taken into account. Decomposition, which is treated as a process with first-order kinetics, results in either mineralization or immobilization of nitrogen, depending on the C/N ratio of the substrate. Following the approach proposed by Burns (1974), water and mineral nitrogen entering a soil layer by leaching and mineralization are completely mixed with water and nitrogen already present. The resulting nitrogen concentration multiplied by the downward water flow, results in the downward transport of nitrogen. Before anthesis crop nitrogen demand is based on the concept of nitrogen deficiency of leaves, stems and roots. As long as the nitrogen content is below its maximum possible value, there will be a sink for nitrogen. The values used for the maximum nitrogen content decrease over time, dependent on the stage of crop development. The actual nitrogen uptake proceeds according to crop demand as long as the soil nitrogen supply is not limiting. After anthesis crop nitrogen may be translocated to the grains which lowers both the nitrogen content and photosynthetic capacity of vegetative tissue.

Direct effect of increase in atmospheric CO_2

This effect was incorporated in the model by increasing the maximum value (AMAX) and the initial angle of the CO_2 assimilation - light response curve of single leaves, by increasing the thickness of leaves, and by decreasing the stomatal conductance. These changes in model parameters were based on studies by Chaudhuri *et al.* (1990), Dijkstra *et al.* (1993), Goudriaan (1990), Goudriaan and Unsworth (1990) and on literature surveys on crop responses to CO_2

doubling by Cure (1985), Cure and Acock (1986) and Kimball (1983). Based on studies by Allen *et al.* (1990), Dijkstra *et al.* (1993) and Idso (1990), the positive effect of increasing CO_2 on AMAX is reduced when day temperatures drop below $20^{\circ}C$.

5.7.3.4   *SIRIUS model*

SIRIUS is a relatively simple wheat model using a daily timestep (Jamieson and Wilson, 1988; Jamieson, 1989). The new version of the model includes soil water and nitrogen submodels so that crop responses to water and nitrogen limitations can be studied (Jamieson *et al.*, 1995).

Crop phenology

The simulation of phenological development is based on leaf appearance and thermal time. Appearance of leaves depends on thermal time and leaf number. The final leaf number is determined by day length and vernalization. After appearance of the flag leaf ligule on the mainstem the rate of phenological development to anthesis and during grain filling is determined by thermal time only.

Crop growth

Leaf area index is determined by thermal time and phenological stage. It is modelled in four stages: an exponential increase with thermal time from emergence to an LAI of 5; a linear increase with thermal time from an LAI of 5 to 8.5; a constant maximum value of 8.5 until anthesis; and a decrease quadratically related to thermal time so that leaf area index reaches zero at the end of grain filling. The fraction of radiation intercepted by the canopy is calculated from Beer's law. Dry matter accumulation is calculated from intercepted radiation with a fixed value for the radiation-use efficiency. All new assimilates are allocated to the grains once grain growth starts. In addition, a pool of 20% of the amount of dry matter at anthesis is bled into the grain at a temperature determined rate.

Water balance

This submodel is based on the Solute Leaching Intermediate Model (SLIM) (Addiscott, 1977;

Addiscott *et al.*, 1986) and the water balance model WATCROSS (Aslyng and Hansen, 1982). Precipitation is partly intercepted by the leaves, the remaining water reaches the soil surface and after infiltration water percolates downwards and is distributed between the soil layers. The model has multiple soil layers, each with their own water storage capacity. To calculate potential crop transpiration the Ritchie (1972) model is used. This model takes into account the main environmental factors (net radiation, temperature and vapour pressure deficit). To derive the actual transpiration, potential transpiration is reduced for incomplete ground cover and soil moisture deficit. Soil evaporation is calculated with either energy or diffusion limited equations, of which the lowest result is used (Tanner and Jury, 1976). The energy limited equation is equal to potential evapotranspiration multiplied by the fraction of incoming radiation received at the soil surface, and the diffusion limited equation is equal to a fixed constant for soil diffusion divided by the square root of the time since the last date the soil surface was completely wet.

Nitrogen uptake and soil nitrogen

The nitrogen submodel is very similar to the NITCROS model (Hansen and Aslyng, 1984). The processes which determine changes in soil inorganic nitrogen are fertilizer nitrogen application, soil mineralization, denitrification, leaching, microbial fixation and nitrogen uptake by the crop. Maximum nitrogen uptake is determined by dry matter production and maximum nitrogen concentration which is a function of the age of the crop. Actual nitrogen uptake depends on both maximum nitrogen uptake and the available amount of inorganic nitrogen in the soil.

Direct effect of increases in atmospheric CO_2

Radiation use efficiency is assumed to increase linearly with atmospheric CO_2 concentration and to become 30% higher with CO_2 doubling.

5.7.3.5   *SOILN model*

SOILN simulates biomass and nitrogen dynamics in a wheat crop and is an application of a general soil-plant model, SOILN-CROP (Eckersten and

Jansson, 1991; Eckersten *et al.*, 1994; Johnsson *et al.*, 1987). The soil can be divided in layers of different thickness. In this study, however, only one layer, the root zone, has been used, because the focus was on plant dynamics of the model and optimum soil water and nutrient status was assumed. The model has a time step of one day. Plant biomass and nitrogen dynamics are based on the relationship between carbon and nitrogen described by Eckersten and Slapokas (1990). This model concept originates from the idea that carbon input is strongly related both to energy input (de Wit, 1965) and to nitrogen input (Ingestad *et al.*, 1981).

Crop phenology

Dates of emergence, end of grain filling and maturity are calculated with a temperature-dependent function that has been taken from AFRCWHEAT. The start of grain filling depends both on temperature and daylength.

Crop growth

Maximum growth is proportional to the radiation intercepted by the canopy leaf area. This proportion decreases during grain filling. Actual growth is the maximum growth reduced by low air temperature and low leaf nitrogen concentration. The plant is divided in two pools for each type of function simulated by the model: one pool for biomass and one for nitrogen. Leaves fix carbon from the atmosphere and roots take up nitrogen from the soil. Stems are used for storage. During grain filling grains are additional storage organs that are supplied with assimilates from stems. The partitioning of assimilates to roots, leaves and stems is governed by two linear functions. The fraction partitioned to roots decreases as total plant biomass increases. The partitioning between leaves and stems depends on the leaf area development. This partitioning is determined by the leaf area to shoot biomass ratio which decreases with increasing shoot biomass. Leaf biomass is calculated from leaf area development and specific leaf area, and stem biomass is the remaining part of the shoot biomass. During grain filling biomass is allocated from stems to grains and stems receive assimilates from roots and leaves. Before old

leaves die, their biomass and nitrogen is translocated to stems.

Nitrogen uptake and soil nitrogen

Nitrogen allocation in the crop is determined by biomass allocation and nitrogen concentration in plant tissue. Maximum nitrogen uptake is the sum of the maximum demands by the different plant organs. The demand equals the daily growth multiplied by the maximum nitrogen concentration of the tissue concerned. Actual nitrogen uptake is the lower value of the demand and the amount of nitrogen available in the soil. This available amount is a fraction of the total mineral nitrogen in the root zone. The amount of mineral nitrogen depends on the rate of decomposition of soil organic matter which is a function of temperature and the C/N ratio of soil organic matter.

Direct effect of increases in atmospheric CO_2

This effect is not included in the model. For comparison with results from the other models it was assumed that biomass production increases by 30% with doubling of atmospheric CO_2.

5.7.4 Model calibration and validation

The ability of each model to reproduce observed data was tested for two sites, Rothamsted, U.K. and Sevilla, Spain. For each site two sets of experimental data were required, one set for model calibration and one set for model validation. The models were calibrated for a single variety at each site to overcome differences in parameterisation conditions between models.

Models were initially run for potential production, ie. assuming no limitations to growth from water or nitrogen availability. Thereafter, models were run for water-limited production where crop growth can be limited by the water supply from precipitation and soil storage.

Calibration was conducted in three steps:

(i) phenological development was calibrated such that modelled dates of emergence, anthesis and maturity were within the experimental error of the observed data;

(ii) simulated maximum green leaf area index was made (as much as possible) identical to observed data;

(iii) simulated biomass and yield were made (as much as possible) identical to the observed data for both potential and the water-limited production.

In both the calibration and validation exercise the models produced output every 10 days from sowing to the end of the growing season. To validate model performance, outputs were compared with both the outputs of the other models and with the experimental data.

5.7.4.1 *Rothamsted*

Data from two experiments, each using the winter wheat variety Avalon, were used for model calibration and validation. The experiments at the IACR-Rothamsted Experimental station investigated the interactive effects of water and nitrogen on crop growth. In this analysis only the results from experiments with large fertilizer-N application have been used. In the experiment used for calibration (Brimstone experiment 1985/86), sown on 10 October 1985, the crop was either fully irrigated (+I) or covered by a rain shelter (-I) from 29 April 1986 until maturity. In the experiment used for validation (Stackyard experiment 1984/85), sown on 5 October 1984, the crop was either growing on a soil maintained to within 25 mm of field capacity by irrigation (+I) or was covered by a rain shelter from 17 April 1985 (-I). Further details on the Brimstone experiments in 1985/86 are given by Weir (1988) and about the Stackyard experiments in 1984/85 by Barraclough *et al.* (1989). Porter (1993) also provides information on these experiments and tests the ability of the AFRCWHEAT model to simulate observed crop growth.

The initial and maximum amounts of available water assumed in all model runs were based on data from J.R. Porter (pers. comm., 1994). Historical sets of weather data were used. As only results from the experiments with large fertilizer N application have been used, it was assumed that N supply was not a limiting factor for crop growth and N uptake in the model runs.

Calibration

An overview of model results and the observed data for the calibration year (1985/86) is given in Table 5.7.1. All results except date of emergence (DE), date of anthesis (DA) and maximum green leaf area index (LAM) are given for the date of maturity. Note that the observed data are mean results from the experiments and the variation in experimental results was not taken into account in these analyses.

Rates of phenological development were calibrated well in most models, resulting in dates of anthesis (DA) and maturity (DM) identical to those observed (Table 5.7.1). Only SIRIUS and SOILN calculated a date of maturity that was too early. The calibration of maximum green leaf area index (LAM) was not as successful as phenology. AFRCWHEAT and SOILN did quite well, but CERES and NWHEAT calculated too low a value. In the SIRIUS model LAM was fixed at 8.5 which was greater than that observed in both the irrigated and water-limited experiments.

The simulated values for total above-ground biomass (TB) and grain yield (GR) were calibrated fairly well in the irrigated trial (Table 5.7.1). Only SIRIUS calculated rather low values for GR. In the water-limited trials (with rain shelter) the reduction of TB by water shortage was reproduced well by CERES and NWHEAT, but the reduction was overestimated by AFRCWHEAT and underestimated by SIRIUS. These over or underestimations were not due to model characteristics but were caused by the input value for soil water storage.

Identical values for harvest index (HI) were observed in both the irrigated and water-limited experiments, although crop growth in the water-limited trials was severely reduced by water stress at the end of the growing season. AFRCWHEAT calculated an identical HI for irrigated and water-limited situations, but CERES, NWHEAT and SIRIUS calculated much lower values in the water-limited situation, due to insufficient redistribution of assimilates to the grains.

Table 5.7.1 Plant characteristics as observed in the Brimstone wheat trials (fully irrigated (+I) or with rain shelter from 29 April (-I)) in 1985/86 at the IACR-Rothamsted Experimental station and as simulated by the different models.

	DE	DA	DM	GR	TB	HI	ET[1]	WUE[1]	RI	RUE	LAM	NB	NUE[2]
Observed +I	-	171	218	9.30	19.22	0.48	326	5.61	-	-	6.83	257	74.8
AFRCWHEAT +I	295	170	219	9.11	19.77	0.46	280	6.73	723	2.73	7.42	202	97.9
CERES Wheat +I	296	171	218	9.27	18.56	0.50	317	5.30	-	-	4.87	244	76.0
NWHEAT +I	295	171	218	9.80	19.56	0.50	319	5.99	720	2.72	4.70	267	73.2
SIRIUS +I	296	171	210	8.17	19.28	0.42	264	5.68	-	2.2	8.50	-	-
SOILN +I	295	-	208	9.04	18.39	0.49	-	-	773	2.38	6.86	221	83.2
Observed -I	-	168	218	7.51	15.70	0.48	219	6.48	-	-	6.28	196	80.1
AFRCWHEAT -I	295	170	219	6.06	13.55	0.45	167	7.56	545	2.49	5.98	139	97.5
CERES WHEAT -I	296	171	218	6.42	15.67	0.41	246	5.65	-	-	4.73	232	67.6
NWHEAT -I	295	171	218	6.07	15.34	0.40	220	6.79	688	2.23	4.49	186	82.6
SIRIUS -I	296	171	210	7.86	19.07	0.41	251	5.90	-	2.2	8.50	-	-

[1] Evapotranspiration and water use efficiency from day 110 to maturity.
[2] For the meaning of the abbreviations see Section 5.7.2.

Observed values for cumulative evapotranspiration (ET) were for the period from day 110 to the date of maturity (Table 5.7.1). In the irrigated situation simulated results from CERES and NWHEAT were almost identical to observed ET, whilst AFRCWHEAT and SIRIUS gave too low values. This resulted in a high water use efficiency (WUE) in the AFRCWHEAT run, but not in the SIRIUS run. This can be explained by the large amount of biomass at day 110 in the SIRIUS run, which resulted in a relatively small increase in biomass from that day until the date of maturity (Figure 5.7.1). In the water-limited runs the estimated soil water supply varied from relatively low in AFRCWHEAT to fairly high in CERES and SIRIUS which strongly influenced the water losses by ET. WUE is higher in the water-limited than in the irrigated situation. This can be explained by lower losses through soil evaporation in the water-limited situation.

AFRCWHEAT and NWHEAT calculated similar values for cumulative intercepted photosynthetically active radiation (RI) and radiation use efficiency (RUE) in the irrigated situation. No experimental data were available for these variables. Lower values of RUE were calculated by the SIRIUS and SOILN models. Simulated RUE decreased in the water-limited, compared to the irrigated, situation.

Observed values of nitrogen content in above-ground biomass (NB) and nitrogen use efficiency (NUE) were simulated reasonably well by CERES and NWHEAT for the irrigated situation (Table 5.7.1). AFRCWHEAT and SOILN calculated a lower NB which resulted in a much and slightly higher NUE, respectively. This may be because the available amount of nitrogen was underestimated. In the water-limited situation NB was reduced because drying of the top soil reduced the availability of soil and fertilizer nitrogen.

The time course of TB and green leaf area index (LAI) as observed in the irrigated Brimstone experiment during the growing season 1985/86 and as simulated with the different models is shown in Figure 5.7.1. TB was calibrated quite well in all models, but growth in the spring was strongly overestimated by SIRIUS and moderately overestimated by CERES. The time course of LAI was calibrated quite well in AFRCWHEAT and SOILN, was strongly overestimated by SIRIUS and strongly underestimated by NWHEAT and CERES. Dry matter production did not change much for LAI values varying between 4 and 8 and, hence, these differences in LAI had little effect on the prediction of TB.

The time course of ET and NB as observed in the irrigated Brimstone experiment during the growing season 1985/86 and as simulated with the different models is shown in Figure 5.7.2. ET was simulated quite accurately by all models. SIRIUS set the date of maturity and thus the end of transpiration too early, and AFRCWHEAT

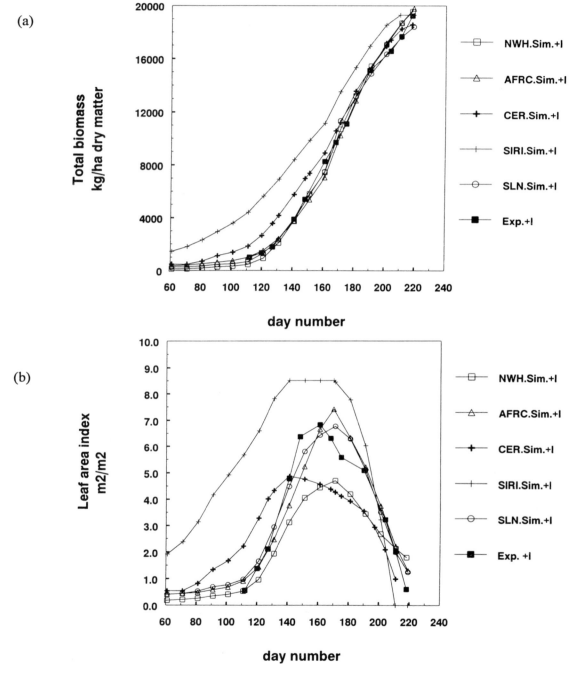

Figure 5.7.1   Time course of (a) total above-ground biomass and (b) green leaf area of winter wheat as observed in the Brimstone field trials (IACR-Rothamsted Experimental station, UK) for the treatment with irrigation (+I) and with a large fertilizer N application in growing season 1985/86 and as simulated with the NWHEAT (NWH.), AFRCWHEAT 3S (AFRC.), CERES-Wheat (CER.), SIRIUS (SIRI.) and SOILN-Wheat (SLN.) models for potential production.

slightly underestimated water losses by ET. Relatively poor calibration of LAI against the field trials for most models did not influence the successful calibration of ET. The time course of NB was simulated well by AFRCWHEAT, NWHEAT and SOILN. The AFRCWHEAT run, and the SOILN run to a lesser extent, showed a

reduction of NB which was too strong at the end of the growing season. This was caused by either an underestimation of the total available amount of soil nitrogen or a decrease too early in the nitrogen uptake process. The overestimation of TB and leaf growth in spring by CERES resulted in nitrogen being taken up too rapidly in

(a)

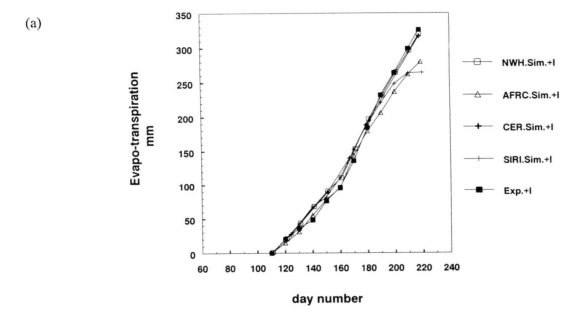

(b)

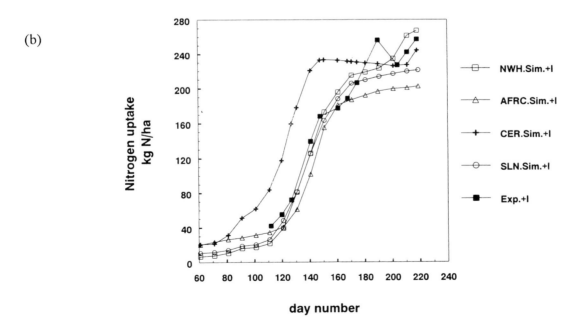

Figure 5.7.2 Time course of (a) evapotranspiration and (b) nitrogen uptake by winter wheat as observed in the Brimstone field trials (IACR-Rothamsted Experimental station, UK) for the treatment with irrigation (+I) and with a large fertilizer N application in growing season 1985/86 and as simulated with the NWHEAT (NWH.), AFRCWHEAT 3S (AFRC.), CERES-Wheat (CER.), SIRIUS (SIRI.) and SOILN-Wheat (SLN.) models for potential production.

spring, but NB at maturity corresponded well to the observed value.

Validation

Results from the Stackyard experiments during the growing season 1984/1985 were used to validate the different models (Table 5.7.2). The simulated and observed dates of anthesis (DA) corresponded reasonably well. The dates of maturity (DM) calculated by CERES and SIRIUS were reasonably close to the observed date, but those calculated with AFRCWHEAT and NWHEAT were approximately a week late. There are two explanations for this difference. First, both AFRCWHEAT and NWHEAT use a rather high base temperature for calculating the rate of post-anthesis phenological development which makes the length of the grain-filling period rather sensitive to changes in temperature. Second, nitrogen limitation in the field trial may have reduced the duration of grain-filling. SOILN needed a second calibration of phenological

development or otherwise the modelled date of maturity would have been one month earlier than the observed date. The observed value for LAM was slightly lower than that in 1985/86. AFRCWHEAT, SOILN and SIRIUS calculated about the same value for LAM as in 1985/86 and NWHEAT and CERES a higher value. This resulted in slightly too low values for LAM in the CERES and NWHEAT runs, and slightly, moderately and much too high values in the SOILN, AFRCWHEAT, and SIRIUS runs, respectively.

Simulated TB and GR were high compared to those in the field trial, except those modelled with SOILN (Table 5.7.2). HI was too low in the SIRIUS run and too high in the NWHEAT run, this high value being mainly the result of a very long period of grain filling. In the water-limited situation, observed and simulated TB corresponded quite well, except for the SIRIUS run, and the CERES run to a lesser extent, in which the available amount of soil water was

Table 5.7.2 Plant characteristics as observed in the Stackyard wheat trials (fully irrigated (+I) or with rainshelter from 17 April (-I)) in 1984/85 at the IACR-Rothamsted Experimental station and as simulated by the different models.

	DE	DA	DM	GR	TB	HI	ET[1]	WUE[1]	RI	RUE	LAM	NB	NUE[2]
Observed +I	-	170	218	8.28	17.66	0.47	268[3]	5.54[3]	-	-	6.23	203	87.0
AFRCWHEAT +I	290	164	224	10.70	21.99	0.49	290	6.87	814	2.70	7.68	204	107.8
CERES Wheat +I	288	166	217	10.12	20.22	0.50	291	5.58	-	-	5.44	269	75.1
NWHEAT +I	290	169	225	11.84	22.33	0.53	309	6.73	849	2.63	5.70	296	75.5
SIRIUS +I	290	175	220	9.05	21.05	0.43	260	5.88	-	2.2	8.50	-	-
SOILN +I[4]	289	-	221	8.35	18.81	0.44	-	-	850	2.21	6.85	222	84.7
Observed -I	-	166	208	6.73	15.44	0.44	200[3]	6.67[3]	-	-	5.72	161	95.9
AFRCWHEAT -I	290	164	224	7.31	15.31	0.48	171	7.75	622	2.46	6.33	139	110.1
CERES Wheat -I	288	166	217	7.80	17.68	0.44	227	6.04	-	-	5.44	255	69.3
NWHEAT -I	290	169	225	5.65	15.82	0.36	197	7.24	798	1.98	5.58	188	84.2
SIRIUS -I	290	175	220	7.78	20.35	0.38	236	6.18	-	2.2	8.50	-	-

[1]   Evapotranspiration and water use efficiency from day 110 to maturity.
[2]   For the meaning of the abbreviations see Section 5.7.2.
[3]   Observed evapotranspiration and water use efficiency from day 110 to day 210.
[4]   This model needed a new calibration of the rate of phenological development against Stackyard data as otherwise the date of maturity would be one month too early.

overestimated. In the experiment water shortage resulted in a slightly lower HI. According to the simulation with AFRCWHEAT, water shortage did not affect HI, and according to those with CERES, SIRIUS and NWHEAT, water shortage reduced HI moderately, moderately and strongly, respectively.

Observed values for ET covered the period from day 110 to day 210, whilst simulated values covered a period which was 7 to 15 days longer (Table 5.7.2). Taking this difference into account, the simulated ET values in the irrigated situation corresponded well to observed values. In the water-limited situation, ET was determined by the soil water supply which was underestimated in the AFRCWHEAT run and overestimated in the CERES and SIRIUS runs. WUE was higher in the water-limited situation than in the irrigated situation because water losses by soil evaporation have been reduced.

In the irrigated trial RUE calculated with AFRCWHEAT and NWHEAT was higher than the RUE calculated with SIRIUS and SOILN. In the AFRCWHEAT run water shortage reduced LAI, and thus RI, more strongly than in the NWHEAT run. This resulted in a smaller decrease in RUE by water shortage in the AFRCWHEAT run.

The observed value for NB in the irrigated trial was simulated well by AFRCWHEAT (Table 5.7.2). SOILN, CERES and NWHEAT calculated slightly, much and much too high values for NB, respectively. It is probable that the nitrogen supply in the field trial was not sufficient to attain the potential yield level. This resulted in reduced TB and a relatively high NUE. In the water-limited field trial the nitrogen supply was reduced by drying of the top soil, which resulted in a lower value for observed NB and an even higher NUE. AFRCWHEAT and NWHEAT also simulated a reduced NB for the water-limited situation.

The time course of TB and LAI as observed in the irrigated Stackyard experiment during the growing season 1984/85 and as simulated with the different models is shown in Figure 5.7.3. TB was simulated reasonably well by AFRCWHEAT, NWHEAT and SOILN up to day

180 when the observed growth curve started to flatten off. This part of the curve was only simulated well by SOILN. Growth in spring was strongly overestimated by SIRIUS and moderately overestimated by CERES. The time course of LAI was simulated well only by SOILN. This was partly caused by the difference between the observed and simulated date of maturity for AFRCWHEAT and NWHEAT (Table 5.7.2). LAI was slightly and strongly overestimated by AFRCWHEAT and SIRIUS respectively and slightly underestimated by both NWHEAT and CERES.

The time course of ET and NB as observed in the irrigated Stackyard experiment during the growing season 1984/85 and as simulated with the different models is shown in Figure 5.7.4. ET was simulated quite accurately by all models. In the field trial, however, crop growth and transpiration stopped at an earlier date. Differences in LAI between simulations and experimental data do not appear to influence these results. The time course of NB was simulated reasonably well by AFRCWHEAT, NWHEAT and SOILN up to day 150. From that date the rate of nitrogen uptake in the field trial became very small because of depletion of the soil supply. This was only simulated well by AFRCWHEAT and SOILN. The overestimation of TB and leaf growth in spring by CERES resulted in nitrogen being taken up too rapidly during this period, but NB at maturity corresponded to values calculated with the NWHEAT model.

5.7.4.2 *Sevilla*

Wheat variety trials were carried out at Tomejil in the neighbourhood of Sevilla. The varieties were grown on a heavy clay (vertisol). Large amounts of fertilizer were applied, but no irrigation water. In the trial carried out during the growing season 1988/89 (RAEA, 1989), and used for calibration, the crop was sown on 7 December 1988. In the trial carried out in 1990/91 (RAEA, 1991), and used for validation, the crop was sown on 29 November 1990. Dates of emergence, anthesis and harvest were recorded in all trials. Grain yields were also available for each variety and the average of the three highest yields was used for comparison against simulated yields.

Other information on the time course of biomass, water use, nitrogen use and leaf area during the growth period was not available. Therefore, such results from the model runs were compared between models, but not against observed data.

The initial and maximum amounts of available water assumed in all model runs were based on data from A. Iglesias (pers. comm., 1995). Historical sets of weather data were used. The initial amounts of available water in the CERES

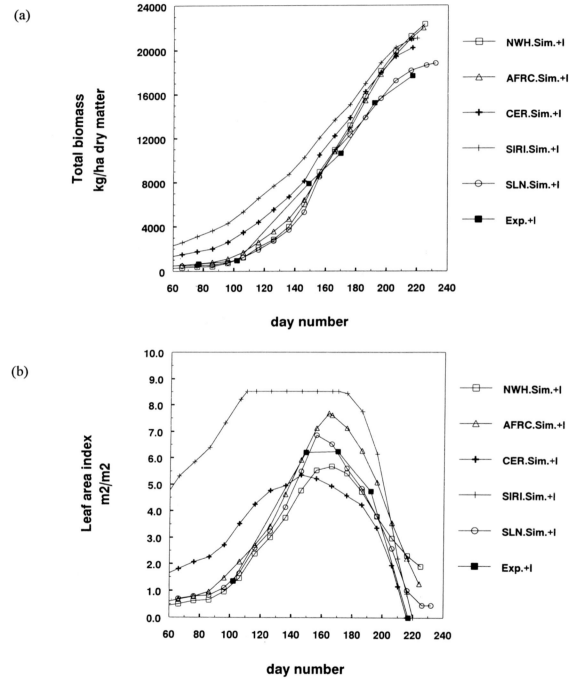

Figure 5.7.3   Time course of (a) total above-ground biomass and (b) green leaf area of winter wheat as observed in the Stackyard field trials (IACR-Rothamsted Experimental station, UK) for the treatment with irrigation (+I) and with a large fertilizer N application in growing season 1984/85 and as simulated with the NWHEAT (NWH.), AFRCWHEAT 3S (AFRC.), CERES-Wheat (CER.), SIRIUS (SIRI.) and SOILN-Wheat (SLN.) models for potential production.

and NWHEAT runs may have been estimated too high as they were set to field capacity at sowing. As large amounts of fertilizer N were applied in the variety trials, it was assumed that in the simulations N supply was not limiting for crop growth and N uptake.

Calibration

An overview of model results and the observed data for the calibration year (1988/89) is given in Table 5.7.3. All results except DE, DA and LAM are given for the date of maturity. The simulated

(a)

(b)

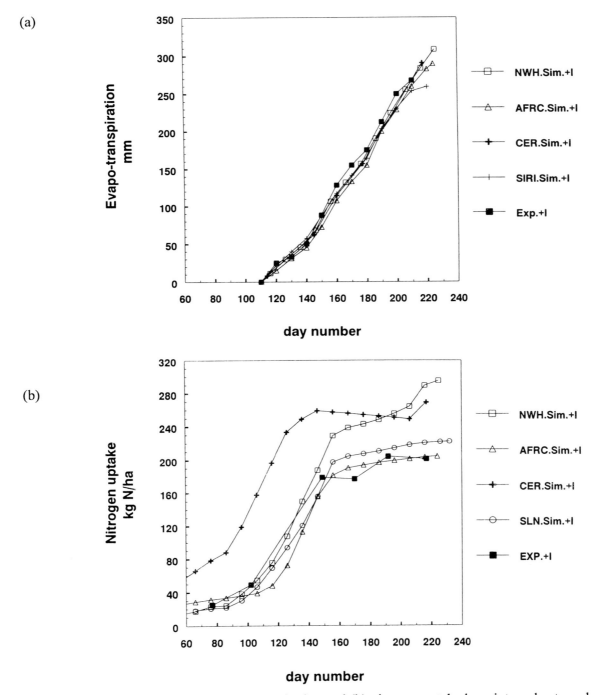

Figure 5.7.4 Time course of (a) evapotranspiration and (b) nitrogen uptake by winter wheat as observed in the Stackyard field trials (IACR-Rothamsted Experimental station, UK) for the treatment with irrigation (+I) and with a large fertilizer N application in growing season 1984/85 and as simulated with the NWHEAT (NWH.), AFRCWHEAT 3S (AFRC.), CERES-Wheat (CER.), SIRIUS (SIRI.) and SOILN-Wheat (SLN.) models for potential production.

dates of emergence (DE) and anthesis (DA) were calibrated well in all models (Table 5.7.3). The date of maturity was not available from the variety trials. A slightly later date of maturity was calculated by AFRCWHEAT and SIRIUS than CERES and NWHEAT. The highest values for LAM were calculated with AFRCWHEAT and SIRIUS and the lowest with CERES and NWHEAT. These differences were also found at Rothamsted. An observed value for LAM was not available.

In the water-limited situation the highest value for TB was calculated with NWHEAT and the lowest value with AFRCWHEAT (Table 5.7.3). HI was higher for the irrigated situation than for the water-limited situation. In water-limited conditions, AFRCWHEAT calculated the highest value for HI and CERES and SIRIUS the lowest values. The calibration of GR was not as accurate as phenology. The CERES model corresponded best, the AFRCWHEAT and SIRIUS results were slightly too low and the NWHEAT result was too high. These differences might be explained by, firstly, the amount of initial soil water at sowing might be overestimated in the simulations (at least for CERES and NWHEAT) and, secondly,

in variety trials yield losses often occur due to ripening diseases and sub-optimum crop management.

Observed values for water losses by ET were not available. Simulated ET in the CERES and SIRIUS runs were relatively high whilst ET from AFRCWHEAT was very low, probably because this model used a much lower estimate for the soil water supply than the other models (Table 5.7.3). This resulted in WUE values that varied from a relatively high value in the AFRCWHEAT run to low values in the CERES and SIRIUS runs.

RI in the AFRCWHEAT run was much lower than in the NWHEAT run. This might explain the low values for TB and ET calculated with AFRCWHEAT. RUE, however, was almost identical in both model runs and in the SIRIUS run.

Calculated values for NB differed mainly because of differences in TB (Table 5.7.3). CERES and NWHEAT calculated identical NUE, with a slightly higher value in the case where soil water supply was non-limiting.

Table 5.7.3   Plant characteristics as simulated by the different models for potential (+I) and water-limited production (-I) for winter wheat growing in 1988/89 at Tomejil near Sevilla and as observed in the wheat variety trials at Tomejil.

	DE	DA	DM	GR	TB	HI	ET[1]	WUE[1]	RI	RUE	LAM	NB	NUE[2]
CERES Wheat +I	358	107	145	7.18	17.45	0.41	425	4.11	-	-	5.59	241.7	72.2
NWHEAT +I	358	105	145	9.47	20.10	0.47	354	5.68	753	2.67	5.30	281.7	71.3
Observed -I	359	105	-	6.27[3]	-	-	-	-	-	-	-	-	-
AFRCWHEAT -I	358	107	151	5.49	12.16	0.45	181	6.72	527	2.31	7.52	221.0	55.0
CERES Wheat -I	358	107	145	5.99	16.09	0.37	355	4.53	-	-	5.59	241.7	66.6
NWHEAT -I	358	105	145	7.57	18.15	0.42	304	5.98	745	2.44	5.26	276.9	65.6
SIRIUS -I	358	106	149	5.60	14.71	0.38	358	4.10	-	2.2	8.50	-	-

[1]   Evapotranspiration and water use efficiency from emergence to maturity.
[2]   For the meaning of the abbreviations see Section 5.7.2.
[3]   Average of three highest grain yields in variety trial.

In the AFRCWHEAT run the water supply was strongly limiting which resulted in the lowest value for NUE.

The time course of TB and LAI as simulated with the different models for water-limited production in the 1988/89 growing season is shown in Figure 5.7.5. The time course of TB was very similar for NWHEAT and CERES up to day number 120, after which the CERES curve flattens off at an earlier date than NWHEAT near maturity.

SIRIUS calculated a smaller increase in TB during the main growth period than the other models. In the AFRCWHEAT run crop growth started at a later date, but from day 70 the rate of increase in TB was almost identical to those in the NWHEAT and CERES runs. However, growth stopped at an earlier date, probably because the soil water supply was more limited. The time courses of LAI as calculated with the different models were similar to those simulated for the field trials in Rothamsted (Figures 5.7.1

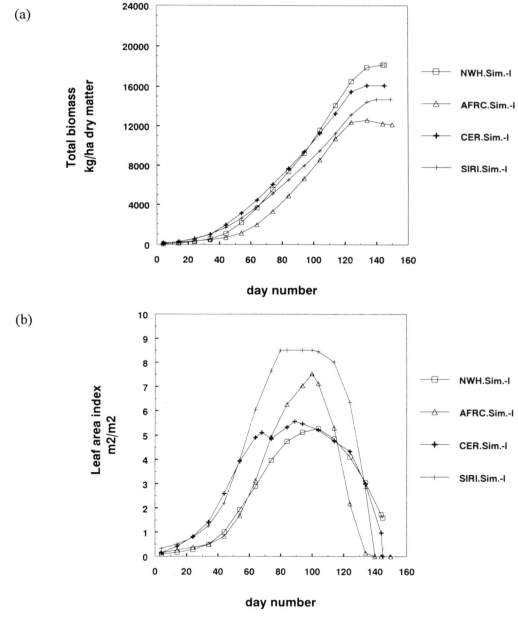

Figure 5.7.5 Time course of (a) total above-ground biomass and (b) green leaf area of winter wheat as simulated with the NWHEAT (NWH.), AFRCWHEAT 3S (AFRC.), CERES (CER.), and SIRIUS (SIRI.) models for water-limited production (-I) in growing season 1988/89 at Tomejil (near Sevilla), Spain.

and 5.7.3). CERES and NWHEAT gave relatively low values for LAI, with an earlier increase in the CERES run. AFRCWHEAT simulated a relatively late start of leaf area growth which resulted in a rather high maximum value, followed by a very early and drastic decrease in LAI, probably because of water shortage. SIRIUS simulated the highest values as LAI is fixed at 8.5 around the time of anthesis.

The time course of ET and NB as simulated with the different models for water-limited production in the 1988/89 growing season is shown in Figure 5.7.6. ET during the initial part of the growing season was relatively high in the SIRIUS and CERES runs, which is explained by the high values for LAI. During the rest of the growing season all models calculated the same rate of ET except for AFRCWHEAT, probably because its

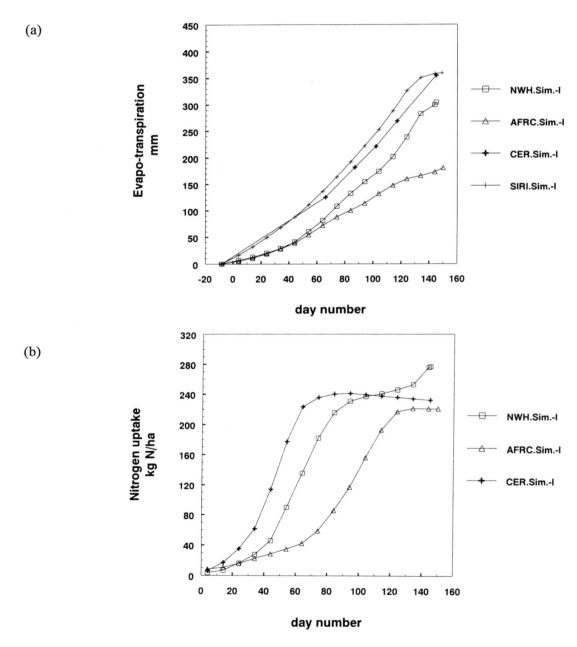

Figure 5.7.6   Time course of (a) evapotranspiration and (b) nitrogen uptake by winter wheat as simulated with the NWHEAT (NWH.), AFRCWHEAT 3S (AFRC.), CERES (CER.), and SIRIUS (SIRI.) models for water-limited production (-I) in growing season 1988/89 at Tomejil (near Sevilla), Spain.

soil water supply was more limiting. The initial rate of increase in NB was greatest in the CERES run, which was partly caused by the early start of crop growth (Figure 5.7.5) and was partly due to model characteristics (Figures 5.7.2 and 5.7.4). NB was lowest in the AFRCWHEAT run because of the late start of crop growth (Figure 5.7.5) and perhaps due to reduced nitrogen availability in the dry soil.

Validation

Results from the wheat variety trials in 1990/91 were too limited for a thorough validation of all crop parameters. For those parameters for which observations were not available, model results were compared between models (Table 5.7.4). All models calculated dates of emergence (DE) that corresponded well to the observed date. The modelled dates of anthesis (DA) were almost identical between models, but were later than the observed date. The date of maturity (DM) was not observed in the variety trials. SIRIUS and AFRCWHEAT calculated slightly later dates of maturity than the CERES and NWHEAT models. The highest value for LAM were again calculated

in the SIRIUS and AFRCWHEAT runs and the lowest in the CERES and NWHEAT runs.

NWHEAT calculated the highest value for TB and AFRCWHEAT the lowest value (Table 5.7.4). Highest HI and GR was calculated by NWHEAT. The other models calculated a lower HI and a much lower GR which corresponded well with the best GR in the variety trials. These observed GR may not be completely comparable to the simulated GR if in the trials GR losses due to ripening diseases and sub-optimum crop management were not negligible.

ET was highest in the CERES and SIRIUS runs and lowest in the AFRCWHEAT run (Table 5.7.4). This resulted in the highest WUE for the AFRCWHEAT run and the lowest for CERES and SIRIUS runs. In irrigated conditions WUE was lower because of increased water losses by soil evaporation. NWHEAT calculated the highest NB because of the high TB (Table 5.7.4). This resulted in a NUE that was slightly lower than that calculated by CERES. In the AFRCWHEAT run water supply was strongly limiting which resulted in the lowest NUE.

Table 5.7.4 Plant characteristics as simulated by the different models for potential (+I) and water-limited production (-I) for winter wheat growing in 1990/91 at Tomejil near Sevilla and as observed in the wheat variety trials at Tomejil.

	DE	DA	DM	GR	TB	HI	ET	WUE[1]	RI	RUE	LAM	NB	NUE[2]
CERES Wheat +I	347	110	150	8.26	18.88	0.44	463	4.08	-	-	5.57	233.8	80.8
NWHEAT +I	349	109	152	10.16	20.87	0.49	351	5.95	824	2.53	5.03	285.9	73.0
Observed -I	348	104	-	6.06[3]	-	-	-	-	-	-	-	-	-
AFRCWHEAT -I	347	108	156	5.49	14.36	0.38	195	7.38	644	2.23	7.86	255.0	56.3
CERES Wheat -I	347	110	150	6.77	17.18	0.39	382	4.50	-	-	5.57	233.8	73.5
NWHEAT -I	349	109	152	8.52	19.21	0.44	296	6.50	818	2.35	5.03	282.5	68.0
SIRIUS -I	349	111	155	6.18	17.06	0.36	394	4.33	-	2.2	8.50	-	-

[1] Evapotranspiration and water use efficiency from emergence to maturity.
[2] For the meaning of the abbreviations see Section 5.7.2.
[3] Average of three highest grain yields in variety trial.

The time course of TB and LAI as simulated with the different models for water-limited production in the 1990/91 growing season is shown in Figure 5.7.7. The time course of TB in the different model runs were similar, except that in the CERES and SIRIUS runs growth started earlier than in the other two model runs. Near maturity growth stopped at a relatively early date in the AFRCWHEAT run, probably because of water shortage, and at a relatively late date in the NWHEAT run. SIRIUS calculated a smaller increase in TB during the main growth period than the other models. The time courses of LAI were similar to those simulated for the other site and/or year.

(a)

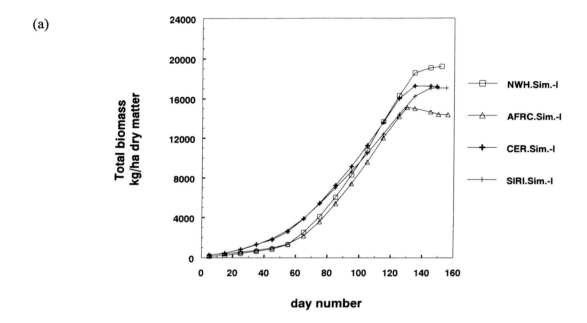

(b)

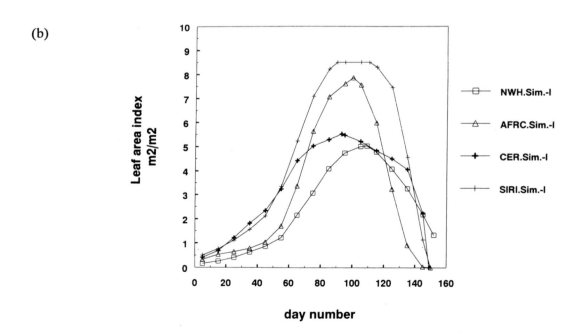

Figure 5.7.7   Time course of (a) total above-ground biomass and (b) green leaf area of winter wheat as simulated with the NWHEAT (NWH.), AFRCWHEAT 3S (AFRC.), CERES (CER.), and SIRIUS (SIRI.) models for water-limited production (-I) in growing season 1990/91 at Tomejil (near Sevilla), Spain.

The time course of ET and NB as simulated with the different models for water-limited production in the 1990/91 growing season is shown in Figure 5.7.8. ET during the initial part of the growing season was relatively high in the SIRIUS and CERES runs, which was caused by the high values for LAI. During the rest of the growing season all models calculated approximately the same rate of ET. In the AFRCWHEAT run ET was reduced strongly from day 100, probably because of limiting soil water supply. The time courses of NB were similar to those simulated for the calibration year.

(a)

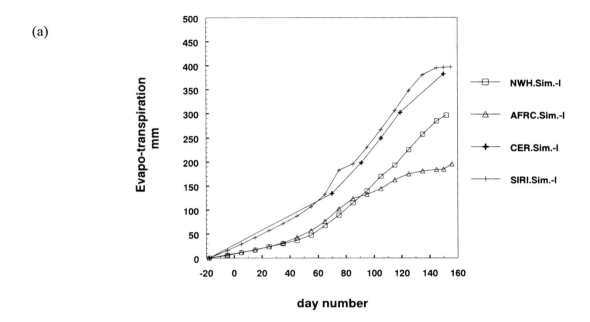

(b)

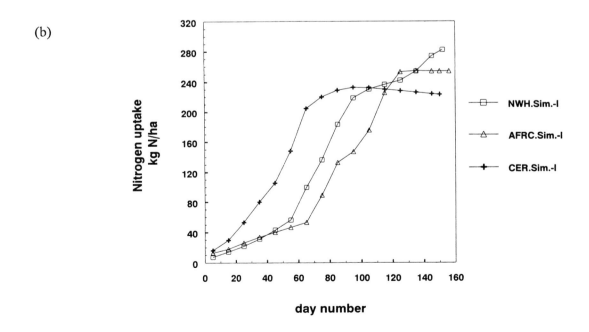

Figure 5.7.8   Time course of (a) evapotranspiration and (b) nitrogen uptake by winter wheat as simulated with the NWHEAT (NWH.), AFRCWHEAT 3S (AFRC.), CERES (CER.), and SIRIUS (SIRI.) models for water-limited production (-I) in growing season 1990/91 at Tomejil (near Sevilla), Spain.

5.7.5   Model sensitivity to systematic changes in climate

A baseline climate data set for a time period of 30 years has been generated on the basis of an historical weather data set using the LARS-WG stochastic weather generator (Racsko *et al.*, 1991; Barrow and Semenov, 1995). Weather variables in the baseline data set were adjusted independently, in a stepwise manner, in order to gauge the sensitivity of model results to changing values of each variable. The following output variables from crop growth simulations were compared: total biomass yield, grain yield, cumulative evapotranspiration (from sowing to maturity) and CV of grain yield. For each output variable, reported values are the mean result of 30 years of crop growth simulations. Five models have been used, of which CERES and NWHEAT calculated results for both potential and water-limited production, whilst SOILN calculated results for only potential production and AFRCWHEAT and SIRIUS calculated results for only water-limited production.

Three climatic variables were systematically adjusted. Firstly, the amount of precipitation was varied which affected the duration and degree of water shortage and, thus, crop growth and transpiration. Secondly, the atmospheric CO_2 concentration was varied which affected both the CO_2 assimilation rate and crop transpiration rate and, hence, crop growth. Finally, temperature was varied which mainly resulted in changes in the rate of phenological development and, thus, in the length of the vegetative and grain-filling periods. These analyses were carried out for the two sites, Rothamsted and Sevilla, and for both mean changes in climatic variables and for changes in climatic variability.

5.7.5.1   *Rothamsted: mean changes in climate*

For winter wheat in Rothamsted, increasing rainfall resulted in an increase in TB and GR in the absence of irrigation (Figure 5.7.9a, b). These increases in TB and GR appeared to be much larger in the NWHEAT run than in the other model runs. This was because the soil water storage assumed in the NWHEAT simulation was

much smaller than in the other models. This also explains why ET increased more strongly with the amount of precipitation in the NWHEAT run than in the other model runs (Figure 5.7.9c). AFRCWHEAT calculated a relatively low value for ET. CV of grain yield almost did not change with the amount of precipitation in the AFRCWHEAT, CERES and SIRIUS runs, probably because of the limited degree of water shortage, but decreased strongly in the NWHEAT run with its much smaller soil water supply.

Increasing concentrations of atmospheric CO_2 resulted in about the same increases in TB and GR in all model runs (Figure 5.7.10a, b). The CO_2 effect on yield was linear in the AFRCWHEAT, CERES and SIRIUS runs but curved according to NWHEAT. The NWHEAT model includes interactions between CO_2 and temperature. At low temperatures the CO_2 effect becomes nil and this interaction limits the CO_2 effect to a greater degree at higher CO_2 concentrations. Secondly, increasing CO_2 changes the CO_2 assimilation - light response curve in a partly non-linear way. CERES showed no sensitivity to a decrease in CO_2 concentration below the present level. ET increased slightly with increasing atmospheric CO_2 in the AFRCWHEAT and SIRIUS runs and decreased slightly and considerably in the NWHEAT and CERES runs, respectively (Figure 5.7.10c). This decrease was caused by the decrease in stomatal conductance with increasing atmospheric CO_2. CV of grain yield did not change with increasing atmospheric CO_2, except in the NWHEAT water-limited run. In this run, water shortage reduced the yield to a large extent resulting in a high CV of grain yield for baseline conditions. Increases in atmospheric CO_2 caused a higher water use efficiency and a smaller yield reduction by water shortage resulting in a lower value for the CV (see Figure 5.7.10d).

Increases in temperature resulted in advancement of the date of maturity and a decrease in the duration of the grain-filling period. At the lowest temperature (-4°C) the date of anthesis was so late that only a short period was available for grain filling and, according to AFRCWHEAT, grains did not become mature in a number of

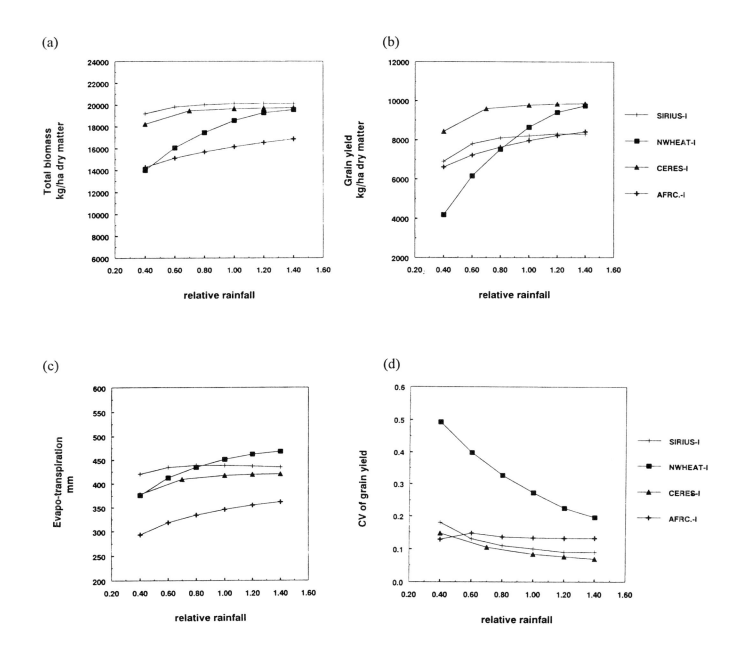

Figure 5.7.9 Sensitivity to precipitation of (a) total biomass (b) grain yield (c) cumulative evapotranspiration (from sowing to maturity) and (d) coefficient of variation (CV) of grain yield of winter wheat in Rothamsted, U.K. as simulated with the SIRIUS, NWHEAT, CERES and AFRCWHEAT 3S (AFRC.) models for water-limited (-I) production.

years. Furthermore, the CO_2 assimilation rate and, hence, the growth rate were reduced at low at low temperatures in some of the models (at least NWHEAT). Therefore, low values for GR and TB were simulated with large increases in temperature and in some models also with large decreases in temperature (Figure 5.7.11a, b: low

yield in NWHEAT run and no yield in AFRCWHEAT run). The SIRIUS run showed a stronger decrease in TB with rising temperature than the other model runs. Yield sensitivity to temperature was similar for all models, both in the potential and the water-limited situation, but considerable differences in yield level occurred.

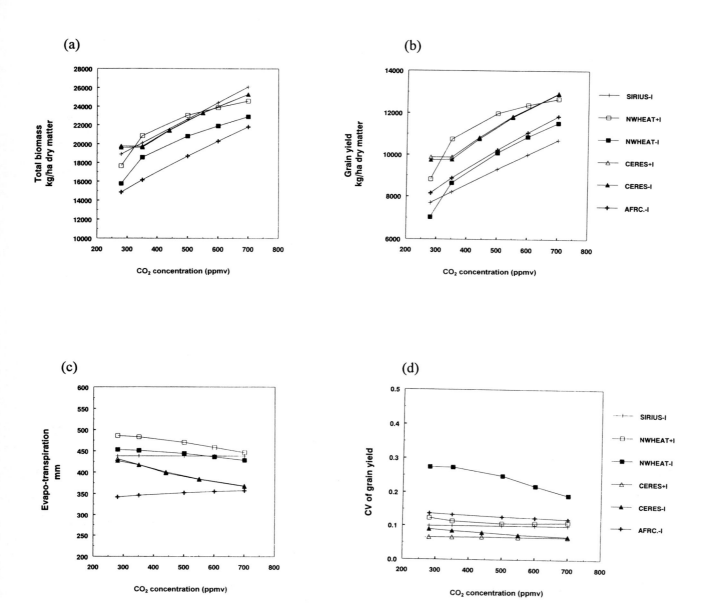

Figure 5.7.10   Sensitivity to atmospheric CO_2 concentration of (a) total biomass (b) grain yield (c) cumulative evapotranspiration (from sowing to maturity) and (d) coefficient of variation (CV) of grain yield of winter wheat in Rothamsted, U.K. as simulated with the SIRIUS, NWHEAT, CERES and AFRCWHEAT 3S (AFRC.) models for potential (+I) and water-limited (-I) production.

Water losses by ET decreased strongly and slightly with rising temperature in the CERES and NWHEAT runs respectively (Figure 5.7.11c), mainly because of advancement of the date of maturity. AFRCWHEAT calculated a relatively low ET that was unaffected by temperature change. SIRIUS calculated a large decrease in ET for decreases in temperature. The coefficient of variation (CV) of grain yield did not change with temperature change (Figure5.7.11d). Only with -4°C change, CV increased in the NWHEAT and SIRIUS runs and at +4°C and +6°C in the AFRCWHEAT run. NWHEAT calculated a higher CV for water-

(a)

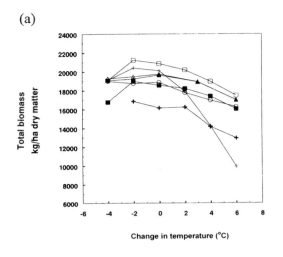

(b)

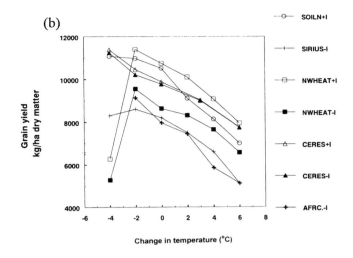

(c)

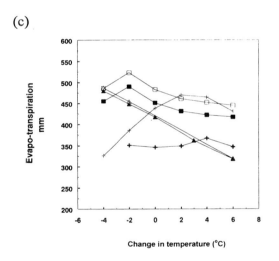

(d)

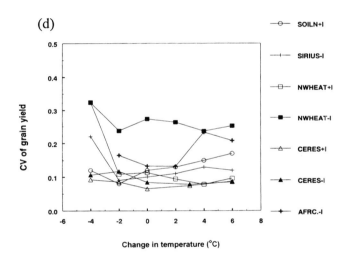

Figure 5.7.11 Sensitivity to temperature of (a) total biomass (b) grain yield (c) cumulative evapotranspiration (from sowing to maturity) and (d) coefficient of variation (CV) of grain yield of winter wheat in Rothamsted, U.K. as simulated with the SOILN, SIRIUS, NWHEAT, CERES and AFRCWHEAT 3S (AFRC.) models for potential (+I) and water-limited (-I) production.

limited production than for potential production, i.e. the increasing risk of water shortage increased the variation in yield.

5.7.5.2 Rothamsted: changes in climatic variability

Two changes in climatic variability have been analysed: a doubling of the daily variability of temperature and a doubling of the length of dry spells. The doubling in temperature variability was applied in conjunction with changes in mean temperature, comparable to those in Section 5.7.5.1. Higher temperatures gave a decrease in TB which was strongest in the SIRIUS run, and a decrease in GR that was about the same in all model runs (Figure 5.7.12 a, b). This decrease can be explained from the advanced date of maturity and the shorter period of grain filling at higher temperatures. Doubled temperature variability

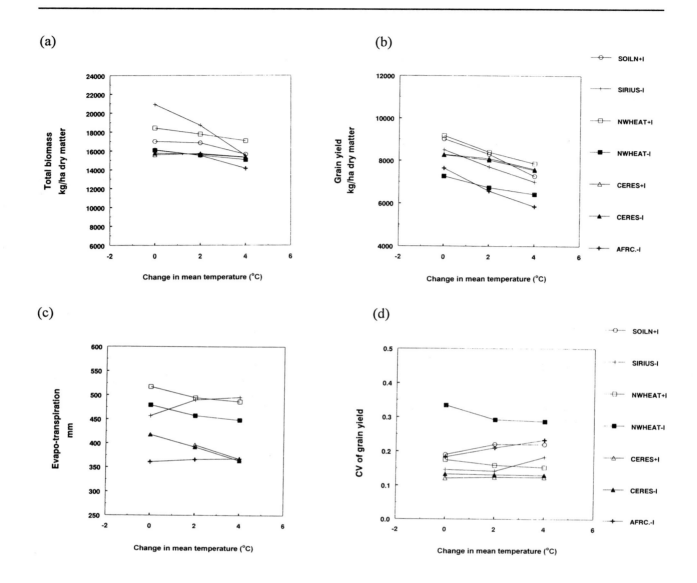

Figure 5.7.12 Sensitivity to changes in mean temperature in conjunction with a doubling of daily temperature variability of (a) total biomass (b) grain yield (c) cumulative evapotranspiration (from sowing to maturity) and (d) coefficient of variation (CV) of grain yield of winter wheat in Rothamsted, U.K. as simulated with the SOILN, SIRIUS, NWHEAT, CERES and AFRCWHEAT 3S (AFRC.) models for potential (+I) and water-limited (-I) production.

did not further reduce TB and GR in the AFRCWHEAT and SIRIUS runs but it considerably further reduced yields in the CERES and NWHEAT runs and in the SOILN run to a lesser extent (compare Figure 5.7.12a, b with 5.7.11a, b). ET increased slightly and considerably with higher temperatures in the AFRCWHEAT and SIRIUS runs respectively and decreased in the CERES and NWHEAT runs (Figure 5.7.12c). ET changed with temperature to about the same extent as in the runs without without doubled temperature variability (Figure

5.7.11c), but ET from the NWHEAT and SIRIUS runs was slightly higher than ET from the same model runs without doubled variability. CV of grain yield changed minimally with increased temperature, with a small increase in the AFRCWHEAT, SIRIUS and SOILN runs and a small decrease in the NWHEAT run (Figure 5.7.12d). Values for CV were slightly higher in all model runs including variability compared to CV in the runs without doubled temperature variability.

Doubling dry spell length gave identical values for TB, GR and ET in the SIRIUS run and slightly smaller values for TB, GR and ET in the AFRCWHEAT, CERES and NWHEAT runs (Figures 5.7.13a, b, c). This indicated that the degree of water stress had not increased much by doubling of the dry spell length. CV of grain yield was low and increased slightly by the doubling of dry spells in the AFRCWHEAT, CERES and SIRIUS runs and was much higher and increased more strongly by doubling of dry spells in the NWHEAT run, indicating a stronger yield-reducing effect of water shortage in this run (Figure 5.7.13d).

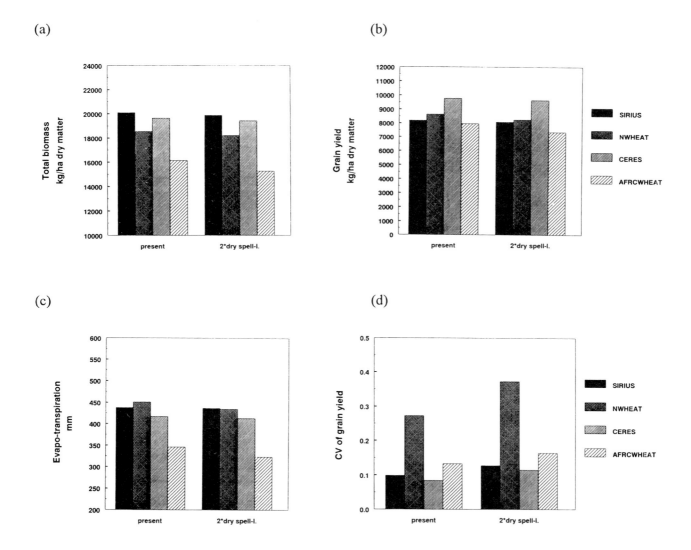

Figure 5.7.13 Sensitivity to a doubling in the length of dry spells of (a) total biomass (b) grain yield (c) cumulative evapotranspiration (from sowing to maturity) and (d) coefficient of variation (CV) of grain yield of winter wheat in Rothamsted, U.K. as simulated with the SIRIUS, NWHEAT, CERES and AFRCWHEAT 3S models for water-limited (-I) production.

5.7.5.3   *Sevilla: mean changes in climate*

Increasing the amount of rainfall at Sevilla resulted in an increase in TB and GR in most water-limited runs (Figure 5.7.14a, b). Yield increase with increasing precipitation was higher in the NWHEAT run than in the CERES and SIRIUS runs, which was indicative of the degree of water shortage. In the AFRCWHEAT run water supply did not limit crop yield. In this run ET was relatively low and increased

considerably with the amount of precipitation which was contrary to expectation (Figure 5.7.14c). In the CERES, NWHEAT and SIRIUS runs ET also increased with increasing precipitation. CV of grain yield was constant and very low in the AFRCWHEAT run indicating no water shortage, and decreased rapidly in the CERES, NWHEAT and SIRIUS runs with increasing precipitation amount due to a reduced risk of water shortage (Figure 5.7.14d).

(a)

(b)

(c)

(d)

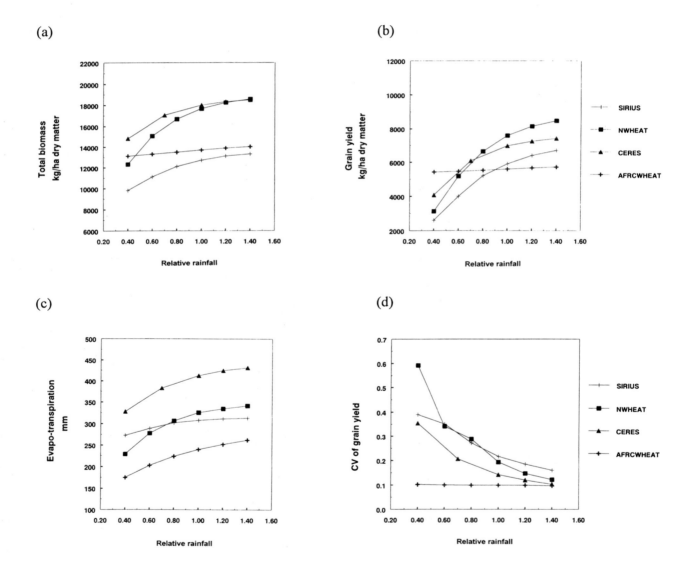

Figure 5.7.14   Sensitivity to precipitation of (a) total biomass (b) grain yield (c) cumulative evapotranspiration (from sowing to maturity) and (d) coefficient of variation (CV) of grain yield of winter wheat in Sevilla, Spain as simulated with the SIRIUS, NWHEAT, CERES and AFRCWHEAT 3S models for water-limited (-I) production.

Increasing concentrations of atmospheric CO_2 resulted in a larger increase in TB in the CERES and NWHEAT runs than in the SIRIUS and AFRCWHEAT runs. The largest relative increase in GR occurred in the NWHEAT run (Figure 5.7.15a, b). This contrasted with results for Rothamsted where the positive effect of increased CO_2 on TB was smallest in the NWHEAT run, resulting from the interaction between increased CO_2 and low temperatures. ET remained constant with increasing atmospheric CO_2 in the AFRCWHEAT and SIRIUS runs and decreased

slightly in the CERES and NWHEAT runs (Figure 5.7.15c). In the AFRCWHEAT run ET is relatively low and in the CERES run ET is relatively high. CV of grain yield did not change with increasing atmospheric CO_2 except for in the CERES and NWHEAT water-limited runs (Figure 5.7.15d). In these runs water shortage reduced GR in many years resulting in a higher CV of grain yield. Increases in atmospheric CO_2 caused a decrease in ET and, hence, less GR reduction by water shortage which resulted in a lower value for CV.

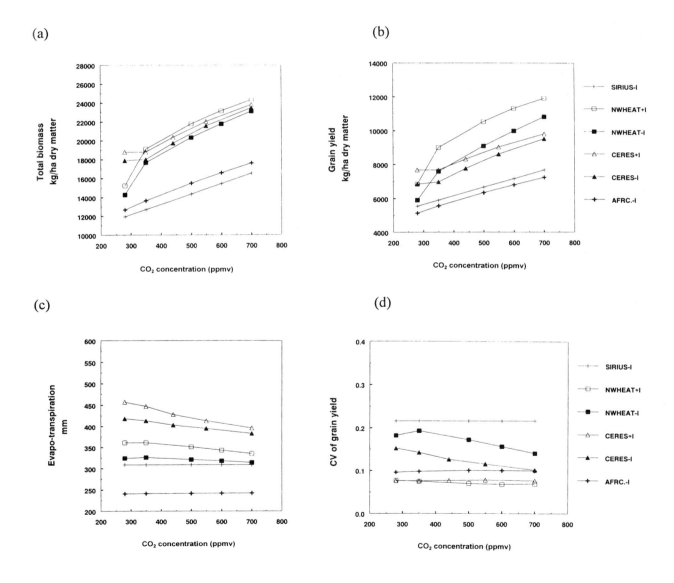

(a)   (b)

(c)   (d)

Figure 5.7.15 Sensitivity to atmospheric CO_2 concentration of (a) total biomass (b) grain yield (c) cumulative evapotranspiration (from sowing to maturity) and (d) coefficient of variation (CV) of grain yield of winter wheat in Sevilla, Spain as simulated with the SIRIUS, NWHEAT, CERES and AFRCWHEAT 3S (AFRC.) models for potential (+I) and water-limited (-I) production.

Increases in temperature resulted in a decrease in TB and GR in all model runs, mainly through advancement of the maturity date, (Figure 5.7.16a, b). SIRIUS calculated a much smaller decrease in GR with warming than the other models, and NWHEAT calculated a stronger decrease in TB. Decreases in temperature resulted in a decrease in TB in the CERES and NWHEAT water-limited runs and a decrease in GR in the CERES, NWHEAT and SIRIUS water-limited runs. This was probably due to the soil water supply which became more limiting for ET during the long period of growth at cooler temperatures (Figure 5.7.16c). ET decreased with increasing temperature, particularly when soil water supply not limiting. Only in the AFRCWHEAT run did ET not change with increasing temperature and its value was relatively low. CERES calculated the highest values for ET. This was different from results for Rothamsted where NWHEAT calculated much higher values for ET than CERES. The CV of grain yield was highest if water shortage affected crop growth relatively severely which was the case in the CERES, NWHEAT and SIRIUS water-limited runs and in particular at cooler temperatures (Figure 5.7.16d). In the AFRCWHEAT run CV of grain yield was low except with a 6°C warming where a strong increase in CV occurred.

(a)

(b)

(c)

(d)

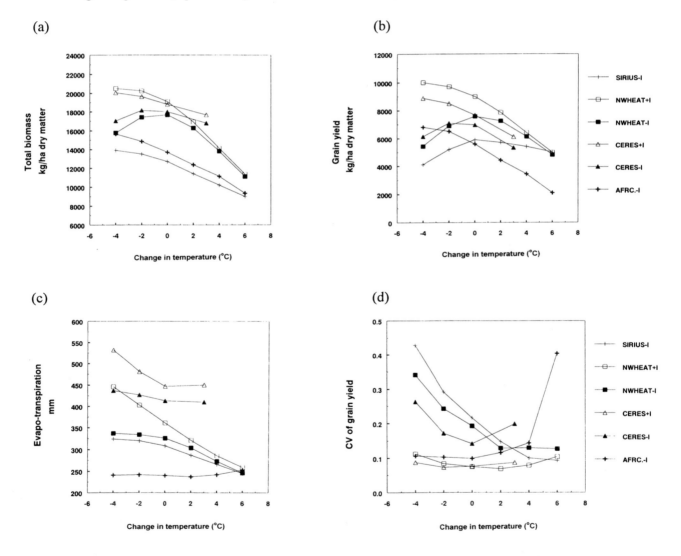

Figure 5.7.16 Sensitivity to temperature of (a) total biomass (b) grain yield (c) cumulative evapotranspiration (from sowing to maturity) and (d) coefficient of variation (CV) of grain yield of winter wheat in Sevilla, Spain as simulated with the SIRIUS, NWHEAT, CERES and AFRCWHEAT 3S (AFRC.) models for potential (+I) and water-limited (-I) production.

5.7.5.4 Sevilla: changes in climatic variability

Simulations have also been conducted for a doubling of daily temperature variability (in conjuction with changes in mean temperature) and a doubling of the length of dry spells. Increases in the both the mean and variability of temperature resulted in a decrease in TB and GR (Figure 5.7.17a, b). This can be explained mainly by the advanced date of maturity at higher temperatures. Exceptions were GR in the SIRIUS run and TB for a limited temperature rise (+2°C) in the AFRCWHEAT run, which slightly increased with temperature. Doubled temperature

variability did not affect TB and GR in the SIRIUS run but it reduced yields considerably in the AFRCWHEAT, CERES and NWHEAT runs and in particular with cooling (compare Figure 5.7.17a, b with 5.7.16a, b). ET decreased with warming in the SIRIUS and NWHEAT runs, remained at a constant low value in the AFRCWHEAT run, and remained constant or even increased in the CERES runs (Figure 5.7.17c). ET changed only minimally with doubled temperature variability compared to values calculated without variability (Figure 5.7.16c).

(a)   (b)

(c)   (d)

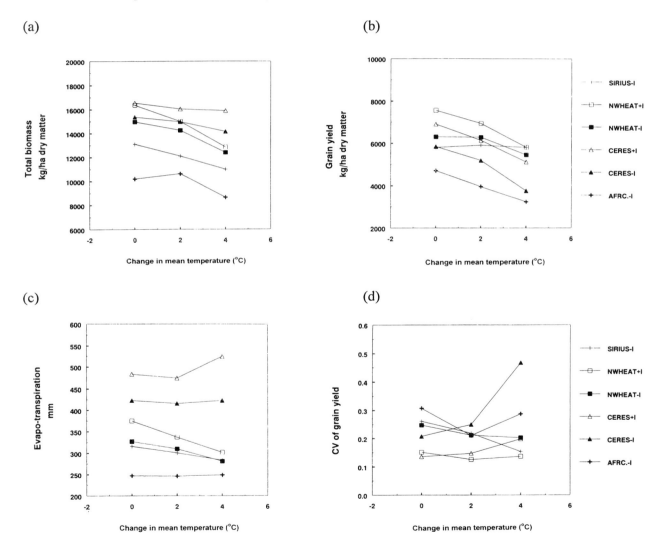

Figure 5.7.17 Sensitivity to changes in mean temperature in conjunction with a doubling of daily temperature variability (a) total biomass (b) grain yield (c) cumulative evapotranspiration (from sowing to maturity) and (d) coefficient of variation (CV) of grain yield of winter wheat in Sevilla, Spain as simulated with the SIRIUS, NWHEAT, CERES and AFRCWHEAT 3S (AFRC.) models for potential (+I) and water-limited (-I) production.

CV of grain yield showed little sensitivity to warming in NWHEAT potential production run, decreased slightly and moderately with warming in the NWHEAT and SIRIUS water-limited runs respectively, was rather variable in the AFRCWHEAT run and increased moderately and strongly in both CERES runs (potential and water-limited) (Figure 5.7.17d). CV of grain yield was slightly to moderately higher with doubled temperature variability than without (Figure 5.7.16d).

Doubling the length of dry spells resulted in lower TB and much lower GR in the CERES, NWHEAT and SIRIUS water-limited runs (Figure 5.7.18a, b). This can largely be explained by the cumulative amount of precipitation during the growth period which was approximately halved by doubling dry spell length. In the AFRCWHEAT run, however, the yield remained the same with doubling of dry spells indicating that water supply was not limiting. In this run, however, ET decreased strongly with doubling

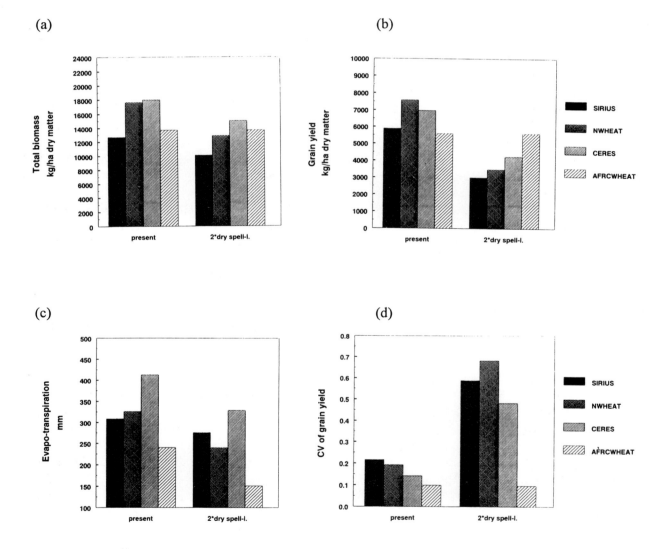

Figure 5.7.18   Sensitivity to a doubling in the length of dry spells of (a) total biomass (b) grain yield (c) cumulative evapotranspiration (from sowing to maturity) and (d) coefficient of variation (CV) of grain yield of winter wheat in Sevilla, Spain as simulated with the SIRIUS, NWHEAT, CERES and AFRCWHEAT 3S models for water-limited production.

of dry spells (Figure 5.7.18c). The reason for this is not known. In the other model runs, ET also decreased with doubling of dry spells as a result of the more limited water supply. CV of grain yield increased strongly with doubling of dry spells in the CERES, NWHEAT and SIRIUS runs, which indicated the strongly increasing risk of yield reduction by water shortage (Figure 5.7.18d). In the AFRCWHEAT run CV of grain yield was low and did not change.

5.7.6 Application of the climate change scenarios

Models have been applied for both current and future climatic conditions at Rothamsted and Sevilla. Future climate data sets for time periods of 30 years have been produced with the LARS-WG stochastic weather generator (Racsko *et al.*, 1991; Barrow and Semenov, 1995) on the basis of output from GCM experiments. Output from two types of GCM models have been used: (i) equilibrium $2xCO_2$ models (UKLO and UKHI); and (ii) transient models (UKTR and GFDL). Two types of scenarios have been constructed on the basis of output from the GCM experiments: (i) scenarios containing monthly mean changes in weather variables only; and (ii) scenarios which include changes in variability, as well as the same monthly mean changes, in weather variables. Scenarios which include changes in climatic variability are denoted by 'V' following the GCM name, eg. UKHIV.

GCM results used for these analyses were those from the UK Met. Office equilibrium low resolution experiment without changes in variability (UKLO), the UK Met. Office equilibrium high resolution experiment, both without (UKHI) and with changed variability (UKHIV), the UK Met. Office transient GCM experiment, both without (UKTR) and with changed variability (UKTRV), and the Geophysical Fluid Dynamics Laboratory transient GCM experiment without changes in variability (GFDL). Calculations were performed mainly for the scenario climate with the corresponding increased level of atmospheric CO_2. From both transient experiments results of two decades have been used, i.e. UKTR decades

31-40 and 66-75, and GFDL decades 25-34 and 55-64. For each of these experiments, the scenario for the earlier decade was applied together with a concentration of atmospheric CO_2 of 454 ppmv CO_2 and that for the second decade with 617 ppmv CO_2. These concentrations correspond to the IPCC IS92a emissions scenario. For the equilibrium scenarios (UKLO and UKHI) the CO_2 concentration was set at 560 ppmv. For more information on the construction of the climate change scenarios and how these GCM and emissions scenarios relate to actual years see Section 2.4.

A higher atmospheric CO_2 concentration resulted in an increase in the CO_2 assimilation rate and in a slight decrease in the transpiration rate in most model runs (see Section 5.7.5). In order to analyse the impact of climate change independent from the direct effect of increased atmospheric CO_2, the model runs for the UKTR scenarios for Rothamsted have been conducted for both present atmospheric CO_2 (353 ppmv) and increased CO_2 concentrations.

Not all models have been applied to all situations and sites. SOILN has been run for the scenarios at Rothamsted and for potential production only. The other models have been used for both sites. CERES and NWHEAT have calculated both potential and water-limited crop yields, whilst AFRCWHEAT and SIRIUS have calculated only water-limited crop yields. Results shown are the mean output of 30 years of crop growth simulations.

5.7.6.1 *Rothamsted: Equilibrium scenarios*

Grain yield: Potential production

The UKLO scenario resulted in a lower GR in the SOILN and NWHEAT runs but not in the CERES run, compared to GR at present (Figure 5.7.19a). The UKHI scenario gave a higher GR in the SOILN and NWHEAT runs but not in the CERES run, compared to the UKLO results. If climate variability has been changed in the UKHI scenario (UKHIV), this gave the same GR in CERES and SOILN runs and a lower GR in the NWHEAT run.

Grain yield: Water-limited production

The UKLO scenario resulted in a lower GR in the SIRIUS run, the same GR in the NWHEAT and AFRCWHEAT runs and a slightly higher GR in the CERES run, compared to GR at present (Figure 5.7.19a). The UKHI scenario gave a higher GR in all runs, compared to UKLO results, and also higher than GR at present, except for the SIRIUS run. Changed variability in the UKHI scenario (UKHIV) gave lower GR in the

NWHEAT run, the same GR in CERES and AFRCWHEAT runs, and a slightly higher GR in the SIRIUS run.

CV of grain yield

CV of grain yield was slightly higher in all equilibrium scenarios, compared, with present, in the CERES and SOILN potential production runs and remained the same in the NWHEAT potential production run (Figure 5.7.19b). In the

(a)

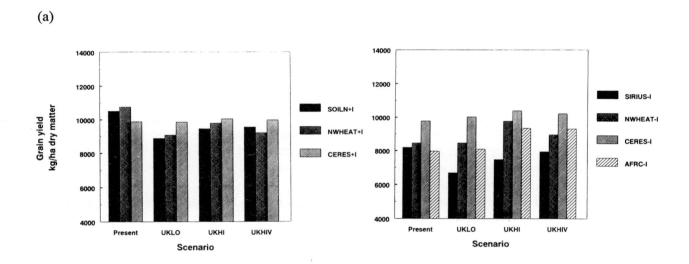

(b)

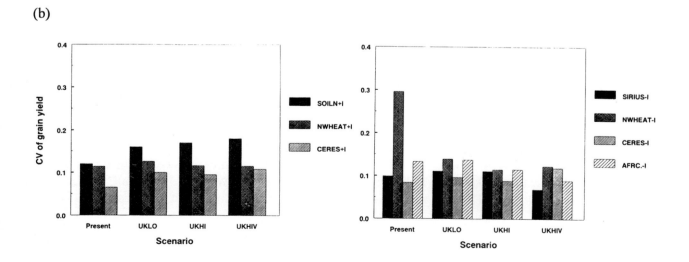

Figure 5.7.19   (a) Average value and (b) coefficient of variation (CV) of grain yield of winter wheat at present and future climatic conditions (including the direct effects of increasing atmospheric CO_2) in Rothamsted, U.K. as simulated with the SOILN, SIRIUS, NWHEAT, CERES and AFRCWHEAT 3S (AFRC.) models for potential (+I) and water-limited (-I) production. 'V' denotes scenarios which include changed variability.

water-limited runs, the UKLO and UKHI scenarios resulted in about the same CV of grain yield as present. Only in the NWHEAT run was the CV of grain yield lower than at present, indicating a decrease in the risk of water shortage in the future. With changed climate variability in the UKHI scenario (UKHIV), CV of grain yield decreased in the SIRIUS and AFRCWHEAT runs. However, it remained almost the same and slightly increased in the NWHEAT and CERES water-limited runs, respectively.

5.7.6.2 *Rothamsted: Transient scenarios*

UKTR scenario without direct CO_2 effect

Grain yield: Potential production

The UKTR3140 and UKTR6675 scenarios gave moderately and slightly lower GR, respectively (Figure 5.7.20a). All model runs gave similar results. With changed climatic variability (UKTR6675V scenario) GR remained similar.

(a)

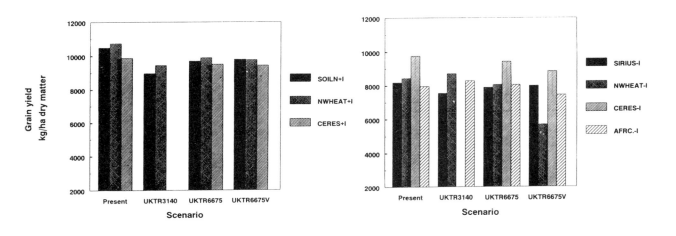

(b)

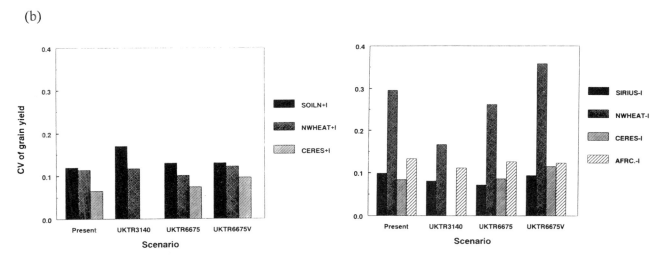

Figure 5.7.20 (a) Average value and (b) coefficient of variation (CV) of grain yield of winter wheat at present and future climatic conditions (not including the direct effects of increasing atmospheric CO_2) in Rothamsted, U.K. as simulated with the SOILN, SIRIUS, NWHEAT, CERES and AFRCWHEAT 3S (AFRC.) models for potential (+I) and water-limited (-I) production. 'V' denotes scenarios which include changed variability.

Grain yield: Water-limited production

For the UKTR3140 scenario GR decreased in the SIRIUS run and increased in the NWHEAT and AFRCWHEAT runs, whilst for the UKTR6675 scenario GR remained similar in all model runs, compared to GR at present (Figure 5.7.20a). With changed climatic variability (UKTR6675V scenario) GR in the SIRIUS run remained almost the same and decreased slightly in the CERES and AFRCWHEAT runs and strongly in the NWHEAT run. These differences in the magnitude of the decrease in GR were caused by different degrees of change in water limitation.

CV of grain yield

CV of potential grain yield was similar to present for all scenarios and increased only marginally with changed climatic variability (Figure 5.7.20b). Only the SOILN model calculated a higher CV than present for the UKTR3140 scenario. In the water-limited situation, CV of grain yield was low in the SIRIUS and CERES runs and did not change with climate change, indicating that water supply was not limiting for crop growth. In the AFRCWHEAT run, CV of grain yield was slightly higher than in the SIRIUS and CERES runs, but did not differ from CV at present for the various scenarios. In the NWHEAT water-limited run, the present CV of grain yield was high and CV was similar for the UKTR6675 scenario, but much lower for the UKTR3140 scenario. With changed climatic variability in the UKTR6675V scenario, CV of grain yield increased slightly in the SIRIUS and CERES runs, increased considerably in the NWHEAT run, and remained the same in the AFRCWHEAT run.

UKTR scenario with direct CO_2 effect

Grain yield: Potential production

The UKTR6675 scenario including the direct effect of increased atmospheric CO_2 resulted in a considerable increase in GR, with the smallest increase occurring in the NWHEAT run (Figure 5.7.21a). Changed climatic variability did not change GR in the different runs. For the UKTR3140 scenario, GR was the same as GR at

present in the CERES runs and smaller in the SOILN and NWHEAT runs.

Grain yield: Water-limited production

The UKTR6675 scenario gave a considerable increase in GR compared to GR at present (Figure 5.7.21a). If the direct effects of increased atmospheric CO_2 were not taken into account in the UKTR6675 scenario, GR generally remained similar to GR at present (Figure 5.7.20a). This indicated the strong contribution of CO_2 enrichment to the increase in GR. Changed climatic variability in the UKTR6675V scenario resulted in the same GR in the SIRIUS run, a slightly lower GR in the CERES run, and a much lower GR in the NWHEAT and AFRCWHEAT runs. For the UKTR3140 scenario GR was the same as GR at present in the SIRIUS run, slightly higher in the CERES run, and much higher in the NWHEAT and AFRCWHEAT runs.

CV of grain yield

CV of potential grain yield was virtually unchanged in the UKTR3140 and UKTR6675 scenarios, compared to CV at present (Figure 5.7.21b). Also with changed climatic variability in the UKTR6675V scenario, CV of grain yield did not increase in these runs. Only in the SOILN run did the UKTR3140 scenario result in a moderately higher value for CV. In the water-limited runs, the UKTR6675 scenario resulted in about the same CV of grain yield as at present in the CERES and AFRCWHEAT runs, and a slightly and moderately lower value for CV in the SIRIUS and NWHEAT runs, respectively. For the UKTR3140 scenario, the decreases in CV were similar or slightly larger. In the NWHEAT water-limited runs, CV of grain yield was much higher than other models, which indicated a higher degree of water shortage. With changed climatic variability in the UKTR6675V scenario CV of grain yield increased slightly in the different water-limited runs.

GFDL scenario with direct CO_2 effect

Grain yield

The GFDL2534 scenario resulted in a slight decrease in GR in the NWHEAT potential and

SIRIUS water-limited runs and in slight and moderate increases in the AFRCWHEAT and NWHEAT water-limited runs respectively. The GFDL5564 scenario resulted in moderate increases in GR in the NWHEAT potential, CERES potential, SIRIUS and CERES water-limited runs and in strong increases in the AFRCWHEAT and NWHEAT water-limited runs (Figure 5.7.22a).

CV of grain yield

For the GFDL scenarios CV of grain yield in the potential runs was the same or slightly lower than that at present (Figure 5.7.22b). In the water-limited situation the GFDL2534 scenario resulted in the same, slightly lower and much lower values for CV of grain yield in the AFRCWHEAT, SIRIUS and NWHEAT water-

(a)

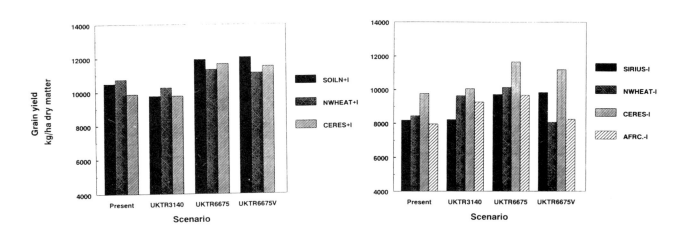

(b)

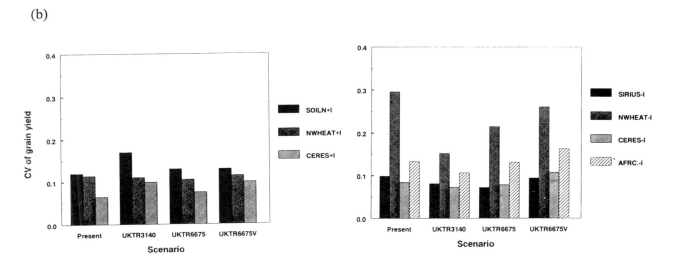

Figure 5.7.21   (a) Average value and (b) coefficient of variation (CV) of grain yield of winter wheat at present and future climatic conditions (including the direct effects of increasing atmospheric CO_2) in Rothamsted, U.K. as simulated with the SIRIUS, NWHEAT, CERES and AFRCWHEAT 3S (AFRC.) models for potential (+I) and water-limited (-I) production. 'V' denotes scenarios which include changed variability.

limited runs respectively, whilst the GFDL5564 scenario resulted in a slightly higher value for CV of grain yield in the CERES water-limited run, a slightly lower value in the AFRCWHEAT and SIRIUS runs, and a much lower value in the NWHEAT water-limited run, all values compared to those at present. The low values of CV of grain yield and the high GR in the water-limited runs indicated that the risk of water shortage and GR reduction by water stress was very low in the GFDL scenario climate.

5.7.6.3   *Sevilla: Equilibrium scenarios*

Grain yield

The UKLO scenario resulted in similar values for GR in the CERES potential and the SIRIUS and NWHEAT water-limited runs, slightly higher GR in the CERES water-limited run, and in slightly and moderately lower GR in the AFRCWHEAT and the NWHEAT potential water-limited runs respectively, compared to GR at present (Figure

(a)

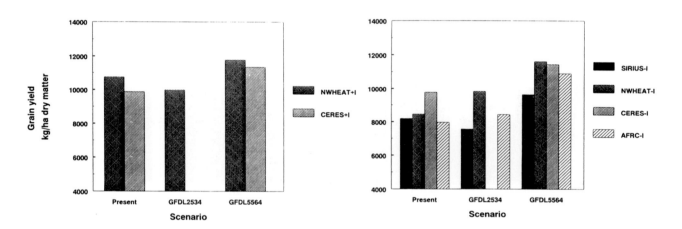

(b)

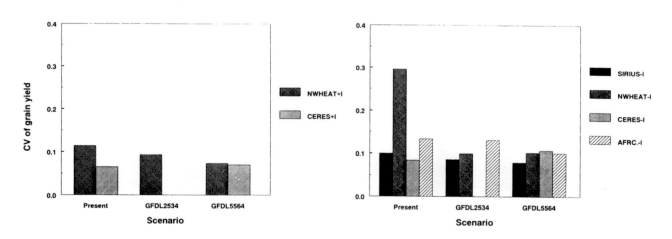

Figure 5.7.22   (a) Average value and (b) coefficient of variation (CV) of grain yield of winter wheat at present and future climatic conditions (including the direct effects of increasing atmospheric CO_2) in Rothamsted, U.K. as simulated with the SIRIUS, NWHEAT, CERES and AFRCWHEAT 3S (AFRC.) models for potential (+I) and water-limited (-I) production.

5.7.23a). The UKHI scenario gave a very low GR in the SIRIUS and NWHEAT water-limited runs, and resulted in a moderately lower GR in the AFRCWHEAT run and approximately the same GR in the NWHEAT potential run, compared to UKLO results. Changed climatic variability in the UKHIV scenario, gave almost no change in GR in all runs. In most water-limited runs the water supply in the UKHI (with and without variability) scenarios appeared to strongly limit GR, but in the present and UKLO scenario water supply was only limiting to a small extent.

CV of grain yield

For the UKLO scenario, CV of grain yield in most model runs was similar to CV at present (Figure 5.7.23b). Only the SIRIUS run gave a lower CV and the CERES water-limited run a higher CV for the UKLO scenario. The UKHI

(a)

(b)

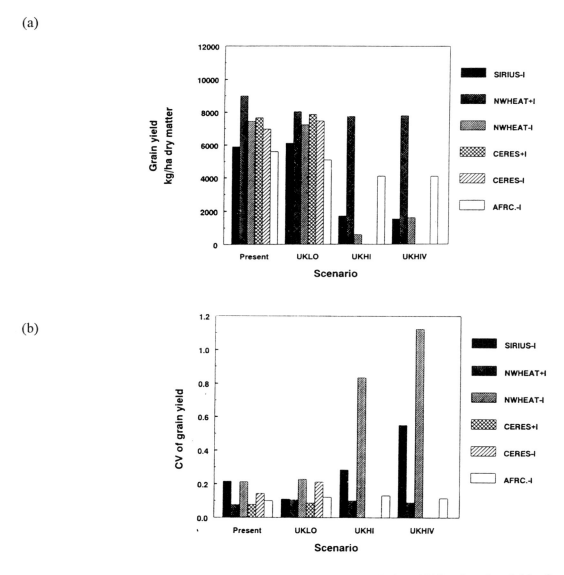

Figure 5.7.23 (a) Average value and (b) coefficient of variation (CV) of grain yield of winter wheat at present and future climatic conditions (including the direct effects of increasing atmospheric CO_2) in Sevilla, Spain as simulated with the SIRIUS, NWHEAT, CERES and AFRCWHEAT 3S (AFRC.) models for potential (+I) and water-limited (-I) production. 'V' denotes scenarios which include changed variability.

scenario produced similar CVs of grain yield in the NWHEAT potential and AFRCWHEAT water-limited runs and a moderately and much higher value for CV in the SIRIUS and NWHEAT water-limited runs respectively, compared to UKLO results. With changed climatic variability in the UKHIV scenario, the CV of grain yield remained the same in the NWHEAT potential and AFRCWHEAT water-limited runs and increased strongly in the SIRIUS and NWHEAT water-limited runs. In most water-limited runs, CV of grain yield for the UKHI (with and without variability) scenarios was much higher than both the CV at present and in the UKLO scenario. This indicated that in a situation without irrigation the risk for water shortage was highest in UKHI and UKHIV scenarios.

5.7.6.4   *Sevilla: Transient scenarios*

UKTR scenario with direct CO$_2$ effect

Grain yield: Potential production

The UKTR6675 scenario, including the direct effect of increased atmospheric CO$_2$, resulted in slight and moderate increases in GR in the CERES and NWHEAT runs respectively, compared to GR at present (Figure 5.7.24a). Changed climatic variability in the UKTR6675V scenario had virtually no effect on GR in both model runs. For the UKTR3140 scenario, GR was similar to GR at present in the CERES run, and slightly higher in the NWHEAT run.

Grain yield: Water-limited production

The UKTR6675 scenario gave no change in GR in the AFRCWHEAT run and slight, moderate and strong increases in GR in the CERES, SIRIUS and NWHEAT runs respectively, compared to GR at present. Changed climatic variability in the UKTR6675V scenario resulted in the same GR in the AFRCWHEAT run, a considerably lower GR in the CERES run and a much lower GR in the SIRIUS and NWHEAT runs. For UKTR3140 scenario, GR was approximately the same as GR at present in all water-limited runs.

CV of grain yield

The UKTR3140 and UKTR6675 scenarios gave almost no change in CV of grain yield in the potential runs (Figure 5.7.24b). Also changed climatic variability in the UKTR6675V scenario did not increase CV of grain yield in these runs. In the water-limited situation, the UKTR6675 scenario resulted in almost the same CV of grain yield as CV at present in the AFRCWHEAT run and a slightly and moderately lower value for CV in the CERES and the SIRIUS and NWHEAT runs respectively. The UKTR3140 scenario gave an increase in CV of grain yield in the SIRIUS and NWHEAT water-limited runs and no change in CV in the AFRCWHEAT and CERES water-limited runs, compared to CV at present. With changed climatic variability in the UKTR6675V scenario, CV of grain yield remained the same in the AFRCWHEAT run, increased strongly in the SIRIUS and CERES water-limited runs and very strongly in the NWHEAT water-limited run. CV of grain yield remained low if the degree of water limitation during crop growth was small, such as in the AFRCWHEAT runs.

The UKTR6675 scenario resulted in higher values for GR and lower values for CV of grain yield in all water-limited runs, except AFRCWHEAT (which showed little sensitivity to water shortage) (Figure 5.7.24). Changed climatic variability in the UKTR6675V scenario resulted in much lower GR and much higher CV of grain yield in all water-limited runs, except AFRCWHEAT. For a more detailed analysis, cumulative probability functions of GR in the SIRIUS and NWHEAT water-limited runs for the UKTR6675 (with and without variability) scenarios are presented in Figure 5.7.25. These functions show that with changed climatic variability the distribution of GR has been split with approximately 50% probability of a very low GR and 50% probability of GR comparable with GR calculated for the UKTR6675 scenario without changed variability.

GFDL scenario with direct CO$_2$ effect

Grain yield

The GFDL2534 scenario resulted in about the same GR in the SIRIUS and NWHEAT water-

(a)

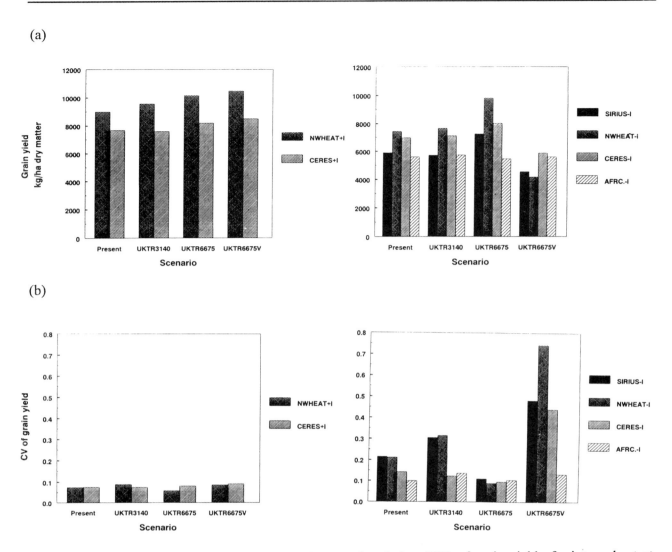

(b)

Figure 5.7.24   (a) Average value and (b) coefficient of variation (CV) of grain yield of winter wheat at present and future climate conditions (including the direct effects of increasing atmospheric CO_2) in Sevilla, Spain as simulated with the SIRIUS, NWHEAT, CERES and AFRCWHEAT 3S (AFRC.) models for potential (+I) and water-limited (-I) production. 'V' denotes scenarios include changed variability.

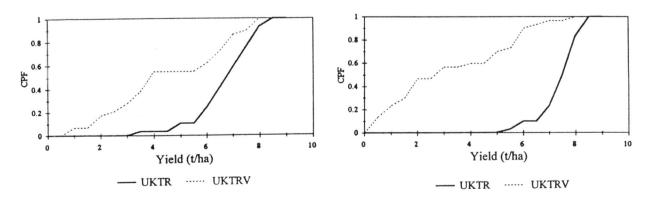

Figure 5.7.25   Cumulative probability function for grain yield of winter wheat at future climatic conditions in Sevilla, Spain as simulated with the (a) SIRIUS and (b) NWHEAT models for water-limited production. 'V' denotes scenarios which include changed variability.

limited runs and a slight and a moderate increase in the AFRCWHEAT water-limited and NWHEAT potential runs respectively (Figure 5.7.26a). The GFDL5564 scenario gave a slight increase in GR in the AFRCWHEAT water-limited and the CERES potential and water-limited runs and a moderate increase in the SIRIUS water-limited and the NWHEAT potential and water-limited runs, all compared to GR at present. GR was relatively high in the NWHEAT runs and relatively low in the AFRCWHEAT and SIRIUS runs.

CV of grain yield

For the GFDL2534 scenario CV of grain yield was slightly higher in NWHEAT potential and AFRCWHEAT water-limited runs and moderately higher in the SIRIUS and NWHEAT water-limited runs (Figure 5.7.26b). For the GFDL5564 scenario CV was slightly higher in the AFRCWHEAT water-limited run, remained the same in the CERES and NWHEAT potential runs, was slightly lower in the SIRIUS and CERES water-limited runs and moderately lower in the NWHEAT water-limited run, all compared to CV at present. The relatively high values for CV of grain yield in water-limited runs for the GFDL2534 scenario indicated an increased

risk for water shortage and yield reduction. For the GFDL5564 scenario the opposite was found.

5.7.7   Discussion

To analyse the main differences between the models and the consequences for their use in climate change studies, the following procedure was applied. Firstly, the wheat growth models compared in this study were calibrated and validated against two field data sets. This was done for Rothamsted and Sevilla, sites which can be considered representative for temperate and Mediterranean climatic zones, respectively. This enabled the ability of each model to simulate observed data from field experiments to be examined. Subsequently, for the same sites, sensitivity analyses of wheat growth and yield to changes in weather variables were carried out with the different models. This revealed correspondences and differences between the models' sensitivity. The models were then run for future climatic conditions, using various climate change scenarios for both sites. Finally, the relative importance of changes in climatic variability, compared to changes in mean values, was assessed in the sensitivity analyses and in the climate change scenarios.

(a)   (b)

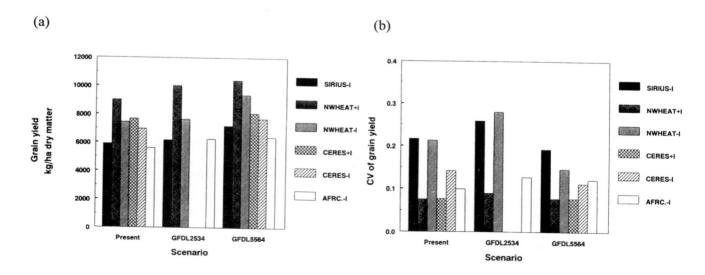

Figure 5.7.26   (a) Average value and (b) coefficient of variation (CV) of grain yield of winter wheat at present and future climatic conditions (including the direct effects of increasing atmospheric CO_2) in Sevilla, Spain as simulated with the SIRIUS, NWHEAT, CERES and AFRCWHEAT 3S (AFRC.) models for potential (+I) and water-limited (-I) production.

The simulated values for TB and GR were quite close to observed values in the irrigated calibration trial at Rothamsted. Only SIRIUS calculated a rather low value for GR. The time course of TB was calibrated quite well in most models, except for the fact that the growth in spring was overestimated strongly in the SIRIUS run and moderately in the CERES run. The time course of LAI was simulated quite well by AFRCWHEAT and SOILN but not correctly by the other models. ET was simulated quite accurately by the different models and also NB was simulated quite well. AFRCWHEAT, and SOILN to a lesser extent, underestimated the total available amount of nitrogen which resulted in a reduction of nitrogen uptake at the end of the growth period. In the CERES run, the overestimated growth in spring resulted in a too rapid nitrogen uptake in spring but NB at maturity corresponded well to the observed value.

Results from the second irrigated trial at Rothamsted were used to validate the models. The simulated and observed dates of anthesis corresponded reasonably well in the different model runs. The date of maturity was only calculated well in the CERES and SIRIUS runs. The date of maturity in the AFRCWHEAT and NWHEAT runs was a week later than the observed date, which was partly a result of the phenology routine in the models and partly an experimental artefact. SOILN needed a second calibration of phenological development. Simulated TB and GR were high compared to those in the field trial, except those modelled with SOILN. The time course of TB was simulated reasonably by AFRCWHEAT, NWHEAT and SOILN up to 40 days before the date of maturity when the observed growth curve started to flatten off. This part of the curve was only simulated well by SOILN. Growth in spring was again overestimated strongly and moderately by SIRIUS and CERES, respectively. The time course of LAI was simulated well by SOILN only. ET was simulated quite accurately by the different models. The course of NB was simulated reasonably well by AFRCWHEAT, NWHEAT and SOILN up to day 150. From that date the rate of nitrogen uptake in the field trial became very small because of depletion of the soil nitrogen supply. This was only simulated well by AFRCWHEAT and SOILN.

For Sevilla only GR from variety trials was available. Results from simulations of water-limited wheat growth could be compared, but a thorough calibration and validation was not possible. The highest value for TB was calculated with NWHEAT, intermediate values with CERES and SIRIUS, and the lowest value with AFRCWHEAT. The time course of TB was almost identical in both NWHEAT and CERES runs, except for the fact that CERES simulated a curve that flattened off at an earlier date. SIRIUS calculated a smaller rate of growth during the main growth period than the other models. In the AFRCWHEAT run the increase in TB started at a later date and stopped at an earlier date than the other models. The time course of LAI as calculated with the different models was similar to values simulated for the field trials at Rothamsted. In the SIRIUS and CERES runs ET during the initial part of the growth period was relatively high which can be explained from the high values for LAI. During the rest of the growth period these models calculated the same increase in ET as NWHEAT. In the AFRCWHEAT run ET was much smaller, probably because in this model the soil water supply was more limiting. Nitrogen uptake started relatively early in the CERES run which was partly caused by the early start of crop growth and was partly a characteristic of the model, and started latest in the AFRCWHEAT run because of the late start of crop growth.

The simulations of water-limited wheat growth in Sevilla were repeated for a second year (validation). TB was 1 to 2 tons higher than TB in the first year, with the highest value again in the NWHEAT run and the lowest in the AFRCWHEAT run. The time course of TB in the different model runs was similar, except that in the CERES and SIRIUS runs crop growth started more rapidly in spring than in the other two model runs. Near maturity growth stopped at a relatively early date in the AFRCWHEAT run, probably because of water shortage, and at a relatively late date in the NWHEAT run. SIRIUS again calculated a relatively small increase in TB during the main growth period. The courses of LAI were about the same as those simulated for the other site and year. For ET and NB the same applied as described for the first run in Sevilla.

In Rothamsted, increasing temperature resulted in a continuous decrease in TB and GR. These decreases were approximately the same in the different model runs except for a stronger decrease in TB in the SIRIUS run. Absolute values for TB and GR, however, were considerably different. CV of grain yield did not change with increasing temperature and was about the same in most model runs. Only if water supply became more limiting was a higher value for CV calculated. ET increased with rising temperature in the SIRIUS run, remained the same in the AFRCWHEAT run and decreased in the CERES and NWHEAT runs. ET was highest in the NWHEAT and SIRIUS runs.

In Sevilla, increasing temperature also resulted in a continuous decrease in TB and GR. These decreases varied moderately between the different model runs, but the absolute values for TB and GR were considerably different. In runs with a severely limiting water supply, decreasing temperature and the resulting longer growth period also resulted in a decrease in TB and GR. CV of grain yield changed in the same way as described for Rothamsted. ET decreased with rising temperature in the CERES and NWHEAT potential production runs and decreased slightly or remained almost constant in the water-limited runs. ET was highest in the CERES runs, which was different from ET in runs for Rothamsted.

In Rothamsted, increasing rainfall resulted in a continuous increase in TB, GR and ET and in a decrease in CV of grain yield. In the NWHEAT water-limited run, the effects of increasing rainfall were much stronger than in the other model runs, indicative of a much more limited water supply. In Sevilla, increasing rainfall resulted in the same changes as found at Rothamsted. In most model runs increasing rainfall gave rise to strong changes, except for the AFRCWHEAT run where water supply appeared to be almost non-limiting.

In Rothamsted, CO_2 enrichment resulted in approximately the same increases in TB and GR in the different model runs. This CO_2 effect on yield was curvilinear in the NWHEAT runs and linear in the other runs, but for the CO_2 range used in the scenario runs this difference did not result in a considerably different effect of

increased CO_2. In general, CV of grain yield did not change with increasing atmospheric CO_2 concentration, except in the NWHEAT water-limited run where CV decreased with increasing CO_2 because the water supply became less limiting for crop growth. ET increased slightly with increasing CO_2 in the AFRCWHEAT and SIRIUS runs as a result of the increasing leaf area and decreased slightly and considerably in the NWHEAT and CERES runs, respectively, because of the decrease in stomatal conductance. In Sevilla, the effect of increasing CO_2 on TB, GR and CV of grain yield was about the same as that observed for Rothamsted, except that larger CO_2 effects on TB and GR occurred in the NWHEAT run. ET did not change with increasing CO_2 in the AFRCWHEAT and SIRIUS runs and slightly decreased in the CERES and NWHEAT runs.

The effect of changes in climatic variability on the models was also examined. A doubling of daily temperature variability at Rothamsted had little effect on TB and GR in the AFRCWHEAT and SIRIUS runs, but they became slightly and considerably less in the SOILN and the CERES and NWHEAT runs respectively. Doubled temperature variability in Sevilla did not affect TB and GR in the SIRIUS run, but it considerably reduced TB and GR in the AFRCWHEAT, CERES and NWHEAT runs. CV of grain yield slightly increased with a doubling of temperature variability in all runs for both sites. Doubling the length of dry spells in the climate data set for Rothamsted gave identical values for TB, GR and ET in the SIRIUS run and slightly smaller values in the AFRCWHEAT, CERES and NWHEAT water-limited runs. CV of grain yield increased slightly by doubling of dry spells in the AFRCWHEAT, SIRIUS and CERES water-limited runs and increased more strongly in the NWHEAT water-limited run, indicative of a stronger yield-reducing effect of water shortage in this run. Doubling of dry spells in Sevilla resulted in lower values for TB, much lower values for GR and ET and much higher values for CV of grain yield in the CERES, NWHEAT and SIRIUS runs, but in no change in TB, GR and CV of grain yield in the AFRCWHEAT run. This can largely be explained by the amount of precipitation, which was approximately halved by doubling of dry spells. Only in the

AFRCWHEAT model was the soil water supply large enough to compensate for this effect.

Simulations of crop growth have been conducted for a number of different scenario climates, derived from transient GCM experiments, i.e. UKTR and GFDL scenarios, and from equilibrium GCM experiments, i.e. UKLO and UKHI scenarios. On the basis of the UKTR and UKHI climate scenarios, scenarios with the same monthly mean changes in variables but with changed temperature variability and length of dry spells have been constructed, i.e. UKTR6675V and UKHIV. An increased level of atmospheric CO_2 that corresponded with the scenario climate change, was taken into account in most simulations. As a higher atmospheric CO_2 concentration resulted in an considerable increase in CO_2 assimilation rate and in a slight decrease in transpiration in most model runs, the impact of climate change was first analysed independent of the direct effect of increased CO_2. This was done for the UKTR scenario at Rothamsted.

In Rothamsted, the UKTR6675 scenario, without the direct effect of increased atmospheric CO_2, resulted in a slight decrease in GR in the potential production runs, compared to GR at present. This can be explained by the shorter growth duration as a result of the higher temperatures in this scenario climate. With changed climatic variability in the UKTR6675V scenario, GR did not change in the potential runs. However, although a change in temperature variability had no effect on crop phenology and growth according to the different models, this may not be true in practice (J.R. Porter, pers. comm., 1995). For the UKTR3140 scenario climate, lower GR was calculated than GR at present and in the UKTR6675 scenario climate. This difference can be explained by the lower amount of irradiation in the UKTR3140 scenario climate. There was virtually no change in the CV of grain yield with climate change on the basis of the UKTR3140 and UKTR6675 scenarios. Only changed climatic variability (UKTR6675V) gave a slightly higher value for CV and SOILN calculated an increase in CV for the UKTR3140 scenario.

In the water-limited runs for Rothamsted, the UKTR6675 scenario resulted in no change in GR and the UKTR3140 scenario resulted in both

higher and lower values for GR, compared to GR at present. With changed climatic variability in the UKTR6675V scenario, GR in the SIRIUS run remained almost the same and decreased slightly in the CERES and AFRCWHEAT runs and strongly in the NWHEAT run. CV of grain yield was approximately the same for both present and UKTR3140 and UKTR6675 scenario climates and was slightly higher with changed climatic variability (UKTR6675V) in most runs. This indicated that the degree of growth reduction caused by water shortage changed very little with climate change. The NWHEAT water-limited runs resulted in relatively high values for CV, both for present and scenario conditions, which indicated the larger risk for yield reduction by water shortage in this model run.

The UKTR6675 scenario for Rothamsted, including the direct effect of increased atmospheric CO_2, resulted in a considerable increase in GR in the potential runs. Changed climatic variability in the UKTR6675V scenario did not change GR in the different runs, as found for the present CO_2 runs. These results were also found for Sevilla, except that the increase in GR was quite small. For the UKTR3140 scenario, GR in Rothamsted was similar or slightly smaller than GR at present. The positive effect on crop growth of CO_2 enrichment was almost counter balanced by the relatively low irradiation in this scenario climate. In Sevilla irradiation was probably less limiting and, hence, similar or slightly higher GR was calculated for the UKTR3140 scenario. CV of grain yield in both Rothamsted and Sevilla did not change in the potential runs for the UKTR scenarios.

In the water-limited runs for Rothamsted, the UKTR6675 scenario resulted in a considerable increase in GR. This was a result of the higher CO_2 concentration. For Sevilla considerable increases were also calculated in the NWHEAT and SIRIUS runs, but in the AFRCWHEAT and CERES runs increases in GR were nil to slight. With changed climatic variability (UKTR6675V), GR at Rothamsted remained almost the same in the SIRIUS and CERES runs and considerably decreased in the NWHEAT and AFRCWHEAT runs, but at Sevilla strong decreases occurred in all runs except for the AFRCWHEAT run where GR remained constant.

These changes in GR depended mainly on the change in the risk of water shortage. A more detailed analysis of the consequences of changed climatic variability (UKTR6675V) in Sevilla showed that the distribution of GR was split with approximately a 50% probability of very low GR and a 50% probability of GR comparable with GR for the UKTR6675 scenario. This illustrated that wheat production may become a risky agricultural activity as a result of climate change, and that the incorporation of climatic variability into climate change scenarios may change the conclusions concerning the future suitability of wheat production in Sevilla. CV of grain yield in Rothamsted was low and did not change with climate change in the SIRIUS and CERES runs. This indicated that water supply was not limiting for crop growth. In the AFRCWHEAT run CV of grain yield was slightly higher and in the NWHEAT run much higher than in the CERES and SIRIUS runs, with the lowest value for CV for the UKTR3140 scenario and the highest values for the present climate and the UKTR6675V scenario. This indicated the relatively high risk for yield reduction by water shortage in the NWHEAT run, in particular, at present or in the UKTR6675V scenario climate. In Sevilla CV of grain yield was low for both present and UKTR scenario conditions in the CERES and AFRCWHEAT runs. In the SIRIUS and NWHEAT runs, CV was low in the UKTR6675 scenario climate and considerably higher for the present and UKTR3140 scenario climate. Changed climatic variability in the UKTR6675V scenario resulted in very high values for CV in all model runs except that of AFRCWHEAT.

The transient scenarios were constructed using the same global mean temperature change and concentration of atmospheric CO_2 and, hence, are directly comparable. In the potential runs for Rothamsted, the GFDL2534 scenario gave a slight decrease in GR and the GFDL5564 scenario resulted in a moderate increase in GR. This was fairly similar to results from both model decades of the UKTR GCM. The decrease in GR in the first decade was caused by the relatively low amount of irradiation and the increase in GR in the second decade was mainly caused by the increase in atmospheric CO_2. It was remarkable that at Rothamsted the scenarios for the first

decade from both transient GCM experiments had a considerably lower level of irradiation than both the level at present and that in the scenario for the second decade. In Sevilla, the GFDL scenario for both decades resulted in slight to moderate increases in GR and the UKTR scenarios in nil to slight increases for the first decade and slight to moderate increases for the second decade. In Sevilla the amount of irradiation in the first decade was less limiting than in Rothamsted which resulted in more positive yield changes. CV of grain yield was rather low in the potential runs and virtually did not change for the GFDL scenarios for both decades. This corresponds with the CV of grain yield determined for the UKTR scenarios.

In the water-limited runs the GFDL2534 scenario gave a slight decrease in GR in the SIRIUS run and slight to moderate increases in the NWHEAT and AFRCWHEAT runs for Rothamsted and nil to slight increases in all runs for Sevilla. If water supply was not limiting, the low amount of irradiation in the first decade resulted in lower GR at Rothamsted. The increase in rainfall and the decrease in potential ET for this decade resulted in higher GR if water supply was currently limiting. For Sevilla the amount of rainfall in the GFDL2534 scenario was less than that at present. This resulted in no change in GR if water supply was limiting (e.g. NWHEAT) and slight increases in the other model runs with a larger water supply. The GFDL5564 scenario gave a considerable increase in GR at Rothamsted and a slight to moderate increase at Sevilla. This was mainly the result of the increase in atmospheric CO_2 which resulted in a higher growth rate and water use efficiency. In Sevilla the positive effect of climate change appeared to be less than in Rothamsted. This can be explained from the increase in temperature which resulted in a considerable decrease in GR at Rothamsted, but in a very strong decrease at Sevilla where temperatures are currently much higher (see Sections 5.7.5.1 and 5.7.5.3). These GFDL results were similar to those for the UKTR scenario in comparable decades. CV of grain yield was low in the CERES and SIRIUS runs for Rothamsted and changed very little with climate change on the basis of both UKTR and GFDL experiments. This indicated that water supply was not limiting in these model runs. In Sevilla the same applied for the CERES and AFRCWHEAT runs. CV of grain yield in Rothamsted was generally slightly higher in the AFRCWHEAT run and much higher in the NWHEAT run. In both model runs CV was generally lower for GFDL and UKTR scenario climates than for the present climate. For both scenarios the lower value for CV was caused by increased rainfall and/or decreased potential ET, compared to present conditions. In Sevilla CV of grain yield was relatively high in the SIRIUS and NWHEAT runs for both present and scenario climates with the highest value for CV calculated for the first decade of both GFDL and UKTR scenarios.

The effects of climate change were also analysed using scenarios based on output from equilibrium $2xCO_2$ GCM experiments. When comparing results for these UKLO and UKHI scenarios, it should be taken into account that both the distribution of climate change over Europe and the global mean temperature changes are different. Higher temperature changes are generally predicted in the UKLO, compared to the UKHI, scenario. For example, in Rothamsted the UKLO scenario gave a temperature rise of 6.6°C averaged over the year and the UKHI scenario a mean temperature rise of about 5.8°C. Further, comparing results from these equilibrium scenarios with those from the transient UKTR6675 scenario the following differences should be considered: (i) they have different distributions of climate change over Europe; (ii) they are standardised on different global mean temperatures (much smaller temperature changes are predicted in the UKTR6675 scenario, eg. 2.7°C averaged over the year for Rothamsted); and (iii) the CO_2 concentration for the equilibrium scenarios is 560 ppmv and for the UKTR6675 scenario is 617 ppmv.

In the potential runs GR at Rothamsted decreased nil to slightly and nil to moderately for UKHI and UKLO scenarios, respectively, and nil to slightly for both scenarios in Sevilla. Compared to the changes in GR for the UKTR6675 scenario which were considerably positive at Rothamsted and slightly to moderately positive at Sevilla, the effects of the UKLO and UKHI scenarios on GR were very small or even negative. This was partly the result of the smaller increase in atmospheric CO_2 in the UKLO and UKHI scenarios and partly

because of the larger temperature rise in these scenarios. CV of grain yield in Rothamsted and Sevilla increased nil to slightly for the UKLO and UKHI scenarios compared to CV at present, which was almost identical to the change in CV found for the UKTR6675 scenario.

In the water-limited runs for Rothamsted, both the UKLO and UKHI scenarios gave decreases in GR in the SIRIUS run and nil and moderate increases, respectively, in the other runs. For Sevilla the UKLO and UKHI scenarios gave nil to slight and moderate to strong decreases in GR respectively. GR at Sevilla for the UKHI scenario was much lower than GR for the UKLO scenario because the amount of rainfall was very low. Compared to the changes in GR for the UKTR6675 scenario which were considerably and slightly to considerably positive at Rothamsted and Sevilla respectively, the effects of the UKLO and UKHI scenarios on GR were small or negative. This was the result of the smaller increase in atmospheric CO_2 in the UKLO and UKHI scenarios, the larger temperature rise and the lower amount of rainfall in these scenarios. CV of grain yield at Rothamsted and Sevilla for the UKLO and UKHI scenarios was similar to CV at present. Exceptions were the NWHEAT run for Rothamsted where CV at present was much higher than CV for the scenarios, and the SIRIUS and NWHEAT runs for the UKHI scenario at Sevilla with a slightly and much higher CV respectively than CV at present. Furthermore, for the UKTR6675 scenario CV of grain yield was the same as CV at present in most runs except for the NWHEAT run at Rothamsted and the SIRIUS and NWHEAT runs at Sevilla which experienced a relatively higher CV than at present.

5.7.8 Conclusions

Total biomass and grain yield were simulated reasonably well by the different models. Even when simulated growth in spring started too early and too fast, a good yield prediction was still possible. The course of leaf area index was not simulated well by most models. Fortunately, dry matter production is not much different for leaf area index values varying between 4 and 10. The courses of leaf area index as calculated for both sites differed only slightly and appeared to be rather characteristic for each model.

Cumulative evapotranspiration was simulated quite accurately by the different models. Differences in evapotranspiration were often caused by the amount of available water and that mainly depended on the assumed soil water storage. Models that overestimated the leaf area index in early spring also overestimated evapotranspiration during this period. The nitrogen uptake by the crop was also simulated quite well by the different models, although the simulated time course was not always the same as the observed. Differences in nitrogen uptake were caused mainly by the amount of mineral nitrogen in the rooted soil profile and its availability for crop uptake. These factors generally limited nitrogen uptake at the end of the growth period.

A broad survey of the sensitivity of grain yield to changes in mean climatic variables, climatic variability and atmospheric CO_2 concentration and to changes in climate as based on equilibrium and transient scenarios is given in Table 5.7.5. These results are based on simulation runs with the different wheat models.

Increasing temperature resulted in a continuous decrease in total biomass and grain yield in the different model runs. If the water supply was severely limiting, an opposite temperature effect occurred. The CV of grain yield did not change with increasing temperature, however cumulative evapotranspiration increased, remained the same or decreased depending on the model.

Increasing rainfall resulted in a continuous increase in total biomass, grain yield and cumulative evapotranspiration, and in a decrease in CV of grain yield. This rainfall effect was found in all model runs and became stronger if water supply was more limiting.

Increasing atmospheric CO_2 resulted in similar increases in total biomass and grain yield and in no change in CV of grain yield in the different model runs. CV of grain yield only decreased if increased CO_2 led to less water limitation. Cumulative evapotranspiration increased or decreased with increasing CO_2 depending on the model.

In the sensitivity analyses the various models calculated considerably different values for cumulative evapotranspiration. These differences in value between model runs for Rothamsted clearly differed from the differences in value between model runs for Sevilla.

By doubling the variability in the temperature data, total biomass and grain yield remained the same or became considerably less, depending on the model and CV of grain yield slightly to moderately increased. Doubling the length of dry spells resulted in smaller values for total biomass, grain yield and evapotranspiration and higher values for CV of grain yield. However, this effect was mainly caused by the decrease in amount of rainfall and only to a limited extent by the change in rainfall distribution.

The UKTR6675 scenario of climate change resulted in considerable increases in grain yield in Rothamsted and in nil to considerable increases in Sevilla for both potential and water-limited runs. This scenario resulted in the same value for CV of grain yield in the potential runs for both sites and in the same or lower value for CV of grain yield in the water-limited runs. Changed climatic variability in UKTR6675V did not change grain yield in the potential runs, but resulted in nil to considerable decreases in water-limited runs for Rothamsted depending on the model and in strong decreases in most water-limited runs for Sevilla. CV of grain yield strongly increased with changed climatic variability in situations with water shortage, in particular, the water-limited runs for Sevilla.

If the direct effect of increased atmospheric CO_2 was not taken into account, the UKTR6675 scenario alone for Rothamsted resulted in a slight decrease in grain yield in potential runs and in no change in grain yield in water-limited runs. This scenario resulted in the same or slightly lower values for CV of grain yield in all runs. The direct effect of increased atmospheric CO_2 on grain yield was strongly positive compared to the effect of the predicted changes in climate. CV of grain yield decreased only with increasing CO_2 if simultaneously water shortage decreased.

Table 5.7.5 Summary table of the sensitivity[1] of grain yield to changes in mean climate variables, climatic variability and atmopheric CO_2 concentration and to changes in climate based on the equilibrium and transient scenarios, both with and without changes in climatic variability. Results are based on simulation runs with the different models for both potential (+I) and water-limited production (-I) at Rothamsted, U.K. and Sevilla, Spain.

	AFRCWHEAT -I	CERES +I	CERES -I	NWHEAT +I	NWHEAT -I	SIRIUS -I	SOILN +I
Rothamsted							
Sensitivity to							
- temperature	- (+)²	-	-	- (+)²	- (+)²	-	-
- precipitation	+	0	+	0	+	+	0
- atmospheric CO_2	+	+	+	+	+	+	+
- doubled variability in temperature	0	-	-	-	-	0	-
- doubled length of dry spells	0	0	0	0	0	0	0
Scenarios[3]							
- UKLO	0	0	0	-	0	-	-
- UKHI	+	0	+	-	+	-	-
- UKHIV	+	0	0	-	0	0	-
- UKTR3140	+	0	0	0	+	0	-
- UKTR6675*	0	0	0	-	0	0	-
- UKTR6675	+	+	+	+	+	+	+
- UKTR6675V	0	+	+	0	0	+	+
- GFDL2534	0	?	?	-	+	-	?
- GFDL5564	+	+	+	+	+	+	?
Sevilla							
Sensitivity to							
- temperature	-	-	- (+)²	-	- (+)²	-/+	?
- precipitation	0	0	+	0	+	+	?
- atmospheric CO_2	+	+	+	+	+	+	?
- doubled variability in temperature	-	-	-	-	-	0	?
- doubled length of dry spells	0	0	-	0	-	-	?
Scenarios[3]							
- UKLO	-	0	+	-	0	0	?
- UKHI	-	?	?	-	-	-	?
- UKHIV	-	?	?	-	-	-	?
- UKTR3140	0	0	0	+	0	0	?
- UKTR6675	0	+	+	+	+	+	?
- UKTR6675V	0	+	-	+	-	-	?
- GFDL2534	+	?	?	+	0	0	?
- GFDL5564	+	0	+	+	+	+	?

[1] + / 0 / - : positive / nil / negative effect of increase in temperature etc. on grain yield. ? : no simulation result.

[2] positive effect at low temperatures.

[3] for information on the scenarios see section 5.7.6 . Simulations were done for scenario climate with the corresponding increased level of atmospheric CO_2, except for the UKTR6675* scenario which assumed ambient CO_2 (353 ppmv).

The GFDL5564 scenario resulted in moderate and slight to moderate increases in grain yield in the potential runs for Rothamsted and Sevilla respectively and in considerable and slight to moderate increases in grain yield in the water-limited runs for Rothamsted and Sevilla respectively. This scenario resulted in a constant CV of grain yield in the potential runs for Rothamsted and Sevilla and the same or lower value for CV in the water-limited runs. Comparing results from the UKTR and GFDL scenarios, these scenarios resulted in almost the same change in grain yield and in CV of grain yield.

The scenarios for the first decade from both the GFDL and UKTR experiments had a considerably lower level of irradiation, in particular for Rothamsted, than the level at present and that in the scenario for the second decade. This resulted in decreases or relatively small increases in yield.

The UKLO and UKHI scenarios resulted in nil to moderate decreases in grain yield in the potential runs and from considerable decreases to moderate increases in grain yield in the water-limited runs. The amount of rainfall in the UKHI scenario for Sevilla was very low and resulted in low yields in most water-limited runs. Compared to the changes in grain yield for the UKTR6675 scenario, the effects of the UKLO and UKHI scenarios on grain yield were small or even negative. These scenarios resulted in a nil to slight increase in CV of grain yield in the potential runs for both Rothamsted and Sevilla and in no change in CV of grain yield in most water-limited runs. Such changes in CV of grain yield were similar to the changes calculated for the UKTR6675 scenario.

Comparison of the distribution of grain yields in Sevilla for the UKTR6675 scenarios with and without changed climatic variability showed that incorporation of climatic variability into climate change scenarios may change the conclusions concerning the future suitability of wheat production at Sevilla. Changes in climatic variability may result in both a lower mean grain yield and a larger yield variation and, thus, a greater risk of very low yields.

For most climate change scenarios the simulation models gave a range of results on grain yield and CV of grain yield that were not too widely apart. If results from the various models were very different, a considerable element of the differences could often be explained on the basis of model sensitivity and input data. Although the models have been calibrated on the same data sets, it became clear from this analysis that there were still differences in input data, for example, the initial and maximum amount of available soil water. This resulted in large differences in model results in growth periods with a low amount of rainfall.

Acknowledgements

Many thanks are due to E.M. Barrow (Climatic Research Unit, University of East Anglia, Norwich, U.K.) for providing the baseline and scenario climate data sets, to the Rothamsted Experimental Station (Harpenden, Herts, U.K.) for providing data from the Brimstone 1985/86 and Stackyard 1984/85 winter wheat experiments, and to all CLAIRE participants who gave valuable comments on this paper. A complete report on this study can be obtained from the first author.

5.8   Effects on cereal weeds

5.8.1   Background

Cropping systems are influenced by the distribution and abundance of weeds. Crop-weed interactions may alter with changes in climate and atmospheric conditions. Current simulation models of crop growth and development do not usually account for competition from weeds.

Avena sterilis is a weed of international importance. It can cause considerable losses of yield in winter cereals, and requires costly methods of chemical and cultural control (Holm *et. al.*, 1977). *A. sterilis* occurs in regions with warm and dry climates, predominately in all Mediterranean countries as well as in eastern Australia (Fernandez-Quintanilla *et. al.*, 1987). The geographical distribution of *A. sterilis* is related to its temperature and water requirements for germination and emergence.

Simulation models of weed-crop competition were first introduced by Spitters and Aerts (1983), and further developed in other studies, such as Kropf and van Laar, 1993. However, these analyses have been conducted for present climatic conditions only.

The objective of this study is to identify the effect of climate change on the distribution of *A. sterilis* and its effect on wheat yield in Spain.

5.8.2 Experimental data

Data on the competitive ability of *A. sterilis* was compiled from different sites (Sevilla, Badajoz, Albacete, Lerida and Zamora). Laboratory experiments were also required to determine the duration from sowing to emergence of *A. sterilis* under various temperature and soil moisture regimes (osmotic potential). The experimental results were used to indicate the extent to which temperature and soil moisture are responsible for the distribution of *A. sterilis*. This information was then used to predict the potential of the weed to spread beyond its present distribution with changing climatic conditions.

5.8.2.1 *Material and methods*

Influence of temperature

Five replicates of twenty dehulled seeds for each species were sown on blotter paper in 100 mm square Petri dishes and moistened with 8 ml of distilled water. The dishes were covered with foil paper to exclude the light and placed in germinators. Six constant temperatures (5, 10, 15, 20, 25 and 30°C) were imposed using separate germinators. Germination and emergence counts were carried out every 12 hours and continued until no further germination or emergence was detected over five consequtive days.

The minimum temperature (t_{min}) and the heat sum (S_{50}) required to achieve 50% germination or emergence were estimated from linear regression of reciprocal median response time versus temperature. This method assumes that a constant

heat sum in degree days is necessary to obtain 50% germination or emergence. This sum is defined according to the following equation:

$$S_{50} = t_{50}(T-T_{min}) \qquad (5.8.1)$$

where S_{50} is the heat sum, t_{50} is the median response time, T is the temperature of the treatment and T_{min} is the minimum temperature for germination and emergence. The time required for emergence was 150 accumulated degree days above a threshold temperature of 1°C.

Influence of osmotic potential

Four solution concentrations ranging from 10 to 40 g of polyethylene glycol (PEG) 20000 in 100 ml of distilled water were prepared and left to equilibriate overnight. The molar concentration of the various solutions were measured using a vapour pressure osmometer. The osmotic potential was calculated using the following equation:

$$OP = M*R*T \qquad (5.8.2)$$

where OP is the osmotic potential in Kpa, M is the molar concentration in moles litre^{-1}, T is the temperature in K and R the gas constant (8.287 l kpa^{-1} K^{-1} mole^{-1})

Twenty five seeds were placed on two Wathman N° 1 papers in 90 mm Petri dishes. Ten millilitres of the PEG solution were added to each Petri dish. A check treatment consisted of seeds germinated in 8 ml of distilled water. Each treatment was replicated five times. The dishes were covered with foil paper and incubated at a constant temperature of 15°C.

5.8.3 Statistical model

The functional relationships between temperature or osmotic potential and seedling emergence were established by non-linear regression using a maximum likelihood computer algorithm (MLP program). The goodness of fit was judged by residual mean squares.

5.8.3.1   *Effect of temperature*

Various types of models were fitted to the experimental data. The Gamma distribution was found to be the best fit for the relationship between percentage of emergence (Y) and incubation temperature (T). The following gamma model was derived:

$$Y = 4.50*exp\,(-0.15*T)*T^{(1.76)} \qquad (5.8.3)$$

5.8.3.2   *Effect of osmotic potential*

The effect of osmotic potential (X) on percentage emergence (Y) of *A. sterilis* was best described by a second order degree polynomial:

$$Y = 85.5 - 0.040X - 0.00002X^{-2} \qquad (5.8.4)$$

5.8.4   Potential distribution of *A. sterilis* in Spain

Figure 5.8.1 shows the current distribution of *A. sterilis* in Spain according to observed records from a total of 52 climatic stations. Only the northern region of Spain is not currently colonised by this weed species. The potential distribution of *A. sterilis* based on the statistical model is shown in Figure 5.8.2. The model indicates that *A. sterilis* is not climatically limited in northern Spain. The potential suitability has not been realised in this region due to other limitations, principally because northern Spain is not a cereal cropping area.

Figure 5.8.2 shows the duration from sowing to emergence for *A. sterilis* assuming a sowing date of 1 October, with emergence occurring between one and two weeks after sowing. A sowing date

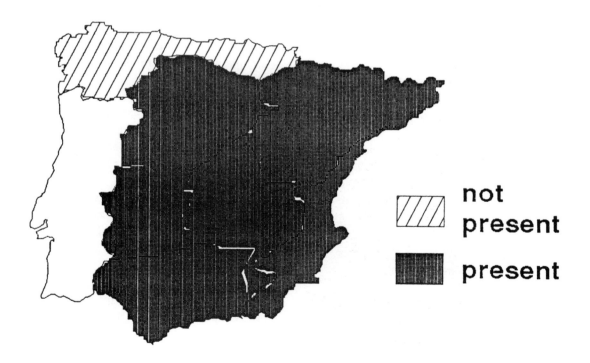

Figure 5.8.1   Current distribution of *Avena sterilis* in Spain.

of one month later considerably alters the timing of emergence, varying from one week after sowing in Andalucia and Extremadura up to approximately two months in Castilla-Leon (Figure 5.8.3).

5.8.5 Winter wheat-weed competition

5.8.5.1 Statistical model

Various types of non linear models have been fitted to the experimental data (wheat grain yield) (Cousens, 1985). A hyperbolic distribution (Gonzalez-Andujar *et. al.*, 1993) fitted the relationship between grain yield (GY, t/ha) and weed density (D, plants m^{-2}) best for the zones considered (Sevilla, Badajoz, Albacete, Lérida and Zamora).

$$GY = GY_{max} \, [1 - aD \, / \, (100(1 + bD))] \quad (5.8.5)$$

where a and b are parameters and GY_{max} is the grain yield in absence of weeds. The parameter values estimated were a=0.39 and b=0.005.

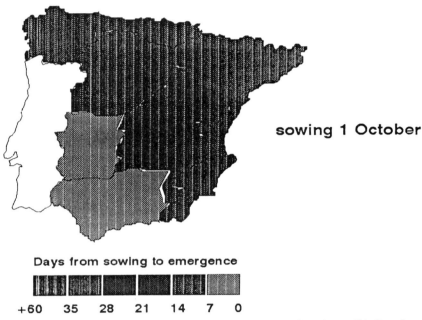

sowing 1 October

Days from sowing to emergence

+60 35 28 21 14 7 0

Figure 5.8.2 Date of emergence of *Avena sterilis*, assuming a sowing date of 1 October.

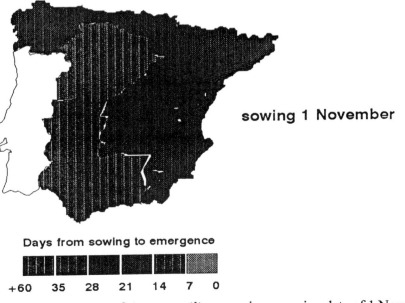

sowing 1 November

Days from sowing to emergence

+60 35 28 21 14 7 0

Figure 5.8.3 Date of emergence of *Avena sterilis*, assuming a sowing date of 1 November.

5.8.6   Winter wheat-*Avena sterilis* competition under climatic scenarios

The CERES-wheat model (see Section 5.7.3.2) and the fitted statistical models were used to calculate grain yield changes at different sites in Spain (Sevilla, Badajoz, Albacete, Lerida and Zamora), considering different climatic scenarios. Two weed infestations were considered: non infestation and a typical infestation of 50 weed plants m^{-2}. Results are presented as percentage changes from the baseline data for the sites.

Generated data from two equilibrium scenarios (UKLO, UKHI) and two transient scenarios (UKTR and GFDL) were used. For the transient scenarios a late model decade was used. For the UKTR scenario this was 66-75, and for GFDL 55-64. The scenario data were produced by a stochastic weather generator. For the UKLO and GFDL scenarios the baseline variability in temperature was retained in the scenario data, whereas for the UKHI and UKTR scenarios both the baseline variability and variability calculated from the GCM experiments were used. The scenarios with changed variability are denoted with a small 'v' in the scenario name, e.g. UKTR6675v.

The atmospheric CO_2 concentration was set to 353 ppmv for the baseline climate, and to 560 ppmv for the equilibrium GCM scenarios. The CO_2 concentration of the late transient model decade was set to 617 ppmv corresponding to the IS92a emissions scenario. The emissions scenario is denoted with a small 'a' in the scenario name, e.g. GFDL5564a. Details of the construction of the site-specific scenarios are given in Section 2.4.

5.8.6.1   *Equilibrium scenarios*

The UKHI scenario without weed infestation produced a crop failure in southern and central regions of Spain (Sevilla, Albacete and Badajoz), possibly because water supply was strongly limiting in this scenario. Otherwise, a strong reduction in grain yield was predicted in the northern region of Zamora (Table 5.8.1).

The UKLO climate change scenario, without weed infestation, resulted in an increase of grain yield at all sites. However, the increase was stronger in the north (Table 5.8.1).

The inclusion of weed competition in both scenarios resulted in a reduction of grain yield at all sites considered, compared to scenario results without infestation. However, at all sites an increase in grain yield is still predicted with a weed infestation of 50 weed plants per m^{-2}, with the exception of Lerida.

5.8.6.2   *Transient scenarios*

Under the GFDL5564a scenario, without weed infestation, grain yield increased at all sites by up to 35% in Zamora (Table 5.8.1). Application of the UKTR6675a scenario without weed infestation resulted in an increase in grain yield (especially in the northern areas of Zamora and Lerida). The opposite effect occurs in the UKTR6675av scenario, where a reduction in grain yield occurred at all sites in northern and central Spain compared to the baseline.

As with the equilibrium scenarios, the introduction of weed infestation caused a reduction in grain yield for most sites and scenarios compared to results without infestation. A relatively larger reduction in yield, up to 15%, is found at the northern sites (Lerid, Zamora), in comparison to a maximum reduction of 7% found at the central and southern sites (Sevilla, Badajoz, Albacete).

5.8.7   Discussion and conclusion

Although this paper has considered the effect of *A. sterilis* only, the results could be representative of other weeds, showing that the inclusion of the competitive effects of weeds produces, under all the climatic scenarios considered, a reduction in crop yield.

The results show that *A. sterilis* is not climatically limited in northern Spain nor, possibly, in other regions of central Europe. However, the potential spread of *A. sterilis* would be limited principally by the extent of the crop cereal areas.

The time to reach emergence varied between sowing times, varying from one or two weeks when sown in October up to approximately

Table 5.8.1   Simulated changes (%) in dryland wheat grain yield from the baseline with the climate change scenarios and with or without weed infestation.

Site	Scenario	Weed density (plants m^{-2})	
		0	**50**
Sevilla	UKLO	+9	+7.0
	UKHI	Crop failure	Crop failure
	GFDL5564a	+15	+8.2
	UKTR6675a	-16	+11.7
	UKTR 6675av	+9	-19.5
Badajoz	UKLO	+10	+8.3
	UKHI	Crop failure	Crop failure
	GFDL5564a	+5	+4.1
	UKTR6675a	+18	+14.9
	UKTR 6675av	-17	+19.9
Albacete	UKLO	+19	+14.8
	UKHI	Crop failure	Crop failure
	GFDL5564a	+14	+10.9
	UKTR6675a	+32	+24.9
	UKTR 6675av	-10	-12.2
Lerida	UKLO	+9	+23.4
	UKHI	Crop failure	Crop failure
	GFDL5564a	+26	+20.2
	UKTR6675a	+15	+34.3
	UKTR 6675av	-16	-18.3
Zamora	UKLO	+42	+34.8
	UKHI	-56	-65.5
	GFDL5564a	+35	+29.0
	UKTR6675a	+85	+70.5
	UKTR 6675av	-20	-23.4

two months when sown in November. These observations may contribute to the design of management strategies for the control of *A. sterilis*.

The crop-weed interaction produced a reduction in the grain yield with most climatic scenarios and sites considered. This study considered a typical infestation of 50 plants m^{-2} (Gonzalez-Andujar *et. al.*, 1993) but for other densities the qualitative results would not vary, but would be reflected in the quantity of the yield reduction.

In general, the work presented shows a further limitation to crop yields besides climatic conditions which should be taken in account in future climate change impact assessments.

References

Acock, B. (1991). Modeling canopy photosynthetic response to carbon dioxide, light interception, temperature and leaf traits. In: Boote, K.J. and Loomis, R.S. (Eds.) *Modelling crop photosynthesis - from biochemistry to canopy*, Crop Science Society of America, Wisconsin, 41-56.

Addiscott, T.M. (1977). A simple computer model for leaching in structured soil. *Journal of Soil Science*, **28**, 554-563.

Addiscott, T.M., Heys, P.J. and Whitmore, A.P. (1986). Application of simple leaching models in heterogeneous soils. *Geoderma*, **38**, 185-194.

Addiscott, T.M. and Whitmore, A.P. (1987). Computer simulation of changes in soil mineral nitrogen and crop nitrogen during autumn, winter and spring. *Journal of Agricultural Science, Cambridge*, **109**, 141-157.

Aguilar, M. (1990). *Influencia de la densidad de plantas en crecimiento, rendimiento y calidad de grano de tres cultivares de maíz (Zea mays L.), ciclos 600, 700, 800 FAO, en el Valle Medio del Guadalquivir*. PhD. Thesis, University of Cordoba, Cordoba.

Aguilar, M. and Rendón, M. (1983). *El Cultivo del Maíz en Regadíos de Climas Cálidos*. Ministerio de Agricultura, Pesca y Alimentación. HD **No. 1/83**.

Allen, S.G., Idso, S.B., Kimball, B.A., Baker J.T., Allen, L.H., Mauney, J.R., Radin, J.W. and Anderson, M.G. (1990). *Effects of air temperature on atmospheric CO_2 - plant growth relationships*. Report TR048. U.S. Department of Energy/ U.S. Department of Agriculture, Washington D.C., 61pp.

Amir, J. and Sinclair, T.R. (1991) A model of the temperature and solar-radiation effects on spring wheat growth and yield. *Field Crop Research*, **28**, 47-58.

Aslyng, H.C. and Hansen, S. (1982). *Water balance and crop production simulation. Model WATCROS for local and regional application*. The Royal Veterinary and Agricultural University, Copenhagen, 200 pp.

Baier, W. and Robertson, G.W. (1968). The performance of soil moisture estimates as compared with the direct use of climatological data for estimating crop yields. *Agricultural Meteorology*, **5**, 17-31.

Baker, J. (1985). *Leaf area development of spring and winter wheat cultivars as affected by temperature, water, growth stage, and plant population*. Ph.D. Thesis, Kansas State University, Manhattan, 210 pp.

Barraclough, P.B., Kuhlmann, H. and Weir, A.H. (1989). The effects of prolonged drought and nitrogen fertilizer on root and shoot growth and water uptake by winter wheat. *Journal of Agronomy and Crop Science*, **163**, 352-360.

Barrow, E.M and Semenov, M.A. (1995). Climate change scenarios with high temporal and spatial resolution for agricultural applications. *Forestry*. (in press).

Bignon, J. (1990). *Agrometeorology and the physiology of maize*. Publication: EUR 13041 EN. Office for Official Publications of the EC, Series: An Agricultural Information System for the EC. Luxembourg.

Bindi M., Gozzini, B. and Orlandini, S. (1994). The combined effects of climate changes and increasing atmospheric CO_2 concentration on potential growth of three grapevine varieties. Proceeding of "International Symposium on Viticulture and Enology: Rootstock, Varieties and New Enological". *ACTA Hortitulturae*. (in press).

Brewster, J.L. (1990). Physiology of crop growth and bulbing. In: Rabinowich, H.D. and Brewster, J.L. (Eds.) *Onions and allied crops. Volume 1: Botany, physiology and genetics*. C.R.C. Press, Boca Ratan, Florida, 53-81.

Brewster, J.L. (1983). Effects of photoperiod, nitrogen nutrition and temperature on inflorescence initiation and development in onion (*Allium cepa L.*) *Annals of Botany*, **51**, 429-440.

Burns, I.G. (1974). A model for predicting the redistribution of salts applied to fallow soils after excess rainfall or evaporation. *Journal of Soil Science*, **25**, 165-178.

Carter, T.R., Parry, M.L. and Porter, J.H. (1991). Climatic change and future agroclimatic potential in Europe. *International Journal of Climatology*, **11**, 251-269.

Charles-Edwards, D.A., Dooley, D. and Rimmington, G.M. (1986). *Modelling plant growth and development*, Academic press, Sydney.

Chaudhuri, U.N., Kirkham, M.B. and Kanemasu E.T. (1990). Carbon dioxide and water level effects on yield and water use of winter wheat. *Agronomy Journal*, **82**, 637-641.

Clough J.M., Peet M.M., Kramer P.J. (1981). Effects of high atmospheric CO_2 and sink size on rates of photosynthesis of a soybean cultivar. *Plant Physiology*, **67**, 1007-1010.

Cousens, R. (1985). An empirical model relating crop yields to weed and crop density and a statistical comparison with other models. *Journal of Agricultural Science Cambridge*, **105**, 513-521.

Crisp, P., Gray, A.R. and Jewell, P.A. (1975). Selection against the bracting defect of cauliflower. *Euphytica*, **24**, 459-465.

Cure, J.D. (1985). Carbon dioxide doubling responses: A crop survey. In: Strain, B.R. and Cure, J.D. (Eds.). *Direct effects of increasing carbon dioxide on vegetation.* DOE/ER-0238. US Department of Energy, Washington DC, USA, 99-116.

Cure, J.D. and Acock B. (1986). Crop responses to carbon dioxide doubling: A literature survey. *Agricultural and Forest Meteorology*, **38**, 127-145.

Dijkstra, P., Schapendonk, A.H.C.M and Groenwold, J. (1993). Effects of CO_2 enrichment on canopy photosynthesis, carbon economy and productivity of wheat and faba bean under field conditions. In: Geijn, S.C. van de, Goudriaan, J. and Berendse, F. (Eds.). *Climate change: Crops and terrestrial ecosystems.* Agrobiological Themes 9, AB-DLO, Wageningen, 23-41.

Eckersten, H. (1994). Modelling daily growth and nitrogen turnover for a short-rotation forest over several years. *Forest Ecology and Management*, **69**, 57-72.

Eckersten, H. (1991). *Simulation model for growth and nitrogen dynamics in short rotation forests. WIGO model description.* Division of Agricutural Hydrotechnics Report **No. 163**. Department of Soil Sciences, Swedish University of Agricultural Science, Uppsala.

Eckersten, H. and Jansson, P.-E. (1991). Modelling water flow, nitrogen uptake and production for wheat. *Fertiliser Research*, **27**, 313-329.

Eckersten, H. and Slapokas, T. (1990). Modelling nitrogen turnover and production in an irrigated short-rotation forest. *Agricultural and Forest Meteorology*, **50**, 99-123.

Eckersten, H., Jansson, P.-E. and Johnsson, H. (1994). *SOILN model version 8.0. User's manual.* Communications, 94. Section of Hydrotechnics, Department of Soil Sciences, Swedish University of Agricultural Sciences, 58 pp.

Eckersten, H., Kowalik, P., Nilsson, L. and Perttu, K. (1983). *Simulation of total willow production.* Energy Forestry Project, Technical Report **No. 32**, Department of Ecology and Environmental Research, Swedish University of Agricultural Science, Uppsala.

Eckersten, H., Lindroth, A., Nilsson, L. (1987). Willow production related to climatic variations in southern Sweden. *Scandanavian Journal of Forest Research*, **2**, 99-110.

Fernandez-Quintanilla, C., Navarrete, L., Torner, C. and Gonzalez-Andujar, J.L. (1987). The influence of herbicide treatments on the population of *Avena sterilis* in winter wheat. *Weed Research*, **27**, 375-383.

Frère, M. and Popov, G.F. (1979). *Agrometeorological crop monitoring and forecasting.* FAO Plant production and protection paper 17. FAO, Rome, Italy, 64 pp.

Gaastra, P. (1962). Photosynthesis of leaves and field crops. *Netherlands Journal of Agricultural Science*, **10**, 311-324.

GCTE (1994). Global Change and Terrestrial Ecosystems Focus 3 Wheat network. *Model and experimental meta data.*

Gifford, R.M. (1995). Whole plant respiration and photosynthesis of wheat grown under increased CO_2 concentration and temperature. *Journal of Experimental Botany*, **46 Supplement**, 2.

Giorgi, F., and Mearns, L.O. (1991). Approaches to the simulation of regional climate change: A review. *Rev. Geophys.*, **29**, 191-216.

Godwin, D., Ritchie, J., Singh, U. and Hunt, L. (1990). *A user's guide to CERES-Wheat - V2.10*. International Fertilizer Development Center. Simulation Manual IFDC-SM-2.

Gonzalez-Andujar, J.L., Fernandez-Quintanilla, C. and Torner, C. (1993). Competencia entre la avena loca (*Avena sterilis*) y el trigo de invierno. Comparación de modelos empirícos. *Investigación Agraría*, **8 (3)**, 425-430.

Goudriaan, J. (1994). Predicting crop yields under global change. In: Walker, B.H. and Mooney, H.A. (Eds.) *Proceedings first GCTE Science Conference.* May 1994, Woodshole, MA, USA.

Goudriaan, J. (1990). Primary productivity and CO_2. In: Goudriaan, J., Keulen, H. van and Laar H.H. van (Eds.). *The greenhouse effect and primary productivity in European agro-ecosystems.* Pudoc, Wageningen, 23-25.

Goudriaan, J. (1986). A simple and fast numerical method for the computation of daily totals of crop photosynthesis. *Agricultural and Forest Meteorology*, **38**, 249-254.

Goudriaan J. and Laar H.H. van (1978). Relations between leaf resistance, CO_2 concentration and CO_2 assimilation in maize, beans, lalang grass and sunflower. *Photosynthetica*, **12**, 241-249.

Goudriaan, J. and Unsworth, M.H. (1990). Implications of increasing carbon dioxide and climate change for agricultural productivity and water resources. In: Kimball B.A., Rosenberg, N.J., Hartwell, Allen L., Heichel, G.H., Stuber, C.W. and Kissel, D.E. (Eds.). *Impact of carbon dioxide, trace gases, and climate change on global agriculture.* ASA Special Publication **No. 53.**, Madison, USA. ASA, Crop Science Society of America, and Soil Science Society of America, 111-130.

Goudriaan, J., van Laar, H.H., van Keulen, H. and Louwerse, W. (1985). Photosynthesis, CO_2 and plant production. In: Day, W. and Atkin, R.K. (Eds.) *Wheat growth and modelling*, NATO ASI Ser., Series A: Life sciences, Plenum Press, New York, **86**, 107-122.

Grace, J. (1988). Temperature as determinant of plant productivity. In: Long, S.P. and Woodward, F.I. (Eds.) *Plants and temperature.* The Company of Biologists Ltd., Cambridge, 91-107.

Grevsen, K. and Olesen, J.E. (1994). Modelling cauliflower development from transplanting to curd initiation. *Journal of Horticultural Science*, **69**, 755-766.

Groot, J.J.R. (1993). NWHEAT; Nitrogen balance in a system of winter wheat and soil. In: Engel, T., Klöcking, B., Priesack, E. and Schaaf, T. (Eds.) *Simulationsmodelle zur Stickstoffdynamik, Analyse und Vergleich.* Agrarinformatik, Band 25, Ulmer, Stuttgart, Germany, 397-411.

Groot, J.J.R. (1987). *Simulation of nitrogen balance in a system of winter wheat and soil.* Simulation reports CABO-TT **No. 13**, Centre for Agrobiological Research and Dept. of Theoretical Production Ecology, Agricultural University, Wageningen, Netherlands, 195 pp.

Groot, J.J.R. and Spiertz, J.H.J. (1991). The role of nitrogen in yield formation and achievement of quality standards in cereals. In: Porter, J.R. and Lawlor, D.W. (Eds.) *Plant growth: Interactions with nutrition and environment.* Society for experimental biology seminar series, Cambridge university press, Cambridge, U.K., 227-247.

Groot, J.J.R. and Willigen, P. de (1991). Simulation of the nitrogen balance in the soil and a winter wheat crop. *Fertilizer Research*, **27**, 261-272.

Gutierrez, A.P. and Baumgärtner, J.U. (1984). A realistic model of plant-herbivore-parasitoid-predator interactions. *The Canadian Entomologist*, **116**, 933-949.

Hansen, S. and Aslyng, H.C. (1984). *Nitrogen balance in crop production. Simulation model NITCROS.* The Royal Veterinary and Agricultural University, Copenhagen, 113 pp.

Hansen, S., Jensen, H.E., Nielsen, N.E. and Svendsen, H. (1990). *DAISY - Soil plant atmosphere system model.* NPo Forskning fra Miljøstyrelsen, Nr A10, Miljøstyrelsen, Copenhagen.

Holm, L. G., Plucknett, D. L., Pancho, J. V. and Herberger, J. P. (1977). *The World's Worst Weeds: Distribution and Biology.* University Press of Hawaii, Honolulu.

Idso, S.B. (1990). Interactive effects of carbon dioxide and climate variables on plant growth. In: Kimball, B.A., Rosenberg, N.J., Hartwell, Allen L., Heichel, G.H., Stuber, C.W. and Kissel, D.E. (Eds.) *Impact of carbon dioxide, trace gases, and climate change on global agriculture.* ASA Special Publication **No. 53**, Madison, USA. Am. Soc. Agron., Crop Sci. Soc. Am., and Soil Sci. Soc. Am., 61-69.

Iglesias, A. and Mínguez, M.I. (1995). Perspectives for maize production in Spain under climate change. In: Harper, L., Hollinger, S., Jones, J. and Rosenzweig, C. *Climate Change and Agriculture.* ASA Special Publication. American Society of Agronomy. Madison, WI. (in press).

Ingestad, T., Aronsson, A. and Ågren, G. (1981). Nutrient flux density model of mineral nutrition in conifer ecosystems. In: Linder, S. (Ed.) Understanding and predicting tree growth. *Studia Forestalia Suecica*, **160**, 61-71.

IPCC (1992). *Climate Change 1992: The Supplementary Report to the IPCC Impacts Assessment.* Tegart, W.J. McG., Sheldan, G.W. and Griffiths, D.C. (Eds). Report prepared for the IPCC Working Group II, Australian Government Publishing Service, Canberra.

ITAP (1985-1993). *Boletines Monográficos de Resultados de los Ensayos de Variedades de Cereales.* Instituto Técnico Agrónomico Provincial, S.A. Albacete.

Jamieson, P.D. (1989). Modelling the interaction of wheat production and the weather. In: Johnson, R.W.M. (Ed.) *Integrated systems analysis and climate impacts.* Proceedings of a workshop on systems analysis, Wellington, November 1989. Rural Policy Unit, MAF-Technology, Wellington, 133-140.

Jamieson, P.D. and Wilson, D.R. (1988). Agronomic uses of a model of wheat growth, development and water use. *Proceedings of the Agronomy Society of New Zealand*, **18**, 7-10.

Jamieson, P.D., Semenov, M.A., Brooking, I. R. and Francis, G.S. (in press). *Sirius: A mechanistic model of wheat response to environmental variation.*

Johnsson, H., Bergström, L., Jansson, P.-E. and Paustian, K. (1987). Simulation of nitrogen dynamics and losses in a layered agricultural soil. *Agriculture, Ecosystems and Environment*, **18**, 333-356.

Jones, C.A. and Kiniry, J.R. (Eds.) (1986). *CERES-Maize: A simulation model of maize growth and development.* Texas A & M University Press. College Station, 194 pp.

Katz, R.W. and Brown, B.G. (1992). Extreme events in a changing climate: Variability is more important than averages. *Climatic Change*, **21**, 289-302.

Kenny, G.J. and Harrison, P.A. (1992a). The effects of climate variability and change on grape suitability in Europe. *Journal of Wine Research*, **3 (3)**, 163-183.

Kenny, G.J. and Harrison, P.A. (1992b). Thermal and moisture limits of grain maize in Europe: Model testing and sensitivity to climate change. *Climate Research*, **2**,113-129.

Kenny, G.J., Harrison, P.A. and Parry, M.L. (Eds.) (1993). *The effect of climate change on agricultural and horticultural potential in Europe*. Research Report **No. 2**, Environmental Change Unit, University of Oxford, 224 pp.

Kenny, G.J., Harrison, P.A., Olesen, J.E. and Parry, M.L. (1993). The effects of climate change on land suitability of grain maize, winter wheat and cauliflower in Europe. *European Journal of Agronomy*, **2**, 325-338.

Keulen, H. van and Laar, H.H. van (1986). The relation between water use and crop production. In: Keulen, H. van and Wolf, J. (Eds.). *Modelling of agricultural production: weather, soils and crops*. Pudoc, Wageningen, 117-129.

Kimball, B.A. (1983). Carbon dioxide and agricultural yield: An assemblage and analysis of 430 prior observations. *Agronomy Journal*, **75**, 779-788.

Kropf, M. J. and van Laar, H. H. (1993). *Modelling Crop-Weed Interactions*. CAB International, Cambridge.

López-Bellido, L. (1991). *Cultivos Herbaceos, Vol. I: Cereales*. Mundi-Prensa, Madrid.

Manetsch, T.J. (1976). Time-varying distributed delays and their use in aggregative models of large systems. *IEEE Transactions on Systems, Man, and Cybernetics*, **SMC-6**, 547-553.

Santa Olalla, M. de, Juan Valero, F.A. de and Tarjuelo Martin-Benito, J.M. (1990). *Respuesta al Agua en Cebada, Girasol y Maíz*. Instituto Técnico Agronómico Provincial, S.A. y Universidad de Castilla-La Mancha, Albacete.

Mearns, L.O., Rosenzweig, C. and Goldberg, R. (1992). Effects of changes in interannual climatic variability on CERES-Wheat yields: Sensitivity and $2xCO_2$ general circulation model scenarios. *Agricultural and Forest Meteorology*, **62**, 159-189.

Mearns, L.O., Schneider, S.H., Thompson, S.L. and McDaniel L.R. (1990). Analysis of climate variability in general circulation models - comparison with observation and changes in variability in $2xCO_2$ experiments. *Journal of Geophysical Research*, **95**, 20469-20490.

Miglietta, F., Gozzini, B. and Orlandini S. (1992). Simulation of leaf appearance in grapevine. *Viticultural and Enological Sciences*, **47**, 41-45.

Mínguez, M.I. and Iglesias, A. (1995). Perspectives of future crop water requirements in Spain: The case of maize as a reference crop. In: A. Angelakis (Ed). *Diachronic Climatic Changes: Impacts on Water Resources*. Springer-Verlag, New York (in press).

Monsi, M. and Saeki, T. (1953). Über der lichtfaktor in den pflanzengesellschaften und seine bedeutung fur die stoffproduktion. *Japanese Journal of Botany*, **14**, 22-52.

Muchow, R.C., Sinclair, T.R. and Bennett, J.M. (1990). Temperature and solar radiation effects on potential maize yield across locations. *Agronomy Journal*, **82**, 338-343.

Nonhebel, S. (1994). The effects of use of average instead of daily weather data in crop growth simulation models. *Agricultural Systems*, **44**, 377-396.

Olesen, J.E. and Grevsen, K. (1994). Simulation of effects of climatic change on cauliflower production. In: Grasman, J. and van Straten, G. (Eds.): *Predictability and nonlinear modelling in natural sciences and economics*. Kluwer, Dordrecht, pp. 127-137.

Olesen, J.E. and Grevsen, K. (1993). Simulated effects of climate change on summer cauliflower production in Europe. *European Journal of Agronomy*, **2**, 313-323.

Orlandini, S., Bindi, M. and Gozzini, B. (1993). Effect of CO_2-induced climatic change on viticultural environments of cool climate regions of Italy. *Viticultural and Enological Science*, **48**, 81-85.

Orlandini, S., Gozzini, B., Miglietta, F., Bindi, M., and Segli, L. (1994). Dry matter allocation in three fruit species during fruit growth. *Proceeding XXIV International Horticultural Congress Kyoto 21-27 August 1994*, 50.

Penning de Vries, F.W.T. (1975). The cost of maintenance processes in plant cells. *Annals of Botany*, **39**, 77-92.

Penning de Vries, F.W.T. and van Laar, H.H. (1982). Simulation of plant growth and crop production. *Simulation monographs*, Pudoc, Wageningen.

Pereira, A.R. and Villa-Nova, N.A. (1992). Analysis of the Priestley-Taylor parameter. *Agricultural Forest and Meteorology*, **61**, 1-9.

Poorter H. (1993). Interspecific variation in the growth response of plants to an elevated CO_2 concentration. In: Rozema, J., Lambers, H., van de Geijn, S.C., Cambridge, M.L., (Eds.) *CO_2 and Biosphere*. Dordrecht: Kluwer Academic Press, 77-98.

Porter, J.R. (1984). A model of canopy development in winter wheat. *Journal of Agricultural Science, Cambridge*, **102**, 383-392.

Porter, J.R. (1993). AFRCWHEAT2: A model of the growth and development of wheat incorporating responses to water and nitrogen. *European Journal of Agronomy*, **2**, 69-82.

Porter J.R., Jamieson P.D. and Wilson, D.R. (1993). Comparison of the wheat simulation models AFRCWHEAT2, CERES-Wheat and SWHEAT for non-limiting conditions of crop growth. *Field Crops Research*, **33**, 131-157.

Pouget, R. (1988). Le debourrement des bourgeons de la vigne: Methode de prevision et principes d'etablissement d'une echelle de precocite de debourrement. *Connaissance de la Vigne et du Vin*, **22**, 105-123.

Pratt, C. and Coombe, B.G. (1978) Shoot growth and anthesis in *Vitis*. *Vitis*, **17**, 125-133.

Priestley, C.H.B. and Taylor, R.J. (1972). On the assessment of surface heat flux and evaporation using large scale parameters. *Monthly Weather Review*, **100**, 81-92.

Racsko, P., Szeidl, L. and Semenov, M.A. (1991). A serial approach to local stochastic weather models. *Ecological Modelling*, **57**, 27-41.

RAEA (1991). *Variedades de trigos campaña 90/91*. Red Andaluza de experimentacion Agraria. Junta de Andalucia, Consejeria de agricultura y pesca, Direccion general de investigacion y extension agrarias, Sevilla.

RAEA (1989). *Variedades de trigos campaña 88/89*. Red Andaluza de experimentacion Agraria. Junta de Andalucia, Consejeria de agricultura y pesca, Direccion general de investigacion y extension agrarias, Sevilla.

Reinink, K., Jorritsma, I. and Darwinkel, A. (1986). Adaptation of the AFRC wheat phenology model for Dutch conditions. *Netherlands Journal of Agricultural Science*, **34**, 1-13.

Rind, D., Goldberg, R., and Ruedy, R. (1989). Changes in climate variability in the 21st century. *Climatic Change*, **14**, 5-37.

Ritchie, J.T. (1972). Model for predicting evaporation from a row crop with incomplete cover. *Water Resources Research*, **8**, 1204-1213.

Ritchie, J. and Otter S. (1985). Description of and performance of CERES_Wheat: A user-oriented wheat yield model. In: Willis W.O. (Ed.) *ARS wheat yield project*. Department of agriculture, Agricultural research service. ARS-38. Washington D.C., 159-175.

Roberts, E.H. and Summerfield, R.J. (1987). Measurement and prediction of flowering in annual crops. In: Atherton, J.G. (Ed.) *Manipulation of flowering,* Butterworths, London, 17-50.

Rosenberg, N.J., Blad, B.L. and Verma, S.B. (1983). *Microclimate, The Biological Environment.* John Wiley and Sons, New York.

Rosenzweig C. and Iglesias, A. (Eds.) (1994). *Implications of climate change for international agriculture: Crop modeling study.* U.S. Environmental Protection Agency, Washington D.C.

Saini, H.S. and Aspinall, D. (1982). Effect of water deficit on sporogenesis in wheat (*Triticum aestivum L.*) *Annals of Botany,* **48,** 623-633.

Salter, P.J. (1960). The growth and development of early summer cauliflower in relation to environmental factors. *Journal of Horticultural Science,* **35,** 21-33.

Santer, B.D., Wigley, T.M.L, Schlesinger, M.E., and Mitchell, J.F.B. (1990). *Developing climate scenarios from equilibrium GCM results.* Report 47, Max-Planck Institut für Meteorologie, Hamburg.

Semenov, M.A. and Porter, J.R. (1995). Climatic variability and the modelling of crop yields. *Agricultural and Forest Meteorology,* **73,** 265-283.

Semenov, M.A., Porter, J.R. and Delécolle, R. (1993). Simulation of the effects of climate change on growth and development of wheat in the UK and France. In: Kenny, G.J., Harrison, P.A. and Parry M.L. (Eds.) *The effect of climate change on the agriculture and horticultural potential in Europe.* Research Report **No. 2,** Environmental Change Unit, Oxford University.

Shouse, P., Jury, W.A. and Stolzy, L.H. (1980). Use of deterministic and empirical models to predict potential evapotranspiration in an advective environment. *Agronomy Journal,* **72,** 994-998.

Smith, M. (1992). *Report of expert consultation on revision of FAO methodologies for crop water requirements.* FAO, Rome, May 1990. FAO, Land and Water Development Division, Rome. 60 pp.

Spaeth, S.C., Sinclair, T.R., Ohnuma, T. and Konno, S. (1987). Temperature, radiation, and duration dependence of high soybean yields: Measurement and simulation. *Field Crops Research,* **16,** 297-307.

Spitters, C.J.T and Aerts, R. (1983). Simulation of competition for light and water in crop weed associations. *Asppects of Applied Biology,* **4,** 467-484.

Spitters, C.J.T, Keulen, H. van and Kraalingen, D.W.G. van (1989). A simple and universal growth simulator: SUCROS87. In: Rabbinge, R., Ward, S.A. and Laar H.H. van (Eds.) *Simulation and systems management in crop production.* Simulation Monographs, Wageningen, The Netherlands, pp. 147-181.

Steer B.T. (1980). The bulbing response to day length and temperature of some Australian cultivars of onion (*Allium cepa* L.). *Australian Journal of Agricultural Research,* **31,** 511-18.

Tanner C.B. and Jury W.A. (1976). Estimating evaporation and transpiration from a row crop during incomplete cover. *Agronomy Journal,* **68,** 239-243.

Terabun M. (1981). Effect of low temperature on bulb formation in onion plants. *Journal of the Horticultural Association of Japan,* **50,** 53-59.

Visser, C.L.M. de (1994). ALCEPAS, an onion growth model based on SUCROS87. I. Development of the model. *Journal of Horticultural Science,* **69,** 501-518.

Weir, A.H. (1988). Estimating losses in the yield of winter wheat as a result of drought in England and Wales. *Soil Use and Management,* **4,** 33-40.

Weir, A.H., Bragg, P.L., Porter, J.R. and Rayner, J.H. (1984). A winter wheat crop simulation model without water or nutrient limitations. *Journal of Agricultural Science, Cambridge*, **102**, 371-382.

Wheeler, T.R and Ellis, R.H. (1992). Seed quality and seedling emergence in onion (*Allium cepa* L.). *Journal of Horticultural Science*, **67**, 319-332.

Wheeler, T.R., Ellis, R.H., Hadley, P. and Morison, J.I.L. (1995). Effects of CO_2, temperature and their interaction on the growth, development and yield of cauliflower (*Brassica oleracea* L. *botrytis*). *Scientia Horticulturae*, **60**, 181-197.

Wit, C.T. de (1965). *Photosynthesis of leaf canopies.* Agricultural Research Report 663, Pudoc, Wageningen, 57 pp.

Wurr, D.C.E., Fellows, J.R. and Hambridge, A.K. (1995). The potential impact of global warming on summer/autumn cauliflower growth in the UK. *Agricultural and Forest Meteorology*, **72**, 181-193.

Wurr, D.C.E., Fellows, J.R. and Hiron, R.W.P. (1990). The influence of field environmental conditions on the growth and development of four cauliflower cultivars. *Journal of Horticultural Science*, **65**, 565-572.

Wurr, D.C.E., Fellows, J.R., Hiron, R.W.P. and Antill, D.D. (1992). The development and evaluation of techniques to predict when to harvest iceberg lettuce heads. *Journal of Horticultural Science*, **67**, 385-393.

Wurr, D.C.E., Fellows, J.R., Sutherland, R.A. and Elphinstone, E.D. (1990). A model of cauliflower curd growth to predict when curds reach a specified size. *Journal of Horticultural Science*, **65**, 555-564.

CHAPTER 6

Modelling the effects of climate change

on crops at the regional scale

SUMMARY

Spatial crop modelling has been undertaken at three scales: regional, country and continental. Several methodologies have been developed to model crop-climate interactions across space. These are reported in four studies, one regional assessment based on the Camargue region in southern France, two country studies in Spain and Finland and one continental scale assessment for a wide European region extending from 11°W to 42°E and from 35 to 71.5°N.

In the regional study, a method for calibrating crop models at the landscape level using remotely sensed data has been developed and verified for durum wheat in the Camargue region, southern France. The Camargue zone is an area of approximately 30 x 30 km with a cropping system of wheat, sunflower, and other dry crops, alternating with flooded rice crops. Ten images were obtained from the earth observation satellite SPOT for the period 6 February to 9 August 1987. A classification was performed over the ten available scenes to identify the crops which were sown in each field. All fields larger than two hectares containing durum wheat were retained and pixel values of reflectances and Normalized Difference Vegetation Index (NDVI) were derived for each field. The satellite measurements of NDVI were compared with observed NDVI values and values simulated using a canopy radiation transfer model and found to be reliable estimates of 'true' crop vegetation index. The radiometric information was used in conjunction with the AFRCWHEAT model to test model calibration across different fields. Results showed that the model was well calibrated for one field, but not for the other. Significant differences in the prediction of grain yield were found when the model was run using observed LAI as a forcing variable compared with the original calibration. In future analyses the satellite information will be used to calibrate the crop model across all durum wheat fields in the study area to derive spatial distribution functions for key crop parameters. The aim will be to produce a stochastic crop model which will be able to simulate crop evolution at the landscape level. Modified climates will then be applied to this stochastic model to quantify regional responses in terms of expected yield distributions.

In the Spanish country study, the productivity of wheat and maize was analysed by extrapolating results from detailed site-based models. The CERES crop simulation models were calibrated for five sites located in the main cereal-growing regions of Spain. These regions have been classified as having similar climatic and soil characteristics according to Elena-Rossello et al. (1990). The climate change scenarios were applied to the crop models along with the associated changes in CO_2 concentration for the IS92a emissions scenario. Maize yields decreased significantly at all five sites for all scenarios due to substantial shortening of the duration of crop growth stages, particularly grain filling, and little benefit from CO_2 enrichment (C_4 crop). The largest yield reductions were found with the UKHI scenario and in the major area of maize production (Albacete). Yield reductions were lowest at the site representing the coldest region (Zamora). Wheat yields increased at all sites for most climate change scenarios due to large direct effects of elevated CO_2 on photosynthesis and water use (C_3 crop), and also due to an increase in the length of the frost free period at northern sites. The largest yield increases were found with the UKTR6675 scenario and in the northern sites. A number of adaptive strategies have been examined for maize to improve the efficiency of water use with climate change. The inclusion of very short growth cycle maize as a second crop sown after barley, lentils or a vetch-barley forage mixture considerably reduced irrigation demand, compared to current practices, as the period of maximum water requirement coincided with a period of both lower temperatures and higher precipitation. However, the shorter season variety produced lower yields than the traditional varieties.

In the Finnish country study, a national scale geographic information system was used in conjunction with crop models to analyse spring wheat and barley suitability on a regular 10 x 10 km grid. Phenological models have been constructed to estimate the growing time and phasic development of a number of spring-sown cereal cultivars. Models were derived by examining the relationships between environmental variables and phenological observations at experimental stations. Definitions of the beginning and end of a favourable growing season were developed based on the gridded spatial climatology. Each phenological model was run within the predefined growing season for the 30 year time series from 1961 to 1990. The estimated suitability under the baseline climate corresponded well with the actual cultivation limit for spring wheat and was slightly to the south of the actual cultivated zone for spring barley.

The sensitivity of crop potential to climate change in Finland was examined using both sensitivity tests and climate change scenarios. All scenarios caused a northward shift in the area of suitability and a shortening of period from heading to yellow ripeness for both spring wheat and barley. Northward shifts of wheat (cv. Kadett) were 570 km in western Finland and 320 km in eastern Finland under the UKTR6675 scenario, and 520 km and 320 km, respectively, under the GFDL5564 scenario. The estimated zone of suitability of spring barley (cv. Arra) moves northwards by about 450 km in the west and 330 km in the east of Finland under the UKTR6675 scenario, and 390 km and 250 km, respectively, under the GFDL5564 scenario. The equilibrium scenarios caused even greater northward shifts than the transient scenarios. The period from heading to yellow ripening reduced by 6 to 14 days for wheat and by 1 to 10 days for barley under the range of scenarios due to increased temperatures. A decreased grain filling period will cause reduced grain size and decreased yields relative to present conditions. Adaptive strategies were investigated to counteract the shortening in the growing period by substituting existing cultivars with others having higher temperature requirements. The longer-season varieties exhibited slightly delayed phenological development relative to a traditional cultivar and were higher yielding under elevated temperature conditions.

In the Europe-wide study, a continental scale geographic information system was used in conjunction with crop models to analyse the suitability and productivity of winter wheat, sunflower and onion on a regular 0.5° latitude/longitude grid. A literature review for grassland was also conducted to assess the feasibility of developing a spatial model of grassland suitability in future analyses. A number of methods for modelling broadscale crop-climate interaction were evaluated. Errors associated with the different methods were quantified and indicate that regional crop modelling need not imply higher levels of uncertainty, at least for the purposes of climate change impact assessment. Model complexity was dependent on the availability of climatic and agronomic data across the study region. Sufficient data were available to simulate water-limited yield in the wheat and sunflower models and potential yield in the onion model.

The sensitivity of crop productivity to climate change in Europe was examined using both sensitivity tests and climate change scenarios. The area of suitability expanded northwards and eastwards for winter wheat and northwards for sunflower and onion. Water-limited yield for wheat increased in all scenarios across most of Europe. The largest increases occurred for the last model decade of the transient GCMs assuming the IS92a emissions scenario and in central Europe. Conversely, water-limited yield for sunflower decreased in most scenarios. The largest decreases occurred in the equilibrium scenarios and in southwest Europe. The lowest decreases were generally found in northern central Europe and for the last model decade of the transient GCMs assuming the IS92a emissions scenario. Yield increases for sunflower were only found in central and eastern Europe under the transient scenarios. Onion potential yields decreased in the equilibrium scenarios and increased in the transient scenarios with no consistent regional pattern. Again, the largest increases occurred in the last model decade of the transient GCMs assuming the IS92a emissions scenario. For all three crops, predictions of both water-limited and potential yield worsened for the IS92d scenario, compared to IS92a.

These differences in yield can be explained by a number of interacting factors. Firstly, higher temperatures caused increased developmental rates and, hence, shorter growing period length. A shorter grain filling (wheat), seed filling (sunflower) or bulb growth (onion) period resulted in less time to accumulate dry matter and, thus, gave lower yields. On the other hand, elevated concentrations of atmospheric CO_2 caused increased assimilation rates and, hence, higher potential yields, counteracting the negative effects of a shorter growing period. Furthermore, in water-limited situations the interaction between increased evapotranspiration, either increased or decreased precipitation (depending on the scenario) and improved water use efficiency from elevated CO_2 further complicated the simulated change in yield. In the case of wheat, relatively small decreases were predicted in the length of the growing period and the beneficial effects from CO_2 were large, compared with sunflower and onion. This resulted in moderate to strong increases in yield for all climate change scenarios. Alternatively, the length of the growing period for sunflower was reduced dramatically and the direct effects of CO_2 were less than for wheat. This resulted in strong decreases in yield for most scenarios. The onion simulations were intermediate between wheat and sunflower. The CO_2 concentration was not sufficient to counterbalance the large decreases in growing period length predicted in the equilibrium scenarios, but it was sufficient in all transient scenarios where the relative increase in developmental rates was lower. A number of adaptive strategies were investigated to improve water-limited yield predictions for wheat and sunflower. Sowing earlier led to an increase in yield for both crops due to a considerable reduction in the shortening of the growing period.

6.1   Introduction

Different scales of assessment reveal different aspects of a problem. For example, at the local scale crop experimental programmes and complex mechanistic crop models provide information on the intricate relationships between weather, atmosphere, soil and crop physiology at a site. At the regional scale interactions between cropping systems and land use planning can be considered spatially. At the country or continental scale broadscale aspects of a problem can be analysed, such as bioclimatic shifts in crop productivity, identification of sensitive areas, comparative advantages between crops and regions and the effects of policy.

However, large scale models can not take account of the level of detail found within small scale models due to data and computing limitations. Hence, certain processes found to be less sensitive to changes in climate may be parameterised or simply ignored. There is a need for models to be developed and tested specifically for regional assessments. Previous large scale modelling studies have relied on the use of semi-empirical indices to identify regions of crop suitability (Carter *et al.*, 1991a; Kenny and Harrison, 1992a). However, the predictive capability of empirical approaches is limited to within the boundaries of the environmental variables from which they were constructed, restricting their value for climate change impact assessment. Methodologies for the development and application of mechanistic-based crop models at the regional scale are required.

The four studies reported in this chapter have developed methodologies for modelling crop-climate interactions at three geographical scales: regional (group of fields), country and continental. The first paper (Section 6.2) describes a method for calibrating mechanistic crop models at the landscape level using remotely sensed data. The approach is verified for a cropping system of wheat, sunflower and other dry crops alternating with flooded rice crops in the Camargue region in southern France. The two studies reported in Sections 6.3 and 6.4 examine different methods of analysing the suitability and productivity of crops at the national scale. Section 6.3 is based on extrapolating results from detailed

site-specific models for the main cereal-growing regions of Spain. Section 6.4 employs a national scale geographic information system to apply crop-climate models to data on a regular 10 x 10 km grid across Finland. The final section in this chapter (Section 6.5) describes three spatial crop models which have been developed at the continental scale for wheat, sunflower and onion. This study also uses a geographical information system to apply the models to a consistent collection of climatic and other relevant environmental data on a regular 0.5° latitude by 0.5° longitude grid across Europe.

The regional scale assessment reported in Section 6.2 was a preliminary study aimed at verifying the approach over a well-studied and sampled test area. Hence, as yet, the approach has not been applied to possible future climates. The studies reported in Sections 6.3, 6.4 and 6.5 have followed guidelines which were established to provide a coherant structure to the crop modelling research. Firstly, methodologies or models were developed and evaluated for the region of interest based on observed meteorological data for the period 1961-1990. This baseline run acted as a reference against which the impacts of sensitivity tests and climate change scenarios were appraised. Following the baseline run, the sensitivity of each model to a range of systematic changes in mean climate was investigated (sensitivity tests). The quantification of crop model responses to independent changes in individual climatic variables as well as changes in CO_2 concentration allowed a more informed interpretation of predicted impacts from GCM scenarios. Scenarios of future climate have been constructed at the appropriate scales (Table 6.1.1; see Section 2.3 for a detailed description). Two equilibrium (UKLO, UKHI) and two transient (UKTR, GFDL) GCM scenarios have been applied to the crop models. For each transient GCM, two model decades have been analysed (UKTR3140, UKTR6675, GFDL2534, GFDL5564). Appropriate concentrations of atmospheric CO_2 have been assumed for each scenario (Table 6.1.1). For the transient GCM scenarios, the CO_2 concentrations for the model decades have been related to two IPCC greenhouse gas emissions scenarios (IS92a, IS92d). Finally, a number of possible farm-level adaptive strategies were evaluated using the

Table 6.1.1   Details of climate change scenarios applied to the spatial crop models.

Emissions scenario	GCM scenario	CO$_2$ concentration (ppmv)
2 x CO$_2$	UKLO	560
2 x CO$_2$	UKHI	560
IS92a	UKTR3140	454
IS92a	UKTR6675	617
IS92a	GFDL2534	454
IS92a	GFDL5564	617
IS92d	UKTR6675	545
IS92d	GFDL5564	545

models, including changes in sowing or transplanting time and changes in crop variety.

6.2   Regional calibration of crop models using remote sensing data

6.2.1   Background

Previous impact studies dealing with the effects of changing climate characteristics on agriculture at a global scale have addressed this problem under the assumption that results from crop models calibrated at the field level could be extended to the regional or continental level through the extension of input (namely weather) variables. This approach can assess broadscale trends in crop production, but it cannot account for responses of local cropping systems (landscapes, small regions) where the choice of crop species, genotypes, sowing dates and cropping practices are correlated and where the resilience of the agrosystem is more manageable. This paper is a first attempt to characterise such agricultural landscapes through the joint use of remotely sensed (satellite) information and crop models. Series of satellite scenes over a test area have been used to derive distributions of crop parameters over a collection of fields. Crop models were applied as integrators of these statistically defined parameters, aiming at a comprehensive simulation of crop evolution at the landscape level. Future studies will introduce modified climates into such stochastic models, leading to

(for instance) local responses in terms of expected yield distributions.

6.2.2   Rationale

In practice, the final production of a given crop in a given region is achieved by a set (mosaic) of fields or groups of homogeneous fields. Each field differs from its neighbours by its sowing date, the variety sown, the soil type and possibly the cropping practices. In the same way as a single shift in the mean values of climate variables is not satisfactory for estimating the possible impacts of climate change, using mean crop conditions for simulating the responses of an entire agricultural region is probably inadequate.

In models the spatial variability of crop conditions can be translated into a distribution of some parameters of the vegetation or a distribution of initial values for some of the vegetation state variables. If this spatial variability of parameters and variables can be introduced into a crop model, and if the time variability of climate variables in a changing climate is then used as an input into this model, the result will be a tool for numerical experiments on the probable evolution of the landscape. Simulations of parameter and weather values according to their respective empirical distribution functions will, for instance, allow estimates of the 'resilience' of a present cropping system to modified climatic conditions.

The estimation of the distribution of crop parameters is not a simple matter. Either it is known by means of surveys or expert knowledge, which is highly improbable, or it must be estimated by some objective technique. In this respect, remote sensing is probably the most adequate tool when used in symbiosis with crop models. From a time series of remote sensing (RS) images over the same region, time profiles of radiometric characteristics can be extracted for a set of fields. Such profiles can be translated into profiles of crop characteristics (Leaf area indices -LAIs-, radiation interception efficiencies) which can be used for a dynamic recalibration of a crop model for each field (Delécolle *et al.*, 1992). This results in observed distributions of model parameters characterising an area (Figure 6.2.1). From observed distributions, theoretical distributions can be estimated (including the covariances between parameters), providing a 'crop generator' comparable with the weather generator, when introduced into the crop model.

In the final phase, the crop model is run a given number of times with parameters drawn at random from the above distributions and with changed climate (from a weather generator) as input. Distributions of yields conditional to the landscape and the future climate can thus be obtained. A further study will examine how the relationships between cropping practices (for instance, the choice of the sowing date) can evolve under changing conditions (Figure 6.2.2).

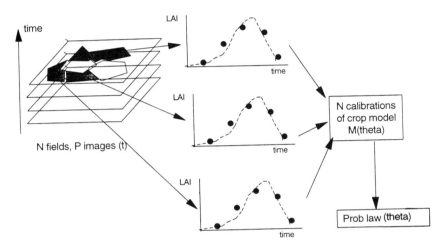

Figure 6.2.1   Principle of the estimation of parameter (theta) distributions in the crop simulation model M, from P satellite images of the same landscape of N fields.

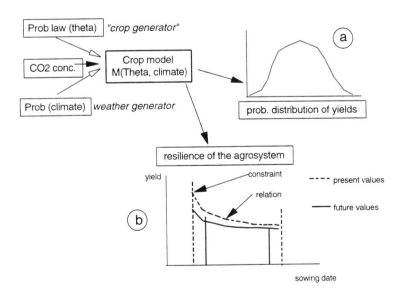

Figure 6.2.2   Principle of the joint use of the estimated distributions of model parameters, weather generator and various hypotheses of CO_2 concentration to simulate (a) expected distributions of final yield over a landscape and (b) variations of yield vs. practice relationships ('resilience' of the crop-environment-practice system). The constraints in the system are illustrated for the yield-sowing date relationship.

This is expected to investigate the resilience of the system of crop species, cropping practices and environment to changing climate and broaden the concept of adaptive strategies.

The present study is a preliminary one, aimed at verifying the feasibility of this approach over a well-studied and sampled test area, the Camargue region in southern France (Delécolle *et al.*, 1992). As a first step it will be limited to the application of remote sensing techniques to derive distribution functions of crop state variables over this area.

6.2.3   The pilot study

6.2.3.1   *Location and methods*

Test site

The Camargue zone is an area of approximately 30 by 30 km. It is located in southern France on the Mediterranean coast. A former zone of salty swamps, it was drained during the last century in order to grow intensive crops. To prevent upward motion of salt water from the bottom soil layers, the soil must be flooded with fresh water every two or three years, and farmers have chosen to grow rice approximately every other year or so to achieve this. The cropping system is therefore very unusual by French standards: wheat, sunflower, and other dry crops alternating with flooded rice crops.

As a flat zone of intricate cultivated fields, it has been chosen as a test area for remote sensing studies including crop identification, ground samples and radiometric measurements. These measurements were performed on nine test fields planted with durum wheat and consisted of: leaf area index (measured with a leaf-area meter); above-ground biomass (oven dried); radiation interception efficiency (estimated with fish-eye photographic) and hand-held radiometry (red and near infrared reflectances) (Guérif *et al.*, 1988).

Satellite information

In the year 1987, many overpasses of the earth observation satellite SPOT were programmed in order to obtain as many scenes of this area as possible. At the end of the season, ten SPOT scenes were available from 6 February to 9 August. These scenes were corrected for atmospheric influences and for the modulation transfer function of the on-board sensor. Finally, they were corrected in order to be mutually superimposable and to allow their projection on a common geographic reference (Lambert projection map). The time series of these scenes is illustrated in Figure 6.2.3. From this map, a canvas of field limits was digitised and this canvas was used to extract the information for each field in each satellite scene. The result was a time profile of radiometric values for all pixels in each field: the area can therefore be described by the individual field radiometric evolutions (mean value and standard deviation for the field).

A classification was performed over the ten available scenes to identify the various crops that were sown in the identified fields (Unpublished results by Guérif, Atzberger and Blöser). This led to the crop classification illustrated in Figure 6.2.4. From fields that were identified as planted with durum wheat, only fields larger than two hectares were retained. To avoid confusion between winter wheat and other winter crops, the time evolution (time profile) of each identified field was examined, and a selection procedure performed with the following criteria: (i) a field should have attained a maximum value of the Normalised Difference Vegetation Index (NDVI)[1] after 5 March and before 6 June; (ii) the maximum NDVI value should range between 0.6 and 0.9. These selection criteria were probably too strict,

---

[1]   Reflectance is the ratio of reflected radiation to incoming radiation in a given bandwidth. SPOT multispectral bands used here are Red (610-680nm) and Near Infrared (790-890nm). Respective reflectances are Rr and Rnir. Vegetation indices are functions of reflectances which are more or less related to crop canopy properties or state variables, such as the radiation interception efficiency or LAI. In this study, the Normalised Difference Vegetation Index NDVI (Rouse *et al.*, 1974), which has been designed to minimise the effect of soil reflectance and is defined as: NDVI = (Rnir-Rr)/(Rnir+Rr), was used.

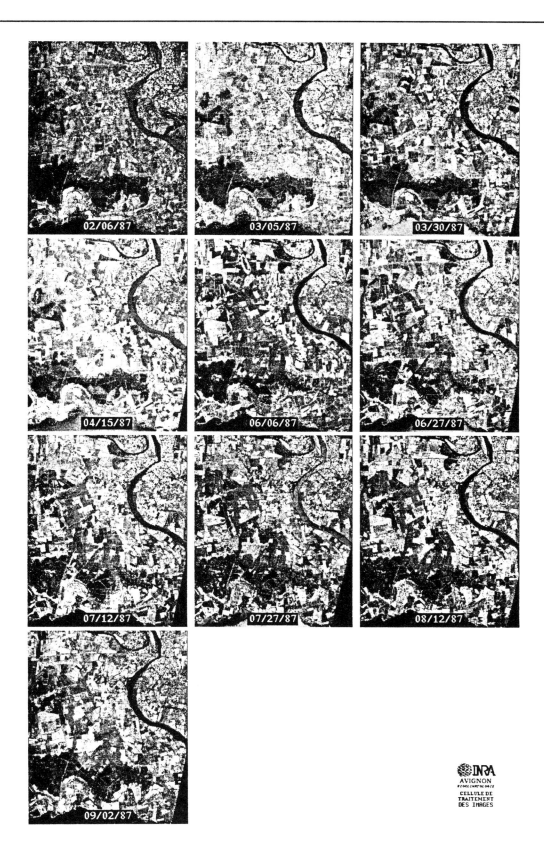

Figure 6.2.3 Evolution of the agricultural landscape in the Camargue area as seen by ten scenes of the SPOT earth observation satellite (Normalised Difference Vegetation Index, year 87). Light grey zones are bare soils, medium grey zones are photosynthetically active canopies and dark grey zones are flooded areas (rice fields in early growth stages and marshes).

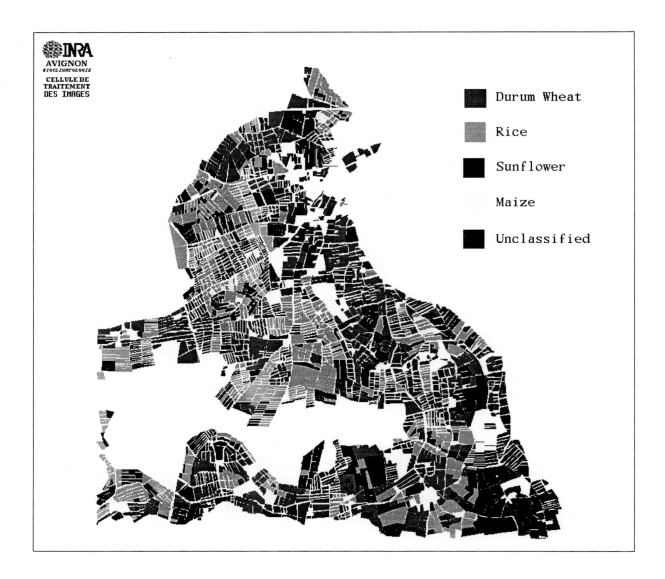

Figure 6.2.4   Classification of crops present in the Camargue area from the ten SPOT scenes (1cm = 0.8km).

and many fields that were presumably planted with durum wheat were rejected, particularly because the series of scenes was interrupted during a period which corresponds to the maximum LAI (and therefore NDVI) values for wheat. Sixty-four fields were nevertheless identified and retained through this procedure: they are represented in Figure 6.2.5. For each field, pixel values of reflectances and NDVI were computed and values of field means and standard deviation were derived.

6.2.3.2   *Results from test fields*

From a radiometric point of view, the homogeneity of field measurements with satellite results was tested by comparing different types of time evolutions which are displayed in Figure 6.2.6. This figure compares the 'observed' NDVIs (computed from hand-held measurements of reflectances) to 'SPOT' NDVIs (averaged values over the field pixels) and 'simulated' NDVIs (obtained from using observed LAIs as input values into the SAIL

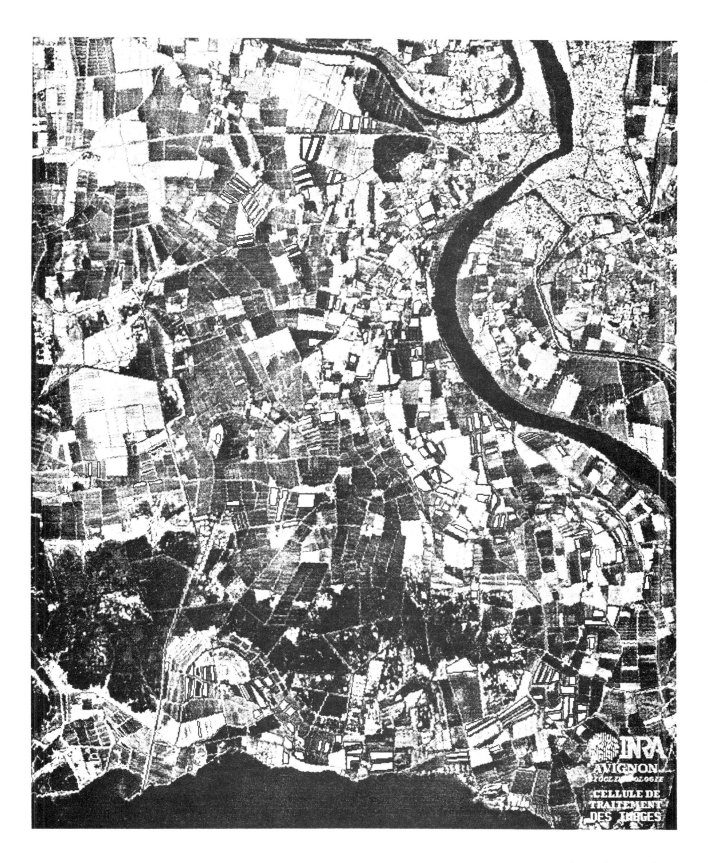

Figure 6.2.5 Locations of the sixty four durum wheat fields (outlined in black) used to characterise the time evolution of the area.

canopy radiation transfer model (Verhoef, 1984) and thus simulating 'biological' reflectances). It can be observed that 'physical' and 'biological' reflectances are very close, indicating that the radiation transfer model works satisfactorily, and also that satellite estimations reasonably follow the ground truth, even if one notices a

critical gap in observations during the phase of maximum crop development. Therefore a first conclusion for our test area is that satellite measurements of NDVI are reliable estimates of 'true' crop vegetation index and can be used for this estimation wherever ground measurements are unavailable.

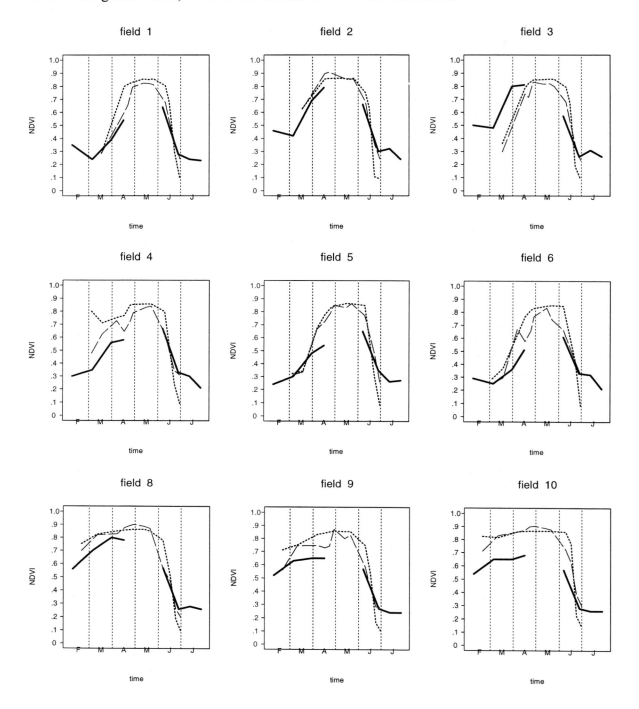

Figure 6.2.6   Time evolution of NDVIs for nine test fields (broken line: observed values from ground level radiometry; dotted line: values simulated from observed LAIs; broad line: observed values from SPOT scenes, averaged over each field).

Radiometric information is nevertheless not sufficient, as it must be converted into biologically meaningful values (crop state variables). As stated by Delécolle *et al.* (1992), neither radiometric estimations nor stand-alone crop simulation models will suffice in estimating intermediate or final production over a large area, but joint use of the two techniques can be fruitful. An illustration of the inaccuracy of crop models to correctly represent the time evolution of a landscape is shown in Figure 6.2.7. In this figure, LAI simulations by the wheat model AFRCWHEAT2 (under non limiting water conditions) for two test fields (differing in sowing date, the genotypes being rather similar) are displayed. Contrasted situations appear, simulations showing respectively good and poor agreement with observed LAI values. Apparently, the model was well calibrated for one field but not for the other one. In fact, the contrast between the two fields is probably due to causes that are not accounted for by the model, such as crop practices or water shortage, and we should speak of 'apparent calibration'. To confirm this, Table 6.2.1 shows the different grain dry matters simulated by AFRCWHEAT2 when using observed LAI (as a forcing variable) and when simulating LAI itself.

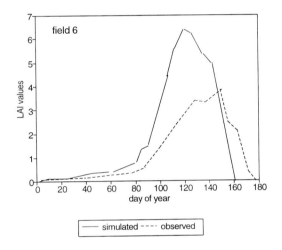
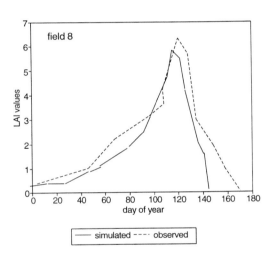

Figure 6.2.7   Observed (dotted line) and simulated (AFRCWHEAT2 results) LAIs for two test fields.

Table 6.2.1   Final grain dry matter (DM) simulated by AFRCWHEAT2 for nine different field conditions when observed green leaf area index values are input into the model (LAI, second column) and when it simulates its own LAIs (third column).

Field number	Grain DM simulated with observed LAI (g m^{-2})	Grain DM simulated with simulated LAI (g m^{-2})
1	731	942
2	714	890
3	658	818
5	759	886
6	619	832
8	932	1008
9	844	990
10	947	991

It appears that the 'actual' yields are much smaller than the 'simulated' yields (and closer to observed yields), thus illustrating the benefit of the joint use of models and images. However, one would be more interested in establishing a real per-field calibration of the model over the whole area to establish distributions of values of major model parameters, rather than restricting the study to well-sampled fields.

6.2.3.3   *Regional results and discussion*

In order to characterise one field, the time profile of the field mean NDVI was considered. At a first level, the evolution and variability of the landscape (conditionally to the durum wheat crop) can therefore be described either by a family of time profiles for mean NDVIs, or the evolution of the distribution curve of mean (per field) NDVIs (Figure 6.2.8). It can be noticed that this distribution evolves over time, both in mean or mode (from mode NDVI = 0.2, low percent cover, to mode NDVI = 0.8, almost full coverage) and in shape. This last point emphasises differential evolutions amongst individual fields due to non-synchronised changes in growth rates. These changes characterise a sort of 'life of the landscape', which could interact (positively or negatively) with a possibly more variable climate through the onset of early or late lethal extreme events.

The next phase of the study will be to calibrate a crop model over the 64 fields to derive distribution functions for key-parameters or initial variables (for instance, sensitivities of development and growth to temperature and sowing date, and distribution functions, including estimates of covariances between parameters, which will probably be the most difficult part of the estimation). This will lead to a stochastic form of the crop model which will represent the landscape (or regional) simulator. A comprehensive representation of all European countries at this scale is of course out of reach for the moment, but several illustrative cases could be chosen, perhaps in agreement with the EC's MARS Project, which manages numerous test-sites in Europe for yield monitoring, with numerous SPOT scenes spanning several years. For most of these sites, it will be necessary to

introduce a calibration of water budget routines from thermal infrared satellite information.

Acknowledgements

The authors are grateful to Sophie Moulin for providing AFRCWHEAT2 simulations and to Jean-Pierre Guinot for processing SPOT images.

6.3   Effects on wheat and maize in Spain

6.3.1   Background

6.3.1.1   *Climatic stress for crops in Spain*

Spanish cereal production is greatly affected by temperature and precipitation fluctuations. As in other semi-arid Mediterranean regions, water deficits and water restrictions are major problems which Spain has to face. In Spain, water consumed for agriculture represents 80% of the total national water consumption (MOPTMA, 1993a). The future law on water use ("Ley del Plan Hidrologico Nacional") aims to increase water availability by increasing the efficiency of its use (MOPTMA, 1993b) with specific water saving programs that deal mainly with improvement of the irrigation systems and more efficient adjustments between crop water demand and supply (MOPTMA, 1993a). The recognised perspective of a changing climate (IPCC, 1990; 1992) would increase the present uncertainties of water availability in Mediterranean regions since higher temperatures will have profound implications on hydrological processes in general and water availability in particular.

The availability of water is a predominant limiting factor to the growth of spring-summer grain crops in southern Europe. For example, virtually all of grain maize in Spain and Greece is irrigated (Bignon, 1990). Knowledge of how factors affecting water availability may change will be critical to planning future use of water resources. Only a few studies in Mediterranean regions have addressed this problem (Santer, 1985; Imerson *et al.*, 1987; Parry *et al.*, 1988, 1992; Carter *et al.*, 1991a, 1991b; Kenny and Harrison, 1992b; Minguez and Iglesias, 1995).

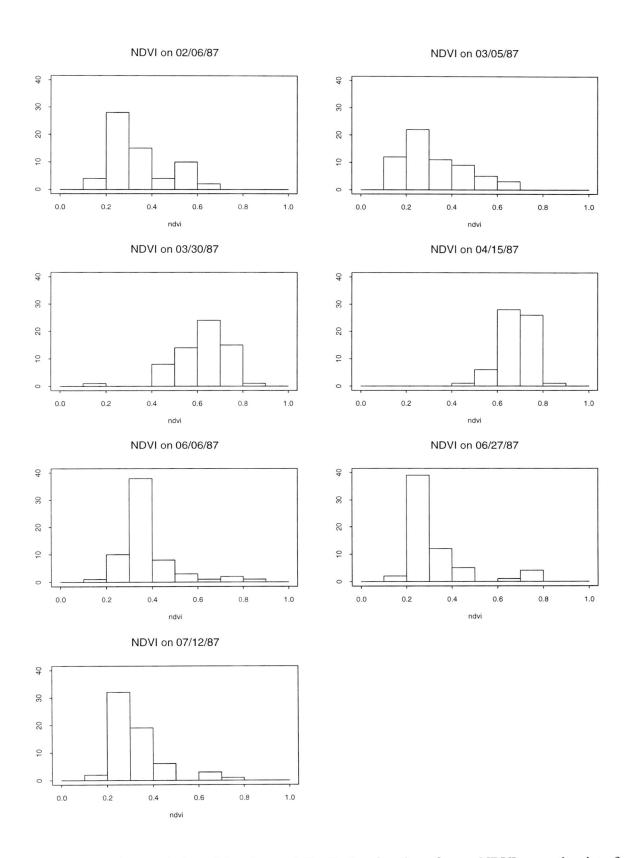

Figure 6.2.8 Time evolution of the observed distribution function of mean NDVIs over the sixty four durum wheat fields.

The growing competition for water and the importance of irrigated agriculture in Spain has provided additional stimulus for such research. In 1992, due to irrigation water restraints, the area sown with irrigated maize diminished by about 20%, the national production dropped to 2.5 million tonnes and imports rose to 1.9 million tonnes (MAPA, 1993). In 1995, the total irrigated agricultural land of Spain has to date been reduced by almost 50% due to water limitations (unofficial data as of June 1995).

6.3.1.2 *Study design*

Most previous studies to evaluate vegetation responses to climate have used output weather variables from general circulation models (GCMs) (Goudriaan and Unsworth, 1990; Rosenzweig and Parry, 1994; Rosenzweig and Iglesias, 1994). The recent IPCC scientific and impacts assessments (IPCC, 1992) endorse this approach.

This study analyses the sensitivity of crop yields and water demand of two representative crops (maize and wheat) to climate change using the CERES crop simulation models (Jones and Kiniry, 1986; Godwin *et al.*, 1990) in conjunction with climate change scenarios derived from equilibrium and transient GCMs (see Chapter 2). There are several reasons for chosing wheat and maize in this study. They are crops well adapted to most Spanish regions, with growing cycles that cover the entire year and represent different agronomic systems. Maize is a high-input irrigated crop whose maximum water requirements occur during the season when there are the largest water shortages and rainfall variability in Spain. The uncertainties of irrigated maize production are large due to high production costs and limited and unreliable water available for irrigation. Wheat is mainly rainfed, sown in winter and very susceptible to drought during the spring. These two crops have been studied extensively and agronomic data for model validation and calibration are available. In addition wheat and maize have different photosynthetic pathways so their responses to increases in atmospheric CO_2 are different.

The study is based on five sites located in the main cereal-growing regions of Spain (Figure 6.3.1). These regions have similar climatic and soil characteristics according to the regional classification of Elena-Rossello *et al.* (1990). Differences in seasonal temperatures and precipitation amounts and their distribution between the sites lead to different crop management practices. Furthermore, only 40% of land in Spain is available for cultivation because of the varied topography of the country, which also includes a diversity of agroecological regions. The climate in Spain is Mediterranean, with hot and dry summers, and cold and wet winters, and it is characterised by large inter-annual variability. In general, precipitation is concentrated between October and April (southern regions) or May (northern regions). Average seasonal temperatures decrease with increasing altitude and latitude, and the weather at all sites is characterised by large inter-annual variability (Font-Tullot, 1983). The low precipitation especially in the summer months (June, July and August) makes irrigation a necessity (Bignon, 1990, Iglesias and Minguez, 1994) for crops such as maize since summer precipitation is well under 100 mm in all regions (Font-Tullot, 1983).

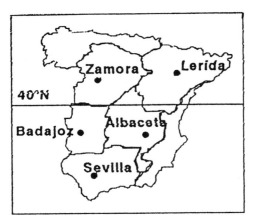

Figure 6.3.1 Spanish agroclimatic regions and location of model simulations:
Sevilla, 37.42° N, 5.88° W, altitude 31 m;
Badajoz, 38.88° N, 6.80° W, altitude 192 m;
Albacete, 38.95° N, 1.85° W, altitude 704 m;
Zamora 41.48° N, 5.75° W, altitude 667 m; and
Lérida, 41.62° N, 0.62° E, altitude 221 m.

6.3.2   Methodology and model validation

6.3.2.1   *Crop models and management variables*

The CERES-Maize and CERES-Wheat models (Jones and Kiniry, 1986; Godwin *et al.*, 1990) are simulation models for maize and wheat that describe daily phenological development and growth in response to environmental factors (soils, weather and management). Description of the models, model calibration and validation and adjustment of the water balance routine are included in Section 5.6. Soil and crop management variables were determined for each site to represent the current conditions according to Lopez-Bellido (1991) (Table 6.3.1). The water demand at all sites was calculated assuming: 100% efficiency of the automatic irrigation system; 1 m irrigation management depth; automatic irrigation when available water was 50% of soil water capacity; and soil water for each layer was re-initialised to 100% capacity at the start of each growing season. Because of these assumptions, only relative changes in water requirements are considered in this study.

6.3.2.2   *Climatic data*

Daily maximum and minimum temperatures, precipitation and hours of sunshine for the period 1971-1990, for the five sites, were obtained from the Instituto Nacional de Meteorologia (Madrid). Daily solar radiation was calculated from a linear relation of n/N (actual daily hours of sunshine/maximum daily hours of sunshine), according to Richardson and Wright (1984).

6.3.2.3   *Climate change scenarios*

To analyse the effects of climate change on wheat and maize suitability, several scenarios of possible future climates were applied to the CERES-Maize and CERES-Wheat models. Scenarios were based on two types of GCM experiments: (i) equilibrium (UKLO and UKHI); and (ii) transient (UKTR and GFDL). Two model decades from the UKTR experiment were applied; an intermediate decade, 31-40, and the last decade, 66-75. Only one model decade from the GFDL experiment was considered, 55-64. All scenarios consisted of 30 years of daily changes in the mean values of all relevant climatic variables. For the UKHI and UKTR6675 scenarios changes in climatic variability were also incorporated as well as changes in the mean. Scenarios including changes in variability are denoted with a small 'v', eg. UKTR6675v. A full description of the construction of climate change scenarios at the site-specific scale is given in Section 2.4.

6.3.2.4   *Simulations*

The CERES-Maize model was run for 30 years of baseline climate and climate change scenarios. Because the climate change scenarios are associated with concomitant higher levels of CO_2 than the current climate GCM simulations (353 ppmv), the physiological effects of CO_2 on crop yield and water use were included in the simulations according to the following concentrations: UKLO, UKHI 560 ppmv; UKTR3140 454 ppmv; UKTR6675, UKTR6675v 617 ppmv; GFDL5564 617 ppmv (see Rosenzweig and Iglesias, 1994 for a

Table 6.3.1   Soil and crop management variables for sites.

Site	Soil	Wheat		Maize	
		Variety	Sowing date	Hybrid	Sowing date
Sevilla	sandy loam	ANZA	1 Dec	700-800	15 Mar
Badajoz	sandy loam	ANZA	1 Dec	700-800	30 Mar
Albacete	silty loam	ANZA	1 Dec	700	15 May
Lérida	silty clay	MARIUS	15 Nov	700	15 May
Zamora	sandy loam	MARIUS	1 Nov	500-600	15 May

description of the methodology). The CO_2 concentrations assumed for the transient scenarios correspond to the IS92a emissions scenario.

Changes were computed as the means and standard deviations of yield, evapotranspiration, water applied for irrigation, and crop flowering and maturity dates. In addition, the study evaluated possible adaptation strategies of crop management to future climate change. Scenarios were created altering some current agricultural practices in order to maximise yield under the conditions of climate change.

6.3.3   Model sensitivity to systematic changes in climate

Crop responses to temperature changes are non-linear, therefore a sensitivity analysis was carried out in Sevilla to characterise changes in yield, evaporative demands and lengths of the crop growth duration associated with changes in temperature and precipitation and their variability (see Section 5.6).

6.3.4   Application of the climate change scenarios

In this section the effects of GCM climate change equilibrium and transient scenarios on the crops are considered, simulated under current crop management conditions. Although this is not a realistic future situation it is an essential part of the analysis because it establishes a base reference for the assessment of climate change and for the design of adaptation strategies.

6.3.4.1   *Crop yield and growing season length*

The simulated changes in crop yield under the GCM climate change scenarios (Tables 6.3.2 and 6.3.3) were driven by two interacting effects, changes in climate and CO_2 enrichment. Although yield changes under the GCM scenarios varied with location and scenario considered, in all cases maize yield (averaged over the 30 year period) significantly decreased, with the largest reductions in the UKHI scenario and the smallest with the GFDL5564 scenario. Yield reductions were particularly significant at

the site that represents the major areas of maize production (Albacete) and least significant in the site representing the coldest region (Zamora). These yield decreases were driven primarily by the increased temperatures, which shorten the duration of crop growth stages, particularly grain filling, (Table 6.3.2). Shortening of the vegetative period has been associated with higher temperatures (Watts, 1974; Dale *et al.*, 1980). Furthermore, grain yield is dependent on both the rate and the duration of the seed filling period. Maturity dates of maize were reached 6 to 26 days earlier than the baseline with the climate change scenarios. Maize is also a C_4 crop and therefore benefits little from CO_2 enrichment.

Wheat yields generally increased in the climate change scenarios at all sites. Wheat yield increases are driven mainly by the direct effects of increased CO_2 on the photosynthesis and water use of the crop, and by the increase in the length of the frost free spring period at the northern sites.

6.3.4.2   *Crop evapotranspiration and water use efficiency*

Daily evaporative rates for wheat and maize increased for most of the crop season at all sites due to temperature increases. Nevertheless, the projected total evapotranspiration (ET) throughout the entire crop season generally decreased due to a combination of factors: the shortening of the vegetative period associated with higher temperatures; and the physiological effects of CO_2 on crop water use efficiency (Tables 6.3.2 and 6.3.3). The reduction in total season ET has to be interpreted in relation to the significant shortening of the crop growing season, associated with the warmer climate, which implies yield reductions.

These simulated evaporative changes are consistent with previous studies. Using a crop specific water balance model, Kenny and Harrison (1992b) reported that a $1^{\circ}C$ rise in temperature increased ET by an average of 32 mm in European regions south of $40^{\circ}N$. An annual increase in potential evapotranspiration of the order of 55 to 70 mm for each $1^{\circ}C$ rise in annual temperature has been estimated for the southern Mediterranean (Le Houerou, 1990).

In general, maize water use efficiency (ratio of crop yield to total crop evapotranspiration) declined at all locations, with the highest reductions occurring in central regions (main production areas) and the lowest reductions in the coldest region (Zamora) and the wettest regions (Sevilla and Badajoz) (Table 6.3.2). Wheat water use efficiency generally increased in all sites with all scenarios considered (Table 6.3.3).

Table 6.3.2   Changes in irrigated maize with climate change scenarios. GY: grain yield; SL: total crop season length; ET: total crop evapotranspiration; IRR: irrigation demand; WUE: water use efficiency (GY/ET); IUE: irrigation use efficiency (GY/IRR).

Site	Scenario	GY (%)	SL (days)	ET (%)	IRR (%)	WUE (%)	IUE (%)
Sevilla	UKLO	-11	-21	+2	-6	-13	-6
	UKHI	-27	-21	+14	+8	-36	-33
	GFDL5564	-5	-7	-6	-11	+1	+7
	UKTR6675	-10	-10	-13	-18	+4	+10
	UKTR6675v	-8	-10	-16	-11	+10	+4
Badajoz	UKLO	-15	-9	-17	+1	+1	0
	UKHI	-16	-11	-24	+12	0	-6
	GFDL5564	-8	-7	-6	-15	+1	+10
	UKTR6675	-12	-9	-10	-19	+1	+12
	UKTR6675v	-14	-9	-20	-2	+5	+2
Albacete	UKLO	-18	-20	-3	-2	-10	-14
	UKHI	-22	-20	-6	+10	-24	-28
	GFDL5564	-10	-13	-8	-4	-7	-9
	UKTR6675	-16	-16	-5	-2	-9	-12
	UKTR6675v	-18	-18	-3	+1	-12	-19
Lerida	UKLO	-14	-10	-5	+3	0	-14
	UKHI	-17	-14	-1	+8	-6	-14
	GFDL5564	-10	-6	-4	-4	-7	-4
	UKTR6675	-12	-10	-6	+1	-7	-12
	UKTR6675v	-16	-11	-7	+2	-1	-12
Zamora	UKLO	-7	-20	-15	-4	-2	-2
	UKHI	-12	-26	-16	+8	-10	-14
	GFDL5564	-2	-14	-9	-10	+2	+7
	UKTR6675	-6	-18	-11	-2	-3	-1
	UKTR6675v	-5	-19	-14	-6	-5	-3

6.3.4.3 *Irrigation demand and irrigation use efficiency*

Changes in maize irrigation requirements with the climate scenarios are shown in Table 6.3.2. Because of the assumptions made for their calculation, only relative changes are considered. Irrigation requirements not only reflect changes in crop evapotranspiration but also predicted changes in precipitation mainly during spring. With climate change, maize irrigation requirements generally decreased except in the UKHI scenario. These irrigation decreases have to be carefully interpreted, since they may only reflect the decrease in crop ET due to the significant shortening of the crop

Table 6.3.3   Changes in dryland wheat with climate change scenarios. GY: grain yield; SL: total crop season length; ET: total crop evapotranspiration; WUE: water use efficiency (GY/ET).

Site	Scenario	GY (%)	SL (days)	ET (%)	WUE (%)
Sevilla	UKLO	+14	-10	-4	+18
	UKHI		crop failure		
	GFDL5564	+10	-5	-2	+12
	UKTR6675	+15	-8	-9	+26
	UKTR6675v	-16	-11	-27	+15
Badajoz	UKLO	+10	-14	-10	+15
	UKHI		crop failure		
	GFDL5564	+5	-8	-7	+2
	UKTR6675	+18	-12	-6	+25
	UKTR6675v	-17	-14	-30	+1
Albacete	UKLO	+19	-18	-8	+40
	UKHI v		crop failure		
	GFDL5564	+14	-10	-11	+31
	UKTR6675	+32	-16	-6	+48
	UKTR6675v	-10	-22	-12	+17
Lerida	UKLO	+30	-30	-14	+34
	UKHI	-56	-22	-16	-1
	GFDL5564	+26	-13	-14	+33
	UKTR6675	+44	-18	-14	+47
	UKTR6675v	-15	-20	-18	+2
Zamora	UKLO	+42	-27	-27	+36
	UKHI	-80	-32	-34	-4
	GFDL5564	+35	-14	-17	+21
	UKTR6675	+85	-22	-25	+56
	UKTR6675v	-20	-19	-22	+13

growing season which is accompanied with significant yield reductions. The irrigation use efficiency (ratio of crop yield to total irrigation water used) generally decreased at all sites under all scenarios considered, compared with the baseline (Table 6.3.2 and Figure 6.3.2).

6.3.5   Possible adaptive responses

The previous section analysed crop responses to the climate change scenarios simulated with current management conditions. This is not a realistic future situation since farmers and agricultural institutions will adapt to changing climatic conditions. An important possible adaptation strategy is sowing earlier under a warmer climate, thereby allowing the crop to develop during a period of the year with cooler temperatures and partially offsetting crop yield reductions.

For maize, earlier sowing dates implied yield increases for present cultivars under the climate change scenarios in regions where crop yield is currently limited by low spring temperatures. However, sowing earlier did not completely offset yield decreases in some regions (Figure 6.3.3). Earlier sowing dates also allowed the

crop to develop during a period of lower ET demand, implying an increase in water use efficiency and a reduction in irrigation demand compared to the current conditions at most sites. A combination of adaptation strategies (such as changes in hybrids and sowing dates), maintained or improved the water and irrigation use efficiencies in most regions under the climate change scenarios (Figure 6.3.2).

A different strategy was tested in order to obtain water use optimisation with alternative management. In Spain, new management strategies are being evaluated in order to assess alternatives that would lower water consumption since water availability is often limited even under the present climate. One strategy considers the inclusion of very short growth cycle maize (200-variety) as a second crop sown after barley, lentils or a vetch-barley forage mixture. A delay in sowing date lowers yield so direct sowing into previous crop residues is being implemented. This allows for planting during the last week in June. The performance of 700-varieties sown 15 March (current strategy) versus 200-varieties sown as a first or second crop was compared in terms of yield and water use. Figure 6.3.4 shows

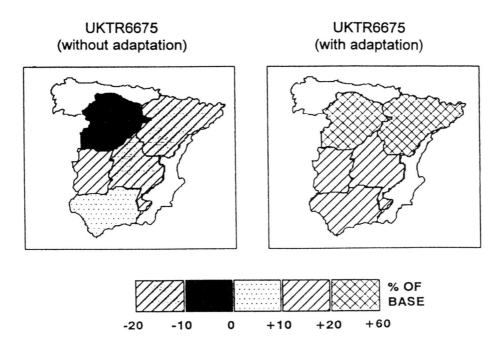

Figure 6.3.2   Simulated regional changes in maize irrigation use efficiency with the UKTR6675 climate change scenario without and with adaptation. The results incorporate the direct effects of CO_2 on the crop.

that a short-season hybrid clearly reduced irrigation demand when sown in the traditional spring season (Short-1 in Figure 6.3.4) and it further reduced irrigation demand if sown later in the year as a second crop (Short-2 in Figure 6.3.4), since in this case maximum crop water requirements coincided with the period of both lower temperatures and higher precipitation (end of summer/beginning of autumn). Nevertheless, a shorter-season variety caused yield reductions when compared with the traditional varieties.

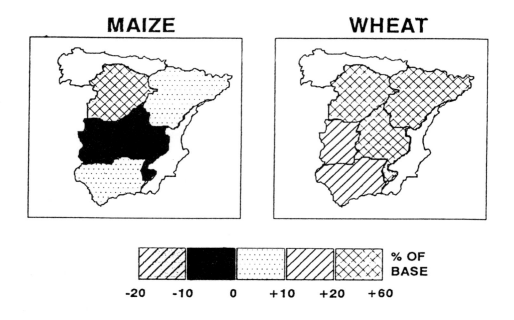

Figure 6.3.3   Simulated regional changes in maize and wheat yields with the UKTR6675 climate change scenario. The results incorporate the direct effects of CO_2 on the crop and adjustments in sowing dates and crop varieties.

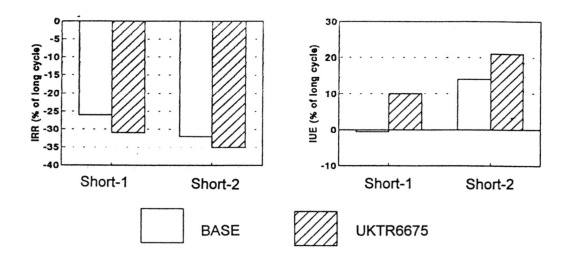

Figure 6.3.4   Simulated changes in maize net irrigation demand (IRR) and irrigation use efficiency (IUE) with alternative management under the base climate and the UKTR6675 climate change scenario.

6.3.6   Discussion and conclusions

This study has evaluated the impact of climate change on yields and water use in two crops that represent different and contrasting agricultural systems in Spain: a highly water consumptive crop (maize) that has the largest water demand during the period of the year with largest water limitations and possible restrictions and a less consumptive crop (wheat) that is grown during the winter/spring. Furthermore, these two crops have different photosynthetic pathways so their response to increased CO_2 is different.

In all cases the effects of a CO_2-induced climate depended on the counteracting effects between higher daily ET rates, shortening of crop growth duration and changes in precipitation patterns as well as the simulated effects of CO_2 on the water use efficiency of the crops. In terms of yields, maize did not benefit from climate change but wheat productivity increased significantly in some regions. Because the large yield and water use efficiency improvements simulated in the case of wheat (a C_3 crop), the results have to be interpreted carefully, since the extent of these effects may not be completely similar outside the enclosed experimental systems in which they have been observed over wide geographical areas and long time periods (Körner, 1990).

For summer crops such as maize, the problems arising from water restrictions and irrigation costs are currently major challenges to agriculture in Spain and may be exacerbated in the future if global climate change projections are realised. The study considered strategies for improving the efficiency of water use, based on the optimisation of crop management decisions in a greenhouse-driven warmer climate.

If current levels of water availability are maintained, there is scope for adaptation to predicted climate change by maintaining similar levels of water and irrigation use efficiencies in some agroecological areas, but even in the best case, crops such as maize would use water for irrigation less efficiently in many regions. Furthermore, since the current water restrictions question the possibility of increasing irrigation in the future, the use of crops and management

systems that minimise water stress during sensitive development phases, as suggested in the adaptation section, may be realistic alternatives, that need to be further evaluated with an economic study. Water and production costs, as well as grain prices, will also delimit the choice of management strategies. Water supply for irrigation and competition from industrial and urban uses are hard to predict but the latter have been constantly increasing, adding another uncertainty factor to future water availability for agricultural purposes. The use of improved irrigation systems, and the application of effective irrigation scheduling minimising water stress during sensitive development phases are also beneficial strategies to be considered.

6.4   Effects on spring wheat and spring barley in Finland

6.4.1   Background

Changes in climate, which are likely to occur during future decades, may affect the suitability and productivity of crops in Finland. This study focuses on spring-sown wheat and barley, aiming first, to specify the environmental constraints restricting their production, second, to map the present pattern of regional crop potential and third, to examine the sensitivity of crop potential to climate changes.

6.4.2   Methods and models

The approach adopted in the study employs a national-scale geographical analysis system in conjunction with crop-climate models (Carter and Saarikko, in press).

6.4.2.1   *The geographical analysis system*

A geographical analysis system has been developed to map the pattern of crop potential in Finland (Figure 6.4.1). The term crop potential refers both to the suitability of a region for crop cultivation and to the productivity or yield of that crop. Crop models ranging from simple agroclimatic indices to complex simulation models are being used to estimate crop potential.

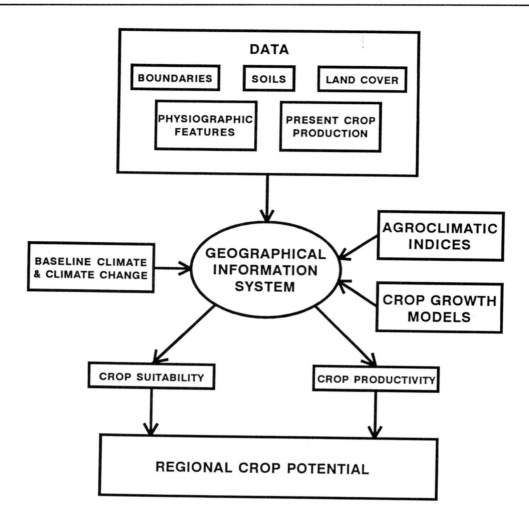

Figure 6.4.1   Schema of the research approach.

The crop models are applied to data on a regular grid (10 x 10 km) across Finland. They require environmental input data such as climate, soils, land use and topography, which are being gathered at the above grid resolution. Regional agricultural data, including cropped area and yields, are also being collected to map the current production pattern and to validate the indices and models. A raster-based geographical information system, IDRISI, is used to combine the data and display the results.

The period 1961-90 represents the baseline climate. For this period, climatic variables have been interpolated at the Finnish Meteorological Institute from station data to the 10 km grid by the kriging method (Henttonen, 1991). The data include monthly mean temperatures, precipitation and solar radiation. The agroclimatic indices and crop growth models are run for the baseline

climate and for changed climates to evaluate the magnitude and rate of change in potential. Changed climates are generated by altering the baseline climate either systematically or according to climatic scenarios.

6.4.2.2   *Models of crop phenological development*

Phenological models have been constructed to estimate the growing time and phasic development of a number of spring-sown cereal cultivars (Saarikko *et al.*, 1993). Models were derived by examining the relationship between environmental factors (daily mean temperature, photoperiod and precipitation) and phenological observations (dates of sowing, heading and yellow ripeness) at experimental stations in Finland during the period 1970-90.

Temperature alone was found to explain the course of phasic development, and a linear relationship between daily mean air temperature and the daily development rate was established. The dominant effect of temperature can be seen in Figure 6.4.2, where the mean temperature during the growing period is plotted against mean development rate for the spring wheat cultivar Ruso (breeder: Plant Breeding Institute, Hankkija, Finland). Similar models were constructed for each cereal cultivar examined and for each of the three phases: sowing to heading, heading to yellow ripeness and the entire phase sowing to yellow ripeness.

6.4.2.3   *Application of the models*

In order to estimate the phasic development of a crop cultivar at any location, the beginning and end of a "favourable growing period" needs to be defined. Sowing of both wheat and barley was assumed to take place on the day when daily mean temperature exceeds 8°C, based on sowing date information from the experimental

sites. This assumption has been tested by comparing observed sowing dates for rural districts in Finland during 1961-85 with predictions based on gridded temperatures over the same period averaged by district. On average, the estimated dates were 0.4 days later than those observed (root mean square difference = 6.4 days) with no systematic differences in prediction accuracy between districts, except in some coastal areas where most of the predictions were too late.

An autumn cut off at the end of the favourable growing period was applied on the basis of a frost risk analysis as the date on which mean daily temperature falls below 12°C. This date approximately corresponds to the 25% probability of first autumn frost occurrence in Finland as computed by Solantie (1987).

When estimating crop development across the 10 km grid, mean monthly air temperatures were available for each year of the baseline period, 1961-90. Smoothed daily mean temperatures

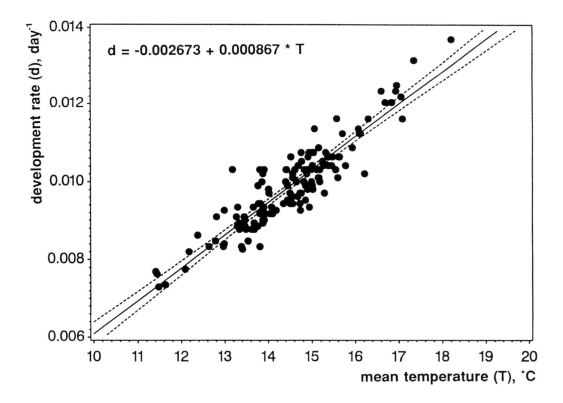

$$d = -0.002673 + 0.000867 * T$$

Figure 6.4.2   The relationship between mean development rate (day^{-1}) and mean temperature (°C) in spring wheat cv. Ruso for the development phase sowing to yellow ripeness. Broken lines are 95% confidence limits. (Data source: Official Variety Trials, Agricultural Research Centre of Finland).

were computed by using a sine curve interpolation method (Brooks, 1943). Development in different phases was computed for two spring wheat cultivars: Ruso (early maturing) and Kadett (late maturing; breeder: W. Weibull, Sweden), and for an early maturing barley cultivar, Arra (breeder: Plant Breeding Institute, Jokioinen, Finland).

The development of each cultivar was computed for individual years during the 30-year baseline period, and during 30-year periods corresponding to different climate change scenarios. A grid box was considered suitable for cereal cultivation when the crop successfully reaches the yellow ripeness stage in at least 24 years out of 30. This represents an 80% probability of success.

6.4.2.4   Validation and uncertainty of the models under the baseline climate

Spring wheat

The estimated suitability of the two spring wheat cultivars under the baseline climate is compared with the actual pattern of cultivation of all spring wheat cultivars in Figure 6.4.3. The calculated northern limit of suitability (for the early maturing cultivar) corresponds well with the actual pattern. Note, however, that the actual cultivation is also strongly influenced by other limiting factors such as soils, drainage and economic profitability, which are not considered in this analysis. Note, further, that farmers may be ready to accept a higher risk of crop failure than the 20% assumed.

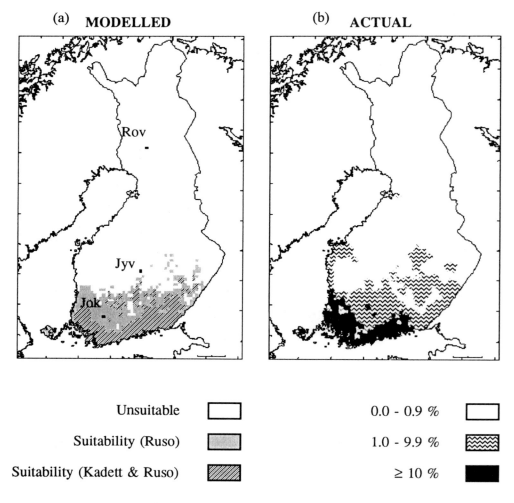

Figure 6.4.3   (a) Estimated suitability (≥ 80% probability of ripening) of late-maturing (Kadett) and early-maturing (Ruso) spring wheat varieties based on temperature for the baseline climate (1961-90). Sites for which temperature scenarios are given in Table 6.4.1 are also shown. (b) Area of spring wheat by commune in 1990 as a percentage of cultivated land (data from Finnish Board of Agriculture).

Spring barley

The computed pattern of suitability for a fast maturing barley cultivar, Arra, is shown in Figure 6.4.4a. Two shading tones are used here, to indicate the spatial expression of uncertainty attributable to the development model (cf. Figure 6.4.2). The lighter shade represents the region of suitability having a 97.5% confidence. The dark shading embraces 95% of the model uncertainty (i.e., between the 2.5 and 97.5 percentiles). Hence, with respect to crop development alone, there is only a 2.5% probability that the limit lies to the north of this region.

The computed baseline limits lie somewhat to the south of the actual cultivated zone (Figure 6.4.4b). This suggests that barley is currently being grown in areas where the risk of crops not ripening is greater than the 20% assumed.

6.4.3 Model sensitivity to systematic changes in climate

Since the phenological models are based on temperature alone, model sensitivity was evaluated for systematic temperature adjustments of +1, +2, +3 and +4°C throughout each year of the 30-year baseline.

(a)   (b)

MODELLED   **ACTUAL**

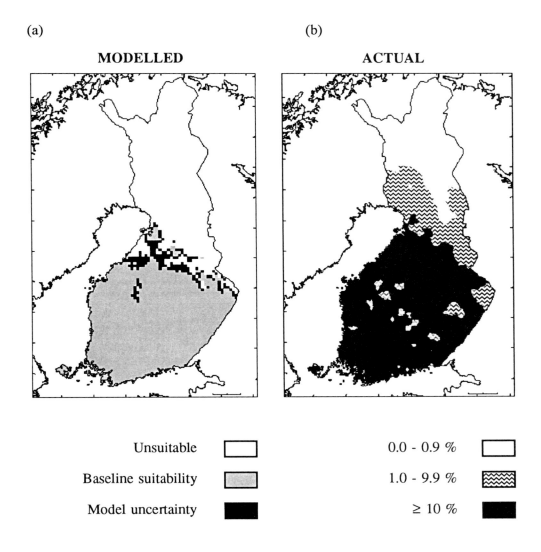

Unsuitable	☐	0.0 - 0.9 %	☐
Baseline suitability	▨	1.0 - 9.9 %	▨
Model uncertainty	■	≥ 10 %	■

Figure 6.4.4   (a) Estimated suitability (≥ 80% probability of ripening) of spring barley (cv. Arra) based on temperature for the baseline climate (1961-90) and model uncertainty (95% confidence limits); (b) area of spring barley by commune in 1990 as a percentage of cultivated land (data from Finnish Board of Agriculture).

6.4.3.1   *Spring wheat*

The sensitivity of spring wheat to systematic temperature changes is shown in Figure 6.4.5a for the late maturing variety, Kadett. The estimated limit of suitability extends northwards by, on average, about 180 km in western and 150 km in eastern Finland per 1°C warming. Since altitudes are low over much of central and southern Finland, this differential regional sensitivity is mainly due to the maritime influence in western Finland, producing milder winters and cooler summers than in the east.

6.4.3.2   *Spring barley*

The northern boundary of barley exhibits a slightly lower sensitivity to warming than that of spring wheat, exhibiting a northward expansion of about 130 km°C^{-1} in all regions for temperature increases up to 3°C. For warming in excess of 3°C expansion into northwestern Lapland is retarded by high altitude, while expansion accelerates on the eastern side (Figure 6.4.5b).

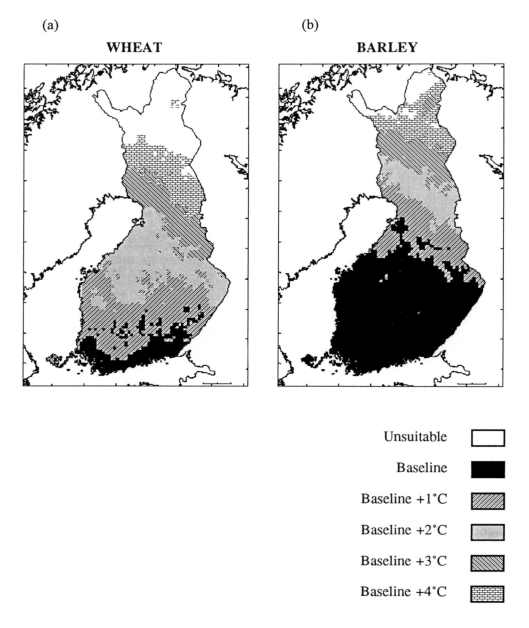

Figure 6.4.5   Sensitivity of estimated suitability to temperature increases of 1, 2, 3, and 4°C relative to the baseline for: (a) spring wheat (cv. Kadett); (b) spring barley (cv. Arra).

6.4.4 Application of the climate change scenarios

Two types of climate change scenario have been applied as adjustments to the baseline climate: equilibrium and transient scenarios. The equilibrium scenario is based on general circulation model equilibrium $2 \times CO_2$ simulations with the United Kingdom Met. Office high resolution (UKHI) model. The grid box outputs of temperature changes from this model ($2 \times CO_2$ minus control) have been linearly interpolated to the 10 km grid over Finland and applied as adjustments to all years of the 30-year baseline climate.

The transient scenarios are from experiments with two coupled ocean-atmosphere models: the United Kingdom Met. Office (UKTR) and the Geophysical Fluid Dynamics Laboratory (GFDL) transient experiments. Decadal mean temperature changes relative to the control for years 66-75 of the UKTR simulation (UKTR6675) and years 55-64 of the GFDL simulation (GFDL5564) were linearly interpolated to the 10 km Finnish grid. These scenarios can be used to represent a range of future dates, depending upon various assumptions about the rate of future warming (see Chapter 2, Table 2.2). They have been used as adjustments to the gridded baseline temperatures

in the same way as for the equilibrium scenario. This procedure is somewhat unrealistic, however, as a transient change in climate can be expected to exhibit a long-term trend which ought to be reflected in the scenario temperatures (i.e., with a warming trend, temperatures would be adjusted by less in the early years of the baseline than in the later years). This problem will be addressed in future work.

Seasonal and annual temperature changes under each scenario are depicted in Table 6.4.1 for grid boxes representing sites in southern, central and northern Finland: respectively, Jokioinen, Jyväskylä and Rovaniemi/Apukka (locations are shown in Figure 6.4.3a). For each scenario climate, two features of crop suitability have been computed. First, the area of suitability is mapped (as in the sensitivity analysis). Second, within the suitable area, the period from heading to yellow ripeness (which approximates to the grain filling period) has also been calculated.

6.4.4.1 *Results for spring wheat*

Suitability maps for late maturing spring wheat (Kadett) under the equilibrium and transient scenarios are depicted in Figure 6.4.6 along with the changes relative to the baseline in the period of development from heading to yellow ripeness.

Table 6.4.1 Seasonal and annual temperature changes (°C) at three locations in Finland under the three GCM-based climate change scenarios. Site locations are shown in Figure 6.4.3a.

Scenario/site	Spring (MAM)	Summer (JJA)	Autumn (SON)	Winter (DJF)	Annual
UKHI					
Jokioinen	7.5	4.0	6.3	7.8	6.4
Jyväskylä	7.1	4.1	7.2	7.5	6.5
Rovaniemi	5.1	4.5	6.7	7.0	5.8
UKTR6675					
Jokioinen	3.6	2.2	2.9	4.4	3.3
Jyväskylä	3.2	2.2	3.2	4.8	3.4
Rovaniemi	2.6	2.3	3.1	4.8	3.2
GFDL5564					
Jokioinen	1.9	2.4	3.4	2.7	2.6
Jyväskylä	1.8	2.4	3.6	2.8	2.6
Rovaniemi	1.2	2.2	3.7	2.4	2.4

UKHI

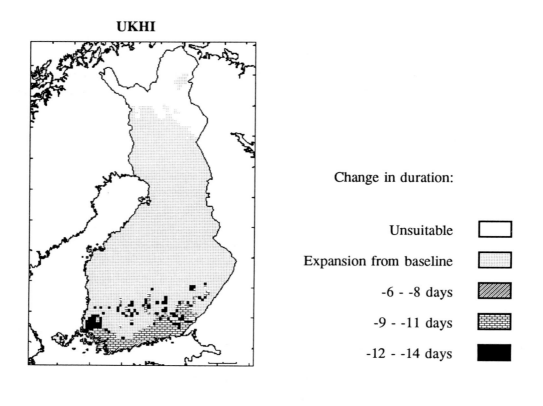

Change in duration:

Unsuitable

Expansion from baseline

-6 - -8 days

-9 - -11 days

-12 - -14 days

UKTR6675   **GFDL5564**

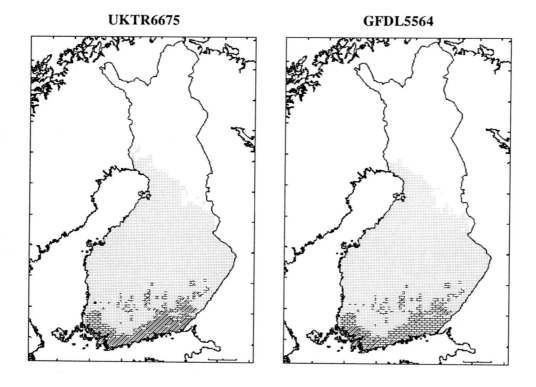

Figure 6.4.6   Change in simulated duration of the phase heading to yellow ripeness relative to the baseline climate for spring wheat (cv. Kadett) under three climate scenarios: (a) UKHI equilibrium; (b) UKTR6675 transient and (c) GFDL5564 transient.

Equilibrium scenario

Temperature changes over the Finnish region under the UKHI equilibrium scenario are very large in winter and early spring (Table 6.4.1), exceeding 8°C in some months. This had a dramatic effect on the predicted sowing date in some grid boxes (some dates in January were obtained). Due to the low light conditions so early in the year, and the certainty of future severe freezing events (which are excluded by the temperature smoothing technique) a limit was placed on the earliest sowing date for both wheat and barley of 15 March, in line with dates commonly observed in central Europe at the present day (Russell and Wilson, 1994).

With this additional constraint, under the UKHI scenario the northern limit of suitability shifts by about 750 km in the west and 590 km in the east of Finland (Figure 6.4.6a). The development rate of a cereal crop is enhanced with rising temperatures. Hence, for the warming assumed under the UKHI scenario, Kadett needs 7-14 days less to develop from heading to yellow ripeness over most of the zone of present-day suitability, the greatest shortening occurring at the northern boundary of suitability, where the phase length is longest under the baseline climate.

Transient scenarios

Northward shifts of Kadett under the transient scenarios are less than those for the equilibrium scenarios (Figures 6.4.6b, c). These shifts are 570 km in western Finland and 320 km in eastern Finland under the UKTR6675 scenario, and 520 km and 320 km, respectively, under the GFDL5564 scenario. The heading to yellow ripeness phase shortens by 6-12 days under the UKTR6675 and 7-11 days under the GFDL5564 scenarios, relative to the baseline. Again, the greatest changes occur at the northern boundary.

6.4.4.2 *Spring barley*

The corresponding results for early maturing spring barley (Arra) are shown in Figure 6.4.7.

Equilibrium scenario

Under the UKHI scenario, the limit of suitability shifts northwards by about 500 km in western Finland and 690 km in eastern Finland (Figure 6.4.7a). The heading to yellow ripeness period shortens by 1-10 days, with the greatest shortening at the northern boundary of baseline suitability.

Transient scenarios

The estimated zone of suitability of spring barley shifts northwards by about 450 km in the west and 330 km in the east of Finland under the UKTR6675 scenario (Figure 6.4.7b), and 390 km and 250 km, respectively, under the GFDL5564 scenario (Figure 6.4.7c). The heading to yellow ripeness phase shortens by 2-7 days under the UKTR6675 and 3-7 days under the GFDL5564 scenarios.

6.4.5 Possible adaptive responses

The preceding results consider crop suitability, but not productivity. Nonetheless, one implication of a shortening of the heading to yellow ripeness development phase under climatic warming is for the grain filling period to be truncated, grain size to be reduced and yields to decrease relative to present conditions (e.g., see Nonhebel, 1993). In such cases, it is advisable to substitute existing cultivars with others having more demanding temperature requirements that better correspond to the warming and lengthening growing season.

In order to investigate the effectiveness of switching cultivars, preliminary variety trial experiments have been conducted with spring wheat cultivars originating from central Europe, where temperatures today are comparable to or in excess of those estimated for Finland under the climatic scenarios described. The performance of these cultivars (two from Germany and one from the Netherlands, along with a domestic cultivar, Polkka) was observed for crop stands grown under conventional farm management at Jokioinen (60°49'N, 23°30'E) in 1994. Three treatments were studied, each having two replicates: (i) open field plots; (ii) outside plots beneath a plastic cover (to approximate the

UKHI

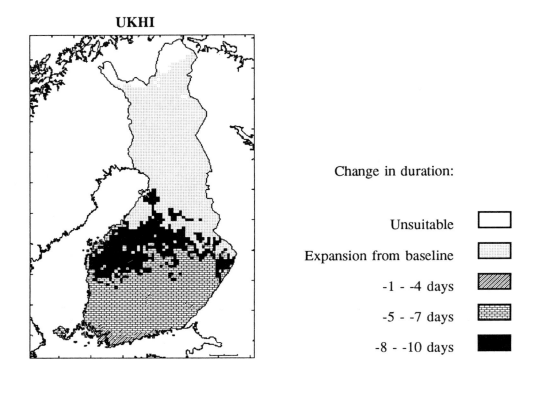

Change in duration:

Unsuitable

Expansion from baseline

-1 - -4 days

-5 - -7 days

-8 - -10 days

UKTR6675   **GFDL5564**

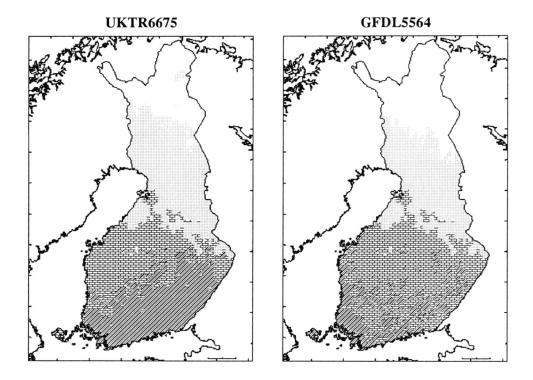

Figure 6.4.7   Change in simulated duration of the phase heading to yellow ripeness relative to the baseline climate for spring barley (cv. Arra) under three climatic scenarios: (a) UKHI equilibrium; (b) UKTR6675 transient and (c) GFDL5564 transient.

radiation conditions inside a greenhouse); and (iii) inside a greenhouse with temperatures 3°C above ambient outside temperatures.

The results are shown in Table 6.4.2. The effect of temperature on crop performance is demonstrated by comparing the greenhouse experiment with the outside plots. The elevated temperature conditions decreased the growing time (phase sowing to yellow ripeness) of the different varieties by 13 to 22 days. This enhanced development led to yield losses of 2 to 32%, which was mainly attributable to the shortened grain filling period, since the individual grain weight was low under the high temperature conditions. The two other components of yield - ear population density and number of grains per panicle - were less affected by the temperature treatment.

As expected for longer-season varieties, the three foreign cultivars exhibited slightly delayed phenological development relative to Polkka, and were somewhat higher yielding under the elevated temperatures. They also out-yielded the domestic variety in the open field, which may be due to the anomalous warmth of the late summer in 1994. Possible photoperiodic effects on the non-domestic cultivars under the long day conditions in Finland were not investigated.

Table 6.4.2 Comparison of the phenology and yield of four spring wheat cultivars under different conditions at Jokioinen. All the experimental plots were sown on 13 May 1994.

Measurement (1994)	Open field	Outside plot, under plastic	Greenhouse (+3 °C)
Polkka (Domestic)			
Phase sowing to anthesis (days)	69	68	59
Phase anthesis to yellow ripening (days)	31	30	26
Grain yield, (dry matter, g/m^2)	452	506	386
Average grain weight (mg)	34.5	33.8	31.4
Average number of ears /m^2	588	504	474
Average number of grains /ear	22	30	30
Munk (Germany)			
Phase sowing to anthesis (days)	71	66	59
Phase anthesis to yellow ripening (days)	35	38	29
Grain yield, (dry matter, g/m^2)	546	566	413
Average grain weight (mg)	40.9	38.9	30.2
Average number of ears /m^2	618	568	612
Average number of grains /ear	22	26	22
Nandu (Germany)			
Phase sowing to anthesis (days)	72	68	59
Phase anthesis to yellow ripening (days)	35	38	30
Grain yield, (dry matter, g/m^2)	460	458	448
Average grain weight (mg)	43.7	45.2	34.7
Average number of ears /m^2	623	464	504
Average number of grains /ear	17	22	26
Jondolar (Netherlands)			
Phase sowing to anthesis (days)	73	72	60
Phase anthesis to yellow ripening (days)	37	40	30
Grain yield, (dry matter, g/m^2)	546	492[1]	453
Average grain weight (mg)	36.8	42.4	32.8
Average number of ears /m^2	619	528	548
Average number of grains /ear	24	22	25

[1] An estimate - part of the grain yield was damaged by vermin

Note that all cultivars were sown on the same date, whereas the non-domestic cultivars are sown one month or more earlier under prevailing climatic conditions in their source regions. An earlier sowing is likely to be possible in Finland if spring temperatures warm in accordance with the climatic scenarios described. Further trials with staggered sowing dates will be necessary before firm conclusions about the adaptive capability of these wheat cultivars can be obtained, and before phenological models can be developed and suitability maps produced.

6.4.6   Conclusions

The results indicate that substantial shifts in suitability and a marked shortening of the grain filling period in spring cereals could occur under the climate changes anticipated for Finland during the next century and beyond. These can be converted to rates of change if calendar dates are attached to the transient scenarios. In Chapter 2, Table 2.2 these dates range from a low emissions/low climate sensitivity projection of later than 2100 to a high emissions/high climate sensitivity projection of 2042. If the former date is assumed, conservatively, to be 2150, this produces rates of northward shift in suitability ranging from approximately 20 to 45 km to 50 to 110 km per decade.

One focus for further study concerns the extrapolation of the development models under the scenario temperatures. In some regions and under certain scenarios, temperatures lie above the range used in constructing the models. Further field experiments are required to determine whether the linear relationship between crop development and temperature is still valid at these higher temperatures.

It is also important to note that the areas of suitability are based on climate alone. Much of the mapped area would be unavailable for crop cultivation due to inappropriate soils or terrain, the presence of lakes and mires, or competing land uses such as forestry and urban development. Subsequent analyses will account for these land types, using digital information from satellite and ground survey.

The implications of climatic warming for cereal yields, as well as other effects of changing water availability and atmospheric carbon dioxide concentrations, will be addressed in future work with crop growth simulation models in conjunction with variety trials and open top chamber experiments.

Acknowledgements

We would like to thank Marjo Pihala for her assistance in the variety trials experiments. This work is a component of the project "The Impacts of Climate Change on Crop Production", which is supported by the Academy of Finland as part of the Finnish Research Programme on Climate Change (SILMU).

6.5   Effects on winter wheat, sunflower, onion and grassland in Europe

6.5.1   Background

Plant developmental rates and growth processes are determined by the interactions of certain climatic and other environmental variables (Table 6.5.1). The availability of the necessary input data over the region of interest is a prerequisite to modelling a particular process or sequence of processes. Further, relevant calibration and validation datasets must be available to thoroughly evaluate the performance of a model across a region before it can be applied with confidence. Thus, a major limitation to model development and application at the broadscale is data availability.

This section describes three spatial crop models for Europe which have been developed from either physical principles or existing site-specific mechanistic models: EuroWheat (winter wheat), EuroSunfl (sunflower) and EuroOnion (onion). The complexity of each model was dependent on data availability and the degree of existing knowledge for the particular crop (see Table 6.5.1). Sufficient information was available for wheat and sunflower to allow the prediction of phenological development, potential yield and water-limited yield. Modelling of onions is not as well advanced and, hence, the EuroOnion model only predicts phenological development and potential yield. A review of existing knowledge on grassland modelling is presented in the final section.

6.5.2 Winter wheat

6.5.2.1 *Methodology*

A spatial model of wheat phenology and growth has been developed for Europe (EuroWheat) and used to assess the potential impacts of climate change. EuroWheat is divided into three integrated submodels, each submodel being based on a different site-specific mechanistic model:

(i) phenological development, based on the AFRCWHEAT simulation model;
(ii) potential growth, based on the SIRIUS simulation model; and

(iii) water-limited growth, based on the FAO crop-specific water balance model.

Phenological development

The AFRCWHEAT simulation model predicts wheat development through the interaction of thermal time, photoperiod and vernalization (Weir *et al.*, 1984). Dates of emergence, floral initiation, double ridges, terminal spikelet, anthesis, beginning of grain filling, end of grain filling and physiological maturity are calculated by the model. Input data are daily minimum and maximum temperature, sowing date and latitude. A spatial climatic database for Europe has been constructed at a resolution of 0.5° latitude x 0.5° longitude (Hulme *et al.*, 1993). This database contains minimum and maximum temperatures but at a monthly temporal resolution. No spatial database of sowing dates throughout Europe exists. Hence, to adapt the AFRCWHEAT model for a broadscale assessment these limitations had to be overcome.

Table 6.5.1   Input data required for modelling specific plant processes.

Process	Model inputs			Model output
	Climatic data	Agronomic data	Other data	
Phenological development	Min. temperature	Sowing date	Photoperiod	Date of specific developmental phases
	Max. temperature	Variety parameters		
Potential growth	Min. temperature	Sowing date	Photoperiod	Potential yield
	Max. temperature	Variety parameters		
	Radiation	CO_2-assimilation response		
Water-limited growth	Min. temperature	Sowing date	Photoperiod	Water-limited yield
	Max. temperature	Variety parameters	Water-holding capacity of the soil	
	Radiation	CO_2-assimilation response		
	Precipitation	CO_2-stomatal conductance response		

A number of methods for estimating daily maximum and minimum temperatures from monthly values were investigated. These included a sine curve interpolation (Brooks, 1943), a sine curve interpolation which includes information on the variability of daily values about their monthly means and two stochastic weather generators (Richardson and Nicks, 1990; Racsko *et al.*, 1991). The ability of each method to provide satisfactory estimates of phenological timing was tested and the associated errors calculated. Full results from this analysis are available in Harrison and Butterfield (1994). The sine curve interpolation routine was adopted as the most appropriate method as only very small improvements in accuracy could be gained using the more complex procedures. This method caused errors for the predicted date of maturity which ranged from 0 to 9.66 days with a mean error of 2.05 days for 219 calculations.

Sowing dates for winter wheat vary widely throughout Europe from early September in Scandinavia to early December in the Mediterranean region. To determine present and possible future optimal sowing dates in Europe a climatic criterion was required. In southern Europe the crop is sown close to the time when vernalization will be most effective due to the relatively short time period over which vernalization can take place (Bindi and Miglietta, pers. comm., 1992). According to the AFRCWHEAT model, vernalization of winter wheat occurs between -4 and 17°C with an optimum temperature range of 3 to 10°C. Sowing time in the EuroWheat model was defined as the first day of autumn when the mean temperature is 11.75°C or lower. The value of 11.75°C is three-quarters between the maximum vernalizing temperature of 17°C and the beginning of the optimum range (10°C). This assumed that temperatures will decrease sufficiently to be within the optimum vernalizing temperature range shortly after sowing. Predicted sowing dates agreed well with observed sowing dates throughout Europe. In southern Finland winter wheat is sown in late August/early September (Mukula and Rantanen, 1989). This corresponded with a simulated date in early September in the model. The average sowing date for winter wheat in the Netherlands

and Hungary is mid October (Wolf, pers. comm., 1994; Harnos, pers. comm., 1994) which fitted with the predicted date. In Spain, Italy and Greece sowing dates vary from late October to early December, which also agreed well with the climatic criterion (Bindi *et al.*, 1993; Narciso *et al.*, 1992).

Potential growth

Potential wheat yields were determined by integrating the potential growth submodels from the site-specific SIRIUS simulation model (Jamieson and Wilson, 1988; Jamieson, 1989) with the phenological development submodel in EuroWheat (originally derived from the AFRCWHEAT simulation model). Canopy development was modelled as a function of leaf area index (LAI). LAI was calculated in four stages throughout the growing season, which are:

(i) an exponential function of thermal time from emergence to an LAI of 5;
(ii) a linear function of thermal time from an LAI of 5 to the maximum LAI of 8.5;
(iii) a constant value from an LAI of 8.5 to anthesis; and
(iv) a quadratic function of thermal time from anthesis to the end of grain filling.

Daily incident solar radiation was estimated from monthly values using a sine curve interpolation routine (Brooks, 1943). The interception of radiation by the canopy was calculated, according to the Monsi-Saeki equation, based on the downward light flux density on a horizontal plane above the crop canopy, the leaf area index and an extinction coefficient (k) of 0.45. Intercepted photosynthetically active radiation (PAR) was assumed to be 50% of the total intercepted radiation to account for the use of global radiation input data. Dry matter was accumulated using a radiation use efficiency (RUE) of 2.2 g MJ^{-1}. Two methods were used to calculate final yield. The first was a simple method using a harvest index (HI) of 0.5. The second method was based on the SIRIUS model, which assumes all dry matter after anthesis goes to the grain plus 20% of the dry matter which has accumulated by anthesis.

The direct effect of elevated concentrations of atmospheric carbon dioxide on RUE were taken from the SIRIUS model (Mitchell and Lawlor, 1993). This assumes a 30% increase in RUE for a doubling of CO_2 from 350 to 700 ppmv. A linear relationship was assumed for lower CO_2 concentrations. It is recognised that there are interactions between temperature and CO_2 which can negate or amplify the direct beneficial effects of CO_2 on crop growth (Wolf and Erickson, 1993). For example, the optimal temperature for photosynthesis is higher at high CO_2 concentrations and this interacts with ambient temperatures and higher leaf temperatures caused by partial closure of stomates. Such interactions have been included in some mechanistic models, eg. NWHEAT (see Section 5.7.3.3). However, they were not included in the EuroWheat model as the main purpose of this study was to evaluate methods of scaling-up existing mechanistic models. If this approach proves successful then such refinements will be included in future research.

Water-limited growth

Water-limited wheat yields were determined by integrating the FAO crop-specific water balance model (FAO, 1986) with the potential growth submodel in EuroWheat. Crop water requirements were calculated by adjusting potential evapotranspiration (PET) according to the crop demand for water over a particular development stage, using a crop coefficient. Crop coefficients were derived from the ratio between potential and actual crop evapotranspiration. The difference between precipitation and available soil water was determined for successive crop phases to assess whether the soil was in deficit or surplus. Crop performance was resolved as the accumulated difference between crop water requirements and deficit expressed as a ratio of the total water requirement. The final output of the model was the water requirement satisfaction index (WRSI). The available water-holding capacity of the soil was estimated using the methodology and database developed by Groenendijk (1989) at a 0.5° latitude x 0.5° longitude spatial resolution. PET was calculated using the Penman method (Penman, 1948). However,

insufficient climatic variables were available to calculate Penman PET for a number of the climate change scenarios. In these cases, the Thornthwaite method of PET calculation was the only available option (Thornthwaite and Mather, 1955). Differences, rather than absolute values, of water-limited yields from a baseline calculated with Thornthwaite PET are presented for scenarios where Thornthwaite PET was used. Nevertheless, the two methods are likely to have different sensitivities to changes in climate and, thus, a comparison between predictions calculated using both Penman and Thornthwaite PET was undertaken where possible.

Spatial precipitation data for Europe were only available at a monthly temporal resolution on the 0.5° latitude/longitude grid. There are many problems and uncertainties in estimating daily precipitation from monthly totals. Hence, the water-limited growth model was run on a monthly time step. Monthly crop coefficients were calculated throughout the growing season based on the development of LAI. FAO (1986) report that crop coefficients for winter wheat are fixed at 0.3 throughout the period of winter dormancy. They begin to increase when the crop resumes active growth, reaching 1.0 when full crop cover is achieved. After anthesis coefficients fall to a value of 0.5 at maturity. The development of leaf area reflects changes in the water demand of wheat throughout the growing season. Hence, in the EuroWheat model, crop coefficients were linearly related to LAI varying between 0.3 and 1.0 as LAI increases and between 1.0 and 0.5 as LAI decreases.

FAO (1986) relate the WRSI to the final yield of a crop based on the correspondence between the percentage of satisfaction of water requirements and the percentage of the maximum foreseeable yield for a given crop and location (Table 6.5.2). In this analysis, the calculation of potential yield was taken to represent the maximum yield foreseeable. The WRSI values and the FAO classification (Table 6.5.2) were used to adjust potential yield to account for water-limitations.

Table 6.5.2   Classification of water-limited crop performance according to the FAO (1986).

Percentage of yield in relation to the maximum (potential) yield	Classification of crop performance	WRSI
> 100	Very good	100
90 - 100	Good	95 - 99
50 - 90	Average	80 - 94
20 - 50	Mediocre	60 - 79
10 - 20	Poor	50 - 59
< 10	Crop failure	< 50

The direct effect of elevated concentrations of atmospheric carbon dioxide on the transpiration rate of wheat was incorporated in the model through an adjustment factor applied to the crop coefficients. Goudriaan and Unsworth (1990) calculated a reduction in daily transpiration of 0.897 for C_3 crops grown under doubled CO_2. Wolf (1993) also used a reduction factor for transpiration of 0.9 for wheat under doubled atmospheric concentrations of CO_2. Hence, in EuroWheat crop coefficients were reduced by 10% for a doubling of CO_2 from 350 to 700 ppmv. This reflects an increased water use efficiency under elevated CO_2. A linear relationship was assumed for lower CO_2 concentrations.

Other constraints

The mechanistic nature of the site-specific models AFRCWHEAT and SIRIUS means that they should be applicable to more than just the sites for which they were originally developed. However, as only selected components of each site-specific model were used in the development of the EuroWheat model, it was necessary to incorporate two further constraints to winter wheat growth and development: severe winters and excessive rainfall.

Winter wheat cultivars vary widely in their resistance to extreme cold winters. A broadly applicable climatic criteria was needed to identify regions where winters are generally too

harsh for the crop to survive. The northern limit to successful winter wheat cultivation in Europe is in Finland, where it is grown in southern and southwestern regions between latitudes 60° and 61°30'N (Mukula and Rantanen, 1989). Beyond this, significant crop losses occur from damage caused by ice and water during winter. The mean minimum January temperature at the margin of suitability in Finland is approximately -11.5°C. Hence, in EuroWheat the probability of significant crop losses due to winter damage was considered to be too great in areas with mean minimum January temperatures less than -11.5°C. This identified mid and northern Scandinavia and much of Russia as unsuitable for winter wheat cultivation due to severe winters.

In areas of excessive rainfall the probability of achieving effective establishment of winter wheat and its subsequent harvest is so low that the risks of crop failure outweigh any benefits of growing wheat (Russell and Wilson, 1994). Therefore, a constraint to wheat suitability was added to the EuroWheat model to extract those regions where there are likely to be problems from excessive rainfall leading to waterlogging of the soil. Bunting *et al.* (1982) reported that wheat cultivation is generally prevented if mean annual precipitation is greater than 1000 mm. However, such a constraint does not take into account the changes in evapotranspiration or soil moisture status that may occur with climate change. Hence, a constraint based on an accumulated soil water surplus throughout the period of crop establishment was developed and calibrated for the present situation against Bunting's precipitation threshold. All areas with an accumulated soil water surplus in excess of 280 mm between sowing and December were classified as unsuitable. This identified western Norway, western Great Britain, western Ireland, northwest Spain and western parts of the former Yugoslavia as unsuitable for winter wheat cultivation due to excessive rainfall.

6.5.2.2 *Baseline results and validation*

The EuroWheat model predicts development for a specified cultivar across Europe. However, many different varieties of wheat are cultivated in different regions of Europe depending on environmental conditions and management practices. Further, cultivars which are considered optimal for a region under the present climate may become sub-optimal with climate change. Existing cultivars from other areas or entirely new cultivars may be more appropriate in the future. Hence, it is not realistic to model a single wheat cultivar for the entire European region. It would be possible to calculate phenology for different cultivars in specified regions, for example, by using the sowing date criterion to distinguish zones where cultivars with different developmental characteristics are grown. However, this does not allow the relative performance of different cultivars in different regions with climate change to be evaluated. Thus, seven wheat varieties were modelled throughout Europe (Table 6.5.3) and each prediction interpreted for the appropriate region and ignored elsewhere.

Phenological development

The date of maturity for the six winter wheat cultivars as predicted by the EuroWheat model is shown in Figure 6.5.1. Avalon, Hustler, Riband, Slepner and Caribo are all northwestern European wheat varieties and hence, results are only described for this region. Physiological maturity was predicted to occur from late July to early August in northwest Europe for Avalon wheat (a fast developing variety), from late July to early August for Riband (a medium-fast developing variety), in early August for Slepner (a slow developing variety) and from early to mid August for Hustler (a slow developing variety). The model calibration for Caribo was based on Reinink *et al.* (1986). This is a modification of the Hustler model which has slightly shorter thresholds for early development stages; a more constricted vernalization curve and requirement where only temperatures

Table 6.5.3 Details of modelled wheat varieties.

Wheat species/cultivar	Region of model calibration data	Cultivar characteristics	Reference
Winter wheat (cv. Avalon)	U.K.	Fast developing	Porter (1991, pers. comm.)
Winter wheat (cv. Riband)	U.K.	Medium-fast developing	Semenov *et al.* (1993)
Winter wheat (cv. Slepner)	U.K.	Slow developing	Semenov *et al.* (1993)
Winter wheat (cv. Hustler)	U.K.	Slow developing	Weir *et al.* (1984)
Winter wheat (cv. Caribo)	Netherlands	-	Reinink *et al.* (1986)
Winter wheat (cv. Alcala)	Spain	Fast developing	Semenov (1995, pers. comm.)
Durum wheat	Southern France	-	Porter (1994, pers. comm.)

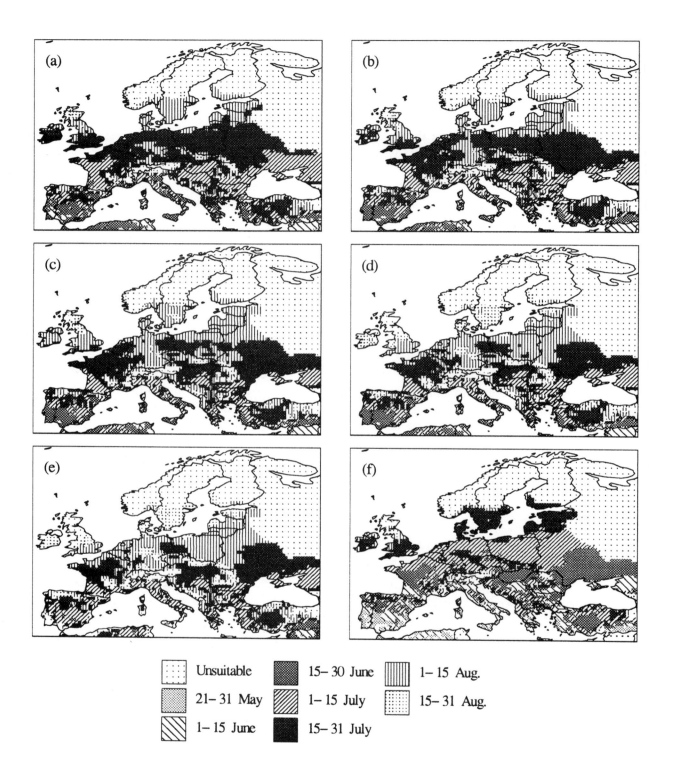

Figure 6.5.1 EuroWheat prediction of date of physiological maturity for six winter wheat varieties for present climate (1961-90).

between -1 to 9°C contribute to vernalization; and the state of vernalization is fixed at the floral initiation stage so that incomplete vernalization has a delaying effect on subsequent stages of development. These alterations led to a later maturity date of early to mid-August compared to the calibrations based on Porter (1991, pers. comm.), Semenov *et al.* (1993) and Weir *et al.* (1984). Furthermore, the varieties Avalon, Riband and Slepner used a base temperature of 0°C from anthesis to maturity, whilst Hustler and Caribo used a base of 9°C. It was found that the 9°C base temperature placed an unrealistic restriction on wheat development in northern latitudes, such as Scotland, due to the use of spatially and temporally averaged climatic data (Porter, 1991, pers. comm.). Finally, calibration parameters for

the cultivar Alcala were derived from variety trials in Sevilla, Spain. Predicted dates of maturity in southern Europe range from mid May to early July.

Potential yield

The distribution of potential yield for cultivar Avalon, based on the SIRIUS model, is shown in Figure 6.5.2. The first method, based on the harvest index, gave slightly lower potential yields than the SIRIUS method. Potential yields were highest in southern Europe, due to higher radiation receipts, where they were up to 12 t/ha and lowest in northeast Europe where they ranged from 7 to 10 t/ha. Across most of central and northwest Europe potential yields ranged from 8 to 10.5 t/ha.

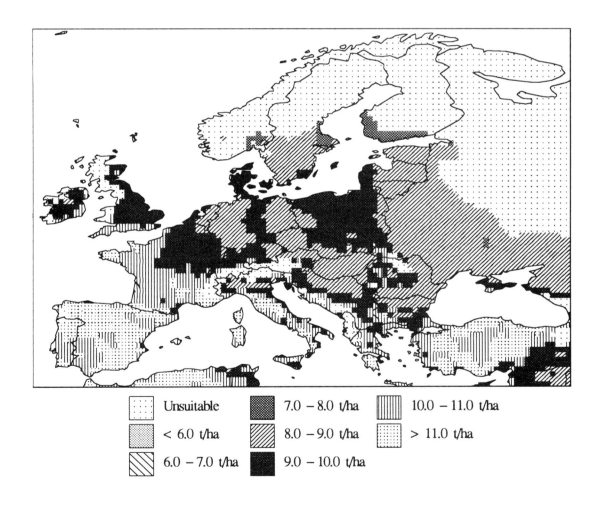

Unsuitable		7.0 – 8.0 t/ha		10.0 – 11.0 t/ha	
< 6.0 t/ha		8.0 – 9.0 t/ha		> 11.0 t/ha	
6.0 – 7.0 t/ha		9.0 – 10.0 t/ha			

Figure 6.5.2 EuroWheat prediction of potential yield for winter wheat (cv. Avalon) for present climate (1961-90).

Water-limited yield

The water requirement satisfaction index (WRSI) predicted very good yields across most of central and northern Europe. This implies that there were no significant water limitations to wheat growth for the average 1961-90 climate. In southern Europe the classification varied from mediocre to poor crop performance. This implies that only 10 to 50% of potential yield will be achieved without irrigation. The distribution of water-limited yield for cultivar Avalon is shown in Figure 6.5.3. The lowest water-limited yields were predicted in southern Europe and varied from 1 to 5 t/ha. In central and eastern Europe yields ranged from 6 to 10 t/ha, whilst in northwest Europe yields of 8 to 10.5 t/ha were predicted.

Validation

EuroWheat was validated in two ways. Firstly, by comparison of model results with output from the original site-based simulation models and, secondly, by comparison with observed and experimental data reported in the literature and from agricultural experimental stations. A system was developed within the ARC/INFO GIS which allows comparisons between site and grid-based model predictions. Details of this comparison are presented in Section 7.4.

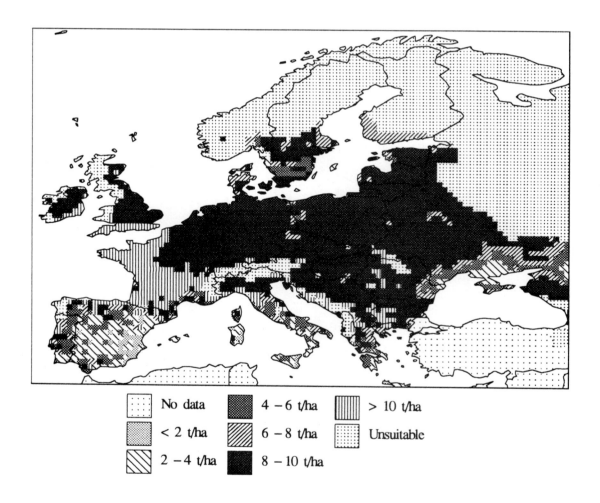

No data	4 – 6 t/ha	> 10 t/ha	
< 2 t/ha	6 – 8 t/ha	Unsuitable	
2 – 4 t/ha	8 – 10 t/ha		

Figure 6.5.3   EuroWheat prediction of water-limited yield for winter wheat (cv. Avalon) for present climate (1961-90).

A database of observed wheat phenology for Europe was developed. It contains 330 observations and covers most of the EU, Scandinavia and eastern Europe. A comparison between observed and predicted phenology indicated that calculated dates from EuroWheat were within the range of observed dates for the appropriate cultivar-regions. Figure 6.5.4 shows the difference between observed dates of harvest and predicted dates of physiological maturity in northwest Europe for a fast- (Avalon), medium- (Slepner) and slow- (Hustler) developing cultivar. Correspondence between observed and predicted dates was good considering physiological maturity occurs 1 to 2 weeks before harvest and the observed dates were averaged over a range of varieties. The predictions of potential growth corresponded with expert opinion and statistics from experimental stations where optimal growing conditions have been maintained throughout the season. Observed yield data were extracted from the FAO, EUROSTAT and national statistics to compare against predicted water-limited yields from EuroWheat. Figure 6.5.5 shows a comparison between FAO and EUROSTAT observed yields and EuroWheat predicted yields at the country level. Actual yields include dry matter losses due to stresses from nutrients,

pests, diseases, etc. as well as from water and, hence, as expected were generally lower than predicted water-limited yields. However, the model captured the correct spatial pattern of yield levels with highest yields occurring in northwest Europe and very low yields in southern Europe.

6.5.2.3 Model sensitivity to systematic changes in climate

Phenological development

The sensitivity of the EuroWheat phenology submodel to incremental increases in temperature was evaluated. As temperatures increase there was a progressive northward and eastward expansion in the area of suitability and a reduction in the length of the growing period. An increase of 1°C caused the duration from sowing to maturity to decrease by 1 to 2 weeks across most of Europe. Further sensitivity tests indicated that for each 1°C increase in temperature the duration from sowing to maturity reduced by, on average, approximately a week. With a 4°C increase the duration decreased by 5 to 6 weeks in northwest Europe and by 3 to 4 weeks in southern and eastern Europe.

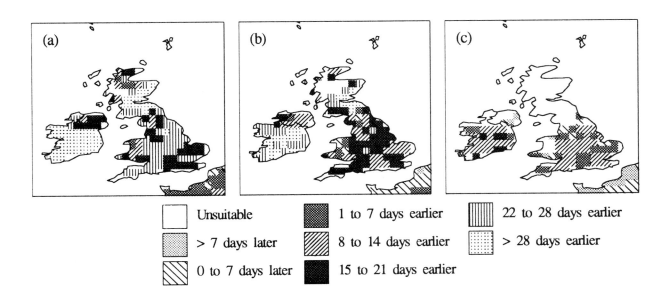

Figure 6.5.4   Observed dates of harvest minus EuroWheat predicted dates of physiological maturity in northwest Europe for three cultivars: (a) Avalon (fast developing); (b) Slepner (medium developing); and (c) Hustler (slow developing).

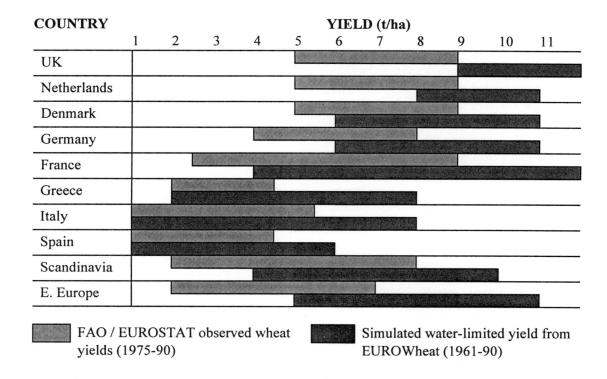

Figure 6.5.5   Comparison of FAO and EUROSTAT observed wheat yields and EuroWheat predicted water-limited wheat yields for a range of European countries.

Potential yield

Similar temperature sensitivity tests were applied to the EuroWheat potential growth submodel. An increase of 1°C led to a slight decrease in potential yield over most of Europe as the shortening of the growing period caused less radiation to be intercepted. The decrease in yield was greatest in western Europe where decreases of up to 0.6 t/ha were predicted. A slight increase in potential yield was indicated in parts of central and northern Europe due to an earlier start to the period of grain filling making it coincide with a time of greater incident radiation. A similar pattern of change was predicted for a 2°C increase in temperature, but decreases of up to 1 t/ha in parts of western Europe were perdicted. A 3°C increase in temperatures caused decreases in potential yield of 0 to 0.6 t/ha in central, northern and eastern Europe, and decreases of 0.8 to 1.4 t/ha in western and southern Europe. A 4°C increase in temperature caused a decrease in yield of up to 2.2 t/ha relative to the baseline (1961-90).

The sensitivity of the potential growth submodel to changes in CO_2 concentration was also examined. For every 100 ppmv increase in CO_2, relative to the present day concentration of 353 ppmv, potential yield increased by 0.6 to 0.9 t/ha. With a CO_2 concentration of 700 ppmv, and no change to current climatic conditions, potential yields were predicted to be approximately 3 t/ha greater in western Europe and 2.5 t/ha greater in eastern Europe.

Water-limited yield

The sensitivity of the water-limited growth submodel of EuroWheat to independent changes in temperature and CO_2 and combined changes in temperature and precipitation was evaluated. A 1°C increase in temperature caused water-limited yields to decrease by 0 to 1 t/ha across most of Europe due to greater water stress from increased evapotranspiration. In central Germany yields increased very slightly reflecting the increase in potential yield described in the previous section. In central Spain and parts of Italy and Greece yields increased by 0 to 1 t/ha as the shortening of the growing period in these regions meant that the period when the crop demands most water was shortened and no longer fell into a time of minimum water availability. A similar pattern of change was apparent for higher temperature sensitivity tests, i.e. water-limited yields increased slightly in parts of southern Europe and decreased across the rest of Europe. Decreases were largest in eastern England and central and eastern Europe, up to 6 t/ha for a 4°C increase in temperature.

Four combinations of changes in temperature and precipitation were assessed (+2°C increase in temperature with ±10 and ±20% precipitation). With -10% precipitation very few regions experienced any increase in yield and decreases ranged from 0 to 6 t/ha. With -20% precipitation yields decreased to a greater extent varying from 0 to 7 t/ha. An increase in precipitation caused yield increases across southern Europe and decreases in central and northern Europe ranging from 0 to 4.5 t/ha for +10% and from 0 to 3 t/ha for +20%. A 10% increase in precipitation was not sufficient to counteract the negative effects of increased evapotranspiration resulting from a 2°C increase in temperature. However, +20% precipitation almost compensated for this level of temperature change.

Increases in the atmospheric concentration of CO_2 led to increased water-limited yields due to improved RUE and reduced transpiration. In northern and central Europe, where there is little water limitation, predicted increases were the same as those described for potential yield. In southern Europe increases in yield were higher than for potential yield due to the added advantage of reduced transpiration, ranging from 3.5 to 6.0 t/ha at 700 ppmv CO_2.

6.5.2.4 *Application of climate change scenarios*

Two equilibrium (UKLO, UKHI) and two transient (UKTR, GFDL) GCM scenarios were applied to the EuroWheat model. For each transient GCM two model decades were

analysed (UKTR3140, UKTR6675, GFDL2534, GFDL5564). As well as different GCM scenarios, two greenhouse gas emissions scenarios were considered (IS92a, IS92d). The atmospheric concentrations of carbon dioxide used in the potential and water-limited growth model runs varied according to the emissions and GCM scenarios. For the equilibrium scenarios a CO_2 concentration of 560 ppmv was assumed. For the IS92a emissions scenarios CO_2 concentrations were: 454 ppmv for UKTR3140 and GFDL2534; and 617 ppmv for UKTR6675 and GFDL5564. For the IS92d emissions scenarios CO_2 concentrations were: 545 ppmv for UKTR6675 and GFDL5564. A description of these climate change scenarios is given in Chapter 2.

The phenological development submodel is not affected by CO_2 concentration and hence, results can be assumed to apply to both emissions scenarios. All results for potential yield are for the IS92a emissions scenario, whilst the water-limited growth sub-model has been run for both the IS92a and IS92d scenarios.

Phenological development

All the climate change scenarios caused faster rates of wheat development, which shortened the length of the growing period. This would lead to an earlier start to crop growth in the spring and a shorter grain filling period, resulting in reduced grain production if management practices are not altered. The magnitude of the shortening of the growing period varied according to the increases in temperature projected by each scenario. The UKLO scenario predicted the greatest increases in temperature and shortened the duration from sowing to maturity by more than 8 weeks in northern Europe and by 4 to 7 weeks in southern Europe. The UKHI scenario predicted smaller reductions by 3 to 5 weeks in southern Europe and 4 to 8 weeks in northern Europe but with a similar pattern to that of the UKLO scenario. Both equilibrium scenarios predicted a large expansion in the area of suitability of winter wheat into northern and eastern Europe.

For the UKTR3140 scenario the duration from sowing to maturity decreased by 1 to 2 weeks across Europe (Figure 6.5.6). This is similar to the predictions for the +1°C sensitivity test. For the second decade (UKTR6675) the duration decreased to a greater extent in eastern Europe, by 4 to 5 weeks, than in western Europe (by 2 to 4 weeks). The GFDL scenarios predicted smaller decreases in growing period length than the UKTR scenarios for both model decades. The GFDL2534 scenario predicted a shortening of the growing period of approximately 1 week across Europe, whilst the GFDL5564 scenario predicted shortenings of 3 to 4 weeks in northern Europe and 1 to 3 weeks in southern Europe. The pattern of change was very different for the UKTR6675 and the GFDL5564 scenarios.

Potential yield

The two equilibrium scenarios predicted increases in potential yield throughout most of Europe as the beneficial effects of elevated CO_2 outweighed the negative effects of increased temperatures. In western Europe increases in yield were greater in the UKHI scenario (0.3 to 1.2 t/ha) compared to the UKLO scenario (0 to 0.6 t/ha). However, in northeast Europe the reverse applied where changes in yield ranged from 0.5 to 1.5 t/ha in the UKLO scenario and from 0 to 1.5 t/ha in the UKHI scenario. Small decreases in potential yield were indicated for some regions in the UKLO scenario (southern England, western France and southern Spain). No decreases in yield were predicted in the UKHI scenario.

All the transient scenarios predicted increases in potential yield (Figure 6.5.7). The UKTR3140 and GFDL2534 scenarios showed similar patterns of change with slightly greater increases predicted by GFDL2534 of up to 2.1 t/ha. The patterns of change in the second model decade of the two transient scenarios were quite different, whilst the magnitude of change was very similar. UKTR6675 predicted the greatest increases in yield in central Europe (up to 3 t/ha) whereas GFDL5564 predicted the greatest increases in southern Europe (up to 3 t/ha) and much lower increases in central Europe (1.2 to 2.1 t/ha). The patterns of change in potential yield also differed considerably between the

time slices of the same transient model. This was particularly pronounced in the GFDL scenarios, where in central Europe relatively large increases in yield were predicted for the first model decade (25-34) and relatively small increases in yield for the second model decade (55-64), compared with other regions.

Water-limited yield: IS92a emissions scenario

All results are firstly discussed based on the Thornthwaite method of calculating PET. A comparison of predicted changes in water-limited yields using the Penman method is then presented for those scenarios containing sufficient climatic variables (UKHI, UKTR).

Both UKLO and UKHI scenarios predicted increases in water-limited yield of between 0 an 2 t/ha throughout most of Europe. Decreases in yield of up to 1 t/ha were predicted in the UKLO scenario for parts of western Europe (England, western France and southern Spain and Portugal) and in the UKHI scenario for small regions of southern Europe.

The transient scenarios predicted increases in water-limited yield throughout most of Europe (Figure 6.5.8). Similar predictions were given by the UKTR3140 and GFDL2534 scenarios in which water-limited yield increased by 0 to 1 t/ha in western Europe and by 1 to 2 t/ha in eastern Europe. The exceptions with the GFDL2534 scenario were a small decrease in yield was predicted in southwest England and western France, and either a small decrease or increase in yield was predicted in Russia. The last model decade of the two transient GCMs showed fairly different patterns of response. The UKTR6675 scenario predicted the greatest increases in yield in central Europe (2 to 3 t/ha) and increases of 1.5 to 2 t/ha in western and eastern Europe. On the other hand, the GFDL5564 scenario predicted the greatest increases in southern Europe (2 to 3.5 t/ha) and increases of 0.5 to 2 t/ha in central and northwest Europe and 2 to 3 t/ha in Scandinavia. The patterns of change between the time slices of the transient models differed considerably for the GFDL scenarios, but differed only slightly for the UKTR scenarios.

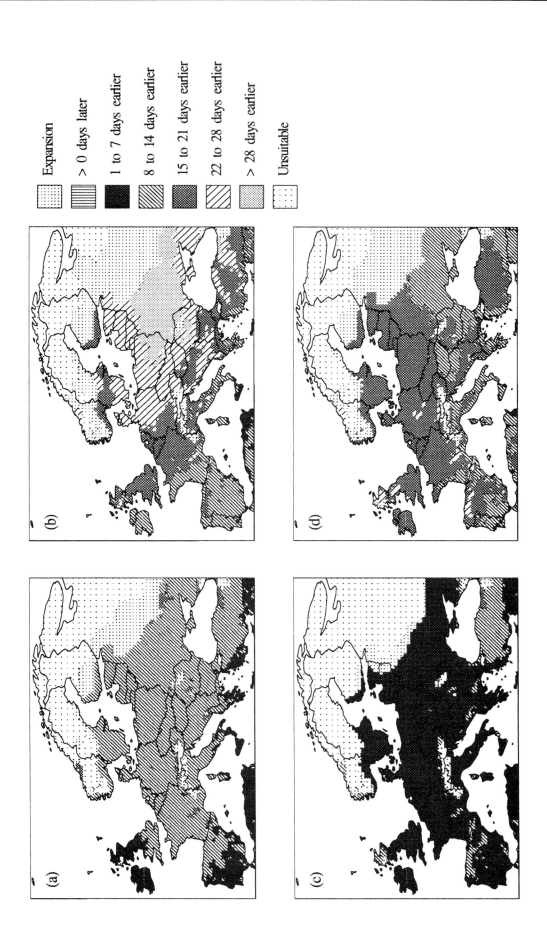

Figure 6.5.6   Change in the duration from sowing to maturity for winter wheat (cv. Avalon) under four transient GCM scenarios: (a) UKTR3140, (b) UKTR6675, (c) GFDL2534, and (d) GFDL5564.

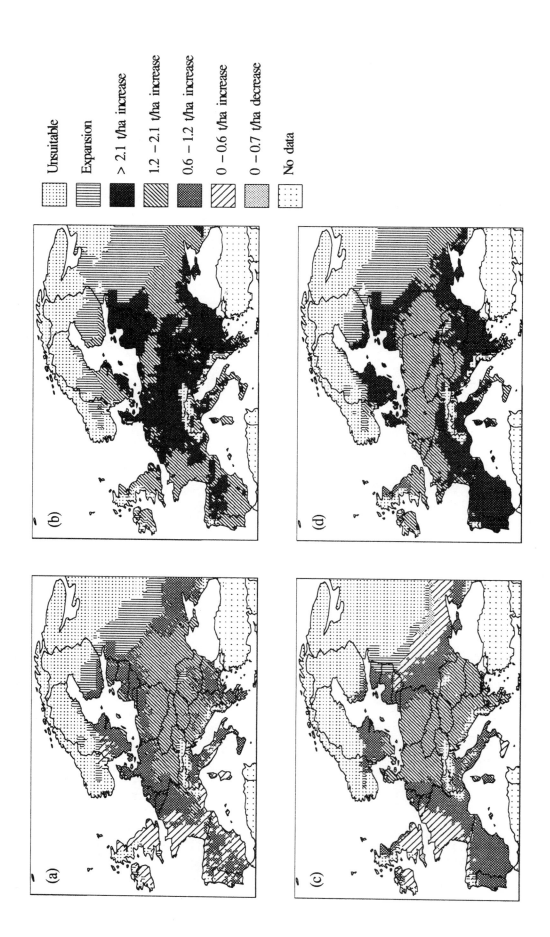

Figure 6.5.7   Change in potential yield for winter wheat (cv. Avalon) for the IS92a emissions scenario with four transient GCM scenarios: (a) UKTR3140, (b) UKTR6675, (c) GFDL2534, and (d) GFDL5564.

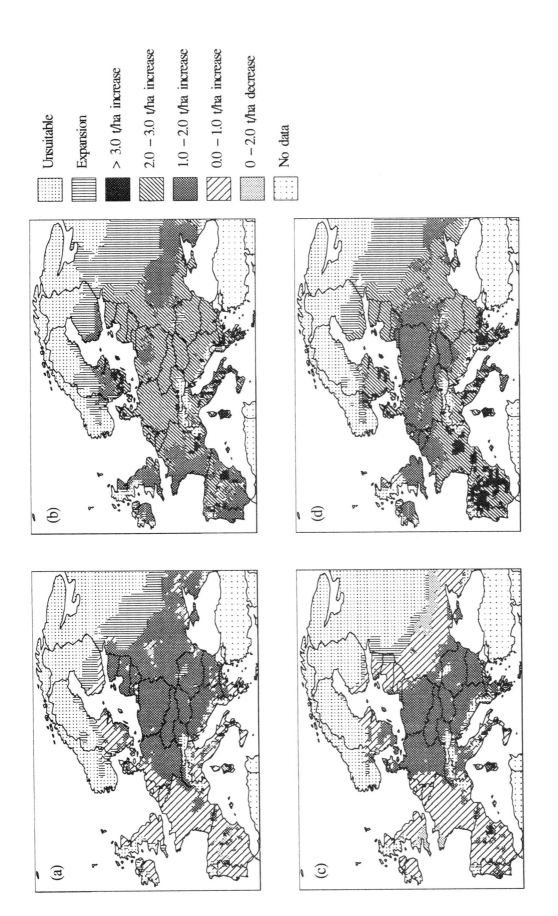

Figure 6.5.8   Change in water-limited yield for winter wheat (cv. Avalon) for the IS92a emissions scenario with four transient GCM scenarios: (a) UKTR3140, (b) UKTR6675, (c) GFDL2534, and (d) GFDL5564.

Similar changes were derived using Penman as opposed to Thornthwaite PET in northwest Europe for all scenarios considered. However, in southern and eastern Europe the Penman predictions generally indicated much lower increases in yield or in some cases decreases. Differences were particularly evident in the Ukraine and eastern Rumania where the Penman predictions were for decreases of up to 1.5 t/ha, whilst the Thornthwaite predictions indicated increases of 1 to 2 t/ha for the UKHI and UKTR3140 scenarios. These differences are consistent with the results of the comparison of three methods for PET calculation discussed in Section 1.2.1.4. in which the Thornthwaite method was found to give the lowest values of PET over the whole southern European region, whilst the Penman method produced the highest values in Russia.

Water-limited yield: IS92d emissions scenario

Lower increases in water-limited yield were predicted for both GFDL5564 and UKTR6675 with the IS92d emissions scenario compared with IS92a. This is to be expected as IS92d assumes lower concentrations of atmospheric CO_2 than IS92a with the same changes in climate and, hence, the benefits from the direct effects of CO_2 are less. In general, yield changes were between 0.5 and 1 t/ha less in the IS92d scenarios. As the climate projections do not change, the pattern of yield change was the same for both emissions scenarios. However, the predictions are expected to be realised at a later date (with a mean climate sensitivity they would occur in 2099 with the IS92d scenario rather than in 2064 with the IS92a scenario).

6.5.2.5   *Possible adaptive responses*

Given current levels of greenhouse gas emissions there is a continuing commitment to warming of the atmosphere. The implication is that there will be some impacts on agriculture in the future, the magnitude of which will depend on emissions over the coming decades. Even with vigorous abatement efforts some adaptation will be required. A possible farm-level adaptive response was been evaluated with the EuroWheat model: changes in the date of sowing.

Sowing dates were altered by ±30 days from present dates and the EuroWheat model rerun for the climate change scenarios. Sowing 30 days earlier considerably reduced the shortening of the growing period. For example, in the UKHI scenario the period between sowing and maturity shortened by 4 to 8 weeks in northern Europe and by 3 to 5 in southern Europe with no change in sowing date. However, if sowing occurs 30 days earlier the reduction in growing period length was only 1 to 4 weeks in northern Europe and 0 to 1 weeks in southern Europe. Hence, there was not such a significant decrease in the length of the grain filling period and higher yields may be expected. This was confirmed in the potential and water-limited growth sub-model runs. Both potential and water-limited yields were predicted to increase throughout Europe by approximately 0.3 to 0.9 t/ha in the UKHI scenario with an earlier sowing date compared to the present sowing date.

Sowing 30 days later than at present caused larger reductions in the length of the growing period throughout Europe according to the UKHI scenario (by 6 to 8 weeks). This led to a general decrease in potential and water-limited yields by 0.1 to 1.2 t/ha compared with those predicted using present sowing dates.

6.5.2.6   *Discussion and conclusions*

A spatial model of wheat phenology and growth (EuroWheat) has been developed based on three existing mechanistic models. A number of methods for scaling-up the site-specific simulations models have been evaluated, including statistical functions, weather generators and monthly reduced-form models. Errors associated with the different methods have been quantified and indicate that broadscale crop modelling need not imply higher levels of uncertainty, at least for the purposes of climate change impact assessment. For example, the root mean square error associated with scaling up the AFRCWHEAT phenology submodel to the European scale was insignificant.

The EuroWheat model has been applied to the range of climate change scenarios described in Chapter 2. The predicted changes in water-limited wheat yields have been summarised for four European regions, defined as follows:

Europe: A large European region extending from Scandinavia in the north to north Africa in the south and from Ireland in the west to the Black Sea in the east.

E.U.: The 15 countries of the European Union (Austria, Belgium, Denmark, Finland, France, Germany, Greece, Ireland, Italy, Luxembourg, Netherlands, Portugal, Spain, Sweden, United Kingdom).

Northern E.U.: All European Union regions north of 45°N latitude.

Southern E.U.: All European Union regions south of 45°N latitude.

Area averaged water-limited yields increased for all regions and scenarios (Tables 6.5.4 and 6.5.5). Table 6.5.4 shows the mean and standard deviation of yields for each of the four regions. The largest increase in yield (+ 26.5% for the European region) was observed with the IS92a emissions scenario and the UKTR6675 GCM scenario. Given a mean climate sensitivity and the IS92a emissions scenario, the changes in climate projected in the UKTR3140 and UKTR6675 GCM scenarios would occur in 2023 and 2064 respectively (see Table 2.2, Chapter 2). This implies a rate of increase in wheat yields of 0.2 t/ha per decade from 1990 to 2023 and 0.36 t/ha per decade from 2023 to 2064 across Europe. With the IS92d emissions scenario, the increase in yield between 2023 and 2064 declines to 0.13 t/ha per decade. In the northern and southern E.U. regions the rate of increase in yield is also greater between the first and second decade of the GCM scenarios than between the present and the first GCM decade. The spatial variability of yields was approximately 2.5 times greater in the southern E.U. region than the northern E.U. region for current conditions and all scenarios.

Changes in total water-limited yield by region are shown in Table 6.5.5 for all scenarios. The two equilibrium models (UKLO and UKHI) predicted similar changes of the order of a 10% increase in production for all regions. Relatively small increases in yield were found for the equilibrium scenarios compared to the transient

scenarios. This was due to the balance between the negative effects of higher temperatures reducing the growing period length and the positive effects of elevated CO_2 concentrations. The CO_2 concentrations assumed in the equilibrium runs (560 ppmv) were only just sufficient to counterbalance the much greater increases in temperature predicted in the UKLO and UKHI models compared to the transient scenarios. A comparison between the same model decades of the two transient models (UKTR and GFDL) indicated very similar changes for the large European region. However, the GFDL scenarios predicted significantly larger increases in yields than the UKTR scenarios for both decades in southern E.U. regions, whilst in northern E.U. regions the UKTR scenarios predicted slightly higher yields. The later model decade of the transient scenarios produced the greatest increases in yield of all scenarios due to the high CO_2 concentration (617 ppmv). This was particularly evident for the southern E.U. region in which 38.3 and 45.3% increases were predicted for UKTR6675 and GFDL5564 respectively. The lower emissions scenario (IS92d) led to about a 10% reduction in the predicted yield increase compared with the IS92a scenario across Europe.

Total wheat production in 1990 in the 15 countries included in the definition of the E.U. region in Tables 6.5.4 and 6.5.5 in 1990 was 89 million tonnes (FAO, 1990). Relating this historic yield to the percentage increases predicted in Table 6.5.5 a crude indication of future wheat yields for the E.U. is given, assuming similar acreage of production. In the first transient model decade yields may increase to between 98.4 and 100.0 million tonnes. This relates to a date of between 2013 to 2036 according to Table 2.2 in Chapter 2 for both emissions scenarios. In the later transient model decade yields may increase to between 114.3 and 115.6 million tonnes. According to Table 2.2 in Chapter 2, this would relate to a date of between 2042 and the early 22nd century using the IS92a emissions scenario.

Despite mainly positive impacts on wheat yields for the majority of scenarios, it is likely that farmers will optimise their management

Table 6.5.4   Mean water-limited wheat yields (and standard deviation) for four predefined regions of Europe for baseline climate (1961-90) and climate change scenarios (in t/ha). NB: calculated using Penman PET.

Emissions scenario (CO$_2$ (ppmv))	GCM scenario	Region			
		Europe	E.U.	Northern E.U.	Southern E.U.
Base (353)	Base	8.07 (2.34)	7.77 (2.86)	9.25 (1.22)	5.94 (3.23)
2 x CO$_2$ (560)	UKHI	8.43 (2.55)	8.50 (2.86)	9.70 (1.37)	6.79 (3.49)
IS92a (454)	UKTR3140	8.74 (2.50)	8.61 (2.69)	9.86 (1.33)	6.91 (3.09)
IS92a (617)	UKTR6675	10.21 (2.22)	10.17 (2.62)	11.13 (1.37)	8.83 (3.28)
IS92d (545)	UKTR6675	9.28 (2.30)	9.21 (2.69)	10.33 (1.32)	7.64 (3.27)

Table 6.5.5   Percentage change in total water-limited wheat yield from baseline (1961-90) for four predefined regions of Europe. NB: calculated using Thornthwaite PET.

Emissions scenario (CO$_2$ (ppmv))	GCM scenario	Region			
		Europe	E.U.	Northern E.U.	Southern E.U.
2 x CO$_2$ (560)	UKLO	13.0	8.7	9.1	7.9
2 x CO$_2$ (560)	UKHI	12.5	9.6	8.7	11.4
IS92a (454)	UKTR3140	12.7	10.6	9.2	13.5
IS92a (617)	UKTR6675	27.4	28.5	23.3	38.3
IS92a (454)	GFDL2534	12.2	12.4	8.9	19.1
IS92a (617)	GFDL5564	27.6	29.9	21.9	45.3
IS92d (545)	UKTR6675	17.4	17.5	15.0	22.4
IS92d (545)	GFDL5564	17.2	18.3	13.2	28.2

practices to adapt to changing climatic and atmospheric conditions. For example, changing to an earlier sowing date or a better suited variety would further improve the yields which could be realised under climate change.

6.5.3   Sunflower

Sunflower (*Helianthus annus* L.) is a dicotyledonous annual having the C$_3$ photosynthetic pathway. It is an unusual C$_3$ plant because its photosynthesis is saturated only with relatively high radiation receipts. Because of its high photosynthetic capacity and relatively high harvest index, sunflower is a viable crop for high-yielding environments (Kiniry *et al.*, 1992). Since its introduction into Europe and the recognition of its food value it has spread throughout Europe, eventually reaching the USSR where it was adapted to diverse environments and no other oil crop was available for production at northern latitudes (Seiler, 1992). Sunflower has become a crop of major economic importance worldwide. It is grown mainly for its oil and now ranks second among all oilseed crops in the world as a source of edible vegetable oil. Major sunflower production areas are now the former USSR,

France, Spain, Rumania, Hungary, former Yugoslavia as well as North America, Argentina, China and South Africa.

6.5.3.1 *Methodology*

A spatial model of sunflower (EuroSunfl) has been developed using information available in the literature and in current mechanistic models. The model was designed to simulate the response of sunflower to changes in climate at a European scale, using monthly gridded climatological data as input driving variables. The model consists of three submodels: (i) a phenological model, (ii) a potential yield model and (iii) a water limited yield model.

The phenology model has a climatological input of mean monthly temperature; the potential yield model requires monthly global radiation and temperature as inputs and the water-limited yield model requires monthly temperature, radiation, precipitation, potential evapotranspiration and information on soil water holding capacity.

Phenological development

In order to accurately represent sowing dates throughout Europe a method of calculating a spatially varying sowing date was required. A sine curve interpolation (Brooks, 1943) was used to estimate daily maximum and minimum temperatures from monthly values. The initial criterion chosen was the first day in the year when mean temperature is greater than 8°C. This is the minimum temperature required for emergence (CETIOM, 1989; Angus *et al.*, 1981). When applied to the European (1961-90 mean) temperature data, sowing dates were predicted to occur in February, March and April throughout Europe, except in the marginal areas in the Ukraine and Russia where they were later. This agreed well with information available for sowing dates in France but dates were early for southern parts of Spain and Italy. Therefore it was assumed that this criterion represented the earliest possible dates of sowing. Sunflower yields well with high radiation and sowing is likely to be timed so that the growing season corresponds to the period of maximum radiation receipt at any location. This can be represented

by identifying the first day with a mean temperature of 10°C (the optimal temperature for sowing, Narciso *et al.*, 1992). This criterion predicted a broader range in sowing dates in the southern European countries presently cultivating sunflower and gave dates more consistent with those reported in the literature for Spain, Italy and Greece. Hence, this criterion was used in all model runs to estimate sowing dates throughout Europe.

The phenological sub-model was based on accumulated thermal time and calculates dates of flowering and physiological maturity. Parameters for several sunflower varieties were determined. These ranged from an early maturing French variety, Cerflor (Merrien, 1986), a later maturing French variety, Topflor (which is not suitable for production in northern France) and a variety grown in the UK, Avante. A base temperature for development of 6°C was chosen for Cerflor, Topflor and Avante based on Kiniry *et al.*'s review (1992). Thermal time thresholds for determining flowering and maturity were 890°C days and 1570°C days respectively (Merrien, 1986) for the early maturing French variety and 1000°C days and 1700°C days respectively for the later maturing variety. Sufficient information was available only to derive the thermal time threshold from sowing to maturity for Avante (1050°C.days, Church, pers. comm., 1994).

Most cultivars of sunflower are classified as insensitive to photoperiod (Merrien, pers. comm., 1995) although it has been reported that short days can accelerate sunflower development (Doyle, 1975). Flowering can occur over a wide range of daylengths and, hence, photoperiod was assumed to be inconsequential when predicting development over a wide range of locations (Kiniry *et al.*, 1992).

Potential growth

Potential yield was calculated by combining the phenological model with a temperature and radiation based model which calculates leaf area, intercepted radiation between sowing and maturity and uses a radiation use efficiency taken from the literature to calculate yield. Leaf area index was calculated using accumulated degree days up to a maximum leaf area index of 3 at anthesis (Chapman *et al.*, 1993). The model was adapted to allow for changes in the value of the extinction coefficient throughout the growing season, based on leaf area index (Zaffaroni and Schneiter, 1989). Radiation intercepted by the canopy was calculated using the Monsi-Saeki equation with inputs of the leaf area index and extinction coefficient. This was converted into yield using a radiation use efficiency of 2.0 gMJ^{-1} and a harvest index of 0.25 (Kiniry *et al.*, 1992).

For climate change experiments it is necessary to include the effects of changes to the physiology of the crop produced by increases in ambient CO_2. Kiniry (pers. comm, 1994) reported an increase in photosynthetically active radiation use efficiency of 20% from present to 660 ppmv CO_2 concentration. In the climate change runs the radiation use efficiency was assumed to increase linearly with atmospheric CO_2 concentration based on this observed change.

Water-limited growth

Water-limited sunflower yields were calculated by integrating the potential yield model with the FAO crop specific water balance model (FAO, 1986). This was calculated specifically for the water requirements of sunflower throughout the modelled duration of growth. It requires inputs of soil water holding capacity, precipitation and potential evapotranspiration. Available water capacity (AWC) was calculated using the methodology and database developed by Groenendijk (1989) at a 0.5° latitude by 0.5° longitude spatial resolution. In the FAO model potential evapotranspiration is adjusted according to the crop's demand for water during the particular development stage using crop coefficients. Crop coefficients are derived from the ratio between potential and actual crop evapotranspiration. For sunflower, crop coefficients ranged from 0.3 at emergence to a maximum of 1.05 at flowering and returned to 0.4 at maturity. The water balance was

calculated monthly to determine whether the soil was in surplus or deficit. The accumulated difference between the crop water requirement and deficit was expressed as a ratio of the total crop water requirement. The final output of the model is the water requirement satisfaction index (WRSI).

FAO (1986) relate the WRSI to the final yield of a crop based on the correspondence between the percentage of satisfaction of water requirements and the percentage of the maximum foreseeable yield for a given crop and location (Table 6.5.2). In this analysis, the calculation of potential yield was taken to represent the maximum yield foreseeable. The WRSI values and the FAO classification (Table 6.5.2) were used to adjust potential yield to account for water-limitations.

Potential evapotranspiration was calculated according to Penman (1948) for the baseline, sensitivity tests and scenarios of UKTR and UKHI and according to Thornthwaite and Mather (1955) for the baseline and all scenarios. In order to calculate Penman PET temperature, radiation, humidity and wind speed data is required which is not available for the GFDL and UKLO scenarios. Thornthwaite potential evapotranspiration can be calculated using temperature data alone so is not considered to be as accurate as Penman. It also gives values consistently lower than Penman in southern Europe.

The direct effect of elevated CO_2 concentrations on transpiration rate (mainly as a result of a decrease in stomatal conductivity due to an increase in internal CO_2 concentration (Kramer, 1983)) of sunflower was incorporated in the model through an adjustment factor applied to the crop coefficients. Goudriaan and Unsworth (1990) calculated a reduction in daily transpiration of 0.897 for C_3 crops grown under doubled CO_2. Hence, in EuroSunfl crop coefficients were reduced by 10% for a doubling of CO_2 from 350 to 700 ppmv. A linear relationship for concentrations between 350 and 700 ppmv was assumed.

6.5.3.2 *Baseline results and validation*

Phenological development

Dates of flowering for the variety Cerflor were predicted to occur mainly in June in the southernmost Mediterranean areas of Portugal, Italy, Sicily and Greece. This corresponded well with dates reported (Narciso, 1992). Simulated dates also agreed with observations in southern Spain where flowering is reported as occurring in May (Narciso, 1992). Further north, in most of France, central Spain and eastern Italy sunflowers are reported to flower in July which was also represented by the model (Narciso, 1992; CARGILL, 1994). In northern France, which had a sowing date of April, flowering was modelled as occurring in August. Maturity dates ranged from June to December (Figure 6.5.9).

At the most northerly limits of the crop's suitability, in Germany, Poland and Russia, maturity dates were very late. A faster maturing variety would probably be more suitable in these areas. Modelled maturity dates were consistent with those reported in central Spain, central France, Italy and Greece (Narciso, 1992; CARGILL, 1994). The longer maturing variety (Topflor) was more suited to the temperature conditions of southern Spain according to the dates of maturity reported. The very early maturing variety Avante showed suitability for production throughout Germany, Czechoslovakia, Bulgaria, Austria, Poland, most of England and as far north as the Baltic states. This is a fairly new variety developed specifically for the UK market, and its temperature requirements are clearly suitable for many other areas in Europe. Lower temperature

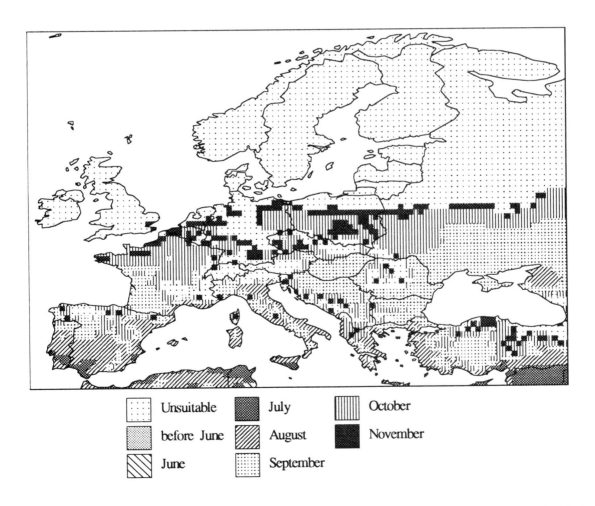

⬚ Unsuitable	▓ July	▥ October
▒ before June	▨ August	■ November
▧ June	⬚ September	

Figure 6.5.9 EuroSunfl prediction of date of maturity of sunflower for present climate (cv. Cerflor).

requiring varieties are currently being developed and production is expanding rapidly in the UK (UKSA, 1994) and Germany (EUROSTAT, 1994).

Though dates of phenological stages are not available for non EU countries, FAO statistics reveal sunflower production in the former Yugoslavia, Rumania, Hungary, Czechoslovakia, Bulgaria, Austria and Albania. These areas were also included within the model's thermal limit for suitability.

Potential yield

The distribution of potential yield for variety Cerflor is shown in Figure 6.5.10. Yields ranged from 2.0 up to 5 t/ha for most of Europe. The highest yields were predicted in areas where the season was long and radiation receipts were high in continental central-eastern Europe. Irrigated sunflower yields in Greece, which are comparable to potential yield predictions were between 2.5 and 4 t/ha (Narciso *et al.*, 1992).

Water-limited yield

The distribution of water-limited yield of Cerflor is shown in Figure 6.5.11. Yields varied widely between and within countries. In areas where crop water requirements could not be met, predicted yields were poor, for example, across most of Spain, southern Italy and Greece and southern USSR (yielding less than 1 t/ha). Low reported yields (EUROSTAT) were consistent with predictions in those parts of Spain where production is not irrigated. Unirrigated yields observed in Greece of 1 t/ha were also comparable to water limited yield predictions.

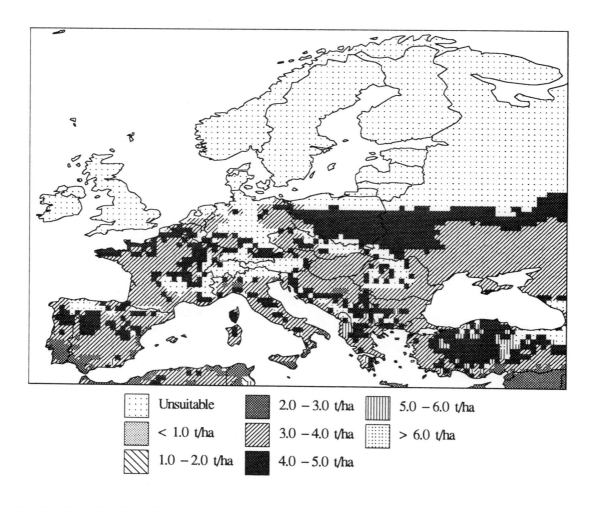

:::: Unsuitable	▓ 2.0 – 3.0 t/ha	▥ 5.0 – 6.0 t/ha
░ < 1.0 t/ha	▨ 3.0 – 4.0 t/ha	▦ > 6.0 t/ha
▧ 1.0 – 2.0 t/ha	■ 4.0 – 5.0 t/ha	

Figure 6.5.10 EuroSunfl prediction of potential yield (in t/ha) for sunflower (cv. Cerflor) for present climate (1961-90).

In Italy, Narciso *et al.* (1992) reported that sunflower was cultivated as a rainfed crop with good results in central areas and as an irrigated crop in the south. This was also distinguished in the water-limited yield predictions. Eastern, more continental climates seemed to have precipitation and evapotranspiration conditions most suitable for high yielding sunflower production. The best yields were predicted in northern Italy, the shared border of Austria and Hungary, western Germany, and parts of Poland and Russia.

Validation

Sources including the EUROSTAT database (EUROSTAT, 1992) and FAO Production Yearbooks supplied information on area, production and yield of sunflower and were used to check the model of suitability of the crop in a region. Unfortunately it was not possible to run the model in order to produce a time series of yields for comparison as not all parameters of the baseline climate datasets were available yearly, rather as mean values for 1961-90 for each grid. Figure 6.5.12(a) and (b) shows the time series of mean sunflower yields over the period 1975 to 1990 for EU (EUROSTAT) and non-EU countries (FAO). The EUROSTAT database gave mean observed yields for 1975 to 1990 at greater detail than country level. When this is plotted spatially it reveals the lowest yields of 0.5 to 1 t/ha in central Spain and most of Portugal; between 1 and 1.5 t/ha in southern Spain, north-eastern Spain, Sicily and Greece; and yields of 2.0 t/ha or greater in most of France, central and northern Italy. Small areas with yields between 3 and 3.5t/ha can be seen in central Portugal and areas surrounding the Italian Alps. Trials data from France

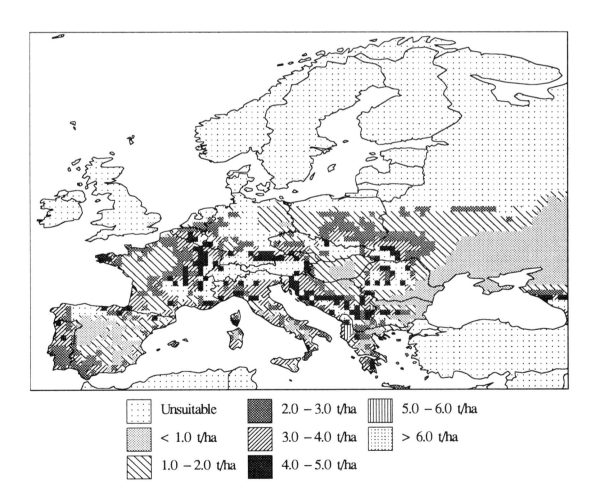

░	Unsuitable	▓	2.0 – 3.0 t/ha	▥	5.0 – 6.0 t/ha
▒	< 1.0 t/ha	▨	3.0 – 4.0 t/ha	⠿	> 6.0 t/ha
▧	1.0 – 2.0 t/ha	■	4.0 – 5.0 t/ha		

Figure 6.5.11   EuroSunfl prediction of water limited yield (in t/ha) for sunflower (cv.Cerflor) for present climate (1961-90) using Thornthwaite PET.

(F. Michaux, Semences, CARGILL, 1994) were also collected and were useful in checking sowing dates, harvest dates and yields. Sowing dates used in French trials in the north-western region were from the third week of April up to early in May and yields over a wide range of (unirrigated) conditions ranged from 2.0 to 3.5 t/ha in 1994, which were better than predictions of water-limited production using the model with 1961-90 baseline data. Maturity dates for trials in1994 were very late September or early October in this region which was consistent with predicted maturity dates for Cerflor.

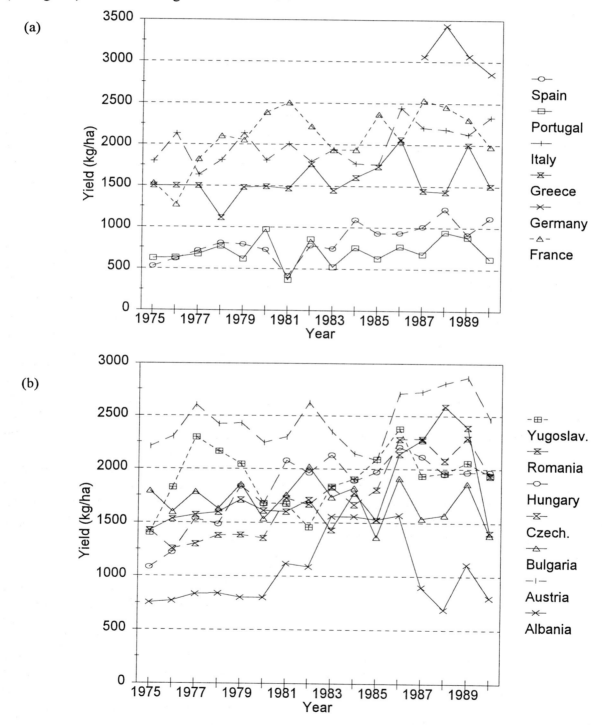

Figure 6.5.12   Time series of observed sunflower yields in kg/ha for (a) EU and (b) non EU countries. Data provide by EUROSTAT database and FAO yearbooks (1975-90).

6.5.3.3 *Model sensitivity to systematic changes in climate*

Phenological development

The response of the development component of the EuroSunfl model to incremental increases in temperature was examined. As temperature increased a progressive northward and eastward expansion in the area of suitability and a reduction in the growing period was observed. With an increase of 1°C the period from sowing to maturity shortened by 3 to 4 weeks in northern Europe to around a week in southern Europe. With 4°C warming the change in duration was up to 10 weeks in northern Europe and between 5 and 7 weeks in southern Europe.

Potential yield

Sensitivity tests were conducted with 2°C and 4°C warming. With 2°C warming potential yield was reduced from the baseline by between 0.5 and 1.0 t/ha throughout most of Europe due to the shortening of the period when radiation could be intercepted (this clearly was more important in lower potential yielding areas). An increase of 4°C caused higher yield losses ranging from 0.5 to 2.0 t/ha. Losses were lowest in southern Europe increasing northwards and eastwards up to 2 t/ha in northern France and Germany. The sensitivity of potential yield to elevated CO_2 concentrations was also evaluated. Increases in potential yield were small at a concentration of 450 ppmv. The spatial pattern varied little from the baseline and the largest increases were 0.3 t/ha. For every further increase in 100 ppmv CO_2 potential yields increased by between 0.2 and 0.3 t/ha. At 700 ppmv yield increases compared with the baseline ranged from 0.8 to 1.2 t/ha.

Water limited yield

The sensitivity of water limited production of a 2°C warming combined with $\pm10\%$ precipitation was evaluated. A 10% increase in precipitation caused yield changes from the baseline of 0.5 to 1.5 t/ha. In only a few areas did the excess rainfall offset the reduction in yield caused by the shortening of the season including small areas in Portugal, southwestern France,

scattered areas in Italy and western Greece. A 10% reduction in precipitation led to further yield reductions of approximately 0.5 t/ha above those predicted for a 10% increase in precipitation.

6.5.3.4 *Application of climate change scenarios*

Two equilibrium (UKLO and UKHI) and two transient (UKTR, GFDL) GCM scenarios were used with the EuroSunfl model. For each transient model two model decades were analysed (UKTR3140, UKTR6675, GFDL2534, GFDL5564). The emissions scenarios IS92a and IS92d have been used as forcing scenarios on UKTR6675 and GFDL5564 models. All climate change scenarios are described in Chapter 2.

Phenological development

All scenarios caused faster development of sunflower which resulted in reduction of the crop duration (Figure 6.5.13). In general, this would be expected to reduce yields if the effects of faster development were not offset by increasing CO_2 or shifts to more fitting management practices. UKLO gave a shortening of duration from 50 days (southern Europe) to 90 days (northern Europe) relative to the baseline and expansion of the area of suitability up to northern Scotland and into Scandinavia. Under the UKHI scenario there was a shortening of the season ranging from 30 to 90 days. Both scenarios showed a strong north-south gradient in change in duration, resulting in a more uniform timing of maturity dates across Europe. These changes were equivalent to the changes induced by a 3°C to 4°C warming in the sensitivity analysis.

Changes in duration under the transient scenarios were less severe than under either of the equilibrium models being closer to changes induced by a warming of 2°C to 3°C in the sensitivity tests. For UKTR3140, maturity dates were between 10 and 50 days earlier, and for UKTR6675 between 10 and 70 days earlier. The smallest changes in duration and the least expansion into new areas occurred under the GFDL2534 scenario. These changes were equivalent to those induced by a 1°C warming

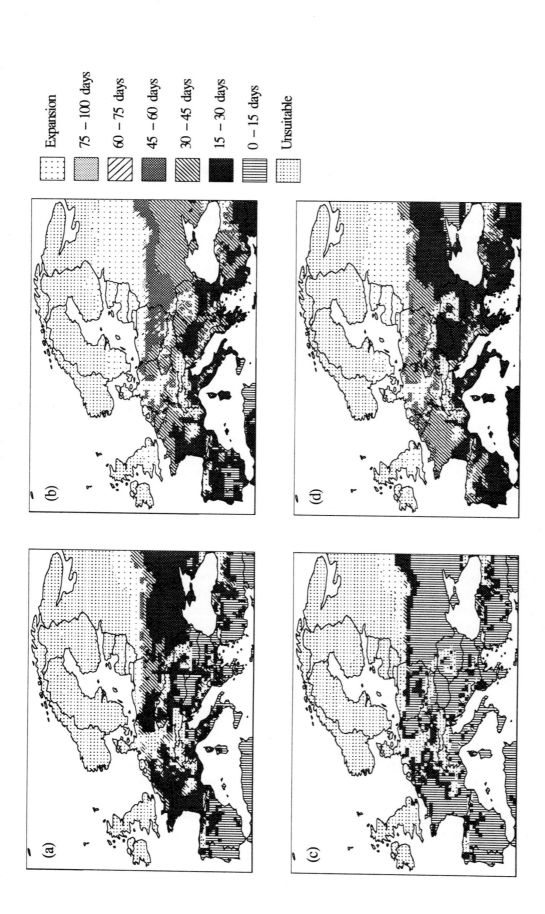

Figure 6.5.13 Change in season duration from baseline duration (in days shorter) for sunflower (cv. Cerflor) four transient scenarios: (a) UKTR3140, (b) UKTR6675, (c) GFDL2534, and (d) GFDL5564.

(which ranged from 5 to 30 days reduction) and around 2°C warming under the GFDL5564 scenario (which ranged from 10 to 50 days reduction).

Duration was at least 10 days shorter at all locations, except in southern Spain, under UKTR3140 compared with the equivalent GFDL2534 scenario. The later model decade of the transient scenarios revealed both similarities and differences in spatial patterns of changes in duration caused by warming. In western Europe the scenarios had similar patterns of change compared with the baseline although under the GFDL5564 scenario there were larger reductions in duration by up to 10 days. Continental, eastern Europe, however, showed lower reductions in duration in the GFDL5564 scenario than the UKTR6675, with reductions which were considerably higher in the former USSR north of the Baltic sea by up to 20 days.

Potential yield

The potential yield models were adapted to include the effects of increased CO_2 on radiation use efficiency as described in Section 6.5.3.1. The IS92a emissions scenario was used with all transient scenario decades. IS92d emissions scenario was used with UKTR6675 and GFDL5564 only. For the equilibrium scenarios a CO_2 concentration of 560 ppmv was assumed. For the IS92a emissions scenarios CO_2 concentrations were: 454 ppmv for UKTR3140 and GFDL2534; and 617 ppmv for UKTR6675 and GFDL5564. For the IS92d emissions scenarios CO_2 concentrations were: 545 ppmv for UKTR6675 and GFDL5564.

Yield changes for both equilibrium models were negative throughout Europe even with the benefit of increased RUE. Losses were severe due to the large reduction in the growing period. The smallest losses were in southern Spain, mainly because baseline potential yields were low in this region and losses increased rapidly under both UKHI and UKLO scenarios moving north and eastwards. UKLO showed the greatest losses of up to 2.5 t/ha in potentially high yielding areas in north eastern Spain, and the

present northern limit of growth in Hungary and the former USSR.

Yield losses were low in most areas for the UKTR3140 scenario (Figure 6.5.14). There were small increases in yield in areas which experienced fairly small changes in duration. This offset was caused by the effect of increased CO_2 concentration in areas with currently long durations (in eastern Germany, Hungary, Czechoslovakia, the former Yugoslavia and Bulgaria). The UKTR6675 scenario showed losses in yield throughout Europe of up to 1.0 t/ha which increased from west to east in a similar pattern to the decrease in crop growing period. There were no areas showing yield benefits in this scenario. The GFDL2534 scenario gave potential yield increases throughout almost the whole of Europe (up to 1 t/ha) which was caused by the small reduction of the growing season length and the increase in RUE (of 17.5%). Under the GFDL5564 scenario there were minor losses of potential yield throughout most of Europe except in the former USSR where a small increase was predicted. The lower CO_2 concentration assumed in the emissions scenario IS92d removed any yield increases and increased the losses in yield predicted by the UKTR6675 and GFDL5564 scenarios.

Water-limited yield: IS92a emissions scenario

Changes in water-limited yield compared with baseline water-limited yield is described for model runs using Thornthwaite PET with scenario data first and then differences between the results using Penman PET compared with Thornthwaite PET will be described for UKHI, UKTR3140 and UKTR6675 scenarios.

Under the equilibrium scenarios there were small yield improvements compared with the baseline in central Spain, Germany, and northern France. All other areas suffered yield losses (up to 1.5 t/ha) under these scenarios. Benefits were larger under the UKLO scenario in central Spain, giving yield increases of between 0.5 and 1.5 t/ha. Benefits in eastern Germany were small under both scenarios at the most 0.5 t/ha.

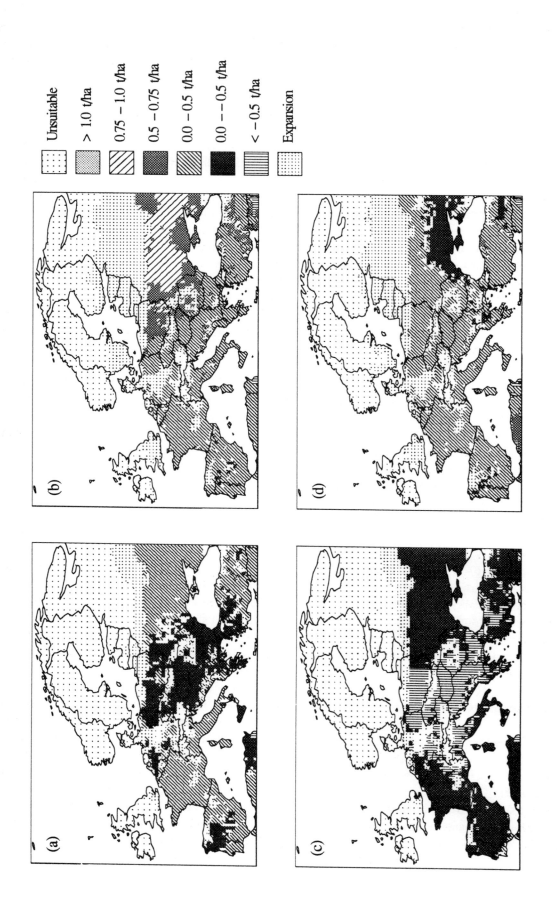

Figure 6.5.14 Change in potential yield for sunflower (cv. Cerflor) from baseline potential yield (presented as yield losses in *t*/ha) under four transient GCM scenarios: (a) UKTR3140, (b) UKTR6675, (c) GFDL2534, and (d) GFDL5564.

Figure 6.5.15 shows the yield losses produced with the transient scenarios, with emissions scenario IS92a and using Thornthwaite PET. Under the UKTR3140 scenario there were yield benefits compared with the baseline in eastern Germany, Poland, Hungary, Czechoslovakia, Belorussia and parts of Russia. Also the east coast of Spain and small areas in southern Italy showed yield benefits, however, these were small in all areas up to only 1 t/ha. All other areas suffered yield losses under this scenario. Under the UKTR6675 scenario yield benefits covered a larger area of Europe particularly further east in Russia and yield benefits were larger (up to a maximum of 2 t/ha). Under the GFDL2534 scenario benefits were higher and more widespread and losses were lower than under UKTR3140. The greatest yield benefits were centred around Poland and Russia and became less to the south and east of this area.

Using Penman PET rather than Thornthwaite PET in the calculation of water-limited yields, produced smaller losses or in some cases gains in yield under the UKTR6675 scenario, when each was compared with its respective yields calculated using the baseline. Portugal in particular showed yield gains with Penman PET where yield losses were predicted with Thornthwaite PET. Under the UKTR3140 scenario yield losses were similar with Penman and Thornthwaite PET. However, small yield benefits were lost in eastern Spain and the most southern parts of Italy when using Penman rather than Thornthwaite PET. Under the UKHI scenario losses were greater using Penman PET in central and eastern Europe but were less in Spain, Portugal (with some yield gains), Italy and Greece. In general, water-limited yields in northern and eastern Europe were affected little by using Penman rather than Thornthwaite PET.

Water-limited yield: IS92d emissions scenario

Under the IS92d scenario for the transient scenarios UKTR6675 and GFDL5564, the spatial pattern of yield losses and gains remained as for IS92a, but the size of the losses and gains changed because ambient CO_2 was lower. With GFDL5564 yield gains in Poland, Hungary, Russia, Rumania and Czechoslovakia were lower (by up to 1 t/ha) and yield losses in

France were larger. This also applied to UKTR6675 in these regions. A comparison between the transient models showed that yield benefits were more widespread in central Europe under GFDL5564 than under UKTR6675.

6.5.3.5 *Possible adaptive responses*

The detrimental effects of climate change on sunflower production may be abated by the use of earlier sowing dates or by switching to longer maturing varieties. Recalculating the sowing date model for the UKHI scenario with variety Cerflor caused sowing dates to occur earlier at all locations and reduced the yield losses in central and eastern Europe. Yield benefits occurred more widely in Germany, Poland and Hungary. However, benefits were small in southern Europe because sowing days under current climate were already early in the year (February).

The use of a longer maturing variety, Topflor resulted in yield improvements in all areas compared with Cerflor under UKHI. Yield losses were offset in Spain, Italy and France and losses were lower compared with the baseline in central and eastern Europe.

6.5.3.6 *Discussion and conclusions*

A spatial model of sunflower phenology and growth has been developed based on existing site models and discussion with experts and growers. The EuroSunfl model has been applied to the range of climate change scenarios described in Chapter 2. The predicted changes in water-limited sunflower yields have been summarised for four European regions defined as follows:

Europe: A large European region extending from Scandinavia in the north to north Africa in the south and from Ireland in the west to the Black Sea in the east.

E.U.: The 15 countries of the European Union (Austria, Belgium, Denmark, Finland, France, Germany, Greece, Ireland, Italy, Luxembourg, Netherlands, Portugal, Spain, Sweden, United Kingdom).

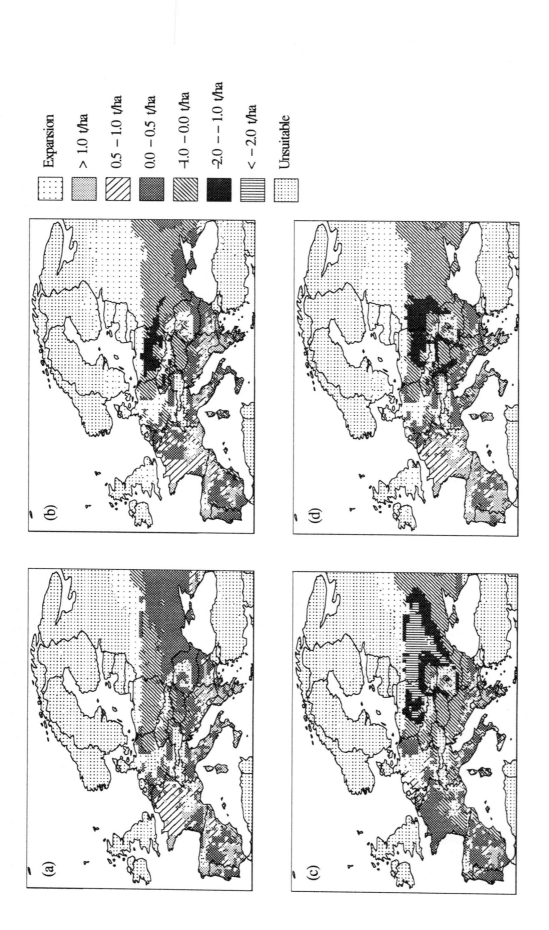

Figure 6.5.15 Change in water-limited yield for sunflower (cv. Cerflor) from baseline potential yield (presented as yield losses in t/ha) under four transient GCM scenarios: (a) UKTR3140, (b) UKTR6675, (c) GFDL2534, and (d) GFDL5564.

Northern E.U.: All European Union regions north of 45°N latitude.

Southern E.U.: All European Union regions south of 45°N latitude.

Table 6.5.6 shows the mean yields for the baseline climate and for applied scenarios when Penman PET was used. It can be seen that the UKTR6675 scenario was the only case which predicted higher yields than the baseline for any of the regions, although it should be noted that standard deviations were large. The figures show that all transient scenarios predicted yield benefits in eastern continental Europe (non EU) but losses in western Europe. With the equilibrium scenarios very small areas showed yield benefits. This is because of the large warming associated with these scenarios which caused severe shortening of the growing season length. The difference in mean yield in northern EU was just over half that of southern EU under the UKTR6675 scenario and southern EU showed benefits compared with the baseline whereas southern EU showed small yield losses compared with the baseline. This relation did not hold out when water-limited yield was calculated using the Thornthwaite method (Table 6.5.6) highlighting the importance of this variable in the model results.

When Thornthwaite PET was used to calculate water-limited sunflower yields for all scenarios (Table 6.5.7) the GFDL2534 was the only scenario which showed any yield increase, and this was only for the whole European region. The equilibrium models showed severe mean

Table 6.5.6 Mean water-limited sunflower yield (and standard deviation) for four predefined regions of Europe for baseline climate (1961-90) and climate change scenarios (in t/ha). NB: calculated using Penman PET.

Emissions scenario (CO_2 (ppmv))	GCM scenario	Region			
		Europe	E.U.	Northern E.U.	Southern E.U.
Base (353)	Base	1.53 (1.27)	1.36 (1.22)	2.41 (1.09)	0.78 (0.84)
2 x CO_2 (560)	UKHI	0.93 (0.77)	0.98 (0.83)	1.46 (0.77)	0.76 (0.74)
IS92a (454)	UKTR3140	1.37 (1.11)	1.24 (1.05)	1.94 (1.11)	0.86 (0.78)
IS92a (617)	UKTR6675	1.59 (1.22)	1.47 (1.16)	2.15 (1.11)	1.10 (1.01)

Table 6.5.7 Mean water-limited sunflower yield (and standard deviation) for four predefined regions of Europe for baseline climate (1961-90) and climate change scenarios (in t/ha). NB: calculated using Thornthwaite PET.

Emissions scenario (CO_2 (ppmv))	GCM scenario	Region			
		Europe	E.U.	Northern E.U.	Southern E.U.
Base (353)	Base	2.01 (1.23)	2.38 (1.12)	2.63 (1.03)	2.24 (1.15)
2 x CO_2 (560)	UKLO	1.24 (0.96)	1.52 (1.03)	1.57 (0.69)	1.49 (1.18)
2 x CO_2 (560)	UKHI	1.12 (0.84)	1.22 (0.89)	1.59 (0.72)	1.01 (0.91)
IS92a (454)	UKTR3140	1.58 (1.09)	1.62 (1.05)	2.10 (1.02)	1.35 (0.96)
IS92a (617)	UKTR6675	1.86 (1.18)	1.93 (1.17)	2.26 (1.02)	1.74 (1.20)
IS92a (454)	GFDL2534	2.34 (1.31)	2.13 (1.21)	2.46 (1.08)	1.94 (1.24)
IS92a (617)	GFDL5564	1.85 (1.28)	1.56 (1.11)	2.11 (1.08)	1.25 (1.10)
IS92d (545)	UKTR6675	1.57 (1.05)	1.60 (1.03)	1.91 (0.90)	1.43 (1.05)
IS92d (545)	GFDL5564	1.59 (1.13)	1.34 (0.96)	1.78 (0.96)	1.09 (0.87)

yield losses in all specified regions and losses were less severe under the transient scenarios. The first model decade of the UKTR scenarios showed smaller yield losses than the second decade, presumably the losses due to shortening of the growing season were offset more by the increases in RUE in the later decade when CO_2 was higher. This, however, did not occur under the GFDL scenario where the later decade predicted lower yields than the earlier decade. This is because season shortening was much greater under the first decade of UKTR than that of GFDL, whereas the later decade of both transient scenarios showed similar reductions.

6.5.4   Onion

A spatial model of onion phenology and growth has been developed for Europe (EuroOnion) and used to assess the potential impacts of climate change. Simulation modelling of field-grown vegetable crops is not as advanced as that for major cereal or legume crops and, hence, this study focuses on the broadscale prediction of potential (ie. neither water- or nutrient-limited) yields. Furthermore, onion crops are generally irrigated and it is likely that observed yields are comparable to modelled potential yields. EuroOnion is based on the site-specific onion model (PELonion) described in detail in Section 5.3.

6.5.4.1   *Methodology*

PELonion consists of a number of interconnected semi-empirical functions describing development, leaf expansion, light interception, assimilation, dry matter accumulation and respiration, partitioning and conversion of dry matter to fresh weight yields (Section 5.3). Input data for the model are daily minimum and maximum temperature, global radiation, sowing date and latitude. PELonion is written in Visual Basic and as such it was relatively simple to incorporate these key functions for direct use in the EuroOnion model.

Monthly minimum and maximum temperature and global radiation data were available for Europe at a 0.5° latitude/longitude spatial resolution for the period 1961-90. A module was written in Visual Basic to estimate daily

values of minimum and maximum temperature and global radiation from the monthly spatial data based on a sine curve interpolation procedure (Brooks, 1943). A further module to calculate a spatially variable sowing date across Europe was written based on information from the literature and a questionnaire which was mailed to onion growers throughout Europe. Data from the questionnaire suggested that most onions are sown in early spring in northern Europe and late autumn/winter in southern Europe (Friis, pers. comm., 1995). In the current version of the EuroOnion model only sowing dates after 1 January were considered. Autumn sowings will be investigated in future analyses. A minimum temperature for onion growth of 6°C has been reported in the literature (Visser, 1994). Hence, sowing was assumed to take place on the first day of the year (from 1 January) when mean temperatures reach 6°C. Based on this criterion sowing was predicted to occur between January and March in southern Europe and in March/April in northern Europe. In the far north of Europe sowing occurred in early May. These dates were consistent with the data on winter/spring sowing dates from the questionnaire (Friis, per. comm., 1995). Both modules, for estimating daily data and sowing dates, were linked to the appropriate functions from the PELonion site model.

To date, the PELonion model has only been calibrated for a single long season cultivar (Hysam). Hence, all subsequent analyses with the EuroOnion model are based on cv. Hysam.

6.5.4.2   *Baseline results and validation*

Phenological development

Dates of emergence, bulbing and bulb maturity were calculated by the model. Emergence occurred later in the north and east of Europe, but generally occurred within a month of sowing. Bulb formation began just after the longest days around the summer solstice (22 June) over large parts of central and eastern Europe. Bulbing was predicted to occur in early July in northwest Europe and in mid to late June throughout most of northern, eastern and southern Europe. Exceptions were in northern Spain, Turkey, parts of the former Yugoslavia,

Albania and Greece where it occurred from mid to late July. The predicted dates of bulb maturity are shown in Figure 6.5.16. Bulb maturity occurred in early to late September in England, late August/early September throughout the rest of northwest Europe and in northern Europe, early to mid August in southern and eastern Europe and late July in the far south and east of Europe (southern Spain, southern Italy, eastern Greece and the Ukraine). These dates were consistent with those reported in the questionnaire (Friis, pers. comm., 1995). For example, the predicted dates of bulb maturity in Hungary from EuroOnion ranged from 1 to 20 August which corresponded with reported dates of harvest ranging from 1 to 25 August. In Denmark reported harvest dates for long season cultivars are September to October, whilst in the Netherlands harvest occurs in September. These corresponded with simulated maturity dates of 1 to 20 September and 21 August to 20 September, respectively. Further, in eastern England EuroOnion predicted bulb maturity to occur between 1 and 20 September which is consistent with reported dates for late maturing onion varieties in the questionnaire (7 to 14 September).

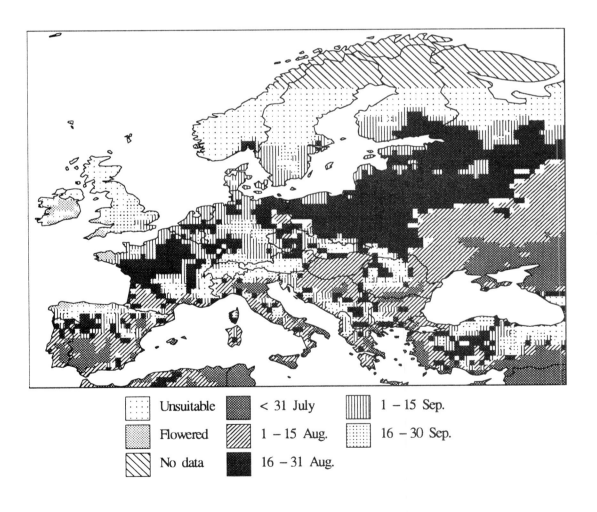

Figure 6.5.16 EuroOnion prediction of date of bulb maturity for present climate (1961-90).

Potential yield

Predicted bulb fresh weights are shown in Figure 6.5.17. Yields were generally greatest in southwest Europe and gradually declined northwards and eastwards, varying from greater than 70 t/ha in Portugal and western France to less than 20 t/ha in southern Finland. Predictions of total dry matter exhibited a similar pattern to bulb fresh weight, varying from 1400 g/m^2 in southwest Europe to less than 300 g/m^2 in northeast Europe.

Validation

The PELonion site model was validated against field trials conducted at Reading, UK (51.45°N) and Årslev, Denmark (55.3°N) in 1994. Details of this validation exercise are reported in Section 5.3. The EuroOnion spatial model was run with monthly meteorological data from the two field trials and the output compared with the field observations and the PELonion model. The EuroOnion model was then run with monthly meteorological data from the 1961-90 spatial

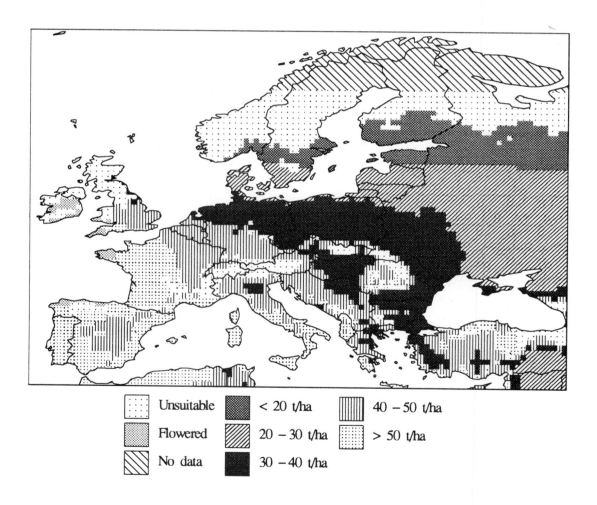

:::: Unsuitable	▓ < 20 t/ha	▦ 40 – 50 t/ha	
▒ Flowered	▨ 20 – 30 t/ha	⋮ > 50 t/ha	
▧ No data	■ 30 – 40 t/ha		

Figure 6.5.17 EuroOnion prediction of bulb fresh weight for present climate (1961-90).

climatic database for the grid squares which contain the sites of Reading and Årslev. Two different sowing dates were used in these runs: the experimental sowing date and the sowing date derived from the climatic criterion described in the previous section. Results from these comparisons are shown in Tables 6.5.8 and 6.5.9.

The performance of the spatial model was tested by comparing the run using the field trial meteorological data against PELonion output and experimental data (column 4 against columns 2 and 3 in Tables 6.5.8 and 6.5.9). The development of the crop at Reading was closely predicted. The date of bulbing was the same as in the experiment and 2 days later than that predicted by the PELonion model, whilst the date of bulb maturity was 11 and 5 days later than the experiment and PELonion model, respectively. The development of the crop at Årslev was predicted less accurately. The date of bulbing was 17 and 1 days earlier than the field observation and PELonion model respectively, whilst bulb maturity was 21 days earlier and 3 days later respectively. The slightly longer growing season predicted at Reading led to a slightly higher prediction of bulb fresh weight by 4.4 t/ha compared with the experiment. Similarly, the shorter growing season predicted for Årslev led to a lower prediction of final yield by 15.3 t/ha and 0.6 t/ha compared to the experiment and PELonion model, respectively.

The differences between model output from the two scales of assessment, site and 0.5° latitude/longitude grid, was determined by comparing the EuroOnion runs using the spatial database (columns 5 and 6 in Tables 6.5.8 and 6.5.9) against the EuroOnion run at each site (column 4 in Tables 6.5.8 and 6.5.9). There are a number of reasons why model output should be expected to vary between the scales: (i) the gridded data represents the average climate over the period 1961-90 whilst both sites refer to the climate in an individual year, 1994; (ii) the gridded data are interpolated from a number of sites of which Reading and Årslev may not be included; and (iii) the altitude of the grid square

and site may be different. The altitude of the Reading site is 46 m compared to a mean grid square altitude of 123 m. This corresponds with slightly lower temperatures in the spatial climatic database compared with the site climatology. These differences resulted in a longer growing season being predicted for the grid square than the site, by 25 days, and a slightly higher yield, by 2.7 t/ha. The altitudes for the Årslev site and the associated grid square are more similar, 48m and 26m respectively. The two climatologies are also very similar, except for maximum temperatures in July where a very high value was recorded at Årslev in 1994, 5.5°C greater than the gridded 1961-90 climate. This explains why a shorter growing season was predicted for the site than the associated grid square, by 18 days, and a marginally lower yield, by 2.4 t/ha.

The behaviour of the EuroOnion model in response to changes in its input parameters was validated against that of the site-based PELonion model (Figures 6.5.18 and 6.5.19). The effect of changes in mean temperature and CO_2 concentration on model output was examined at the two sites (Reading and Årslev) using the 1994 season as the baseline climate. An increase in temperature shortened the time of all developmental stages at both sites with both the EuroOnion and the PELonion model. Model output of EuroOnion was more disparate from that of PELonion at Årslev than Reading. This may be due to inaccuracies which occur when interpolated temperatures are close to base temperatures. At temperatures 2°C cooler than the baseline, the crops at both Reading and Årslev were predicted to flower rather than form harvestable bulbs. Bulb fresh weight progressively decreased with increasing temperature at both sites probably because of the decrease in the length of the growing period. An increase in CO_2 concentration from 355 to 700 ppmv increased bulb fresh weight (Figure 6.5.19). A constant difference was observed between the output from EuroOnion and PELonion, hence, both models responded in an identical fashion to the change in CO_2 and the small difference in yield was due to the effects of interpolating the climatic data.

Table 6.5.8   Site (PELonion) and spatial (EuroOnion) model output and field observations.

Parameter	[1]Field observation	[1]Site model (PELonion)	[1]Spatial model (EURO-ONION)	[2]Spatial model (EURO-ONION)	[3]Spatial model (EURO-ONION)
Emergence (DOY)	[4]n.d.	89	90	104	116
Bulbing (DOY)	185	183	185	191	191
Bulb maturity (DOY)	229	235	240	265	265
Bulb dry weight at bulb maturity (gm^{-2})	702	705	764	802	690
Total dry weight at bulb maturity (gm^{-2})	851	873	938	918	787
Yield; Bulb fresh weight (tha^{-1})	50.3	50.2	54.7	57.4	49.3

[1] a single sowing of onion cv. Hysam at Reading, UK in 1994 on day of the year 62.
[2] a single sowing of onion cv. Hysam for the 1961-90 average climate at the 0.5° latitude/longitude grid which Reading falls within on day of the year 62.
[3] a single sowing of onion cv. Hysam for the 1961-90 average climate at the 0.5° latitude/longitude grid which Reading falls within on day of the year 84 (sowing date determined by a climatic criterion, cf. Section 6.5.4.1).
[4] n.d. indicates not determined.

Table 6.5.9   Site (PELOnion) and spatial (EuroOnion) model output and field observations.

Parameter	[1]Field observation	[1]Site model (PELonion)	[1]Spatial model (EURO-ONION)	[2]Spatial model (EURO-ONION)	[3]Spatial model (EURO-ONION)
Emergence (DOY)	134	133	137	139	134
Bulbing (DOY)	200	184	183	183	181
Bulb maturity (DOY)	258	234	237	255	252
Bulb dry weight at bulb maturity (gm^{-2})	[4]n.d.	331	323	356	384
Total dry weight at bulb maturity (gm^{-2})	n.d.	399	384	402	436
Yield; Bulb fresh weight (tha^{-1})	38.4	23.7	23.1	25.5	27.5

[1] a single sowing of onion cv. Hysam at Årslev, Denmark in 1994 on day of the year 116.
[2] a single sowing of onion cv. Hysam for the 1961-90 average climate at the 0.5° latitude/longitude grid which Årslev falls within on day of the year 116.
[3] a single sowing of onion cv. Hysam for the 1961-90 average climate at the 0.5° latitude/longitude grid which Årslev falls within on day of the year 107 (sowing date determined by a climatic criterion, cf. Section 6.5.4.1).
[4] n.d. indicates not determined.

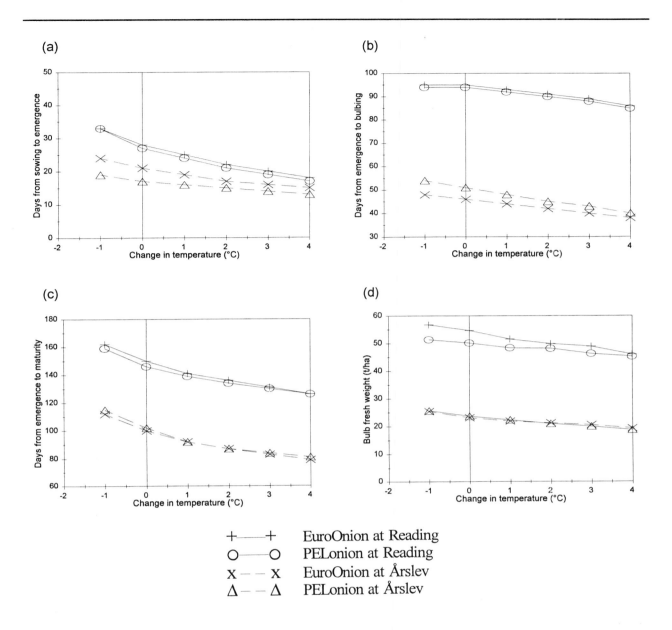

Figure 6.5.18 Sensitivity of EuroOnion and PELonion models to systematic changes in mean temperature at Reading and Årslev of: (a) time from sowing to emergence; (b) time from emergence to bulbing; (c) time from emergence to bulb maturity; and (d) bulb fresh weight at bulb maturity.

To conclude, the validation exercise indicated that the EuroOnion model performed satisfactorily in northern Europe. There was less confidence in the capability of the model in southern Europe due to lack of validation data for this region. Furthermore, it is unlikely that potential yields will be obtained in southern Europe due to water limitations. However, onion crops are generally irrigated and, hence, observed yields may be comparable to modelled potential yields.

6.5.4.3 Model sensitivity to systematic changes in climate

Phenological development

The sensitivity of onion development to incremental increases in temperature was evaluated. As temperatures increase there was a progressive northward and westward expansion in the area of suitability for onions. Only small changes in temperature were necessary for onion production to become viable, in terms of

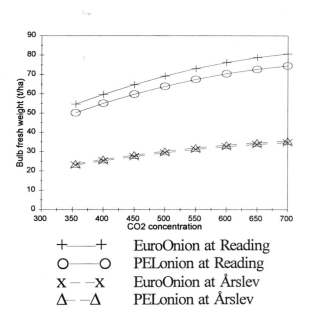

+——+   EuroOnion at Reading
O——O   PELonion at Reading
X– –X   EuroOnion at Årslev
Δ– –Δ   PELonion at Årslev

Figure 6.5.19 Sensitivity of EuroOnion and PELonion models to systematic changes in CO_2 concentration at Reading and Aarslev of bulb fresh weight at bulb maturity.

crop development at least, in currently marginal regions. For example, a 1°C increase in temperature enabled onions to be produced throughout most of Ireland. Flowering occurred less as temperatures increased; with +1°C it only occurred in small areas of western Ireland and western England and with +2°C or greater flowering was not found in most regions of Europe. The duration of development stages progressively decreased with increasing temperature. A temperature rise of 1°C reduced the growing period by 1 to 2 weeks across most of Europe and 2 to 3 weeks in England and southern Scandinavia. Further sensitivity tests indicated that for each 1°C increase in temperature the duration from sowing to bulb maturity decreased by approximately 7 to 10 days. With a 4°C increase the duration was reduced by 3 to 5 weeks in southern Europe, 4 to 6 weeks in central and northern Europe and 5 to 7 weeks in England.

Potential yield

Temperature sensitivity tests from +1 to +4°C were applied to the model of potential onion growth. A 1°C increase in temperature caused potential yield to decrease throughout Europe with the exception of Scandinavia and northern Russia. Decreases ranged from 0 to 6 t/ha for +1°C, 0 to 10 t/ha for +2°C, 0 to 14 t/ha for +3°C and 0 to 20 t/ha for +4°C. There was a north-south pattern to the predicted changes with larger decreases in yield occurring in southern Europe compared with northern Europe.

The sensitivity of potential growth to changes in CO_2 concentration was also examined. For each 100 ppmv increase in CO_2, relative to the present day concentration of 353 ppmv, potential yield increased by 2 to 6 t/ha. With a CO_2 concentration of 700 ppmv, and no change to current climatic conditions, potential yields were predicted to be approximately 20 to 30 t/ha greater in southern and western Europe, 12 to 18 t/ha greater in eastern Europe and 2 to 12 t/ha greater in northern Europe.

6.5.4.4 *Application of climate change scenarios*

Two equilibrium (UKLO, UKHI) and two transient (UKTR, GFDL) GCM scenarios were applied to the EuroOnion model. For each transient GCM two model decades were analysed (UKTR3140, UKTR6675, GFDL2534, GFDL5564). As well as different GCM scenarios, two greenhouse gas emissions scenarios were considered (IS92a, IS92d). The atmospheric concentrations of carbon dioxide used to predict potential yield varied according to the emissions and GCM scenarios. For the equilibrium scenarios a CO_2 concentration of 560 ppmv was assumed. For the IS92a emissions scenarios CO_2 concentrations were: 454 ppmv for UKTR3140 and GFDL2534; and 617 ppmv for UKTR6675 and GFDL5564. For the IS92d emissions scenarios CO_2 concentrations were: 545 ppmv for UKTR6675 and GFDL5564. A description of these climate change scenarios is given in Chapter 2.

Phenological development is not affected by CO_2 concentration and hence, results can be assumed to apply to both emissions scenarios. Results for potential yield are for both the IS92a and IS92d emissions scenarios.

Phenological development

All the climate change scenarios caused faster rates of onion development, which shortened the length of the growing period. The greatest decrease in the duration from sowing to bulb maturity was observed with the equilibrium scenarios as these predicted the largest changes in temperature. The duration reduced by 4 to 8 weeks with the UKLO scenario and 3 to 7 weeks with the UKHI scenario. The pattern of change was similar between the two scenarios with the lowest reductions in growing period length occurring in southeast Europe and the greatest in northwest Europe, in particular England. Both equilibrium scenarios predicted a large expansion in the area of suitability of onions into northern and western Europe.

The transient scenarios predicted smaller reductions in the length of the growing period compared to the equilibrium scenarios (Figure 6.5.20). For both the UKTR3140 and GFDL2534 scenarios the duration from sowing to bulb maturity decreased by 1 to 2 weeks across Europe. This decrease was slightly less in the GFDL2534 scenario compared to the UKTR3140 scenario. The second model decade of the transient scenarios (UKTR6675, GFDL5564) predicted decreases from 1 to 5 weeks across Europe. The two GCMs predicted similar magnitudes of change but slightly different patterns. In the UKTR6675 scenario the lowest decreases occurred in southern Spain and the greatest in northern and northwest Europe. On the other hand, in the GFDL5564 scenario the lowest decreases occurred in the Ukraine, whilst the largest also occurred in northern and northwest Europe.

Potential yield: IS92a emissions scenario

A shorter growing period results in less time to accumulate radiation and, thus, lower bulb fresh weights might be expected. However, increased rates of photosynthesis at elevated concentrations of CO_2 may potentially compensate for such a decrease. In the UKLO scenario the reduction in duration from sowing to bulb maturity was too great to be compensated by the beneficial effects of CO_2 over most of Europe, and decreases in yield of between 0 and 15 t/ha were predicted. The only regions to experience an increase in yield were northwest and northern Europe where increases up to 8 t/ha were predicted. In the UKHI scenario northwest, central and northern Europe showed increases in yield from 0 to 12 t/ha. Decreases in potential yield were indicated for southern and eastern Europe, ranging from 0 to 12 t/ha. The two equilibrium scenarios exhibited similar patterns of change, showing a gradient from yield increases in northwest Europe to decreases in southeast Europe, but the magnitude of change was very different.

The transient scenarios predicted increases in potential yield throughout most of Europe (Figure 6.5.21). In the first model decade increases in yield of 0 to 8 t/ha were predicted for both the UKTR3140 and GFDL2534 scenarios. Both scenarios had a similar pattern, as well as magnitude, of change. Increases in yield were greatest in central Europe and slightly lower in northern and southern Europe. Small decreases in yield were predicted in central Spain, parts of Turkey and the former Yugoslavia in the UKTR3140 scenario and in central Spain, parts of Turkey and southern Russia in the GFDL2534 scenario. In the second model decade the magnitude of yield change was similar for the two GCMs, but the spatial differences were much greater than in the first decade. In the UKTR6675 scenario yields increased by 8 to 16 t/ha in northwest and central Europe and parts of Spain and Italy, by 4 to 8 t/ha in eastern Europe, Scandinavia and Germany and decreased by 0 to 8 t/ha in northeast Spain, Turkey and parts of the former Yugoslavia. In the GFDL5564 scenario yields increased by 12 to 20 t/ha in Italy, by 8 to 12 t/ha in northwest Europe, by 4 to 8 t/ha across most of northern, central and eastern Europe and decreased by 0 to 10 t/ha in northern Spain and parts of Turkey.

Potential yield: IS92d emissions scenario

Lower increases in potential yield were predicted for both GFDL5564 and UKTR6675 with the IS92d emissions scenario compared with IS92a. Many regions were on the margins of change. In general, increases of 0 to 8 t/ha were predicted for northwest, northern and

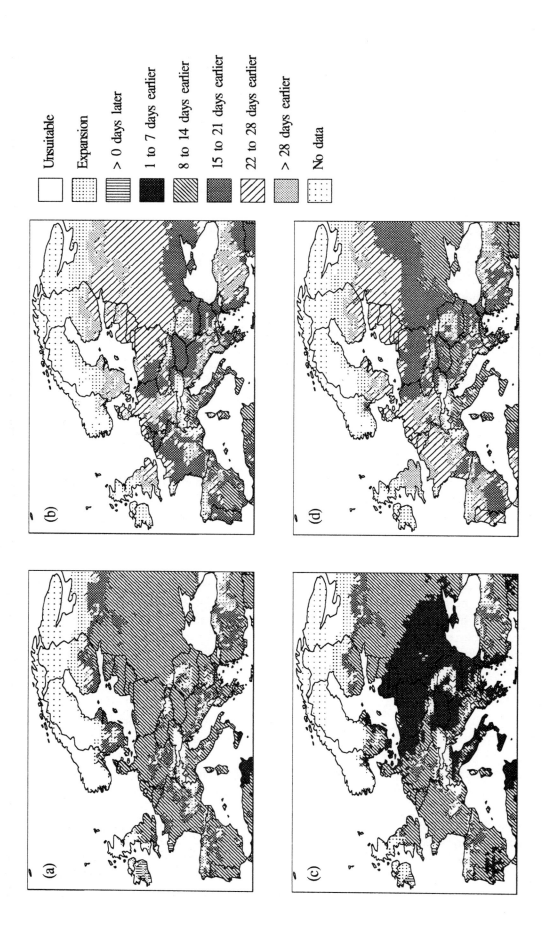

Figure 6.5.20 Change in the duration from sowing to bulb maturity for onion under four transient GCM scenarios: (a) UKTR3140, (b) UKTR6675, (c) GFDL2534, and (d) GFDL5564.

Legend:
- Unsuitable
- Expansion
- > 0 days later
- 1 to 7 days earlier
- 8 to 14 days earlier
- 15 to 21 days earlier
- 22 to 28 days earlier
- > 28 days earlier
- No data

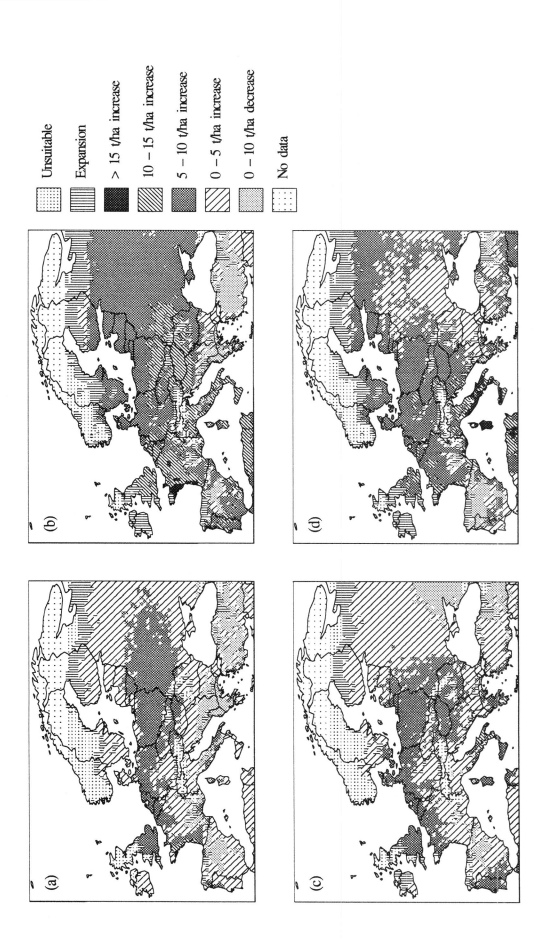

Figure 6.5.21 Change in potential yield for onion for the IS92a emissions scenario with four transient GCM scenarios: (a) UKTR3140, (b) UKTR6675, (c) GFDL2534, and (d) GFDL5564.

central Europe. Decreases of up to 12 t/ha were observed in Spain, southern France and Turkey with both GCMs and in the former Yugoslavia with the UKTR6675 GCM. The lower CO_2 concentrations projected in the IS92d scenario meant that the compensatory effect for the shortening of the growing season was diminished. These predictions are also expected to be realised several decades beyond the estimated dates for the IS92a emissions scenario (with a mean climate sensitivity they would occur in 2099 with the IS92d scenario rather than in 2064 with the IS92a scenario).

6.5.4.5 *Discussion and conclusions*

A site-based model of onion development and growth (PELonion) has been scaled up to analyse the effects of climate change on European onion production. The broadscale model (EuroOnion) was validated against data from two field trials in northern Europe and model output from the original site-based model, PELonion. The EuroOnion model performed satisfactorily in northern Europe, but there was less confidence in its predictions for southern Europe due to lack of validation data for this region.

The EuroOnion model has been applied to the range of climate change scenarios described in Chapter 2. The predicted changes in potential onion yields have been summarised for four European regions, defined below:

Europe: A large European region extending from Scandinavia in the north to north Africa in the south and from Ireland in the west to the Black Sea in the east.

E.U.: The 15 countries of the European Union (Austria, Belgium, Denmark, Finland, France, Germany, Greece, Ireland, Italy, Luxembourg, Netherlands, Portugal, Spain, Sweden, United Kingdom).

Northern E.U.: All European Union regions north of 45°N latitude.

Southern E.U.: All European Union regions south of 45°N latitude.

In general, area average potential yields decreased in the equilibrium scenarios and increased in the transient scenarios (Table 6.5.10). Yield decreases occurred in the equilibrium scenarios as the positive effects of elevated CO_2 concentrations were insufficient to counterbalance negative effects from the

Table 6.5.10 Mean potential onion yields (and standard deviation) for four predefined regions of Europe (in t/ha).

Emissions scenario (CO₂ (ppmv))	GCM scenario	Region			
		Europe	**E.U.**	**Northern E.U.**	**Southern E.U.**
Base (353)	Base	39.4 (15.7)	47.6 (16.7)	37.5 (16.1)	57.5 (10.0)
2 x CO₂ (560)	UKLO	31.2 (15.8)	40.4 (17.0)	35.4 (18.5)	47.4 (11.5)
2 x CO₂ (560)	UKHI	36.6 (17.2)	45.5 (19.2)	38.8 (19.7)	54.6 (14.0)
IS92a (454)	UKTR3140	41.7 (17.4)	49.2 (19.9)	39.2 (19.7)	60.2 (13.0)
IS92a (617)	UKTR6675	45.1 (19.6)	53.2 (22.3)	44.1 (23.0)	65.0 (14.5)
IS92a (454)	GFDL2534	42.6 (18.2)	50.9 (19.9)	40.6 (19.2)	62.9 (12.7)
IS92a (617)	GFDL5564	44.7 (19.7)	52.9 (22.1)	44.0 (22.5)	64.4 (15.3)
IS92d (545)	UKTR6675	41.2 (18.1)	48.7 (20.6)	40.2 (21.1)	59.8 (13.4)
IS92d (545)	GFDL5564	40.9 (18.2)	48.4 (20.5)	40.2 (20.7)	59.2 (14.1)

predicted changes in climate. Decreases in yield were greatest in the UKLO scenario compared to the UKHI scenario. Yields were predicted to decrease by 21% in UKLO and 7% in UKHI for the entire European region. The E.U. experienced relatively smaller decreases in yield than the rest of Europe; in the UKLO scenario the area average yield for the northern and southern E.U. regions decreased by 6% and 18% respectively. The largest increase in potential yield was observed with the UKTR6675 GCM scenario and the IS92a emissions scenario in all regions. In the northern E.U. region yields were predicted to increase by 15% for both the UKTR6675 and GFDL5564 GCM scenarios with the IS92a emissions scenario. With the lower CO_2 concentrations associated with the IS92d emissions scenario this increase was reduced to 7% for both GCM scenarios. Wider differences in the predicted increases in yield were apparent in the earlier model decade of the two transient GCM scenarios for the northern E.U. region. Increases of 4% and 8% were predicted for the UKTR3140 and GFDL2534 scenarios, respectively.

6.5.5 Grassland

6.5.5.1 *Introduction*

Grassland is one of the most important types of agricultural land use in Great Britain and northern Europe representing more than 50% of agricultural land use in 1992 (MAFF, 1992). Grassland usually comprises more than one species and occurs at a wide range of scales and management units (GCTE, 1995). There are thus a number of different grassland types occupying a wide range of habitats, their distribution being determined primarily by temperature and precipitation regimes. The primary controls on plant growth in grassland systems are i) precipitation and ii) nutrient availability, particularly nitrogen (Parton *et al.*, 1994). Grassland types present in the UK include uncultivated grassland (namely the downs, heaths and fens) and cultivated grasslands (both permanent pastures and temporary leys).

This brief review covers aspects of grassland production which need to be considered in modelling the crop at a spatial scale; what methods and scale are presently used to model production and what issues need to be addressed before embarking on site and spatial model development.

6.5.5.2 *Grasslands and climate change*

Grassland is likely to be sensitive to climate change. Its sensitivity to changes in precipitation and temperature suggest that small climatic changes could reduce productive potential and usability of grasslands (Parton *et al.*, 1994). This could in turn have significant implications for livestock and dairy farming. Sensitivity of grassland to changes in precipitation and temperature regimes were evident following the drought in 1995 which reduced grass production on lowland farms. Grass shortages and thus reduced grazing forced many farmers to supplement feed with winter forage. Concerns regarding livestock condition, possible forage shortages and nutritional deficiencies during the winter have been raised (Farmers Weekly, 1995; Davies, 1995). The economic importance of grassland, its sensitivity to changing environmental conditions and the range of possible responses to climate change underlie the value of trying to assess implications of global climate change on grassland productivity and distribution.

6.5.5.3 *Experimental results: grasslands and climate change*

Much experimental work has been conducted on the effects of altered CO_2, temperature and nitrogen regimes on grass productivity and species composition. Hebeisen *et al.* (1994) and Clark *et al.* (1995), for example, investigated the dynamics of a perennial ryegrass and white clover community to changed conditions and revealed that white clover has a competitive advantage over ryegrass when grown under elevated CO_2 concentrations. Hebeisen *et al.* (1994) results revealed, however, that management systems were more important than increased CO_2 in determining the relative responses of each species. Investigations into the competitive reactions between grasses, non-legume dicotyledonous and legume species in a grassland system by Lüscher *et al.* (1994)

supported findings that increased CO_2 concentrations will lead to important changes in the relative composition of grassland communities.

Comparisons of C_3 and C_4 responses to raised CO_2 and increased temperature regimes by Morgan *et al.* (1994) revealed C_3 plants showed a greater increase in CO_2 assimilation than C_4 plants. However, the photosynthetic capacity of the C_3 leaves was reduced in plants grown at higher CO_2 concentrations, but assimilation was 41% greater at higher CO_2 levels.

The ESPACE-GRASS project which has also been funded under the Environment programme of the EC was designed as a programme of coordinated experiments and mathematical modelling (using the Hurley pasture model) at sites across Europe aiming to establish the impacts of climate change on both managed and natural grassland vegetation. Their results indicated that by 2030 grassland production in temperate Europe will be 18% higher than at present owing to temperature increase, and a further 10-15% higher owing to direct CO_2 effects (Jones *et al.*, 1993). Other effects of climate changes observed were in the pattern of seasonal growth and changes in carbon/nitrogen ratios of tissues, shoot/root ratios and canopy transpiration. Their experiments were mainly conducted on a monoculture of perennial ryegrass in open-topped chambers. However, they noted that grass swards in Europe are normally a mixture of grasses and broad-leaved herbaceous species and it might be expected that they would show differential responses to elevated CO_2.

6.5.5.4   *Approaches to modelling*

Grassland systems are difficult to model as they comprise more than one species and occur at a variety of management units (GCTE, 1995). A review of the literature revealed that no models have yet been developed to assess the potential impact of global climate change on managed grassland at a regional scale in Europe. Most modelling efforts to date have considered:

- natural grassland ecosystems in warm temperate areas of America (e.g. Hanson *et*

al., 1985; Hunt *et* al., 1991) and Australia (e.g. GCTE, 1995);
- species-specific models (e.g. Davies *et al*'s perennial ryegrass model);
- site-based models (e.g. Olesen, 1990);
- the effects of increased CO_2 concentration and altered temperature and precipitation regimes on various species under experimental conditions (e.g. Clark *et al.*, 1995; Morgan *et al.*, 1994); and
- generic water-balance based models such as Biopot (CRU, 1992)

Modelling approaches can be categorised as follows:

(i)   Yield models provide information on herbage production. These are generally species specific and site specific and have some use in climate change impact assessment.

(ii) Management models are essentially yield models which allow for changes in management options; they may be used for climate change impact assessment.

(iii) Land use potential models are based on land use (LU) suitability which relate spatial datasets to grassland production. These methods are species non-specific and have wide application.

(iv) Statistical techniques are not species specific and relate LU to environmental factors.

6.5.5.5   *Models available*

Spatial models

Hunt (1991) studied the response of temperate grasslands to climate change using a grassland ecosystem model which simulated seasonal dynamics of shoots, roots, soil water, mycorrhizal fungi, saprophytic microbes, soil fauna, inorganic nitrogen, plant residues and soil organic matter. Forty year simulations were done for several scenarios. The model was driven by observed weather and combinations of increased CO_2, increased temperature and increased/decreased precipitation.

Precipitation and CO_2 changes caused most variation amongst the treatments. A doubling of

CO_2 led to an increased production even with N limitations and increased C storage in plant residues and soil organic matter. Increased temperatures were found to have little net effect on annual primary production as increased production owing to the extended growing season was offset by reduced photosynthesis during summer.

Hunt developed the Grassland Ecosystem Model (GEM) based largely on the PHOENIX and BAHUDE models with the specific objective of predicting seasonal /yearly biomass dynamics of primary producers, and the effects of CO_2 and climate change on these dynamics. This included:

- predicting ecosystem level effects of climate change in shortgrass steppe (in the U.S.);
- identifying the most important component of climate change; and
- interpreting processes and feedbacks responsible for model responses.

Both crested wheatgrass (C_3) and shortgrass steppe (C_4) were modelled. Results showed that precipitation levels, CO2 concentration and species type accounted for 89% of variation in net primary production (NPP): 50% less precipitation resulted in more than 50% loss in NPP (too dry); 50% more precipitation increased NPP by less than 50% as N becomes limiting relative to water. C_3 were generally more productive than C_4 plants, and the ratio of above- to below-ground NPP was greater for C_3 than C_4 - a pattern that increased with rainfall. Variation of precipitation by 50% had a greater effect than doubling of CO2 and a much greater effect than raising temperature by 3^0C.

Brignall and Rounsevell (1994) developed a grassland suitability model based on work by Harrod (1979). This model sought to characterise the spatial variation in grassland potential for large geographical areas expressed as grassland suitability. Six suitability classes were qualitatively defined based on the optimum response of grass production systems found in England and Wales. The model requires information on soils, topography and climate with the controlling influence on

suitability being soil moisture - which may be in deficit (yield class) or excess (poaching/ trafficability risk). It is not species specific. Yield class was estimated from dryness subclass (via the difference between soil available water and potential soil water deficit), climatic zone and length of growing season (ie. when soil temperatures are constantly above 6^oC).

Poaching/trafficability risk was defined as the potential for soil structure to be damaged by trampling or vehicles. This was measured by soil variables, wetness class and climatic factors determining length of fallow period.

The model was run under current and altered climatic conditions. Suitability in the eastern and western U.K. was limited by yield in dry conditions and trafficability in wet conditions. Results showed that very little of England is ill-suited to grassland; south west England, southern Wales, Cheshire, the north west and east coast of England were best suited. Areas currently moderately to well-suited decrease with a 1^oC temperature increase, but increase with both temperature and precipitation increases. With a 2^oC temperature increase, most of England and Wales becomes marginal - too dry (yield decrease) or too wet (trafficability is reduced). A 1^oC temperature increase was offset by a 10% increase in precipitation, but a temperature increase of more than 2^oC had a significant negative effect on grassland suitability.

Davies *et al.* (1994) developed a grassland yield model. Management of grass-based farming is determined by duration of herbage production throughout the year with yield being determined by the timing of fertilizer application, composition of sward and timing of defoliation. This model predicted the growth of perennial ryegrass using temperature and solar radiation. The model estimateed growth by assuming a theoretical maximum growth rate which was modified daily by sub-optimal conditions of temperature, radiation and soil moisture deficit (SMD). Results showed that the best yields came from the wetter west; cooler, wetter areas produced lower yields. Increased temperature lengthened the growing season but limited production in drier areas owing to increased evaporation. The study concurs with Brignall and Rounsevell's findings (1994) that increases in both temperature and precipitation increase production.

Van de Geijn *et al.* (1994) developed a model describing the regrowth of grass after defoliation which was calibrated and validated with a 40 year dataset of 7 varieties of perennial ryegrass. The model described yield well, but not regrowth after drought. Results supported experimental evidence that the affect of CO_2 is heavily influenced by management decisions. Furthermore, rising temperatures were shown to strongly decrease the effect of elevated CO_2. A better description of the carbon economy of grassland systems is required if implications of climate change are to be better understood. Model results from Armstrong and Castle (1995) indicate the impacts of climate change on grass growth is dominated by temperatures

effects. Changes in winter and summer runoff will have important management implications for grass growth. Climate change scenarios applied in their study indicated that the length of the growing season and the total amount of grass available will increase, but farmers' ability to exploit such responses will depend on the development of appropriate management strategies as waterlogging in winter will reduce accessibility for grazing.

Site models

Olesen (1989) worked with two models WATCROS and HEJMDAL (Table 6.5.11) which were validated for ryegrass in Danish summer conditions. Site models have also been run for Mullinger (Ireland) by McWilliams (1991). Results of all model runs are summarised in Table 6.5.12.

Table 6.5.11   Data requirements of WATCROS and HEJMDAL.

Model	Characteristics	Requirements
WATCROS	mechanistic model for simulating water use efficiency and crop production	daily temperature, global solar radiation and precipitation
HEJMDAL	process model for simulating water use and crop production of vegetative crops	hourly temperature, vapour pressure, wind velocity, global radiation, net radiation and precipitation.

Table 6.5.12   Simulated changes in dry matter yield of grassland in a changed climate.

Model	Climatic conditions	Soil	Yield change (%)	Site	Source
WATCROS	3°C temperature incr	Sand	-5	Sterns, Denmark	Olesen (1990)
	3°C temperature incr	Loam	-2		
	30% rainfall incr	Sand	+20		
	30% rainfall incr	Loam	-8		
HEJMDAL	3°C temperature incr		-27	Sterns, Denmark	Olesen (1990)
	30% rainfall incr		+32		
	CO_2 incr. (325 ppmv)		+54		
Hurley pasture model	2°C temperature incr		-6		Thornley *et al.* (1991)
	CO_2 incr. (250 ppmv)		+65		
Johnstown Castle Model	1°C temperature incr		+12	Mullinger, Ireland	McWilliams (1991)
	3°C temperature incr & 30% rainfall incr		+38		

Source: Proceedings of the 14th General Meeting of the EGF, Finland, 1994.

The disparate model results and their differing sensitivity to climatic change scenarios highlights the need for further model development.

6.5.5.6 *Factors for consideration in modelling grasslands*

In order to assess the impacts of climate change on grassland on a large spatial scale an approach is needed that is robust, cross-cutting and integrative across a spectrum of agroecosystems and not only for one system (GCTE, 1995). To predict the effects of global change on pasture systems the effects of climate change (in particular temperature, CO_2 and precipitation changes) on a range of pasture species vegetative growth and composition, soil processes and animal developments need to be understood (GCTE, 1995). The differential responses of different species to CO_2 may change their competitive ability and therefore influence the percentage of individual species in pasture swards. The influence of such changes will be crucial in determining the optimum management regime for pastures under future conditions. Changes in the seasonal growth of pasture species due to elevated CO_2 will also need to be considered in relation to the management of cutting regimes. It is necessary to decide whether cultivated grassland should be modelled alone or natural grassland ecosystems should be included also. Long term feedbacks on soil structure, soil fertility and nutrient recycling must also be considered.

6.5.6 Overall discussion and conclusions

Europe-wide models of crop productivity have been developed for wheat, sunflower and onion and used to assess the potential impacts of climate change. A literature and modelling-based review of climate-grassland interactions has been conducted to assess the feasibility of developing a Europe-wide grassland model in future analyses.

Sufficient climatic data were available to model water-limited yield for all crops. However, the available climatology was at a monthly resolution and, thus, models were limited to either functioning at this temporal scale or developing methods for interpolating data to a daily resolution. Errors associated with downscaling temperature and radiation data were small and the phenological models and potential yield models were run at a daily time step. However, errors associated with interpolating precipitation data were large and, hence, the water-limited yield models were run at a monthly time interval.

The main limitation to model development was the availability of adequate agronomic data at the regional scale for model parameterisation and validation. Wheat is a well studied crop and, as such, there is a relatively plentiful supply of experimental and observed statistics for different regions of Europe. This allowed models of phenology, potential yield and water-limited yield to be developed for a range of European cultivars. The models were thoroughly validated by comparison with output from detailed site-based models and with observed and experimental data reported in the literature and from agricultural experimental stations. Sunflower is not as well studied as wheat and less experimental data is available for the European region. Sufficient agronomic data were available to develop models of phenology, potential yield and water-limited yield for a single cultivar. However, model validation was limited to comparison with country level observed statistics, sporadic trials data and expert opinion. Simulation modelling of field-grown vegetable crops is not as advanced as for cereals and oilcrops and very few experiments have been conducted in Europe. Only sufficient agronomic data were available to develop models of phenology and potential yield for a single cultivar and validation was limited to comparison with output from a site-based model and with field trials at two northern European sites. Grassland is a complex cropping system often comprising more than one species with diverse management practices. Hence, to date, analyses have been limited to a survey of available knowledge to identify the key considerations, and feasibility, of broadscale modelling.

The sensitivity of crop productivity to climate change has been examined using a range of climate change scenarios (Table 6.5.13). Water-limited yield for wheat increased in all scenarios. The largest increases occurred for the last model decade of the transient GCMs assuming the IS92a emissions scenario. Conversely, water-limited yield for sunflower decreased in most scenarios. The largest decreases occurred in the equilibrium scenarios and the lowest decreases were generally found for the last model decade of the transient GCMs assuming the IS92a emissions scenario. Onion potential yields decreased in the equilibrium scenarios and increased in the transient scenarios. Again, the largest increases occurred in the last model decade of the transient GCMs assuming the IS92a emissions scenario. All crops predictions of both water-limited and potential yield were worse for the IS92d scenario, compared with IS92a.

These differences in yield can be explained by a number of interacting factors. Firstly, higher temperatures cause increased developmental rates and, hence, shorter growing period length. A shorter grain filling (wheat), seed filling (sunflower) or bulb growth (onion) period results in less time to accumulate dry matter and, thus, lower yields. On the other hand,

elevated concentrations of atmospheric CO_2 cause increased assimilation rates and, hence, higher potential yields, counteracting the negative effects of a shorter growing period. Furthermore, in water-limited situations the interaction between increased PET, either increased or decreased precipitation (depending on the scenario) and improved water use efficiency from elevated CO_2 further complicates the simulated change in yield. In the case of wheat, relatively small decreases were predicted in the length of the growing period and the beneficial effects from CO_2 were large, compared to sunflower and onion. This resulted in moderate to strong increases in yield for all climate change scenarios. Alternatively, the length of the growing period for sunflower was reduced dramatically and the direct effects of CO_2 were less than for wheat. This resulted in strong decreases in yield for most scenarios. The onion simulations were intermediate between wheat and sunflower. The CO_2 concentration was not sufficient to counterbalance the large decreases in growing period length predicted in the equilibrium scenarios, but it was sufficient in all transient scenarios where the relative increase in developmental rates is lower.

Table 6.5.13 Relative changes in water-limited yield for wheat and sunflower and potential yield for onion across Europe for all climate change scenarios. + / − refers to 0 to 5% yield increase/decrease; ++ / − − refers to 5 to 20% yield increase/decrease; +++ / − − − refers to greater than 20% yield increase/decrease.

Emissions scenario (CO$_2$ (ppmv))	GCM scenarios	Winter wheat		Sunflower		Onion
		[1]Thw. PET	[2]Pen. PET	Thw. PET	Pen. PET	-
2xCO$_2$ (560)	UKLO	++	[3]n.d.	− − −	n.d.	− − −
2xCO$_2$ (560)	UKHI	++	+	− − −	− − −	− −
IS92a (454)	UKTR3140	++	++	− − −	− −	++
IS92a (617)	UKTR6675	+++	+++	− −	+	++
IS92a (454)	GFDL2534	++	n.d.	++	n.d.	++
IS92a (617)	GFDL5564	+++	n.d.	− −	n.d.	++
IS92d (545)	UKTR6675	++	++	− − −	n.d.	+
IS92d (545)	GFDL5564	++	n.d.	− − −	n.d.	+

[1] Thw. indicates yield calculated using Thornthwaite PET.
[2] Pen. indicates yield calculated using Penman PET.
[3] n.d. indicates not determined

It was not possible to use the Penman method to compute PET for all scenarios. Where possible a comparison between the predicted changes in water-limited yields calculated using Penman and Thornthwaite PET was undertaken (Table 6.5.13). In general, across Europe predicted changes in yield were slightly lower using Penman PET compared to Thornthwaite PET. Analysing the spatial pattern showed that similar changes were derived for northwest Europe. However, in southern and eastern Europe the Penman method tended to indicate substantially worse changes in yield due to higher PET values.

Acknowledgement

The authors are grateful to John Orr for producing the figures in this section. Thanks are also due to Paul Prignall for his contribution to Section 6.5.5.

References

Angus, J.F., Cunningham, R.B., Moncur, M.W. and MacKenzie, D.H. (1981). Phasic development in field crops. I. Thermal response in the seedling phase. *Field Crops Research*, **3**, 365-378.

Armstrong, A.C. and Castle, D.A. (1995). Potential effects of climate change on agricultural production and the hydrology of drained grassland in the UK. In: McGregor, D.F.M. and Thompson, D.A. (Eds.). *Geomorphology and land management in a changing environment.* Wiley, Chichester. 139-151.

Bignon, J. (1990). *Agrometeorology and the physiology of maize.* Publication: EUR 13041 EN. Office for Official Publications of the EC, Series: An Agricultural Information System for the EC. Luxembourg.

Bindi, M., Maracchi, G. and Miglietta, F. (1993). Effects of climate change on the ontomorphogenetic development of winter wheat in Italy. In: Kenny, G.J, Harrison, P.A. and Parry, M.L. (Eds.) *The effect of climate change on agricultural and horticultural potential in Europe.* Research Report 2, Environmental Change Unit, University of Oxford, 67-92.

Brignall, A.P. and Rounsevell, M.D.A. (1994). *The effects of future climate change on crop potential and soil tillage opportunities in England and Wales.* Environmental Change Unit Research Report No. 4. Environmental Change Unit, Oxford.

Brooks, C.E.P. (1943). Interpolation tables for daily values of meteorological elements. *Quarterly Journal of the Royal Meteorological Society*, **69**, 160-162.

Bunting, A.H., Dennett, M.D., Elston, J. and Speed, C.B. (1982). Climate and crop distribution. In: Blaxter, K. and Fowder, L. (Eds.) *Food, nutrition and climate.* Applied Science Publishers, London. 43-74.

Carter, T.R. and Saarikko, R.A. (in press). Estimating regional crop potential in Finland under a changing climate. *Agricultural and Forest Meteorology.*

Carter, T.R., Parry, M.L. and Porter, J.R. (1991a). Climatic change and future agroclimatic potential in Europe. *International Journal of Climatology*, **11**, 251-269.

Carter, T.R., Porter, J.R. and Parry, M.L. (1991b). Climatic warming and crop potential in Europe: Prospects and uncertainties. *Global Environmental Change*, **1**, 291-312.

CETIOM (1989). *La culture du Tournesol.* Centre technique Interprofessionel des Oleagineux Metropolitans, Paris.

Chapman, S.C., Hammer, G.L. and Holger, M. (1993). A sunflower simulation model: I. Model development. *Agronomy Journal*, **85**, 725-735.

Cook, S.K. (1993). An evaluation of the growth and yield of sunflower varieties. Annals of Applied Biology 122 (Supplement). *Test of Agrochemicals and Cultivars*, **14**, 180-181.

Cook, S.k. (1993). An evaluation of the growth and yield of sunflower varieties. Annals of Applied Biology 122 (Supplement). *Test of Agrochemicals and Cultivars*, **14**, 180-181.

Clark, H., Newton, P.C.D., Bell, C.C. and Glasgow, E.M. (1995). The influence of elevated CO_2 and simulated seasonal changes in temperature on tissue turnover in pasture turves dominated by perennial ryegrass (*Lolium perenne)* and white clover (*Trifolium repens)*. *Journal of Applied Ecology,* **32,** 128-136.

CRU (Climatic Research Unit) and ERL (Environmental Resources Limited). (1992). *Development of a framework for the evaluation of policy options to deal with the greenhouse effect. A scientific description of the ESCAPE model: Version 1.1.* Climatic Research Unit, University of East Anglia, Norwich, 93-101.

Dale, R.F., Coelho, D.T. and Gallo, K.P. (1980). Prediction of daily green leaf area index for corn. *Agronomy Journal*, **72**, 999-1005.

Davies, A., Shao, J., Bardgett, R.D., Brignall, A.P., Parry, M. L. and Pollock, C.J. (1994). *Specification of Climatic Sensitivity for UK Farming Systems.* IGER and Environmental Change Unit.

Davies, R. (1995). Now grass keep men warn of a fodder famine. *Farmers Weekly,* 15 - 21 September, 41.

Delécolle, R., Maas, S.J., Guérif, M., Baret, F. (1992). Remote sensing and crop production models: present trends. *ISPRS Journal of Photogrammetry and. Remote Sensing,* **47,** 145-161.

Doyle, A.D. (1975). Influence of temperature and daylength on phenology of sunflowers in the field. *Australian Journal of Experimental Agriculture and Animal Husbandry*, **15**, 88-92.

Elena-Rosselló, R., Tella-Ferreiro, G., Allué-Andrade, J.L. and Sanchez-Palomares, O. (1990). Clasificación Biogeoclimática Territorial de España: Definición de Eco-regiones. *Ecología*, Fuera de Serie N. **1**, 59-79.

EUROSTAT (1992). *Regio regional databank.* Statistical Office of the European Communities, Luxembourg.

FAO (1986). *Early agrometeorology crop yield assessment,* Plant Production and Protection Paper 73, Food and Agricultural Organisation of the United Nations, Rome, 150pp.

FAO Production Yearbook (1975-1990). Food and Agricultural Organisation of the United Nations, Rome.

Farmers Weekly (1995). *Welsh away-wintering hit by grass shortage.* 8 - 14 September.

Font-Tullot, I. (1983). *Climatología de España.* Instituto Nacional de Meteorología. MOPT. España.

Global Change and Terrestrial Ecosystems (1995*). Global Change Impats on Pastures and Rangelands. Implementation Plan.* GCTE Report No. 3. GCTE, Canberra.

Godwin, D., Ritchie, J., Singh, U. and Hunt, L. (1990). *A Users Guide to CERES Wheat, version 2.10.* International Fertilizer Development Center. Muscle Shoals. Alabama. 94 pp.

Goudriaan, J. and Unsworth, M.H. (1990). Implications of increasing carbon dioxide and climate change for agricultural productivity and water resources. In: Kimball, B.A., N.J Rosenberg, L.H. Allen Jr. (Eds.) *Impact of Carbon Dioxide, Trace Gases, and Climate Change on Global Agriculture.* American Society of Agronomy Special Publication Number 53. American Society of Agronomy, Inc. pp. 71-82.

Goudriaan, J. and Unsworth, M.H. (1990). Implications of increasing carbon dioxide and climate change for agricultural productivity and water resources. In: Kimball, B.A., N.J Rosenberg, L.H. Allen Jr. (Eds.) *Impact of carbon dioxide, trace gases and climate change on global agriculture.* ASA Special publication no. 53, Crop Science Society of America and Soil Science Society of America, Madison, USA, 111-130.

Groenendijk, H. (1989). *Estimation of the water-holding capacity of soils in Europe. The compilation of a soil dataset*, Simulation Report CABO-TT 19, Department of Theoretical Production Ecology, Agricultural University, Wageningen.

Guérif, M., Delécolle, R., Gu, X.F., Guinot, J.P., Jappiot, M., Steinmetz, S. (1988). Estimation de la biomasse et du rendement de cultures de blé dur à partir d'indices de végétation SPOT. *4th. Int. Coll. on Spectral Signatures of Objects in Remote Sensing, Aussois, France*, ESA.

Hanson, J.D., Parton, W.J. and Innis, G.S. (1985). Plant Growth and Production of Grassland Ecosystems: A Comparison of Modelling Approaches. *Ecological Modelling*, **29**, 131-144.

Harrison, P.A. and Butterfield, R.E. (1994). Europe-wide crop modelling. In: Harrison, P.A., Butterfield, R.E. and Downing, T.E. (Eds.) *Climate change and agriculture in Europe: Assessment of impacts and adaptation*. Annual report to the European Commission, Contract number: EV5V-CT93-0294, 146-161.

Harrod, T.R. (1979). *Soil suitability for grassland*. In: Jarvis, M.G. and Mackney, D. (Eds.). Soil survey applications. Soil Survey Technical Monograph No. **13**, 51-69.

Hebeisen, T., Lüscher, A., Blum, H. and Nösberger, J. (1994). Response of biomass and species composition to CO_2 and management in a model system of *Lolium perenne/Trifolium repens*. In: Blum, H. (Ed.) *Effect of atmospoheric CO_2-increase on carbon fluxes in grassland ecosystems*. Report of the meeting of COST ACTION 619, Lindau, 25-27 October 1994.

Henttonen, H. (1991). Kriging in interpolating July mean temperatures and precipitation sums. *Reports from the Department of Statistics*, **12/1991**, University of Jyväskylä, Finland, 41 pp.

Hulme, M., Jiang, T., Turney, C. and Barrow, E. (1993). A 1961-90 baseline climatology and future climate change scenarios for Great Briatain and Europe. Part II: 1961-90 European baseline climatology. A report accompanying the datasets prepared for the "Landscape dynamics and climate change" TIGER IV consortium, Climatic Research Unit, University of East Anglia, 49pp.

Hunt, H.W., Trilca, M.J., Redente, E.F., Moore, J.C., Detling, J.K., Kittel, T.G.F., Walter, D.E., Fowler, M.C., Klein, D.A. and Elliott, E.T. (1991). Simulation model for the effects of climate change on temperate grassland ecosystems. *Ecological modelling*, **53**, 205-246.

Iglesias, A. and Mínguez, M.I. (in press). Perspectives for maize production in Spain under climate change. In: L. Harper, S. Hollinger, J. Jones and C. Rosenzweig. (Eds.) *Climate Change and Agriculture*. ASA Special Publication No. American Society of Agronomy. Madison, WI.

Imerson, A., Dumont, H. and Sekliziotis, S. (1987). Impact analysis of climatic change in the mediterranean region. Volume F: *European Workshop on Interrelated Bioclimatic and Land Use Changes*. Noordwijkerhout, The Netherlands, October 1987.

IPCC (1992). *Climate Change 1992: the supplementary report to the IPCC Impacts Assessment*. Tegart, W.J. McG., Sheldan, G.W. and Griffiths, D.C. (Eds). Report prepared for the IPCC Working Group II, Australian Government Publishing Service, Canbera, Australia.

IPCC. (1990). *Climate Change. The IPCC Impacts Assessment*. Tegart, W.J. McG., Sheldon, G.W. and Griffiths, D.C. (Eds.) Intergovernmental Panel on Climate Change, World Meteorological Organisation and United Nations Environmental Program. Bracknell.

Jamieson, P.D. (1989). Modelling the interaction of wheat production and the weather. In: Johnson, R.W.M. (Ed.) *Integrated systems analysis and climate impacts*. Proceedings of a workshop on systems analysis, Wellington, November 1989. Rural Policy Unit, MAF-Technology, Wellington, 133-140.

Jamieson, P.D. and Wilson, D.R. (1988). Agronomic uses of a model of wheat growth, development and water use. *Proceedings of the Agronomy Society of New Zealand*, **18**, 7-10.

Jones, C.A. and Kiniry, J.R. (Eds.). (1986). *CERES-Maize: A simulation model of maize growth and development*. Texas A&M University Press. College Station, TX. 194 pp.

Jones, M. B., Ashenden, T., Parsons, A.J., Payer, H., Raschi, A. and Thornley, J.H.M. (1993). *The effects of rising CO_2 and changing climate on grassland communities in Europe*. In: I.Troen (Ed). Global Change: Climate change and climate change impacts, Proceedings of the symposium held in Copenhagen, Denmark, 6-10 September 1993. EC, Brussels, 247-258.

Kenny, G.J. and Harrison, P.A. (1992a). The effects of climate variability and change on grape suitability in Europe. *Journal of Wine Research*, **3(3)**, 163-183.

Kenny, G.J. and Harrison, P.A. (1992b). Thermal and moisture limits of grain maize in Europe: Model testing and sensitivity to climate change. *Climate Research*, **2,** 113-129.

Kiniry, J.R., Blanchet, R., Williams, J.R., Texier, V., Jones, C.A. and Cabelguenne, M., 1992. Sunflower simulation using the EPIC and ALMANAC models. *Field Crops Research*, **30,** 403-423.

Körner, C. (1990). CO_2 fertilization: The great uncertainty in future vegetation development. In: A. Salomon and D. Reidel. *Global Vegetation Change*. Hingham.

Kramer, P.J. (1983). *Water Relations of Plants*. Academic press, Orlando.

Le Houerou, H.N. (1990). Global change: Vegetation, ecosystems and land use in the Mediterranean basin by the mid twenty-first century. *Israel Journal of Botany,* **39,** 481-508.

López-Bellido, L. (1991). *Cultivos Herbaceos, Vol. I: Cereales*. Mundi-Prensa, Madrid.

Lüscher, A., Blum, H. and Nösberger, J. (1994). *Interspecific and intraspecific variability in the response of grassland species to CO_2 enrichment*. In: Blum, H. (Ed.) *Effect of atmospheric CO_2-increase on carbon fluxes in grassland ecosystems*. Report of the meeting of COST ACTION 619, Lindau, 25-27 October 1994.

MAFF (1992). *Digest of agricultural census statistics United Kingdom 1992.* HMSO, London.

MAPA. (1993). *Manual de Estadística Agraria*. Secretaría General Técnica. Servicio de Publicaciones del Ministerio de Agricultura, Pesca y Alimentación de España. Madrid, Spain.

McWilliams, B.E. (1991). (Ed.) *Climate change: studies on the implications for Ireland*. Environment Action Programme, Department of the Environment, Ireland.

Mearns, L.O., Rosenzweig, C. and Goldberg, R. (in press). The effect of changes in interannual variability on CERES-Wheat yields: Sensitivity and $2xCO_2$ GCM studies. *Journal of Agricultural and Forest Meteorology*.

Merrien, A. (1986). Cahier technique physiologie tournesol. CETIOM, Paris, 46pp.

Mínguez, M.I. and Iglesias, A. (in press). Perspectives of future crop water requirements in Spain: the case of maize as a reference crop. In: A. Angelakis (Ed). *Diachronic Climatic Changes: Impacts on Water Resources*. Springer-Verlag, New York.

Mitchell, R.A.C. and Lawlor, D.W. (1993). The effect of increased temperature and CO_2 concentration on winter wheat: Test of model prediction. *Journal of Experimental Botany*, **44** (Supplement), 15.

MOPTMA (Ministerio de Obras Públicas, Transportes y Medio Ambiente). (1993a). *Plan Hidrológico Nacional. Memoria.* Ministerio de Obras Publicas y Transportes. Secretaria de Estado para las Políticas del Agua y el Medio Ambiente. Madrid.

MOPTMA (Ministerio de Obras Públicas, Transportes y Medio Ambiente). (1993b). *Anteproyecto de Ley del Plan Hidrológico Nacional.* Ministerio de Obras Publicas y Transportes. Secretaria de Estado para las Políticas del Agua y el Medio Ambiente. Madrid.

Morgan, J.A., Hunt, H.W., Monz, C.A. and Lecain, D.R. (1994). Consequences of growth at two carbon dioxide concentrations and two temperatures for leaf gas exchange in *Pascopyrum smithii* (C_3) and *Bouteloua gracilis* (C_4). *Plant, Cell and Environment,* **17,** 1023-1033.

Mukula, J. and Rantanen, O. (1989). Climatic risks to the yield and quality of field crops in Finland IV. Winter wheat 1969-1986. *Annaes Agriculturae Fenniae,* **28,** 13-19.

Narciso, G., Ragni, P. and Venturi, A. (1992). *Agrometeorological aspects of crops in Italy, Spain and Greece: A summary review of common and durum wheat, barley, maize, rice, sugarbeet, sunflower, soybean, rape, potato, tobacco, cotton, olive and grape crops.* Publication EUR 14124 of the Office for Official Publications of the European Communities, Luxembourg, 438 pp.

Nonhebel, S. (1993). The effects of changes in temperature and CO_2 concentration on spring wheat yields in The Netherlands. *Climatic Change,* **24,** 311-329.

Olesen, J.E. (1990). Evaluating the effect of climatic change on productivity of agricultural crops in Denmark. In: Goudriaan, J., ven Keulen, H. and van Laar, H.H. (Eds.). *The greenhouse effect and primary productivity in European agro-ecosystems.* Pudoc, Wageningen.

Olesen, J.E. (1989). Development in Environmental Modelling 15. In: Fenhan, J. *et al.* (Ed.) *RisR International conference on environmental Models; Emissions and consequences.* RisR International Laboratory, Denmark, 22-25 May, 1989.

Parry, M.L., Carter, T.R. and Konijn, N.T. (1988). *The Impact of Climatic Variations on Agriculture. Vol 1 Assessments in Cool Temperate and Cold Regions. Vol 2 Assessments in semi-arid regions.* Kluwer, Dordecht.

Parton. W.J., Ojima, D.S. and Schimel, D.S. (1994). Environmental change in grasslands: Assessment using models. *Climatic Change* **28,** 111-141.

Penman, H.L. (1948). Natural evaporation from open water, bare soil, and grass. *Proceedings of the Royal Society, London A.,* **193,** 120-146.

Racsko, P., Szeidl, L. and Semenov, M. (1991). A serial approach to local stochastic weather models. *Ecological Modelling* **57,** 27-41.

Rawson, H.M. and Hindmarsh, J.H. (1982). Effects of temperature on leaf expansion in sunflower. *Australian Journal of Plant Physiology,* **9,** 209-219.

Reinink, K., Jorritsma, I. and Darwinkel, A. (1986). Adaptation of the AFRC wheat phenology model for Dutch conditions. *Netherlands Journal of Agricultural Science,* **34,** 1-13.

Richardson, C.W. and Nicks, A.D. (1990). Weather generator description. In: Sharpley, A.N. and Williams, J.R. (Eds.) *EPIC - Erosion/productivity impact calculator: 1.Model documentation,* U.S. Department of Agriculture, 93-103.

Richardson, C.W. and Wright, D.A. (1984). *WGEN: A Model for Generating Daily Weather Variables.* ARS-8. U.S. Department of Agriculture, Agricultural Research Service. Washington, DC. 83 pp.

Rosenzweig, C. and Iglesias, A. (Eds). (1994). *Implications of Climate Change for International Agriculture: Crop Modelling Study*. U.S. Environmental Protection Agency. Washington DC.

Rosenzweig, C. and Parry, M.L. (1994). Potential impact of climate change on world food supply. *Nature*, **367**, 133-138.

Rouse, J.W., Haas, R.H., Schell, J.A., Deering, D.W., Harlan, J.C. (1974). Monitoring the vernal advancement and retrogradation of natural vegetation. Greenbelt, MD, NASA/GFC Report Type III 371pp.

Russell, G. and Wilson, G.W. (1994). *An agro-pedo-climatological knowledge-base of wheat in Europe.* Publication EUR 15789 EN of the Office for Official Publications of the European Communities; Series 'Agriculture', Luxembourg, 158 pp.

Saarikko, R.A., Carter, T.R. and Kleemola, J. (1993). Determining temperature and photoperiod effects on the phenological development of spring cereals under northern conditions, in D. Wilson, H. Thomas and K. Pithan (Eds). *Cold Adaptation to Cool, Wet Climates*, COST Workshop, Aberystwyth, UK, 23-24 March 1993, 167-174.

Santer, B. (1985). The use of general circulation models in climate impact analysis: A preliminary study of the impacts of a CO_2-induced climatic change on western European agriculture. *Climatic Change*, **7**, 71-93.

Seiler G.J. (1992). Introduction. Sunflower Edition. *Field Crops Research*, **30**, 191-194.

Semenov, M.A., Porter, J.R. and Delecolle, R. (1993). Simulation of the effects of climate change on growth and development of wheat in the UK and France. In: Kenny, G.J, Harrison, P.A. and Parry, M.L. (Eds.) *The effect of climate change on agricultural and horticultural potential in Europe*. Research report 2, Environmental Change Unit, University of Oxford, 121-136.

Solantie, R. (1987). Hallojan loppuminen keväällä ja alkaminen syksyllä (Last spring frosts and first autumn frosts in Finland). *Meteorological Publications No. 6*, Finnish Meteorological Institute, Helsinki, 60 pp. (in Finnish, with English summary).

Thornley, J.H.M., Fowler, D. and Cannell, M.G.R. (1991). Terrestrial carbon storage resulting from CO_2 and nitrogen fertilization in temperate grasslands. *Plant, Cell and Environment*, **14**(9), 1007-1011.

Thornthwaite, C.W. and Mather, J.R. (1955). The water balance. *Climatology*, **8**, 1-104.

van de Geijn, S., Schapendonk, Ad., Ammerlaan, I., Dijkstra, P., de Visser, R., Pot, S. and Gorissen, T. (1994). Grassland productivity under climate change: Combined experimental and modelling efforts. In: Blum, H. (Ed.) *Effect of atmospheric CO_2-increase on carbon fluxes in grassland ecosystems.* Report of the meeting of COST ACTION 619, Lindau, 25-27 October 1994.

Verhoef, W. (1984). Light scattering by leaf layers with application to canopy reflectance modeling: the SAIL model. *Remote Sensing of Environment*, **16**, 125-141.

Visser, C.L.M. de (1994). ALCEPAS, an onion growth model based on SUCROS87. I. Development of the model. *Journal of Horticultural Science*, **69 (3)**, 501-518

Watts, W.R. (1974). Leaf Extension in *Zea mays*. III. Field measurements of leaf extension in response to temperature and leaf water potential. *Journal of Exerimental Botany*, **25**, 1085-1096.

Weir, A.H., Bragg, P.L., Porter, J.R. and Rayner, J.H. (1984). A winter wheat crop simulation model without water or nutrient limitations. *Journal of Agricultural Science*, **102**, 371-382.

Wolf, J. (1993). *Effects of climate change on the wheat production potential in the E.C.* Department of Theoretical Production Ecology, Wageningen Agricultural University, 64.

Wolf, J., Semenov, M.A., Eckersten, H., Evans, L., Iglesias, A. and Porter, J.R. (1995). Wheat: A comparison of five mechanistic crop models. In: Harrison, P.A., Butterfield, R.E. and Downing, T.E. (Eds.) *Climate change and agriculture in Europe: Assessment of impacts and adaptation*, Final Report to the Commission of the European Communities.

Wolfe, D.W. and Erickson, J.D. (1993). Carbon dioxide effects on plants: Uncertainties and implications for modelling crop response to climate change. In: Kaiser, H.M. and Drennen, T.E. (Eds.) *Agricultural dimensions of global climate change*. St. Lucie Press, Florida, 153-178.

CHAPTER 7

Integration of crop model results:
Study recommendations for
policy and further research

7.1   Objectives and achievements

The project undertook four objectives. For each objective, major achievements have been accomplished:

The first objective was to compile a database of relevant environmental data and state-of-the-art climate scenarios. The present database incorporates site (daily) and spatial (monthly) climate data, an evaluation of different methods of calculating potential evapotranspiration, two coupled ocean-atmosphere transient GCM scenarios, two equilibrium GCM scenarios, agricultural statistics interpolated to the spatial grid, soils data, topographic data, and administrative boundaries and features. A weather generator was used to produce scenarios at the daily temporal scale. This integration of geographically referenced data will facilitate future work on resource sensitivity to climatic variations in Europe.

The second objective was to assess the impact of climate change on crop development, growth, yield and yield quality through controlled experiments and simulation models. Twelve crops were studied at different scales using a variety of methods. Experiments were conducted for seven crops; site models were developed and applied for seven crops; country level spatial models were constructed for two crops; and pan-European spatial models were implemented for three crops. The research process has resulted in guidelines for agricultural impact assessment on: site-based model development, intercomparison and validation; methodologies for scaling up to the regional scale; techniques for analysing impacts of climatic variability and extreme events; site and broadscale sensitivity testing; and site and broadscale scenario evaluation. Methods and results for model intercomparison of five winter wheat models at two sites are a major contribution to the IGBP.

The third objective was to evaluate appropriate farm-level adaptive responses and prospects for sustainability. At both the site and broadscale, changes in sowing date and cultivar were tested. In addition, the site-based models simulated changes in fertilizer and irrigation requirements.

The fourth objective was to develop a geographical information system (GIS) for climate change impact assessment that integrates the project components and spans spatial and temporal scales. Relevant experimental, site and broadscale results have been incorporated into one platform. The interface and results have been reviewed by the specialists in the project consortium.

This chapter describes the use of the GIS to integrate across scales, beginning with a review of the rationale for, and various approaches to, integration. Methods implemented in the project are described. Finally, the conclusion summarises the major results and their implications for European research and policy on climate change.

7.2   Rationale for site and regional scale integration

Different scales of assessment have been used to investigate different aspects of the crop-environment system. Site-based mechanistic crop models were used to analyse detailed physiological responses of crops to changes in climate at individual sites located in different agricultural and climatic zones throughout Europe (Chapter 5). Broadscale models were used to analyse bioclimatic shifts in crop suitability and productivity. These were applied at the regional and national scale at resolutions varying from individual fields to 10 x 10 km grids (Sections 6.2 to 6.4), and at the continental scale at a resolution of 0.5° latitude/longitude (Section 6.5).

Site-based mechanistic models allow the complex interactions between weather, crop growth and management gained from experimental programmes to be untangled enhancing understanding of the underlying principles of mechanisms of crop development, growth and yield formation. However, assessments of global climate change require large scale crop models for at least four reasons:

(i)   Spatial variability: Detailed site-based models provide no information on the spatial variability of crop responses, for example, due to soil variations, topography and climate.

(ii) Interactions over space: In some cases, flows of information need to be modelled across spatial units. The most obvious for crops are water, nutrients and wind (including advection of humidity). For agricultural systems and land use, spatial dependence on infrastructure and markets are important.

(iii) Regional policy: Climate change policy is dependent on the scale of decision making. Site models can provide information for specific fields or typical fields in a local area. However, at the regional level, policy concerns may include changes in the aggregate supply, spatial shifts in crop productivity, identification of sensitive areas, and comparative advantages between crops and regions.

(iv) Data and computational requirements: At present spatial data bases to run site models are not available. This is partly due to the volume of data required. However, many of the variables required are discrete and cannot readily be interpolated over space from existing primary data. For example, correlation of daily rainfall between two sites is extremely sensitive to distance, topography, oceanicity and synoptic conditions. The requirements for local calibration of site models are further constraints. However, large scale models are temporally constrained because available interpolated climate data is generally at a monthly resolution and lacks time series for some necessary variables.

Hence, a full understanding of the possible responses of the crop-environment system to climate change can only be gained through the consideration of crop-climate interactions at both the site and broad scale. Integration of these scales attempts to overcome the limitations of the different modelling approaches to understand the full range of crop responses for the European region.

Most approaches to combining different scales are limited to either using sites representative of the study region, and ignoring spatial patterns, or defining homogenous areas within which model sites are located. Wolf and van Diepen (1991) used a series of representative sites within the Rhine Basin to look at the impacts of climate change on agriculture. The benefits of this method are that detailed modelling techniques can be applied to the sites. The disadvantages are that little information on the spatial patterns of change can be determined. Papajorgji *et al.* (1994) defined zones which were homogenous in terms of climate and soils, and using this detail mapped crop model outputs at the regional level. For this method to be successful, the defined zones have to be small and homogenous. In an alternative approach, Easterling *et al.* (1993) used information on agricultural suitability within a region to scale up site-based results.

These approaches are subject to several constraints. Regions are seldom homogeneous across all of the relevant variables. For example, the climate spaces defined for Europe (reported below) show that unique combinations represent quite small areas and similar climates may not be the geographically proximate cells. In addition, future climate-soil spatial relationships may not be the same as the present interactions, for example, if climatic warming caused a reduction in frost hazard. If representative sites are chosen, spatial patterns within regions are lost, and the choice of sites becomes very important.

The concept of embedding site-based models within a broad-scale modelling environment is new and provides substantial benefits. The broadscale modelling allows spatial patterns of change to be analysed, whilst the site scale modelling provides information on detailed crop responses over time. The broadscale approach is limited by the assumption that the climate is homogenous over 0.5° latitude/longitude cells. Application of a higher resolution dataset would improve this to the detriment of model performance. The important assessments which can be made are in terms of relative changes in performance for larger regions and countries.

Integrating results from a wide range of models requires novel techniques. A geographic information system (GIS) enabled the development of techniques for integration based on the geographical location of results. This chapter presents two methods which have been developed using a GIS to bring together results from the site-based and broadscale crop models. The first required construction of an interface for direct comparison of crop model output between sites and the associated 0.5° latitude/longitude cells. The second method aimed to identify areas with similar climatic characteristics in the European climate dataset in order to allow comparison of a range of cell-based results with the associated sites. Selected examples from the comparison are presented for wheat and onion.

7.3   Methods for site and regional scale integration

A single analytical system was required to integrate the wealth of site-based and Europe-wide crop model results produced in this research project. The ARC/INFO GIS (on an RS6000 with the AIX operating system) was chosen for its ability to handle a range of spatially referenced datasets, including point-based and cell-based data. As well as providing the capability to compare crop model output across scales, the GIS was used to aid the inter-comparison of five site-based models for wheat. Programs have been generated to import and export data from the GIS. Visual tools have been developed to display model results. The system for comparing different site-based models is described in Section 7.3.1, whilst two methods for comparing results across scales are discussed in Section 7.3.2.

In the following discussion the term *cell* refers to individual 0.5° latitude/longitude units and *broadscale* refers to results from the Europe-wide models run on data at this resolution.

7.3.1   Comparison of site-based models

The site-based assessment for wheat involved five different models. The GIS was used to support this comparison by ensuring results were presented in consistent formats. The wheat

models have been run for a range of scenarios to analyse the direct and indirect effects of climate change and climatic variability.

A demonstration tool was developed in ARC/INFO to display results from all the site-based wheat models in comparable formats. The following crop model output was imported to the GIS: date of anthesis, date of maturity, total dry matter and grain yield. The site-based data were held as relational geo-referenced database files. The basic function of the system was to present graphs of model results over a 30-year period, enabling comparison of model performance between models and under different climates. The main menu for the comparison is shown in Figure 7.1. Two types of graph can be drawn, time series or cumulative probability functions. The menu allows the user the flexibility to choose the type of graph, the model, the crop variable (eg. potential or water limited yield), the site and the climate change scenario (with or without variability for UKHI and UKTR6675) for presentation. Several selections can be chosen for presentation on the same graph. For example, the user may wish to display water-limited yield at Rothamsted for all five models for the baseline climate. Alternatively, the user may display water-limited yield at Rothamsted for only one model for the complete range of climate change scenarios. In addition to the graphs, a summary statistics window is provided for each selection which presents the mean and standard deviation of the time series for the four crop variables.

7.3.2   Comparison of site-based and regional models

Two methods have been developed to compare results from the site-based and continental scale crop models. The first method involved construction of an interface for direct comparison of crop model output between sites and the associated 0.5° cells (Section 7.3.2.1).

The second method identified areas with similar climatic characteristics in the European climate dataset to allow comparison of a range of cell-based results with the associated sites (Section 7.3.2.2).

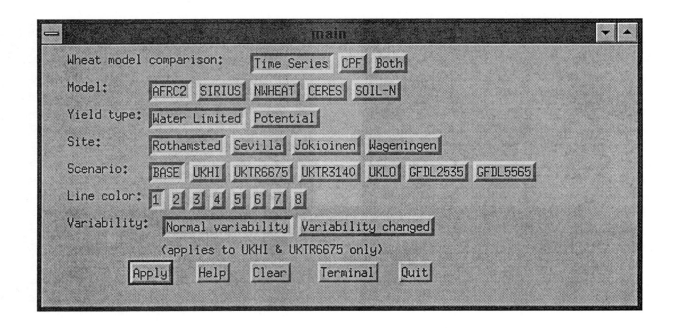

Figure 7.1   Menu for presenting site-based wheat model results.

7.3.2.1 *Direct comparison*

A menu based system has been developed to enable comparison of site-based and broadscale model predictions. The interface provides the ability to view the results from site-based models and relate them to the equivalent broadscale model results for a range of individual crops. The system presents the broadscale results as maps and allows the user to graph selected site-based results on the same display screen. The user has the ability to cross-reference the site within a broadscale context, allowing comparison of results from different scales at the same geographic location. The system also provides the flexibility to allow further development of programs required for the analysis and presentation of results at the regional and national scale. This will allow models at a hierarchy of scales to be compared and the inherent links between them quantified.

The system is described for two illustrative crops: wheat and onion.

Wheat

The wheat demonstration system has been developed to show results from five site-based models (AFRCWHEAT, CERES-Wheat, NWHEAT, SIRIUS and SOILN; see Section 5.7) and one broadscale model (EuroWheat; see Section 6.5).

All models estimate dates (as day of year) for a number of development stages, including emergence, floral initiation, double ridges, terminal spikelet, anthesis, beginning of grain filling, end of grain filling and physiological maturity. The models also predict yield and biomass for potential and water-limited production. The site-based models produce output based on 30 year daily time series climate data for selected sites, whilst EuroWheat produces output based on the average 1961-90 European climate dataset.

EuroWheat results are displayed as maps of a selected development stage, potential yield or water-limited yield and site-based results are displayed as frequency distributions or cumulative probability functions of the day of year of a development stage or yield. The system links the site-based results to the broadscale results through their relative geographic position. In this respect, it presents the corresponding cell-based broadscale result on the frequency distribution of results for each site.

The benefit of the system is the integration of data derived from different temporal and spatial scales. EuroWheat provides broadscale assessments, for example, timing of winter wheat development stages across Europe. It cannot provide information on temporal variation, for example, the expected range of dates over a number of years at a cell location. The site based models provide such information and by linking the two model output datasets by geographical position, it is possible to present both broadscale patterns of spatial variability together with an indication of temporal variability.

Onions

The onion demonstration system uses the same techniques as the wheat demonstration system and shows results from one site-based model (PELonion; see Section 5.3) and one broadscale model (EuroOnion; see Section 6.5).

Both onion models estimate dates (as day of year) for a number of development stages, including seedling emergence, bulbing and bulb maturity. The models also predict total dry matter and bulb fresh weight for potential production. PELonion produces output based on 30 year daily time series climate data for selected sites, whilst EuroOnion produces output based on the average 1961-90 European climate dataset.

7.3.2.2 *Defining areas with similar climates*

In the 'direct comparison' approach only a single cell-based value is available from the broadscale model for comparison with a range of values from the site model. Furthermore, the site climatology may not be representative of the climate at the scale of the cell as this represents an interpolated average climate. A method has been developed to allow comparison of a range of cell-based results based on the identification of cells within the European climatology with similar climatic characteristics to the sites. This study is a preliminary one, aimed at assessing the feasibility of the

approach for the European region. As a first step, it was limited to determining the best method for classifying similar cells and deriving their distribution for the selected sites. In future analyses the method will be applied to the broadscale crop model output.

The method involved locating cells in the 0.5° latitude/longitude European climate dataset which have similar climatic characteristics to the eleven sites at which the site-based crop models were applied (see Chapter 5; Figure 5.1.1). This method of linking site and broadscale results through their shared use of climatic data allows the following techniques to be explored:

- potential extrapolation of site-based model results to a wider area based on a less detailed climate;
- grouping broadscale model results from cells sharing similar climatic characteristics to allow frequency analysis of the model results; and
- association of site-based model results in terms of climate to examine any similarities or differences in response to temporal variations of climate.

Just as the geographical proximity of two sites (distance or angle at the earth's surface) may be determined by their relative positions in geographic space, defined by their latitude and longitude coordinates, so the climatic proximity of two sites can be determined by using climatic variables as coordinates in 'climate space'. For example if a series of sites or cells are plotted on a graph based on their temperature and precipitation characteristics, those which are close to each other in the distribution have similar values for these variables, and their similarity can be expressed in terms of the distance between them. This concept is not new; climate space has been used successfully in ecological modelling for determining the potential distribution of plant species in Europe (Huntley *et al.*, 1989) and for analysing the impacts of climate change in Scotland (Aspinall and Matthews, 1994). However, climate space has previously been determined by examining the spatial distribution of a variable (e.g., presence/absence of a plant species), whilst the approach proposed in this study is to determine the distance in climate space from a single site. This requires a different methodology.

In order to define the climatic similarity of points it is necessary to calculate the distance between them in climate space. In the case shown in Figure 7.2, the geographical proximity of two points, A and B, is evaluated as the Euclidean distance (i.e., $AB = (AC^2 + BC^2)^2$, where C is a point sharing X coordinates with A and Y coordinates with B), and the resultant distance AB is in the same units as the original distances AC and BC. However, in the case of climate space variables do not all have the same units (e.g., AC in mm and BC in °C), so distance cannot be calculated by combining the

variables in this way. To overcome this, distance was calculated using the percentage difference between values rather than the absolute difference. Temperature was converted to Kelvin for this analysis.

By transforming each variable into a range from 0 to 100, meaningful comparison could be made about the differences. Thus, if the range in value of a variable across the European climatology was 0 to 50 units, the percentage difference between points of values 30 and 40 units would be 20%. For example, in Figure 7.2 if AC is 5% of the total range of the X variable and BC is 2% of the range of the Y variable the resultant 'distance' is $(5^2 + 2^2)^2$ or 5.385. This is not an 'average percentage' but an indication of the distance on the graph in percentage terms. When this distance is calculated from a site (or 'seed cell') to all of the other cells in the European climate dataset, using all of the necessary variables, a selection of 'similar' cells can be made.

There is no known range of values which are similar or may occur at a site, hence an arbitrary limit was chosen. For example, if a limit of 5% is chosen (using two variables) the cells within a distance of $(5^2 + 5^2)^2 = 7.07$ of the site will be selected, (shown by the dashed circle in Figure 7.3). This radius selects sites or cells which have values for both variables less than 5% different from the seed cell, those which have values for

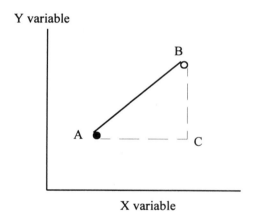

Figure 7.2   Method   for   calculation   of distance between points.

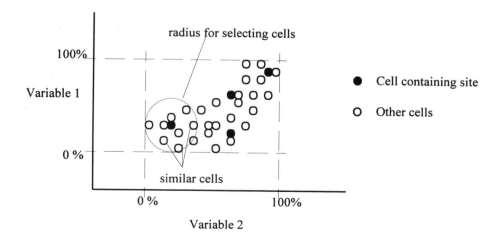

Figure 7.3   Method for selection of cells with similar values to the seed cell.

both variables of exactly 5% and those which have 0% difference for one variable and a difference of 7.07% for the other.

Initially, two variables were used to define similarity: growing degree days (> 10°C); and precipitation minus potential evapotranspiration (P-PET) for June, July and August. These variables were chosen because annual averages and totals of climatic variables are not significant in terms of agricultural crops nor take account of important seasonal differences between regions. The variables were calculated for all 5209 cells in the European climatology and the distance from a seed cell (containing the site of Oxford) to each of the other cells was calculated. The selection radius was taken as ±5% for both variables and the values within this radius chosen (Figure 7.4). The cells selected in climate space were then mapped in geographical space, showing the locations of cells which are climatically similar to Oxford (Figure 7.5). This method showed similar areas occurring in Denmark, southern Sweden and the Baltic Republics.

In this example only two variables were used to describe similarities in climate, which enables the climate space to be plotted on a graph. However, as any two variables may not fully capture the factors which are important for crop growth, two improvements were investigated:

- the incorporation of additional agroclimatic indices which can be related to crop performance; and
- the results of a principal components analysis.

Agroclimatic indices

Four agroclimatic indices were chosen for assessment:

- potential maximum moisture deficit;
- annual growing degree days above 5°C;
- mean temperature of the warmest month; and
- mean temperature of the coldest month.

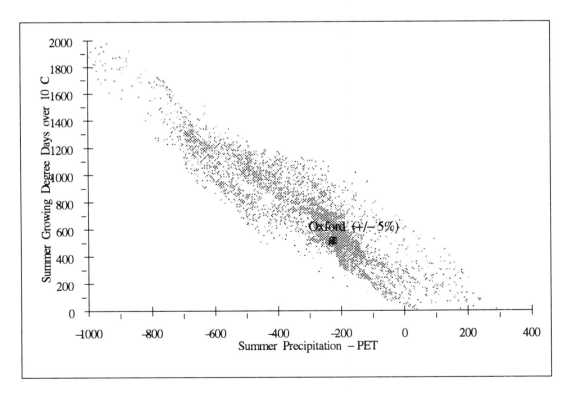

Figure 7.4   The distribution of cells in the 1961-90 European climatology according to summer growing degree days (>10°C) and summer precipitation minus potential evapotranspiration defined climate space. The cells similar to Oxford are darker.

Potential maximum moisture deficit is defined as the maximum accumulated value of P-PET, accumulated for all months when P-PET is negative. An additional variable, oceanicity, was incorporated. Oceanicity was calculated as the difference between January and December temperature divided by the difference between January and December radiation (Driscoll and Fong, 1992). Although oceanicity is not an obvious agroclimatic variable, such an index provides critical extra information on the variation in climate throughout Europe.

The method for calculating the distance between each of the cells in terms of more than two variables is the same as that used for two variables. The percentage difference between the seed cell (or site) and the other cells for all of the variables is calculated, and the differences combined to a single value which is the square root of the sum of the squares. There is no rigorous method for selecting a radius to indicate an appropriate extent of similarity.

Hence, several search radii were examined: limits of 5, 10 and 30% of the values for the seed cell. Because these radii left many cells unselected, all were compared with a dataset where each cell in the European climate dataset was assigned to the nearest seed cell.

Principal components analysis

The principal components analysis (PCA) results were conducted on the 1961-90 European climate dataset by the Institute of Terrestrial Ecology, UK (Bunce, 1994, pers. comm.) in collaboration with the Environmental Change Unit with the aim of defining a climatic land classification of Europe. The purpose of the method is to summarise the variability contained in a multi-dimensional dataset by attempting to describe most of the variability with a lesser number of variables. Conceptually this is done by redrawing orthogonal axes through the space formed by the scatter of the plot of all the variables.

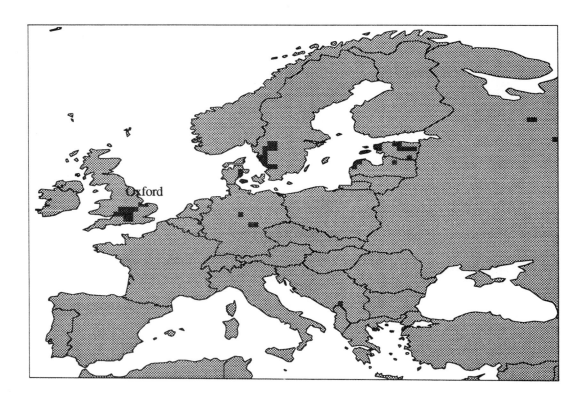

Figure 7.5   The geographical distribution of cells in the 1961-90 European climatology which are similar to Oxford in terms of summer growing degree days (>10°C) and summer precipitation minus potential evapotranspiration defined climate space.

For example, in a two dimensional dataset (Figure 7.6) the method would take as the first principal axis a line through the longest axis of the plot, and the PCA score of the points can be given as a single value, giving its distance along this new axis. These scores could perhaps, if the variables are well correlated, describe over 95% of the variability in the dataset in a single value rather than the two values of the two original axes. The amount of variability contained in the new axis is given in terms of an eigen value. The second principal axis is the longest line orthogonal to the first principal axis which can be drawn through the data and the centre of the point scatter. Points are also given a score for this axis. If the first axis described 95% of the variability then in a two dimensional dataset the scores on the second would describe the remaining 5% of the variability within the data. This would be reflected in a much lower eigen value. The method also outputs the rank correlation coefficient of the original variable's axis with each of the new principal axes. This describes how similar the original axis is to each of the derived principal axes.

There were three stages to the analysis carried out, with the number of variables being reduced at each stage to find those containing the most variability.

Firstly, PCAs were carried out on each of the individual climate variables (except mean temperature) using the 12 monthly values as parameters (a total of 96 variables). On the basis of the PCA output for these parameters the months which describe most of the variability contained within each climate variable were chosen (Table 7.1; columns 2 and 7). These months were selected for each climate variable in the following way. Firstly, the principal component axes containing the most variability were selected (i.e., those having an eigen value greater than 1.0 in column 1), e.g., for frost days components 1 and 2. The monthly variables which had the maximum and minimum eigen vector values for these components (columns 2 and 5) were then selected. This means that the months selected are at opposite ends of the axis in question.

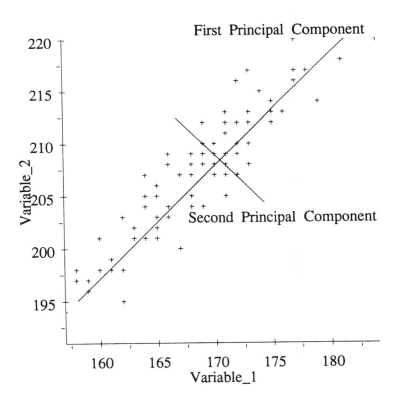

Figure 7.6   Example PCA of two variables, showing principal component axes.

Table 7.1   Results of initial PCA of climate variables (Bunce, 1994, pers. comm.).

Column	1	2	3	4	5	6	7
	Eigen Value	Max. Eigen Vector	Eigen Vector Value	Rank Corr. Coeff.	Min. Eigen Vector	Eigen Vector Value	Rank Corr. Coeff.
Frost Days							
Component 1	8.44	Dec	0.295	0.856	Jul	0.160	0.463
Component 2	2.24	Aug	0.402	0.602	Jan	-0.359	-0.538
Precipitation							
Component 1	7.72	Nov	0.340	0.944	Jul	0.138	0.383
Component 2	2.92	Jul	0.518	0.886	Feb	-0.271	-0.463
Rain Days							
Component 1	9.232	Nov	0.310	0.943	May	0.245	0.743
Component 2	1.245	Apr	0.446	0.497	Sep	-0.375	-0.418
Sun							
Component 1	10.054	Mar	0.306	0.970	Jun	0.240	0.762
Component 2	1.320	Jun	0.551	0.632	Dec	-0.294	-0.337
Temp. Min.							
Component 1	10.844	Sep	0.300	0.987	Jun	0.273	0.897
Temp. Max.							
Component 1	10.548	Oct	0.306	0.993	Jun	0.278	0.882
Component 2	1.264	Jun	0.407	0.458	Jan	-0.393	-0.442
Vap. Press.							
Component 1	10.716	Oct	0.302	0.990	Jul	0.266	0.869
Component 2	1.050	Jul	0.462	0.473	Jan	-0.381	-0.390
Wind Speed							
Component 1	10.941	Sep	0.294	0.972	Jul	0.273	0.901

Secondly, the 28 variables selected from stage 1 (e.g., December, August, July and January frost days in Table 7.1) were included in another PCA, and the most significant variables were selected in the same way. These were found to be:

- frostdays in July;
- wind speed in July;
- raindays in May;
- minimum temperature in September;
- frostdays in April;
- precipitation in November; and
- sunshine duration in June.

Thirdly, these seven variables plus minimum, mean and maximum altitude for each cell were included in a final PCA. The first four principal axes were found to have eigen values greater than 1.0 (Table 7.2).

Table 7.2   Eigen values of the four final principal components.

Principal component	Eigen value
1	12.638
2	3.636
3	2.238
4	1.427

The spatial variation of the first principal component is shown in Figure 7.7. It appears to contain the influence of altitude and latitude. Each of the cells in the European climatology has a value for its position on each of these four axes, which is held in ARC/INFO. These values were used as variables to define similarity.

Results

For each of the two sets of variables (agroclimatic and PCA scores) the method described in Section 7.2.2.2 was applied to give values related to the distance between each of the 5209 cells in the European climatology and the eleven sites chosen to act as seed cells. Here, the results are given for Oxford alone as an example of the analysis. Figure 7.8 and Figure 7.9 show the relationship between Oxford and all the other cells for agroclimatic variables and PCA scores respectively. The shading shows the calculated distance, lighter shading being equivalent to smaller distance or a greater degree of similarity. It can be seen that the patterns on both maps do show some relationship in their pattern, in defining similar areas in southern England, and dissimilar areas in Turkey and north Africa. However the PCA shows a greater number of areas in mainland Europe which may be climatically similar to Oxford and also appears to be more sensitive to the effect of altitude, with the Alps being darker. This may be a result of the inclusion of three altitude variables in the final stage of the derivation of the PCA scores.

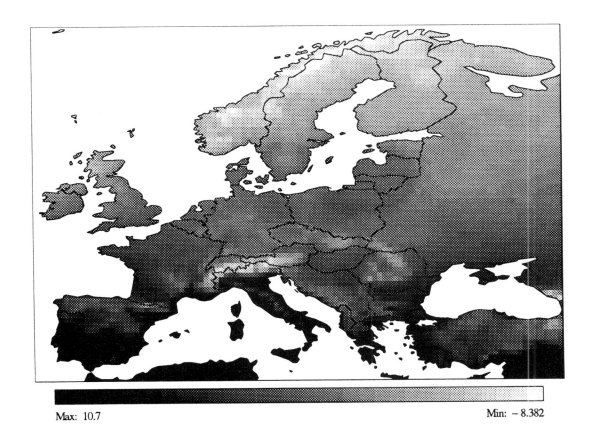

Max: 10.7   Min: − 8.382

Figure 7.7   Map showing the spatial variation of the first principal component.

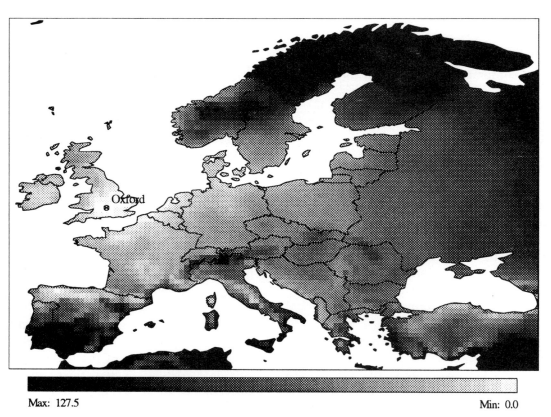

Max: 127.5   Min: 0.0

Figure 7.8   Cumulative distance from Oxford in agroclimatic variable climate space. There is no data above 65.5° N.

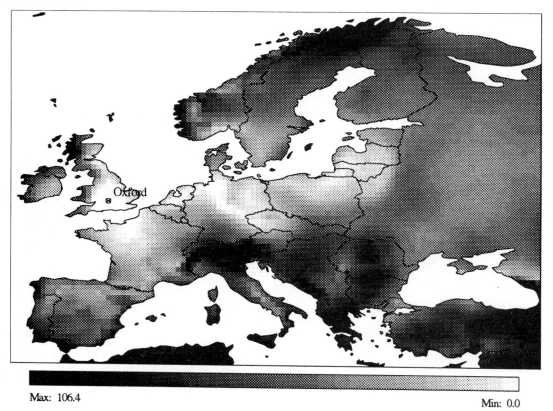

Max: 106.4   Min: 0.0

Figure 7.9   Cumulative distance from Oxford in PCA (4 variable) climate space.

The information in these maps may be reduced to more clearly show the areas which are similar to Oxford. Figure 7.10 and Figure 7.11 show the points selected using 5%, 10% and 30% search radii. These maps exclude any points which are closer to another of the 10 sites for which the analysis was performed (the sites used for site-based modelling). This also shows that the areas defined by agroclimatic indices tend to be confined to the British Isles, whereas the PCA defined areas spread into central Europe even at the low (5%) level, and show greater variation in the British Isles. It should be noted that neither of the sets of variables show areas in Denmark and the Baltic coast to be similar to Oxford at these levels in contrast with the results from the areas defined by the initial use of only two variables (Figure 7.5).

It is difficult to define which of the variables are having the greatest effect in the patterns shown, especially for the areas selected by the PCA scores, as these are an abstract combination of variables which are not necessarily related to those important for crop growth. However, for the areas defined by agroclimate it appears that oceanicity may be eliminating possible similarities in mainland Europe, which may not be realistic. Both methods could be weighted to an unrealistic extent by the use of redundant or unnecessary variables, or ones which are not well correlated with crop responses to climatic variations. The PCA and agroclimatic methods require further study to evaluate their sensitivity to the choice of the input variables.

There are advantages and disadvantages to the use of both methods. The PCA scores are derived in a way which captures the variability of the European climatology and independently chooses the significant variables. However, this method does not allow the use of expert knowledge to define the variables chosen. This makes the interpretation of the final results difficult. The choice of agroclimatic variables allows more simple interpretation of the results as the inputs are known, but makes the omission of an important variable in the climate space more likely, as well as the possible weighting in favour of certain types of variables, for example those based on temperature. The ideal approach

may well be to perform a PCA on a set of well-defined agroclimatic variables.

The choice of a search radii is arbitrary at present. Further analysis may provide a better indication of suitable values as it is clear that this determines what areas are marked 'similar' to the seed cell. Choice of limits could be made more complex by scaling the search radii to meet the range of the indicator variables found in the time series climate for the site. For current purposes, the selection of the nearest 20 cells is sufficient.

7.4 Results from site and regional scale integration

7.4.1 Comparison of site-based models

7.4.1.1 *Baseline climate*

An illustration of the site-based wheat model comparison for the baseline climate is shown in Figure 7.12. This shows time series graphs for date of sowing, date of anthesis, date of maturity, water-limited total dry matter and water-limited grain yield for two crop models applied at the site of Sevilla.

For most years the dates of anthesis and maturity are similar for the AFRCWHEAT and NWHEAT models. This is because both models use very similar approaches for simulating phenological development. The NWHEAT model predicted higher grain yield and total dry matter than AFRCWHEAT (by 1.5 and 3.2 t/ha, on average, respectively). The inter-annual variation in yield was larger in the NWHEAT model that in AFRCWHEAT, due to a higher sensitivity to water-limitation in NWHEAT. A similar result, but with a greater difference, is apparent for grain yield. For example, the standard deviation of grain yield was over three times greater in the NWHEAT model run compared with the AFRCWHEAT model run. The larger standard deviation in NWHEAT is explained by a relatively larger reduction in dry matter production and harvest index due to water shortage. A full discussion of the wheat model comparison for baseline climate is given in Section 5.7.4.

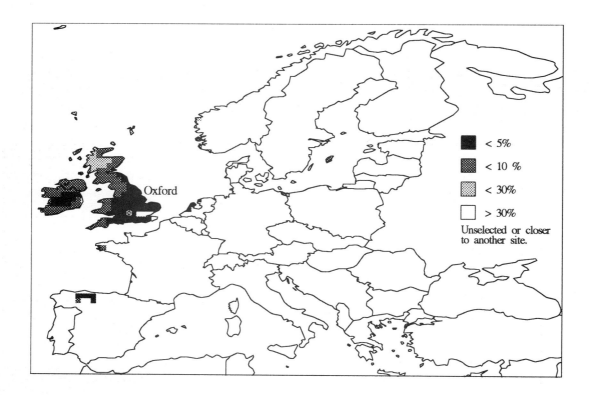

Figure 7.10   Areas within 5%, 10% and 30% limits of Oxford in agroclimatic variable climate space. There is no data above 65.5°N.

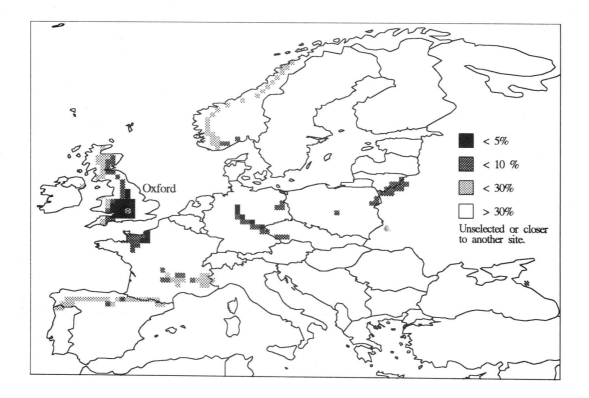

Figure 7.11   Areas within 5%, 10% and 30% limits of Oxford in PCA (4 variable) climate space.

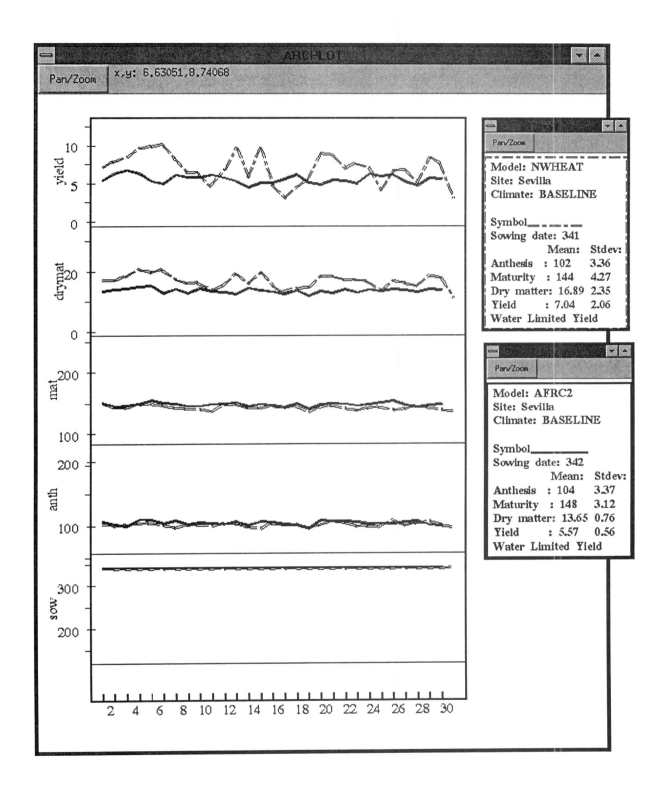

Figure 7.12   Example output from the site model comparison demonstration system: Time series graphs for water-limited wheat production under the baseline climate (1961-90) at Sevilla.

7.4.1.2 *Climate change scenarios*

An illustration of the site-based wheat model comparison for the climate change scenarios is shown in Figure 7.13. This shows cumulative probability functions (CPFs) for date of anthesis, date of maturity, water-limited total dry matter and water-limited grain yield for three crop models applied at Sevilla under the UKTR6675 scenario (with variability).

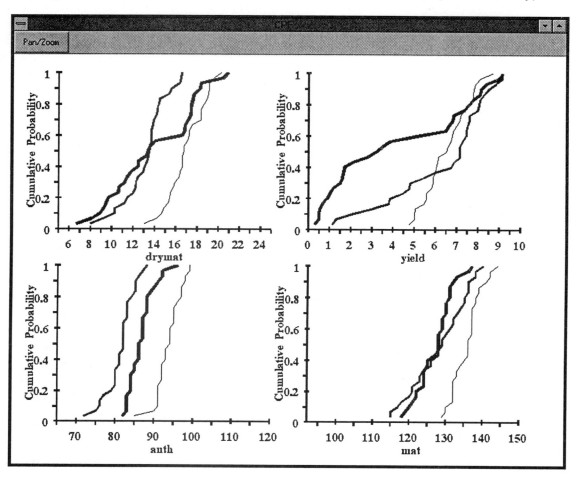

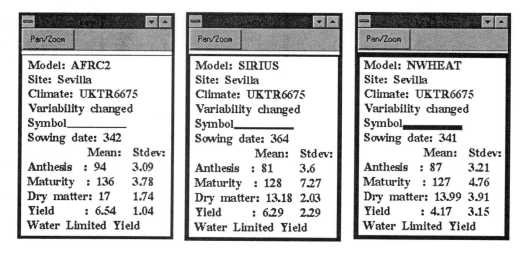

Figure 7.13 Example output from the site model comparison demonstration system: Cumulative probability functions for water-limited wheat production under the UKTR6675 (with variability) scenario at Sevilla.

The range of predictions for the dates of anthesis and maturity between the AFRCWHEAT, NWHEAT and SIRIUS models is 20 and 10 days respectively. The duration to these stages varied little between the 30 modelled seasons, represented by the steepness of the curves. The SIRIUS model predicted the largest variance in dates of anthesis and maturity.

Predictions of total dry matter and grain yield showed greater variability between the models. AFRCWHEAT exhibited the least inter-annual variability (i.e., has the steepest CPF) for both dry matter and yield due to a very low sensitivity to water shortage. The SIRIUS model had a fairly constant CPF for dry matter, but its yield distribution was quite variable with a wide range of yields for 40% of years, followed by a conservative increase up to a maximum of 9 t/ha. NWHEAT showed the greatest risks to production as the CPF was the least steep and constant out of all the models. In fact, it appeared to exhibit a bimodal distribution for both total dry matter and grain yield. This is supported by the standard deviation of grain yield which in NWHEAT was approximately 3 and 1.4 times greater than AFRCWHEAT and SIRIUS respectively. SIRIUS yield predictions were relatively high compared to its predictions of dry matter. This is a result of the use of photosynthate accumulated before anthesis being used to fill grain. A full discussion of the wheat model comparison for the complete range of climate change scenarios is given in Section 5.7.6.

7.4.2   Comparison of site-based and regional models

7.4.2.1   *Baseline climate*

An illustration of the site-based and broadscale model comparison for the baseline climate is shown in Figure 7.14. This shows a comparison of the predicted date of anthesis by the broadscale model (EuroWheat) with three site-based models (AFRCWHEAT, NWHEAT and SIRIUS) at Rothamsted. Broadscale results are presented in map form. The site-based results are presented in three histograms on which the

mean from the 30 year time series and the associated cell value are indicated.

The predicted date of anthesis for the cell containing Rothamsted was day 161. This is slightly earlier than the predictions from the site-based models by approximately 4, 6 and 10 days, on average, for AFRCWHEAT, NWHEAT and SIRIUS respectively. Comparison of the climatic data for the cell and site showed that temperatures for the cell were about 0.5°C greater than at the site for all months except October, which was 4°C greater. Higher temperatures caused faster development rates and, thus, an earlier anthesis date for the cell would be expected. However, the cell predictions still fell within the range of dates predicted for the 30 year time series from the AFRCWHEAT and NWHEAT models. For all site-based models there was a fairly wide temporal distribution of dates, with a range of up to 23 days.

7.4.2.2   *Climate change scenarios*

An illustration of the site-based and broadscale model comparison for the climate change scenarios is shown in Figure 7.15. This shows a comparison of potential bulb fresh weight (yield) predicted by the broadscale model, EuroOnion, and the site-based model, PELonion, for two sites under the GFDL5564d scenario. The two sites (Oxford and München) are indicated on the broadscale map.

At Oxford the mean of the site model results were very close to the cell value, differing by only 1 t/ha. With the exception of one outlier the inter-annual variability was small, with yields ranging from 45 to 56 t/ha over the 30 year period. At Munchen the broadscale and mean site model results differed to a greater extent (by approximately 6 t/ha), but both predicted lower yields than at Oxford. The temporal variation in yield was greater at München than Oxford. This may be explained by the München site being situated on the margins of a high altitude zone. Better correspondence in yields would be expected for the Oxford site compared to München as both models were originally developed and calibrated in England and the spatial variability within the 0.5° cell is likely to

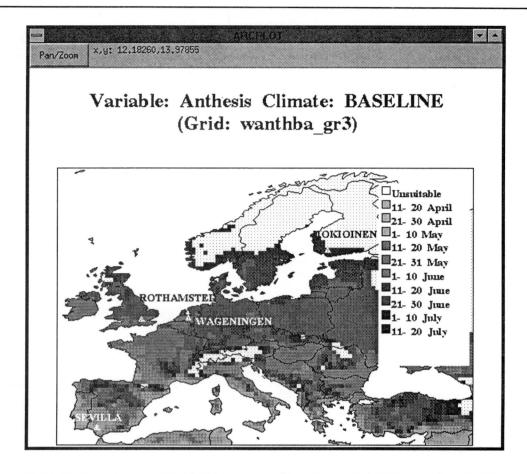

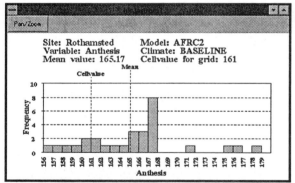

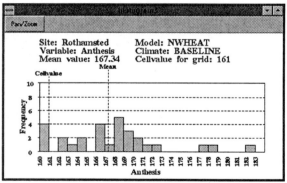

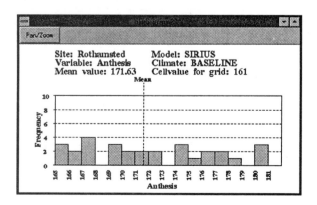

Figure 7.14   Example output from the broadscale and site model comparison demonstration system: Date of anthesis for winter wheat under the baseline climate (1961-90) at Rothamsted.

be lower at the lower altitude cell (Oxford) and, hence, more representative of the site. In summary, results from the broadscale and the site-based models show good agreement, with the cell value falling well within the temporal yield distributions for both sites.

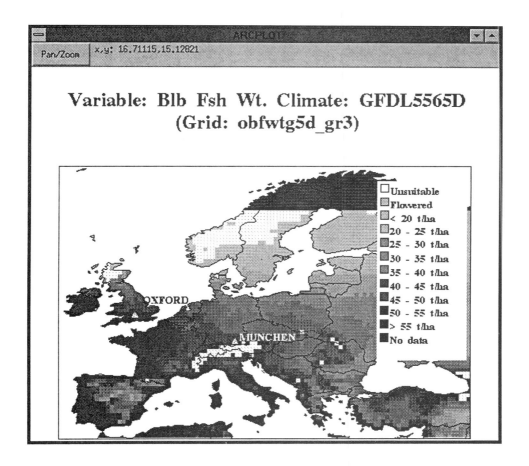

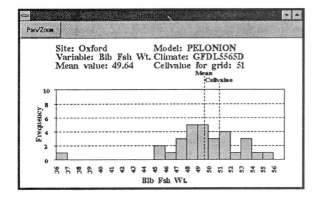

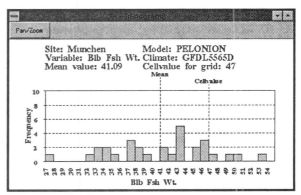

Figure 7.15 Example output from the broadscale and site model comparison demonstration system: Potential bulb fresh weight for onion under the GFDL5564d scenario at two sites.

7.5 Conclusions: Relevance for European climate change policy

7.5.1 Summary of major findings

The research reported in this volume of papers represents a substantial contribution to the body of literature on the potential agricultural impacts of climate change. The substantive results that appear to be of wide interest are summarised below.

Projections of climate change in Europe, based on transient GCM scenarios with no abatement of greenhouse gas emissions, suggest that annual-average warming will be 0.7 to 1.3°C by the 2030s and 1.9 to 2.5°C by the 2060s. The lower number is approximately equivalent to global-mean warming, as reported for Europe in the GFDL transient experiment. The higher range is 40 to 80 per cent greater than the global mean, from the UKTR experiment. These projections are substantially lower than the scenarios of equilibrium warming used for impact assessments over the past few years.

The GCM results for precipitation show wide ranges, from -20 to +20 per cent, across Europe and even between future decades. While there is some convergence in the projections of warming, the results for precipitation must be treated as scenarios. There is even some disagreement as to the conventional wisdom that southern Europe tends to get drier and northern Europe tends to get wetter. This outcome appears to vary between GCM experiments to some degree.

Prospects for improved, local projections and scenarios of climate change may be quite promising. The most recent GCM models are more reliable at matching global climate over the historical record. High resolution limited area models embedded in GCMs should provide daily data for small areas that overcomes many of the difficulties of downscaling from coarse resolution global models.

Modelling of the probability of agriculturally significant extreme events emphasises the importance of relatively small changes in mean

climates. The probability of exceeding 40°C in Montpellier is almost zero at present, but would begin to occur (with a probability of 5% or higher) in some scenarios of climate change. In contrast, the frost free period in Oxford, currently 150 to 200 days per year, would increase by about 50 days with some scenarios of climate change.

Based on a detailed study of agroclimatic risk in Hungary, unfavourable climate-types have increased in the past several decades resulting in decreased potential yields of 5-10%. At least one scenario of climate change implies that this trend would continue.

The experimental programme provided numerous results, designed to support development of robust crop models. For broccoli and cauliflower, development is strongly influenced by temperature. For onion, CO_2 stimulates early growth, but not later stages. Mini-FACE experiments on grapes showed increased fruit weight. For spring wheat, CO_2 enhances net photosynthesis and total dry matter, although nutrient limitations may reduce this effect. The interactions of temperature, CO_2 and plant stresses (nutrients and water in particular) need a systematic experimental programme to evaluate responses involving partitioning of dry matter and the balance of carbohydrate storage and utilisation.

Intercomparison of the site models demonstrated the need to evaluate a range of appropriate models when designing climate change impact assessments. When compared against the experimental results, the site models tended to perform reasonably well, except for the development of the leaf area index over the growing season. Scenario results showed a consistent increase in wheat yield at Rothamsted, but a range of responses at Sevilla. Incorporating weeds into the wheat models tended to reduce yield gains expected with climate change. Inclusion of extreme events in agricultural impact models is essential and will be a task for the next round of model development.

At the European scale, broadscale modelling of wheat showed increases in yields across most of the continent with climate change. In contrast, sunflower yields decreased in most scenarios and regions due to water limitations and significant shortening of the growing period. Changes in the potential yield of onions varied between regions and scenarios. The outcome for individual crops depends on the balance of faster developmental rates, shorter periods for seed filling (wheat and sunflower) or bulb growth (onion), higher potential yields due to increased assimilation of CO_2, and increased water use efficiency due to enhanced regulation of transpiration with elevated CO_2.

In addition to optimising responses to CO_2, yields can be improved or the adverse impacts of climate change can be ameliorated, through selection of crops and cultivars, or changing the sowing date and crop rotation. In Spain, for example, the efficiency of water use can be improved by using a short season maize variety in a barley and lentil rotation.

In summary, maize in southern Europe shows the most detrimental responses to climate change, while other crops (wheat, cauliflower, broccoli, onion and grapevine) benefit from the interaction of CO_2 and higher temperatures throughout Europe. Yield increases are less, and variability in yields is greater, in southern Europe where water stress influences production.

7.5.2 Implications for climate change policy

This research was not commissioned to evaluate specific policy issues. However, it would be remiss not to try and draw together the major achievements and their relevance to climate change policy. Perhaps the best starting point is to relate the potential impact of climate change on agriculture in Europe to policies to abate greenhouse gas emissions. At least this comparison between impacts and costs of abatement is common, as reported in the IPCC Working Group 3 report on the social costs of climate change (Pearce *et al.*, 1994). This is a dangerous comparison – the sciences of climate systems, plant responses, and economic valuation are too coarse, as yet, to provide reliable global cost-benefit comparisons. For regional studies, the reliability is even more problematic. Certainly, the cost of climate change related to agricultural impacts is likely to be relatively minor compared to costs for biodiversity, ecosystems and health. Probably all of the contributors of this volume would be reluctant to have their results interpreted in such comparisons without further analysis.

If the global cost-benefit analysis is problematic, what can be reliably said for the regional prospects in Europe? Again, the results are dependent on the scenarios of climate change, the interactions of complex plant processes, and responses by agriculturalists and the agricultural economy. Over the past five years of research and scenario evaluation, the most robust conclusion is that the northern limits of agricultural suitability are limited by temperature and this constraint is likely to be reduced with climate change. The common wisdom of a 200 km per 1°C advancement of agroclimatic suitability still seems appropriate. In central and southern Europe, however, the situation is more complex. Many aspects of plant dynamics are poorly modelled at present, so it would not be surprising to see future impact assessments that vary considerably from the present set of experimental and simulated results.

One of the major improvements in the current research is the evaluation of CO_2 effects at the site and broad scale. The outcome of plant responses to CO_2 enrichment, temperature stress and water availability is not fully understood. At present, the CO_2 effects tend to offset some of the temperature and water stresses. Two factors combine to provide some optimism. Many of the transient models result in lower levels of warming than the equilibrium scenarios used previously. Yet, CO_2 concentrations will continue to increase and projections for 2050 are fairly consistent for a range of emission scenarios.

Thus, plants will have the benefit of CO_2 enrichment while coping with (or taking advantage of) fairly modest changes in temperature and precipitation. If these scenarios and projections prove reliable, the impacts of climate change in Europe may be less adverse than previously believed. Annual crops are likely to benefit more than perennial vegetation. Unresolved issues concern effects on yield quality, down regulation of photosynthesis with high levels of CO_2, and interactions with specific stresses.

The development of spatial models for wheat, sunflower and onion has demonstrated that spatial models need not have higher errors than site models. Over the whole of Europe, the growing season from sowing to maturity for winter wheat can be predicted with an error of only several days based on monthly data. Such reduced form models focus on the processes most sensitive to climatic variations. They still require detailed, mechanistic modelling at the site scale, calibration and scaling up to the regional level.

An example of the benefit of a systematic approach to multi-level modelling and integration of the results in a GIS is demonstrated in the analysis of winter wheat yields for Europe. By using an area-weighted index of yield, percentage changes with climate change can be applied to current production levels. By the 2030s wheat production could exceed 100 Million tonnes, even without improvements in agricultural technology.

Notwithstanding the above substantive results, the major focus of this research is improving methodologies for climate change impact assessment. The research has demonstrated the fruitful interaction across countries and disciplines to compile data bases, conduct and review experiments, develop modelling tools and contribute expert analyses to a singular issue. The integration is not simply a question of hardware and software; multi-level modelling is matched by multidisciplinary contributions.

The resulting data bases and their interpretation lay the necessary foundation for evaluating the impact of climatic, economic, political and social change on land use. With the addition of more crop models and data on economic activities, scenarios of the future landscapes of Europe could be evaluated. A promising innovation is the integration of remote sensing data and dynamic crop models to assess crop responses for the present distribution of fields. Such areas as regional demand for water by cropping systems, the full cost of adapting agricultural systems to new climates, and implications for meeting greenhouse gas emission targets could be evaluated based on robust understanding of the dynamics of land cover and land utilisation.

Climate system research is increasingly bridging the near and long term. Weather forecasting is already based on general circulation models; prediction of climates over the medium term, for example related to ENSO events, and for decadal (ten-year) trends is progressing for many parts of the world. The approaches adopted here would be invaluable to forecast potential impacts and effective responses.

Future developments in climate change impact assessment in Europe should focus on more dynamic linkages between the site and broad scales of analysis. Formal evaluation of uncertainty is required to understand crop responses within fields and across space resulting from the chain of uncertainty in projections of climate change, plant metabolism, climate-environment interactions, and agricultural responses. Incorporating extreme events and climatic variability at the site and broad scales will begin to identify local and regional thresholds for significant changes in the risk of crop failure and the probability of economic yields. Many of these issues will be taken up in the next phase of this research, the CLIVARA project funded by the European Commission.

References

Aspinall, R.J. and Matthews, K.B. (1994). Climate change impact on distribution and abundance of wildlife species: An analytical approach using GIS. *Environmental Pollution*, **86(2)**, 217-223.

Driscoll, D.M. and Fong, J.M.Y., (1992). Continentality: A basic climatic parameter re-examined. *International Journal of Climatology*, **12**, 185-192.

Easterling, W.E., Crosson, P.R., Rosenberg, N.J. McKenney, M.S. Katz, L.A. and Lemon, K.M. (1993). Agricultural impacts and responses to climate change in the Missouri-Iowa-Nebraska-Kansas (MINK) region. *Climatic Change,* **24,** 23-61.

Huntley, B., Bartlein, P.J. and Prentice, I.C., (1989). Climatic control of the distribution of and abundance of Beech (*Fagus* L.) in Europe and North America. *Journal of Biogeography,* **16,** 551-560.

Kenny, G.J. and Harrison, P.A., (1992). The effects of climate variability and change on grape suitability in Europe. *Journal of Wine Research,* **3**(3), 163-183.

Kenny, G.J. and Shao, J., (1992). An assessment of a latitude-temperature index for predicting climate suitability of grapes in Europe. *Journal of Horticultural Science,* **67,** 239-246.

Papajorgji, P., Jones, J.W., Peart, R.M. and Curry, B (1994). Using crop models and geographic information systems to study the impact of climate change in the southeastern USA. *Soil and Crop Science Society of Florida Proceedings,* **53,** 82-86.

Pearce, D.W., Cline, W.R., Achanta, A.N., Fankhauser, S, Pachauri, R.K., Tol, R.S.J. and Vellinga, P. (1994). *The social costs of climate change: greenhouse damage and the benefits of control.* Intergovernmental Panel on Climate Change, Geneva, (manuscript).

Wolf, J. and van Diepen, C.A. (1991). *Effects of climate change on crop production in the Rhine basin. Wageningen* (The Netherlands), DLO-The Winand Staring Centre.

APPENDIX I

Authors' Addresses

E. Barrow	Climatic Research Unit, University of East Anglia, Norwich, NR4 7TJ, UK
M. Bindi	IATA-CNR, P.le delle Cascine 18, 50144 - Florence, Italy
A.P. Brignall	Environmental Change Unit, University of Oxford, 1a Mansfield Road, Oxford, OX1 3TB, UK
R.E. Butterfield	Environmental Change Unit, University of Oxford, 1a Mansfield Road, Oxford, OX1 3TB, UK
T.R. Carter	Agricultural Research Centre of Finland, c/o Finnish Meteorological Institute, PO Box 503, FIN-00101 Helsinki, Finland
A.J. Daymond	Department of Horticulture, University of Reading, Reading, RG6 2AS, UK
R. Delécolle	Bioclimatologie, INRA, Avignon, France
T.E. Downing	Environmental Change Unit, University of Oxford, 1a Mansfield Road, Oxford, OX1 3TB, UK
H. Eckersten	Department of Soil Science, Swedish University of Agricultural Sciences, S-75007 Uppsala, Sweden
R.H. Ellis	Department of Agriculture, University of Reading, Reading, RG6 2AT, UK
L.G. Evans	IACR - Long Ashton Research Station, University of Bristol, Bristol, BS18 9AF, UK
L. Fibbi	CeSIA - Accademia dei Georgofili, Logge Uffizi Corti, 50122 - Florence, Italy
M.J. Gawith	Environmental Change Unit, University of Oxford, 1a Mansfield Road, Oxford, OX1 3TB, UK
J-L. González-Andújar	CSIC - Instituto de Agricultura Sostenible, Aptdo. 4084, 14080 Cordoba, Spain
B. Gozzini	CeSIA - Accademia dei Georgofili, Logge Uffizi Corti, 50122 - Florence, Italy
K. Grevsen	Danish Institute of Plant and Soil Science, Research Centre for Horticulture, Kirstinebjergvej 6, DK-5792 Årslev, Denmark
M.O. Guérif	Bioclimatologie - Agronomie, INRA, Laon, France
P. Hadley	Department of Horticulture, University of Reading, Reading, RG6 2AS, UK

K. Hakala — Agricultural Research Centre of Finland, Institute of Crop and Soil Science, FIN-31600 Jokioinen, Finland

Zs. Harnos — Department of Mathematics and Informatics, University of Horticulture and Food Industry, H-1118 Budapest, Hungary

P.A. Harrison — Environmental Change Unit, University of Oxford, 1a Mansfield Road, Oxford, OX1 3TB, UK

M. Hulme — Climatic Research Unit, University of East Anglia, Norwich, NR4 7TJ, UK

A. Iglesias — Department de Sistemas Forestales, INIA, 28040 Madrid, Spain

T.S. Karacostas — Department of Meteorology and Climatology, Aristotelian University of Thessaloniki, Thessaloniki 540 06, Greece

T. Mela — Agricultural Research Centre of Finland, Institute of Crop and Soil Science, FIN-31600 Jokioinen, Finland

F. Miglietta — IATA-CNR, P.le delle Cascine 18, 50144 - Florence, Italy

J.I.L. Morison — Department of Biology, University of Essex, Colchester, CO4 3SQ, UK

J.E. Olesen — Danish Institute of Plant and Soil Science, Research Centre Foulum, P.O. Box 23, DK-8830 Tjele, Denmark

S. Orlandini — CeSIA - Accademia dei Georgofili, Logge Uffizi Corti, 50122 - Florence, Italy

J.L. Orr — Environmental Change Unit, University of Oxford, 1a Mansfield Road, Oxford, OX1 3TB, UK

J.R. Porter — Department of Agricultural Sciences, Royal Agricultural and Veterinary University, Agrovej 10, 2630 Taastrup, Denmark

R. Saarikko — Agricultural Research Centre of Finland, c/o Finnish Meteorological Institute, PO Box 503, FIN-00101 Helsinki, Finland

J. Schellberg — Institut für Pflanzenbau, Friedrich Wilhelms Universität, 5300 Bonn 1, Germany

M.A. Semenov — IACR - Long Ashton Research Station, University of Bristol, Bristol, BS18 9AF, UK

T.R. Wheeler — Plant Environment Laboratory, Department of Agriculture, University of Reading, Reading, RG2 9AD, UK

K. Wilbois — Institut für Pflanzenbau, Friedrich Wilhelms Universität, 5300 Bonn 1, Germany

J. Wolf — Department of Theoretical Production Ecology, Wageningen Agricultural University, Wageiningen 6700 AK, The Netherlands